Paper P3

Business Analysis

EXAM KIT

KAPLAN

PUBLISHING

British Library Cataloguing-in-Publication Data

A catalogue record for this book is available from the British Library.

Published by:

Kaplan Publishing UK

Unit 2 The Business Centre

Molly Millar's Lane

Wokingham

Berkshire

RG41 2QZ

ISBN: 978-1-78415-836-1

Acknowledgements

The past ACCA examination questions are the copyright of the Association of Chartered Certified Accountants. The original answers to the questions from June 1994 onwards were produced by the examiners themselves and have been adapted by Kaplan Publishing.

We are grateful to the Chartered Institute of Management Accountants and the Institute of Chartered Accountants in England and Wales for permission to reproduce past examination questions. The answers have been prepared by Kaplan Publishing.

CONTENTS

Section

Key features in this edition

In addition to providing a wide ranging bank of real past exam questions, we have also included in this edition:

- An analysis of all of the recent new syllabus examination papers.

- Paper specific information and advice on exam technique.

- Our recommended approach to make your revision for this particular subject as effective as possible.

  This includes step by step guidance on how best to use our Kaplan material (Study text, pocket notes and exam kit) at this stage in your studies.

- Enhanced tutorial answers packed with specific key answer tips, technical tutorial notes and exam technique tips from our experienced tutors.

- Complementary online resources including full tutor debriefs and question assistance to point you in the right direction when you get stuck.

You will find a wealth of other resources to help you with your studies on the following sites:

www.mykaplan.co.uk

www.accaglobal.com/students/

Quality and accuracy are of the utmost importance to us so if you spot an error in any of our products, please send an email to mykaplanreporting@kaplan.com with full details, or follow the link to the feedback form in MyKaplan.

Our Quality Co-ordinator will work with our technical team to verify the error and take action to ensure it is corrected in future editions.

KAPLAN PUBLISHING

INDEX TO QUESTIONS AND ANSWERS

INTRODUCTION

The P3 examination starts with a strategic case study (see the scenario based questions) and strategic implementation has formed the majority of the option questions. However there has been a slight change in the way that the syllabus has been examined – strategic implementation has begun to feature as one part of the scenario question, whilst strategic analysis (such as the value chain) has begun to appear in the option questions. The exam kit tries to reflect this by having all three strategic planning areas (analysis, choice and action/implementation) reflected in both the scenario based questions section and the option question section.

Note that the majority of the questions within the kit are past ACCA exam questions – though, since the change of the examiner in 2007 and the change in syllabus this year, some new topics have been introduced to the syllabus and there are fewer past exam questions in these areas.

KEY TO THE INDEX

PAPER ENHANCEMENTS

We have added the following enhancements to the answers in this exam kit:

Key answer tips

Most answers include key answer tips to help your understanding of each question.

Tutorial note

Most answers include more tutorial notes to explain some of the technical points in detail.

Top tutor tips

For selected questions, we "walk through the answer" giving guidance on how to approach the questions with helpful 'tips from a top tutor', together with technical tutor notes.

These answers are indicated with the "footsteps" icon in the index.

ONLINE ENHANCEMENTS

🕐 *Timed question with Online tutor debrief*

For selected questions, we recommend that they are to be completed in full exam conditions (i.e. properly timed in a closed book environment).

In addition to the examiner's technical answer, enhanced with key answer tips and tutorial notes in this exam kit, online you can find an answer debrief by a top tutor that:

- works through the question in full

- points out how to approach the question

- how to ensure that the easy marks are obtained as quickly as possible, and

- emphasises how to tackle exam questions and exam technique.

- These questions are indicated with the "clock" icon in the index.

📌 *Online question assistance*

Have you ever looked at a question and not known where to start, or got stuck part way through?

For selected questions, we have produced "Online question assistance" offering different levels of guidance, such as:

- ensuring that you understand the question requirements fully, highlighting key terms and the meaning of the verbs used

- how to read the question proactively, with knowledge of the requirements, to identify the topic areas covered

- assessing the detail content of the question body, pointing out key information and explaining why it is important

- help in devising a plan of attack.

With this assistance, you should then be able to attempt your answer confident that you know what is expected of you.

These questions are indicated with the "signpost" icon in the index.

Online question enhancements and answer debriefs will be available on MyKaplan

www.mykaplan.co.uk

PRACTICE QUESTIONS

STRATEGIC ANALYSIS

			Question	Answer	Past exam
			Page number		
1	CTC Telecommunication		1	185	–
2	3C Pharmaceuticals		2	188	–
3	ICOM		3	191	S/D 15
4	Swift		5	194	Jun 10
5	Bowland		7	197	Dec 95
6	McGeorge Holdings plc		8	200	Jun 03
7	NESTA		9	202	Jun 13
8	ATD		10	206	Dec 13
9	Retail World		12	209	S/D 16
10	Moor Farm		14	212	Dec 12
11	One Energy plc		16	216	Jun 09
12	Independent Living		18	219	Dec 09
13	Noble Pets		20	223	Dec 14

STRATEGIC CHOICE

14	Graffoff		22	226	Dec 12
15	Environment Management Society		24	230	Pilot 11
16	MMI		25	233	Dec 08
17	Bluesky		27	238	–

ORGANISATIONAL STRUCTURE

18	ALG Technology		30	242	Dec 01
19	ICC Organisation		31	245	Dec 96
20	Frigate Limited		32	247	Dec 10
21	Yvern Trinkets Regional		33	250	Jun 15

BUSINESS PROCESS CHANGE

22	Country Car Club		35	253	Jun 08
23	Stella Electronics		36	258	Dec 14
24	TMP		39	260	Dec 10
25	Institute of Analytical Accountants		40	264	Jun 11
26	Flexipipe		42	268	Jun 12

INFORMATION TECHNOLOGY

E-MARKETING

PROJECT MANAGEMENT

SCENARIO-BASED QUESTIONS

ANALYSIS OF PAST PAPERS

The table below summarises the key topics that have been tested in recent examinations.

The references are to the number of the question in this edition of the Exam Kit.

Note that, from September 2015, ACCA will only make public hybrid papers which combine the March and June exams and the September and December exams.

	Jun 14	Dec 14	Jun 15	S/D 15	M/J 16	S/D 16
Strategic planning						
PESTEL			Q80			Q87
5 FORCES			Q80			Q87
Forecasting		Q13				Q9
Strengths/weaknesses						
Value chain		Q13			Q86	
SWOT	Q71					
Stakeholders/mission			Q80	Q3	Q32	
Strategy evaluation		Q72				
Strategic choice	Q71	Q72	Q21			
Methods of strategic development		Q72		Q81		Q87
Organisational structure			Q21			Q68
Business process change	Q33	Q23			Q63	
Project management	Q44	Q45	Q48			
Information technology					Q32	Q40
Marketing	Q39				Q35	Q40
Financing/cost accounting				Q56	Q86	
Strategy and people			Q59		Q63	
Change management	Q71			Q81		Q68

APPROACH TO EXAMINING THE SYLLABUS

The syllabus is assessed by a three-hour paper-based examination.

Section A

Section A contains one multi-part question based on a case study scenario. This question is worth 50 marks.

Section B

Section B will consist of three discrete questions each worth 25 marks. Candidates must answer two questions from this section.

EXAM TECHNIQUE

- **Divide the time** you spend on questions in proportion to the marks on offer:

  - there are 1.8 minutes available per mark in the examination (this allows for an initial 15 minutes in the exam hall for previewing the exam paper and choosing option questions)

  - within that, try to allow time for reading the long scenarios, and at the end of each question to review your answer and address any obvious issues

  Whatever happens, always keep your eye on the clock and **do not over run on any part of any question!**

- Spend the last **five minutes** of the examination:

  - reading through your answers, and

  - **making any additions or corrections**.

- If you **get completely stuck** with a question:

  - leave space in your answer book, and

  - **return to it later.**

- Stick to the question and **tailor your answer** to what you are asked.

  - pay particular attention to the verbs in the question.

- If you do not understand what a question is asking, **state your assumptions**.

  Even if you do not answer in precisely the way the examiner hoped, you should be given some credit, if your assumptions are reasonable.

- You should do everything you can to make things easy for the marker.

  The marker will find it easier to identify the points you have made if your **answers are legible**.

- **Your answer should have:**

  - a clear structure

  - a brief introduction, a main section and a conclusion.

  Be concise.

  It is better to write a little about a lot of different points than a great deal about one or two points.

- **Reports, memos and other documents**:

  Some questions ask you to present your answer in the form of a report, a memo, a letter or other document.

  Make sure that you use the correct format – there could be easy marks to gain here.

EXAM TECHNIQUE

PAPER SPECIFIC INFORMATION

THE EXAM

FORMAT OF THE EXAM

	Number of marks
1 compulsory questions	50
A choice of 2 from 3 option questions worth 25 marks each	50
Total time allowed: 3 hours 15 minutes.	

Note that:

- All syllabus areas will be examined.

- The exam may contain one question from each syllabus area. However, some exam questions have examined more than one syllabus area in the same question.

- Questions will be based around a long scenario. It is important to refer back to this scenario when answering the question.

PASS MARK

The pass mark for all ACCA Qualification examination papers is 50%.

KAPLAN GUIDANCE

As all questions are compulsory, there are no decisions to be made about choice of questions, other than in which order you would like to tackle them.

Therefore, in relation to P3, we recommend that you take the following approach with your reading and planning time:

- **Skim through the whole paper**, assessing the level of difficulty of each question.

- **Write down** on the question paper next to the mark allocation **the amount of time you should spend on each part.** Do this for each part of every question.

- **Decide the order** in which you think you will attempt each question:

  This is a personal choice and you have time on the revision phase to try out different approaches, for example, if you sit mock exams.

  A common approach is to tackle the question you think is the easiest and you are most comfortable with first.

  Psychologists believe that you usually perform at your best on the second and third question you attempt, once you have settled into the exam, so not tackling the most difficult question first may be advisable.

  It is usual however that students tackle their least favourite topic and/or the most difficult question in their opinion last.

  Whatever you approach, you must make sure that you leave enough time to attempt all questions fully and be very strict with yourself in timing each question.

- **For each question** in turn, read the requirements and then the detail of the question carefully.

  Always read the requirement first as this enables you to **focus on the detail of the question with the specific task in mind**.

  Models:

  Most questions will require you to use a model from the syllabus as the structure for your answer. You therefore need to be clear as to which model(s) are required in each question. If you cannot determine which model to use it may be better for you to choose an alternative question.

  For written questions:

  Take notice of the format required (e.g. letter, memo, notes) and identify the recipient of the answer. You need to do this to judge the level of financial sophistication required in your answer and whether the use of a formal reply or informal bullet points would be satisfactory.

  Plan your beginning, middle and end and the key areas to be addressed and your use of titles and sub-titles to enhance your answer.

  For all questions:

  Spot the easy marks to be gained in a question and parts which can be performed independently of the rest of the question. For example, discussing the problems with a numerical technique might be easier than actually performing the calculations.

  Make sure that you do these parts first when you tackle the question.

Don't go overboard in terms of **planning time** on any one question – you need a good measure of the whole paper and a plan for all of the questions at the end of the 15 minutes.

By covering all questions you can often help yourself as you may find that facts in one question may remind you of things you should put into your answer relating to a different question.

- With your plan of attack in mind, **start answering your chosen question** with your plan to hand, as soon as you are allowed to start.

Always keep your eye on the clock and do not over run on any part of any question!

DETAILED SYLLABUS

The detailed syllabus and study guide written by the ACCA can be found at:

www.accaglobal.com/students/

KAPLAN'S RECOMMENDED REVISION APPROACH

QUESTION PRACTICE IS THE KEY TO SUCCESS

Success in professional examinations relies upon you acquiring a firm grasp of the required knowledge at the tuition phase. In order to be able to do the questions, knowledge is essential.

However, the difference between success and failure often hinges on your exam technique on the day and making the most of the revision phase of your studies.

The **Kaplan study text** is the starting point, designed to provide the underpinning knowledge to tackle all questions. However, in the revision phase, pouring over text books is not the answer.

Kaplan Online fixed tests help you consolidate your knowledge and understanding and are a useful tool to check whether you can remember key topic areas.

Kaplan pocket notes are designed to help you quickly revise a topic area, however you then need to practice questions. There is a need to progress to full exam standard questions as soon as possible, and to tie your exam technique and technical knowledge together.

The importance of question practice cannot be over-emphasised.

The recommended approach below is designed by expert tutors in the field, in conjunction with their knowledge of the examiner and their recent real exams.

The approach taken for the fundamental papers is to revise by topic area. However, with the professional stage papers, a multi topic approach is required to answer the scenario based questions.

You need to practice as many questions as possible in the time you have left.

OUR AIM

Our aim is to get you to the stage where you can attempt exam standard questions confidently, to time, in a closed book environment, with no supplementary help (i.e. to simulate the real examination experience).

Practising your exam technique on real past examination questions, in timed conditions, is also vitally important for you to assess your progress and identify areas of weakness that may need more attention in the final run up to the examination.

In order to achieve this we recognise that initially you may feel the need to practice some questions with open book help and exceed the required time.

The approach below shows you which questions you should use to build up to coping with exam standard question practice, and references to the sources of information available should you need to revisit a topic area in more detail.

Remember that in the real examination, all you have to do is:

- attempt all questions required by the exam

- only spend the allotted time on each question, and

- get them at least 50% right!

Try and practice this approach on every question you attempt from now to the real exam.

EXAMINER COMMENTS

We have included the examiners comments to the specific new syllabus examination questions in this kit for you to see the main pitfalls that students fall into with regard to technical content.

However, too many times in the general section of the report, the examiner comments that students had failed due to:

- "not answering the question"

- "a poor understanding of why something is done, not just how it is done"

- "simply writing out numbers from the question. Candidates must understand what the numbers tell them about business performance"

- "a lack of common business sense" and

- "ignoring clues in the question".

Good exam technique is vital.

THE KAPLAN PAPER P3 REVISION PLAN

Stage 1: Assess areas of strengths and weaknesses

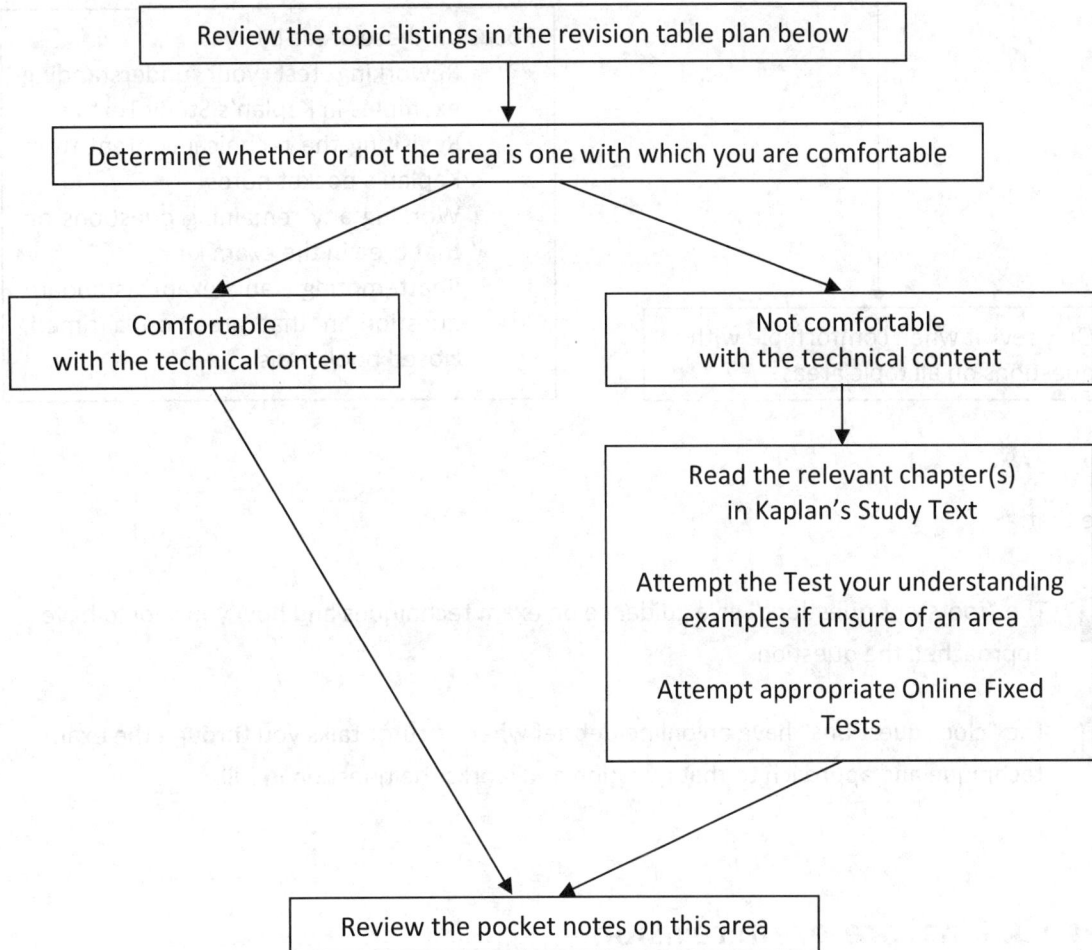

```
┌─────────────────────────────────────────────────────────────┐
│   Review the topic listings in the revision table plan below │
└─────────────────────────────────────────────────────────────┘
                              │
                              ▼
┌─────────────────────────────────────────────────────────────┐
│ Determine whether or not the area is one with which you are   │
│                      comfortable                              │
└─────────────────────────────────────────────────────────────┘
```

```
┌──────────────────────┐              ┌──────────────────────┐
│     Comfortable       │              │    Not comfortable    │
│ with the technical    │              │ with the technical    │
│      content          │              │      content          │
└──────────────────────┘              └──────────────────────┘
```

```
┌──────────────────────────────────────┐
│   Read the relevant chapter(s)         │
│   in Kaplan's Study Text               │
│                                        │
│   Attempt the Test your understanding  │
│   examples if unsure of an area        │
│                                        │
│   Attempt appropriate Online Fixed     │
│   Tests                                │
└──────────────────────────────────────┘
```

```
┌──────────────────────────────────────┐
│   Review the pocket notes on this area │
└──────────────────────────────────────┘
```

Stage 2: Practice questions

Follow the order of revision of topics as recommended in the revision table plan below and attempt the questions in the order suggested.

Try to avoid referring to text books and notes and the model answer until you have completed your attempt.

Try to answer the question in the allotted time.

Review your attempt with the model answer and assess how much of the answer you achieved in the allocated exam time.

Fill in the self-assessment box below and decide on your best course of action.

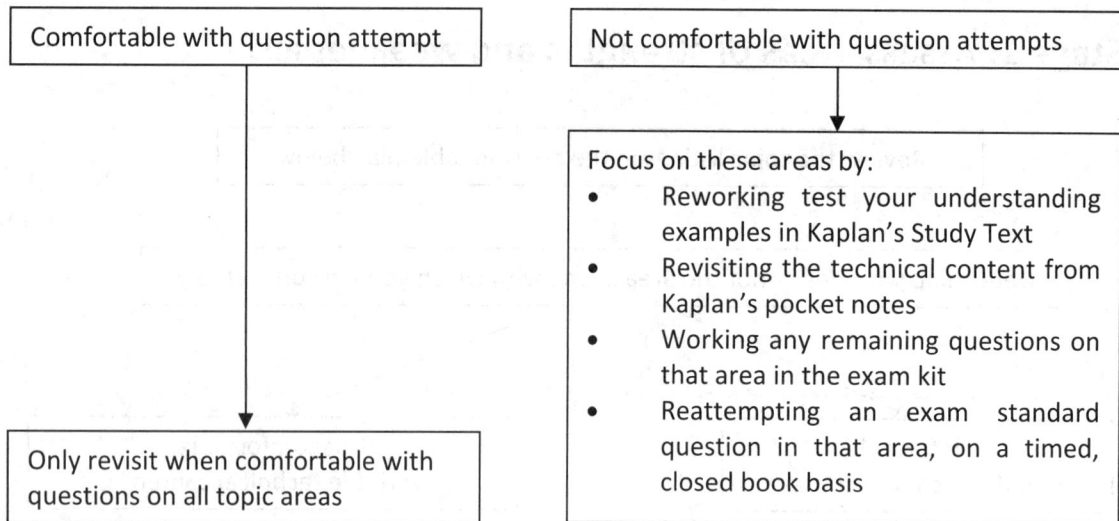

Comfortable with question attempt

Not comfortable with question attempts

Focus on these areas by:
- Reworking test your understanding examples in Kaplan's Study Text
- Revisiting the technical content from Kaplan's pocket notes
- Working any remaining questions on that area in the exam kit
- Reattempting an exam standard question in that area, on a timed, closed book basis

Only revisit when comfortable with questions on all topic areas

Note that:

The "footsteps questions" give guidance on exam techniques and how you should have approached the question.

The "clock questions" have an online debrief where a tutor talks you through the exam technique and approach to that question and works the question in full.

Stage 3: Final pre-exam revision

We recommend that you **attempt at least one three hour mock examination** containing a set of previously unseen exam standard questions.

It is important that you get a feel for the breadth of coverage of a real exam without advanced knowledge of the topic areas covered – just as you will expect to see on the real exam day.

Ideally this mock should be sat in timed, closed book, real exam conditions and could be:

- a mock examination offered by your tuition provider, and/or

- the pilot paper in the back of this exam kit, and/or

- the last real examination paper (available shortly afterwards on MyKaplan with "enhanced walk through answers" and a full "tutor debrief").

KAPLAN'S DETAILED REVISION PLAN

Topic	Complete Text Chapter	Pocket note Chapter	Questions to attempt	Tutor guidance	Date attempted	Self assessment
Strategic position						
– strategic planning	1	1		This chapter pulls all the other chapters together. It means that strategic planning could be combined with a question on almost any other topic. It is important that you understand the two key models: J, S & W, and the strategy lenses.		
– external analysis	2	2	7, 8, 70, 87	Key models are the PESTEL and 5 Forces. Forecasting also forms part of this chapter and Q8 should illustrate the nature of the question that you could face on this topic. Q70 will help revise the strategy lenses from chapter 1.		
– internal analysis	3	3	11, 69	A key skill in this chapter will be the ability to perform good quantitative analysis. These questions will ensure you can do this well.		
– objectives	4	4	3, 77	The key model in this chapter is Mendelow's matrix. In any question on stakeholders you should aim to apply this model to the scenario.		

Topic	Complete Text Chapter	Pocket note Chapter	Questions to attempt	Tutor guidance	Date attempted	Self assessment
Strategic choice						
– competitive strategies and strategy evaluation	5 – 6	5 – 6	75, 87	Competitive strategies are tested in Q75. Strategy evaluation appears in almost every compulsory question and it is vital that you can apply the J, S &W technique.		
– strategic development	7	7	15, 81, 84	It is important in these types of question that you do not just regurgitate the lists that are presented in the pocket notes. You need to apply the lists to the scenario and ensure you focus on the actual requirement in the scenario.Q71 provides a good question on portfolio management.		
Strategy in action						
– Organisational structure	8	8	18	There are few recent exam questions on this area. But Q18 should test your application of the pocket note material to a question scenario. The key in this question is to spot the most appropriate type of structure.		
– Business process change	9	9	22, 23	Harmon's models are the key models in this chapter. The first model helps decide which processes should be redesigned, the second model helps explain how the redesign should happen. Q22 is a good test of the first model, whilst the second model is covered again in Q23.		

KAPLAN PUBLISHING

Topic	Complete Text Chapter	Pocket note Chapter	Questions to attempt	Tutor guidance	Date attempted	Self assessment
– Information technology	10	10	27, 30, 32	The examiner is likely to focus on supply chain management – an area covered well in Q27 (whilst Q30 goes into more details on e-procurement). Q32 covers IT controls – recent additions to the syllabus.		
– Marketing	11	11	34, 40	This area is deceptively tough. The knowledge seems straightforward and common sense, and a lot of it is carried forward from paper F1. But you will only score in this area of the syllabus if you use the appropriate models and make your answers as relevant and specific to the scenario as possible.		
– Project management	12 & 13	12 & 13	42, 43, 44, 47, 49	Covering two chapters, this is a very important and significant part of the syllabus. Q44 will test the numerical aspects, whilst the other questions will test different elements of the project management process. It is strongly advised that you attempt all of these questions.		

Topic	Complete Text Chapter	Pocket note Chapter	Questions to attempt	Tutor guidance	Date attempted	Self assessment
– Financing	14	14	14, 55, 57	This chapter focuses primarily on cost accounting techniques. You should focus on areas of weakness rather than doing questions on topics that you are comfortable with. Questions 54 and 56 are the most exam focused questions in this section. Q14 will test your knowledge on raising finance (the other element within this topic).		
– Strategy and people	15	15	58, 63	You may benefit in this area if you can remember some of your brought forward knowledge from paper F1 on leadership and motivation (though you will not lose out in any way if you cannot remember this material). This question will show you how to apply the chapter to a real world scenario.		

Topic	Complete Text Chapter	Pocket note Chapter	Questions to attempt	Tutor guidance	Date attempted	Self assessment
– Managing strategic change	16	16	65, 85	This is another chapter that can be linked to almost any other chapter. For example, launching new strategies, changing organisational structure, redesigning processes etc. will all require good change management. There are a lot of models in the chapter but the examiner is keen for you to have quite a broad syllabus knowledge so it is important that you are familiar with them all. The suggested questions focus on key models such as the cultural web, types of change, and the contextual features of change.		

Note that not all of the questions are referred to in the programme above. We have recommended a large number of exam standard questions and successful completion of these should reassure you that you have a good grounding of all of the key topics and are well prepared for the exam.

The remaining questions are available in the kit for extra practice for those who require more question on some areas.

Section 1

PRACTICE QUESTIONS

STRATEGIC ANALYSIS

1   CTC TELECOMMUNICATION

CTC, a telecommunications company, has recently been privatised by the government of C after legislation was passed which removed the state monopoly and opened up the communications market to competition from both national and overseas companies – a process known as deregulation.

Prior to the deregulation, CTC was the sole, protected, supplier of telecommunications and was required to provide 'the best telecommunications service the nation can afford'. At that time the government dictated the performance levels required for CTC, and the level of resources it would be able to bring to bear to meet its objectives.

The shares were floated on the C Stock Exchange with 80% being made available to the population of C and up to 20% being made available to foreign nationals. The government of C retained a 'golden share' to prevent the acquisition of CTC by any foreign company. However, the privatisation meant that many of the traditional ways in which the industry had operated would need to change under the new regulations. Apart from the money received from the flotation, the government privatised CTC in recognition of both the changing global environment for telecommunications companies, and the overseas expansion opportunities that might exist for a privatised company. The government recognises that foreign companies will enter the home market but feels that this increased competition is likely to make CTC more effective in the global market.

You have recently been appointed as the management accountant for CTC and have a background in the commercial sector. The Board of Directors is unchanged from CTC's pre-flotation days.

Required:

(a)   **Explain to the Board of Directors why the objectives of CTC will need to change as a result of the privatisation of CTC and the deregulation of the market.   (10 marks)**

(b)   **Produce two examples of suitable strategic objectives for CTC, following its privatisation and the deregulation of the market, and explain why each would be an appropriate long term objective.   (4 marks)**

(c)   **Advise the Board of Directors on the stages of an appropriate strategic planning process for CTC in the light of the privatisation and deregulation.   (11 marks)**

(Total: 25 marks)

2 3C PHARMACEUTICALS

3C is a medium-sized pharmaceutical company. It is based in Asia, but distributes and sells its products world-wide.

In common with other pharmaceutical companies, 3C has a large number of products in its portfolio, though most of these are still being developed. The success rate of new drugs is very low, as most fail to complete clinical trials or are believed to be uneconomic to launch. However, the rewards to be gained from a successful new drug are so great that it is only necessary to have a few successful drugs on the market to be very profitable.

At present 3C have 240 drugs at various stages of development, being tested or undergoing clinical trials prior to a decision being made whether to launch the drug. 3C has only three products that are actually 'on the market':

- Epsilon is a drug used in the treatment of heart disease. It has been available for eight months and has achieved significant success. Sales of this drug are not expected to increase from their current level.

- Alpha is a painkiller. It was launched more than ten years ago, and has become one of the leading drugs in its class. In a few months the patent on this drug will expire, and other manufacturers will be allowed to produce generic copies of it. Alpha is expected to survive a further twelve months after it loses its patent, and will then be withdrawn.

- Beta is used in the hospital treatment of serious infections. It is a very specialised drug, and cannot be obtained from a doctor or pharmacist for use outside the hospital environment. It was launched only three months ago, and has yet to generate a significant sales volume.

The directors of 3C meet every month to review the product portfolio and to discuss possible investment opportunities. At their next meeting, they are to be asked to consider three investments. Due to a limited investment budget, the three investments are mutually exclusive. The options are as follows:

- The directors can invest in a new version of Alpha, Alpha2, which offers improved performance. This will allow 3C to apply for a new patent for Alpha2, and maintain the level of sales achieved by Alpha for an additional five years. Alpha2 has successfully completed all its clinical trials, and can be launched immediately.

- The directors can invest in a major marketing campaign to promote the use of Beta to specialist hospital staff. While this investment should lead to a significant growth in the sales of Beta, 3C is aware that one of its competitors is actively promoting a rival product with similar performance to that of Beta.

- The directors can invest in the final stage of clinical trials for Gamma. This is a 'breakthrough' drug, as it has no near rivals on the market. Gamma is used in the treatment of HIV, and offers significantly better success rates than any treatment currently available. The team of 3C specialists managing the development of Gamma is confident it can successfully complete clinical trials within six months. The team also believes that Gamma should be sold at the lowest price possible, to maximise the benefits of Gamma to society. However, the marketing department of 3C believes that it would be possible to earn very large profits from Gamma, due to its success rate and breakthrough status.

Required:

(a) Briefly explain how the product life cycle model can be used to analyse the current product portfolio of 3C (that is, BEFORE the planned investment). **(8 marks)**

(b) Evaluate the potential impact of each of the three investment options on the product portfolio of 3C, referring to your answer to part (a) above. **(9 marks)**

(c) Discuss the social responsibility implications of each of the three investment options, for the directors of 3C. **(8 marks)**

(Total: 25 marks)

3 ICOM

The Institute of Certified Operations Managers (ICOM) has a professional scheme of examinations, completed and supported by an acceptable portfolio of practical experience. ICOM also supports full members (those who have achieved certification, or have completed examinations and are in the process of gaining relevant experience) by offering a range of member services, including professional development courses. Similar services are offered by their close rival, the Operational Management Institute (OMI).

ICOM has experienced a decline in both full membership and student membership in the last five years, despite there being an increased demand for operations managers in organisations. In contrast, OMI has published data showing that it has increased student membership by 27% and full membership by 12% in the same time period. The revenue and profitability of ICOM, a company limited by guarantee, have also declined over the last five years.

There are opposing views within ICOM about the reason for the decline. Some directors, including John Turvey, believe that the absence of a formal strategic plan, identifying critical areas for success, has meant a lack of direction and focus. However, another member of the senior management team has suggested that the main reason for ICOM's problems is the inefficiency of the student recruitment process. He feels that the company needs to understand how other organisations (such as OMI) do this and to put changes in place to improve the process at ICOM.

Strategic planning

To support his viewpoint, John Turvey was asked to write a strategic plan to address how to regain lost membership and to grow market share, to compete with OMI. A mission statement, critical success factors (CSFs) and key performance indicators (KPIs) were to be included within the plan. As he had not completed a strategic plan before, John has asked for your views on the draft plan, part of which is shown below, which he intends to share with senior management.

Mission statement

I suggest that we replace our current mission statement 'Simply the best in operations management' with a more focused statement which states that 'Our mission is to satisfy the needs of our members, to inspire our student members and to motivate our staff to provide the best possible service'.

CSFs

These are the things we are going to focus on in the long term to help us to achieve growth and fulfil our mission statement. Altogether I have identified 35 critical success factors. The full list is available on our staff intranet, but the most important ones are shown below:

1   To satisfy our members

2   To grow membership by 5% year on year for the next five years

3   To maximise profits within acceptable risk

4   To ensure that the syllabus is in line with the current operations management environment

KPIs

Here are the KPIs which we should measure to help us assess the CSFs listed above:

1   95% of members rate us as excellent in an externally administered customer satisfaction survey

2   To implement a vigorous marketing campaign

3   Return on capital employed (ROCE) and margin of safety

4   To recruit an examinations manager to rewrite the syllabus

We should also adopt an integrated reporting approach so that stakeholders understand our mission, our strategy and all aspects of our business performance.

Required:

(a)   Critically evaluate the mission statement, critical success factors and key performance indicators suggested by John Turvey.   **(15 marks)**

(b)   Discuss how benchmarking could be used at ICOM, identifying any limitations in its application.   **(5 marks)**

(c)   Discuss the role of integrated reporting in relation to communicating strategy and business performance at ICOM.   **(5 marks)**

(Total: 25 marks)

4   SWIFT   📌 *Online question assistance*

Ambion is the third largest industrial country in the world. It is densely populated with a high standard of living. Joe Swift Transport (known as Swift) is the largest logistics company in Ambion, owning 1500 trucks. It is a private limited company with all shares held by the Swift family. It has significant haulage and storage contracts with retail and supermarket chains in Ambion. The logistics market-place is mature and extremely competitive and Swift has become market leader through a combination of economies of scale, cost efficiencies, innovative IT solutions and clever branding. However, the profitability of the sector is under increased pressure from a recently elected government that is committed to heavily taxing fuel and reducing expenditure on roads in favour of alternative forms of transport. It has also announced a number of taxes on vehicles which have high carbon emission levels as well as reducing the maximum working hours and increasing the national minimum wage for employees. The company is perceived as a good performer in its sector. The 20X9 financial results reported a Return on Capital Employed of 18%, a gross profit margin of 17% and a net profit margin of 9.15%. The accounts also showed a current liquidity ratio of 1.55 and an acid test ratio of 1.15. The gearing ratio is currently 60% with an interest cover ratio of 8.

10 years ago the northern political bloc split up and nine new independent states were formed. One of these states was Ecuria. The people of Ecuria (known as Ecurians) traditionally have a strong work ethic and a passion for precision and promptness. Since the formation of the state, their hard work has been rewarded by strong economic growth, a higher standard of living and an increased demand for goods which were once perceived as unobtainable luxuries. Since the formation of the state, the government of Ecuria has pursued a policy of privatisation. It has also invested heavily in infrastructure, particularly the road transport system, required to support the increased economic activity in the country.

The state haulage operator (EVM) was sold off to two Ecurian investors who raised the finance to buy it from a foreign bank. The capital markets in Ecuria are still immature and the government has not wished to interfere with or bolster them. EVM now has 700 modern trucks and holds all the major logistics contracts in the country. It is praised for its prompt delivery of goods. Problems in raising finance have made it difficult for significant competitors to emerge. Most are family firms, each of which operates about 20 trucks making local deliveries within one of Ecuria's 20 regions.

These two investors now wish to realise their investment in EVM and have announced that it is for sale. In principle, Swift are keen to buy the company and are currently evaluating its possible acquisition. Swift's management perceive that their capabilities in logistics will greatly enhance the profitability of EVM. The financial results for EVM are shown in Figure 1. Swift has acquired a number of smaller Ambion companies in the last decade, but has no experience of acquiring foreign companies, or indeed, working in Ecuria.

Joe Swift is also contemplating a more radical change. He is becoming progressively disillusioned with Ambion. In a recent interview he said that 'trading here is becoming impossible. The government is more interested in over regulating enterprise than stimulating growth'. He is considering moving large parts of his logistics operation to another country and Ecuria is one of the possibilities he is considering.

Figure 1 – Extract from financial results: EVM 20X9

Extract from the statement of financial position

	$million
Assets	
Non-current assets	
Intangible assets	2,000
Property, plant, equipment	6,100
	8,100
Current assets	
Inventories	100
Trade receivables	900
Cash and cash equivalents	200
	1,200
Total assets	9,300

	$million
Equity and liabilities	
Equity	
Share capital	5,700
Retained earnings	50
Total equity	5,750
Non-current liabilities	
Long-term borrowings	2,500
Current liabilities	
Trade payables	1,000
Current tax payable	50
	1,050
Total liabilities	3,550
Total equity and liabilities	9,300

Extract from statement of profit or loss

	$million
Revenue	20,000
Cost of sales	(16,000)
Gross profit	4,000
Administrative expenses	(2,500)
Finance cost	(300)
Profit before tax	1,200
Income tax expense	(50)
Profit for the year	1,150

Required:

(a) Assess, using both financial and non-financial measures, the attractiveness, from Swift's perspective, of EVM as an acquisition target. **(15 marks)**

(b) Porter's Diamond can be used to explore the competitive advantage of nations and could be a useful model for Joe Swift to use in his analysis of countries that he might move his company to.

Examine using Porter's Diamond (or an appropriate alternative model/framework) the factors which could influence Swift's decision to move a large part of its logistics business to Ecuria. **(10 marks)**

(Total: 25 marks)

> **Online question assistance**

5 BOWLAND

> **Timed question with Online tutor debrief**

Bowland Carpets Ltd is a major producer of carpets within the UK. The company was taken over by its present parent company, Universal Carpet Inc., in 20X3. Universal Carpet is a giant, vertically integrated carpet manufacturing and retailing business, based within the USA but with interests all over the world.

Bowland Carpets operates within the UK in various market segments, including the high value contract and industrial carpeting area – hotels and office blocks, etc. – and in the domestic (household) market. Within the latter the choice is reasonably wide, ranging from luxury carpets down to the cheaper products. Industrial and contract carpets contribute 25% of Bowland Carpets' total annual turnover which is currently $80 million. Up until 15 years ago the turnover of the company was growing at 8% per annum, but since 20X2 sales revenue has dropped by 5% per annum in real terms.

Bowland Carpets has traditionally been known as a producer of high quality carpets, but at competitive prices. It has a powerful brand name, and it has been able to protect this by producing the cheaper, lower quality products under a secondary brand name. It has also maintained a good relationship with the many carpet distributors throughout the UK, particularly the mainstream retail organisations.

The recent decline in carpet sales revenue, partly recession induced, has worried the US parent company. It has recognised that the increasing concentration within the European carpet manufacturing sector has led to aggressive competition within a low growth industry. It does not believe that overseas sales growth by Bowland Carpets is an attractive proposition as this would compete with other Universal Carpet companies. It does, however, consider that vertical integration into retailing (as already practised within the USA) is a serious option. This would give the UK company increased control over its sales and reduce its exposure to competition. The president of the parent company has asked Jeremy Smiles, managing director of Bowland Carpets, to address this issue and provide guidance to the US board of directors. Funding does not appear to be a major issue at this time as the parent company has large cash reserves on its balance sheet.

Required:

Acting in the capacity of Jeremy Smiles you are required to outline the various issues which might be of significance for the management of the parent company. Your answer should cover the following:

(a)   **To what extent do the distinctive competences of Bowland Carpets conform with the key success factors required for the proposed strategy change?   (10 marks)**

(b)   **In an external environmental analysis concerning the proposed strategy shift what are likely to be the key external influences which could impact upon the Bowland Carpets' decision?   (15 marks)**

(Total: 25 marks)

Calculate your allowed time, allocate the time to the separate parts...............

6   MCGEORGE HOLDINGS PLC

McGeorge Holdings plc is a large, international consumer goods company specialising in household cleaning products and toiletries. It has many manufacturing and sales facilities throughout the world. Over several years it has offered an increasingly wide range of products appealing to differing market segments based on both socio-demographic and geographic criteria. However this product spread has not only resulted in increased sales volume but production, marketing and distribution costs have also increased disproportionately. McGeorge's costs are now about 20% higher than those of its nearest competitors. In such a competitive market it is difficult to pass on these extra costs to the customer.

In order to regain a competitive position Adrian Reed, the Managing Director of McGeorge Holdings, has been advised to reduce the range of products and the product lines. Advisors have suggested that a cut back in the product mix by about 20% could increase profits by at least 40%. Reed is keen to implement such a product divestment strategy but he fears that this cutting back could alienate customers. He needs to know which products need to be removed and which products are important to the survival of the company. He is unhappy about the overall performance of his company's activities. Benchmarking has been recommended as a method of assessing how his company's performance compares with that of his competitors.

Required:

(a) **Using appropriate analytical models discuss how Adrian Reed might select the products to be removed from the portfolio as part of his product divestment strategy.** **(13 marks)**

(b) **Examine how benchmarking can be carried out and discuss its limitations.**

(12 marks)

(Total: 25 marks)

7   NESTA

NESTA is a large chain of fixed-price discount stores based in the country of Eyanke. Its stores offer ambient goods (goods that require no cold storage and can be kept at room temperature, such as cleaning products, stationery, biscuits and plastic storage units) at a fixed price of one dollar. Everything in the store retails at this price. Fixed-price discount chains focus on unbranded commodity goods which they buy from a number of small suppliers, for which the dollar shops are the most significant customers. Profit margins on the products they sell are low and overheads are kept to a minimum. The target price is fixed. The products tend to be functional, standardised and undifferentiated.

NESTA has observed the long-term economic decline in the neighbouring country of Eurobia, where a prolonged economic recession has led to the growth of so-called 'dollar shops'. Three significant dollar shop chains have developed: ItzaDollar, DAIAD and DollaFellas (see Table One). The shops of these three chains are particularly found on the high streets of towns and cities where there is significant financial hardship. Many of these towns and cities have empty stores which are relatively cheap to rent. Furthermore, landlords who once required high rents and long leases are increasingly willing to rent these stores for a relatively short fixed-term lease. The fixed-price dollar shop chains in Eurobia advertise extensively and continually stress their expansion plans. Few weeks go by without one of the chains announcing plans for a significant number of new shops throughout the country.

NESTA has recognised the growth of fixed-price discount retailers in Eurobia and is considering entering this market.

NESTA recently commissioned a brand awareness survey in Eurobia. The survey results showed that NESTA was relatively well-known to respondents who work in the consumer goods retail market. Most of these respondents correctly identified the company as a discount fixed-price company with a significant presence in Eyanke. However, amongst general consumers, only 5% of the respondents had heard of NESTA. In contrast, the three current fixed-price dollar shop discounters in Eurobia were recognised by more than 90% of the respondents.

NESTA itself has revenue of $120,000 million. It has cash reserves which could allow it to lease a significant number of shops in Eurobia and establish a credible market presence. It has recognised competencies in effective supplier selection and management, supported by effective procurement systems. Its logistics systems and methods are core strengths of the company.

There are also many conventional supermarket chains operating in Eurobia. The largest of these has annual revenue of $42,500 million. Supermarkets in Eurobia tend to increasingly favour out-of-town sites which allow the stores to stock a wide range and quantity of products. Customer car parking is plentiful and it is relatively easy for supplying vehicles to access such sites. As well as stocking non-ambient goods, most supermarkets do also stock a very wide range of ambient goods, often with competing brands on offer. However, prices for such goods vary and no supermarkets have yet adopted the discount fixed-price sales approach. In general, the large supermarket chains largely compete with each other and pay little attention to the fixed-price dollar shop discounters. Many supermarkets also have internet-based home ordering systems, offering (usually for a fee of $10) deliveries to customers who are unable or unwilling to visit the supermarket.

Table One shows the relative revenue of the three main discount fixed-price chains in Eurobia.

	20X2 ($million)	20X1 ($million)	20X0 ($million)
ItzaDollar	330	300	275
DAIAD*	310	290	250
DollaFellas	290	235	200
Total	930	825	725

*Don't Ask it's A Dollar

Table One: Revenue of three main discount fixed-price chains in Eurobia

Required:

(a) Use Porter's five forces framework to assess the attractiveness, to NESTA, of entering the discount fixed-price retail market in Eurobia. **(15 marks)**

(b) Discuss the potential use of scenarios by NESTA's managers as part of their analysis of NESTA's possible entry into the discount fixed-price retail market in Eurobia.

(10 marks)

(Total: 25 marks)

8 ATD

ATD is a medium-sized engineering company providing specialist components for the marine engineering market. The sales manager is currently under pressure from the other departmental managers to explain why his sales revenue forecasts are becoming increasingly unreliable. Errors in his forecasts are having consequential effects on production, inventory control, raw materials purchasing and, ultimately, on the profitability of the company itself. He uses a 'combination of experience, intuition and guesswork' to produce his sales forecast, but even he accepts that his forecasts are increasingly inaccurate.

Consequently, he has asked a business analyst to investigate more rigorous, appropriate ways of forecasting. The business analyst has suggested two possible alternatives. The first (summarised in Figure 1) is least squares regression. The second (summarised in Figure 2) is time series analysis. The actual sales figures in both of these examples are for ATD, so the company is currently in quarter 3 − 2013. However, the business analyst has left the company before completing and explaining either the basis for, or implications of, these two alternative approaches to forecasting.

Figure 1: Least squares analysis

Year/quarter	x	y	x^2	xy	y^2
	Quarter sales ($000)				
20X0 quarter 1	1	110	1	110	12,100
20X0 quarter 2	2	160	4	320	25,600
20X0 quarter 3	3	155	9	465	24,025
20X0 quarter 4	4	96	16	384	9,216
20X1 quarter 1	5	116	25	580	13,456
20X1 quarter 2	6	160	36	960	25,600
20X1 quarter 3	7	153	49	1,071	23,409
20X1 quarter 4	8	100	64	800	10,000
20X2 quarter 1	9	128	81	1,152	16,384
20X2 quarter 2	10	180	100	1,800	32,400
20X2 quarter 3	11	169	121	1,859	28,561
20X2 quarter 4	12	99	144	1,188	9,801
20X3 quarter 1	13	137	169	1,781	18,769
20X3 quarter 2	14	180	196	2,520	32,400
		1,943	1,015	14,990	281,721

Other data:

b	1.84
a	125.022
r	0.253

The equation of a straight line is y = a + bx

Figure 2: Time series analysis

Quarter	Sales ($000)	Trend	Deviation	Svar (1)	Residual	Sadj (2)
20X0 quarter 1	110					124.70
20X0 quarter 2	160					127.77
20X0 quarter 3	155	131.00	24.00	22.55	1.45	132.45
20X0 quarter 4	96	131.75	−35.75	−40.08	4.33	136.08
20X1 quarter 1	116	131.50	−15.50	−14.70	−0.80	130.70
20X1 quarter 2	160	131.75	28.25	32.23	−3.98	127.77
20X1 quarter 3	153	133.75	19.25	22.55	−3.30	130.45
20X1 quarter 4	100	137.75	−37.75	−40.08	2.33	140.08
20X2 quarter 1	128	142.25	−14.25	−14.70	0.45	142.70
20X2 quarter 2	180	144.13	35.88	32.23	3.64	147.77
20X2 quarter 3	169	145.13	23.88	22.55	1.33	146.45
20X2 quarter 4	99	146.25	−47.25	−40.08	−7.17	139.08
20X3 quarter 1	137					151.70
20X3 quarter 2	180					147.77

Analysis of seasonal variation		*1*	*2*	*3*	*4*	
				24.00	−35.75	
		−15.50	28.25	19.25	−37.75	
		−14.25	35.88	23.88	−47.25	
Totals		−29.75	64.13	67.13	−120.75	
Average		−14.88	32.06	22.38	−40.25	−0.69
Adjustment		0.17	0.17	0.17	0.17	
Svar (1)		−14.70	32.23	22.55	−40.08	

Note 1: Svar: seasonal variation

Note 2: Sadj: seasonally adjusted figures

The failure of the company to meet sales targets for quarters 1 and 2 of 2013 has prompted the Chief Executive Officer (CEO) to put into place a broad cost-cutting policy. He has banned business travel, cancelled a number of marketing initiatives and introduced a complete freeze on recruiting for posts which become vacant on the resignation of the current post holder. He claims that 'our failure to meet sales targets means we must ruthlessly cut costs'. However, many of the departmental managers are critical of such an indiscriminate approach and believe that the measures might be counter-productive.

This cost-cutting has particularly demotivated the production manager and the inventory manager, who both blame the sales director for setting unrealistic targets. The production manager has commented that, 'I am working tirelessly to keep costs down, but my only reward is that I cannot replace one of my best purchasing administrators who left last month'. In general, departmental managers at the company feel 'powerless and undervalued'.

The company currently does not have a formal budgeting process in place. The production manager is sure that such a process, particularly if senior managers were involved in the budget setting process, would help address issues around forecast reliability, the low morale of departmental managers and the seemingly indiscriminate cost-cutting of the CEO.

Required:

(a) Explain and analyse the data in the least squares regression and time series analysis spreadsheets (Figure 1 and 2) left by the business analyst and evaluate the appropriateness of both techniques to sales forecasting at ATD. **(15 marks)**

(b) Analyse how introducing a formal budgeting process would address the issues of inaccurate forecasting, low morale and indiscriminate cost cutting at ATD.

(10 marks)

(Total: 25 marks)

9 RETAIL WORLD

Retail World (RW) is a major international retail chain, selling groceries, clothing, electronic items, toiletries and homeware items. It has grown rapidly across a number of different countries, offering a broad product range to suit a wide range of customer segments. Growth has been through the expansion of existing stores, in addition to the opening of new stores.

The new finance director, whose background is in a non-retail environment, is keen to understand the sales trends of the organisation, as well as the industry, in order to help develop a strategy which can take advantage of these trends in the future. A business analyst has provided summarised internal sales data for this purpose. The company's IT systems are fully integrated and associated controls are rigorous, allowing the data to be manipulated in many ways. The analyst has provided time series analysis (Figure 1) and regression analysis (Figures 2 and 3). He wanted to explore the possibility of identifying different causal relationships, carrying out least squares regression analysis linking sales to both time (Figure 2) and number of stores in operation (Figure 3).

The number of stores has grown annually and the analyst believes that this is a better indicator of the expected future revenue than simply the passage of time. The average number of stores expected to be in operation in 2017 is 3,700 rising to 4,000 in 2018.

Figure 1 – Time series analysis

Year/quarter	Sales ($m)	Trend (T)	Deviation	Svar (1)	Res	Sadj (2)
2013 2	88					116.25
2013 3	110					121.38
2013 4	134	121.38	12.63	14.60	−1.98	119.40
2014 1	150	122.50	27.50	25.02	2.48	124.98
2014 2	95	123.25	−28.25	−28.25	0.00	123.25
2014 3	112	123.75	−11.75	−11.38	−0.38	123.38
2014 4	138	124.38	13.63	14.60	−0.98	123.40
2015 1	150	126.00	24.00	25.02	−1.02	124.98
2015 2	100	128.63	−28.63	−28.25	−0.38	128.25
2015 3	120	131.38	−11.38	−11.38	0.00	131.38
2015 4	151	134.00	17.00	14.60	2.40	136.40
2016 1	159	136.00	23.00	25.02	−2.02	133.98
2016 2	112					140.25
2016 3	124					135.38

Notes:

(1) Svar is the expected seasonal variation, calculated by averaging the variations of each quarter.

(2) Sadj is the sales total, adjusted for average seasonal variation.

Figure 2 – Least squares regression analysis (time)

An extract of the values used in the calculation of this is shown below. This illustrates the basis of the regression analysis. All values were used in the calculation of the least squares regression formula.

Year/quarter	quarter (x)	revenue (y)
2016 1	12	159
2016 2	13	112
2016 3	14	124

The least squares regression formula derived from **all data** was found to be:

$$Y = 110.93 + 1.81x \qquad\qquad r = 0.33$$

Figure 3 – Least squares regression analysis (number of stores)

The values used in the calculation of this are shown below:

Year	stores (x)	average quarterly sales (y)
2013	2,400	111
2014	2,750	124
2015	3,200	130
2016	3,512	132

The least squares regression formula derived from this data was found to be:

Y = 69.50 + 0.02x   r = 0.94

The finance director was interested to receive the analysis, saying, 'We can use this to estimate what our revenues might be in the future, both quarterly and annually.' However, he also stated that it was not quite as useful as he would have hoped for, commenting, 'I have been hearing a lot about big data at industry meetings I have attended. I think we should investigate the ways in which we could use this, and the benefits we might hope to obtain from it.'

Required:

(a) Analyse the data given above in the time series analysis and least squares regression analysis (Figures 1, 2 and 3) and evaluate the appropriateness of each technique in forecasting future sales and developing strategic plans.   **(15 marks)**

(b) Discuss how three 'Vs' of big data (volume, velocity and variety) could be used to enhance strategic development within RW.   **(10 marks)**

(Total: 25 marks)

10   MOOR FARM

Moor Farm is a large estate in the rural district of Cornaille. The estate covers a large area of forest, upland and farmland. It also includes two villages, and although many of the properties in these villages have been sold off to private homeowners, the estate still owns properties which it rents out. The estate also has a large mansion house set inside a landscape garden designed in the 19th century by James Kent. The garden, although now overgrown and neglected, is the only surviving example of his work in the district. The estate was left as a gift to a charitable trust ten years ago. The trust is based at the estate. A condition of the gift to the trust was that the upland and forest should be freely accessible to visitors.

The estate has a manager, four full-time staff and 45 volunteers. These volunteers undertake most of the work on the estate, including the continuing excavation of Kent's original garden design. They are happy, well-motivated and fully support the current manager who is due to retire in the very near future. Three of the volunteers have become acknowledged experts on land management, through their work on the estate. Government grants for initiatives such as tree planting, protected pasture land and rural employment have been received by the estate in the past. However, a recent change in government means that this funding is unlikely to continue. This will also affect funding for the maintenance of the mansion. It was built almost 80 years ago when the climate of the area was much colder and drier. Recent warm wet winters have caused the fabric of the building to decay and increased the cost of maintaining it.

The estate has appointed a new manager who is due to take over the estate when the current manager retires. She is working alongside the current manager so that she understands her responsibilities and how the estate works. As a one-off project, she has commissioned a stakeholder survey which has requested information on the visitor experience to help with a planned re-design of the estate's website. The website is generally thought to be well structured and presented, but it receives fewer visitors than might reasonably be expected. It provides mainly static information about the estate and forthcoming events but currently users cannot interact with the site in anyway.

Here are some extracts from the survey:

'I live in one of the villages and I am angry about visitors crowding around the village attractions – the tearooms, the craft shops, the souvenir stalls. We feel that we are prisoners in our own village and the traffic is terrible.' **Homeowner, from a village on the estate**

'We had a good day, but the weather was awful. If we had known it was going to rain all day, then we probably would have postponed the visit until a fine day. It spoilt a family day out.' **Visitor with small family**

'We were very disappointed, on arrival, to find that the family fun day was fully booked.' **Visitor who had travelled 100 kms with two small children to visit a special event**

'We all love it here, but we didn't know you had a website!! We almost had to type in the complete website address before we found it! I am sure more people would come if they could only find the website!' **Visitor aged mid-20s**

'As usual, we had a great time here and took great photos. It would have been nice to be able to share our pleasure with other people. We would recommend it to anyone who loves the outdoors.' **Visitor – family with teenage children**

'We met the volunteers who were excavating the buildings in the landscape garden. They were so helpful and knowledgeable. They turned something that looked like a series of small walls into something so much more tangible.' **Visitor – elderly couple**

'I was disappointed that I was not allowed into the farmland with my dog. As a human being, I have the right to roam. It is a basic human right.' **Visitor – elderly female dog-walker**

'We are regular visitors and we really want to know what is going on! There are many of us who would like to really be involved with the estate and help it thrive. We need more than just occasional questionnaires.' **Visitor – hiking group**

'We came out for a nice walk and ended up dodging cyclists. Next time we will go somewhere where they are not welcome.' **Visitor – hiking group**

'As a farmer, I am appalled with the reckless attitude of some dog walkers. Last week, I lost two sheep, ravaged by dogs that should not have been off their leads.' **Farmer – estate tenant**

'I'm a volunteer and I love it here. We are a happy, social group of people. I hope the new manager is not going to change things.' **Volunteer**

Required:

(a) Evaluate the strategic position of the estate with specific reference to the expectations of stakeholders, to the external environmental factors beyond the control of the estate and to the strategic capabilities of the estate itself. **(15 marks)**

(b) Discuss how the website could be further developed to address some of the issues highlighted in the survey. **(10 marks)**

(Total: 25 marks)

11   ONE ENERGY PLC   *Walk in the footsteps of a top tutor*

OneEnergy plc supplies over half of the electricity and gas in the country. It is an expanding, aggressive company which has recently acquired two smaller, but significant, competitors.

Just over a year ago, OneEnergy purchased the RitePay payroll software package from RiteSoftware. The recently appointed Human Resources (HR) director of OneEnergy recommended the package because he had used it successfully at his previous employer – a major charity. His unreserved recommendation was welcomed by the board because the company was currently running three incompatible payroll systems. The purchase of the RitePay payroll system appeared to offer the opportunity to quickly consolidate the three separate payroll systems into one improved solution. The board decided to purchase the software without evaluating alternative solutions. It was felt that payroll rules and processes were relatively standard and so there was no need to look further than a package recommended by the HR director. The software was purchased and a project initiated for converting the data from the current systems and for training users in the features and functions of the new software.

However, it soon became apparent that there were problems with the suitability of the RitePay software package. Firstly, OneEnergy had a wide variety of reward and pay schemes to reflect previous employment in the acquired companies and to accommodate a wide range of different skills and grades. Not all of these variations could be handled by the package. Consequently, amendments had to be commissioned from the software house. This led to unplanned costs and also to delays in implementation. Secondly, it also became clear that the software was not as user-friendly as the previous systems. Users had problems understanding some of the terminology and structure of the software. 'It just does not work like we do', commented one frustrated user. Consequently users made more errors than expected and training costs exceeded their budget.

Three months ago, another set of amendments was requested from RiteSoftware to allow one of the acquired companies in OneEnergy to pay bonuses to lorry drivers in a certain way. Despite repeated requests, the amendments were not received. Two weeks ago, it was announced that RiteSoftware had filed for bankruptcy and all software support was suspended. Just before this was announced the HR director of OneEnergy left the company to take up a similar post in the public sector.

OneEnergy has engaged W&P consultants to advise them on the RitePay project. An interim report from W&P suggests that OneEnergy should abandon the RitePay package. 'It is clear to us that RitePay never had the functionality required to fulfil the variety of requirements inevitable in a company the size of OneEnergy.' They also commented that this could have been avoided if the project had followed the competitive procurement policy defined in company operating procedures.

W&P also reports that:

- The procurement department at OneEnergy had requested two years of accounts from RiteSoftware. These were provided (see Figure 1) but not interpreted or used in the selection process in any way. W&P concluded 'that there were clear signs that the company was in difficulty and this should have led to further investigation'.

- They discovered that the former HR director of OneEnergy was the brother of the managing director of RiteSoftware.

Figure 1: RiteSoftware Accounts

Extract from the statement of financial position

	$000	
Assets		
Non-current assets	*20X8*	*20X7*
Property, plant and equipment	30	25
Goodwill	215	133
	245	158
Current assets		
Inventories	3	2
Trade receivables	205	185
	208	187
Total assets	453	345
Liabilities		
Current liabilities		
Trade payables	257	178
Current tax payable	1	2
Bank overdraft	10	25
	268	205
Non-current liabilities		
Long-term borrowings	80	35
Total liabilities	348	240
Equity		
Share capital	105	105
Total equity and liabilities	453	345

Extract from the statement of statement of profit and loss

	$000	
Revenue	2,650	2,350
Cost of sales	(2,600)	(2,300)
Gross profit	50	50
Other costs	(30)	(20)
Finance costs	(10)	(4)
Profit before tax	10	26
Income tax expense	(1)	(2)
Profit for the year	9	24

Extract from the annual report

Number of staff	90	70

Required:

(a)   W&P concluded in their report 'that there were clear signs that the company (RiteSoftware) was in difficulty and this should have led to further investigation'.

Assess, using the financial information available, the validity of W&P's conclusion.

(13 marks)

(b)   Examine FOUR ways in which OneEnergy failed to follow a proper evaluation procedure in the selection of the RitePay software package. Include in your examination a discussion of the implication of each failing.   (12 marks)

(Total: 25 marks)

12   INDEPENDENT LIVING

Introduction

IL (Independent Living) is a charity that provides living aids to help elderly and disabled people live independently in their own home. These aids include walkers, wheelchairs, walking frames, crutches, mobility scooters, bath lifts and bathroom and bedroom accessories.

IL aims to employ people who would find it difficult or impossible to work in a conventional office or factory. IL's charitable aim is to provide the opportunity for severely disabled people to 'work with dignity and achieve financial independence'. IL currently employs 200 severely disabled people and 25 able bodied people at its premises on an old disused airfield site. The former aircraft hangars have been turned into either production or storage facilities, all of which have been adapted for severely disabled people.

Smaller items (such as walking frames and crutches) are manufactured here. These are relatively unsophisticated products, manufactured from scrap metal bought from local scrap metal dealers and stored on-site. These products require no testing or training to use and they are packaged and stored after manufacture. IL uses its own lorry to make collections of scrap metal but the lorry is old, unreliable and will soon need replacing.

Larger and more complex items (such as mobility scooters and bath lifts) are bought in bulk from suppliers and stored in the hangars. Delivery of these items to IL is organised by their manufacturers. These products are stored until they are ordered.

When an order is received for such products, the product is unpacked and tested. An IL transfer logo is then applied and the product is re-packaged in the original packing material with an IL label attached. It is then dispatched to the customer. Some inventory is never ordered and last year IL had to write-off a significant amount of obsolete inventory.

All goods are sold at cost plus a margin to cover wages and administrative costs. Prices charged are the same whether goods are ordered over the web or by telephone. Customers can also make a further voluntary donation to help support IL if they wish to. About 30% of customers do make such a donation.

Ordering and marketing

IL markets its products by placing single-sided promotional leaflets in hospitals, doctors' surgeries and local social welfare departments. This leaflet provides information about IL and gives a direct phone number and a web address. Customers may purchase products by ringing IL directly or by ordering over their website. The website provides product information and photos of the products which are supplied by IL. It also has a secure payment facility. However, customers who ring IL directly have to discuss product requirements and potential purchases with sales staff over the phone. Each sales discussion takes, on average, ten minutes and only one in two contacts results in a sale. 20% of sales are through their website (up from 15% last year), but many of their customers are unfamiliar with the Internet and do not have access to it. Goods are delivered to customers by a national courier service. Service and support for the bought-in products (mobility scooters, bath lifts) are supplied by the original manufacturer.

Commercial competitors

IL is finding it increasingly difficult to compete with commercial firms offering independent living aids. Last year, the charity made a deficit of $160,000, and it had to sell some of its airfield land to cover this. Many of the commercial firms it is competing with have sophisticated sales and marketing operations and then arrange delivery to customers directly from manufacturers based in low labour cost countries.

Required:

IL fears for its future and has decided to review its value chain to see how it can achieve competitive advantage.

(a) **Analyse the primary activities of the value chain for the product range at IL.**

(10 marks)

(b) **Evaluate what changes IL might consider to the primary activities in the value chain to improve their competitiveness, whilst continuing to meet their charitable objectives.**

(15 marks)

(Total: 25 marks)

13   NOBLE PETS

Noble Pets is one of four companies which dominate the pet food market in the country of Brellia. Between them, these four companies share 90% of the market. Noble Pets was established in 1930 in the market town of Milton. Its factory (plant) was updated in 1970 with new canning and labelling technology. However, further developments and expansion to the factory site were prevented by the rapid growth of housing in Milton. The factory, which was once on the edge of the town, is now surrounded by modern housing development. The town is also relatively remote from the motorway network which has been developed in Brellia since 1960. Trucks transporting goods in and out of the plant have to negotiate relatively minor rural roads and also have to pass through the town centre of Milton, which is often very congested. Furthermore, the large 44 tonne trucks which Noble Pets and its competitors use, wherever possible, to distribute cans of pet food to wholesalers and supermarket distribution centres are banned from the centre of the town. Thus distribution out of the Milton plant is undertaken with smaller 36 tonne trucks, which are less cost-effective. However, residents find even this size of truck too large, complaining that they keep them awake at night.

The Milton plant is solely concerned with the production of moist pet food. Raw foodstuff and empty unlabelled cans are brought into the plant, where the foodstuff is cooked and put into cans which are then labelled and distributed to wholesalers or supermarket distribution centres. Many of these distribution centres, like Noble Pets' competitors, are now located on or near the motorway network. Although the recipe for the pet food is very similar to its competitors, Noble Pets has a reputation for producing a quality product. This quality has been promoted ever since the company's formation by clever marketing campaigns which stress the importance of giving your pet good food, and the superior nature of Noble Pets' products to its competitors. This has traditionally been supported by free fact guides and information promoting responsible pet ownership and nutrition. The company now has a website dedicated to giving advice and guidance. This advice appears to be unbiased, although recommended solutions to pet problems often involve Noble Pets' products.

Noble Pets is currently reviewing its operations and has asked external consultants to assess the Milton plant from a value chain perspective. It has provided the following table (Table One) to help in that analysis. Average figures for its competitors are also provided.

Production cost of a six can pack of moist pet food All figures in $	Milton Factory	Competitor A	Competitor B	Competitor C
Raw foodstuff costs	0.10	0.10	0.09	0.15
Cost of cans	0.05	0.10	0.06	0.05
Direct labour costs	0.25	0.25	0.30	0.24
Production costs	0.30	0.25	0.20	0.26
Transport costs (good inward)	0.15	0.10	0.10	0.12
Transport costs (good outward)	0.10	0.05	0.05	0.08
Sales price (to customer)	**1.25**	**1.15**	**1.10**	**1.20**

Table One: Direct costs of the Milton plant compared to major competitors

Dry pet food is an alternative to moist pet food. It is packaged in bags and it is in the form of a biscuit. Many people who buy pet food prefer the dry food because it does not smell and can be left in the pet's bowl for longer. Noble Pets also produces dry pet food, but not at its Milton plant. It would like to reduce costs at Milton but it is concerned that the demand for moist pet food will not justify such investment. Consequently, it has also asked the consultants to look at the pet food market as a whole and to forecast demand for moist pet food for the next three years (20X7, 20X8 and 20X9). It is aware that new technology is available (and is already being used by its competitors) which offers more efficient and reliable canning, but it is not sure that it is worth investing in.

The consultants have identified the following information provided by the Pet Food Industry Group.

Years	Year (x)	Moist pet food (000s tonnes) (y)	Dry pet food (000s tonnes)
20X0	1	370	292
20X1	2	350	307
20X2	3	331	321
20X3	4	325	329
20X4	5	315	341
20X5	6	310	351
20X6	7	310	359

Table Two: Production of pet food (20X0–20X6)

A linear regression analysis has been conducted for the moist food production. Time (years) is represented as x (the independent variable) and moist pet food volume as y. The linear regression analysis has identified the following values of a, b and r for the relationship between time and moist pet food production.

a	b	r
369.5714	−9.86	−0.94432

Noble Pets currently has a market share of 30% of the moist food market, a share which has remained unchanged since 20X0. It has three sites. As well as the Milton plant it has two other plants. These two plants combined have an annual maximum capacity of 40,000 tonnes of moist pet food.

Required:

(a) Evaluate the strengths and weaknesses of the Milton plant from the perspective of the primary activities of a value chain analysis. **(15 marks)**

(b) (i) Analyse trends in the pet food industry **(5 marks)**

(ii) Forecast demand for moist pet food for the next three years, as required by Noble Pets, using the regression formula given and comment on the validity and implications of that forecast. **(5 marks)**

(Total: 25 marks)

STRATEGIC CHOICE

14   GRAFFOFF

Emile Gonzalez is an industrial chemist who worked for the government of Pablos for more than 20 years. In his spare time, he continually experimented with formulating a product that could remove graffiti from all surfaces. Graffiti is a particular problem in Pablos and all previous removal methods were expensive, dangerous to apply and did not work on all surfaces. After many years of experimentation, Emile formulated a product that addressed all these issues. His product can be applied safely without protective clothing, it removes graffiti from all surfaces and it can be produced economically in small, as well as large, volumes.

Three years ago, Emile left his government job to focus on refining the product and bringing it to market. He formed a limited liability company, Graffoff, with initial share capital funded by his savings, his family's savings and a legacy from a wealthy relative. He is the sole shareholder in the company, which is based in a factory in central Pablos. The company has filed two years of results (see Figure 1 for extracted information from year (2), and it is expected to return similar net profit figures in its third trading year. Emile takes a significant dividend out of the company each year and he wishes that to continue. He also wishes to remain the sole owner of the company.

Four years ago, Emile was granted a patent for the formula on which his product is based and a further patent on the process used to produce the product. In Pablos, patents are protected for ten years and so Emile has six further years before his formula becomes available to his competitors. Consequently, he wants to rapidly expand the company and plans to lease premises to create 30 new graffiti removal depots in Pablos, each of which will supply graffiti removing services in its local region. He needs $500,000 to finance this organic growth of his company.

Emile does have mixed feelings about his proposed expansion plan. Despite the apparent success of his company, he prefers working in the laboratory to managing people. 'I am just not a people person', he has commented. He is aware that he lacks business experience and, despite the technical excellence of the product, he has failed to build a highly visible brand. He also has particular problems in the accounts receivables department, where he has failed to address the problems of over-worked and demotivated employees. Emile dislikes conflict with customers and so he often offers them extended payment terms to the dismay of the accounts receivables section, who feel that their debt collecting effectiveness is being constantly undermined by his concessions. In contrast, Graffoff pays bills very promptly, due to a zealous administrator in accounts payable who likes to reduce creditors. Emile is sanguine about this. 'I guess we have the money, so I suppose we should pay them.'

In Pablos, all goods are supplied to customers on 30 days credit. However, in the services sector that Graffoff is trading in, the average settlement period for payables (creditors) is 40 days. One supplier commented that 'Graffoff is unique in its punctuality of payment.'

Emile is currently reviewing how to finance his proposed organic growth. He is unwilling to take on any further external debt and consequently he has also recently considered franchising as an alternative to organic growth. In his proposed arrangement, franchisees would have responsibility for leasing or buying premises to a specification defined in the franchise agreement. The franchise would have exclusive rights to the Graffoff product in a defined geographical region.

The Equipment Emporium has 57 superstores throughout the country selling tools and machines such as air compressors, generators and ventilation systems. It is a well-recognised brand with a strong marketing presence. It focuses on selling specialist products in bright, well-lit superstores. It has approached Graffoff to ask whether it can sell the Graffoff product through its superstores. Emile has rejected this suggestion because he feels that his product requires proper training if it is to be used efficiently and safely. He sees Graffoff as offering a complete service (graffiti removal), not just a product (graffiti removal equipment) and so selling through The Equipment Emporium would be inappropriate.

Figure 1: Extracted financial data for Graffoff's second year of trading, reported at 31 December 20X1

Extract from the statement of financial position: as at 31 December 20X1		*Extracts from the income statement:* as at 31 December 20X1	
All figures in $000:		All figures in $000	
ASSETS		Revenue	1,600
Non-current assets		Cost of sales	(1,375)
Property, plant and equipment	1,385	Gross profit	225
Intangible assets	100	Administrative expenses	(100)
Total non-current assets	1,485	Finance costs	(15)
Current assets		Profit before tax	110
Inventories	100	Income tax expense	(20)
Trade receivables	260	Profit for the period	90
Cash and cash equivalents	30		
Total current assets	390		
Total assets	1,875		
EQUITY AND LIABILITIES			
Share capital	1,500		
Retained earnings	30		
Total equity	1,530		
Non-current liabilities			
Long-term borrowings	250		
Total non-current liabilities	250		
Current liabilities			
Trade and other payables	75		
Current tax payable	20		
Total current liabilities	95		
Total liabilities	345		
Total equity and liabilities	1,875		

Required:

(a)   Evaluate the franchising option being considered by Graffoff, highlighting the advantages and disadvantages of this approach from Emile's perspective.

(10 marks)

(b)   Johnson, Scholes and Whittington have identified franchising as a form of strategic alliance.

Evaluate how other forms of strategic alliance might be appropriate approaches to strategy development at Graffoff.   (7 marks)

(c)   A consultant has suggested that Graffoff should be able to completely fund its proposed organic expansion (at a cost of $500,000) through internally generated sources of finance.

Evaluate this claim.   (8 marks)

(Total: 25 marks)

15   ENVIRONMENT MANAGEMENT SOCIETY

The Environment Management Society (EMS) was established in 1999 by environment practitioners who felt that environmental management and audit should have its own qualification. EMS has its own Board who report to a Council of eight members. Policy is made by the Board and ratified by Council. EMS is registered as a private limited entity.

EMS employs staff to administer its qualification and to provide services to its members. The qualification began as one certificate, developed by the original founding members of the Society. It has since been developed, by members and officers of the EMS, into a four certificate scheme leading to a Diploma. EMS employs a full-time chief examiner who is responsible for setting the certificate examinations which take place monthly in training centres throughout the country. No examinations are currently held in other countries.

If candidates pass all four papers they can undertake an oral Diploma examination. If they pass this oral they are eligible to become members. All examinations are open-book one hour examinations, preceded by 15 minutes reading time. At a recent meeting, EMS Council rejected the concept of computer-based assessment. They felt that competence in this area was best assessed by written examination answers.

Candidate numbers for the qualification have fallen dramatically in the last two years. The Board of EMS has concluded that this drop reflects the maturing marketplace in the country. Many people who were practitioners in environmental management and audit when the qualification was introduced have now gained their Diploma. The stream of new candidates and hence members is relatively small.

Consequently, the EMS Board has suggested that they should now look to attract international candidates and it has targeted countries where environmental management and audit is becoming more important. It is now formulating a strategy to launch the qualification in India, China and Russia.

However, any strategy has to recognise that both the EMS Board and the Council are very cautious and notably risk-averse. EMS is only confident about its technical capability within a restricted definition of environmental management and audit. Attempts to look at complementary qualification areas (such as soil and water conservation) have been swiftly rejected by Council as being non-core areas and therefore outside the scope of their expertise.

Required:

Internal development, acquisitions and strategic alliances are three development methods by which an organisation's strategic direction can be pursued.

(a)   Explain the principles of internal development and discuss how appropriate this development method is to EMS.   **(8 marks)**

(b)   Explain the principles of acquisitions and discuss how appropriate this development method is to EMS.   **(8 marks)**

(c)   Explain the principles of strategic alliances and discuss how appropriate this development method is to EMS.   **(9 marks)**

(Total: 25 marks)

16   MMI   *Walk in the footsteps of a top tutor*

In 20X2 the board of MMI met to discuss the strategic direction of the company. Established in 1952, MMI specialised in mineral quarrying and opencast mining and in 20X2 it owned fifteen quarries and mines throughout the country. However, three of these quarries were closed and two others were nearing exhaustion. Increased costs and falling reserves meant that there was little chance of finding new sites in the country which were economically viable. Furthermore, there was significant security costs associated with keeping the closed quarries safe and secure.

Consequently the Chief Executive Officer (CEO) of MMI suggested that the company should pursue a corporate-level strategy of diversification, building up a portfolio of acquisitions that would 'maintain returns to shareholders over the next fifty years'. In October 20X2 MMI, using cash generated from their quarrying operations, acquired First Leisure, a company that owned five leisure parks throughout the country. These leisure parks provided a range of accommodation where guests could stay while they enjoyed sports and leisure activities. The parks were all in relatively isolated country areas and provided a safe, car-free environment for guests.

The acquisition was initially criticised by certain financial analysts who questioned what a quarrying company could possibly contribute to a profitable leisure group. For two years MMI left First Leisure managers alone, letting them get on with running the company. However, in 20X4 a First Leisure manager commented on the difficulty of developing new leisure parks due to increasingly restrictive government planning legislation. This gave the CEO of MMI an inspired idea and over the next three years the five quarries which were either closed or near exhaustion were transferred to First Leisure and developed as new leisure parks. Because these were developments of 'brown field' sites they were exempted from the government's planning legislation. The development of these new parks has helped First Leisure to expand considerably (see table 1). The company is still run by the managers who were in place when MMI acquired the company in 20X2 and MMI plays very little role in the day-to-day running of the company.

In 20X4 MMI acquired two of its smaller mining and quarrying competitors, bringing a further five mines or quarries into the group. MMI introduced its own managers into these companies resulting in a spectacular rise in revenues and profits that caused the CEO of MMI to claim that corporate management capabilities were now an important asset of MMI.

In 20X6 MMI acquired Boatland, a specialist boat maker constructing river and canal boats. The primary rationale behind the acquisition was the potential synergies with First Leisure. First Leisure had experienced difficulties in obtaining and maintaining boats for its leisure parks and it was expected that Boatland would take on construction and maintenance of these boats. Cost savings for First Leisure were also expected and it was felt that income from the First Leisure contract would also allow Boatland to expand its production of boats for other customers. MMI perceived that Boatland was underperforming and it replaced the current management team with its own managers. However, by 20X8 Boatland was reporting poorer results (see table 1). The work force had been used to producing expensive, high quality boats to discerning customers who looked after their valued boats. In contrast, the boats required by First Leisure were for the casual use of holiday makers who often ill-treated them and certainly had no long-term investment in their ownership. Managers at First Leisure complained that the new boats were 'too delicate' for their intended purpose and unreliability had led to high maintenance costs. This increase in maintenance also put Boatland under strain and its other customers complained about poor quality workmanship and delays in completing work. These delays were compounded by managers at Boatland declaring First Leisure as a preferred customer, requiring that work for First Leisure should take precedence over that for established customers. Since the company was acquired almost half of the skilled boat builders employed by the company have left to take up jobs elsewhere in the industry.

Three months ago, InfoTech – an information technology solutions company approached MMI with a proposal for MMI to acquire them. The failure of certain contracts has led to falling revenues and profits and the company needs new investment. The Managing Director (MD) of InfoTech has proposed that MMI should acquire InfoTech for a nominal sum and then substantially invest in the company so that it can regain its previous profitability and revenue levels. However, after its experience with Boatland, the CEO of MMI is cautious about any further diversification of the group.

Table 1: Financial and market data for selected companies (all figures in $millions)

MMI Quarrying and Mining	20X8	20X6	20X4	20X2
Revenue	1,680	1,675	1,250	1,275
Gross profit	305	295	205	220
Net profit	110	105	40	45
*Estimated Market Revenue	6,015	6,050	6,200	6,300
First Leisure	20X8	20X6	20X4	20X2
Revenue	200	160	110	100
Gross profit	42	34	23	21
Net profit	21	17	10	9
*Estimated Market Revenue	950	850	770	750
Boatland	20X8	20X6	20X4	20X2
Revenue	2.10	2.40	2.40	2.30
Gross profit	0.30	0.50	0.50	0.60
Net profit	0.09	0.25	0.30	0.30
*Estimated Market Revenue	201	201	199	198

InfoTech	20X8	20X6	20X4	20X2
Revenue	21	24	26	25
Gross profit	0.9	3	4	4
Net profit	−0.2	2	3	3
*Estimated Market Revenue	560	540	475	450

*The estimated size of the market (estimated market revenue) is taken from Slott's Economic Yearbooks, 20X2–20X8.

Required:

(a) **In the context of MMI's corporate-level strategy, explain the rationale for MMI acquiring First Leisure and Boatland and assess the subsequent performance of the two companies.** **(15 marks)**

(b) **Assess the extent to which the proposed acquisition of InfoTech represents an appropriate addition to the MMI portfolio.** **(10 marks)**

(Total: 25 marks)

17 BLUESKY

Dr John Clarkson is currently Managing Director of BlueSky Analysis Ltd, a research company which obtains data gathered from satellite observations, analyses this data and then sells the information to client organisations. Twenty years ago Clarkson had been employed by the United Kingdom's Ministry of Defence, to interpret military data obtained from satellite surveillance. He set up BlueSky Analysis Ltd to utilise the technology which he understood, and to adapt it for peaceful applications. Together with four other scientists he formed the company in 1996. These five scientists were the only shareholders. Most of the work was then focused on obtaining new customers, and as the technology had, until then, been primarily used for highly confidential military information gathering there were few other potential competitors. It was now possible to buy from both military and civil satellite owners data obtained from a variety of sources. This data could be usefully interpreted and could provide valuable information on a wide range of topics including climate change, crop forecasts, soil conditions and mineral deposits. The potential customers for such information were mainly governmental agencies, operating both nationally and internationally, including organisations such as the United Nations Food and Agricultural Organisation. Many mining and oil exploration companies also found the information invaluable in helping to select geographical locations for exploration and development.

The initial growth was rapid. The company had to employ more scientists and within two years the company had grown to number about 45 employees including 15 clerical staff. It was an attractive company for the scientists to work for. There was little management structure. Each analyst worked on an individual client's project, specialising on either a geographical area or on a specific industry such as mining, helping to identify the location of mineral deposits. The analysts could concentrate solely on scientific work and were not diverted into administrative activities involving long meetings and planning programmes. Staff turnover was very low. All the scientists required was a project to work on and secretarial support to prepare reports for clients. Otherwise they usually worked alone. Clarkson was the Managing Director, but all five shareholders took it in turn to carry out the necessary but, in their opinion, mundane administrative tasks required in any company – personnel, purchasing, finance and marketing activities.

They did employ some junior staff or used outside agencies to carry out the routine tasks such as payroll and book-keeping. Even recruitment was contracted out to an agency. These five senior managers were also totally responsible for the critical tasks of obtaining contracts. However they, like most of the scientists, were at their happiest when they were focusing on the analytical work for clients and not being managers.

Unfortunately this informal style and structure did not run smoothly. Although the company provided a good social and challenging work environment, it was inevitable that this analyst-led approach should lack direction and that errors in administration would create problems with clients. There was inadequate integration and teamwork within the company, with most of the scientists working independently on their own projects. The five senior scientists began to spend much of their time 'fire-fighting' – correcting mistakes which should never have occurred. Fortunately the company was still a leader in this small specialist field and so did not lose much business to emerging competitors.

However by late 20X7 it was apparent that this loose management structure was inhibiting the growth of the company. The market for data collection and analysis was becoming more global and competitors were eroding BlueSky's market position. Its projects were frequently going over budget and many were taking too long to complete. A lack of cohesion and cooperation between the analysts within the company meant that when such delays occurred other staff members could not help to sort out the problems. Furthermore, as the senior managers acted as intermediaries between the client and the scientist responsible for their particular research contract, any negotiations for changes in requirements tended to be lengthy and confusing. The problem was that a move towards greater discipline and structure, necessary for keeping work on target and profitable, was likely to alienate the analysts who enjoyed their independence.

In early 20X8 the senior management, now facing declining orders, decided that they could not continue in such as undisciplined manner. They were approached by a much larger company from the USA, United Data System (UDS), whose main business was as a software company, providing information systems for major clients throughout the world. These contracts were with both public and private sector clients ranging from automobile manufacturers to governmental tax agencies. UDS was accustomed to dealing with multi-million pound contracts, serviced by specialist teams, and accordingly had the infrastructure and systems to suit such a business. The company employed in excess of 3,000 employees worldwide, with almost half being in support but non-operational roles, compared with a total of 90 employees at BlueSky in 20X8. Recognising their lack of interest in administration, Clarkson and his four fellow shareholders agreed to the acquisition by UDS, but still maintained a significant share of the equity. Although technically UDS now own BlueSky it was not seeking to absorb it. The larger company, seeking to diversify into more innovative areas, saw BlueSky as providing the expertise and access into a rapidly expanding and lucrative market. They did not wish to destroy the research-centred culture of BlueSky because the company's success depended upon the scientists' continued goodwill and commitment.

They agreed to allow the smaller company to continue operating as a subsidiary company in an innovative manner – no large company bureaucracy being imposed upon the scientists. However UDS would now require that all new contracts be investigated by themselves for financial attractiveness. A charge was levied from the centre for this service. This meant that all contracts, regardless of size were now sent to the headquarters in the USA. This was intended to ensure that BlueSky did not accept contracts which they could not complete on time or which were not profitable.

However, this fusion of cultures did generate unforeseen problems. BlueSky had been accustomed to managing smaller contracts with lower margins but now UDS was seeking to impose financial criteria on them which were more suitable for a larger company with a bigger infrastructure to support. UDS also had a more formalised system of contract vetting which took time to complete. There was dissatisfaction in both BlueSky and UDS as BlueSky's scientists were seeing contracts being lost and the parent company was not seeing the growth it had expected when it acquired the subsidiary. In addition some of BlueSky's long-standing clients were becoming increasingly worried by the further reduction in quality and service they were receiving. Clarkson was summoned to the USA headquarters to discuss the future of BlueSky. He feared that the proposed solution would be to integrate BlueSky more closely into UDS, by making it an operating division, with both strategy and operations being dependent upon UDS's central control, rather than by allowing it the greater freedom it currently had as a subsidiary company.

Details of the performance and financial position of BlueSky Ltd can be found in Table 1 below.

Table 1: Financial Data ($000)

	20X8	20X9
Sales revenue	4,400	4,350
Cost of sales	3,400	3,250
Gross profit	1,000	1,100
Expenses	300	480
Of which – marketing	100	80
– administration	200	400
Operating profit	700	620
Value of contracts in progress or on order book (31 December)	1,300	750
Employees	85	93
Non-current assets	750	600
Average value of contracts	45	90
% of contracts overrunning on cost or time	37	45

Note: 20X8 was the last full year as an independent company and 20X9 was the first year as a subsidiary of UDS.

Required:

(a) **Identify and explain the problems which are now being faced by BlueSky Analysis Ltd, operating as a subsidiary company of UDS.** **(15 marks)**

(b) **If BlueSky is integrated fully into UDS it is probable that there will be a clash of cultures**

    (i) **using the cultural web, or a similar model, comment on the current differences in culture, explaining the main factors which cause these differences** **(5 marks)**

    (ii) **explain the ways in which the management at UDS might minimise the conflict which may arise from the cultural differences.** **(5 marks)**

(Total: 25 marks)

ORGANISATIONAL STRUCTURE

18 ALG TECHNOLOGY   *Online question assistance*

John Hudson is the Managing Director of ALG Technology, a medium-sized high tech company operating in several geographic markets. The company provides software and instrumentation, mainly for military projects but it also does have civilian interests. It currently has four key projects – (1) a command, communication and control system for the army's gunnery regiments, (2) avionics for the fighter aircraft within the air force, (3) an air traffic control system for a regional airport and (4) radar installations for harbour authorities in the Middle East. All these projects were expected to have a life expectancy of at least five years before completion. However, Hudson was worried because each of these projects was increasingly falling behind schedule and the contracts which he had negotiated had late delivery penalties.

Hudson is convinced that a significant cause of the problem is the way that the company is organised. It has been shown that a competitive advantage can be obtained by the way a firm organises and performs its activities. Hudson's organisation is currently structured on a functional basis, which does not seem to work well with complex technologies when operating in dynamic markets. The functional structure appears to result in a lack of integration of key activities, reduced loyalties and an absence of team work. Hudson has contemplated moving towards a divisionalised structure, either by product or by market so as to provide some element of focus, but his experience has suggested that such a structure might create internal rivalries and competition which could adversely affect the performance of the company. Furthermore, there is a risk that such a structure may lead to an over-emphasis on either the technology or the market conditions. He is seeking a structure which encourages both integration and efficiency. Any tendency towards decentralisation, whilst encouraging initiative and generating motivation may result in a failure to pursue a cohesive strategy, whereas a move towards centralisation could reduce flexibility and responsiveness.

The company is already relatively lean and so any move towards delayering, resulting in a flatter organisation is likely to be resisted. Furthermore the nature of the market – the need for high technical specifications and confidentiality – is likely to preclude outsourcing as a means of achieving both efficiency and rapidity of response.

Required:

(a) Provide an alternative organisational structure for ALG Technology, discussing both the benefits and problems which such a structure might bring. **(13 marks)**

(b) Evaluate the main factors which can influence organisational design relating these, where possible, to ALG Technology. **(12 marks)**

(Total: 25 marks)

> *Online question assistance*

19 ICC ORGANISATION

International Computer Corporation (ICC) has two major world-wide customer functions. The sales and marketing (S&M) function which sells the product and the sales engineering support (SES) function which installs the product and provides customer technical support and maintenance. Within each country functional management (S&M, SES and other functions such as Finance) report to the country Vice President (Operations) and also to the functional Vice President located at the Head Office in the USA. For example, the ICC country Finance Manager for Germany reports and provides support to the German Vice President (Operations) but also has a line responsibility to the Vice President (Finance) located at head office in the USA.

Within each country however S&M and SES are organised as independent divisions. The S&M division organises its sales teams on the basis of product groups, for example, printers or network hardware. S&M product specialisation is seen as essential if sales staff are to develop the level of product technical expertise deemed necessary to sell advanced technologies to computing professionals. The SES division on the other hand organises on the basis of customers not products. The intention being that the customer has only one SES contact for any hardware or software problem and the SES teams are equipped to deal with any aspect of technical support. SES activity is seen as a means of assisting product sales as potential sales leads are picked up by SES staff and passed on to the S&M sales teams. Recently there have been a growing number of country based problems in co-ordination between S&M and SES. One result has been a number of instances of sales leads not being passed by SES to S&M. Another has been instances of hardware being sold by S&M which later proved unsuitable in performance terms. This created significant workload problems for SES engineers in re-configuring to a specification which met the customers' performance criteria.

Required:

(a)   The 'international to country' functional management at ICC provides an example of the matrix form of organisational structure.

Briefly explain why you feel that ICC has chosen to manage its international operations in this way. **(8 marks)**

(b)   Suggest how the adoption of a country-based matrix structure combining S&M and SES could assist in resolving the apparent co-ordination problems between the two divisions. **(9 marks)**

(c)   The matrix organisational form has been described as 'no place for a middle manager seeking security and stability'.

Examine the issues which organisation design must address if the matrix form is to function effectively. **(8 marks)**

(Total: 25 marks)

20 FRIGATE LIMITED

Frigate Limited is based in the country of Egdon. It imports electrical components from other countries and distributes them throughout the domestic market. The company was formed twenty years ago by Ron Frew, who now owns 80% of the shares. A further 10% of the company is owned by his wife and 5% each by his two daughters.

Although he has never been in the navy, Ron is obsessed by ships, sailing and naval history. He is known to everyone as 'The Commander' and this is how he expects his employees to address him. He increasingly spends time on his own boat, an expensive motor cruiser, which is moored in the local harbour twenty minutes drive away. When he is not on holiday, Ron is always at work at 8.00 am in the morning to make sure that employees arrive on time and he is also there at 5.30 pm to ensure that they do not leave early. However, he spends large parts of the working day on his boat, although he can be contacted by mobile telephone. Employees who arrive late for work have to immediately explain the circumstances to Ron. If he feels that the explanation is unacceptable then he makes an appropriate deduction from their wages. Wages, like all costs in the company, are closely monitored by Ron.

Employees, customers and suppliers

Frigate currently has 25 employees primarily undertaking sales, warehousing, accounts and administration. Although employees are nominally allocated to one role, they are required to work anywhere in the company as required by Ron. They are also expected to help Ron in personal tasks, such as booking holidays for his family, filling in his personal tax returns and organising social events.

Egdon has laws concerning minimum wages and holidays. All employees at Frigate Ltd are only given the minimum holiday allocation. They have to use this allocation not only for holidays but also for events such as visiting the doctor, attending funerals and dealing with domestic problems and emergencies. Ron is particularly inflexible about holidays and work hours. He has even turned down requests for unpaid leave. In contrast, Ron is often away from work for long periods, sailing in various parts of the world.

Ron is increasingly critical of suppliers ('trying to sell me inferior quality goods for higher prices'), customers ('moaning about prices and paying later and later') and society in general ('a period working in the navy would do everyone good'). He has also been in dispute with the tax authority who he accused of squandering his 'hard-earned' money. An investigation by the tax authority led to him being fined for not disclosing the fact that significant family expenditure (such as a holiday for his daughters overseas) had been declared as company expenditure.

Company accountant

It was this action by the tax authority that prompted Ron to appoint Ann Li as company accountant. Ann had previously worked as an accountant in a number of public sector organisations, culminating in a role as a compliance officer in the tax authority itself. Ron felt that 'recruiting someone like Ann should help keep the tax authorities happy. After all, she is one of them'.

Ann was used to working in organisations which had formal organisational hierarchies, specialised roles and formal controls and systems. She tried to install such formal arrangements within Frigate. As she said to Ron 'we cannot have everyone working as if they were just your personal assistants. We need structure, standardised processes and accountability'. Ron resisted her plans, at first through delaying tactics and then through explicit opposition, tearing up her proposed organisational chart and budget in front of other employees. 'I regret the day I ever made that appointment', he said. After six months he terminated her contract. Ann returned to the tax authority as a tax inspector.

Required:

The cultural web allows the business analyst to explore 'the way things are done around here'.

(a)   Analyse Frigate Ltd using the cultural web or any other appropriate framework for understanding organisational culture.   **(15 marks)**

(b)   Using appropriate organisation configuration stereotypes identified by Henry Mintzberg, explain how an understanding of organisation configuration could have helped predict the failure of Ann Li's proposed formalisation of structure, controls and processes at Frigate Ltd.   **(10 marks)**

(Total: 25 marks)

21   YVERN TRINKETS REGIONAL

Yvern is large region in the country of Gaulle. It is ethnically and culturally distinct from the rest of the country and it has aspirations for independence. The desire for this independence is reflected by consumers in Yvern preferring to buy products which have been produced in the region.

Yvern Trinkets Regional (YTR) is a manufacturer of giftware products aimed at the Yvern market. Its products are bought primarily by residents of Yvern and visitors to the Yvern region. It is the third largest company of its type in the region, and the 50th largest producer of giftware in Gaulle. Its marketing message stresses the regional identity of the company and its employment of local skills and labour. It currently manufactures four products, designated here as products A, B, C and D. The company does not sub-contract or outsource any element of production and it has never done so. Data concerning products A, B, C and D are given in Table one.

	A	B	C	D
Monthly production (in units)	2,000	5,500	4,000	3,000
Direct materials cost ($ per unit)	3	5	2	4
Direct labour cost ($ per unit)	9	6	9	6
Variable production overheads ($ per unit)	2	3	1	2

Table one: Production and marginal cost data for the YTR product range

YTR recently appointed a new managing director, born outside the region. He has been tasked with improving the profitability of the company.

After a short period of consultation, the new managing director produced a proposal for the board. Here is an extract of his proposal.

'First of all, we need to be clear about our generic strategy. Strategists have suggested that we have four alternatives. I have reproduced them in this slide (shown here as Table two).

Cost Leadership	Differentiation
Cost Focus	Differentiation Focus

Table two: Generic strategies

My vision for YTR is that we should pursue a cost leadership strategy. I have already established that our products can be produced by an established company in the distant country of Tinglia at the following prices (see Table three). These costs include the delivery of products to our warehouse here in Yvern.

	A	B	C	D
Buy-in price ($ per unit)	11.5	16.5	12.5	13.5

Table three: Contract prices per unit from the external supplier in Tinglia

Our financial director of YTR has also estimated that we have company-wide fixed overheads of $75,000 per month. He assures me that $16,000 per month of these is directly attributable to the production of products A, B, C and D, evenly split across the four products, each having $4,000 of fixed overheads. So, we could save overheads of $16,000 per month by outsourcing all of our products to the Tinglia supplier.

I realise that this leaves us with $59,000 per month fixed overheads, but I will be looking for savings there also. The information technology of YTR is outdated and inefficient. Productivity benefits will follow from harnessing the power of modern technology.

However, returning to my main concern: production costs. My view is that increased profitability can only be achieved if we take advantage of the cheaper production costs now available to us. All four products can be produced more cheaply by the supplier in Tinglia. So, this strategy of outsourcing is the one we should pursue to achieve our cost leadership strategy.'

Required:

(a) Evaluate the claim that 'all four products can be produced more cheaply by the supplier in Tinglia' and discuss the issues raised by outsourcing the production of YTR's products to Tinglia. **(15 marks)**

(b) Examine the relevance of each of the four generic strategies shown in Table two to the competitive environment in which YTR operates and evaluate the choice of a cost leadership strategy by YTR's managing director. **(10 marks)**

(Total: 25 marks)

BUSINESS PROCESS CHANGE

22 COUNTRY CAR CLUB

Introduction

The Country Car Club (3C) was established fifty years ago to offer breakdown assistance to motorists. In return for an annual membership fee, members of 3C are able to phone for immediate assistance if their vehicle breaks down anywhere in the country. Assistance is provided by 'service patrol engineers' who are located throughout the country and who are specialists in vehicle repair and maintenance. If they cannot fix the problem immediately then the vehicle (and its occupants) are transported by a 3C recovery vehicle back to the member's home address free of charge.

Over the last fifteen years 3C has rapidly expanded its services. It now offers vehicle insurance, vehicle history checks (to check for previous accident damage or theft) as well as offering a comprehensive advice centre where trained staff answer a wide range of vehicle-related queries. It also provides route maps, endorses hotels by giving them a 3C starred rating and lobbies the government on issues such as taxation, vehicle emissions and toll road charging. All of these services are provided by permanent 3C employees and all growth has been organic culminating in a listing on the country's stock exchange three years ago.

However, since its stock market listing, the company has posted disappointing results and a falling share price has spurred managers to review internal processes and functions. A Business Architecture Committee (BAC) made up of senior managers has been charged with reviewing the scope of the company's business activities. It has been asked to examine the importance of certain activities and to make recommendations on the sourcing of these activities (in-house or outsourced). The BAC has also been asked to identify technological implications or opportunities for the activities that they recommend should remain in-house.

First review

The BAC's first review included an assessment of the supply and maintenance of 3C's company vehicles. 3C has traditionally purchased its own fleet of vehicles and maintained them in a central garage. When a vehicle needed servicing or maintenance it was returned to this central garage. Last year, 3C had seven hundred vehicles (breakdown recovery vehicles, service patrol engineer vans, company cars for senior staff etc) all maintained by thirty staff permanently employed in this garage. A further three permanent employees were employed at the garage site with responsibility for the purchasing and disposal of vehicles. The garage was in a residential area of a major town, with major parking problems and no room for expansion.

The BAC concluded that the garage was of low strategic importance to the company and, although most of the processes it involved were straightforward, its remoteness from the home base of some vehicles made undertaking such processes unnecessarily complicated. Consequently, it recommended outsourcing vehicle acquisition, disposal and maintenance to a specialist company. Two months ago 3C's existing vehicle fleet was acquired by AutoDirect, a company with service and repair centres nationwide, which currently supplies 45,000 vehicles to companies throughout the country. It now leases vehicles back to 3C for a monthly payment. In the next ten years (the duration of the contract) all vehicles will be leased from AutoDirect on a full maintenance basis that includes the replacement of tyres and exhausts. 3C's garage is now surplus to requirements and all the employees that worked there have been made redundant, except for one employee who has been retained to manage the relationship with AutoDirect.

Second review

The BAC has now been asked to look at the following activities and their supporting processes. All of these are currently performed in-house by permanent 3C employees.

- *Attendance of repair staff at breakdowns* – currently undertaken by permanent 'service patrol engineers' employed at locations throughout the country from where they attend local breakdowns.

- *Membership renewal* – members must renew every year. Currently renewals are sent out by staff using a bespoke computer system. Receipts are processed when members confirm that they will be renewing for a further year.

- *Vehicle insurance services* providing accident insurance which every motorist legally requires.

- *Membership queries* handled by a call-centre. Members can use the service for a wide range of vehicle-related problems and issues.

- *Vehicle history checks*. These are primarily used to provide 'peace of mind' to a potential purchaser of a vehicle. The vehicle is checked to see if it has ever been in an accident or if it has been stolen. The check also makes sure that the car is not currently part of a loan agreement.

Required:

(a) **The Business Architecture Committee (BAC) has been asked to make recommendations on the sourcing of activities (in-house or outsourced). The BAC has also been asked to identify technological implications or opportunities for the activities that they recommend should remain in-house.**

Suggest and justify recommendations to the BAC for each of the following major process areas:

(i) **Attendance of repair staff at breakdowns**

(ii) **Membership renewal**

(iii) **Vehicle insurance services**

(iv) **Membership queries; and**

(v) **Vehicle history checks.** **(15 marks)**

(b) **Analyse the advantages that 3C will gain from the decision to outsource the purchase and maintenance of their own vehicles.** **(10 marks)**

(Total: 25 marks)

23 STELLA ELECTRONICS

Stella Electronics (SE) owns a chain of electrical retail stores throughout the country of Arborium. The company sells to the general public through its stores and website. It has outsourced three areas of a business process to Terra Call Generale (TCG), a call centre specialist based overseas. They handle, on behalf of SE, the following calls:

- Customers requesting service contracts.

- Customers requesting refunds for goods purchased from the SE website.

- Customers with technical queries about the products they have bought.

The business process for handling these calls is given in Figure 1.

SE is currently reviewing the renewal of the TCG contract in the light of customer complaints about:

- The time taken to complete a query

- The frustration caused by the need to provide a reference number and password

- The problem of understanding the accents of the people in the call centre.

Unemployment is rising in Arborium and there is increased resistance to services being outsourced and offshored to companies such as TCG. SE is aware of the growing hostility of customers to such arrangements.

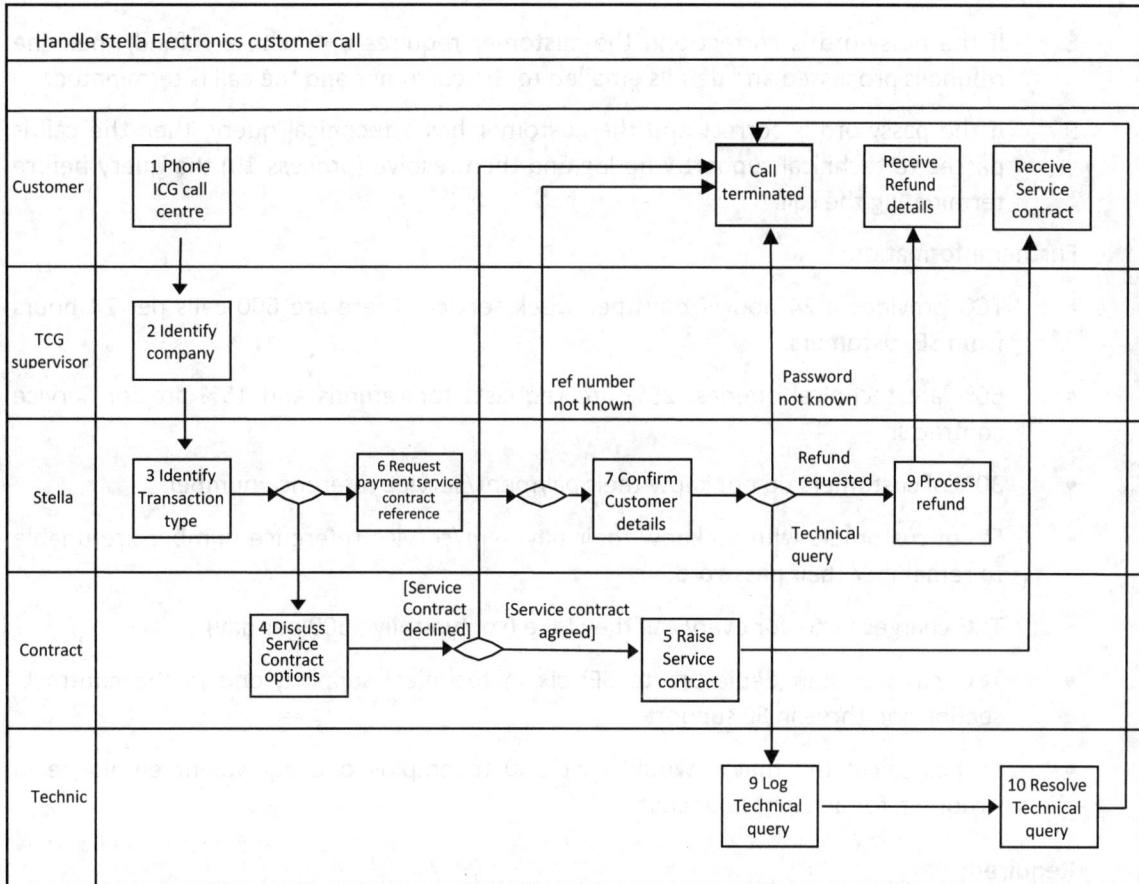

Figure 1: Business process for handling a Stella Electronics customer call

Call centre processing (TCG) – to be read in conjunction with Figure 1

1   The process is initiated by a customer phoning the TCG call centre.

2   TCG offers call centre services to a number of companies. The supervisor asks the customer which company they are phoning about. Calls for SE are routed to Stella support. Calls for other companies are routed to other support teams (not shown here).

3   The TCG support operator asks the customer what their call is about. Three transaction types are possible.

4   Callers who wish to discuss a service contract are passed immediately to the contracts section. Service contract options are discussed and if the caller decides to buy a service contract, then this is raised in the next activity in the process (5: Raise service contract).

5   Raise service contract and details are emailed to the customer. If the caller decides not to have a service contract, then the call is terminated.

6   For all other transaction types, Stella support asks the customer for their payment reference number or service contract reference number. If the customer cannot supply either of these, then the call is terminated. If the reference number is provided, then the support team member enters it into the computer system.

7   The computer system retrieves customer details and these are confirmed by the support team member with the customer. These details include a password which the customer has to give. Failure to give the correct password leads to the call being terminated.

8   If the password is correct and the customer requires a purchase refund, then the refund is processed and details emailed to the customer and the call is terminated.

9   If the password is correct and the customer has a technical query, then the call is passed to technical support who log and then resolve (process 10) the query before terminating the call.

Further information:

- TCG provides a 24 hour/7 days per week service. There are 600 calls per 24 hours from SE customers.

- 60% are technical queries, 25% are requests for refunds and 15% are for service contracts.

- 30% of customers do not know their payment/service reference number.

- 5% of customers who do know their payment/service reference number are unable to remember their password.

- TCG charges SE $1 for every call they take (so, typically $600 per day).

- TCG has ten staff dedicated to SE: six in technical support, one in the contracts section and three in SE support.

- SE has calculated that it would cost $50 to employ one equivalent employee in Arborium for an eight hour shift.

Required:

(a)   **Evaluate the current process for handling SE's customer calls at TCG and suggest improvements to that process at TCG.**   **(15 marks)**

(b)   **Discuss whether SE should continue outsourcing its customer call handling process to TCG or should it bring the process in-house.**   **(10 marks)**

(Total: 25 marks)

24   TMP

TMP (The Management Press) is a specialist business publisher; commissioning, printing and distributing books on financial and business management. It is based in a small town in Arcadia, a high-cost economy, where their printing works were established fifty years ago. 60% of the company's sales are made through bookshops in Arcadia. In these bookshops TMP's books are displayed in a custom-built display case specifically designed for TMP. 30% of TMP's sales are through mail order generated by full-page display advertisements in magazines and journals. Most of these sales are to customers based outside Arcadia. The final 10% of sales are made through a newly established website which offers a restricted range of books. These books are typically very specialised and are rarely featured in display advertising or stocked by general bookshops. The books available on the website are selected to avoid conflict with established supply channels. Most of the online sales are to customers based in Arcadia. High selling prices and high distribution costs makes TMP's books expensive to buy outside Arcadia.

Business changes

In the last decade costs have increased as the raw materials (particularly timber) used in book production have become dearer. Paper is extremely expensive in Arcadia and the trees used to produce it are becoming scarcer. Online book sellers have also emerged who are able to discount prices by exploiting economies of scale and eliminating bookshop costs. In Arcadia, it is estimated that three bookshops go out of business every week. Furthermore, the influential journal 'Management Focus', one of the journals where TMP advertised their books, also recently ceased production. TMP itself has suffered three years of declining sales and profits. Expenditure on marketing has been reduced significantly in this period and further reductions in the marketing budget are likely because of the weak financial position of the company. Overall, there is increasing pressure on the company to increase profit margins and sales.

Despite the poor financial results, the directors of TMP are keen to maintain the established supply channels. One of them, the son of the founder of the company, has stated that 'bookshops need all the help they can get and management journals are the heart of our industry'.

However, the marketing director is keen for the company to re-visit its business model. He increasingly believes that TMP's conventional approach to book production, distribution and marketing is not sustainable. He wishes to re-examine certain elements of the marketing mix in the context of the opportunities offered by e-business.

A young marketing graduate has been appointed by the marketing director to develop and maintain the website. However, further development of the website has not been sanctioned by the Board. Other directors have given two main reasons for blocking further development of this site. Firstly, they believe that the company does not have sufficient expertise to continue developing and maintaining its own website. It is solely dependent on the marketing graduate. Secondly, they feel that the website will compete with the established supply channels which they are keen to preserve.

However, the marketing director is convinced that investing in e-business is essential for the survival of TMP. 'We need to consider what unique opportunities it offers for pricing the product, promoting the product, placing the product and providing physical evidence of the quality of the product. Finally, we might even re-define the product itself'. He feels if the company fails to grasp these opportunities, then one of its competitors will, and 'that will be the end of us'.

Required:

(a)   Determine the main drivers for the adoption of e-business at TMP and identify potential barriers to its adoption.   **(5 marks)**

(b)   Evaluate how e-business might help TMP exploit each of the five elements of the marketing mix (price, product, promotion, place and physical evidence) identified by the marketing director.   **(20 marks)**

(Total: 25 marks)

25   INSTITUTE OF ANALYTICAL ACCOUNTANTS

The Institute of Analytical Accountants (IAA) offers three certification programmes which are assessed through examinations using multiple choice questions. These questions are maintained in a computerised question bank. The handling process for these questions is documented in Figure 1 and described in detail below. The IAA is currently analysing all its processes seeking possible business process re-design opportunities. It is considering commissioning a bespoke computer system to support any agreed re-design of the business processes. The IAA is keen to implement a new solution fairly quickly because competitors are threatening to move into their established market.

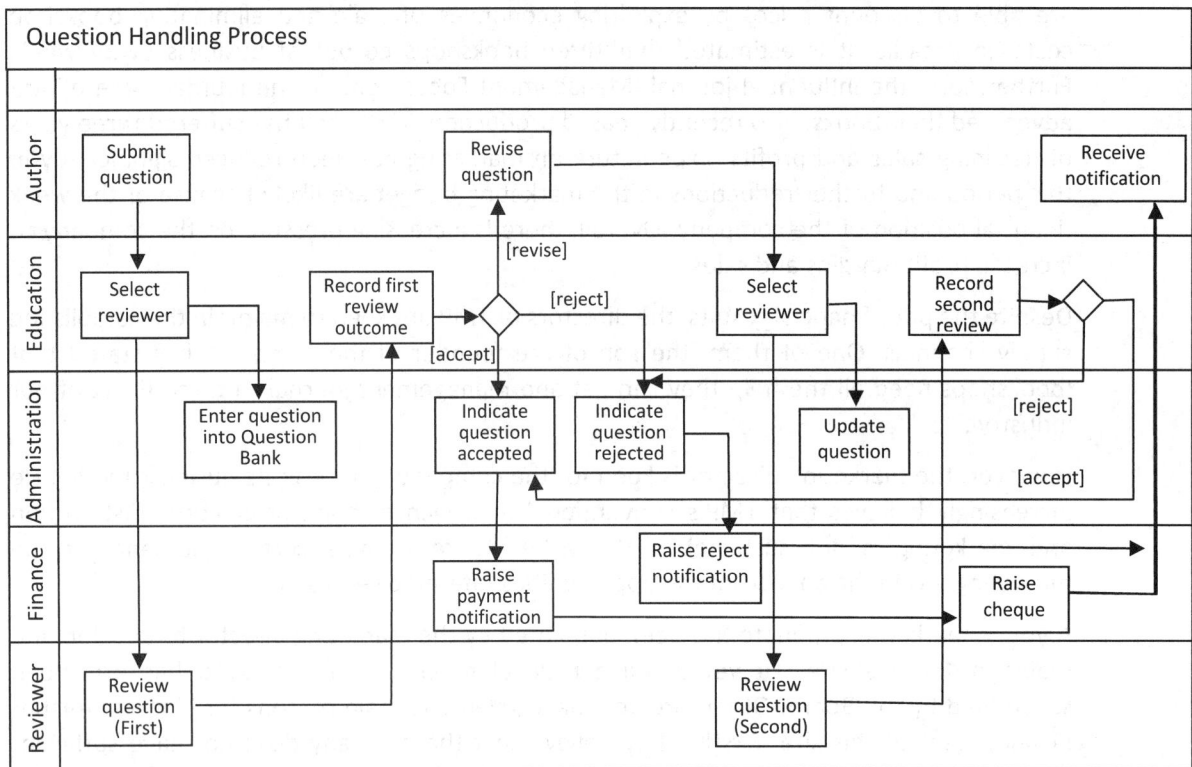

Figure 1: Question handling process at IAA

The author (the question originator) submits the question to the IAA as a password protected document attached to an email. The education department of the IAA (which is staffed by subject matter experts) select an appropriate reviewer and forward the email to him or her. At no point in the process does the author know the identity of the reviewer. A copy of the email is sent to the administration department where administrators enter the question in a standard format into a computerised question bank. These administrators are not subject matter experts and sometimes make mistakes when entering the questions and answers. A recent spot-check identified that one in ten questions contained an error. Furthermore, there is a significant delay in entering questions. Although five administrators are assigned to this task, they also have other duties to perform and so a backlog of questions has built up. Administrators are paid less than education staff.

The reviewer decides whether the question should be accepted as it is, rejected completely, or returned to the author for amendment. This first review outcome is recorded by the education department before the administration department updates the database with whether the question was accepted or rejected. On some occasions it is not possible to find the question which needs to be updated because it is still in the backlog of questions waiting to be entered into the system. This causes further delay and frustration.

The finance department is notified of all accepted questions and a payment notification is raised which eventually leads to a cheque being issued and sent to the author.

The amended question is returned by the author to the education department who forward this onto the reviewer. A copy is again sent to the administration department so that they can amend the question held on the database.

On the second review, the question is accepted or rejected. Rejected questions (irrespective of when they are rejected) are notified to the finance department who raise a reject notification and send it back to the author.

Currently, 20% of questions are immediately rejected by the reviewer and a further 15% are sent back to the author for revision. Of these, 30% are rejected on the second review.

Required:

(a)   The IAA would like to consider a number of re-design options, ranging from very simple improvements to radical solutions.

Identify a range of re-design options the IAA could consider for improving their question handling process. Evaluate the benefits of each option.   (15 marks)

(b)   Eventually, the IAA decided not to develop a bespoke solution but to use an established software package to implement its multiple choice question management and examination requirements. The selected package, chosen from a shortlist of three, includes the delivery of tests, question analysis, student invoicing and student records. It is already used by several significant examination boards in the country.

Explain the advantages of fulfilling users' requirements using a software package solution and discuss the implications of this solution for process re-design at IAA.
(10 marks)

(Total: 25 marks)

26   FLEXIPIPE

Introduction

Flexipipe is a successful company supplying flexible pipes to a wide range of industries. Its success is based on a very innovative production process which allows the company to produce relatively small batches of flexible pipes at very competitive prices. This has given Flexipipe a significant competitive edge over most of its competitors whose batch set-up costs are higher and whose lead times are longer. Flexipipe's innovative process is partly automated and partly reliant on experienced managers and supervisors on the factory floor. These managers efficiently schedule jobs from different customers to achieve economies of scale and throughput times that profitably deliver high quality products and service to Flexipipe's customers.

A year ago, the Chief Executive Officer (CEO) at Flexipipe decided that he wanted to extend the automated part of the production process by purchasing a software package that promised even further benefits, including the automation of some of the decision-making tasks currently undertaken by the factory managers and supervisors. He had seen this package at a software exhibition and was so impressed that he placed an order immediately. He stated that the package was 'ahead of its time, and I have seen nothing else like it on the market'.

This was the first time that the company had bought a software package for something that was not to be used in a standard application, such as payroll or accounts. Most other software applications in the company, such as the automated part of the current production process, have been developed in-house by a small programming team. The CEO felt that there was, on this occasion, insufficient time and money to develop a bespoke in-house solution. He accepted that there was no formal process for software package procurement 'but perhaps we can put one in place as this project progresses'.

This relaxed approach to procurement is not unusual at Flexipipe, where many of the purchasing decisions are taken unilaterally by senior managers. There is a small procurement section with two full-time administrators, but they only become involved once purchasing decisions have been made. It is felt that they are not technically proficient enough to get involved earlier in the purchasing lifecycle and, in any case, they are already very busy with purchase order administration and accounts payable. This approach to procurement has caused problems in the past. For example, the company had problems when a key supplier of raw materials unexpectedly went out of business. This caused short-term production problems, although the CEO has now found an acceptable alternative supplier.

The automation project

On returning to the company from the exhibition, the CEO commissioned a business analyst to investigate the current production process system so that the transition from the current system to the new software package solution could be properly planned. The business analyst found that some of the decisions made in the current production process were difficult to define and it was often hard for managers to explain how they had taken effective action. They tended to use their experience, memory and judgement and were still innovating in their control of the process. One commented that 'what we do today, we might not do tomorrow; requirements are constantly evolving'.

When the software package was delivered there were immediate difficulties in technically migrating some of the data from the current automated part of the production process software to the software package solution. However, after some difficulties, it was possible to hold trials with experienced users. The CEO was confident that these users did not need training and would be 'able to learn the software as they went along'. However, in reality, they found the software very difficult to use and they reported that certain key functions were missing. One of the supervisors commented that 'the monitoring process variance facility is missing completely. Yet we had this in the old automated system'. Despite these reservations, the software package solution was implemented, but results were disappointing. Overall, it was impossible to replicate the success of the old production process and early results showed that costs had increased and lead times had become longer.

After struggling with the system for a few months, support from the software supplier began to become erratic. Eventually, the supplier notified Flexipipe that it had gone into administration and that it was withdrawing support for its product. Fortunately, Flexipipe were able to revert to the original production process software, but the ill-fated package selection exercise had cost it over $3m in costs and lost profits. The CEO commissioned a post-project review which showed that the supplier, prior to the purchase of the software package, had been very highly geared and had very poor liquidity. Also, contrary to the statement of the CEO, the post-project review team reported that there were at least three other packages currently available in the market that could have potentially fulfilled the requirements of the company. The CEO now accepts that using a software package to automate the production process was an inappropriate approach and that a bespoke in-house solution should have been commissioned.

Required:

(a) Critically evaluate the decision made by the CEO to use a software package approach to automating the production process at Flexipipe, and explain why this approach was unlikely to succeed. **(12 marks)**

(b) The CEO recommends that the company now adopts a formal process for procuring, evaluating and implementing software packages which they can use in the future when a software package approach appears to be more appropriate.

Analyse how a formal process for software package procurement, evaluation and implementation would have addressed the problems experienced at Flexipipe in the production process project. **(13 marks)**

(Total: 25 marks)

INFORMATION TECHNOLOGY

27 PERFECT SHOPPER ## *Walk in the footsteps of a top tutor*

Local neighbourhood shops are finding it increasingly difficult to compete with supermarkets. However, three years ago, the Perfect Shopper franchise group was launched that allowed these neighbourhood shops to join the group and achieve cost savings on tinned and packaged goods, particularly groceries. Perfect Shopper purchases branded goods in bulk from established food suppliers and stores them in large purpose-built warehouses, each designed to serve a geographical region. When Perfect Shopper was established it decided that deliveries to these warehouses should be made by the food suppliers or by haulage contractors working on behalf of these suppliers. Perfect Shopper places orders with these suppliers and the supplier arranges the delivery to the warehouse. These arrangements are still in place. Perfect Shopper has no branded goods of its own.

Facilities are available in each warehouse to re-package goods into smaller units, more suitable for the requirements of the neighbourhood shop. These smaller units, typically containing 50–100 tins or packs, are usually small trays, sealed with strong transparent polythene. Perfect Shopper delivers these to its neighbourhood shops using specialist haulage contractors local to the regional warehouse. Perfect Shopper has negotiated significant discounts with suppliers, part of which it passes on to its franchisees. A recent survey in a national grocery magazine showed that franchisees saved an average of 10% on the prices they would have paid if they had purchased the products directly from the manufacturer or from an intermediary – such as cash and carry wholesalers.

As well as offering savings due to bulk buying, Perfect Shopper also provides, as part of its franchise:

(i) Personalised promotional material. This usually covers specific promotions and is distributed locally, either using specialist leaflet distributors or loosely inserted into local free papers or magazines.

(ii) Specialised signage for the shops to suggest the image of a national chain. The signs include the Perfect Shopper slogan 'the nation's local'.

(iii) Specialist in-store display units for certain goods, again branded with the Perfect Shopper logo.

Perfect Shopper does not provide all of the goods required by a neighbourhood shop. Consequently, it is not an exclusive franchise. Franchisees agree to purchase specific products through Perfect Shopper, but other goods, such as vegetables, fruit, stationery and newspapers they source from elsewhere. Deliveries are made every two weeks to franchisees using a standing order for products agreed between the franchisee and their Perfect Shopper sales representative at a meeting they hold every three months. Variations to this order can be made by telephone, but only if the order is increased. Downward variations are not allowed. Franchisees cannot reduce their standing order requirements until the next meeting with their representative.

Perfect Shopper was initially very successful, but its success has been questioned by a recent independent report that showed increasing discontent amongst franchisees. The following issues were documented.

(i) The need to continually review prices to compete with supermarkets.

(ii) Low brand recognition of Perfect Shopper.

(iii) Inflexible ordering and delivery system based around forecasts and restricted ability to vary orders (see above).

As a result of this survey, Perfect Shopper has decided to review its business model. Part of this review is to re-examine the supply chain, to see if there are opportunities for addressing some of its problems.

Required:

(a)   Describe the primary activities of the value chain of Perfect Shopper.   **(5 marks)**

(b)   Explain how Perfect Shopper might re-structure its upstream supply chain to address the problems identified in the scenario.   **(10 marks)**

(c)   Explain how Perfect Shopper might re-structure its downstream supply chain to address the problems identified in the scenario.   **(10 marks)**

(Total: 25 marks)

28   JAYNE COX DIRECT   *Online question assistance*

Jayne Cox Direct is a company that specialises in the production of bespoke sofas and chairs. Its products are advertised in most quality lifestyle magazines. The company was started ten years ago. It grew out of a desire to provide customers with the chance to specify their own bespoke furniture at a cost that compared favourably with standard products available from high street retailers. It sells furniture directly to the end customer. Its website allows customers to select the style of furniture, the wood it is to be made from, the type of upholstery used in cushion and seat fillings and the textile composition and pattern of the covering. The current website has over 60 textile patterns which can be selected by the customer. Once the customer has finished specifying the kind of furniture they want, a price is given. If this price is acceptable to the customer, then an order is placed and an estimated delivery date is given. Most delivery dates are ten weeks after the order has been placed. This relatively long delivery time is unacceptable to some customers and so they cancel the order immediately, citing the quoted long delivery time as their reason for cancellation.

Jayne Cox Direct orders wood, upholstery and textiles from long-established suppliers. About 95% of its wood is currently supplied by three timber suppliers, all of whom supplied the company in its first year of operation. Purchase orders with suppliers are placed by the procurement section. Until last year, they faxed purchase orders through to suppliers. They now email these orders. Recently, an expected order was not delivered because the supplier claimed that no email was received. This caused production delays. Although suppliers like working with Jayne Cox Direct, they are often critical of payment processing. On a number of occasions the accounts section at Jayne Cox Direct has been unable to match supplier invoices with purchase orders, leading to long delays in the payment of suppliers.

The sofas and chairs are built in Jayne Cox Direct's factory. Relatively high inventory levels and a relaxed production process means that production is rarely disrupted. Despite this, the company is unable to meet 45% of the estimated delivery dates given when the order was placed, due to the required goods not being finished in time. Consequently, a member of the sales team has to telephone the customer and discuss an alternative delivery date.

Telephoning the customer to change the delivery date presents a number of problems. Firstly, contacting the customer by telephone can be difficult and costly. Secondly, many customers are disappointed that the original, promised delivery date can no longer be met. Finally, customers often have to agree a delivery date much later than the new delivery date suggested by Jayne Cox Direct. This is because customers often get less than one week's notice of the new date and so they have to defer delivery to much later. This means that the goods have to remain in the warehouse for longer.

A separate delivery problem arises because of the bulky and high value nature of the product. Jayne Cox Direct requires someone to be available at the delivery address to sign for its safe receipt and to put the goods somewhere secure and dry. About 30% of intended deliveries do not take place because there is no-one at the address to accept delivery. Consequently, furniture has to be returned and stored at the factory. A member of the sales staff will subsequently telephone the customer and negotiate a new delivery date but, again, contacting the customer by telephone can be difficult and costly.

Delivery of furniture is made using the company's own vans. Each of these vans follow a defined route each day of the week, irrespective of demand.

The company's original growth was primarily due to the innovative business idea behind specifying competitively priced bespoke furniture. However, established rivals are now offering a similar service. In the face of this competition the managing director of Jayne Cox Direct has urged a thorough review of the supply chain. She feels that costs and inventory levels are too high and that the time taken from order to delivery is too long. Furthermore, in a recent customer satisfaction survey there was major criticism about the lack of information about the progress of the order after it was placed. One commented that 'as soon as Jayne Cox Direct got my order and my money they seemed to forget about me. For ten weeks I heard nothing. Then, just three days before my estimated delivery date, I received a phone call telling me that the order had been delayed and that the estimated delivery date was now 17 June. I had already taken a day off work for 10 June, my original delivery date. I could not re-arrange this day off and so I had to agree a delivery date of 24 June when my mother would be here to receive it'.

People were also critical about after-sales service. One commented 'I accidently stained my sofa. Nobody at Jayne Cox Direct could tell me how to clean it or how to order replacement fabrics for my sofa'. Another said 'organising the return of a faulty chair was very difficult'.

When the managing director of Jayne Cox Direct saw the results of the survey she understood 'why our customer retention rate is so low'.

Required:

(a) **Analyse the existing value chain, using it to highlight areas of weakness at Jayne Cox Direct.** **(12 marks)**

(b) **Evaluate how technology could be used in both the upstream and the downstream supply chain to address the problems identified at Jayne Cox Direct.** **(13 marks)**

(Total: 25 marks)

> *Online question assistance*

29   PROTECH-PUBLIC

Ergo city authority administers environmental, social care, housing and cultural services to the city of Ergo. The city itself has many social problems and a recent report from the local government auditor criticised the Chief Executive Officer (CEO) for not spending enough time and money addressing the pressing housing problems of the city.

Since 1970 the authority has had its own internal Information Technology (IT) department. However, there has been increasing criticism of the cost and performance of this department. The CEO has commented that 'we seem to expand the department to cope with special demands (such as the millennium bug) but the department never seems to shrink back to its original size when the need has passed'. Some employees are lost through natural wastage, but there have never been any redundancies in IT and the labour laws of the nation, and strong trade unions within the authority, make it difficult to make staff redundant.

In the last few years there has been an on-going dispute between managers in the IT department and managers in the finance function. The dispute started due to claims about the falsification of expenses but has since escalated into a personal battle between the director of IT and the finance director. The CEO has had to intervene personally in this dispute and has spent many hours trying to reconcile the two sides. However, issues still remain and there is still tension between the managers of the two departments.

A recent internal human resources (HR) survey of the IT department found that, despite acknowledging that they received above average pay, employees were not very satisfied. The main complaints were about poor management, the ingratitude of user departments, ('we are always being told that we are overheads, and are not core to the business of the authority') and the absence of promotion opportunities within the department. The ingratitude of users is despite the IT department running a relatively flexible approach to fulfilling users' needs. There is no cross-charging for IT services provided and changes to user requirements are accommodated right up to the release of the software. The director of IT is also critical of the staffing constraints imposed on him. He has recently tried to recruit specialists in web services and 'cloud computing' without any success. He also says that 'there are probably other technologies that I have not even heard of that we should be exploring and exploiting'.

The CEO has been approached by a large established IT service company, ProTech, to form a new company ProTech-Public that combines the public sector IT expertise of the authority with the commercial and IT knowledge of ProTech. The joint company will be a private limited company, owned 51% by ProTech and 49% by the city authority. All existing employees in the IT department and the IT technology of the city authority will be transferred to ProTech who will then enter into a 10 year outsourcing arrangement with the city authority. The CEO is very keen on the idea and he sees many other authorities following this route.

The only exception to this transfer of resources concerns the business analysts who are currently in the IT department. They will be retained by the authority and located in a new business analysis department reporting directly to the CEO.

The CEO has suggested that the business analysts have the brief to 'deliver solutions that demonstrably offer benefits to the authority and to the people of the city, using information technology where appropriate'. They need to be 'outward looking and not constrained by current processes and technology'. They will also be responsible for liaising between users and the newly outsourced IT company and, for the first time, defining business cases with users.

In principle, the creation of the new company and the outsourcing deal has been agreed. One of the conditions of the contract, inserted by the finance director, is that the new company achieves CMMI level 5 within three years. The current IT department has been recently assessed as CMMI level 2. ProTech has recently been assessed at CMMI level 3.

Required:

(a) Evaluate the potential benefits to the city authority and its IT employees, of outsourcing IT to ProTech-Public. **(12 marks)**

(b) The role of the business analyst is currently being re-designed.

Analyse what new or enhanced competencies the business analysts will require to undertake their proposed new role in the city authority. **(7 marks)**

(c) This question element is no longer examinable. **(6 marks)**

(Total: 25 marks)

30 GOOD SPORTS

> *Timed question with Online tutor debrief*

Good Sports Limited is an independent sports goods retailer owned and operated by two partners, Alan and Bob. The sports retailing business in the UK has undergone a major change over the past ten years. First of all the supply side has been transformed by the emergence of a few global manufacturers of the core sports products, such as training shoes and football shirts. This consolidation has made them increasingly unwilling to provide good service to the independent sportswear retailers too small to buy in sufficiently large quantities. These independent retailers can stock popular global brands, but have to order using the Internet and have no opportunity to meet the manufacturer's sales representatives. Secondly, UK's sportswear retailing has undergone significant structural change with the rapid growth of a small number of national retail chains with the buying power to offset the power of the global manufacturers. These retail chains stock a limited range of high volume branded products and charge low prices the independent retailer cannot hope to match.

Good Sports has survived by becoming a specialist niche retailer catering for less popular sports such as cricket and hockey. They are able to offer the specialist advice and stock the goods that their customers want. Increasingly since 2000 Good Sports has become aware of the growing impact of e-business in general, and e-retailing in particular. They employed a specialist website designer and created an online purchasing facility for their customers. The results were less than impressive, with the Internet search engines not picking up the company website. The seasonal nature of Good Sports' business, together with the variations in sizes and colours needed to meet an individual customer's needs, meant that the sales volumes were insufficient to justify the costs of running the site.

Bob, however, is convinced that developing an e-business strategy suited to the needs of the independent sports retailer such as Good Sports will be key to business survival. He has been encouraged by the growing interest of customers in other countries to the service and product range they offer. He is also aware of the need to integrate an e-business strategy with their current marketing, which to date has been limited to the sponsorship of local sports teams and advertisements taken in specialist sports magazines. Above all, he wants to avoid head-on competition with the national retailers and their emphasis on popular branded sportswear sold at retail prices that are below the cost price at which Good Sports can buy the goods.

Required:

(a) Provide the partners with a short report on the advantages and disadvantages to Good Sports of developing an e-business strategy and the processes most likely to be affected by such a strategy. **(15 marks)**

(b) Good Sports Limited has successfully followed a niche strategy to date. Assess the extent to which an appropriate e-business strategy could help support such a niche strategy. **(10 marks)**

(Total: 25 marks)

🕐 *Calculate your allowed time, allocate the time to the separate parts...............*

---

31   CRONIN AUTO RETAIL

Cronin Auto Retail (CAR) is a car dealer that sells used cars bought at auctions by its experienced team of buyers. Every car for sale is less than two years old and has a full service history. The company concentrates on small family cars and, at any one time, there are about 120 on display at its purpose-built premises. The premises were acquired five years ago on a 25 year lease and they include a workshop, a small cafe and a children's playroom. All vehicles are selected by one of five experienced buyers who attend auctions throughout the country. Each attendance costs CAR about $500 per day in staff and travelling costs and usually leads to the purchase of five cars. On average, each car costs CAR $10,000 and is sold to the customer for $12,000. The company has a good sales and profitability record, although a recent economic recession has led the managing director to question 'whether we are selling the right type of cars. Recently, I wonder if we have been buying cars that our team of buyers would like to drive, not what our customers want to buy?' However, the personal selection of quality cars has been an important part of CAR's business model and it is stressed in their marketing literature and website.

Sales records show that 90% of all sales are to customers who live within two hours' drive of CAR's base. This is to be expected as there are many competitors and most customers want to buy from a garage that they can easily return the car to if it needs inspection, a service or repair. Consequently, CAR concentrates on display advertising in newspapers in this geographical area. It also has a customer database containing the records of people who have bought cars in the last three years. All customers receive a regular mail-shot, listing the cars for sale and highlighting any special offers or promotions. The company has a website where all the cars are listed with a series of photographs showing each car from a variety of angles. The website also contains general information about the company, special offers and promotions, and information about its service, maintenance and repair service.

CAR is keen to expand the service and mechanical repair side of its business. It would particularly like customers who have purchased cars from them to bring them back for servicing or for any mechanical repairs that are subsequently required. However, although CAR holds basic spare parts in stock, it has to order many parts from specialist parts companies (called motor factors) or from the manufacturers directly. Mechanics have to raise paper requisitions which are passed to the procurement manager for reviewing, agreeing and sourcing. Most parts are ordered from regular suppliers, but there is an increasing backlog and this can cause a particular problem if the customer's car is in the garage waiting for the part to arrive. Customers are increasingly frustrated and annoyed by repairs taking much longer than they were led to expect.

Another source of frustration is that the procurement manager only works from 10.00 to 16.00. The mechanics work on shifts and so the garage is staffed from 07.00 to 19.00. Urgent requisitions cannot be processed when the procurement manager is not at work. The backlog of requisitions is placing increased strain on the procurement manager who has recently made a number of clerical mistakes when raising a purchase order.

Requests for stationery and other office supplies also go through the same requisitioning process, with orders placed with the office supplier who is offering the best current deal. Finding this deal can be time consuming and so employees are increasingly submitting requisitions earlier so that they can be sure that new supplies will be received in time.

The managing director is aware of the problems of the requisitioning system but is reluctant to appoint a second procurement manager because he is trying to keep staff overheads down during a difficult trading period. He is keen to address 'more fundamental issues in the marketing and procurement processes'. He is particularly interested in how the 'interactivity, intelligence, individualisation and independence of location offered by e-marketing media can help us at CAR'.

Required:

(a) **Evaluate how the principles of interactivity, intelligence, individualisation and independence of location might be applied in the e-marketing of the products and services of CAR.** **(16 marks)**

(b) **Explain the principles of e-procurement and evaluate its potential application at CAR.** **(9 marks)**

(Total: 25 marks)

32 SRO

Shop Reviewers Online (SRO) was founded in 2010 by Amy Needham. She felt that many customers buying from online stores were misled by advertising and that too often, purchased products turned out to be unreliable, faulty or failed to meet the customers' expectations. Amy believed that the online retail industry was increasingly acting unethically, caring only for profits at the expense of the needs and expectations of customers.

Consequently, she set up SRO to 'provide an unbiased review of online stores to ensure the customer has all available information'. The company offers reviews of current online stores and provides direct links for customers to shop at the stores featured on its site. The reviews include price comparisons, provided by SRO, as well as general reviews provided by registered users of the site. The company has two main revenue streams. The first is advertising revenue from online stores who place advertisements on the SRO site. The second revenue stream is commission from sales by online stores to customers who have clicked on the sponsored links provided on the SRO website. This commission is only paid by stores who have entered into such a commission arrangement with SRO.

SRO relies upon its website being available online 24 hours a day, 7 days a week. For this reason it has backup servers running concurrently with the main servers on which data is processed and stored. The servers are directly linked so that any update to the main servers automatically occurs on the backup. The servers are all housed in the same computer centre in the company head office. The computer centre has enhanced its security by implementing a fingerprint recognition system for controlling access to the site. However, as the majority of staff at headquarters are IT personnel, and often temporary staff are hired to cover absentees, the fingerprint recognition system is not comprehensive and, to save time, is often bypassed. Similarly, to save time needed to set up new permanent staff with passwords to access the company's systems, a general 'administrator' user has been created, with the password 'password'. Many temporary staff access the system in this way.

SRO has an intelligent software application which constantly searches the internet for product price changes, uploading these into the reviews of the online store in question. Sometimes, however, there have been problems. Usually this is when the application has not recognised an outdated page and has replaced the correct latest price with an old price found on the outdated page. Furthermore, this intelligent software application needs permanent continual access to the internet, and SRO has identified a problem with its firewall which has prevented the software application from sometimes updating the internal systems. For this reason, it has removed the firewall protection to help ensure that the correct up-to-date prices of all online stores are shown on the website.

SRO rarely generates other elements of reviews (such as product experience), leaving this to registered users of the site. However, it will, occasionally, submit its own review to help boost a store which pays a higher commission rate than its competitors. SRO is always honest in its reviews, but the more reviews a store has, the higher up the search list it appears, when a customer searches for a specific product.

Registered users can submit as many reviews as they wish. Unregistered users may also submit reviews, which will be published under the name 'anonymous', but these reviewers will be unable to comment on the reviews of others. SRO checks reviews for appropriate content, but does not contact the store to verify the accuracy of the review.

SRO is about to undertake an audit of the adequacy of its general and application IT controls. In addition, SRO is currently undertaking an internal ethical governance audit, which has identified two main areas of concern:

(1)   Commercial conflicts of interest

As mentioned earlier, SRO's business objective is to 'provide an unbiased review of online stores to ensure the customer has all available information'. However, the audit has revealed that both SRO's revenue streams may cause an ethical dilemma with regards to this objective.

(2)   Company offices

SRO has little need for traditional offices, as it does not have a direct customer-facing role. It mainly requires IT technicians to support its automated services. The company has carried out research which suggests that the IT skills it requires could be sourced at a much lower rate overseas. It is considering relocation to one such country. This country has low rates of corporation tax and cheaper labour costs. However, the country itself is poorly regulated and does not have legislation concerning the quality of information systems or the security of data contained within them, particularly relating to personal data. The culture of the country is such that accepting unauthorised payments for services is also not unusual. Whilst SRO does not condone this in its code of conduct, it is aware that such issues exist in the country under consideration.

Required:

(a) Evaluate the adequacy of the general and application controls in place within SRO, with respect to its information technology and information systems. Suggest any improvements you consider to be necessary. **(15 marks)**

(b) Assess the corporate governance and ethical dilemmas identified by SRO in its possible relocation to the foreign country and discuss the implications of these on organisational mission, purpose and strategy. **(10 marks)**

(Total: 25 marks)

33 BRIDGE CO

Introduction

The following is an interview with Mick Kazinski, a senior marketing executive with Bridge Co, a Deeland-based construction company. It concerns their purchase of Custcare, a Customer Relationship Management (CRM) software package written by the Custcare Corporation, a software company based in Solland, a country some 4,000 km away from Deeland. The interview was originally published in the Management Experiences magazine.

Interviewer: Thanks for talking to us today Mick. Can you tell us how Bridge Co came to choose the Custcare software package?

Mick: Well, we didn't choose it really. Teri Porter had just joined the company as sales and marketing director. She had recently implemented the Custcare package at her previous company and she was very enthusiastic about it. When she found out that we did not have a CRM package at Bridge Co, she suggested that we should also buy the Custcare package as she felt that our requirements were very similar to those of her previous company. We told her that any purchase would have to go through our capex (capital expenditure) system as the package cost over $20,000. Here at Bridge Co, all capex applications have to be accompanied by a formal business case and an Invitation to Tender (ITT) has to be sent out to at least three potential suppliers. However, Teri is a very clever lady. She managed to do a deal with Custcare and they agreed to supply the package at a cost of $19,995, just under the capex threshold. Teri had to cut a few things out. For example, we declined the training courses (Teri said the package was an easy one to use and she would show us how to use it) and also we opted for the lowest level of support, something we later came to regret. Overall, we were happy. We knew that Custcare was a popular and successful CRM package.

Interviewer: So, did you have a demonstration of the software before you bought it?

Mick: Oh yes, and everyone was very impressed. It seemed to do all the things we would ever want it to do and, in fact, it gave us some ideas about possibilities that we would never have thought of. Also, by then, it was clear that our internal IT department could not provide us with a bespoke solution. Teri had spoken to them informally and she was told that they could not even look at our requirements for 18 months. In contrast, we could be up and running with the Custcare package within three months. Also, IT quoted an internal transfer cost of $18,000 for just defining our requirements. This was almost as much as we were paying for the whole software solution!

Interviewer: When did things begin to go wrong?

Mick: Well, the implementation was not straightforward. We needed to migrate some data from our current established systems and we had no-one who could do it. We tried to recruit some local technical experts, but Custcare pointed out that we had signed their standard contract which only permitted Custcare consultants to work on such tasks. We had not realised this, as nobody had read the contract carefully. In the end, we had to give in and it cost us $10,000 in fees to migrate the data from some of our internal systems to the new package. Teri managed to get the money out of the operational budget, but we weren't happy.

We then tried to share data between the Custcare software and our existing order processing system. We thought this would be easy, but apparently the file formats are incompatible. Thus we have to enter customer information into two systems and we are unable to exploit the customer order analysis facility of the Custcare CRM.

Finally, although we were happy with the functionality and reliability of the Custcare software, it works very slowly. This is really very disappointing. Some reports and queries have to be aborted because the software appears to have hung. The software worked very quickly in the demonstration, but it is painfully slow now that it is installed on our IT platform.

Interviewer: What is the current situation?

Mick: Well, we are all a bit deflated and disappointed in the package. The software seems reasonable enough, but its poor performance and our inability to interface it to the order processing system have reduced users' confidence in the system. Because users have not been adequately trained, we have had to phone Custcare's support desk more than we should. However, as I said before, we took the cheapest option. This is for a help line to be available from 8.00 hrs to 17.00 hrs Solland time. As you know, Solland is in a completely different time zone and so we have had to stay behind at work and contact them in the late evening. Again, nobody had closely read the terms of the contract. We have taken legal advice, but we have also found that, for dispute resolution, the contract uses the commercial contract laws of Solland. Nobody in Bridge Co knows what these are! Our solicitor said that we should have asked for this specification to be changed when the contract was drawn up. I just wish we had chosen a product produced by a company here in Deeland. It would have made it much easier to resolve issues and disputes.

Interviewer: What does Teri think?

Mick: Not a lot! She has left us to rejoin her old company in a more senior position. The board did ask her to justify her purchase of the Custcare CRM package, but I don't think she ever did. I am not sure that she could!

Required:

(a) Suggest a process for evaluating, selecting and implementing a software package solution and explain how this process would have prevented the problems experienced at Bridge Co in the Custcare CRM application. **(15 marks)**

(b) The CEO of Bridge Co now questions whether buying a software package was the wrong approach to meeting the CRM requirements at Bridge Co. He wonders whether they should have commissioned a bespoke software system instead.

Explain, with reference to the CRM project at Bridge Co, the advantages of adopting a software package approach to fulfilling business system requirements compared with a bespoke software solution. **(10 marks)**

(Total: 25 marks)

E-MARKETING

34   AEC   *Walk in the footsteps of a top tutor*

Introduction

The Accounting Education Consortium (AEC) offers professional accountancy education and training courses. It currently runs classroom-based training courses preparing candidates for professional examinations in eight worldwide centres. Three of these centres are also used for delivering continuing professional development (CPD) courses to qualified accountants. However, only about 30% of the advertised CPD courses and seminars actually run. The rest are cancelled through not having enough participants to make them economically viable.

AEC has developed a comprehensive set of course manuals to support the preparation of its candidates for professional examinations. There is a course manual for every examination paper in the professional examination scheme. As well as being used on its classroom-based courses, these course manuals are also available for purchase over the Internet. The complete set of manuals for a professional examinations scheme costs $180.00 and the web site has a secure payment facility which allows this to be paid by credit card. Once purchased, the manuals may be downloaded or they may be sent on a CD to the home address of the purchaser. It is only possible to purchase the complete set of manuals for the scheme, not individual manuals for particular examinations. To help the student decide if he or she wishes to buy the complete manual set, the web site has extracts from a sample course manual. This sample may be accessed, viewed and printed once a student has registered their email address, name and address on the web site.

AEC has recently won a contract to supply professional accountancy training to a global accounting company. All students working for this company will now be trained by AEC at one of its worldwide centres.

Web site

The AEC web site has the following functionality:

Who we are: A short description of the company and its products and services.

Professional education courses: Course dates, locations and standard fees for professional examination courses. This schedule of courses is printable.

Continuing professional development: Course dates, locations and standard fees for CPD courses and seminars. This schedule is also printable.

CPD catalogue: Detailed course and seminar descriptions for CPD courses and seminars.

Downloadable study material: Extracts from a sample course manual. Visitors to the site wishing to access this material must register their email address, name and address. 5,500 people registered last year to download study material.

Purchase study material: Secure purchase of a complete manual set for the professional scheme. Payment is by credit card. On completion of successful payment, the visitor is able to download the manuals or to request them to be shipped to a certain address on a CD. At present, 10% of the people who view downloadable study material proceed to purchase.

Who to contact: Who to contact for booking professional training courses or CPD courses and seminars. It provides the name, email address, fax number, telephone number and address of a contact at each of the eight worldwide centres.

Marketing strategy

The marketing manager of AEC has traditionally used magazines, newspapers and direct mail to promote its courses and products. Direct mail is primarily used for sending printed course catalogues to potential customers for CPD courses and seminars. However, she is now keen to develop the potential of the Internet and to increase investment in this medium at the expense of the traditional marketing media. Table 1 shows the percentage allocation of her budget for 20X8, compared with 20X7. The actual budget has only been increased by 3% in 20X8.

Table 1

Percentage allocation of marketing budget (20X7–20X8)

	20X8	20X7
Advertising	30%	40%
Direct mail	10%	30%
Sponsorship	10%	10%
Internet	50%	20%

Required:

(a) **Explain, in the context of AEC, how the marketing characteristics of electronic media (such as the Internet) differ from those of traditional marketing media such as advertising and direct mail.** **(10 marks)**

(b) **Evaluate how the marketing manager might use electronic marketing (including the Internet) to vary the marketing mix at AEC.** **(15 marks)**

(Total: 25 marks)

35 THE HOLIDAY COMPANY

The Holiday Company (HC) currently offers travel agency services by giving travel advice and making travel bookings for customers who physically visit the offices located in most major towns in the country. However, it is progressively reducing this part of the business while simultaneously trying to achieve a greater proportion of its revenue online.

To help meet this objective, HC is in the process of forming a new business unit to market and sell luxury holidays. The holiday product range marketed by this new business unit will be named Inspirations. It is intended that Inspirations will provide a high quality, bespoke holiday service for discerning clients. HC has decided that this new business unit will have its own mission statement of 'delivering a high quality service for discerning travellers'. The new managing director of Inspirations has stated that it has an objective of achieving annual revenue of $100m by 2018. This would be approximately 25% of the total forecast revenue for HC that year, but it is expected to represent only about 5% of the total number of holidays sold by HC. The type of holidays offered by Inspirations is already provided by some of HC's competitors.

Dilip Kharel, the new director of marketing of Inspirations, has stated that the internet should be increasingly used as the main source of marketing and selling the holidays, as 'the days are almost gone when families visit a 'high street' travel agency to plan their holiday; it's all done now from the comfort of the home'. He believes that potential customers of Inspirations will not want to visit high street travel agencies.

HC currently makes extensive use of traditional marketing techniques, sending out travel brochures containing all of its holidays to potential customers. However, as Dilip has recognised, 'the problem is that we don't even know if our customers bother opening these, or if they put them directly into the dustbin.' These brochures are often produced months in advance, and may advertise holidays which are no longer available. Customers will not discover this until they visit one of the travel agents. The company currently does make some use of targeted emails, but it has been accused of sending spam mail in the past and mass mailing a weekly email of all current holiday offers to everyone registered on its database.

Dilip is keen to embrace the opportunities offered by electronic marketing and believes that Inspirations can benefit greatly by exploiting the principles of intelligence, individualisation, interactivity, integration and independence of location which are central to electronic marketing.

Inspirations will offer holidays in a wide variety of locations, including the Caribbean, Africa and Asia, and plan to offer 'themed' trips, such as gourmet food holidays and heritage trips. Different countries may have different requirements for visiting tourists, such as visa regulations. Inspirations does not own hotels or aircraft and therefore the majority of holidays offered will be provided by third-party suppliers, such as hotel and airline companies. This means that Inspirations can lack control over some elements such as passenger taxes. Inspirations will have representatives on site in all resorts to meet guests at airports and to address any issues they have with the holiday. However, the hotels and excursions will not be solely or exclusively offered to Inspirations guests. For example, there will be other guests at a hotel who have not booked through Inspirations.

Dilip is concerned about this. He feels that the company needs to be able to differentiate itself, either in the overall holiday experience itself or in the marketing of it, so that customers are more likely to book such holidays through Inspirations, rather than through a competitor, or indeed through booking with the hotel directly. He also recognises the importance of adopting an appropriate pricing strategy which meets the needs of the organisation (HC and Inspirations) and customers alike.

Required:

(a) **Evaluate how the principles of intelligence, individualisation, interactivity, integration and independence of location could be exploited when marketing the new range of holidays to be offered by Inspirations.** **(15 marks)**

Dilip Kharel recognises the importance of a pricing strategy which supports the overall corporate and business strategies of the organisation.

Required:

(b) **Describe a strategic approach to establishing prices in the context of Inspirations. You should recognise both economic and non-economic factors in your approach.**
   (10 marks)

   (Total: 25 marks)

36   HGT

Housham Garden is a large garden in the country of Euphorbia, where gardening and visiting gardens is a popular pastime. For many years the garden was neglected, until bought by the Popper family who painstakingly restored the garden and four years ago opened it to the public. The garden is now owned and operated by a charitable trust set up by the Popper family – the Housham Garden Trust (HGT) – with initial funding provided by a legacy from the late Clive Popper.

However, HGT is finding it difficult to meet its costs and it is gradually spending the legacy. It is estimated that fixed costs are currently $60,000 per annum. The price of entry into the garden is $5 per visit. At present, there are approximately 1,000 visits per month and the garden is open for eight months a year. It is closed for a period when the weather is usually much colder and few plants are flowering. HGT feels that few people would wish to visit the garden and so they have always closed it for the four 'cold' months.

There is a café in the garden and it is estimated that 60% of visitors visit the café and buy drinks and food. However, each purchase is relatively modest. The current trust administrator estimates that the average contribution is $1.25 per visitor using the café.

A recent survey undertaken by a local university revealed that most consumers felt that the admission price for a garden such as Housham was too high. It revealed that the average consumer would be willing to pay an entry fee of $3.25, and indeed similar gardens in Euphorbia charge about this amount.

HGT currently advertises the garden in the monthly magazine 'Heritage Gardens'. Each display advertisement costs $500 per issue. Adverts have been booked for the next six months, but it is possible to cancel the last three of these without incurring cancellation charges. The advertisements, like HGT's brochure, stress the historical nature of the garden (it is the only surviving garden designed by William Wessex) and the painstaking nature of the restoration. However, these were not factors that figured highly in a recent visitor survey. Table 1 shows the most common primary reasons for visitors visiting the garden. Two hundred visitors were surveyed and they were only allowed to choose one reason for visiting Housham Gardens

Table 1: Primary reasons for visiting the gardens: one day survey on 13 March 2012

Reason for visiting Housham Garden	Number of respondents
To walk in a peaceful, beautiful, safe environment	100
To enjoy the plants and flowers of the garden	70
To see the restoration work carried out by the trust	20
To visit the café and shop	5
To observe the work of William Wessex	5

Respondents were critical of the food offered by the café. One respondent commented that quality 'had gone down since the café was moved into the garden. Really, there is very little choice, and I could not find anything substantial enough for lunch'. Her reference to the relocation of the café into the garden refers to the fact that the café used to be in the gatehouse of the garden. At this time, many people just visited Housham to use the café and did not pay for admission into the garden. It was decided that moving the café inside the garden would encourage people to pay for garden entry. However, this has not occurred. It is estimated that the café has lost about 500 visits per month and this has had an adverse effect on staff morale and food quality. The gatehouse area where the café was originally situated is still empty.

In the recent consumer survey, 20% of the respondents said that they would buy an annual (calendar year) ticket giving access to the garden for eight months if it were offered for $9. The customer survey also asked visitors where they had heard of the garden. Table 2 summarises their responses. Again, the 200 respondents were only allowed to make one choice for how they heard about Housham Gardens.

Table 2: How visitors heard about the gardens: one day survey on 13 March 2012

How did you hear of Housham Gardens?	Number of respondents
Personal recommendation from a friend	110
Recent articles in the local newspaper	50
Internet	10
Heritage Gardens magazine	10
Other	20

The reference in Table 2 to recent articles in the local newspaper concerns a series of articles written by the HGT administrator outlining the problems of the trust and the fact that short-term cash flow problems might cause the garden's temporary closure. One visitor commented that 'we had never heard of Housham Gardens until then, and we only live four kilometres away'.

HGT also has a simple informative web site showing the location of the garden, giving opening times, showing pictures of the restoration and providing a biography of William Wessex.

You are a business analyst who undertakes voluntary work for the trust. You have been asked to suggest immediate short-term changes as well as long-term marketing initiatives for the trust. Short-term changes should be proposals which can be implemented immediately or within three months and will generate quantifiable income or savings. Long-term marketing initiatives are proposals which will take longer than three months to implement.

Required:

(a) Using the data provided, show why HGT is losing money and recommend immediate and other short-term (within three months) changes for HGT, quantifying the increased income or cost savings that these changes should bring.

(15 marks)

(b) Recommend, with justifications, longer-term marketing strategies (longer than three months) for HGT.

(10 marks)

(Total: 25 marks)

37   BA TIMES

The country of Umboria has two professional business analysis associations, both running certification examination schemes for business analysts worldwide. These are the Association of Benefits Consultants (ABC) and the Institute of Consultants, Finance and Commerce (ICFC). Many private and public sector learning providers run accredited training courses to prepare candidates for the examinations. Some learning providers provide courses for both associations, whilst others focus on niche markets. Umboria itself is a wealthy country with high labour costs and property prices, particularly in the capital city of Ambosium.

Victor is the editor of the *BA Times*, a subscription magazine, published once a month, which provides news and articles preparing students for the examinations of both business analysis associations. The magazine is edited and printed in offices and an adjoining factory in Ambosium. The offices and factory are leased and the magazine currently employs 20 people, all of whom live close to the offices. It is the only independent magazine in the sector. Each association has its own magazine and website, but relatively tight control is maintained over their editorial policy. Victor was the editor of the ABC magazine (*Business Analysis Today*) for 16 years before establishing the *BA Times* nine years ago. Because of its independence, the *BA Times* can be a little more controversial and provocative than its rivals and it is popular with students and well respected by the profession.

However, despite such recognition, the magazine is currently unprofitable due to increased production, distribution and office costs, falling subscriptions and reduced advertising. Changing reading habits in Umboria, particularly amongst the young, has led to less reading of printed media. All of the traditional media providers are experiencing financial problems. The sales of printed magazines and the profits of publishers are both falling dramatically throughout Umboria. Furthermore, advertisers are increasingly unconvinced about the effectiveness of advertising in printed magazines and so the advertising revenues of these magazines are also falling.

The *BA Times* currently has a website but its role is to convince the visitor to order the printed magazine. The website offers extracts of news and articles, often with provocative headlines, which may only be read in full in the printed magazine.

Recent survey

A recent survey of people who had decided not to renew their *BA Times* subscription revealed the following comments:

> I am studying the ABC syllabus and so in-depth articles on ICFC topics and examinations are not relevant to me. I quite enjoy reading the news parts, but not the in-depth analysis of examinations that I am not taking. *ABC student*

> I have reached the final stage of my examinations. I do not want to read articles about the stages I have already passed. I reckon only about 15% of *BA Times* is relevant to me now. *ABC Final Stage student*

> Some of the readers' letters are really irritating or just plain wrong, but the editor seldom makes a comment! It really annoys me! *ICFC student*

> I became a business analyst to get a job, not just to sit examinations and read about examining bodies. *ICFC student*

The examinations are getting more demanding and Victor is under pressure to increase the number of technical examination articles in the magazine, despite the fact that this will make the magazine longer and heavier and so increase print and distribution costs.

Victor is aware that new technology and new media offer opportunities for changing the business model and the financial performance of the *BA Times*. However, he likes the physical, tactile feel of printed magazines and he feels that some of his subscribers do as well. Also, he cannot see how harnessing new technology will make him money, particularly if it leads to decreasing sales of the printed magazine. He is also concerned about how his subscribers and advertisers will react to technological change. He feels that some subscribers will not have access to online technology and that many advertisers would prefer to continue with display advertisements in a printed magazine.

Required:

(a) Analyse how the principles of interactivity, individualisation, intelligence and independence of location offered by the internet and other new media could be exploited by Victor in his development of a new business model for the *BA Times*.

(15 marks)

(b) Write a short report which addresses the specific concerns Victor has about the effect of any potential technology or media change on his subscribers, on his advertisers and on the financial viability of his company. (10 marks)

(Total: 25 marks)

38 CHEMICAL TRANSPORT

Chemical Transport (CT) is a specialist haulage company providing transport services for several chemical wholesalers. Despite these wholesalers being in competition with each other, many of them have outsourced their distribution to CT, recognising the company's expertise in this area and its compliance with stringent and emerging legislation. This legislation is at both national and international level and concerns the transportation and handling of chemicals, as well as the maintenance of trucks and trailers and the health, competencies, safety and driving hours of drivers. There are also chemical wholesalers in the country who either organise their own distribution or outsource to one of CT's competitors.

CT handles the distribution of chemicals from either the port of importation or point of production to the wholesaler's depots or directly to the end customers of the wholesaler. The chemical wholesalers are increasingly attempting to minimise their own storage costs, so many of CT's deliveries are now directly from the point of production (or port of importation) to the end customer. Most of these end customers are manufacturing companies with limited chemical storage capacity.

The complex and changing nature of legislation has led to CT engaging a specialist legal consultancy to provide it with advice. They have found this advice to be both useful and proactive. The consultancy has identified the potential effect of employment, tax and health and safety legislation in advance and has notified CT of its likely implications. CT has benefited from this advice but it is concerned that it is expensive and it is considering employing a full-time legal expert, instead of using the legal consultancy.

The chemical wholesalers have asked CT to provide an internet-based system which would allow them to request and track deliveries. CT does currently have a website, but it only contains information about the company: its structures, history, key contacts and case studies. CT has agreed to provide such a system because it is aware that failure to do so will lead to wholesalers looking for an alternative distributor. CT does have an internal IT capability with some expertise in building web-based systems. The internal IT team have also developed a bespoke payroll system.

Drivers at CT are rewarded with basic pay, together with a complex set of bonuses and deductions which have been developed and enhanced over the last few years. There are bonuses for certain skills and attainments and deductions for missed or delayed deliveries or mistakes. The drivers themselves find the pay arrangements very confusing. One commented that 'we find it almost impossible to check if we have been paid correctly and it confuses us rather than motivates us!' Changes in national tax legislation are also continually affecting the payroll calculation. Indeed, recent changes in legislation led to the IT team being fully occupied for three months, developing and testing the required modifications to the payroll system.

(a)   Three significant business process areas have been identified in the scenario: (1) payroll, (2) legal advice and (3) an enhanced web service allowing wholesalers to request and track deliveries.

Required:

Use Harmon's process-strategy matrix to analyse the characteristics of each of the three process areas defined above and suggest how each should be sourced and implemented at CT. **(15 marks)**

(b)   Requesting and tracking information could be the first part of a comprehensive customer relationship management (CRM) system

Required:

Evaluate how CT could use a CRM system to acquire and retain customers.

(10 marks)

(Total: 25 marks)

39   ITTRAIN

For 11 years, Marco was a senior salesman at AQT, a company specialising in IT certification courses. During that time, AQT became the most successful and dominant training provider in the market.

Marco has now left AQT and established his own training company, iTTrain, aimed at the same IT certification market as his former employers. He wishes to offer premium quality courses in a high quality environment with high quality teaching. He has selected a number of self-employed lecturers and he has agreed a daily lecturing fee of $450 per day with them. He has also selected the prestigious CityCentre training centre as his course venue. It has a number of training rooms which hold up to nine delegates. Each training room costs $250 per day to hire. There is also a $10 per day per delegate charge for lunch and other refreshments. Although not a lecturer, Marco is an IT expert and he has already produced the relevant documentation for the courses iTTrain will run. He sees this as a sunk cost and is not concerned about recovering it. However, printing costs mean that there is also a $20 cost for the course manual which is given to every course delegate.

Marco has scheduled 40 courses next year, as he is limited by the availability of lecturers. Each course will have a maximum of nine delegates (determined by the room size) and a minimum of three delegates. Each course is three days long.

iTTrain has been set up with $70,000 of Marco's own money. He currently estimates that fixed annual costs will be $65,000 (which includes his own salary) and he would like the company to return a modest profit in its first year of operation as it establishes itself in the market.

Marco is currently considering the price he wishes to charge for his courses. AQT charges $900 per delegate for a three-day course, but he knows that it discounts this by up to 10% and a similar discount is also offered to training brokers or intermediaries who advertise AQT courses on their own websites. Some of these intermediaries have already been in touch with Marco to ask if he would be prepared to offer them similar discounts in return for iTTrain courses being advertised on their websites. There are also a number of cheaper training providers who offer the same courses for as little as $550 per delegate. However, these tend to focus on self-financing candidates for whom price is an issue. These courses are often given in poor quality training premises by poorly motivated lecturers. Marco is not really interested in this market. He wants to target the corporate business market, where quality is as important as price and the course fee is paid by the delegate's employer. He is currently considering a price of $750 per delegate.

During his employment at AQT, Marco collected statistics about courses and delegates. Figure 1 shows the data he collected showing the attendance pattern over 1,000 courses.

Number of delegates attending the course	Number of courses
3	150
4	210
5	250
6	190
7	70
8	80
9	50
Total	1,000

Figure 1: Analysis of attendance at 1,000 AQT courses

Required:

(a) Suggest a pricing strategy for iTTrain, including an evaluation of the initial price of $750 per delegate suggested by Marco. Your strategy should include both financial and non-financial considerations. **(16 marks)**

(b) Physical evidence, people and process are three important elements of the marketing mix for services.

Analyse the contribution each of these three elements could make to the success of iTTrain's entry into the IT certification market. **(9 marks)**

(Total: 25 marks)

40 MARATEC

Maratec is a bespoke furniture company, making unique pieces of furniture to clients' specifications. The products are manufactured using a combination of highly technical machinery and skilled craftsmen. Maratec's current clients are wealthy individuals who want a custom-built piece of furniture for their own homes. The company has one showroom where samples of bespoke pieces of furniture are displayed. These sample pieces are not for sale.

The company wishes to implement a planned growth strategy. To enable this, the company has increased its manufacturing capacity with the aim of selling to corporate clients such as hotels. Producing a greater number of bespoke pieces for the same client would deliver some economies of scale. The production manager claims this strategy would reduce set up times and increase procurement discounts, as raw materials would be bought in bulk.

Procurement

High quality materials are used in bespoke furniture manufacture and Maratec uses a specialist procurement company to source specific materials, such as high quality pieces of oak wood of given dimensions. This is an expensive method of procurement and can also delay production, as Maratec cannot confirm an order with the procurement company until a design is agreed with a client. As order to delivery time is already high, Maratec is keen to reduce this procurement time.

The production manager has suggested the implementation of e-procurement, to support planned business growth. He is considering moving to e-procurement, but is keen to ensure that such a move will not lead to a lower quality of raw materials. If e-procurement is adopted, the company will recruit a full-time procurement manager and cancel its agreement with the specialist procurement company.

Marketing

Until now, Maratec has relied predominantly on word-of-mouth marketing. Most new clients have commissioned pieces of furniture after seeing a bespoke piece in an existing client's home. High quality brochures are produced annually and are available on request. They are also placed on display at exhibitions and in the showroom. A new marketing manager has been recruited and has been tasked with analysing whether e-marketing could enhance the current marketing mix. The marketing manager has also identified the following issues:

Visualisation of the product – Because the products are bespoke, it is difficult for a client to visualise what the finished product will look like. This can sometimes lead to a failure to make a sale, as the customer is not sure what they are getting.

Pricing – As materials are not sourced until a design is agreed, it is difficult to provide accurate up-front prices. Maratec currently uses cost plus pricing, but the marketing manager understands that this may deter some clients.

Showroom – There is only one showroom and it is not considered worthwhile opening more as more pieces of furniture would have to be created especially to furnish it. Therefore it is not possible for many potential clients to see the quality of the furniture.

After-sale support

As there is no guaranteed delivery time for the products, Maratec provides production progress updates to their clients on request. When the client phones or emails, the production team photograph the work-in-progress and send the pictures to the client. The client can also visit the manufacturing plant to check on progress, but this requires prior arrangement due to legal health and safety requirements.

Maratec intends to remain a producer of bespoke furniture items. It does not wish to produce standard products or produce to inventory. The only non-commissioned pieces of furniture it produces are for display in the showroom.

Required:

(a) Evaluate the use of e-marketing at Maratec to enhance each of following five elements of the marketing mix: price, promotion, place, processes and physical evidence. **(15 marks)**

(b) Describe the principles of e-procurement and explain the benefits and risks to Maratec. **(10 marks)**

(Total: 25 marks)

PROJECT MANAGEMENT

41 HOMEDELIVER

HomeDeliver is a nationwide company that sells small household goods to consumers. It produces an attractive, comprehensive catalogue which it distributes to staff known as catalogue supervisors. There are 150 of these supervisors in the country. Each supervisor has approximately 30 part-time home-based agents, who then deliver the catalogue to consumers in their homes. Agents subsequently collect the catalogue and any completed order forms and forward these forms to their supervisor. Payment is also taken when the order is collected. Payment is by cash or cheque and these payments are also forwarded to the supervisor by the agent. At the end of the week the supervisor returns completed order forms (and payments) to HomeDeliver. Order details are then entered into a computer system by order entry administrators at HomeDeliver and this starts an order fulfilment process that ends with goods being delivered directly to the customer. The supervisors and the agents are all self-employed. HomeDeliver rewards supervisors on the basis of how many agents they manage. Agents' reward packages are based on how many catalogues they deliver and a commission based on orders received from the homes they have collected orders from.

In August 2010 HomeDeliver decided to replace the physical ordering system with a new electronic ordering system. Agents would be provided with software which would allow them to enter customer orders directly into the computer system using their home personal computer at the end of each day. Payments would also be paid directly into a HomeDeliver bank account by agents at the end of each day.

The software to support the new ordering system was developed in-house to requirements provided by the current order entry administrators at HomeDeliver and managers concerned with order fulfilment and invoicing. The software was tested internally by the order entry administrators. At first, both the specification of requirements and initial software testing progressed very slowly because order administrators were continuing with their normal operational duties. However, as project delays became more significant, selected order administrators were seconded to the project full-time. As a result the software was fully acceptance tested by the end of July 2011, two months behind schedule.

In August 2011 the software was rolled out to all supervisors and agents. The software was claimed to be easy to use, so no formal training was given. A large comprehensive manual with colour screenshots was attached as a PDF to an email sent to all supervisors and agents. This gave detailed instructions on how to set up and use the software.

Unfortunately, problems began to appear as soon as the agents tried to load and use the software. It was found to be incompatible with one particular popular browser, and agents whose computers used that browser were advised to use an alternative browser or computer. Agents also criticised the functionality of the software because it did not allow for the amendment of orders once they had been submitted. It emerged that customers often contacted agents and supervisors to amend their order prior to it being sent to HomeDeliver. This was no longer possible with the new system. Many agents also claimed that it was not possible to enter multiple orders for one household. However, HomeDeliver confirmed that entering multiple orders was possible; it was just not clear from the software, or from the instructions provided, how this could be achieved.

Most of the agents were reluctant to print off the manual (preferring to read it on screen) and a significant number claimed that they did not receive the email with the manual attachment. Agents also found quite a number of spelling and functionality errors in the manual. At certain points the software did not perform in the way the manual stated that it would. Internal standards at HomeDeliver require both a post-project and a post-implementation review.

Required:

(a) Explain the purpose of each of the following: a post-project review, a post-implementation review and a benefits realisation review. **(6 marks)**

(b) Evaluate the problems and the lessons that should be learned from a post-project review and a post-implementation review of the electronic ordering system at HomeDeliver. **(12 marks)**

(c) HomeDeliver does not have a benefits management process and so a benefits realisation review is inappropriate. However, it does feel that it would be useful to retrospectively define the benefits to HomeDeliver of the new electronic ordering system.

Identify and discuss the potential benefits to HomeDeliver of the new electronic ordering system. **(7 marks)**

(Total: 25 marks)

42 ASW 👣 *Walk in the footsteps of a top tutor*

ASW is a software house which specialises in producing software packages for insurance companies. ASW has a basic software package for the insurance industry that can be used immediately out of the box. However, most customers wish ASW to tailor the package to reflect their own products and requirements. In a typical ASW project, ASW's business analysts define the gap between the customer's requirements and the basic package. These business analysts then specify the complete software requirement in a system specification. This specification is used by its programmers to produce a customised version of the software. It is also used by the system testers at ASW to perform their system tests before releasing it to the customer for acceptance testing.

One of ASW's new customers is CaetInsure. Initially CaetInsure sent ASW a set of requirements for their proposed new system. Business analysts from ASW then worked with CaetInsure staff to produce a full system specification for CaetInsure's specific requirements. ASW do not begin any development until this system specification is signed off. After some delay (see below), the system specification was eventually signed off by CaetInsure.

Since sign-off, ASW developers have been working on tailoring the product to obtain an appropriate software solution. The project is currently at week 16 and the software is ready for system testing. The remaining activities in the project are shown in figure 1. This simple plan has been put together by the project manager. It also shows who has responsibility for undertaking the activities shown on the plan.

The problem that the project manager faces is that the plan now suggests that implementation (parallel running) cannot take place until part way through week 28. The original plan was for implementation in week 23. Three weeks of the delay were due to problems in signing off the system specification. Key CaetInsure employees were unavailable to make decisions about requirements, particularly in the re-insurance part of the system. Too many requirements in this module were either unclear or kept changing as users sought clarification from their managers. There have also been two further weeks of slippage since the sign-off of the system specification.

The CaetInsure contract had been won in the face of stiff competition. As part of securing the deal, the ASW sales account manager responsible for the CaetInsure contract agreed that penalty clauses could be inserted into the contract. The financial penalty for late delivery of the software increases with every week's delay. CaetInsure had insisted on these clauses as they have tied the delivery of the software in with the launch of a new product. Although the delay in signing off the system specification was due to CaetInsure, the penalty clauses still remain in the contract. When the delay was discussed with the customer and ASW's project manager, the sales account manager assured CaetInsure that the 'time could be made up in programming'.

The initial planned delivery date (week 23) is now only seven weeks away. The project manager is now under intense pressure to come up with solutions which address the project slippage.

The project plan is presented in Figure 1:

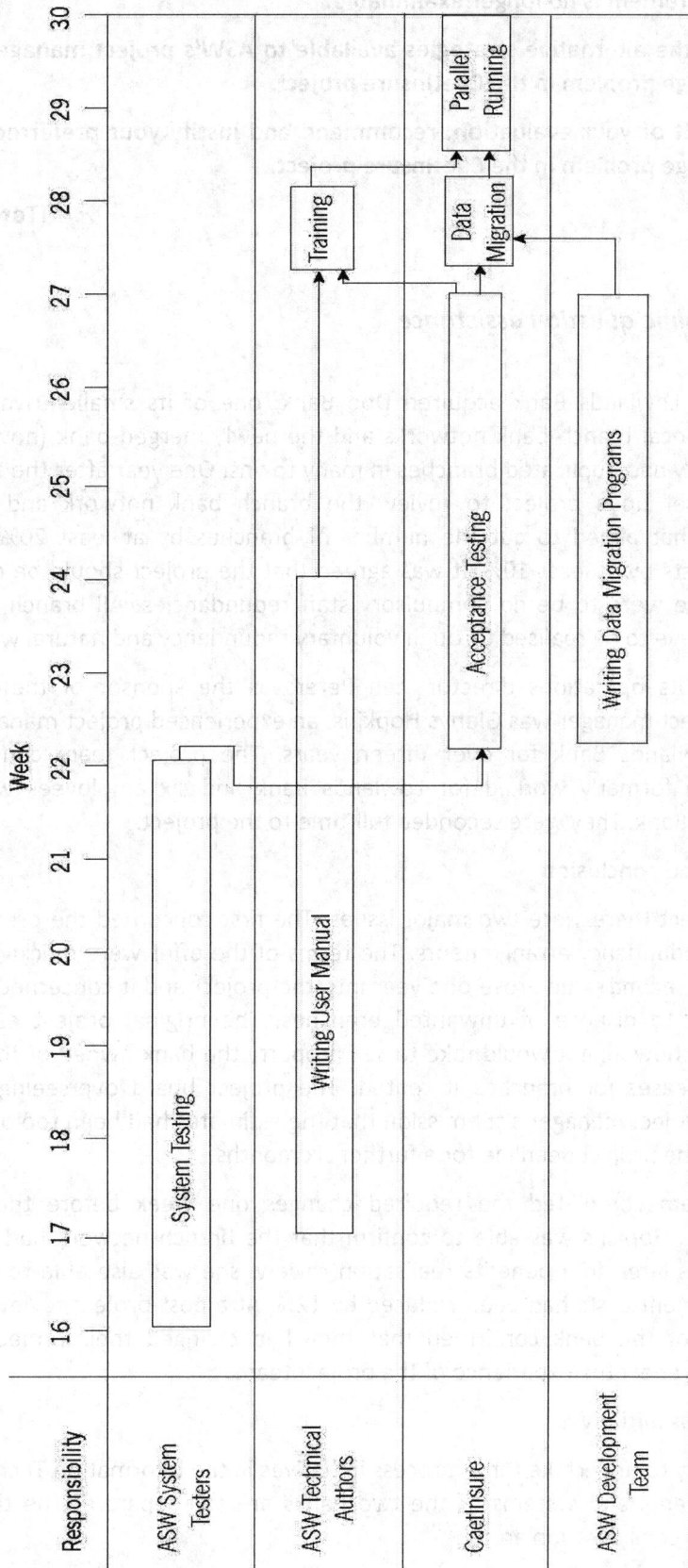

Figure 1: Project Plan – ASW: CaetInsure Contract

Required:

(a)   This requirement is no longer examinable.

(b)   Evaluate the alternative strategies available to ASW's project manager to address the slippage problem in the CaetInsure project.   **(10 marks)**

(c)   As a result of your evaluation, recommend and justify your preferred solution to the slippage problem in the CaetInsure project.   **(6 marks)**

(Total: 16 marks)

43   LDB   *Online question assistance*

Four years ago Lowlands Bank acquired Doe Bank, one of its smaller rivals. Both had relatively large local branch bank networks and the newly merged bank (now called LDB) found that it now had duplicated branches in many towns. One year after the takeover was finalised, LDB set up a project to review the branch bank network and carry out a rationalisation that aimed to cut the number of branches by at least 20% and branch employment costs by at least 10%. It was agreed that the project should be completed in two years. There were to be no compulsory staff redundancies. All branch employment savings would have to be realised through voluntary redundancy and natural wastage.

LDB appointed its operations director, Len Peters as the sponsor of the project. The designated project manager was Glenys Hopkins, an experienced project manager who had worked for Lowlands Bank for over fifteen years. The project team consisted of six employees who formerly worked for Lowlands Bank and six employees who formerly worked for Doe Bank. They were seconded full-time to the project.

Project issues and conclusion

During the project there were two major issues. The first concerned the precise terms of the voluntary redundancy arrangements. The terms of the offer were quickly specified by Len Peters. The second issue arose one year into the project and it concerned the amount of time it took to dispose of unwanted branches. The original project estimates had underestimated how long it would take to sell property the bank owned or to re-assign or terminate the leases for branches it rented. The project board overseeing the project agreed to the project manager's submission that the estimates had been too optimistic and they extended the project deadline for a further six months.

The project team completed the required changes one week before the rearranged deadline. Glenys Hopkins was able to confirm that the branch network had been cut by 23%. Six months later, in a benefits realisation review, she was also able to confirm that branch employment costs had been reduced by 12%. At a post-project review the project support office of the bank confirmed that they had changed their project estimating assumptions to reflect the experience of the project team.

Potential process initiatives

LDB is now ready to undertake three process initiatives in the Information Technology area. The IT departments and systems of the two banks are still separate. The three process initiatives under consideration are:

(1)   The integration of the two bespoke payroll systems currently operated by the two banks into one consolidated payroll system. This will save the costs of updating and maintaining two separate systems.

(2)   The updating of all personal desktop computer hardware and software to reflect contemporary technologies and the subsequent maintenance of that hardware. This will allow the desktop to be standardised and bring staff efficiency savings.

(3)   The bank has recently identified the need for a private personal banking service for wealthy customers. Processes, systems and software have to be developed to support this new service. High net worth customers have been identified by the bank as an important growth area.

The bank will consider three solution options for each initiative. These are outsourcing or software package solution or bespoke development.

Required:

(a)   The branch rationalisation was a successful project.

Identify and analyse the elements of good project management that helped make the branch rationalisation project successful.   (12 marks)

(b)   The bank has identified three further desirable process initiatives (see above).

(i)   Explain, using Harmon's process-strategy matrix, how the complexity and strategic importance of process initiatives can be classified.   (4 marks)

(ii) Recommend and justify a solution option for each of the three process initiatives.   (9 marks)

(Total: 25 marks)

Online question assistance

44   8-HATS PROMOTIONS

8-Hats Promotions was formed twenty years ago by Barry Gorkov to plan, organise and run folk festivals in Arcadia. It soon established itself as a major events organiser and diversified into running events for the staff and customers of major companies. For example, for many years it has organised launch events, staff reward days and customer experiences for Kuizan, the car manufacturer. 8-Hats has grown through a combination of organic growth and acquiring similar and complementary companies. Recently, it purchased a travel agent (now operated as the travel department of 8-Hats) to provide travel to and from the events that it organised.

Barry Gorkov is himself a flamboyant figure who, in the early years of the company, changed his name to Barry Blunt to reflect his image and approach. He calls all the events 'jobs', a terminology used throughout the company. A distinction is made between external jobs (for customers) and internal jobs (within 8-Hats itself). The company is organised on functional lines. The sales and marketing department tenders for external jobs and negotiates contracts. Sales managers receive turnover-related bonuses and 8-Hats is known in the industry for its aggressive pricing policies. Once a contract is signed, responsibility for the job is passed to the events department which actually organises the event. It is known for its creativity and passion. The operations department has responsibility for running the event (job) on the day and for delivering the vision defined by the events department. The travel department is responsible for any travel arrangements associated with the job. Finally, the finance department is responsible for managing cash flow throughout the job, raising customer invoices, paying supplier invoices and chasing any late payments.

However, there is increasing friction between the departments. The operations department is often unable to deliver the features and functionality defined by the events department within the budget agreed by the sales manager. Finance is unaware of the cash flow implications of the job. Recently, an event was in jeopardy because suppliers had not been paid. They threatened to withdraw their services from the event. Eventually, Barry Blunt had to resolve friction between finance and other departments by acquiring further funding from the bank. The event went ahead, but it unsettled Kuizan which had commissioned the job. The sales and marketing department has also complained about the margins expected by the travel department, claiming that they are making the company uncompetitive.

There has been a considerable amount of discussion at 8-Hats about the investment appraisal approach used to evaluate internal jobs. The company does not have sufficient money and resources to carry out all the internal jobs that need doing. Consequently, the finance department has used the Net Present Value (NPV) technique as a way of choosing which jobs should be undertaken. Figure 1 shows an example comparison of two computer system applications that had been under consideration. Job One was selected because its Net Present Value (NPV) was higher ($25,015) than Job Two ($2,090).

'I don't want to tell you about the specific details of the two applications, so I have called them Job One and Job Two' said Barry. 'However, in the end, Job One was a disaster. Looking back, we should have gone with Job Two, not Job One. We should have used simple payback, as I am certain that Job Two, even on the initial figures, paid back much sooner than Job One. That approach would have suited our mentality at the time – quick wins. Whoever chose a discount rate of 8% should be fired – inflation has been well below this for the last five years. We should have used 3% or 4%. Also, calculating the IRR would have been useful, as I am sure that Job Two would have shown a better IRR than Job One, particularly as the intangible benefits of improved staff morale appear to be underestimated. Intangible benefits are just as important as tangible benefits. Finally, we should definitely have performed a benefits realisation analysis at the end of the feasibility study. Leaving it to after the project had ended was a ridiculous idea.'

Figure 1: NPV calculation for two projects at 8-Hats (with a discount rate of 8%)

Job One

Costs

		Year 0	Year 1	Year 2	Year 3	Year 4	
				$000s			
	Hardware costs	50	0	0	0	0	
	Software costs	50	0	0	0	0	
	Maintenance costs	10	10	10	10	10	
	Total	110	10	10	10	10	
Benefits	Staff savings	0	40	5	0	0	
	Contractor savings	0	20	10	10	10	
	Better information	0	0	0	20	30	
	Improved staff morale	0	0	10	20	30	
	Total	0	60	25	50	70	
	Cash flows	−110	50	15	40	60	
	Discount factor at 8%	1.000	0.926	0.857	0.794	0.735	**NPV**
	Discounted CF	−110.000	46.300	12.855	31.760	44.100	25.015

Job Two $000s

Costs		Year 0	Year 1	Year 2	Year 3	Year 4
	Hardware costs	50	0	0	0	0
	Software costs	30	10	10	0	0
	Maintenance costs	10	10	10	10	10
	Total	90	20	20	10	10
Benefits	Staff savings	0	30	10	5	0
	Contractor savings	0	30	15	15	15
	Better information	0	0	0	10	10
	Improved staff morale	0	0	10	10	10
	Total	0	60	35	40	35

	Year 0	Year 1	Year 2	Year 3	Year 4	NPV
Cash flows	−90	40	15	30	25	
Discount factor at 8%	1.000	0.926	0.857	0.794	0.735	
Discounted CF	−90.000	37.040	12.855	23.820	18.375	2.090

Required:

(a) Barry Blunt has criticised the investment appraisal approach used at 8-Hats to evaluate internal jobs. He has made specific comments on payback, discount rate, IRR, intangible benefits and benefits realisation.

Critically evaluate Barry's comments on the investment appraisal approach used at 8-Hats to evaluate internal jobs. **(15 marks)**

(b) Discuss the principles, benefits and problems of introducing a matrix management structure at 8-Hats. **(10 marks)**

(Total: 25 marks)

45   INSTITUTE OF INDEPENDENT ANALYSTS

The Institute of Independent Analysts (IIA), an examining body, is considering replacing its conventional assessment process with computer-based assessment which produces instant results to the candidate. A business case has been developed for the computer-based assessment project. Figure 1, extracted from the business case, shows the financial appraisal of the project. It uses a discount rate of 8%. The NPV of the project is $10,925.

All figures in $000s

Year	0	1	2	3	4	5	6	7
Costs								
Initial software	200	200						
Software maintenance			40	40	40	40	40	40
Question bank	50	50	5	5	5	5	5	5
Security			20	20	20	20	20	20
Disruption		15	15					
Total costs	250	265	80	65	65	65	65	65

Income/Savings

Marker fees			125	125	125	125	125	125
Admin saving		20	30	30	30	30	30	30
Extra income			10	20	30	30	40	40
Total benefits		20	165	175	185	185	195	195
Benefits – costs	(250)	(245)	85	110	120	120	130	130
Discount factor	1	0.926	0.857	0.794	0.735	0.681	0.630	0.583
Present value	(250)	(226.870)	72.845	87.340	88.200	81.720	81.900	75.790
							NPV	10.925

Figure 1: Financial cost/benefit of the computer-based assessment project

An explanation of the costs and benefits is given below.

Initial software – refers to the cost of buying the computer-based assessment software package from the vendor. The software actually costs $375,000, but a further $25,000 has been added to reflect bespoke changes which the IIA requires. These changes are not yet agreed, or defined in detail. Indeed, there have been some problems in actually specifying these requirements and understanding how they will affect the administrative processes of the IIA.

Software maintenance – This will be priced at 10% of the final cost of the delivered software. This is currently estimated at $400,000; hence a cost of $40,000 per annum.

Question bank – refers to the cost of developing a question bank for the project. This is a set of questions which the software package stores and selects from when producing an examination for an individual candidate. Questions will be set by external consultants at $50 for each question they successfully deliver to the question bank. It is expected that further questions will need to be added (and current ones amended) in subsequent years.

Security – refers to security provided at computer-based assessment centres. This price has already been agreed with an established security firm who have guaranteed it for the duration of the project.

Disruption – refers to an expected temporary decline in IIA examinations staff productivity and staff morale during the implementation of the computer-based assessment solution.

Marker fees – manual marking is undertaken in the current conventional assessment process. There will no longer be any requirement for markers to undertake this manual marking. All examinations will be automatically marked.

Admin saving – concerns reduction in examinations staff at IIA headquarters. The actual savings will partly depend on the detailed requirements currently being discussed with the software package provider. It is still unclear how this will affect the administrative process.

Extra income – the IIA expects candidates to be attracted by the convenience of computer-based assessment. Other competing institutions do not offer this service. The extra income is the IIA's best guess at the amount of income which will result from this new assessment initiative.

The IIA is also putting in place a benefits management process for all projects. The IIA director is concerned that project managers are just moving on to other projects and not taking responsibility for the benefits initially established in the business case.

Required:

(a) Critically evaluate the financial case (cost/benefit) of the computer-based assessment project. **(15 marks)**

(b) Benefit owners, benefits maps and benefits realisation are important concepts in benefits management process.

Explain each of these concepts and their potential application to the computer-based assessment project. **(10 marks)**

(Total: 25 marks)

46 TKP

This information was taken from an internal newsletter of The Knowledge Partnership LLP (TKP), a company which offers project and software consultancy work for clients based in Zeeland. The newsletter was dated 2 November 20X1 and describes two projects currently being undertaken by the partnership.

Project One

In this project, one of our clients was just about to place a contract for a time recording system to help them monitor and estimate construction contracts when we were called in by the Finance Director. He was concerned about the company supplying the software package. 'They only have an annual revenue of $5m', he said, 'and that worries me.' TKP analysed software companies operating in Zeeland. It found that 200 software companies were registered in Zeeland with annual revenues of between $3m and $10m. Of these, 20 went out of business last year. This compared to a 1% failure rate for software companies with revenues of more than $100m per year. We presented this information to the client and suggested that this could cause a short-term support problem. The client immediately re-opened the procurement process. Eventually they bought a solution from a much larger well-known software supplier. It is a popular software solution, used in many larger companies.

The client has now asked us to help with the implementation of the package. A budget for the project has been agreed and has been documented in an agreed, signed-off, business case. The client has a policy of never re-visiting its business cases once they have been accepted; they see this as essential for effective cost control. We are currently working with the primary users of the software – account managers (using time and cost data to monitor contracts) and the project support office (using time and cost data to improve contract estimating) – to ensure that they can use the software effectively when it is implemented. We have also given 'drop in' briefing sessions for the client's employees who are entering the time and cost data analysed by the software. They already record this information on a legacy system and so all they will see is a bright new user interface, but we need to keep them informed about our implementation. We are also looking at data migration from the current legacy system. We think some of the current data might be of poor quality, so we have established a strategy for data cleansing (through offshore data input) if this problem materialises. We currently estimate that the project will go live in May 20X2.

Project Two

In this project, the client is the developer of the iProjector, a tiny phone-size projector which is portable, easy to use and offers high definition projection. The client was concerned that their product is completely dependent on a specialist image-enhancing chip designed and produced by a small start-up technology company. They asked TKP to investigate this company. We confirmed their fears. The company has been trading for less than three years and it has a very inexperienced management team. We suggested that the client should establish an escrow agreement for design details of the chip and suggested a suitable third party to hold this agreement. We also suggested that significant stocks of the chip should be maintained. The client also asked TKP to look at establishing patents for the iProjector throughout the world. Again, using our customer contacts, we put them in touch with a company which specialises in this. We are currently engaged with the client in examining the risk that a major telephone producer will launch a competitive product with functionality and features similar to the iProjector.

The iProjector is due to be launched on 1 May 20X2 and we have been engaged to give advice on the launch of the product. The launch has been heavily publicised, a prestigious venue booked and over 400 attendees are expected. TKP have arranged for many newspaper journalists to attend. The product is not quite finished, so although orders will be taken at the launch, the product is not expected to ship until June 20X2.

Further information:

TKP only undertakes projects in the business culture which it understands and where it feels comfortable. Consequently, it does not undertake assignments outside Zeeland.

TKP has $10,000,000 of consultant's liability insurance underwritten by Zeeland Insurance Group (ZIG).

Required:

(a) Analyse how TKP itself and the two projects described in the scenario demonstrate the principles of effective risk management. **(15 marks)**

(b) Describe the principle of the triple constraint (scope, time and cost) on projects and discuss its implications in the two projects described in the scenario. **(10 marks)**

(Total: 25 marks)

47 A CLOTHING COMPANY

A clothing company sells 40% of its goods directly to customers through its website. The marketing manager of the company (MM) has decided that this is insufficient and has put a small team together to re-design the site. MM feels that the site looks 'amateur and old-fashioned and does not project the right image'. The board of the company has given the go-ahead for the MM 'to re-design the website'. The following notes summarise the outcomes of the meetings on the website re-design. The team consists of the marketing manager (MM), a product range manager (RP),a marketing image consultant (IC) and a technical developer (TD).

Meeting 1: 9 July attended by MM, RP, IC and TD

The need for a re-designed website to increase sales volume through the website and to 'improve our market visibility' was explained by MM. IC was asked to produce a draft design.

Meeting 2: 16 August attended by MM, RP, IC and TD

IC presented a draft design. MM and RP were happy with its image but not its functionality, suggesting that it was too similar to the current site. 'We expected it to do much more' was their view.

Meeting 3: 4 September attended by MM, RP and IC

IC produced a re-drafted design. This overall design was agreed and the go-ahead was given for TD to produce a prototype of the design to show to the board.

Meeting 4: 11 September attended by RP, IC and TD

TD explained that elements of the drafted re-design were not technically feasible to implement in the programming language being used. Changes to the design were agreed at the meeting to overcome these issues and signed off by RP.

Meeting 5: 13 October attended by MM, RP, IC and TD

The prototype re-design was demonstrated by TD. MM was unhappy with the re-design as it was 'moving too far away from the original objective and lacked functionality that should be there'. TD agreed to write a technical report to explain why the original design (agreed on 4 September) could not be adhered to.

Meeting 6: 9 November attended by MM, IC and TD

It was agreed to return to the 4 September design with slight alterations to make it technically feasible. TD expressed concerns that the suggested design would not work properly with all web browsers.

At the board meeting of 9 December the board expressed concern about the time taken to produce the re-design and the finance director highlighted the rising costs (currently $25,000) of the project. They asked MM to produce a formal cost-benefit of the re-design. The board were also concerned that the scope of the project, which they had felt to be about re-design, had somehow been interpreted as including development and implementation.

On 22 December MM produced the following cost-benefit analysis of the project and confirmed that the word 'redesign' had been interpreted as including the development and implementation of the website.

	Year 1	Year 2	Year 3	Year 4	Year 5
Costs	$50,000	$10,000	$10,000	$10,000	$10,000
Benefits*	0	$15,000	$25,000	$35,000	$35,000

*These benefits are extra sales volumes created by the website's extra functionality and the company's increased visibility in the market place.

On 4 January the board gave the go ahead for the development and implementation of the website with a further budget of $25,000 and a delivery date of 1 March. TD expressed concern that he did not have enough developers to deliver the re-designed website on time.

Meeting 7: 24 February attended by MM, RP, IC and TD

A partial prototype system was demonstrated by TD. RP felt that the functionality of the re-design was too limited and that the software was not robust enough. It had crashed twice during the demonstration. He suggested that the company delay the introduction of the re-designed website until it was complete and robust. MM declared this to be impossible.

Conclusion

The re-designed website was launched on 1 March. MM declared the re-design a success that 'had come in on time and under budget'. On 2 and 3 March, numerous complaints were received from customers. The website was unreliable and did not work with a particular popular web browser. On 4 March an emergency board meeting decided to withdraw the site and reinstate the old one. On 5 March, MM resigned.

Required:

Most project management methods have an initiation or definition stage which includes the production of a document that serves as an agreement between the sponsors and deliverers of the project. This may be called a project initiation document or a project charter. Defining the business case is also an important part of the initiation or definition stage of the project.

(a)   Explain how a business case and a project initiation document would have helped prevent some of the problems that emerged during the conduct of the website re-design project.   **(15 marks)**

(b)   Analyse how effective project management could have further improved both the process and the outcomes of the website re-design project.   **(10 marks)**

(Total: 25 marks)

48   PAA

Introduction

The country of Mahem is in a long and deep economic recession with unemployment at its highest since the country became an independent nation. In an attempt to stimulate the economy the government has launched a Private/Public investment policy where the government invests in capital projects with the aim of stimulating the involvement of private sector firms. The building of a new community centre in the industrial city of Tillo is an example of such an initiative. Community centres are central to the culture of Mahem. They are designed as places where people can meet socially, local organisations can hold conferences and meetings and farmers can sell their produce to the local community. The centres are seen as contributing to a vibrant community life. The community centre in Tillo is in a sprawling old building rented (at $12,000 per month) from a local landowner. The current community centre is also relatively energy inefficient.

In 2010 a business case was put forward to build a new centre on local authority owned land on the outskirts of Tillo. The costs and benefits of the business case are shown in Figure 1. As required by the Private/Public investment policy the project showed payback during year four of the investment.

All figures in $	Year 1	Year 2	Year 3	Year 4	Year 5
Costs: Initial	600,000				
Costs: Recurring	60,000	60,000	60,000	60,000	60,000
Benefits: Rental savings	144,000	144,000	144,000	144,000	144,000
Benefits: Energy savings	30,000	30,000	30,000	30,000	30,000
Benefits: Increased income	20,000	20,000	70,000	90,000	90,000
Benefits: Better staff morale	25,000	25,000	25,000	25,000	25,000
Cumulative net benefits	(441,000)	(282,000)	(73,000)	156,000	385,000

Figure 1: Costs and benefits of the business case for the community centre at Tillo

New buildings built under the Private/Public investment policy must attain energy level targets and this is the basis for the estimation, above, of the *energy savings*. It is expected that the new centre will attract more customers who will pay for the centre's use as well as increasing the use of facilities such as the cafeteria, shop and business centre. These benefits are estimated, above, under *increased income*. Finally, it is felt that staff will be happier in the new building and their motivation and morale will increase. The centre currently employs 20 staff, 16 of whom have been with the centre for more than five years. All employees were transferred from the old to the new centre. These benefits are shown as *better staff morale* in Figure 1.

Construction of the centre 2010–2011

In October 2010 the centre was commissioned with a planned delivery date of June 2011 at a cost of $600,000 (as per Figure 1). Building the centre went relatively smoothly. Progress was monitored and issues resolved in monthly meetings between the company constructing the centre and representatives of the local authority. These meetings focused on the building of the centre, monitoring progress and resolving issues. Most of these issues were relatively minor because requirements were well specified in standard architectural drawings originally agreed between the project sponsor and the company constructing the centre. Unfortunately, the original project sponsor (an employee of the local authority) who had been heavily involved in the initial design, suffered ill health and died in April 2011. The new project sponsor (again an employee of the local authority) was less enthusiastic about the project and began to raise a number of objections. Her first concern was that the construction company had used sub-contracted labour and had sourced less than 80% of timber used in the building from sustainable resources. She pointed out the contractual terms of supply for the Private/Public policy investment initiatives mandated that sub-contracting was not allowed without the local authority's permission and that at least 80% of the timber used must come from sustainable forests. The company said that this had not been brought to their attention at the start of the project. However, they would try to comply with these requirements for the rest of the contract. The new sponsor also refused to sign off acceptance of the centre because of the poor quality of the internal paintwork. The construction company explained that this was the intended finish quality of the centre and had been agreed with the previous sponsor. They produced a letter to verify this. However, the letter was not counter-signed by the sponsor and so its validity was questioned. In the end, the construction company agreed to improve the internal painting at their own cost. The new sponsor felt that she had delivered 'value for money' by challenging the construction company. Despite this problem with the internal painting, the centre was finished in May 2011 at a cost of $600,000. The centre also included disability access built at the initiative of the construction company. It had found it difficult to find local authority staff willing and able to discuss disability access and so it was therefore left alone to interpret relevant legal requirements. Fortunately, their interpretation was correct and the new centre was deemed, by an independent assessor, to meet accessibility requirements.

Unfortunately, the new centre was not as successful as had been predicted, with income in the first year well below expectations. The project sponsor began to be increasingly critical of the builders of the centre and questioned the whole value of the project. She was openly sceptical of the project to her fellow local authority employees. She suggested that the project to build a cost-effective centre had failed and called for an inquiry into the performance of the project manager of the construction company who was responsible for building the centre. 'We need him to explain to us why the centre is not delivering the benefits we expected', she explained.

Required:

(a)   The local authority has commissioned the independent Project Audit Agency (PAA) to look into how the project had been commissioned and managed. The PAA believes that a formal 'terms of reference' or 'project initiation document' would have resolved or clarified some of the problems and issues encountered in the project. It also feels that there are important lessons to be learnt by both the local authority and the construction company.

Analyse how a formal 'terms of reference' (project initiation document) would have helped address problems encountered in the project to construct the community centre and lead to improved project management in future projects.   **(13 marks)**

(b)   The PAA also believes that the four sets of benefits identified in the original business case (rental savings, energy savings, increased income and better staff morale) should have been justified more explicitly.

Draft an analysis for the PAA that formally categorises and critically evaluates each of the four sets of proposed benefits defined in the original business case.

(12 marks)

(Total: 25 marks)

49   BRIGHTTOWN

The town of Brighttown in Euraria has a mayor (elected every five years by the people in the town) who is responsible for, amongst other things, the transport policy of the town.

A year ago, the mayor (acting as project sponsor) instigated a 'traffic lite' project to reduce traffic congestion at traffic lights in the town. Rather than relying on fixed timings, he suggested that a system should be implemented which made the traffic lights sensitive to traffic flow. So, if a queue built up, then the lights would automatically change to green (go). The mayor suggested that this would have a number of benefits. Firstly, it would reduce harmful emissions at the areas near traffic lights and, secondly, it would improve the journey times for all vehicles, leading to drivers 'being less stressed'. He also cited evidence from cities overseas where predictable journey times had been attractive to flexible companies who could set themselves up anywhere in the country. He felt that the new system would attract such companies to the town.

The Eurarian government has a transport regulation agency called OfRoad. Part of OfRoad's responsibilities is to monitor transport investments and it was originally critical of the Brighttown 'traffic lite' project because the project's benefits were intangible and lacked credibility. The business case did not include a quantitative cost/benefit analysis. OfRoad has itself published a benefits management process which classifies benefits in the following way.

Financial:	A financial benefit can be confidently allocated in advance of the project. Thus if the investment will save $90,000 per year in staff costs then this is a financial benefit.
Quantifiable:	A quantifiable benefit is a benefit where there is sufficient credible evidence to suggest, in advance, how much benefit will result from the project. This benefit may be financial or non-financial. For example, energy savings from a new building might be credibly predicted in advance. However, the exact amount of savings cannot be accurately forecast.

Measurable benefit:	A measurable benefit is a benefit which can only be confidently assessed post-implementation, and so cannot be reliably predicted in advance. Increase in sales from a particular initiative is an example of a measurable benefit. Measurable benefits may either be financial or non-financial.
Observable benefit:	An observable benefit is a benefit which a specific individual or group will decide, using agreed criteria, has been realised or not. Such benefits are usually non-financial. Improved staff morale might be an example of an observable benefit.

One month ago, the mayoral elections saw the election of a new mayor with a completely distinct transport policy with different objectives. She wishes to address traffic congestion by attracting commuters away from their cars and onto public transport. Part of her policy is a traffic light system which gives priority to buses. The town council owns the buses which operate in the town and they have invested heavily in buses which are comfortable and have significantly lower emissions than the conventional cars used by most people in the town. The new mayor wishes to improve the frequency, punctuality and convenience of these buses, so that they tempt people away from using their cars. This will require more buses and more bus crews, a requirement which the mayor presents as 'being good for the unemployment rate in this town'. It will also help the bus service meet the punctuality service level which it published three years ago, but has never yet met. 'A reduction in cars and an increase in buses will help us meet our target', the mayor claims.

The mayor has also suggested a number of initiatives to discourage people from taking their cars into the town. She intends to sell two car parks for housing land (raising $325,000) and this will reduce car park capacity from 1,000 to 800 car spaces per day. She also intends to raise the daily parking fee from $3 to $4. Car park occupancy currently stands at 95% (it is difficult to achieve 100% for technical reasons) and the same occupancy rate is expected when the car park capacity is reduced.

The new mayor believes that her policy signals the fact that Brighttown is serious about its green credentials. 'This', she says, 'will attract green consumers to come and live in our town and green companies to set up here. These companies and consumers will bring great benefit to our community.' To emphasise this, she has set up a Go Green team to encourage green initiatives in the town.

The 'traffic lite' project to tackle congestion proposed by the former mayor is still in the development stage. The new mayor believes that this project can be modified to deliver her vision and still be ready on the date promised by her predecessor.

Required:

(a) A 'terms of reference' (project initiation document, project charter) was developed for the 'traffic lite' project to reduce traffic congestion.

Discuss what changes will have to be made to this 'terms of reference' (project initiation document, project charter) to reflect the new mayor's vision of the project. **(5 marks)**

(b) The new mayor wishes to re-define the business case for the project, using the benefits categorisation suggested by OfRoad.

Identify costs and benefits for the revised project, classifying each benefit using the guidance provided by OfRoad. **(14 marks)**

(c)   Stakeholder management is the prime responsibility of the project manager.

Discuss the appropriate management of each of the following three stakeholders identified in the revised (modified) project.

(i)   The new mayor

(ii)   OfRoad

(iii)   A private motorist in Brighttown who uses his vehicle to commute to his job in the town.   **(6 marks)**

(Total: 25 marks)

FINANCING

50   WOODS EDUCATIONAL INSTITUTION

You are a newly appointed Finance Manager of the Woods Educational Institution (WEI) that is mainly government funded, having moved from a similar post in a service company in the private sector. WEI is a large education establishment which has traditionally focused on providing academic qualifications for under-graduates. It has over 300 full time teaching staff and 60 support staff, with facilities to provide 100 lectures at any one time within the institutions own buildings.

The objective, or mission statement, of this Institution is shown in its publicity material as:

'to achieve recognised standards of excellence in the provision of teaching and research.'

The only financial performance measure evaluated by the government is that the Institution has to remain within cash limits. The cash allocation each year is determined by a range of non-financial measures such as the number of research publications the Institution's staff have achieved and official ratings for teaching quality.

However, almost 20% of total cash generated by WEI is now from the provision of courses and seminars to private sector companies. These customers are aiming to improve their skills base rather than achieve academic qualifications. They are largely unconcerned about research ratings and lecturer qualifications and are more concerned with course content and flexibility. Courses can often be facilitated in WEI's own buildings, but some clients prefer for courses to be provided in their own offices.

WEI's Head of Education aims to increase the percentage of income coming from the private sector to 50% over the next five years.

Required:

(a)   Evaluate whether a financial objective, or objectives, could or should be determined by WEI   **(5 marks)**

(b)   The following is a list of financial and non-financial performance measures that were in use in your *previous company*:

FINANCIAL	NON-FINANCIAL
Value added	Customer satisfaction
Profitability	Competitive position
Return on investment	Market share

Required:

Choose *two of each* type of measure, explain their purpose and advise on how they could be used by WEI over the next five years to assess how it is meeting the Head of Education's aims.

(16 marks)

(c) Explain the role of integrated reporting in communicating strategy and strategic performance.

(4 marks)

(Total: 25 marks)

51 POTATO-TO-GO INC

Potato-to-go Inc ('PTG'), a quoted company, owns and operates a chain of fast food outlets in Europe selling baked potatoes with a range of healthy fillings.

Company background

Since being set up in 1983, PTG has expanded rapidly through organic growth and the acquisition of some smaller competing companies. The expansion was originally financed from retained profits but the company was floated in 1994 to enable larger sums to be raised.

51% of PTG's ordinary share capital is currently owned by the founding Edwards family (who also control the Board of Directors), 35% by large institutions, and the remaining shares by private investors.

The company's five-year record can be summarised as follows:

Years to 31 December	20X2	20X3	20X4	20X5	20X6
Turnover ($m)	370	440	450	420	400
Profit before tax ($m)	120	150	110	66	42
Number of outlets	690	740	770	790	800

Summary statement of profit or loss for 20X6

	$m	$m
Turnover		400
Operating costs	350	
Interest paid	8	
		(358)
Profit before tax		42
Taxation		(14)
Dividends		20
Retained profit		8

Summary statement of financial position (balance sheet) at 31 December 20X6

	$m
Non-current assets	180
Net current assets	60
Less 10% loan stock 20X7	(80)
	____
	160
	____
Ordinary $1 shares	24
Reserves	136
	____
	160
	____

Note: PTG's P/E ratio at the end of 20X6 was 9 compared to an industry average of 10.

Current issues facing the firm

(1) **Redemption of loan stock**

Internally generated funds will be insufficient to enable the loan stock to be redeemed at the end of 20X7 and no sinking fund has been set up. Further finance is thus required. The Edwards family have indicated that they are unwilling to subscribe further equity.

(2) **Overseas expansion**

The directors of PTG believe that their current markets have reached saturation and that there is a potential new market in North America. An initial strategy would be to open 50 outlets early in 20X8 in New York and New England. The total investment required is estimated to be $130m.

Required:

Prepare briefing notes on the following:

(a) **PTG's financial performance.** (7 marks)

(b) **The proposed expansion in the USA.** (8 marks)

(c) **Financing the overseas expansion.** (10 marks)

(Total: 25 marks)

52 DAVID SILVESTER

Timed question with Online tutor debrief

David Silvester is the founder and owner of a recently formed gift packaging company, Gift Designs Ltd. David has spotted an opportunity for a new type of gift packaging. This uses a new process to make waterproof cardboard and then shapes and cuts the card in such a way to produce a container or vase for holding cut flowers. The containers can be stored flat and in bulk and then simply squeezed to create the flowerpot into which flowers and water are then put. The potential market for the product is huge. In the UK, in hospitals alone there are 200,000 bunches of flowers bought each year for patients. David's innovative product does away with the need for hospitals to provide and store glass vases. The paper vases are simple, safe and hygienic. He has also identified two other potential markets. Firstly, the market for fresh flowers supplied by florists, and secondly, the corporate gift market where clients such as car dealers present a new owner with an expensive bunch of flowers when the customer takes delivery of a new car. The vase can be printed using a customer's design and logo, and creates an opportunity for real differentiation and impact at sales conferences and other high profile PR events.

David anticipates a rapid growth in Gift Designs as its products become known and appreciated. The key question is how quickly the company should grow and the types of funding needed to support its growth and development. The initial financial demands of the business have been quite modest but David has estimated that the business needs $500k to support its development over the next two years and is uncertain as to the types of funding best suited to a new business as it looks to grow rapidly. He understands that business risk and financial risk are not the same thing and is looking for advice on how he should organise the funding of the business. He is also aware of the need to avoid reliance on friends and family for funding and to broaden the financial support for the business. Clearly the funding required would also be affected by the activities David decides to carry out himself and those activities better provided by external suppliers.

Required:

(a) Provide David with a short report on the key issues he should take into account when developing a strategy for funding Gift Designs' growth and development.

(15 marks)

(b) Using models where appropriate, what are likely to be the critical success factors (CSFs) as the business grows and develops? **(10 marks)**

(Total: 25 marks)

Calculate your allowed time, allocate the time to the separate parts...............

53 SATELLITE NAVIGATION SYSTEMS

Satellite Navigation Systems (SNS) installs complex satellite navigation systems in cars, at a very large national depot. The standard cost of an installation is shown below. The budgeted volume is 1,000 units installed each month. The operations manager is responsible for three departments, namely: purchasing, fitting and quality control. Satellite Navigation Systems Limited purchases navigation systems and other equipment from different suppliers, and most items are imported. The fitting of different systems takes differing amounts of time, but the differences are not more than 25% from the average, so a standard labour time is applied.

Standard cost of installation of one navigation system

	$	Quantity	Price ($)
Materials	400	1 unit	400
Labour	320	20 hours	16
Variable overheads	140	20 hours	7
Fixed overheads	300	20 hours	15
Total standard cost	1,160		

The Operations Department has gathered the following information over the last few months. There are significant difficulties in retaining skilled staff. Many have left for similar but better paid jobs and as a result there is a high labour turnover. Exchange rates have moved and commentators have argued this will make exports cheaper, but SNS has no exports and has not benefited from these movements. Some of the fitters have complained that one large batch of systems did not have the correct adapters and would not fit certain cars, but this was not apparent until fitting was attempted. Rent, rates, insurance and computing facilities have risen in price noticeably.

The senior management team of SNS want the finance department to lend more support for the business and provide information that will help them to understand why costs appear to be spiralling out of control in the last few months and what the organisation can do to improve its position in the future.

The financial results for September to December are shown below.

Operating statement for SNS for September to December

	September $	October $	November $	December $	4 months $
Standard cost of actual output	1,276,000	1,276,000	1,102,000	1,044,000	4,698,000
Variances materials					
Price	5,505 F	3,354 F	9,520 A	10,340 A	11,001 A
Usage	400 A	7,200 A	800 A	16,000 A	24,400 A
Labour rate	4,200 A	5,500 A	23,100 A	24,000 A	56,800 A
Efficiency	16,000 F	0	32,000 A	32,000 A	48,000 A
Variable overheads					
Expenditure	7,000 A	2,000 A	2,000 F	0	7,000 A
Efficiency	7,000 F	0	14,000 A	14,000 A	21,000 A
Fixed overheads					
Expenditure	5,000 A	10,000 A	20,000 A	20,000 A	55,000 A
Volume	30,000 F	30,000 F	15,000 A	30,000 A	15,000 F
Actual costs	1,234,095	1,267,346	1,214,420	1,190,340	4,906,201

A = adverse variance   F = favourable variance

Required:

(a) Assess the performance of SNS for the period from September to December and suggest probable causes for the key variances. **(15 marks)**

(b) Suggest what extra information could be provided by the finance function and how the finance function can support the business in its development and implementation of new business strategies. **(10 marks)**

(Total: 25 marks)

54 X PLC

X plc manufactures specialist insulating products that are used in both residential and commercial buildings. One of the products, Product W, is made using two different raw materials and two types of labour. The company operates a standard absorption costing system and is now preparing its budgets for the next four quarters. The following information has been identified for Product W:

Sales

Selling price	$220 per unit

Sales demand

Quarter 1	2,250 units
Quarter 2	2,050 units
Quarter 3	1,650 units
Quarter 4	2,050 units
Quarter 5	1,250 units
Quarter 6	2,050 units

Costs

Materials

A	5 kgs per unit @ $4 per kg
B	3 kgs per unit @ $7 per kg

Labour

Skilled	4 hours per unit @ $15 per hour
Semi-skilled	6 hours per unit @ $9 per hour
Annual overheads	$280,000
	40% of these overheads are fixed and the remainder varies with total labour hours. Fixed overheads are absorbed on a unit basis.

Inventory holding policy	
Closing inventory of finished goods	30% of the following quarter's sales demand
Closing inventory of materials	45% of the following quarter's materials usage

The management team is concerned that X plc has recently faced increasing competition in the marketplace for Product W. As a consequence there have been issues concerning the availability and costs of the specialised materials and employees needed to manufacture Product W, and there is concern that these might cause problems in the current budget-setting process.

Required:

(a)   Prepare the following budgets for each quarter for X plc:

   (i)   Production budget in units

   (ii)   Raw material purchases budget in kgs and value for Material B.   (8 marks)

(b)   X plc has just been informed that Material A may be in short supply during the year for which it is preparing budgets.

   Discuss the impact this will have on budget preparation as well as the strategic planning and decision making within X plc.   (12 marks)

The same company is also considering investing in one of three marketing campaigns to increase its profitability. All three marketing campaigns have a life of five years, require the same initial investment and have no residual value. The company has already evaluated the marketing campaigns taking into consideration the range of possible outcomes that could result from the investment. A summary of the calculations is shown below:

Marketing campaign	J	K	L
Expected net present value	$400,000	$800,000	$400,000
Standard deviation of net present value	$35,000	$105,000	$105,000

(c)   Explain

   (i)   the meaning of the data shown above

   (ii)   how the data may be used by the company when choosing between alternative investments.   (5 marks)

(Total: 25 marks)

55   WORLD ENGINES   *Online question assistance*

World Engines (WE) is one of the largest producers of aircraft and ship engines in the world. It has assets in excess of $600bn. It is currently considering improvements to its marine engine production facilities. These improvements include the introduction of specialist hardware and software engine testing technology. Two companies have been shortlisted for supplying this technology.

Amethyst is a well-established company whose product provides sophisticated testing facilities and costs $7m. The software that supports the product is written in a conventional programming language. The solution is widely used, but it is relatively inflexible and it has an out-of-date user interface. Amethyst has been trading profitably for 20 years and currently has an annual turnover of $960m.

Topaz is a relatively new company (formed three years ago) whose product is more expensive ($8m) but it offers significant advantages in high volume performance and stress testing. It has a modular software design that allows it to be easily maintained and upgraded. It is written in a relatively new powerful programming language and it also has an attractive and contemporary user interface. Topaz currently has a turnover of $24m per year. Some WE executives are concerned about purchasing from such a young, relatively small company, although externally commissioned credit reports show that Topaz is a profitable, liquid and lightly geared company.

On a recent evaluation visit to Amethyst, WE's complete evaluation team of five people, including the financial specialist, were killed when their aircraft crashed on its approach to landing. It was a small, 12 seat commuter aircraft that was flying the WE team on a short 100 km flight from the international airport to a small rural airport close to Amethyst's base. It later emerged that small commuter airlines and aircraft were subject to less stringent safety procedures than larger aircraft used by established airlines.

Later that year, one of the divisional directors of WE was given responsibility for picking up and running the testing technology evaluation project. He has found the following table (Figure 1) produced by the financial specialist in the evaluation team who was killed in the air crash. The divisional director recalls that these returns were based on 'tangible benefits resulting from the two options. The returns reflect the characteristics of the two products. Topaz produces better returns if demand for testing is high, but is less effective in low demand circumstances. This is a reflection of the fact that the two solutions differ slightly in terms of their functional scope and power'.

Figure 1: expected returns for three demand and supplier combinations.

Option	Supplier	IF High demand	IF Low demand
A	Amethyst	$3m per annum	$0.5m per annum
B	Topaz	$4m per annum	$0.1m per annum

The divisional director also recalls a workshop convened to consider future market demand.

'Demand in the marine industry is currently affected by global economic uncertainty and it is increasingly difficult to predict demand. I remember that we were also asked to estimate demand for our marine products for the next six years. We eventually came up with the following figures, although it was relatively hard to get everyone to agree and debate at the workshop became a little heated'.

- High demand for six years: probability $p = 0.4$

- Low demand for six years: probability $p = 0.4$

- High demand for three years, followed by low demand for three years: probability $p = 0.2$

These figures are confirmed by a document also recovered from the air crash site. 'As I recall', said the divisional director, 'the financial specialist intended to develop a decision tree to help us evaluate the Amethyst and Topaz alternatives. However, there is no evidence that he ever constructed it, which is a pity because we could have taken the procurement decision on the basis of that decision tree'.

Required:

(a)   Develop a decision tree from the information given in the scenario and discuss its implications and shortcomings.

Ignore the time value of money in your analysis.   **(9 marks)**

(b)   The divisional director suggests that the procurement decision could have been taken on the evidence of the decision tree.

Discuss what other factors (not considered by the decision tree analysis) should also be taken into consideration when deciding which option to select.   **(6 marks)**

(c)   WE executives are concerned about the risk of Topaz, as a relatively new company, going out of business. They have also expressed concern about the loss of the evaluation team in a fatal accident and they believe that this should lead to a review of the risks associated with employee travel.

Discuss how EACH of the above risks (supplier business failure and employee travel) might be avoided or mitigated.   **(10 marks)**

(Total: 25 marks)

Online question assistance

---

56   COOLFREEZE

CoolFreeze construct refrigeration systems for supermarkets, food processing plants, warehouses and other industrial premises. It has a sales forecasting committee consisting of the company's sales manager, procurement manager, production manager and the head of administration. The committee produces annual sales forecasts for the company which they review quarterly. Historically, these forecasts have been reasonably accurate.

In the second quarter of 2009 they revised/produced their estimates for the next four quarters. The predicted unit sales volume and prices are given in figure one.

Figure one: Sales forecast 2009–2010

Year	Quarter	Predicted sales	Predicted sales price	Revenue
2009	3	81	$1,000	$81,000
	4	69	$1,000	$69,000
2010	1	62	$1,000	$62,000
	2	83	$1,000	$83,000

At the meeting that agreed this forecast the sales manager expressed some doubts about the figures. "My team are telling me that it is very tough out there. Companies are not replacing old equipment or constructing new plants. Furthermore, cheaper foreign products are becoming available – undercutting our prices by 10%". Despite these reservations, the sales manager agreed the sales forecasts produced by the committee.

Actual sales performance

The actual sales for the four projected quarters were as follows (figure two).

Figure two: Actual sales 2009–2010

Year	Quarter	Predicted sales	Actual sales
2009	3	81	82
	4	69	68
2010	1	62	61
	2	83	50

The sudden drop in quarter 2 sales caused consternation in the boardroom, particularly as it was a quarter when high demand and profits were anticipated. An analysis of the quarter 2 trading is shown in figure three.

The managing director of CoolFreeze has called you in to review the forecasting model used by the sales forecasting team. "It must be very flawed to go so badly wrong. I have the feeling that the model is not based on a well-accepted approach". He has obtained a copy of the spreadsheet used by the sales forecasting team (see figure four) to help you in your analysis.

The managing director recognises that the actual quarter 2 performance has to be analysed against the budgeted one. "I think everyone here has made mistakes – the sales manager, procurement manager, production manager, administration manager. They all have to take responsibility. We are in this together and now we must pull together to get out of this mess".

Figure three: Analysis of quarter 2 trading; budget and actual

Quarter 2 – 2010	Budget	Actual
Units	83	50
Revenue	$83,000.00	$45,000.00
Raw materials	($29,050.00)	($15,000.00)
Labour	($26,975.00)	($15,750.00)
Fixed overheads	($18,000.00)	($18,000.00)
Operating profit	$8,975.00	($3,750.00)

Figure four: Forecasting spreadsheet

A	B	C	D	E	F	G	H	I
Part 1								
Year	Quarter	Units		Trend	Variation	Seasonal	Residual	Check
2006	1	56						
	2	70						
	3	74	524	65.50	8.50	7.35	1.15	74.00
	4	60	538	67.25	−7.25	−4.73	−2.52	60.00
2007	1	60	554	69.25	−9.25	−11.65	2.40	60.00
	2	80	570	71.25	8.75	9.02	−0.27	80.00
	3	80	582	72.75	7.25	7.35	−0.10	80.00
	4	70	586	73.25	−3.25	−4.73	1.48	70.00
2008	1	62	588	73.50	−11.50	−11.65	0.15	62.00
	2	82	588	73.50	8.50	9.02	−0.52	82.00
	3	80	586	73.25	6.75	7.35	−0.60	80.00
	4	70	586	73.25	−3.25	−4.73	1.48	70.00
2009	1	60	590	73.75	−13.75	−11.65	−2.10	60.00
	2	84	590	73.75	−10.25	9.02	1.23	84.00
	3	82						
	4	68						

Part 2

	1	2	3	4	
2006			8.50	−7.25	
2007	−9.25	8.75	7.25	−3.25	
2008	−11.50	8.50	6.75	−3.25	
2009	−13.75	10.25			
Total	−34.50	27.50	22.50	−13.75	
Average	−11.50	9.17	7.50	−4.58	0.58
Adj	−0.15	−0.15	−0.15	−0.15	
New Avg	−11.65	9.02	7.35	−4.73	0.00

Forecast

2009	3	73.50	7.35	81
	4	73.50	−4.73	69
2010	1	73.65	−11.65	62
	2	74.00	9.02	83

Required:

Write a briefing paper for the managing director that:

(a)   Explains and evaluates the spreadsheet used by the sales forecasting team.

(12 marks)

(b)   Analyses the quarter 2 – 2010 performance of CoolFreeze.   (13 marks)

(Total: 25 marks)

57   MANTIS & GEAR

Mantis & Gear (M&G) was formed over 50 years ago to manufacture branded electrical and electronic goods for other companies. These goods are made to the specification required by these companies, whose own brand logos are attached to the products during the production process. M&G currently manufactures hundreds of products, although some are very similar in specification, with slight differences due to the requirements of each customer. M&G does not sell its own products to individual domestic consumers. Sales teams therefore focus on high volume sales to large companies.

The electrical and electronic goods market is increasingly competitive, with overseas companies entering the market. M&G's customers have responded to this by demanding lower prices and better quality products from M&G. As the electrical and electronic goods market is technologically innovative, there is also a requirement to continually develop new products or enhance existing ones.

The sales manager, James Slater, has revealed his sales team figures for the year 2014 and is excited to announce that the team has exceeded sales volume targets. However, his enthusiasm is not shared by the business controller, Furzana Khan, who has written a report to the chief executive officer (CEO) suggesting that there are fundamental performance problems in the company.

An extract of her report is given below:

Business performance

'In a period of increased competition and growing product ranges, we are failing to keep control of the profitability of our business. Table 1 presents a summary of our performance for 2014, showing problems with our pricing and/or our cost control. This has affected profitability.

	Budget	Actual
	Units	Units
Sales volume	243,000	270,000

	Budget	Actual
	$000s	$000s
Sales revenue	36,450	36,450
Direct materials	(15,795)	(18,630)
Direct labour	(3,402)	(4,725)
Fixed overheads	(8,250)	(11,450)
Operating profit	9,003	1,645

Table 1 – Budgeted versus actual performance for 2014

I recommend that we move from our traditional absorption costing system to that of activity based costing (ABC) in order to better understand our costs and to introduce an appropriate strategy to turn around our business performance. Specifically, we should ensure that we incorporate both product and customer costing into our ABC analysis to determine our profitable and unprofitable products and customers.'

James Slater has seen the report and has angrily confronted Furzana. 'We are in a period of increased competition and have successfully managed to grow our sales in difficult times. We even managed to fulfil some special orders with very short lead times. We should be celebrating these successes, not treating them as poor performance. We should expect some fall in profitability as our customers are able to shop around, so we have to make our products and our prices more attractive to them. The new costing system that you are proposing will just be a paper exercise for you to criticise the efforts of the sales and production teams. I will do everything I can to stop the introduction of this costing system.'

(a) It is clear that the business controller and the sales manager have different opinions about the current performance of the company.

Required:

Analyse the data shown in Table 1, suggesting possible reasons why performance may not be as positive as that portrayed by the sales manager. **(15 marks)**

(b) The sales manager, James Slater, described activity based costing as 'a paper exercise for you to criticise the efforts of the sales and production teams'.

Required:

Briefly explain the principles of activity based costing and the reasons for its development. Evaluate whether it may be beneficial to M&G, making reference to any benefits and limitations of activity based costing and any problems associated with its implementation. **(10 marks)**

(Total: 25 marks)

STRATEGY AND PEOPLE

58   ROCK BOTTOM   *Walk in the footsteps of a top tutor*

This scenario summarises the development of a company called Rock Bottom through three phases, from its founding in 1965 to 20X8 when it ceased trading.

Phase 1 (1965–1988)

In 1965 customers usually purchased branded electrical goods, largely produced by well-established domestic companies, from general stores that stocked a wide range of household products. However, in that year, a recent university graduate, Rick Hein, established his first shop specialising solely in the sale of electrical goods. In contrast to the general stores, Rick Hein's shop predominantly sold imported Japanese products which were smaller, more reliable and more sophisticated than the products of domestic competitors. Rick Hein quickly established a chain of shops, staffed by young people who understood the capabilities of the products they were selling. He backed this up with national advertising in the press, an innovation at the time for such a specialist shop. He branded his shops as 'Rock Bottom', a name which specifically referred to his cheap prices, but also alluded to the growing importance of rock music and its influence on product sales. In 1969, 80% of sales were of music centres, turntables, amplifiers and speakers, bought by the newly affluent young. Rock Bottom began increasingly to specialise in selling audio equipment.

Hein also developed a high public profile. He dressed unconventionally and performed a number of outrageous stunts that publicised his company. He also encouraged the managers of his stores to be equally outrageous. He rewarded their individuality with high salaries, generous bonus schemes and autonomy. Many of the shops were extremely successful, making their managers (and some of their staff) relatively wealthy people.

However, by 1980 the profitability of the Rock Bottom shops began to decline significantly. Direct competitors using a similar approach had emerged, including specialist sections in the large general stores that had initially failed to react to the challenge of Rock Bottom. The buying public now expected its electrical products to be cheap and reliable. Hein himself became less flamboyant and toned down his appearance and actions to satisfy the banks who were becoming an increasingly important source of the finance required to expand and support his chain of shops.

Phase 2 (1989–20X2)

In 1988 Hein considered changing the Rock Bottom shops into a franchise, inviting managers to buy their own shops (which at this time were still profitable) and pursuing expansion though opening new shops with franchisees from outside the company. However, instead, he floated the company on the country's stock exchange. He used some of the capital raised to expand the business. However, he also sold shares to help him throw the 'party of a lifetime' and to purchase expensive goods and gifts for his family. Hein became Chairman and Chief Executive Officer (CEO) of the newly quoted company, but over the next thirteen years his relationship with his board and shareholders became increasingly difficult. Gradually new financial controls and reporting systems were put in b3place. Most of the established managers left as controls became more centralised and formal.

The company's performance was solid but unspectacular. Hein complained that 'business was not fun anymore'. The company was legally required to publish directors' salaries in its annual report and the generous salary package enjoyed by the Chairman and CEO increasingly became an issue and it dominated the 20X2 Annual General Meeting (AGM). Hein was embarrassed by its publication and the discussion it led to in the national media. He felt that it was an infringement of his privacy and civil liberties.

Phase 3 (20X3–20X8)

In 20X3 Hein found the substantial private equity investment necessary to take Rock Bottom private again. He also used all of his personal fortune to help re-acquire the company from the shareholders. He celebrated 'freeing Rock Bottom from its shackles' by throwing a large celebration party. Celebrities were flown in from all over the world to attend. However, most of the new generation of store managers found Hein's style to be too loose and unfocused. He became rude and angry about their lack of entrepreneurial spirit. Furthermore, changes in products and how they were purchased meant that fewer people bought conventional audio products from specialist shops. The reliability of these products now meant that they were replaced relatively infrequently. Hein, belatedly, started to consider selling via an Internet site. Turnover and profitability plummeted. In 20X7 Hein again considered franchising the company, but he realised that this was unlikely to be successful. In early 20X8 the company ceased trading and Hein himself, now increasingly vilified and attacked by the press, filed for personal bankruptcy.

Required:

(a)   Analyse the reasons for Rock Bottom's success or failure in each of the three phases identified in the scenario. Evaluate how Rick Hein's leadership style contributed to the success or failure of each phase. **(18 marks)**

(b)   Rick Hein considered franchising the Rock Bottom brand at two points in its history – 1988 and 20X7. Explain the key factors that would have made franchising Rock Bottom feasible in 1988, but would have made it 'unlikely to be successful' in 20X7. **(7 marks)**

(Total: 25 marks)

59   ARC

Ten years ago Sully Truin formed the Academic Recycling Company (ARC) to offer a specialised waste recycling service to schools and colleges. The company has been very successful and has expanded rapidly. To cope with this expansion, Sully has implemented a tight administrative process for operating and monitoring contracts. This administrative procedure is undertaken by the Contracts Office, who track that collections have been made by the field recycling teams. Sully has sole responsibility for obtaining and establishing recycling contracts, but he leaves the day-to-day responsibility for administering and monitoring the contracts to the Contracts Office. He has closely defined what needs to be done for each contract and how this should be monitored. 'I needed to do this', he said, 'because workers in this country are naturally lazy and lack initiative. I have found that if you don't tell them exactly what to do and how to do it, then it won't get done properly.' Most of the employees working in the Contracts Office like and respect Sully for his business success and ability to take instant decisions when they refer a problem to him. Some of ARC's employees have complained about his autocratic style of leadership, but most of these have now left the company to work for other organisations.

A few months ago, conscious that he was a self-taught manager, Sully enrolled himself on a week's course with Gapminding, a training consultancy which actively advocates and promotes a democratic style of management. The course caused Sully to question his previous approach to leadership. It was also the first time, for three years, that Sully had been out of the office during working hours for a prolonged period of time. However, each night, while he was attending the course, he had to deal with emails from the Contracts Office listing problems with contracts and asking him what action they should take. He became exasperated by his employees' inability to take actions to resolve these issues. He discussed this problem with his course tutors. They suggested that his employees would be more effective and motivated if their jobs were enriched and that they were empowered to make decisions themselves.

On his return from the course, Sully called a staff meeting with the Contracts Office where he announced that, from now on, employees would have responsibility for taking control actions themselves, rather than referring the problem to him. Sully, in turn, was to focus on gaining more contracts and setting them up. However, problems with the new arrangements arose very quickly. Fearful of making mistakes and unsure about what they were doing led to employees discussing issues amongst themselves at length before coming to a tentative decision. The operational (field) recycling teams were particularly critical of the new approach. One commented that 'before, we got a clear decision very quickly. Now decisions can take several days and appear to lack authority.' The new approach also caused tensions and stress within the Contracts Office and absenteeism increased.

At the next staff meeting, employees in the Contracts Office asked Sully to return to his old management style and job responsibilities. 'We prefer the old Sully Truin', they said, 'the Noproblems are again referred up to him. However, he is unhappy with this return to the previous way of working. He is working long hours and is concerned about his health. Also, he realises that he has little time for obtaining and planning contracts and this is severely restricting the capacity of the company to expand.

Required:

(a)   **Analyse Sully Truin's leadership style before and immediately after the training course and explain why the change of leadership style at ARC was unsuccessful.**

(15 marks)

(b)   **Describe the principles of job enrichment and evaluate its potential application in the Contracts Office at ARC.**   (10 marks)

(Total: 25 marks)

60   TMZ

Note: Consider 'now' to be 2015.

TMZ is a music company based in the developed country of Artazia. It was founded in 1963 when it started to sign emerging rock and roll artists to its record label. TMZ offers a contract in which the artists receive royalties based on the sales of their music. As part of this contract, TMZ record the music, distribute it and promote it. Most of the contracts are for a defined number of songs or records. For example, in 1980, TMZ contracted the heavy metal band, Vortex31, to produce ten albums, to be delivered over seven years. Extracted financial data for the period 1965–2000 is given in Table one. During these years TMZ successfully signed bands offering different and emerging types of music (pop, punk, garage, grunge, patio) and also successfully altered the physical media of distribution, from vinyl records to tape cassette and subsequently to compact disc (CD).

All figures in $million	1965	1970	1980	1990	2000
Revenue	10	70	120	150	170
Gross profit	4	30	45	50	50
Net profit	3	22	30	30	25

Table one: Revenue and profit information: TMZ (1965–2000)

The company remained profitable in this period, despite musicians taking longer to produce albums and senior management adopting a relaxed and indulgent approach to their creative artists.

In 1999, the first file sharing company was formed in Artazia, allowing people to easily share their music files with each other. During the next decade, numerous file sharing and digital downloading companies were launched. As early as 2003, the possible implications of this growth in file sharing and digital downloading were highlighted by a number of employees in TMZ. However, senior management at TMZ were dismissive of this threat, suggesting that the contracts with their artists were 'watertight'. Table two shows revenue and profit information for 2003–2007.

All figures in $million	2003	2004	2005	2006	2007
Revenue	165	150	130	100	80
Gross profit	45	30	10	0	(10)
Net profit	20	5	(15)	(20)	(30)

Table two: Revenue and profit information: TMZ (2003–2007)

Senior management at TMZ believed that this decline in performance was due to them providing the 'wrong music, promoted to the wrong people at the wrong price'. During this period the company signed new artists, increased advertising and cut prices. However, this did not halt its decline.

Losses were also made in 2008 and 2009 and the company was only kept afloat by fresh injections of shareholder capital. During these years, the company took legal action against what they considered illegal downloading and file sharing. It won a number of small cases but its actions angered many music fans, who felt that music labels had been greedy in the past. It also upset some of its artists who now benefited from the opportunity the internet gave them to sell music directly to their fans.

In 2009, a new CEO was appointed from outside the music industry. In 2010 he announced a new strategy. TMZ was no longer interested in contracting new artists to the label. Instead it would focus on deriving profit from its established artists and music catalogue. He came to licensing agreements with some large digital downloading operators and stores, allowing them to access or sell the music of established artists. However, he continued litigation against others. He also began to generate revenue from licensing the music for use in computer games, television advertisements and personalised ringtones.

In 2011 the company reported a gross profit for the first time since 2005. In 2013 and 2014 it recorded a small net profit. The CEO stated that TMZ was now a 'slimmer, fitter company. We are a learning organisation, developing the resilience needed to trade successfully in the ever-changing digital music age'. However, he warned that TMZ, like others in the industry, would continue to pursue actions against the illegal downloading of music. 'There is a generation where many people consider music and all creative content should be free. However, we see signs that this assumption is becoming less widely held. The next generation is questioning it. Like many others, we continue to seek ways of distributing music which is fair to both the consumer and the artist. We are constantly monitoring trends and patterns in consumer behaviour. We will not get caught out like we were ten years ago. We won't be fooled again!'

Required:

(a) Analyse the performance of TMZ from 1965 to the present. Include in your analysis reference to the principles and any evidence of strategic drift.   **(15 marks)**

(b) The current CEO claims that TMZ is a learning organisation. Discuss the principles of a learning organisation and its implications for TMZ.   **(5 marks)**

(c) Knowledge management is closely related to the concept of the learning organisation. Explain knowledge management and its relevance to TMZ.   **(5 marks)**

(Total: 25 marks)

61   NATIONAL COLLEGE

Judy Sodhi is in her first teaching year at the National College, a private college offering short courses in accounting, auditing and management. In her first year Judy has primarily taught the Certificate in Managerial Finance. This is a three-day short course which ends in an externally set examination, marked and invigilated by staff employed by the Institute of Managerial Finance (IMF). The IMF also defines the syllabus, the length of the course and accredits colleges to run the course. There are no pre-conditions for candidates who wish to attend the course. Last year Judy ran the course 20 times with an average of nine students on each running of the course. At the end of each course every student has to complete a post-course evaluation questionnaire. Judy does not see these questionnaires and has received no feedback about her performance.

As the college is a virtual organisation using serviced training rooms, Judy rarely sees her manager Blake Jones. However, he contacted her recently to suggest that they should conduct her first appraisal and a date and time was agreed. Blake explained that 'it would be just a general chat looking at how the year had gone. We need to do one to satisfy the college and the IMF'. The time of the appraisal was set for 3.00 pm, finishing at 5.00 pm.

The appraisal did start with a general discussion. Blake outlined the plans of the organisation and his own promotion hopes. Judy was surprised to see that Blake was not following any standard list of questions or noting down any of the answers she made. She told him that one of her main problems was the numeracy level of some of the candidates. She recognised that the course had no pre-conditions, 'but it does require some basic mathematical skills that some of our candidates just do not have'.

After listening to Judy for a while Blake produced a statistical summary of the feedback questionnaires from the courses she had run in the last year. He said that the organisation expected its lecturers to attain an acceptable result in all 10 questions given in the post-course questionnaire. An acceptable result 'is that 90% of all candidates said that they were 'satisfied or very satisfied' with key aspects of the course'. Judy had achieved this on seven of the questions but specifically failed on the following performance measures.

- Percentage of candidates who felt that the course was relevant to their current job – *only 65% of your candidates felt that the course was relevant to their current job.*

- Percentage of candidates who passed the examination – *only 88.88% of your candidates passed the examination.*

- Percentage of candidates who felt that the course pace was satisfactory – *only 75% of your candidates felt that the pace of the course was satisfactory.*

After expressing her surprise that she had not been given this information before, she immediately returned to the problem of numeracy skills. 'As I told you' she said 'some of these students lack the mathematical skills to pass. That's not my fault, it is yours – you should not have let them on the course in the first place. You are just filling the places to make money'.

After a heated discussion, Blake then turned to the 'last thing on my agenda'. He explained that it was only college policy to give pay increases to lecturers who had achieved 90% in all 10 questions, so there would be no increase for Judy next year. However, he also needed to discuss her workload for next year. He produced a spreadsheet and had just begun to discuss course planning and locations in great detail when his mobile phone rang. 'I am sorry, Judy, I have to collect the children from school – I must go. I will write down your planned course assignments and e-mail them to you. I think that was a very useful discussion. Overall we are very happy with you. See you at the end-of-year party, and of course at next year's appraisal.' He left at 4.30 pm.

Required:

(a)   **This requirement is no longer examinable.** (15 marks)

(b)   **Explain the concept and purpose of competency frameworks for organisations, assessing their potential use at the National College and the Institute of Managerial Finance.** (10 marks)

(Total: 25 marks)

62   COOPER UNIVERSITY

Cooper University is situated in the country of Mowria, which has over 300 universities. University tuition fees have increased in the last few years and students are expecting a better level of service as a consequence of this. Results of student satisfaction surveys are published by the Mowrian government, and can greatly influence the students' choice of university.

At Cooper University, students are assessed in two ways: by examinations and coursework. Both types of assessment contribute towards the degree classification awarded to students. In a recent, internally commissioned, student experience report, Cooper University received some negative feedback from students on the coursework organisation, submission and feedback process. Consequently, the university is keen to rectify problems in this process.

Details of the coursework organisation, submission and feedback process are described in the next section and summarised in Figure One.

Coursework organisation, submission and feedback process

At the start of a new semester, an administrator distributes term dates and coursework guidance to lecturers. There are many different subjects within a course and each subject is managed by a different lecturer. The guidance includes a stipulation that coursework should be marked and returned to students within two teaching weeks of the submitted coursework being collected from the course administration office by the lecturer. Lecturers write their own coursework requirements and set their own deadlines, informing the head of department so that a consolidated course schedule can be produced.

Coursework requirements are uploaded by lecturers onto a virtual learning environment (VLE) system, which is accessed by students. Lecturers release these requirements at the beginning of the course, in accordance with the administrative guidelines. Students download the requirements and then complete and submit their work.

Students are required to submit two copies of their completed coursework: a hard copy to the administration office and a soft copy uploaded into the VLE system. The VLE system produces an automatic receipt showing the date and time coursework was submitted, as proof of the upload. An administrator periodically sorts the submitted hard copies by subject, ready for lecturers to collect. Lecturers collect the coursework when they have some free time in their schedule for marking.

Once collected, lecturers mark the coursework and type their feedback into a new word processed document, and then upload that document against the student profile on the VLE. The VLE issues an automatic email to students informing them that feedback is available. The lecturer also collates total marks onto a spreadsheet and emails this to the administrators. The administrators input these marks manually into a computerised administration system and then send a report to the head of department, who records the marks against the individual student's assessment profile.

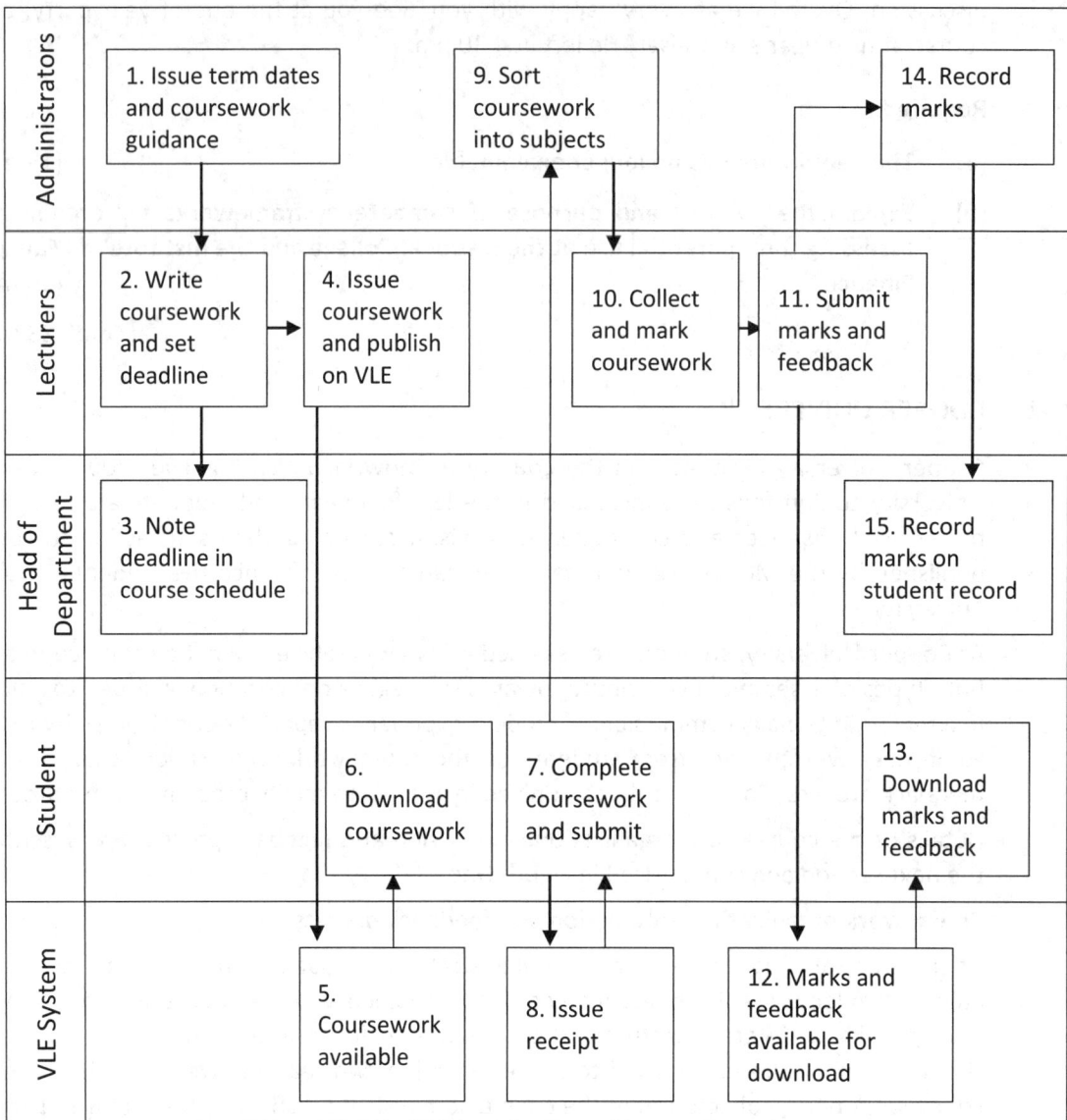

Administrators	1. Issue term dates and coursework guidance		9. Sort coursework into subjects		14. Record marks
Lecturers	2. Write coursework and set deadline	4. Issue coursework and publish on VLE	10. Collect and mark coursework	11. Submit marks and feedback	
Head of Department	3. Note deadline in course schedule				15. Record marks on student record
Student		6. Download coursework	7. Complete coursework and submit		13. Download marks and feedback
VLE System		5. Coursework available	8. Issue receipt	12. Marks and feedback available for download	

Figure One – Coursework organisation, submission and feedback process

Student feedback

The following extracts from the student experience report are representative of the feedback received from students:

'I received one mark from the VLE system, but when my end-of-year results were released the mark was different' 'My feedback was on a separate document so I found it difficult to relate to the coursework submitted'

'I accidentally submitted an unfinished piece of coursework to the administration office but submitted the correct one to the system. The lecturer marked the unfinished piece'

'It takes weeks to receive my marks, by which time I've forgotten what the coursework was about. When I asked the lecturer she said she had marked it within the time allowed'

'We always have about four pieces of coursework to submit at the same time, and then weeks where nothing is required. I wish the university would manage our programme better'

'The lecturer said he did not receive the hard copy of my coursework but I know I handed it in. This was counted as a non-submission'

'There were errors in the initial coursework requirements, which were subsequently significantly changed. I had already started the assignment so this time was wasted'

'I completed and submitted my coursework early in order to manage my workload better, but then the lecturer gave an additional lecture to help us with our coursework. This contained very useful information, which we had not previously covered. I was not allowed to resubmit my work and so suffered from being efficient'

'My lecturer wasn't very supportive when I had personal problems.'

'My course didn't seem well coordinated. Some topics were repeated and others failed to cover the syllabus, making it difficult to move up from one year to the next'

With increases in student tuition fees and therefore student expectations, the role of university lecturers is changing. They are expected to play a more proactive role in the development of students and in monitoring students' well-being. There is a need for lecturers to assist in the development of new courses and subjects and to work closely with each other to ensure that the link between subjects is rational and appropriate.

Currently, there is an extensive guidance document for lecturers, mapping out the way in which all activities should be carried out within their role; the coursework organisation, submission and feedback process is just one of many process maps. There is a high turnover of lecturing staff, some of whom have stated that they are getting little job satisfaction from what should be a rewarding and challenging job.

Required:

(a)   **Identify, and explain, four problems in the current coursework organisation, submission and feedback process and suggest appropriate solutions to address each of these problems.** **(16 marks)**

(b)   **Changes in organisational processes often require the redesign of jobs.**

   Discuss how the jobs of lecturers at Cooper University could be redesigned, using relevant approaches to job design, so that they better meet the needs of their students and the university. **(9 marks)**

(Total: 25 marks)

63   WPHA

The country of Westoria has a well-respected public health service funded primarily through general taxation. The Westoria Public Health Authority (WPHA) is responsible for delivering this health service through a network of hospitals in Westoria.

WPHA is under increasing pressure to demonstrate to taxpayers that it is using public finances wisely and so it wishes to accurately monitor and control health service expenditure. However, it is proving difficult to confidently track the budgeted and actual finances of individual hospitals, as each is operating its own form of budgeting and cash management. Consequently, WPHA has decided to introduce a single computer-based system which will allow all hospitals to enter and manage financial information in a standard way. This system will be part of an authority-wide enterprise resource planning system (ERPS) which will allow WPHA to monitor and control the finances of the entire authority. Currently, the input and consolidation of WPHA information is a time-consuming process, importing data from individual hospitals into a series of spreadsheets to provide total figures for the authority as a whole.

At a recent WPHA board meeting, the head of the authority suggested that the scope of the ERPS should be widened to incorporate other elements of operational and management information. She pointed out that some previous commercial off-the-shelf (COTS) software solutions which the authority selected and implemented had not worked well. She gave two specific examples:

–   The payroll system does not support payment increments for non-standard working, such as overtime rates. To allow this, payroll staff currently have to change the employee's standard hourly rate for the time period in question and then change it back again. This is time-consuming and payment errors have been made when payroll staff have forgotten to change the rate back again.

–   The human resource management system does not support the temporary transfer of staff between hospital departments. To compensate for this, human resource staff have to action a permanent move for a short time period and then action a reverse move at the end of that period.

She therefore felt that the introduction of the ERPS would be an opportunity to address outstanding problems and to improve and standardise the systems in use.

The board agreed the ERPS should, as a minimum, also include payroll and human resource management modules within the overall product. However, given budget limitations, the board decided that a commercial off-the-shelf ERPS solution should be selected and implemented. They all agreed that this would be a cheaper solution than a bespoke system and would be well suited to their needs, as it should fulfil the standard requirements they envisaged. Furthermore, it had always been the policy of WPHA not to employ internal IT system developers. Currently, the IT support team consists of one operational member of staff at each hospital and a central team of ten staff who assist in addressing major IT problems encountered at any of the hospitals. The IT support team has also produced ways to bypass issues with previously implemented COTS package solutions.

This lack of internal IT resource, and the recognition that previous COTS implementations had been less successful than predicted, has prompted WPHA to seek the advice of an external software systems consultant.

The consultant has suggested that the evaluation and implementation of the ERPS package should follow a four-stage process:

- Evaluate whether a COTS solution is an appropriate approach

- Define the requirements for the new software

- Evaluate competing packages

- Implement the selected package

However, the head of the authority believes that the external consultant is being over-cautious in his advice and approach and that the first two stages are not needed. In her words: 'We know that a COTS solution is the right approach for us as we have little alternative, so why spend time doing the first step? We also know that we've been pretty poor at defining what we want in the past; so why not recognise our deficiencies and go straight to stage three and look at competing packages to see which products provide the best features?'

The HR director, who has experienced the problems of the human resource and payroll systems at first hand, disagrees. He feels that the consultant's four-stage process is insufficient. He believes that, 'it is important that we consider all four elements of the POPIT (four view) model, which provides four key areas to be considered when a process is to change. These four key areas are people, organisation, processes and information technology. Only the last of these will be considered in the consultant's four-stage process. If we ignore the remaining three areas we are in danger of another failed software project, which is likely to further upset taxpayers and, perhaps, threaten the future of the authority itself.'

Required:

(a) The external consultant suggested a four-stage process for the evaluation and implementation of the proposed commercial off-the-shelf ERPS package.

Discuss the four-stage process for the evaluation and implementation of a software package, and the significance of each stage in the context of the previous and proposed COTS solutions at WPHA. **(16 marks)**

(b) The HR director has suggested that all elements of the POPIT model should be considered.

Explain, in the context of WPHA, the need for considering the people, the organisation and the processes involved when carrying out a business change project. **(9 marks)**

(Total: 25 marks)

MANAGING STRATEGIC CHANGE

64   PSI

Introduction

Retail pharmacies supply branded medicinal products, such as headache and cold remedies, as well as medicines prescribed by doctors. Customers expect both types of product to be immediately available and so this demands efficient purchasing and stock control in each pharmacy. The retail pharmacy industry is increasingly concentrated in a small number of nationwide pharmacy chains, although independent pharmacies continue to survive. The pharmacy chains are increasingly encouraging their customers to order medicinal products online and the doctors are being encouraged to electronically send their prescriptions to the pharmacy so that they can be prepared ready for the patient to collect.

Pharmacy Systems International (PSI)

Pharmacy Systems International (PSI) is a privately owned software company which has successfully developed and sold a specialised software package meeting the specific needs of retail pharmacies. PSI's stated objective is to be a 'highly skilled professional company providing quality software services to the retail pharmacy industry'. Over the last three years PSI has experienced gradual growth in turnover, profitability and market share (see Figure 1).

Figure 1: PSI Financial information

	20X7	20X6	20X5
Turnover ($000)	11,700	10,760	10,350
Profits ($000) (pre-tax)	975	945	875
Estimated market share	26%	24%	23%
Number of employees	120	117	115

PSI has three directors, each of whom has a significant ownership stake in the business. The chief executive is a natural entrepreneur with a past record of identifying opportunities and taking the necessary risks to exploit them. In the last three years he has curbed his natural enthusiasm for growth as PSI has consolidated its position in the market place. However, he now feels the time is right to expand the business to a size and profitability that makes PSI an attractive acquisition target and enables the directors to realise their investment in the company. He has a natural ally in the sales and marketing director and both feel that PSI needs to find new national and international markets to fuel its growth. The software development director, however, does not share the chief executive's enthusiasm for this expansion.

The chief executive has proposed that growth can best be achieved by developing a generic software package which can be used by the wider, general retail industry. His plan is for the company to take the current software package and take out any specific references to the pharmaceutical industry. This generic package could then be extended and configured for other retail sectors. The pharmaceutical package would be retained but it would be perceived and marketed as a specialised implementation of the new generic package.

This proposed change in strategic direction is strongly resisted by the software development director. He and his team of software developers are under constant pressure to meet the demands of the existing retail pharmacy customers. On-line ordering of medicinal products and electronic despatch of prescriptions are just two examples of the constant pressure PSI is under from their retail customers to continuously update its software package to enable the pharmacies to implement technical innovations that improve customer service.

Ideally, the software development director would like to acquire further resources to develop a more standardised software package for their current customers. He is particularly annoyed by PSI's salesmen continually committing the company to producing a customised software solution for each customer and promising delivery dates that the software delivery team struggle to meet. Frequently, the software contains faults that require expensive and time consuming maintenance. Consequently, PSI is being increasingly criticised by customers. A recent user group conference expressed considerable dissatisfaction with the quality of the PSI package and doubted the company's ability to meet the published deadline for a new release of the software.

Required:

(a)   **The proposal to develop and sell a software package for the retail industry represents a major change in strategy for PSI. Analyse the nature, scope and type of this proposed strategic change for PSI.**   **(10 marks)**

(b)   **The success of any attempt at managing change will be dependent on the context in which that change takes place. Identify and analyse, using an appropriate model, the internal contextual features that could influence the success or failure of the chief executive's proposed strategic change for PSI.**   **(15 marks)**

(Total: 25 marks)

65   ICOMPUTE

iCompute was founded twenty years ago by the technology entrepreneur, Ron Yeates. It initially specialised in building bespoke computer software for the financial services industry. However, it has expanded into other specialised areas and it is currently the third largest software house in the country, employing 400 people. It still specialises in bespoke software, although 20% of its income now comes from the sales of a software package designed specifically for car insurance.

The company has grown based on a 'work hard, play hard work ethic' and this still remains. Employees are expected to work long hours and to take part in social activities after work. Revenues have continued to increase over the last few years, but the firm has had difficulty in recruiting and retaining staff. Approximately one-third of all employees leave within their first year of employment at the company. The company appears to experience particular difficulty in recruiting and retaining female staff, with 50% of female staff leaving within 12 months of joining the company. Only about 20% of the employees are female and they work mainly in marketing and human resources.

The company is currently in dispute with two of its customers who claim that its bespoke software did not fit the agreed requirements. iCompute currently outsources all its legal advice problems to a law firm that specialises in computer contracts and legislation. However, the importance of legal advice has led to iCompute considering the establishment of an internal legal team, responsible for advising on contracts, disputes and employment legislation.

The support of bespoke solutions and the car insurance software package was also outsourced a year ago to a third party. Although support had been traditionally handled in-house, it was unpopular with staff. One of the senior managers responsible for the outsourcing decision claimed that support calls were 'increasingly varied and complex, reflecting incompetent end users, too lazy to read user guides.' However, the outsourcing of support has not proved popular with iCompute's customers and a number of significant complaints have been made about the service given to end users. The company is currently reviewing whether the software support process should be brought back in-house.

The company is still regarded as a technology leader in the market place, although the presence of so many technically gifted employees within the company often creates uncertainty about the most appropriate technology to adopt for a solution. One manager commented that 'we have often adopted, or are about to adopt, a technology or solution when one of our software developers will ask if we have considered some newly released technology. We usually admit we haven't and so we re-open the adoption process. We seem to be in a state of constant technical paralysis.'

Although Ron Yeates retired five years ago, many of the software developers recruited by him are still with the company. Some of these have become operational managers, employed to manage teams of software developers on internal and external projects. Subba Kendo is one of the managers who originally joined the company as a trainee programmer. 'I moved into management because I needed to earn more money. There is a limit to what you can earn here as a software developer. However, I still keep up to date with programming though, and I am a goalkeeper for one of the company's five-a-side football teams. I am still one of the boys.'

However, many of the software developers are sceptical about their managers. One commented that 'they are technologically years out of date. Some will insist on writing programs and producing code, but we take it out again as soon as we can and replace it with something we have written. Not only are they poor programmers, they are poor managers and don't really know how to motivate us.' Although revenues have increased, profits have fallen. This is also blamed on the managers. 'There is always an element of ambiguity in specifying customers' requirements. In the past, Ron Yeates would debate responsibility for requirements changes with the customer. However, we now seem to do all amendments for free. The customer is right even when we know he isn't. No wonder margins are falling. The managers are not firm enough with customers.'

The software developers are also angry that an in-house project has been initiated to produce a system for recording time spent on tasks and projects. Some of the justification for this is that a few of the projects are on a 'time and materials' basis and a time recording system would permit accurate and prompt invoicing. However, the other justification for the project is that it will improve the estimation of 'fixed-price' contracts. It will provide statistical information derived from previous projects to assist account managers preparing estimates to produce quotes for bidding for new bespoke development contracts.

Vikram Soleski, one of the current software developers, commented that 'managers do not even have up-to-date mobile phones, probably because they don't know how to use them. We (software developers) always have the latest gadgets long before they are acquired by managers. But I like working here, we have a good social scene and after working long hours we socialise together, often playing computer games well into the early hours of the morning. It's a great life if you don't weaken!'

Required:

(a) Analyse the culture of iCompute, and assess the implications of your analysis for the company's future performance. **(13 marks)**

(b) iCompute is currently re-considering three high level processes:

   (i) Advice on legal issues (currently outsourced)

   (ii) Software support (currently outsourced)

   (iii) Time recording (in-house, bespoke software development).

   Evaluate, using an appropriate framework or model, the suitability of iCompute's current approach to EACH of these high level processes. **(12 marks)**

   (Total: 25 marks)

66 ZOOMBA

Zoomba is a national chain of restaurants. Zoomba competes with other rival chains by targeting mainly 18–25 year olds and providing healthy food options in a spacious restaurant using organically grown ingredients and served by staff who are in the same age group. It has 100 permanent locations spread across the country. The chain has traditionally performed well and continues to make high levels of profits. However, these profits have levelled off in the last two years and the first quarter of this year saw the first year-on-year, like-for-like drop in sales that the company has experienced in its ten year life.

The company's CEO, Grace Grove, believes that this is due to a number of factors such as a recent downturn in the economy, the market becoming saturated with rivals and limited space for further expansion. She also feels that the company hasn't taken advantage of the growing trend for pop-up restaurants. These restaurants are often created for very short periods, such as during a music festival or national events and public holidays, using temporary locations such as food trucks, disused premises or market stalls. The aim is to maximise sales during a small time frame whilst minimising costs. Reservations are not taken and the restaurants are therefore more accessible to a wider range of customers and can be an important step in breaking into new market segments.

Grace Grove therefore put together a team of staff to manage a project aimed at exploiting this growth opportunity. The team was headed by Elise Hazelwood who had been working in the company's IT function. The project launched in the second quarter of the year and the new pop-up restaurants opened in the third quarter of the year.

The team's first job was to design the process for setting up and running the pop ups. Processes were designed for venue location, asset management, food production, material supplies, marketing and sales. Work was put in to ensure that each process worked as efficiently as possible and, because of Elise Hazelwood's background, there was as much automation and e-processing as possible. Elise was able to ensure that adequate IT systems and controls were in place for elements such as e-procurement, social media marketing, sales recording, staff monitoring and inventory management. Social media marketing was particularly successful as Zoomba gained many followers who would not only act as a feedback and a word of mouth marketing service for the pop ups, but were also useful in suggesting venues and occasions for the pop ups.

Specialist team roles were created for pop up restaurants within the organisational structure. These teams would be managed by a member of the project team who would ensure that the new processes were followed and applied. Staff for the pop ups would be seconded from the nearest permanent location and would return to that location when the pop up closed.

Everything seemed set for success and both Grace Grove and Elise Hazelwood had high expectations for the venture. But having run the first two pop ventures (one to coincide with a large weekend music festival and the other situated at a major tourist resort for three months) profits and feedback have not been as good as expected. Elise Hazelwood was confident that all of the systems were in place to make the pop ups a success. The IT system worked well, premises were sourced and furbished to expectations, all food and service materials were at the venues, and social marketing was a particular success. Onsite project managers understood the processes well and were experienced in team management.

Feedback from customers was no better than average. Many customers were happy that they could now access Zoomba at a point that would not be available to them. But others were unhappy with the level of service provided. Some regular Zoomba visitors complained that the pop ups were disorganised with slower than usual service, whilst first time visitors had comments such as 'surly staff', 'lack of co-ordination' and 'messy premises'.

But the greatest resistance appeared to come from pop up staff. The following are samples of comments gathered as part of a lessons learnt review:

> I turned up at my normal location one day but was told I'd be spending the weekend working on the van at the music festival. It took me an extra half hours travel to get there each day.

> I volunteered for the tourist resort pop up thinking it would be good for my career. But there was little chance to get involved in decision making and when I returned to my normal location I found that someone else had gotten a promotion that I was hoping for.

> I enjoyed my time at the pop up but we seemed to spend most of it learning the new processes which were very different to what we were used to. They worked well once we were used to them but there were many mistakes at first.

Grace Grove is committed to make the pop ups a success and wants to learn from the mistakes of these initial trials. She intends to meet with Elise Hazelwood to discuss how the project can best move forward.

Required:

(a) Explain the type of strategic change that Zoomba appear to be going through with the new pop up venture. **(8 marks)**

(b) Describe the stages that Zoomba will have to undergo if it is to successfully realise the changes necessary to accomplish this strategic alignment. **(10 marks)**

(c) Using a suitable model, assess the reasons for the failures in the pop up venture.

(7 marks)

(Total: 25 marks)

67   STRATEGIES

Honda is a leading manufacturer of motorbikes. The company is credited with identifying and targeting an untapped market for small 50cc bikes in the US, enabling it to expand, overwhelm European competition and severely damage US bike manufacturers. By the late 60s, Honda had more than 60% of the US market. But this occurred by accident.

On entering this market, Honda had wanted to compete with the larger European and American bikes of 250ccs and over. These bikes had a defined market, and were sold through dedicated motorbike dealerships. Disaster struck when Honda's larger machines developed faults – they had not been designed for the hard wear and tear imposed by US motorcyclists. Honda had to recall them. Up until then Honda had made little effort to sell their small 50cc motorbikes – their staff rode them on errands around Los Angeles. Sports goods shops and ordinary bicycle and department stores had expressed an interest, but Honda did not want to confuse its image in its 'target' market of men who bought the larger bikes.

The faults in Honda's larger machines meant that reluctantly, Honda had to sell the small 50cc bikes just to raise money. They proved very popular with people who would never have bought motorbikes before. Eventually the company adopted this new market with enthusiasm with the slogan: 'You meet the nicest people on a Honda'. The strategy had emerged, against managers' conscious intentions, but they eventually responded to the new situation.

Required:

(a)   Explain why the actual strategy pursued by a company over a three- to five-year period may diverge from the deliberate strategy that the company initiated at the outset of that period.   **(13 marks)**

(b)   Discuss how big data could play a role in informing and implementing deliberate business strategies.   **(12 marks)**

(Total: 25 marks)

68   WEBFILMS

Webfilms was originally a film rental organisation, offering DVD rentals which were sent to customers and returned using parcel couriers. Webfilms enrolled members who paid a monthly fee and could rent as many films as they liked, receiving their next choice as soon as a previous film was returned. However, Webfilms found this model was not as successful as it had hoped. It struggled to gain a large customer base and high courier fees made it difficult for the company to make a reasonable profit.

The company underwent a radical strategic change and remodelled itself as an internet television network screening films and drama series. This service is now available in over 25 countries worldwide. All programmes are original and so have not been previously shown on any television channel in any country. The programmes are all produced by a creative team at Webfilms, headed by Paolo Butterfield, and all are only available in English. Members pay a monthly subscription charge and have access to unlimited viewing. Webfilms relies entirely on member subscriptions for funding as, to enhance the customer experience, its programmes do not carry advertising. Webfilms considers itself to be a focused differentiator, offering only programmes which it feels will attract a younger audience (the teens and twenties).

Until recently, Webfilms had no close competitors in this form of internet television. Indeed, it was the main substitute for traditional television channels, causing a downturn in that industry. However, its success has been noted and this has led to the emergence of a number of competitors in different countries. These competitors have recognised and capitalised on any perceived weakness of Webfilms. So, for example, some of them include programmes which are not in English and others also include popular programmes which have also been shown on other television channels. This means that customers need to only subscribe to one television service.

The CEO of Webfilms, who previously transformed the organisation from a postal to internet-based service, has recognised that strategic change is required in order for Webfilms to continue competing effectively in a dynamic market environment. Her proposal to the board included the following key points:

- The creation of a wider range of new programmes, including documentaries and current affairs programmes

- The inclusion of popular programmes which were created for one country's viewers being shown in other countries

- Broadening the types of programmes so that the company can appeal to all age ranges

- Introduction of on-screen advertisements to create another revenue stream

- Translation of the most popular programmes into languages other than English

- The introduction of new services including broadband provision and online gaming

- A focus on efficiency, using the existing customer base to expand and to gain economies of scale, before any new competitors can gain a large market share

- The drive for efficiency should not be at the cost of quality, allowing the company to operate a hybrid strategy

The CEO is keen to pursue a boundary-less organisational model. Three options are presented in her proposal:

Hollow – where *non-core processes* are outsourced to external providers.

Modular – a hollow organisation which outsources some elements of the production process.

Virtual – an organisation with no formal geographical structure, but operates through a series of linked IT systems, partnerships and collaborative agreements.

She further stated that it would be imperative to set **all** the new key points of the strategy in place as soon as possible, to be implemented on a pre-announced date, with a large marketing campaign to support it.

At a meeting with the creative director, Paolo Butterfield expressed concerns about many of the changes being suggested: 'This is an effective demotion for me and my team. Customers pay their monthly fees because they love what we do, and yet you want to change it. Why are we following the crowd, when our existing business model is successful?' The CEO responded, 'There is no demotion. You will still be responsible for the creative element, just not producing all the programmes. This will allow you to take a much more strategic view of what we show, where and in what language. Argue as much as you like, but this is going to happen, it's up to you whether you want to be involved in deciding how such change will take place.'

The meeting ended with some disharmony and a further meeting was arranged to determine which form of boundary-less working would be the most appropriate for Webfilms.

Required:

(a)   Balogun and Hope Hailey developed a change model which examines the contextual features which can influence the success or failure of strategic change.

Assess how five of the internal contextual features defined in Balogun and Hope Hailey's model (time, scope, readiness, preservation and power) would influence the likely success or failure of the strategic change proposed by the CEO for Webfilms. **(16 marks)**

(b)   **Discuss how the different models of boundary-less working (hollow, modular and virtual) might be used to deliver parts of the CEO's future strategy for Webfilms.** **(9 marks)**

(Total: 25 marks)

Section 2

SCENARIO-BASED QUESTIONS

69 OCEANIA NATIONAL AIRLINES (ONA) *Walk in the footsteps of a top tutor*

The island of Oceania attracts thousands of tourists every year. They come to enjoy the beaches, the climate and to explore the architecture and history of this ancient island. Oceania is also an important trading nation in the region and it enjoys close economic links with neighbouring countries. Oceania has four main airports and until ten years ago had two airlines, one based in the west (OceaniaAir) and one based in the east (Transport Oceania) of the island. However, ten years ago these two airlines merged into one airline – Oceania National Airlines (ONA) with the intention of exploiting the booming growth in business and leisure travel to and from Oceania.

Market sectors

ONA serves two main sectors. The first sector is a network of routes to the major cities of neighbouring countries. ONA management refer to this as the regional sector. The average flight time in this sector is one and a half hours and most flights are timed to allow business people to arrive in time to attend a meeting and then to return to their homes in the evening. Twenty five major cities are served in the regional sector with, on average, three return flights per day. There is also significant leisure travel, with many families visiting relatives in the region. The second sector is what ONA management refer to as the international sector. This is a network of flights to continental capitals. The average flight time in this sector is four hours. These flights attract both business and leisure travellers. The leisure travellers are primarily holiday-makers from the continent. Twenty cities are served in this sector with, on average, one return flight per day to each city.

Image, service and employment

ONA is the airline of choice for most of the citizens of Oceania. A recent survey suggested that 90% of people preferred to travel ONA for regional flights and 70% preferred to travel with ONA for international flights. 85% of the respondents were proud of their airline and felt that it projected a positive image of Oceania. The company also has an excellent safety record, with no fatal accident recorded since the merging of the airlines ten years ago.

The customer service of ONA has also been recognised by the airline industry itself. In 20X5 it was voted Regional Airline of the Year by the International Passenger Group (IPG) and one year later the IPG awarded the ONA catering department the prestigious Golden Bowl as provider of the best airline food in the world.

The courtesy and motivation of its employees (mainly Oceanic residents) is recognised throughout the region. 95% of ONA employees belong to recognised trade unions. ONA is perceived as an excellent employer. It pays above industry average salaries, offers excellent benefits (such as free health care) and has a generous non-contributory pension scheme. In 20X4 ONA employed 5400 people, rising to 5600 in 20X5 and 5800 in 20X6.

Fleet

Fleet details are given in Table 1. Nineteen of the Boeing 737s were originally in the fleet of OceaniaAir. Boeing 737s are primarily used in the international sector. Twenty-three of the Airbus A320s were originally part of the Transport Oceania fleet. Airbuses are primarily used in the regional sector. ONA also used three Embraer RJ145 jets in the regional sector.

Table 1: Fleet details

	Boeing 737	Airbus A320	Embraer RJ145
Total aircraft in service			
20X6	21	27	3
20X5	21	27	3
20X4	20	26	2
Capacity (passengers)	147	149	50
Introduced	October 1991	November 1988	January 1999
Average age	12.1 years	12.9 years	6.5 years
Utilisation (hrs per day)	8.70	7.41	7.50

Performance

Since 20X4 ONA has begun to experience significant competition from 'no frills' low-cost budget airlines, particularly in the international sector. Established continental operators now each offer, on average, three low fares flights to Oceania every day. 'No frills' low-cost budget airlines are also having some impact on the regional sector. A number of very small airlines (some with only one aircraft) have been established in some regional capitals and a few of these are offering low-cost flights to Oceania. A recent survey for ONA showed that its average international fare was double that of its low-cost competitors. Some of the key operational statistics for 20X6 are summarised in Table 2.

Table 2: Key operational statistics for ONA in 20X6

	Regional	International	Low-cost competitor average
Contribution to revenue ($m)			
Passenger	400	280	Not applicable
Cargo	35	15	Not applicable
Passenger load factor			
Standard class	73%	67%	87%
Business class	90%	74%	75%
Average annual pilot salary	$106,700	$112,500	$96,500
Source of revenue			
On-line sales	40%	60%	84%
Direct sales	10%	5%	12%
Commission sales	50%	35%	4%
Average age of aircraft	See Table 1		4.5 years
Utilisation (hrs per day)	See Table 1		9.10

ONA have made a number of operational changes in the last few years. Their website, for example, now allows passengers to book over the internet and to either have their tickets posted to them or to pick them up at the airport prior to travelling. Special promotional fares are also available for customers who book on-line. However, the website does not currently allow passengers to check-in on-line, a facility provided by some competitors.

Furthermore, as Table 2 shows, a large percentage of sales are still commission sales made through travel agents. Direct sales are those sales made over the telephone or at the airport itself.

Most leisure travellers pay standard or economy fares and travel in the standard class section of the plane. Although many business travellers also travel in standard class, some of them choose to travel business class for which they pay a price premium.

In the last three years, the financial performance of ONA has not matched its operational success. The main financial indicators have been extracted and are presented in Table 3. In a period (20X4–20X6) when world-wide passenger air travel revenue increased by 12% (and revenue from air travel to Oceania by 15%) and cargo revenue by 10%, ONA only recorded a 4.6% increase in passenger revenue.

Table 3: Extracted Financial Information (All figures in $m)

Extracted from the Statement of Financial Position (Balance Sheet)

	20X6	20X5	20X4
Non-current assets			
Property, plant and equipment	788	785	775
Other non-current assets	60	56	64
Total	848	841	839
Current assets			
Inventories	8	7	7
Trade receivables	68	71	69
Cash and cash equivalents	289	291	299
Total	365	369	375
Total assets	**1,213**	**1,210**	**1,214**
Total shareholders' equity	250	259	264
Non-current liabilities			
Interest bearing long-term loans	310	325	335
Employee benefit obligations	180	178	170
Other provisions	126	145	143
Total non-current liabilities	616	648	648
Current liabilities			
Trade payables	282	265	255
Current tax payable	9	12	12
Other current liabilities	56	26	35
Total current liabilities	347	303	302
Total equity and liabilities	**1,213**	**1,210**	**1,214**

Extracted from the income statement

Revenue		20X6	20X5	20X4
Passenger		680	675	650
Cargo		50	48	45
Other revenue		119	112	115
	Total	849	835	810
Cost of sales				
Purchases		535	525	510
Gross profit		314	310	300
Wages and salaries		215	198	187
Directors' salaries		17	16	15
Interest payable		22	21	18
	Total	254	235	220
Net profit before tax		60	75	80
Tax expense		18	23	24
Net profit after tax		42	52	56

Future strategy

The management team at ONA are keen to develop a strategy to address the airline's financial and operational weaknesses. One suggestion has been to re-position ONA itself as a 'no frills' low-cost budget airline. However, this has been angrily dismissed by the CEO as likely to lead 'to an unnecessary and bloody revolution that could cause the death of the airline itself'.

Required:

(a) Using the information provided in the scenario, evaluate the strengths and weaknesses of ONA and their impact on its performance. Please note that opportunities and threats are NOT required in your evaluation. **(20 marks)**

(b) The CEO of Oceania National Airways (ONA) has already strongly rejected the re-positioning of ONA as a 'no frills' low-cost budget airline.

    (i) Explain the key features of a 'no frills' low-cost strategy. **(4 marks)**

    (ii) Analyse why moving to a 'no frills' low-cost strategy would be inappropriate for ONA.

    Note: Requirement (b) (ii) includes 3 professional marks **(16 marks)**

(c) Identify and evaluate other strategic options ONA could consider to address the airline's current financial and operational weaknesses.

    Note: Requirement (c) includes 2 professional marks **(10 marks)**

                                                (Total: 50 marks)

70   THE NATIONAL MUSEUM   *Walk in the footsteps of a top tutor*

Introduction

The National Museum (NM) was established in 1857 to house collections of art, textiles and metal ware for the nation. It remains in its original building which is itself of architectural importance. Unfortunately, the passage of time has meant that the condition of the building has deteriorated and so it requires continual repair and maintenance. Alterations have also been made to ensure that the building complies with the disability access and health and safety laws of the country. However, these alterations have been criticised as being unsympathetic and out of character with the rest of the building. The building is in a previously affluent area of the capital city. However, what were once large middle-class family houses have now become multi-occupied apartments and the socio-economic structure of the area has radically changed. The area also suffers from an increasing crime rate. A visitor to the museum was recently assaulted whilst waiting for a bus to take her home. The assault was reported in both local and national newspapers.

Thirty years ago, the government identified museums that held significant Heritage Collections. These are collections that are deemed to be very significant to the country. Three Heritage Collections were identified at the NM, a figure that has risen to seven in the intervening years as the museum has acquired new items.

Funding and structure

The NM is currently 90% funded by direct grants from government. The rest of its income comes from a nominal admission charge and from private sponsorship of exhibitions. The direct funding from the government is based on a number of factors, but the number of Heritage Collections held by the museum is a significant funding influence. The Board of Trustees of the NM divide the museum's income between departments roughly on the basis of the previous year's budget plus an inflation percentage. The division of money between departments is heavily influenced by the Heritage Collections. Departments with Heritage Collections tend to be allocated a larger budget. The budgets for 20X8 and 20X9 are shown in Figure 1.

Collection Sections	Number of Heritage Collections	Budget ($000s) 20X8	Budget ($000s) 20X9
Architecture	2	120.00	125.00
Art	2	135.00	140.00
Metalwork	1	37.50	39.00
Glass		23.00	24.00
Textiles	1	45.00	47.50
Ceramics		35.00	36.00
Furniture		30.00	31.50
Print and books		35.00	36.50
Photography		15.00	15.50
Fashion		10.00	10.50
Jewellery	1	50.00	52.50
Sculpture		25.00	26.00
Administration		60.50	63.00
Total		621.00	647.00

The head of each collection section is an important position and enjoys many privileges, including a large office, a special section heads' dining room and a dedicated personal assistant (PA). The heads of sections which have 'Heritage Collections' also hold the title of professor from the National University.

The departmental structure of the NM (see Figure 2) is largely built around the twelve main sections of the collection. These sections are grouped into three departments, each of which has a Director. The Board of Directors is made up of the three directors of these departments, together with the Director of Administration and the Director General. The museum is a charity run by a Board of Trustees. There are currently eight trustees, two of whom have been recently appointed by the government. The other six trustees are people well-known and respected in academic fields relevant to the museum's collections.

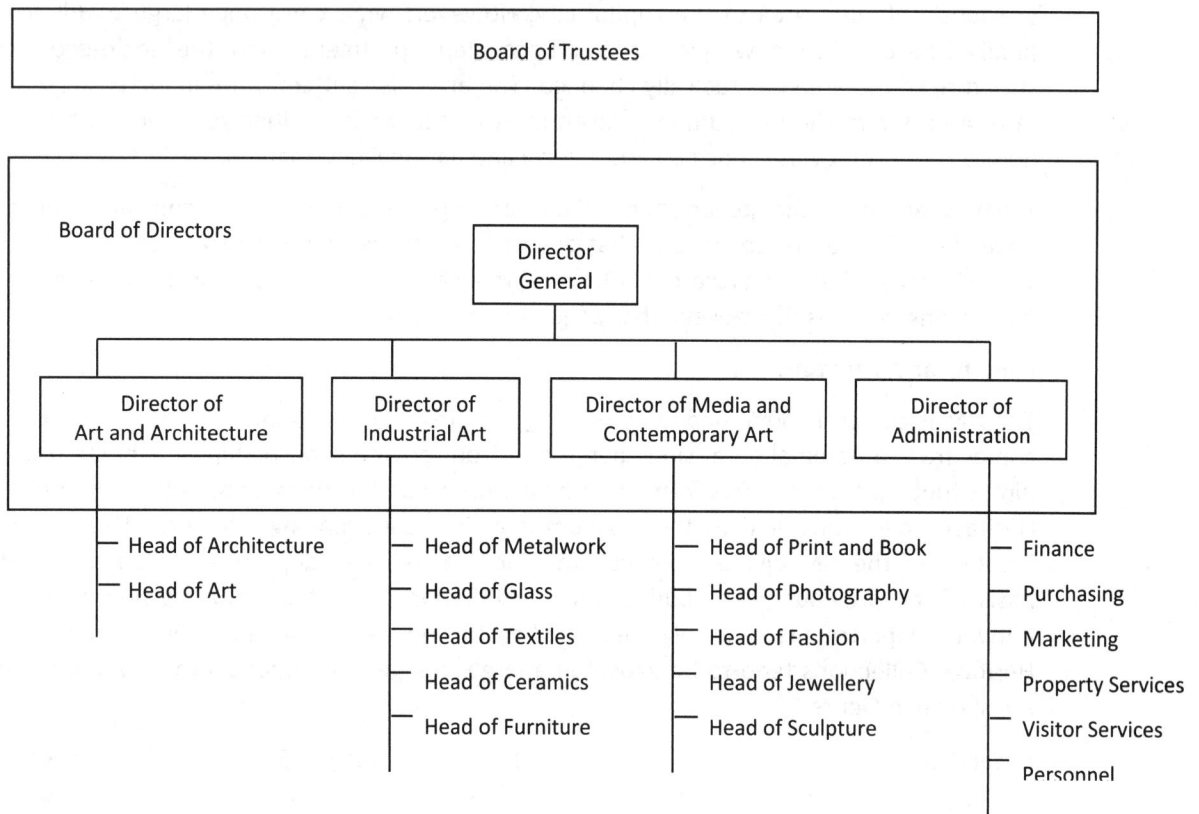

```
                        ┌──────────────────────────────────────┐
                        │          Board of Trustees           │
                        └──────────────────────────────────────┘
                                          │
  ┌──────────────────────────────────────────────────────────────────────┐
  │  Board of Directors              ┌──────────────┐                     │
  │                                  │   Director   │                     │
  │                                  │   General    │                     │
  │                                  └──────────────┘                     │
  │   ┌────────────────┐  ┌────────────────┐  ┌────────────────┐  ┌────────────────┐
  │   │  Director of   │  │  Director of   │  │ Director of Media│ │  Director of   │
  │   │Art and Architecture│ │Industrial Art │  │and Contemporary Art│ │ Administration │
  │   └────────────────┘  └────────────────┘  └────────────────┘  └────────────────┘
  └──────────────────────────────────────────────────────────────────────┘
```

Head of Architecture	Head of Metalwork	Head of Print and Book	Finance
Head of Art	Head of Glass	Head of Photography	Purchasing
	Head of Textiles	Head of Fashion	Marketing
	Head of Ceramics	Head of Jewellery	Property Services
	Head of Furniture	Head of Sculpture	Visitor Services
			Personnel

Figure 2: Current organisational structure

Government change

One year ago, a new national government was elected. The newly appointed Minister for Culture implemented the government's election manifesto commitment to make museums more self-funding. The minister has declared that in five year's time the museum must cover 60% of its own costs and only 40% will be directly funded by government. This change in funding will gradually be phased in over the next five years. The 40% government grant will be linked to the museum achieving specified targets for disability access, social inclusion and electronic commerce and access. The government is committed to increasing museum attendance by lower socio-economic classes and younger people so that they are more aware of their heritage. Furthermore, it also wishes to give increasing access to museum exhibits to disabled people who cannot physically visit the museum site. The government have asked all museums to produce a strategy document showing how they intend to meet these financial, accessibility and technological objectives. The government's opposition has, since the election, also agreed that the reliance of museums on government funding should be reduced.

Traditionally, the NM has provided administrative support for sections and departments, grouped together beneath a Director of Administration. The role of the Director General has been a part-time post. However, the funding changes introduced by the government and the need to produce a strategy document, has spurred the Board of Trustees to appoint a full-time Director General from the private sector. The trustees felt they needed private industry expertise to develop and implement a strategy to achieve the government's objectives. The new Director General was previously the CEO of a major chain of supermarkets.

Director General's proposal

The new Director General has produced a strategic planning document showing how the NM intends to meet the government's objectives. Proposals in this document include:

(1) Allocating budgets (from 20Y0) to sections based on visitor popularity. The most visited collections will receive the most money. The idea is to stimulate sections to come up with innovative ideas that will attract more visitors to the museum. Visitor numbers have been declining (see Figure 3) since 20X4.

Visitor numbers (000s)	20X7	20X6	20X5	20X4
Age 17 or less	10	12	15	15
Age 18–22	5	8	12	10
Age 23–30	10	15	20	20
Age 31–45	20	20	18	25
Age 46–59	35	35	30	30
Age 60 or more	40	35	35	30
Total	120	125	130	130

Figure 3: Visitor numbers 20X4–20X7

(2) Increasing entrance charges to increase income, but to make entry free to pensioners, students, children and people receiving government benefit payments.

(3) Removing the head of sections' dining room and turning this into a restaurant for visitors. An increase in income from catering is also proposed in the document.

(4) Removing the head of sections' personal assistants and introducing a support staff pool to reduce administrative costs.

(5) Increasing the display of exhibits. Only 10% of the museum's collection is open to the public. The rest is held in storage.

(6) Increasing commercial income from selling posters, postcards and other souvenirs.

The Director General has also suggested a major re-structuring of the organisation as:

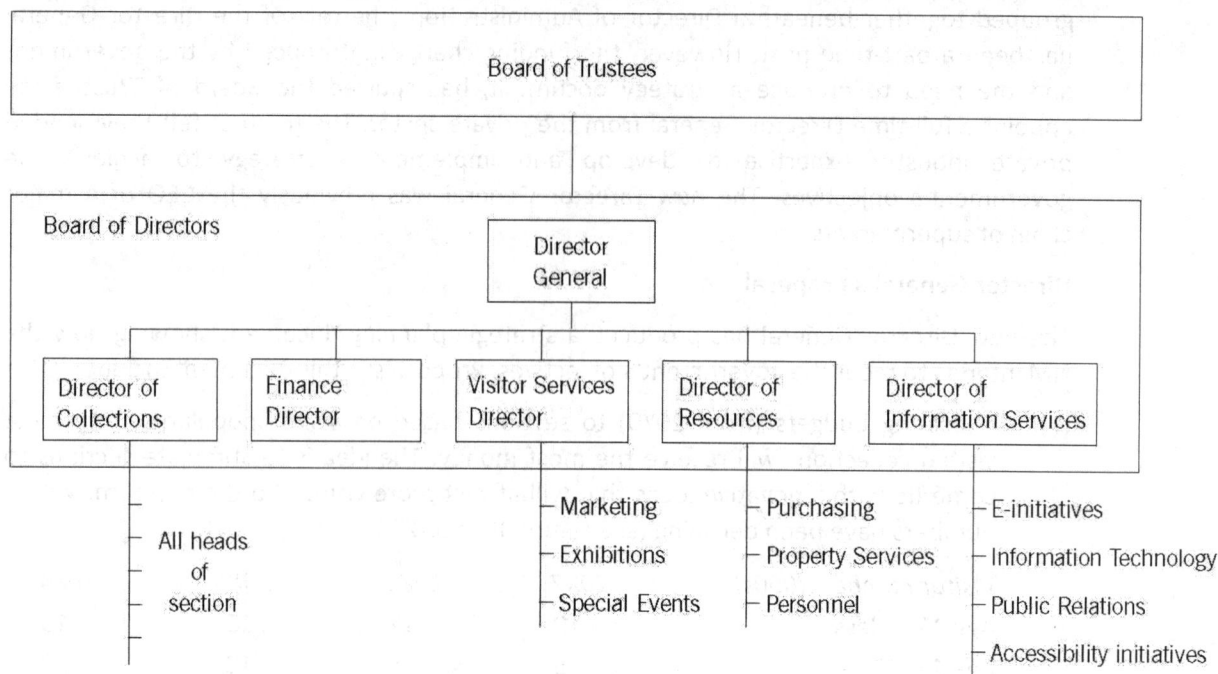

Figure 4: Proposed organisational structure

Reaction to the proposals

Employees have reacted furiously to the Director General's suggestions. The idea of linking budgets to visitor numbers has been greeted with dismay by the Director of Art and Architecture. 'This is a dreadful idea and confuses popularity with historical significance. As previous governments have realised, what is important is the value of the collection. Heritage Collections recognise this significance by putting the nation's interests before those of an undiscerning public. As far as I am concerned, if they want to see fashion, they can look in the high street shops. Unlike fashion, great art and architecture remains.' The Director of Art and Architecture and the two professors who hold the Head of Architecture and Head of Art posts have also lobbied individual members of the Board of Trustees with their concerns about the Director General's proposals.

The Director of Industrial Arts and the Director of Media and Contemporary Art have contacted powerful figures in both television and the press and as a result a number of articles and letters critical of the Director General's proposals have appeared. A recent television programme called 'Strife at the NM' also featured interviews with various heads of collections criticising the proposed changes. They were particularly critical of the lack of consultation; 'these proposals have been produced with no input from museum staff. They have been handed down from on high by an ex-grocer', said one anonymous contributor.

Eventually, the criticism of staff and their lack of cooperation prompted the Director General to ask the Board of Trustees to publicly back him. However, only the two trustees appointed by the government were prepared to do so. Consequently, the Director General resigned. This has prompted an angry response from the government which has now threatened to cut the museum's funding dramatically next year and to change the composition of the Board of Trustees so that the majority of trustees are appointed directly by the government. The Minister of Culture has asked the museum to develop and recommend a new strategy within one month.

Required:

(a) Analyse the macro-environment of the National Museum using a PESTEL analysis.

(20 marks)

(b) The failure of the Director General's strategy has been explained by one of the trustees as 'a failure to understand our organisational culture; the way we do things around here'.

Assess the underlying organisational cultural issues that would explain the failure of the Director General's strategy at the National Museum.

Note: requirement (b) includes 2 professional marks. (20 marks)

(c) Johnson, Scholes and Whittington identify three strategy lenses; design, experience and ideas.

Examine the different insights each of these lenses gives to understanding the process of strategy development at the National Museum.

Note: requirement (c) includes 2 professional marks. (10 marks)

(Total: 50 marks)

71 SHOAL PLC

Shoal plc is a well-known corporate organisation in the fish industry. It owns 14 companies concerned with fishing and related industries.

This scenario focuses on three of these companies:

- ShoalFish Ltd – a fishing fleet operating in the western oceans

- ShoalPro Ltd – a company concerned with processing and canning fish

- ShoalFarm Ltd – a company with saltwater fish farms.

Shoal plc is also finalising the purchase of the Captain Haddock chain of fish restaurants.

ShoalFish

Shoal plc formed ShoalFish in 20X2 when it bought three small fishing fleets and consolidated them into one fleet. The primary objective of the acquisition was to secure supplies for ShoalPro. 40% of the fish caught by ShoalFish are currently processed in the ShoalPro factories. The rest are sold in wholesale fish markets. ShoalFish has recorded modest profits since its formation but it is operating in a challenging market-place. The western oceans where it operates have suffered from many years of over-fishing and the government has recently introduced quotas in an attempt to conserve fish stocks.

ShoalFish has 35 boats and this makes it the sixth largest fleet in the western oceans. Almost half of the total number of boats operating in the western oceans are individually owned and independently operated by the boat's captain. Recent information for ShoalFish is given in Figure 1.

ShoalPro

ShoalPro was acquired in 20W2 when Shoal plc bought the assets of the Trevarez Canning and Processing Company. Just after the acquisition of the company, the government declared the area around Trevarez a 'zone of industrial assistance'. Grants were made available to develop industry in an attempt to address the economic decline and high unemployment of the area. ShoalPro benefited from these grants, developing a major fish processing and canning capability in the area. However, despite this initiative and investment, unemployment in the area still remains above the average for the country as a whole.

ShoalPro's modern facilities and relatively low costs have made it attractive to many fishing companies. The fish received from ShoalFish now accounts for a declining percentage of the total amount of fish processed and canned in its factories in the Trevarez area. Recent information for ShoalPro is given in Figure 1.

ShoalFarm

ShoalFarm was acquired in 20X4 as a response by Shoal plc to the declining fish stocks in the western oceans. It owns and operates saltwater fish farms. These are in areas of the ocean close to land where fish are protected from both fishermen and natural prey, such as sea birds. Fish stocks can be built up quickly and then harvested by the fish farm owner. Shoal plc originally saw this acquisition as a way of maintaining supply to ShoalPro.

Operating costs at ShoalFarm have been higher than expected and securing areas for new fish farms has been difficult and has required greater investment than expected. Recent information for ShoalFarm is given in Figure 1.

All figures in $m

ShoalFish	20X7	20X8	20X9
Turnover of market sector	200.00	198.50	190.00
Turnover of ShoalFish	24.00	23.50	21.50
Gross profit	1.20	1.10	1.05

ShoalPro	20X7	20X8	20X9
Turnover of market sector	40.00	40.10	40.80
Turnover of ShoalPro	16.00	16.20	16.50
Gross profit	1.60	1.65	1.75

ShoalFarm	20X7	20X8	20X9
Turnover of market sector	10.00	11.00	12.00
Turnover of ShoalFarm	1.00	1.10	1.12
Gross profit	0.14	0.14	0.15

Figure 1: Financial data on individual companies 20X7–20X9

Captain Haddock

The Captain Haddock chain of restaurants was founded in 20W2 by John Dory. It currently operates one hundred and thirty restaurants in the country serving high quality fish meals. Much of Captain Haddock's success has been built on the quality of its food and service. Captain Haddock has a tradition of recruiting staff directly from schools and universities and providing them with excellent training in the Captain Haddock academy. The academy ensures that employees are aware of the 'Captain Haddock way' and is dedicated to the continuation of the quality service and practices developed by John Dory when he launched the first restaurant. All management posts are filled by recruiting from within the company, and all members of the Captain Haddock board originally joined the company as trainees. In 20W9 the Prime Minister of the country identified Captain Haddock academy as an example of high quality in-service training. In 20X0, Captain Haddock became one of the thirty best regarded brands in the country.

In the past few years, the financial performance of Captain Haddock has declined significantly (see Figure 2) and the company has had difficulty in meeting its bank covenants. This decline is partly due to economic recession in the country and partly due to a disastrous diversification into commercial real estate and currency dealing. The chairman and managing director of the company both resigned nine months ago as a result of concern over the breaking of banking covenants and shareholder criticism of the diversification policy. Some of the real estate bought during this period is still owned by the company. In the last nine months the company has been run by an interim management team, whilst looking for prospective buyers. At restaurant level, employee performance still remains relatively good and the public still highly rate the brand. However, at a recent meeting one of the employee representatives called for a management that can 'effectively lead employees who are increasingly demoralised by the decline of the company'.

Shoal plc is currently finalising their takeover of the Captain Haddock business. The company is being bought for a notional $1 on the understanding that $15 million is invested into the company to meet short-term cash flow problems and to improve liquidity. Shoal plc's assessment is that there is nothing fundamentally wrong with the company and that the current financial situation is caused by the failed diversification policy and the cost of financing this. The gross profit margin in the sector averages 10%.

Captain Haddock currently buys its fish and fish products from wholesalers. It is the intention of Shoal plc to look at sourcing most of the dishes and ingredients from its own companies; specifically ShoalFish, ShoalPro and ShoalFarm. Once the takeover is complete (and this should be within the next month), Shoal plc intends to implement significant strategic change at Captain Haddock so that it can return to profitability as soon as possible. Shoal plc has implemented strategic change at a number of its acquisitions. The company explicitly recognises that there is no 'one right way' to manage change. It believes that the success of any planned change programme depends on an understanding of the context in which the change is taking place.

Captain Haddock (all figures in $m)	20X7	20X8	20X9
Turnover	115.00	114.50	114.00
Gross profit (loss)	0.20	(5.10)	(6.20)

Figure 2: Financial information for Captain Haddock 20X7–20X9

Required:

(a) **In the context of Shoal plc's corporate-level strategy, assess the contribution and performance of ShoalFish, ShoalPro and ShoalFarm. Your assessment should include an analysis of the position of each company in the Shoal plc portfolio.**

(15 marks)

Shoal plc explicitly recognises that there is no 'one right way' to manage change. It believes that the success of any planned change programme will depend on a clear understanding of the context within which change will take place.

(b) (i) **Identify and analyse, using an appropriate model, the contextual factors that will influence how strategic change should be managed at Captain Haddock.**

(13 marks)

Professional marks will be awarded in part (b) (i) for the identification and justification of an appropriate model.

(2 marks)

Once the acquisition is complete, Shoal plc wish to quickly turnaround Captain Haddock and return it to profitability.

> (ii) **Identify and analyse the main elements of strategic change required to achieve this goal.** **(8 marks)**
>
> **Professional marks will be awarded in part (b) (ii) for the cogency of the analysis and for the overall relevance of the answer to the case study scenario.** **(2 marks)**

Portfolio managers, synergy managers and parental developers are three corporate rationales for adding value.

> (c) **Explain each of these separate rationales for adding value and their relevance to understanding the overall corporate rationale of Shoal plc.** **(10 marks)**
>
> **(Total: 50 marks)**

72   AUTOFONE

Introduction

AutoFone was established almost twenty years ago at the beginning of the mobile telephone boom. It was formed by a dynamic Chief Executive Officer (CEO) who still remains a major shareholder of the company.

AutoFone brought two new concepts to the market. Firstly, it established retail shops where customers could go and handle the products and discuss mobile phone options with trained sales people. Before AutoFone, all mobile telephones were sold through the customer directly contacting the telephone network provider (like conventional home land line services) and were generally aimed at business rather than leisure users. Secondly, AutoFone sold products and services from all the four major network providers licensed by the government to provide telecommunications services in the country. Previously, customers could only choose products and services from within one network provider's range. AutoFone allowed customers to choose products and services across the range of the four providers and reflected this in the company's motto 'ethical advice: the customer's choice'.

Ten years ago, AutoFone signed a thirty-year supply contract with each provider. Although, in retrospect, these deals were on commercially favourable terms for AutoFone, the network providers were happy to agree these deals because none of them believed that mobile telephones could be successfully sold through retail shops. However, speaking in 20X3, the managing director of one of the networks suggested 'that AutoFone had got away with incredible profit margins' when they signed the deals in 1990. The four network providers themselves had re-signed twenty-five year licence deals with the government. Under the terms of these deals, licences will be restricted to the four current providers until their renewal date in 15 years' time.

Retail shops division

AutoFone currently has 415 shops around the country. To reduce costs most shops are on the edge of (but not in) the main shopping area of the town they serve. It is usual for AutoFone to sign a fifty-year shop lease in return for low initial annual rental and a rent-free period at the start of the lease while the company fits out the shop to reflect AutoFone's corporate image. Eleven years ago, AutoFone floated on the country's stock market to assist the funding of further shops and so continue its organic growth. The national coverage of its shops, the publicity generated by its CEO and a successful television advertising campaign culminated, in 20X5, with it being rated by consumers as one of the top 20 brands in the country.

The CEO of AutoFone established the retail shops along, in his words, 'entrepreneurial lines'. He regards each shop as an independent business, having to achieve a profit target but without being closely monitored within these targets. He believes that the company is 'about providing opportunity to its employees, providing them with autonomy and responsibility to achieve their goals. It is not about monitoring them every hour of the day, stifling creativity and enthusiasm.' To support this approach, sales staff are given a relatively low basic salary with a substantial element of profit-related pay linked to the profit targets of the shop. Commission is also paid to sales staff who successfully sell mobile phone insurance to the customer. Each shop is relatively small, usually employing three or four people.

In recent years the CEO has been increasingly involved in television, sports promotion and charity work. At AutoFone he has established a strategic planning committee of senior headquarters managers to develop and implement the company's business strategy. This committee includes the two longest serving board directors. The strategy still continues to have at its heart the central business idea of giving independent and impartial advice to customers so that they can choose the best equipment and network for their needs.

Marketplace trends

Since AutoFone's arrival into the market, two significant trends have emerged:

(i)   The licensed network providers have opened their own retail stores, usually in city centres. AutoFone has reacted to the opening of these shops by stressing AutoFone's independence and impartiality. Only at AutoFone can impartial advice be received on all four competing networks and their supporting services. The CEO now refers to this as 'our central business idea' and, as well as being core to their strategy, it is heavily emphasised in all their promotional material.

(ii)   Mobile phones have become more sophisticated. Many now offer integrated cameras, mp3 players, web browsers and e-mail facilities. AutoFone offers these products in both its shops and through its Internet operation. Mobile phones are either purchased outright or provided on monthly contracts. The minimum contract period with the network provider is usually twelve months.

AutoFone has itself established its own Internet division, AFDirect, as a separate division within the group. It has also established an insurance division (AFInsure) offering insurance to cover loss or damage to mobile phones purchased from the company. Revenue earned from each division, analysed by the age of the customer, is shown in table 1.

Table 1: Analysis of AutoFone Sales: 20X7 (all figures in $m)

Division	Age of customer					
	Under 15	15–25	26–40	41–60	Over 60	Total
AutoFone retail shops	5	90	60	120	65	340
AFDirect	0	15	20	8	2	45
Total sales of mobile phones						385
AFInsure	0	1	3	7	3	14
Group total						399

Analysts agree that growth in the mobile phone business is slowing down and this is supported by the figures given in table 2 showing revenue from sales (both retail and Internet) for AutoFone and its competitors, the four licensed network providers, for the period 20X3–20X7.

Table 2: Market analysis (all figures in $m) of sales of mobile phones

Company	20X7	20X6	20X5	20X4	20X3
AutoFone	385	377	367	340	320
NetAG	350	348	345	340	305
09Net	390	388	380	365	350
PhoneLine	315	315	315	305	300
NetConnex	295	295	294	290	285
Total	1,735	1,723	1,701	1,640	1,560

However, while the AFDirect and AFInsure divisions are prospering, there are increasing problems in the retail shops division. Profitability has been declining over the last few years (see table 3) and this has had a demoralising effect on shop employees. One shop manager commented, in his exit interview, that the profit targets were unattainable in the current market. 'They might have been appropriate in 1997, but they are not in 20X7.' Staff are particularly demoralised by spending time explaining a particular product to a customer who then leaves the shop and buys the product cheaper on the Internet. They have to wait for it to be delivered (usually two or three days) but they are prepared to do this to gain the lower prices offered by the direct Internet-based companies, including AFDirect. It is also increasingly common for customers who have bought from AFDirect to take their phones to AutoFone's retail shops for support and service. This activity is not recognised in the shop employee's reward package.

AutoFone's central city branch

Despite the overall decline in the profitability of the shops, one branch has continually met or exceeded its profitability targets and is held up by the CEO as an example of best practice – proof that the company's approach to mobile phone selling can still be profitably applied. This is the central city branch in one of the country's most prosperous cities.

The CEO arranged for three members of the strategic planning committee to visit the shop, posing as customers, to investigate the reasons for the shop's success. They found the staff very friendly and helpful. However, they also found that they were guided towards products and services which had higher profit margins. Further investigation showed this always to be the case and so customers were sold products which were profitable to the shop, rather than those best suited to the customer's needs. On receiving this information, AutoFone's board concluded that this was unethical as it compromised their central business idea which stressed impartial advice to guide the 'customer's choice'. The manager of the shop was reprimanded and asked to adhere to company policy. He resigned soon afterwards, followed by his two assistants. The shop is currently run by temporary staff and profitability has significantly dropped.

Future strategy

The two longest serving directors on the strategic planning committee are increasingly concerned about the company's decline in profitability (see table 3). They have written an internal paper suggesting that the retail division should be sold off and that AutoFone should re-position itself as an on-line retailer of phones. They believe that the retail shops business model is no longer appropriate. They argue that a company concentrating solely on Internet sales and insurance would be a 'smaller but more profitable and focused' business. The CEO is strongly opposed to this suggestion because it was the shop-based approach to selling mobile phones that formed the original business model of the company. He has a strong emotional attachment to the retail business. The two directors claim that this attachment is clouding his judgement and hence he is unable to see the logic of an 'economically justifiable exit from the retail business'.

Table 3: Extracted Financial Information for AutoFone (retail shops division only)

Extracted Financial Information (all figures in $m)

Extracted from the Statement of Financial Position (Balance Sheet)

	20X7	*20X6*	*20X5*	*20X4*	*20X3*
Total non-current assets	143	140	134	128	123
Current assets:					
Inventories	345	340	335	320	298
Trade receivables	1,386	1,258	1,216	1,174	1,120
Cash and cash equivalents	345	375	390	400	414
Total current assets	**2,076**	**1,973**	**1,941**	**1,894**	**1,832**
Total assets	2,219	2,113	2,075	2,022	1,955
Total shareholder's equity	150	155	160	165	169
Non-current liabilities:					
Interest bearing long-term loans	55	50	45	40	35
Other provisions	16	15	13	13	10
Total non-current liabilities	71	65	58	53	45
Total current liabilities	1,998	1,893	1,857	1,804	1,741
Total equity and liabilities	2,219	2,113	2,075	2,022	1,955

Extracted from the Income Statement

	20X7	*20X6*	*20X5*	*20X4*	*20X3*
Revenue	340	337	332	320	305
Cost of sales	250	252	230	220	205
Gross profit	90	85	102	100	100
Wages and salaries	39	38	37	35	33
Other expenses	40	38	35	30	30
Interest payable	4	4	3	3	3
Total	83	80	75	68	66
Net profit before tax	7	5	27	32	34
Tax	2	3	5	4	4
Net profit after tax	**5**	**2**	**22**	**28**	**30**

Extracted from annual reports

Number of employees	1,400	1,375	1,325	1,300	1,275

Required:

(a) **Using an appropriate model or models, analyse the competitive environment of AutoFone's retail shops division. Note: requirement (a) includes 2 professional marks.** **(20 marks)**

(b) **AutoFone's CEO is anxious to develop a rational and well argued case for retaining the retail shops division.**

Write a briefing paper for the CEO to submit to the strategy planning committee explaining why the retail shops division should continue to form a key part of AutoFone's future strategy.

Note: Requirement (b) includes 3 professional marks. **(15 marks)**

(c) **This requirement is no longer examinable.** **(15 marks)**

(Total: 50 marks)

73   WET

> 🕐   *Timed question with Online tutor debrief*

Introduction

Arcadia is a country with great mineral wealth and a hard-working, well-educated population. It has recently enjoyed sustained economic growth generated by the expansion of its manufacturing industry. The population has grown as well and, as a result, agricultural output has increased to satisfy this population, with much previously marginal land converted to arable and pasture land. However, after 10 years of sustained economic growth the country, in 20X9, began to experience economic problems. Gross Domestic Product (GDP) has declined for three successive quarters and there is increasing unemployment. Surveys have shown that wages are stagnant and retail sales are falling. There are also increasing problems with servicing both personal and business debt leading to business bankruptcy and homelessness.

The climate of the country is also changing, becoming drier and windier. Last year, for the first time, the government had to ration water supply to domestic homes.

The formation of WET

In 20X2, the environmental campaigner Zohail Abbas published a book on the Wetlands of Arcadia. The Wetlands of Arcadia are areas of natural habitat made up of land that is saturated with moisture, such as a swamp, marsh or bog. Dr Abbas' book chronicled the systematic destruction of the wetlands due to population growth, increased economic development and climate change. Water had been progressively drained from the wetlands to provide land for farming and to provide water for the increasing population and industry of the country. Wetlands also provide an important habitat for wildlife. Dr Abbas showed that in the period from 1970 to 2000, there had been a dramatic decline in birds, mammals and fish dependent upon the wetland habitat. Some species had become extinct.

In 20X3, Dr Abbas formed the WEtland Trust (WET), with the aim of preserving, restoring and managing wetlands in Arcadia. Since its formation, the Trust has acquired the four remaining wetland sites left in the country. The Trust's work is funded through donations and membership fees. Donations are one-off contributions. Membership is through an annual subscription which gives members the right to visit the wetlands. Each wetland site is managed by volunteers who provide access and guidance to members. The wetlands are not currently open to the general public. Dr Abbas' work on the wetlands has brought him to the attention of the Arcadian public and he is now a popular television presenter. WET is also a strong brand, recognised by 85% of Arcadians in a recent green consumer survey.

GiftHelp

WET is a registered charity. Charities within Arcadia have to be registered with the Commission of Charities which regulates charities within the country. The number of charities has increased significantly in the last few years leading to widespread criticism from established charities, politicians and the public, who believe that many of these charities have been formed to exploit taxation advantages. Dr Abbas is a vociferous critic, particularly after the Commission of Charities gave permission for the establishment of a rival wetland charity (WWTFT) despite the fact that all wetlands in Arcadia are under WET's control. WWTFT promised to create new wetlands artificially in Arcadia. They have so far only raised $90,000 of the $151,000,000 required for a pilot site. Dr Abbas was part of a group that lobbied the government for the reform of the Commission of Charities, but the government has rejected their advice.

The government of Arcadia has recently changed the rules on charity taxation. Previously, once the charity's accounts had been audited, the government paid the charity a sum of 20% of the total value of donations and membership fees. This reflected the income tax the donor would have paid on the amount they had given to the charity. However, the government has now declared that this is unfair as not all donations or membership fees are from Arcadian taxpayers or from people in Arcadia who actually pay tax. Consequently, in the future, charities will have to prove that a donation or membership fee was from an Arcadian tax payer. Only donations or fees supported by this proof will receive the 20%, so called GiftHelp, refund. Research and evidence from other countries suggests that 30% of donors will not give the GiftHelp details required and so the charity will not be able to reclaim tax from these donors. An analysis of WET's income for 20X8 is given in Figure 1 and an analysis of income for all charities is given in Figure 2. Research has also shown that 55% of members and 85% of donors also give money to other charities.

Figure 1 – WET's income sources; year 20X8

	Members	Donors
Arcadian Taxpayers	$650,000	$100,000
Arcadian Non-taxpayers	$100,000	$50,000
Non-Arcadian	$50,000	$50,000
Total	$800,000	$200,000

Figure 2 – Income for all Arcadian charities; year 20X8 (in $millions)

	Amount donated to charity
Health charities	775.0
Social Care charities	275.5
International charities	149.8
Environmental charities (including WET)	45.6

WET 20X3–20X9

WET was originally a vehicle for promoting the vision and ideology of Dr Abbas. Volunteers were recruited to manage and administer the wetland sites and the number of members gradually increased (see Figure 3). Many of these volunteers have become acknowledged experts in wetlands and their knowledge and experience is valued by members. However, as the charity expanded a number of issues emerged.

1   Administrative costs rose at a faster rate than subscriptions and donations. Administrative staff are all full-time paid employees of the charity. However, despite an increase in staff numbers, there is a substantial backlog of cleared applications in the Membership Department which have not yet been entered into the membership computer system. The membership computer system is one of the systems used to support administration. However, the functionality of this software is relatively restricted and cumbersome and there have been complaints about its accuracy. For example, members claim that renewal reminders are often sent out to people who have already paid and that members who should have received renewal invoices have never received them. As a result 'we seem to be wasting money and losing members'.

2   Members have become increasingly frustrated by their limited access to the wetlands and many wish to participate more in determining the policies of the organisation. They feel that the wetland sites should also have better facilities, such as toilets and concealed positions for bird watching. There were increasing criticisms of Dr Abbas' domineering style and cavalier disregard for the members. Membership is currently falling and very little money is spent on sales and marketing to arrest this fall.

3   Volunteers have also become disgruntled with Dr Abbas' management style. They feel patronised and undervalued. The number of volunteers is declining (see Figure 3) which in itself is reducing the access of members to the wetlands. A recent decision not to pay travelling expenses to volunteers led to further resignations.

Figure 3 – Membership and volunteer statistics WET 20X2–20X9

	20X2	20X3	20X4	20X5	20X6	20X7	20X8	20X9
Members	12,000	14,000	15,000	20,000	22,000	25,000	23,000	20,000
Volunteers	30	35	35	45	50	52	50	40

At the 20X9 Annual General Meeting (AGM) Dr Abbas stood down and announced the appointment of a new Chief Executive Officer (CEO). Dr Abbas admitted in an emotional resignation speech that he had not sufficiently taken into account the views of members, donors or volunteers. 'It is a matter of deep regret that I spent more time focusing on wetlands rather than people'. He was made honorary president of WET in recognition of his work in establishing and expanding the charity.

The new CEO, Sheila Jenkins, wishes to pursue a more inclusive strategy, and immediately set about consulting the membership and voluntary staff about what they expected from WET. The two clearest messages that came from this consultation exercise were that:

•   Members wanted much better access to wetlands and they were more interested in the wildlife that used the wetlands (particularly the birds) than the wetlands sites themselves. This was not a view shared by Dr Abbas who wanted the wetlands preserved for their own sake.

•   Volunteers wished to be much more involved in the running of the organisation and wanted to be treated by management in a way that recognised their voluntary commitment.

System review

Sheila Jenkins is particularly keen to improve the technology that supports WET. She has stated that the better acquisition and management of members, volunteers and donors is an important objective of WET. WET's current website is very rudimentary, but she sees 'e-mail and website technology as facilitating the acquisition, retention and satisfaction of our customers' needs. And by customers, I mean both prospective and existing members, volunteers and donors of WET.' She also wishes to gain increased revenue from each member and donor.

The current membership renewal process has come under instant review and it is shown in the swim lane diagram (flowchart) of Figure 4. A narrative to support this diagram is given below.

Membership renewal process

One month before the date of membership renewal, the computer system (Membership System) sends a renewal invoice to a current (not lapsed) member giving subscription details and asking for payment. A copy of this invoice is sent to the Membership Department who file it away. Approximately 80% of members decide to renew and send their payment (either by providing credit card details (60%) or as a cheque (40%)) to WET. The Membership Department matches the payment with the renewal invoice copy. The invoice copy (stamped paid) is sent to Sales and Marketing who use it to produce a membership card and send this card together with a Guide to Sites booklet, to the member. The Membership Department passes the payment to the Finance Department.

Finance now submits payments to the bank. It currently takes the Finance Department an average of five days from the receipt of renewal to notifying the Membership Department of the cleared payment. Once cleared, Finance notifies the Membership Department by e-mail and they update the Membership System to record that the payment has been made. As mentioned before, there is a backlog in entering these details into the computer system.

Some cheques do not clear, often because they are filled in incorrectly (for example, they are unsigned or wrongly dated). In these circumstances, Finance raises a payment request and sends it to the member. Once the member re-submits a replacement cheque, it again goes through the clearing process.

Credit card payments are cleared instantly, but again there may be problems with the details. For example, incorrect numbers and incorrect expiry dates will lead to the transaction not being authorised and so, in these circumstances, Finance again raises a payment request.

The members' response to payment requests is very low (about 5%). The finance manager has described this as scandalous and 'an unethical response from supposedly ethical people'.

Also, not shown on the diagram: One week before renewal, the Membership System produces a renewal reminder and sends it to the member. Some members pay as a result of this reminder. If payment is not received then the member details are recorded as 'lapsed'.

Figure 4 – Membership renewal process

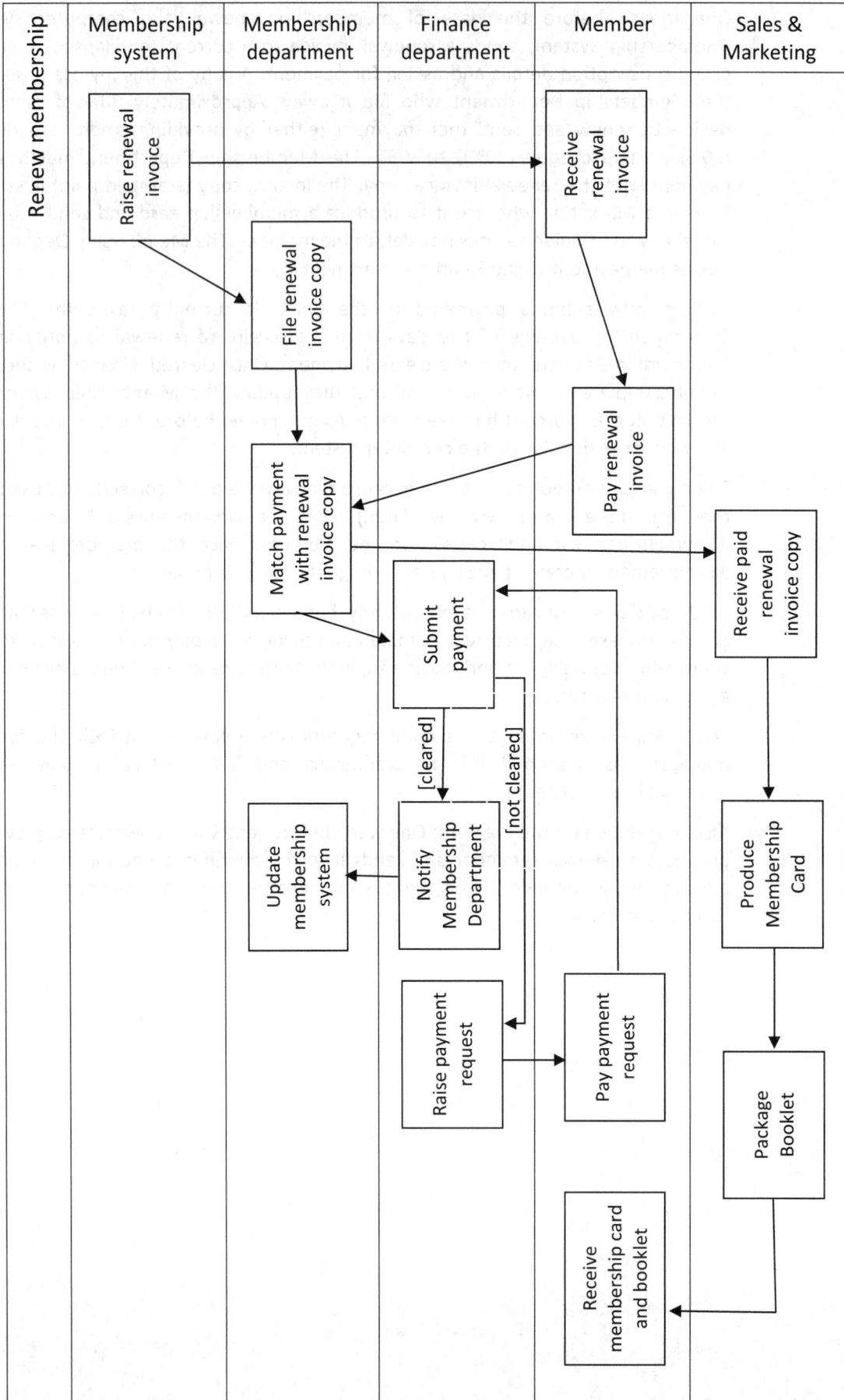

Required:

(a) The new CEO, Sheila Jenkins, recognises that she should understand the strategic position of WET before considering strategic options and changes. She wants a concise assessment of the strategic position; covering environment, strategic capability, stakeholder expectations and organisational mission.

Undertake the assessment, required by Sheila Jenkins, of the strategic position of WET. **(21 marks)**

Professional marks will be awarded in part (a) for the scope, structure and tone of the answer. **(4 marks)**

(b) Problems with the current membership renewal process include:

- the low response to payment requests

- the despatch of renewal reminders for people who have already paid

- the failure to send renewal invoices to some members.

Analyse faults in the current membership renewal process that cause the problems identified above. Suggest solutions that would remedy these faults. **(15 marks)**

(c) Sheila Jenkins sees customers as 'both prospective and existing members, volunteers and donors of WET'. She also wishes to gain increased revenue from each member and donor.

Evaluate how email and website technology might facilitate the acquisition and retention of WET's customers and support WET's aim to gain increased revenues from members and donors. **(10 marks)**

(Total: 50 marks)

🕐 *Calculate your allowed time, allocate the time to the separate parts...............*

---

74 REINK CO

Eland – the country

Eland is an industrial country with a relatively high standard of living. Most commercial and domestic consumers have computers and printers. However, the economic performance of the country has declined for the last seven years and there are large areas of unemployment and poverty. The economic problems of the country have led to a significant decline in tax revenues and so the government has asked its own departments (and the public sector as a whole) to demonstrate value-for-money in their purchases. The government is also considering privatising some of its departments to save money. The Department of Revenue Collections (DoRC), which is responsible for collecting tax payments in the country, has been identified as a possible candidate for future privatisation.

The people of Eland are enthusiastic about the principles of reuse and recycling. There has been a notable rise in the number of green consumers. Mindful of this, and aware of the economic benefits it delivers, the government is also encouraging its departments (and the economy as a whole) to recycle and reuse products.

The printer consumables market

There is a significant computer printer market in Eland, dominated by Original Equipment Manufacturers (OEMs). Many of these are household names such as Landy, IPD and Bell-Tech. OEMs also dominate the printer consumables market, which is worth about $200m per year. However, there are also independent companies who only supply the printer consumables (printer cartridges and toner cartridges) market, offering prices which significantly undercut the OEMs. The printer and printer consumables markets are both technology driven, with companies constantly looking for innovations which make printing better and cheaper.

The emergence of independent printer consumables suppliers has not been welcomed by the OEMs. They have brought legal actions against the independents in an attempt to make refilling their branded products illegal. However, they have not succeeded. The government in Eland has ruled this to be anti-competitive. However, the OEMs continue to promote their case with political parties, claiming that they need the revenues from printer consumables to fund innovations and advances in printer technology. They also regularly issue statements which worry consumers, claiming that printers may be harmed by using ink which is not from the OEM. Landy has been particularly aggressive in this regard. It continues to pursue legal claims against the independents and has also issued a statement which makes clear that if one of their printers is found to be faulty whilst using non-Landy ink, then the printer's warranty will be void.

It is relatively easy to enter the independent printer consumables market and so companies tend to compete on price. There is little brand loyalty amongst consumers, who regularly change their choice of brand. The independent companies constantly focus on finding technologies which make the print cartridges cheaper to buy and are of better quality. Used print cartridges can be reused for their material alone (recycled), or reused by being refilled with ink. However, there are still printing products on the market which can only be used once, or are expensive to recycle.

ReInk Co

ReInk Co (ReInk) was formed five years ago by Dexter Black, a technology entrepreneur with expertise in printer technologies. He still remains the only shareholder. He set up ReInk to produce and market his designs for reusable ink systems. ReInk is focused primarily on the reuse of printer cartridges by using a process to refill them with ink. Key technical elements of ReInk's innovative process for refilling cartridges have been patented, but in Eland, such patents only last for eight years. The current patent has a further six years to run.

The company was established in a declining industrial town in Eland with high unemployment. Government grants were available for two years to help support hi-tech industry and purpose built factories were cheap, readily available and, initially, rent free. Although the company now pays rent for its factory and offices, the annual rent is relatively low. The area has a good supply of people suitable for administrative and factory jobs in the company. ReInk's location is also close to an attractive area of countryside, which Dexter felt would appeal to the technology experts needed to help him exploit and develop his printer technology ideas. It would help provide a good standard of living and relatively cheap property and so he could attract good staff for modest salaries. His assumption proved correct. He has been able to attract an expert team of technologists who have helped him develop a unique approach to printer cartridge reuse. As one of them commented, 'I took a pay cut to come here. But now I can afford a bigger house and my children can breathe fresh country air.'

ReInk is an attractive company to work for and the team of technologists are enthusiastic about working with such an acknowledged industry expert, where technical innovation is recognised and rewarded. Both his staff and competitors acknowledge Dexter's technical expertise, but his commercial expertise is less well regarded. Dexter recognised this as a weakness and it was the prime driver behind his decision to recruit two new directors to the company.

To fund the development of the printer refilling technology, ReInk has needed significant bank loans and a substantial overdraft. Although the company has made a small operating profit for the last three years, interest repayments have meant that it has recorded a loss every year. It currently has revenues of $6m per year, 20% of which are derived from a long-term contract with the DoRC. ReInk is not one of the independent companies currently being sued by Landy.

To help him address these continuing financial losses, Dexter recently recruited a sales director to attempt to increase revenue through improved sales and marketing and a human resources (HR) director to review and improve staffing practices. Together with the financial director and Dexter himself, they make up the board of ReInk.

Although both of these recently appointed directors had the commercial expertise which Dexter lacked, neither has been a success. The technologists within the company are particularly scathing about the two new appointments. They claim that the sales director has never really made the effort to understand the market and that 'he does not really understand the product we are selling'. There has been no evidence so far that he has been able to generate more sales revenue. The HR director upset the whole company by introducing indiscriminate cost cutting and attempting to regrade staff to reduce staff costs. The technologists believe that the HR director 'clearly has no experience of dealing with professional staff'.

Despite the appointment of the new sales director, ReInk is still not recognised by the majority of the consumers who were surveyed in a recent brand awareness survey. No significant marketing is undertaken outside of the development and promotion of ReInk's website. In search results, it often appears alongside companies which appear to offer similar services and usually have very similar trading names.

ReInk continues to struggle financially, and its bank, Firmsure, in response to its own financial difficulties, has recently reduced ReInk's overdraft facility, creating a cash flow crisis which threatens the company's very existence. At present, it does not have enough cash to meet next month's payroll payments.

The employees of the company are well aware of the company's financial position and although they are proud of the company's technical achievements, they believe that the company may soon go into administration and so many are actively looking for other jobs in the industry or in the area. A combination of poor management (particularly from the new directors) and the company's uncertain financial position has demotivated many of the employees, particularly the technologists who have created the company's vital technical edge over its competitors.

Vi Ventures (VV)

Vi Ventures are venture capitalists who inject money and management expertise into struggling companies, in exchange for a certain degree of control, ownership and dividend reward. They have acknowledged financial and management competencies which they have used in a variety of commercial environments. They are experienced change managers.

VV have been introduced to ReInk by Firmsure and they are considering some form of involvement. Actual arrangements are still under consideration and will only be discussed after they have made their standard assessment of ReInk's strategic position. This standard assessment report contains three elements:

- A SWOT analysis

- An assessment of the contextual factors of strategic change. They need to understand what factors will affect the change which they may need to bring to the company. The framework they use is shown in Figure 1 and is derived from the work of Balogun and Hope Hailey.

- A TOWS matrix analysis to identify strategic options which might be pursued if VV invest in the company.

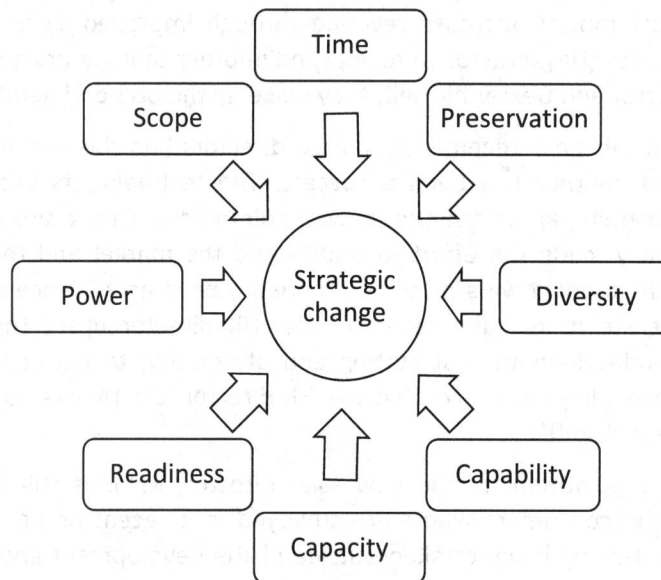

Figure 1: Contextual features in strategic change

Required:

You have been asked to write the standard assessment report of the strategic position of ReInk required by Vi Ventures. Write a report for Vi Ventures which:

(a) **Undertakes a SWOT analysis of ReInk Co.**   **(20 marks)**

(b) **Evaluates the effect of contextual features on the introduction of strategic change at ReInk Co.**   **(14 marks)**

(c) **And, in the light of your analysis above, recommends possible strategic options for each quadrant of a TOWS matrix of ReInk Co.**   **(12 marks)**

Professional marks will be awarded for the overall quality, construction, fluency and professionalism of the complete standard assessment report required by Vi Ventures.

(4 marks)

(Total: 50 marks)

75 ROAM GROUP CO

Roam Group Co (The Roam Group) was formed in 20X1 when the owners of Stuart Roam Road Transport decided to create a group structure to facilitate the acquisition of companies. The CEO of The Roam Group is Sir John Watt, a highly experienced businessman and he has a financial director and an operations director to assist him. The objectives of The Roam Group is to acquire companies which fit well with its existing companies, which would benefit from being part of the Group and which would also bring benefits to companies already in the Group. The Roam Group is a very lean operation. Besides the three full-time directors, it only has two full-time administrative employees. There are currently three operating companies in the Group: Stuart Roam Road Transport, Stuart Roam Warehousing and Stuart Roam Rail. The managing directors of all three operating companies also sit on the board of The Roam Group. Each of these operating companies has significant autonomy within the Group.

The Roam Group, like all the operating companies in the Group, has the majority of its shares owned by the Roam family. Financial information for the operating companies is given in Table One. The Roam Group and its operating companies are all based in the country of Meeland.

Stuart Roam Road Transport

Stuart Roam Road Transport (SRRT) was founded 60 years ago by Stuart Roam. It has grown to be the largest road freight company in Meeland, with over 2,000 trucks. It specialises in the haulage of consumer food and drink and it has significant contracts with most of the large supermarket chains. There are no toll roads in Meeland. Taxes for roads are levied through a fuel tax and an annual road fund licence. The managing director of SRRT is Stuart Roam junior, who was originally employed by his father as a driver. He still drives a truck for one day every month, so that 'he never loses touch with the business'. SRRT's distinctive red and white trucks are seen all over the country, and all carry the company's catchphrase 'All roads lead to Roam'. They have attracted a fan club, whose members spot the trucks on the road and record their movements on a dedicated internet site. These so-called 'New-Roamantics' have themselves become famous and, partly as a result of this, Stuart Roam has become a household name and is the most recognisable brand in the road transport industry. To maintain a modern fleet, SRRT replaces its trucks every three years. It wants to ensure that they are reliable, efficient and that they project a modern image which is attractive to their customers.

Stuart Roam Warehousing

The growth of company outsourcing and consumer internet purchasing made it increasingly clear that SRRT's customers wanted an integrated transport and storage solution. The Roam Group acquired a number of warehouses from its customers who wished to divest themselves of this part of their operations. In 20X1, it consolidated these, together with a number of small warehousing companies it had acquired, into a company called Stuart Roam Warehousing (SRW). The 20X2 figures shown in Table One represent the first year that the company traded in its current form. Nationwide, it owns 4 million square metres of warehousing, with its warehouses painted red and white and prominently displaying the Stuart Roam logo. The warehouses are efficient and highly automated. However, development land for warehouses is getting more difficult to find and acquisition costs of the land are also increasing. The average price for warehouse development land in Meeland is now $20,000 per hectare. A hectare is 10,000 square metres.

Stuart Roam Rail

Increasing fuel costs, increasing road congestion and concern about the environmental consequences of road transport caused The Roam Group to look at opportunities offered by rail transport.

In 20X2 The Roam Group purchased the Freight Direct Rail Company (FDRC). FDRC was formed in 2000 when the government of Meeland privatised the rail freight business. FDRC had struggled to survive in a business dominated by two large companies who shared the lucrative bulk freight contracts (coal, iron ore and oil) between them. The FDRC board welcomed The Roam Group acquisition and the locomotives were quickly painted in the red and white corporate colours and FDRC was renamed Stuart Roam Rail. However, despite experienced managers being transferred into the company from other companies in the Group, Stuart Roam Rail (like FDRC) has struggled to make a significant impact in the rail freight sector. Most of its customers are at locations which are not directly accessible by rail. Furthermore, the lucrative bulk rail freight contracts (coal, iron ore and oil) are in products which companies within The Roam Group have no experience in. It is still unclear whether the movement of consumer food and drink to multiple locations (The Roam Group's core business) is suited to rail transport. Furthermore, it has also been difficult for The Roam Group's senior management to understand the culture and economics of the rail freight business. The railway tracks, which are still owned by the state, are subject to very close control and monitoring and Stuart Roam Rail's use of these tracks is directly charged. There has also been a failure to recognise that train driving requires far greater skills and training than truck driving.

However, on the positive side, Stuart Roam Rail has developed an innovative mini-container system which can easily transfer goods between trucks and trains and it also effectively uses warehouse space. Furthermore, most of the supermarkets, attracted by a green image, are very supportive of the rail initiative and wish to be associated with it.

	20X5		20X4		20X3		20X2		20X1	
	Roam	Industry	Roam	Industry	Roam	Industry	Roam	Industry	Roam	Industry
Stuart Roam Road Transport										
Revenue	575	2,050	565	2,025	550	2,015	520	2,050	500	2,000
Operating profit	10.80%	9.98%	10.75%	9.95%	10.80%	9.93%	10.45%	9.50%	10.25%	9.57%
ROCE	12.25%	11.50%	12.15%	11.45%	12.05%	11.45%	11.95%	11.30%	11.95%	11.35%
Stuart Roam Warehousing										
Revenue	315	3,200	275	3,010	270	3,050	255	2,950	250	2,850
Operating profit	14.55%	14.50%	14.25%	14.15%	14.20%	14.25%	14.00%	14.25%	13.85%	14.15%
ROCE	14.50%	14.15%	14.25%	14.10%	14.15%	14.10%	13.95%	13.90%	13.95%	13.85%
Stuart Roam Rail										
Revenue	112	3,150	110	3,000	105	2,850	105	2,650	105	2,500
Operating profit	4.75%	12.45%	4.50%	12.35%	4.85%	12.25%	4.95%	12.75%	5.15%	12.85%
ROCE	3.50%	8.75%	3.65%	8.55%	3.75%	8.55%	3.85%	8.35%	3.85%	8.25%

Table One: Financial data for operating companies in The Roam Group.

The performance of the company is shown under the columns headed Roam. Industry figures (provided by Freight Line International) are shown under the columns headed Industry. Operating profit and ROCE figures are averages for the industry while revenue figures are totals. All revenue figures are in $million.

Note 1: Stuart Roam Warehousing first traded in 20X2. The 20X1 figure is compiled from companies which were consolidated into Stuart Roam Warehousing.

Note 2: Stuart Roam Rail was formed after the takeover of FDRC. 20X3 was the first reporting period for Stuart Roam Rail. The 20X1 and 20X2 figures are for FDRC.

Note 3: The standard payment terms in Meeland is payment within 30 days of the invoice date. Godiva airport

The Godiva airport is situated on the outskirts of Boleyn town where SRRT already has three transport depots and warehouses. The airport occupies a site of 450 hectares and it has two tarmac runways, four hangers and a small terminal/flying club facility. The airfield is exclusively used by private flyers and two flying clubs. The airport is adjacent to the motorway which connects North and South Meeland. Financial information for Godiva airport is given in Table Two.

All figures in $000s

Assets

Non-current assets

Property, plant and equipment	6,000
Goodwill	250
Total non-current assets	6,250

Current assets

Inventory	550
Trade receivables	80
Cash	370
Total current assets	1,000
Total assets	7,250

Equity and liabilities

Share capital	2,550
Retained earnings	250
Total equity	2,800

Non-current liabilities

Long-term borrowings	4,050

Current liabilities

Trade payables	120
Short-term borrowings	250
Current tax payable	30
Total current liabilities	400
Total liabilities	4,450
Total equity and liabilities	7,250

Statement of profit or loss

Revenue	975
Cost of sales	(700)
Gross profit	275
Administrative expenses	(125)
Finance costs	(100)
Profit before tax	50
Tax expense	(10)
Profit for the period	40

Table Two: Godiva airport – extracts from financial statements – 20X5

The Roam Group has recently issued the following press release from Sir John Watt:

'The Roam Group is pleased to announce that it has signed an initial agreement to purchase Godiva airport from the Godiva Airport Company for the sum of $7m, funded from retained profits from within the Group. We see this as a natural extension of our transport capabilities. Road, rail and air have long been complementary forms of transport and we are pleased to be able to offer our customers all three, using our innovative mini-container system as an effective transhipment method between transport modes. We also hope to attract a no-frills airline to the airport, encouraged by low landing fees and a population of over 150, 000 people living within 20 miles of the airport. Godiva Airport Company will become an operating company within The Roam Group, and renamed Stuart Roam Air.'

In a critical article on the proposed airport acquisition in the financial press, an independent aviation consultant has provided national performance statistics for airports of a similar size and type to Godiva airport (see Table Three).

Operating profit margin	Return on capital employed	Current ratio	Acid test ratio	Gearing ratio
17.5%	8.5%	2.25	1.50	40%

Table Three: Average national performance figures for medium-sized light aviation airports: 20X5

He has also cast doubt on Sir John Watt's statement about attracting a no-frills airline to the airport. He says that a local regional population of at least 500,000 people is required to make such a service attractive. He believes that the population of the Boleyn area is much too small to make passenger services economical.

Required:

(a)   Write an independent report which:

(i)   Evaluates the current performance and contribution of each of the three current operating companies in The Roam Group portfolio and assesses their relative significance in its future strategy.   **(21 marks)**

(ii)   Evaluates the proposed acquisition of Godiva airport.   **(15 marks)**

Professional marks will be allocated in part (a) for the clarity, structure, logical flow and appropriate tone of your answer.   **(4 marks)**

(b) A Business Analysis research student has suggested that Stuart Roam Road Transport (SRRT) pursues a hybrid strategy of offering a price lower than its competitors, whilst simultaneously attempting to achieve differentiation.

Required:

Discuss how both elements of this route to competitive advantage (price and differentiation) might be achieved by Stuart Roam Road Transport. **(10 marks)**

(Total: 50 marks)

76 HAMMOND SHOES

Introduction

Hammond Shoes was formed in 1895 by Richard and William Hammond, two brothers who owned and farmed land in Petatown, in the country of Arnland. At this time, Arnland was undergoing a period of rapid industrial growth and many companies were established that paid low wages and expected employees to work long hours in dangerous and dirty conditions. Workers lived in poor housing, were largely illiterate and had a life expectancy of less than forty years.

The Hammond brothers held a set of beliefs that stressed the social obligations of employers. Their beliefs guided their employment principles – education and housing for employees, secure jobs and good working conditions. Hammond Shoes expanded quickly, but it still retained its principles. Today, the company is a private limited company whose shares are wholly owned by the Hammond family. Hammond Shoes still produce footwear in Petatown, but they now also own almost one hundred retail shops throughout Arnland selling their shoes and boots. The factory (and surrounding land) in Petatown is owned by the company and so are the shops, which is unusual in a country where most commercial properties are leased. In many respects this policy reflects the principles of the family. They are keen to promote ownership and are averse to risk and borrowing. They believe that all stakeholders should be treated fairly. Reflecting this, the company aims to pay all suppliers within 30 days of the invoice date. These are the standard terms of supply in Arnland, although many companies do, in reality, take much longer to pay their creditors.

The current Hammond family are still passionate about the beliefs and principles that inspired the founders of the company.

Recent history

Although the Hammond family still own the company, it is now totally run by professional managers. The last Hammond to have operational responsibility was Jock Hammond, who commissioned and implemented the last upgrade of the production facilities in 1991. In the past five years the Hammond family has taken substantial dividends from the company, whilst leaving the running of the company to the professional managers that they had appointed. During this period the company has been under increased competitive pressure from overseas suppliers who have much lower labour rates and more efficient production facilities. The financial performance of the company has declined rapidly and as a result the Hammond family has recently commissioned a firm of business analysts to undertake a SWOT analysis to help them understand the strategic position of the company.

SWOT analysis: Here is the summary SWOT analysis from the business analysts' report.

Strengths

Significant retail expertise: Hammond Shoes is recognised as a successful retailer with excellent supply systems, bright and welcoming shops and shop employees who are regularly recognised, in independent surveys, for their excellent customer care and extensive product knowledge.

Excellent computer systems/software expertise: Some of the success of Hammond Shoes as a retailer is due to its innovative computer systems developed in-house by the company's information systems department. These systems not only concern the distribution of footwear, but also its design and development. Hammond is acknowledged, by the rest of the industry, as a leader in computer-aided footwear design and distribution.

Significant property portfolio: The factory in Petatown is owned by the company and so is a significant amount of the surrounding land. All the retail shops are owned by the company. The company also owns a disused factory in the north of Arnland. This was originally bought as a potential production site, but increasingly competitive imports made its development unviable. The Petatown factory site incorporates a retail shop, but none of the remaining retail shops are near to this factory, or indeed to the disused factory site in the north of the country.

Weaknesses

High production costs: Arnland is a high labour cost economy.

Out-dated production facilities: The actual production facilities were last updated in 1991. Current equipment is not efficient in its use of either labour, materials or energy.

Restricted internet site: Software development has focused on internal systems, rather than internet development. The current website only provides information about Hammond Shoes; it is not possible to buy footwear from the company's website.

Opportunities

Increased consumer spending and consumerism: Despite the decline of its manufacturing industries, Arnland remains a prosperous country with high consumer spending. Consumers generally have a high disposable income and are fashion conscious. Parents spend a lot of money on their children, with the aim of 'making sure that they get a good start in life'.

Increased desire for safe family shopping environment: A recent trend is for consumers to prefer shopping in safe, car-free environments where they can visit a variety of shops and restaurants. These shopping villages are increasingly popular.

Growth of the green consumer: The numbers of 'green consumers' is increasing in Arnland. They are conscious of the energy used in the production and distribution of the products they buy. These consumers also expect suppliers to be socially responsible. A recent television programme on the use of cheap and exploited labour in Orietaria was greeted with a call for a boycott of goods from that country. One of the political parties in Arnland has emphasised environmentally responsible purchasing in its manifesto. It suggests that 'shorter shipping distances reduce energy use and pollution. Purchasing locally supports communities and local jobs'.

Threats

Cheap imports: The lower production costs of overseas countries provide a constant threat. It is still much cheaper to make shoes in Orietaria, 4000 kilometres away, and transport the shoes by sea, road and train to shops in Arnland, where they can be offered at prices that are still significantly lower than the footwear produced by Hammond Shoes.

Legislation within Arnland: Arnland has comprehensive legislation on health and safety as well as a statutory minimum wage and generous redundancy rights and payments for employees. The government is likely to extend its employment legislation programme.

Recent strategies

Senior management at Hammond Shoes have recently suggested that the company should consider closing its Petatown production plant and move production overseas, perhaps outsourcing to established suppliers in Orietaria and elsewhere. This suggestion was immediately rejected by the Hammond family, who questioned the values of the senior management. The family issued a press release with the aim of re-affirming the core values which underpinned their business. The press release stated that 'in our view, the day that Hammond Shoes ceases to be a Petatown company, is the day that it closes'. Consequently, the senior management team was asked to propose an alternative strategic direction.

The senior management team's alternative is for the company to upgrade its production facilities to gain labour and energy efficiencies. The cost of this proposal is $37.5m. At a recent scenario planning workshop the management team developed what they considered to be two realistic scenarios. Both scenarios predict that demand for Hammond Shoes' footwear would be low for the next three years. However, increased productivity and lower labour costs would bring net benefits of $5m in each of these years. After three years the two scenarios differ. The first scenario predicts a continued low demand for the next three years with net benefits still running at $5m per year. The team felt that this option had a probability of 0.7. The alternative scenario (with a probability of 0.3) predicts a higher demand for Hammond's products due to changes in the external environment. This would lead to net benefits of $10m per year in years four, five and six. All estimated net benefits are based on the discounted future cash flows.

Financial information: The following financial information (see Figure 1) is also available for selected recent years for Hammond Shoes manufacturing division.

Figure 1: Extracts from the financial statements of Hammond Shoes (20X1–20X5)

Extracted from the income statements (all figures in $m)	20X5	20X3	20X1
Revenue	700	750	850
Cost of sales	(575)	(600)	(650)
Gross profit	125	150	200
Administration expenses	(95)	(100)	(110)
Other expenses	(10)	(15)	(20)
Finance costs	(15)	(10)	(5)
Profit before tax	5	25	65
Income tax expense	(3)	(7)	(10)
Profit for the year	2	18	55

Extracted from statements of financial position (all figures in $m)			
Trade receivables	70	80	90
Share capital	100	100	100
Retained earnings	140	160	170
Long term borrowings	70	50	20

In 20X1, Hammond Shoes paid, on average, their supplier invoices 28 days after the date of invoice. In 20X3 this had risen to 43 days and in 20X5, the average time to pay a supplier invoice stood at 63 days.

Required:

(a) **Analyse the financial position of Hammond Shoes and evaluate the proposed investment of $37.5 million in upgrading its production facilities.** **(14 marks)**

(b) **Using an appropriate framework (or frameworks) examine the alternative strategic options that Hammond Shoes could consider to secure its future position.**

(20 marks)

Professional marks will be awarded in part (b) for the clarity, structure and style of the answer. **(4 marks)**

(c) **Advise the Hammond family on the importance of mission, values and objectives in defining and communicating the strategy of Hammond Shoes.** **(12 marks)**

(Total: 50 marks)

77 ABC LEARNING

Introduction

ABC Learning plc (ABCL) is a large training company based in Arcadia. It specialises in professional certification training for accountants, lawyers, business analysts and business consultants. ABCL delivers training through face-to-face courses and e-learning, mainly using full-time lecturing staff. Thirty percent of its revenue is from e-learning solutions. It is constantly seeking new markets and acquisitions to improve shareholder value. It has become aware of the expanding business analysis certification training industry (BACTI) in the neighbouring country of Erewhon. ABCL has commissioned Xenon, a market intelligence company to undertake an analysis of the BACTI market in Erewhon with the aim of assessing its attractiveness and profitability before deciding whether or not to expand into Erewhon. ABCL is aware that an Arcadian competitor, Megatrain, has previously tried to establish itself in this market in Erewhon. Established providers in the BACTI industry in Erewhon responded by price cutting and strengthened promotional campaigns. This was supported by a campaign to discredit the CEO of Megatrain and to highlight its foreign ownership. Within six months Megatrain had withdrawn from the market in Erewhon.

Xenon interim report on the BACTI market in Erewhon – January 20X9

Introduction

The BACTI market in Erewhon is dominated by three suppliers; CATalyst, Batrain and Ecoba (collectively known as the 'big three'). CATalyst is a wholly owned subsidiary of the Tuition Group, a public limited company quoted on the Erewhon stock market. The last annual report of the Tuition Group identified CATalyst as core to their strategy and a source of significant growth. Batrain is a private limited company, with the shares equally divided between the eight founding directors. Four of these directors are under 40. Ecoba is also a private limited company with 95% of the shares owned by Gillian Vari. The other 5% are owned by her business partner Willy Senterit. Gillian is approaching retirement age.

Delivery model

Both CATalyst and Batrain have similar delivery models. They employ mainly full-time lecturing staff who are offered attractive salary packages, share options and generous benefits; such as ten weeks paid holiday. Even with these packages they find it hard to recruit. Teaching vacancies are advertised on both of their websites. CATalyst and Batrain both stress their 'brand' in their marketing material. On their websites there is no specific reference to the lecturers who will present each module. In contrast, Ecoba specifically identifies lecturers in both its advertisements (supported by photographs of the lecturers) and on their website, where the lecturer taking the module is specified. All the lecturers are 'high profile' names in the business analysis training community. None of these are directly employed by Ecoba. They are all on fixed-term contracts and are paid a premium daily rate for lecturing and assignment marking. Xenon interviewed Mike Wilson, a named management lecturer and asked him about the arrangement. He said that he felt relatively secure about it. 'Students are attracted to Ecoba because they know I will be teaching a particular module. I suppose I could be substituted by a cheaper lecturer but the students would soon complain that they had been misled.' Mike had also worked as a sub-contractor for CATalyst but no longer did so because he found that a booking could be cancelled at short notice if full-time staff became available. 'Gillian Vari (the MD of Ecoba) is much more transparent and straightforward in her treatment of sub-contract staff. The only problem is the time it takes to pay our invoices. We are always complaining about that.'

The 'big three' are recognised and established brands in the industry. Although the 'big three' are competitors there does appear to be a degree of mutual tolerance of each other. For example, they appear to have co-ordinated their response to the attempted entry of Megatrain into the industry. Three of the directors of Batrain used to work as lecturers for CATalyst and Gillian Vari (the MD of Ecoba) was a director of the company that spawned CATalyst. Mike Wilson has lectured for all of the 'big three' providers. However, there are also, approximately, twenty other providers in the industry in Erewhon (accounting for 20% of the total industry revenue).

Students and providers

The fees of 60% of students are paid for by their employers. There are around 15 major corporate clients who place significant contracts for certification training with providers. Most (but not all) of these are placed with the 'big three'. CATalyst is particularly strong in managing these contracts, setting up dedicated training sessions and a personalised website to support each contract. However, there is increasing evidence that providers are being played off against each other by the major corporate customers who are seeking to drive down costs. One of the large insurance companies recently moved all of its training to Ecoba after several years of using CATalyst as its sole provider. Another large customer has also recently moved their training contract to Ecoba because they were impressed by the 'named' lecturers that Ecoba used. Interestingly, in a new move for the industry, WAC, a major supplier of business analysis consultancy services, recently bought one of the smaller business analysis training providers and thus is now able to deliver all of its business analysis training in-house for its own staff.

Business Analysis certification in Erewhon is administered by the EIoBA (Erewhon Institute of Business Analysts) which sets the examination. There is no requirement for students to attend a certified training course. In fact 40% of students prepare themselves for the examinations using self-study. One of the smaller BACTI providers has gained some success by offering a blended learning solution that combines tutor support with e-learning modules. Interestingly, the 'big three' all appear to acknowledge the possibilities of e-learning but do not promote it. All three have invested money in specially designed training venues and so they seem committed, at least in the short term, to their classroom-based model.

EIoBA runs a certification scheme for providers of training. This operates at three levels; bronze, silver and gold. The 'big three' all have the highest level of certification (gold). Xenon recognises that gold certification offers a significant competitive advantage and that it will take any new entrant more than one year to achieve this level of certification.

Ecoba Ltd: Background

Ecoba is a private limited company. As well as being its managing director and majority shareholder, Gillian Vari is the only full-time lecturer. Mike Wilson told Xenon that Gillian is averse to employing full-time lecturing staff because 'they have to be paid if courses do not run and also during the long vacations'. Her policy appears to be to minimise overhead training and administrative costs. This may contribute to the slow payment of lecturers. Mike Wilson did comment that the 'full-time administrative staff seem to be under increasing pressure'.

Figure 1 provides comparative data for CATalyst and Batrain. Financial information for Ecoba is presented in Figure 2.

Figure 1: Financial Analysis (all 20X8)

	CATalyst	Batrain
Revenue	$35,000,000	$25,000,000
Cost of sales as a percentage of revenue	65%	63%
Average payables settlement period	65 days	60 days
Average receivables settlement period	30 days	35 days
Sales revenue to capital employed	3.36	3.19
Gross profit margin	35%	37%
Net profit margin	6%	8%
Liquidity ratio	0.92	0.93
Gearing ratio	30%	25%
Interest cover ratio	3.25	4.75

Figure 2: Financial Analysis: Ecoba Ltd (All figures in $000)

Extract from the statement of financial position

	20X8	20X7
Assets		
Non-current assets		
Intangible assets	5,800	5,200
Property, plant, equipment	500	520
	6,300	5,720
Current assets		
Inventories	70	90
Trade receivables	4,300	3,000
Cash and cash equivalents	2,100	1,500
	6,470	4,590
Total assets	12,770	10,310
Current liabilities		
Trade payables	6,900	4,920
Current tax payable	20	15
	6,920	4,935
Non-current liabilities		
Long-term borrowings	200	225
	7,120	5,160
Equity		
Share capital	5,100	5,100
Retained earnings	550	50
Total equity and liabilities	12,770	10,310

Extract from the statement of profit or loss

Revenue	22,000	17,000
Cost of sales	(17,500)	(13,750)
Gross profit	4,500	3,250
Overhead expenses	(3,500)	(2,500)
Profit before tax and finance costs	1,000	750
Finance costs	(20)	(20)
Profit before tax	980	730
Tax expense	(30)	(25)
Profit for the year	950	705

Required:

Xenon usually analyses an industry using Porter's five forces framework.

(a)   Using Porter's framework, analyse the business analysis certification industry (BACTI) in Erewhon and assess whether it is an attractive market for ABCL to enter.

(20 marks)

After considering Xenon's interim report, ABCL decided to enter the business analysis certification training industry (BACTI) in Erewhon through the acquisition of one of the three main providers. In March 20X9 they asked Xenon to write a short report to evaluate Ecoba Ltd and to analyse whether it was the most appropriate and attractive of the three possible acquisition targets. You are a business analyst with Xenon and were given the task of writing this report.

(b)   Write the requested short report evaluating Ecoba Ltd and analysing whether it was the most appropriate and attractive of the three possible acquisition targets for ABCL.   (16 marks)

Professional marks will be awarded in part (b) for clarity and format of your report

(4 marks)

In November 20X9 ABCL acquired Ecoba Ltd. Gillian Vari agreed to stay on for two years to assist the management of the ownership transition. However, her business partner became seriously ill and ABCL have agreed, on compassionate terms, for her to leave the company immediately. ABCL, from experience, know that they must manage stakeholders very carefully during this transition stage.

(c)   Identify the stakeholders in Ecoba Ltd and analyse how ABCL could successfully manage them during the ownership transition.   (10 marks)

(Total: 50 marks)

78   GREENTECH   *Walk in the footsteps of a top tutor*

greenTech was established in 1990 and is still run by the management team that founded it. The company began by specialising in the supply of low voltage, low emission, quiet, recyclable components to the electronic industry. Its components are used in the control systems of lifts, cars and kitchen appliances. Two medium-sized computer manufacturers use *greenTech* components in selected 'green' (that is, environmentally-friendly) models in their product range. Recent market research showed that 70% of the global electronics industry used *greenTech* components somewhere in its products.

In 1993 the company began a catalogue mail order service (now Internet-based) selling 'green' components to home users. Most of these customers were building their own computers and they required such components on either environmental grounds or because they wanted their computers to be extremely quiet and energy efficient. From 20X5, *greenTech* also offered fully assembled computer systems that could be ordered and configured over the Internet. All *greenTech*'s components are purchased from specialist suppliers. The company has no manufacturing capability, but it does have extensive hardware testing facilities and it has built up significant technical know-how in supplying appropriate components.

Finance and revenue

The company has traded profitably since its foundation and has grown steadily in size and revenues. In 20X8, its revenues were $64 million, with a pre-tax profit of $10 million. The spread across the three revenue streams is shown in Figure 1:

All figures in $million	20X8	20X7	20X6
Component sales to electronics industry	40	36	34
Component sales to home users	20	18	16
Fully assembled green computers	4	3	2
Total	64	57	52

Figure 1: Turnover by revenue stream 20X6–20X8

The company has gradually accumulated a sizeable cash surplus. The board cannot agree on how this cash should be used. One beneficiary has been the marketing budget (see Figure 2), but the overall spend on marketing still remains relatively modest and, by April 20X8, the cash surplus stood at $17 million.

All figures in $	20X8	20X7	20X6
Internet development and marketing	100,000	70,000	60,000
Display advertising (manufacturers)	50,000	40,000	30,000
Display advertising (domestic customers)	20,000	15,000	15,000
Exhibitions and conferences	30,000	20,000	15,000
Marketing literature	10,000	5,000	5,000
Total	210,000	150,000	125,000

Figure 2: Marketing budget 20X6–20X8

Company Doctor

In 20X8 a television company wrote to *greenTech* to ask whether it would consider taking part in a television programme called 'Company Doctor'. In this programme three teams of consultants spend a week at a chosen company working on a solution to a problem identified by the company. At the end of the week all three teams present their proposal for dealing with the problem. A panel of experts, including representatives from the company, pick the winner and, in theory, implement the winning proposal. *greenTech* agreed to take part in the programme and selected their future strategic direction as the problem area to be analysed. Their cash surplus would then be used to fund the preferred option. The show was recorded in September 20X8 to be transmitted later in the year. A brief summary of the conclusions of each team of consultants is given below.

The accountants Lewis-Read suggested a strategic direction that planned to protect and build on greenTech's current strategic position. They believed that the company should invest in marketing the fully assembled 'green' computers to both commercial and home customers. They pointed out that the government had just agreed a preferential procurement policy for energy efficient computers with high recyclable content. 'This segment of the market is rapidly expanding and is completely under-exploited by greenTech at the moment', Lewis-Read concluded.

The corporate recovery specialists, Fenix, put forward a strategic direction that essentially offered more services to *greenTech*'s current customers in the electronics industry. They suggested that the company should expand its product range as well as being able to manufacture components to respond to special requirements. They also believed that potential supply problems could be avoided and supply costs could be cut if *greenTech* acquired its own manufacturing capability. 'You need to secure the supply chain, to protect your future position.' They felt that the surplus cash in the company should be used to acquire companies that already had these manufacturing capabilities.

The third team was led by Professor Ag Wan from MidShire University. Their main recommendation was that *greenTech* should not see itself as a supplier of components and computers but as a supplier of green technology. They suggested that the company should look at many other sectors (not just electronics) where quietness, low emissions and recyclable technology were important. 'The company needs to exploit its capabilities, not its products. It is looking too narrowly at the future. To compete in the future you need to develop your markets, not your products', concluded the professor.

Figure 3, which was shown on the television show, illustrates how each solution came from a different part of an amended Ansoff product/market matrix.

		Products	
		Existing	**New**
Markets	**Existing**	Protect/Build *Lewis-Read (option 1)*	Product development with new capabilities *Fenix (option 2)*
	New	Market development with new uses and capabilities *Professor Ag Wan (option 3)*	No team chose this option Diversification

Figure 3: Adapted Ansoff matrix showing the position of the three solutions

In the television programme, the panel chose option 3 (as suggested by Professor Ag Wan's team) as being the most appropriate strategic direction and, much to everyone's surprise, the company began to pursue this direction with much vigour. Objectives and goals were established and a set of processes was designed to facilitate business-to-business transactions with potential new customers. These processes allow customers, by using computer-aided design software, to view the specification of products available, to assemble them and to integrate their own components into the design. This means that they are able to construct virtual prototypes of machines and equipment. This process design, delivered through a web service, is still under development.

Tackling operational problems

In parallel, *greenTech* has decided to make tactical changes to current processes where the company has received poor customer feedback. One of these is the ordering of fully assembled green computers. The current Internet-based process for ordering and configuring these computers is described below. A swim-lane diagram (flowchart) showing the process is also included as Figure 4.

On-line customers use the *greenTech* web site to enter the specific computer configuration they require. These details are fed through to the sales department at *greenTech* which then e-mails Xsys – *greenTech*'s Korean manufacturer – to ask for a delivery date for the requested computer. Xsys e-mails the date back to *greenTech* which then e-mails the customer with delivery and cost details. The customer then decides whether they wish to proceed with their order. Currently, 40% of enquiries proceed no further, which is of concern to *greenTech* as it means that time and effort have been wasted.

For those enquiries that do proceed, customers are invited to enter their payment details (credit card only). These details are sent directly to Equicheck – a specialist credit checking agency. About 20% of orders are rejected at this point because the potential customer has a poor credit rating. For orders that pass the credit check, a payment confirmation is raised by *greenTech* and sent to the customer and *greenTech* place a confirmed order with Xsys for the computer.

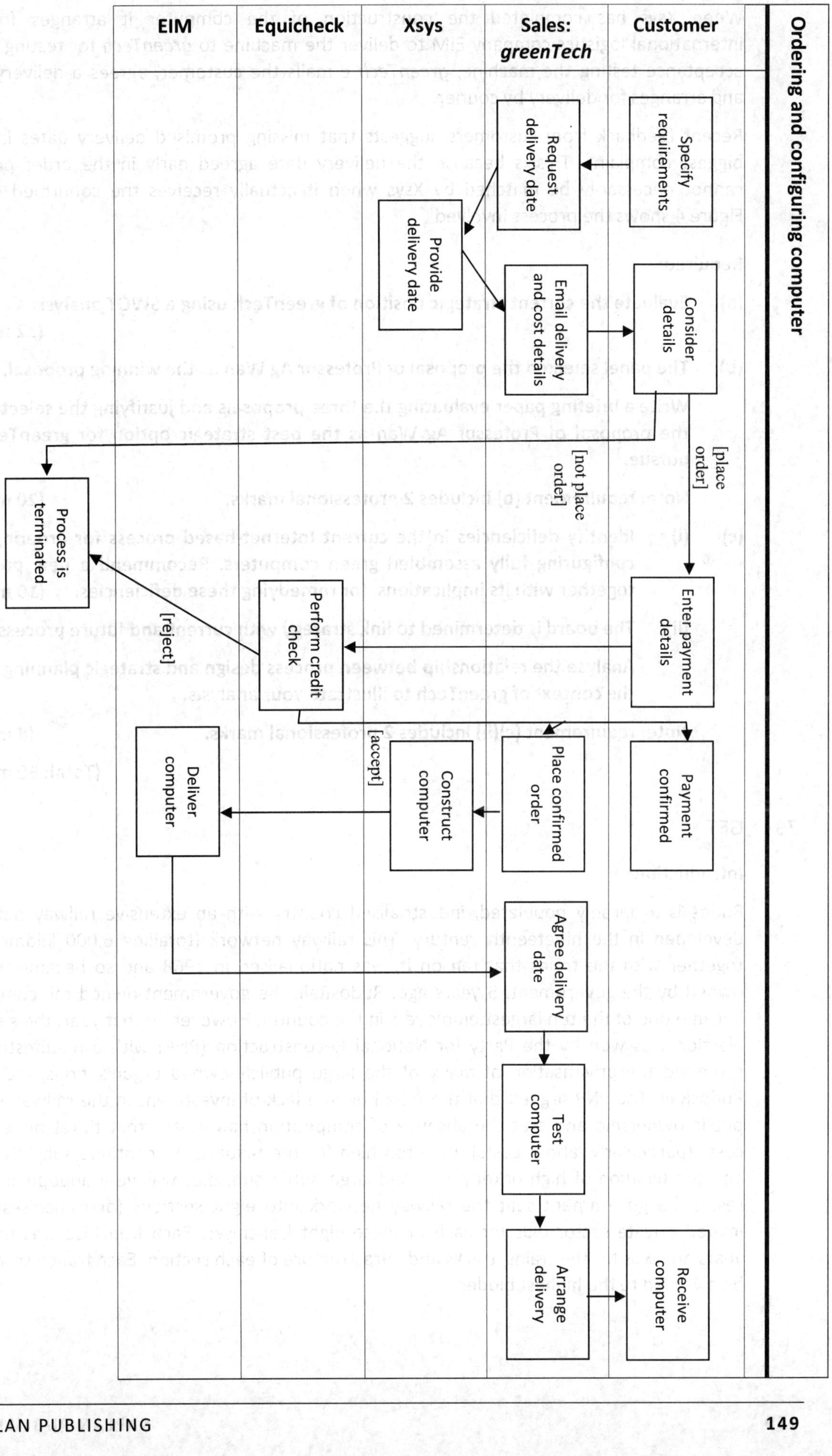

Figure 4: The process of ordering and configuring a computer

When Xsys has completed the construction of the computer it arranges for the international logistics company EIM to deliver the machine to *greenTech* for testing. After acceptance testing the machine, *greenTech* e-mails the customer, agrees a delivery date and arranges for delivery by courier.

Recent feedback from customers suggests that missing promised delivery dates is their biggest complaint. This is because the delivery date agreed early in the order process cannot necessarily be matched by Xsys when it actually receives the confirmed order. Figure 4 shows the process involved.

Required:

(a)   Evaluate the current strategic position of greenTech using a SWOT analysis.

(12 marks)

(b)   The panel selected the proposal of Professor Ag Wan as the winning proposal.

Write a briefing paper evaluating the three proposals and justifying the selection of the proposal of Professor Ag Wan as the best strategic option for greenTech to pursue.

Note: requirement (b) includes 2 professional marks.   (20 marks)

(c)   (i)   Identify deficiencies in the current Internet-based process for ordering and configuring fully assembled green computers. Recommend a new process, together with its implications, for remedying these deficiencies.   (10 marks)

        (ii)   The board is determined to link strategy with current and future processes.

                Analyse the relationship between process design and strategic planning using the context of greenTech to illustrate your analysis.

                Note: requirement (c)(ii) includes 2 professional marks.   (8 marks)

(Total: 50 marks)

79   GET

Introduction

Rudos is a densely populated, industrialised country with an extensive railway network developed in the nineteenth century. This railway network (totalling 6,000 kilometres), together with the trains that ran on it, was nationalised in 1968 and so became wholly owned by the government. 5 years ago, RudosRail, the government-owned rail company, became one of the ten largest employers in the country. However, in that year, the general election was won by the Party for National Reconstruction (PNR) with a manifesto that promised the privatisation of many of the large publicly-owned organisations, including RudosRail. The PNR argued that there had been a lack of investment in the railway under public ownership and that the absence of competition had meant that ticket prices and costs (particularly labour costs) were too high for the taxpayer to continue subsidising it. The combination of high ticket prices and large public subsidies was very unpopular. As a result the government split the railway network into eight sections (or franchises) and invited private sector bids for each of these eight franchises. Each franchise was for ten years and was for the trains, tracks and infrastructure of each section. Each franchise would be awarded to the highest bidder.

The East Rudos franchise, one of the eight franchises, was awarded to Great Eastern Trains (GET), a company specifically set up to bid for the franchise by former members of RudosRail's management. It was the only independent company to win a franchise. The other seven franchises were awarded to companies who were subsidiaries of global transport groups and, initially, were largely financed through investment from the parent companies. In contrast, GET was primarily financed through loans from the government-owned Bank of Rudos. The ten-year franchise started in 20X0. GET is an unquoted company, owned by its management team.

GET – the early years

The first three years of the GET franchise were extremely successful, both in terms of profits and passenger satisfaction. This was partly due to government subsidies to help ease the transition of the network from public to private ownership. However, it was also due to the skill and knowledge of the management team. This team already had significant operating experience (gained with RudosRail) and they adapted quickly to the new private sector model. GET was the most profitable of the new franchises and it was held up as an example of successful privatisation. Its investment in new trains and excellent reliability record meant that it quickly built up a well-respected image and brand. GET uses a series of television advertisements to promote its services. These feature an old lady arriving at various stations and texting her family that she has 'arrived safe & on time!' In a recent consumer survey these advertisements were rated as both memorable and effective.

In the newly privatised rail system many passenger journeys crossed franchise boundaries, so that a journey often involved the use of two or more franchise operators. GET developed an innovative booking and payment system that also automatically reallocated revenue from fares between franchise holders. It also allowed Internet booking and gave discounts for early booking. This system was so successful that GET now uses the system to process the bookings of three of the other franchise operators. GET is paid on a transaction basis for the bookings that it processes on behalf of these other franchisees.

The fourth and fifth years of GET's operation were not as successful. No government subsidies were paid in those years and economic problems in the country led to a fall in passenger numbers. Financial information for GET for 20X4 is provided in Figure 1. Figure 2 provides data for the rail industry as a whole in Rudos.

Figure 1: Selected information for GET in 20X4

Extract from the statement of financial position: All financial figures in $m

ASSETS
Non-current assets

		$m
Property, plant, equipment		2,175
Intangible assets		100
	Total	2,275
Current assets		
Inventories		275
Trade receivables		10
Cash and cash equivalents		300
	Total	585
Total assets		2,860

EQUITY AND LIABILITIES

Share capital	550
Retained earnings	110
Total equity	660
Non-current liabilities	
Long-term borrowings	2,000
Total non-current liabilities	2,000
Current liabilities	
Trade and other payables	199
Current tax payable	1
Total current liabilities	200
Total liabilities	2,200
Total equity and liabilities	2,860

Extract from the statement of comprehensive income

All financial figures in $m

Revenue	320
Cost of sales	(210)
Gross profit	110
Administrative expenses	(40)
Profit before tax and interest	70
Finance cost	(60)
Profit before tax	10
Tax expense	(1)
Profit for the year	9
Extract from the annual report	
Number of employees	3,010
Number of rail kilometres	920

Figure 2: Financial information for the Rudos rail industry as a whole

Measure	National rail industry average
ROCE	4.50%
Operating profit margin	10.00%
Gross profit margin	22.00%
Current ratio	2.1
Acid test ratio	1.2
Gearing ratio	48%
Revenue/employee per year	$85,000
Number of employees per rail kilometre	4.1

Current position

Despite the apparent success of GET, there has been considerable criticism of the overall privatisation of the railway. Much of this criticism is concentrated in two of the geographical areas where the franchisees have struggled to provide an efficient and economic service. The government has appointed auditors who are reviewing the operation of these two franchises and a government minister has stated that 'terminating the franchise and opening it up to re-bidding has not been ruled out as an option'. A major rail accident in Rudos (with many fatalities) has also led to concerns about safety and led to new legislation being enacted. Further safety legislation is expected concerning the relaying of track and all franchisees will be expected to implement the requirements immediately.

In 20X3, the PNR was returned to power, but with a reduced majority. The leader of the main opposition party originally suggested that the railways might be re-nationalised if he were to gain power. However, he has since moderated his view, although he suggests that 'they should return a significant percentage of their profits to the taxpayer'. Road transport has also suffered under the PNR government, with many of the roads in the country heavily congested. Fuel costs have increased to reflect increasing scarcity, causing many companies to face spiralling transport and storage costs. For the first time in the country's history, an ecology (green) party has won seats in government, capitalising on the growth of the 'green consumer', particularly in urban areas.

International rail developments

The pioneering privatisation initiatives in Rudos have been observed by other countries and many have adopted similar policies. Recently, the Republic of Raziackstan announced that it intended to privatise its railway network. Raziackstan is approximately five hours' flying time from Rudos and is part of the former eastern trading bloc. It is a country where there is currently very little health and safety legislation. Although there is also little employment legislation, public service jobs are traditionally viewed as safe, and employees perceive that a 'railway job is a job for life'. At present the railway network, which is 1,500 kilometres long, employs 8,000 employees generating revenues of $180,000,000. The country itself still has a limited technological and financial infrastructure, with only an estimated 20% of the population having access to the Internet. However, all political parties are united in their desire to privatise the railways so that money can be invested elsewhere in the country, for example, for providing better health care.

Because of the poor condition of the railway, the proposal is to retain and upgrade the rail tracks under public ownership. However, the trains and infrastructure, such as stations, will be privatised. The government is looking for letters of intent from private companies who are willing to take over the complete network (excluding the tracks).

A stipulation of the contract is that the bidder should have a significant industrial presence in the country. For some time GET has been interested in acquiring the company that undertakes most of the track and train maintenance in Raziackstan. This company SOFR (SOciety Fabrication de Raziackstan) was established in 1919 and has a long tradition of engineering. GET has used the company to refurbish some of its equipment and they have been delighted with the results.

The board of GET now senses a great opportunity. It would like to combine the speedy acquisition of SOFR with a bid to run the rail network in Raziackstan. In fact, early informal indications from the Raziackstan government suggest that the bid will be successful if SOFR has been acquired by GET as no other prospective bidders for the network have yet come forward.

Required:

(a)   Using appropriate models and frameworks, analyse GET's current strategic position from both an internal and external perspective.   **(20 marks)**

(b)   GET's proposed strategy is firstly to acquire SOFR and then the franchise to run the rail network of Raziackstan. You have been asked to provide an independent assessment of this proposed strategy.

        Write a report evaluating GET's proposed strategy.   **(16 marks)**

        Professional marks will be awarded in part (b) for appropriate structure, style and fluency of the report.   **(4 marks)**

(c)   Critical Success Factors (CSFs) and Key Performance Indicators (KPIs) are important business concepts in the context of franchising rail services.

        Explain and discuss these concepts in the context of GET and the rail industry.

        (10 marks)

(Total: 50 marks)

80   MIDSHIRE HEALTH   *Online question assistance*

Introduction

In 20X1 Terry Nagov was appointed as Chief Executive Officer (CEO) of MidShire Health, a public authority with responsibility for health services in Midshire, a region with a population of five million people in the country of Etopia. Like all health services in Etopia, MidShire Health is funded out of general taxation and is delivered free of charge. Terry Nagov was previously the CEO of a large private company making mobility appliances for disabled people. He had successfully held a number of similar executive positions in companies producing consumer products and goods for the consumer market. He was appointed to bring successful private sector practices and procedures to MidShire Health. Etopia had experienced a prolonged economic recession and such appointments were encouraged by the government of Etopia who were faced with funding increased health care costs. They perceived that private sector expertise could bring some order and greater control to the functioning of public sector services. One of the government ministers publicly commented on the apparent 'anarchy of the health service' and its tendency to consume a disproportionate amount of the money collected through general taxation. The government was keen on establishing efficiencies in the public sector, by demonstrating 'value for money' principles.

Vision and strategic planning

Terry Nagov believed that all organisations need to be firmly focused on a visionary objective. He stated that 'our (MidShire Health) mission is to deliver health to the people of Midshire and, by that, I don't just mean hospital services for the sick, but a wider vision, where health is a state of complete physical, mental and social well-being and not merely the absence of disease or infirmity.'

He believed that this vision could only be achieved through a comprehensive strategic planning process which set objectives, policies and standards at a number of levels in the organisation. In the strategic plan, the high-level objectives and policies of the organisation would be cascaded down to operational levels in a series of lower-level plans, where departments and functions had specific objectives that all contributed to the overall strategic vision.

Terry Nagov had successfully implemented such strategic planning systems at previous organisations he had worked for. He believed that centralised, senior management should decide strategy, and that line managers should be given power and responsibility to achieve their defined objectives. This approach had worked well in the heavily automated industries he had worked in, with semiskilled employees closely following standards and procedures defined by senior managers in the organisation.

Terry Nagov believed that a project should be put in place to establish a formal strategic planning system at MidShire Health and that this should be supported by a comprehensive computer-based information system which recorded the outcomes and activities of the organisation. He immediately engaged the commercial IT consultants, Eurotek, to develop and implement this information system using a standard software package that they had originally developed for the banking sector. The overall strategic planning system project itself would be owned by a small steering group of two senior hospital doctors, two hospital nursing managers and two workers from the health service support sector. Health service support employees provide health services to the wider community in the form of health education and public health information and initiatives. Their inclusion in the steering group was not welcomed by the hospital doctors, but the CEO wanted a wide range of professional input. 'Collectively', Terry declared, 'the steering group has responsibility for delivering health to the Midshire community'.

Initial meeting of the steering group (meeting 1)

The initial meeting of the steering group was not attended by the two senior hospital doctors. In Etopia, it is accepted that hospital doctors, although employed by the health authority on full-time contracts, also have the right to undertake paid private work (practice) where they deliver services for private hospitals to fee-paying patients. This right was negotiated by their professional body, the Institute of Hospital Doctors (IOHD), many years ago. Many of the patients they treat in private practice have paid for private health insurance so that they can be treated quickly and thus avoid the long waiting times associated with the free, public service. The initial meeting of the steering group coincided with a day when both doctors were undertaking private work. In their absence, the steering group approved the overall vision of the CEO and agreed to the initiation of an information system project to generate the detailed planning and control information to support this vision. The exact nature and contents of this information system would be determined by a small multi-disciplinary team reporting to the steering group and referred to as the 'implementation team'. It was made up of three administrative staff employed by MidShire Health supported by four technical consultants from Eurotek, experienced in implementing their software package solution. The composition of the implementation team and steering group is shown in Figure 1.

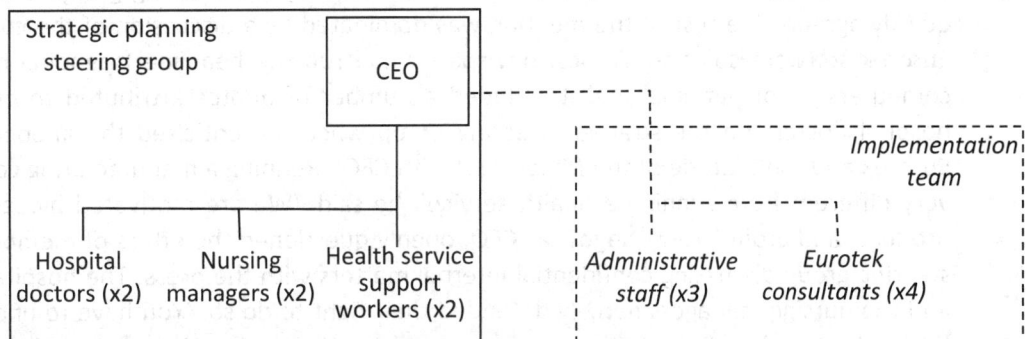

Figure 1: Composition of the steering group and the implementation team

Second meeting of the steering group (meeting 2)

The second meeting was attended by the two senior hospital doctors, but one of the health service support sector workers could not attend. At the start of the meeting, the two hospital doctors questioned the wide definition of health agreed at the previous meeting. One of the hospital doctors suggested that delivering health in this wider context was completely beyond the resources and capabilities of MidShire Health. 'You have to realise', he said, 'that poor health is often caused by poverty, bad housing and social dislocation. You cannot expect MidShire Health to solve such problems. We can advise and also treat the symptoms, but prevention and cure for these wider issues are well beyond us.' The nursing managers, who had previously approved the wider definition of health, now voiced their support for a narrower definition of health and sided with the hospital doctors. One of them commented that 'our real work is treating the sick and we must recognise this'. The CEO, outnumbered and outmanoeuvred in the meeting, had to agree to a modification of his initial vision, narrowing the overall objective to 'effectively and efficiently treating disease'. 'And, as we all know', stated one of the doctors, 'efficiency can only be achieved through giving control and budgets to the doctors, not to the administrators who are an unwanted overhead. This is the very first step we should take.' The nursing managers agreed and the meeting came to a slightly acrimonious and early conclusion.

Meeting three of the steering group (meeting 3)

At the third meeting, a presentation was made by the IT consultants, Eurotek, where they demonstrated their software for recording business activities and showed how these activities could be measured against agreed targets. A great deal of discussion took place on the targets that could be set for measuring health efficiency. After a long heated debate, three measures were agreed for hospitals. It was suggested that similar measures should be discussed and developed for health service support services, such as health education. However, at this point, the two senior doctors declared that they had to leave the meeting to 'return to our real job of treating patients'. The CEO agreed that the health service support workers could establish their own measures before the next meeting. One of these representatives commented that 'in my day-to-day job I am confronted by many people who have preventable illnesses. Their problems are due to poor diet and unhealthy habits. Preventing such problems must be better than curing them!' The CEO agreed; this was what he wanted to hear!

Meeting four of the steering group (meeting 4)

The fourth meeting of the steering group began with a discussion of the preventative perspective of health raised by one of the health service support workers at the end of the previous meeting. Both the hospital doctors and nursing managers suggested that this did not come under the revised definition of health used by the steering group, and the CEO quickly agreed. The rest of the meeting was dominated by a discussion of the costs of the Eurotek software solution. A local newspaper had run the headline 'spending money on computers – not patients' and it included a number of quotes attributed to one of the hospital doctors on the strategic steering group where he criticised the appointment of Eurotek and the attitude of the MidShire Health CEO. 'Running a manufacturing company is very different from running a health service', he said. 'We are motivated by service, not products and profit.' Terry Nagov, as CEO, openly questioned the ethics of members of the steering group discussing confidential internal matters with the press. The hospital doctors and the nursing managers fiercely defended their right to do so. 'You have to understand', they said, 'our loyalty is to the profession and to the public. We must act in the public interest.' Nevertheless, the CEO raised the possibility of disciplinary action against the hospital doctor.

At this point, the senior hospital doctors and the nursing managers left the meeting. The health service support workers stayed and pledged their support to the CEO. They revealed that the autocratic behaviour of hospital doctors often resulted in their work being both unrewarding and unrecognised. One commented, 'We have little professional autonomy, we feel controlled by the agenda of the hospital doctors.'

Meeting five of the steering group (meeting 5)

The possibility of disciplinary action against the hospital doctor had been published in the press and the Institute of Hospital Doctors (IOHD) had made a formal complaint about the CEO's behaviour to Etopia's health minister. Faced with pressure from within the hospital sector, Terry Nagov was forced to retract his threat of disciplinary action and to issue a public apology, but meeting five was boycotted by the hospital doctors and nursing manager representatives due to 'the lack of respect shown by the CEO'. Consequently, meeting five was cancelled.

Meeting six of the steering group (meeting 6)

This meeting received a report from the implementation team working on the specification of the information system for MidShire Health. They reported that the software suggested by Eurotek was excellent for time recording, analysis and reporting, but had very few features to aid the planning and control of activities. 'I suspected this all along', said one of the hospital doctors. 'I think this report shows that you are more interested in finding out what we are doing. The strategic planning exercise is really about cost reduction.' It was agreed that Eurotek should be contacted to provide a price for developing a bespoke solution for the information system requirements envisaged by the MidShire implementation team. 'I realise', the CEO said, 'this will affect the viability of the whole strategic planning project but I ask you all to pull together for the good of MidShire Health and its image within the community.'

Just prior to the next planned meeting, the implementation team specifying the information system reported that Eurotek had quoted a price of $600,000 to develop a software solution that integrated planning and control of hospital activities into their software package solution. This was additional to the $450,000 it was charging for the basic software package. The CEO reacted immediately by cancelling the information system project 'on cost grounds' and disbanding the steering group. He stated that 'from now on, I will personally specify and develop the targets required to bring health to the people of Midshire. I will focus on using the current systems to bring these into place'. Emails were sent to the steering committee members informing them of the dissolution of the steering group, stating that no further meetings would be held and no comments were invited. However, the costs of paying penalty charges to Eurotek were soon released to the press and Terry Nagov resigned from his post as CEO of MidShire Health to return to his previous company as chairman. The Institute of Hospital Doctors (IOHD) took the opportunity to issue the following press release:

'Once again, the government has failed to realise that managing public sector services is not the same as managing a private sector profit making company. Money and time have been wasted, and reputations needlessly damaged. Doctors and nurses, people at the cutting edge of the service, know what needs to be done. But time after time our views are disregarded by professional managers and administrators who have little understanding of health care delivery. The public deserve better and we, the IOHD, remain committed to delivering services in the public interest.'

Required:

(a) (i) **Identify and analyse mistakes made by the CEO in the project management process (initiation, conduct and termination) in his attempt to introduce strategic planning, and an associated information system, at MidShire Health.** **(18 marks)**

(ii) **Explain how an understanding of organisational culture and organisational configuration would have helped the CEO anticipate the problems encountered in introducing a strategic planning system, and an associated information system, at MidShire Health.** **(18 marks)**

Professional marks will be allocated in part (a) for the clarity, structure and logical flow of your answer. **(4 marks)**

(b) **Johnson, Scholes and Whittington identify three strategy lenses: design, experience and ideas.**

Evaluate the strategic planning project at MidShire Health through each of these three strategy lenses. **(10 marks)**

(Total: 50 marks)

Online question assistance

---

81 MACHINESHOP

Arboria is a prosperous industrial country with an established consumer culture that is distinguished by demanding and assertive consumers. Many companies find it difficult to compete successfully in the country but MachineShop is a notable exception. MachineShop sells small electrical machines and tools to both trade (people who use the machines/tools in their work) and domestic customers (people who use the machines/tools at home). For example, it sells a range of paint strippers retailing from $100 to $3,500. These paint strippers are bought by both tradesmen (for example, decorators) and ordinary domestic customers who use them to maintain their own home. It is estimated that 65% of sales are to domestic customers. MachineShop currently has 50 brightly decorated stores throughout Arboria. On average, a further two stores are opened every month. The company has no direct competitors. Most firms offering similar machines only sell them to tradesmen. In many respects MachineShop has defined a new market and it is the only company which, at present, seems to understand the dynamics of this market.

MachineShop is a private company still wholly owned by its directors. The board is headed by Dave Deen, a dynamic entrepreneur who enjoys a high national media profile. He likes the excitement of business and is determined to rapidly grow MachineShop – an ambition shared by his fellow directors. In 20X6, on a turnover of $50m, MachineShop recorded a gross profit margin of 28% and an operating margin of 17%. It delivered a Return on Capital Employed (ROCE) of 17.5%. It currently has a gearing ratio (defined as long-term loans/capital employed) of 15% and an interest cover ratio of 3.5.

Dave Deen has an ambitious growth plan, which he intends to achieve through a combination of internal growth, acquisition and, possibly, strategic alliances. The opening of further stores in Arboria is providing internal (organic) growth. Much of this drive for growth is fuelled by a desire to exploit MachineShop's unique competencies before the idea is copied, both within Arboria and elsewhere in the world. However, the company is having difficulty finding companies to acquire, as there are few equivalent companies to target, either in Arboria or elsewhere in the world. Although MachineShop has never traded outside Arboria, the search for acquisitions is worldwide, with Dave Deen particularly keen to explore international markets in his desire to build a worldwide brand. He has specifically identified the developing country of Ceeland as a potential target, because macroeconomic trends suggest that a consumer society is emerging there, which is similar to the one in Arboria.

Ceeland

The government of Ceeland has spent the last decade building an effective road transport system, supported by low fuel and road taxes which make it cheap to use. The government has also installed a fast digital communication network, providing broadband internet access to all of the population. This is important to MachineShop because internet order placement (either for collection or delivery) is an important part of their business model. The government has also lifted certain restrictions which had been in place under its predecessor. For example, it has removed the need for companies trading in the country to be registered in Ceeland and to have at least one Ceelander citizen on the board. Until recently, there were restrictions on what machines could be used by domestic customers. However, these restrictions have also been removed, as part of a government initiative to encourage the development of light manufacturing in the country. Indeed, one brand of products already stocked by MachineShop is made by a company based in Ceeland.

Fabrique Regle de Garrido (FRG)

Dave Deen has identified Fabrique Regle de Garrido (FRG) as a potential acquisition or strategic partner. FRG currently has 30 depots in Ceeland supplying large machine tools solely to trade customers. It does not sell products to domestic customers. It has an effective distribution network and a sales team which is experienced in selling to Ceeland businesses. MachineShop has the finance (in the form of bank loans and retained earnings) in place for an acquisition or a strategic partnership. Dave Deen has not yet opened up negotiations with FRG, but he has extracted some financial information from the company's most recently filed accounts (see Figure 1). He has also discovered that FRG is a privately owned company, with 30 shareholders, including a local trade union. Dave Deen sees the potential acquisition of FRG as an opportunity to introduce the MachineShop business model into Ceeland. He fully expects the country to become increasingly similar to Arboria and so it will be suitable for the sort of service and products which MachineShop offers. 'Achieving quick, substantial growth through acquisition will give us a powerful bargaining position. It will allow us to develop economies of scale, including purchasing in bulk to further drive down product prices. This will help us erect barriers to potential competition', he said.

Figure 1 – Extracted financial information for FRG

All figures in $000	*20X6*
Revenue	9,000
Cost of sales	(7,500)
Gross profit	1,500
Other expenses	(700)
Finance costs	(300)
Profit before tax	500
Income tax expense	(100)
Profit for the year	400

Non-current liabilities

Share capital	9,500
Retained profit	400
Long-term loans	2,500

MachineShop acquisitions

MachineShop does have some experience in acquisitions. In 20X4 it acquired two companies based in Arboria which still trade as independent companies. The purchase of LogTrans was prompted by the need for MachineShop to have a dedicated and reliable logistics supplier. The post-acquisition performance of the company was spoilt by a dispute between Dave Deen and the senior management of LogTrans. This was due to a personality clash, caused by a different way of doing business. Eventually, the senior management of LogTrans was removed and replaced by people more aligned with the corporate culture of MachineShop. EngSup was also acquired in 20X4 to provide an enhanced service facility to people who had purchased machines from MachineShop. Customer feedback showed that many customers were unimpressed by MachineShop's after sales service. EngSup already provided support for many domestic electrical products and so MachineShop bought the company with the intention of using it to provide support for MachineShop's customers. However, initial feedback was negative because EngSup's service engineers provided a poor level of service, coupled with an arrogant approach to the customer. A retraining scheme, together with selected redundancies, has now addressed these problems. Extracts from the current year's figures for both companies, compared with the last full pre-acquisition period of the company, are shown in Figure 2.

Figure 2 – Extracted financial information for LogTrans and EngSup

All figures in $000	LogTrans		EngSup	
Extracted data	*20X6*	*20X3*	*20X6*	*20X3*
Revenue	700	650	350	325
Cost of sales	(575)	(510)	(275)	(250)
Gross profit	125	140	75	75
Other expenses	(60)	(70)	(35)	(30)
Finance costs	(30)	(15)	(10)	(8)
Profit before tax	35	55	30	37
Income tax expense	(15)	(10)	(7)	(10)
Profit for the year	20	45	23	27
Non-current liabilities				
Share capital	500	400	250	100
Retained profit	80	70	40	170
Long-term loans	100	50	30	20

Required:

(a) Internal growth, acquisition and strategic alliances are three methods of pursuing growth.

Explain and evaluate each of these three methods of pursuing growth in the context of MachineShop's development to date and its ambitions for future growth and development. **(18 marks)**

(b) MachineShop is considering the acquisition of FRG. They have asked you, as a business analyst, to write a report which advises them on this potential acquisition.

Write a report, using the criteria of suitability, acceptability and feasibility, which evaluates the potential acquisition of FRG, concluding with whether you would recommend MachineShop to acquire FRG. **(18 marks)**

Professional marks will be awarded in part (b) for the structure of the report, the clarity of the analysis and the soundness of the conclusion or recommendation. **(4 marks)**

(c) Dave Deen has heard about Porter's 'diamond' and wants an explanation of the principles, relevance and application of this model.

Explain the principles of Porter's 'diamond' and use it to assess the relative attractiveness of Ceeland and Arboria in providing an environment in which MachineShop's growth ambitions could be achieved. **(10 marks)**

(Total: 50 marks)

82   ECOCAR

The EcoCar Company was formed six years ago to commercially exploit the pioneering work of Professor Jacques of Midshire University, a university in the country of Erewhon. Over a number of years he had patented processes that allowed him to use Lithium-ion batteries to power an electric car, which could travel up to 160 kilometres before it needed recharging. Together with two colleagues from the university, he set up EcoCar to put the car into commercial production.

Coincidentally, an area in the south of Midshire was suffering from major industrial decline. This area was centred on the former Lags Lane factory of Leopard Cars, which had recently been shut down by its parent company, bringing to an end 60 years of continuous vehicle manufacture on that site. Many skilled car production workers had been made redundant in an area that already suffered significant unemployment. Grants from the regional council and interest-free loans from the government allowed EcoCar to purchase and re-furbish part of the Lags Lane site and take on a hundred of the skilled workers made redundant by Leopard Cars.

The company now manufactures three car models: the original Eco, the EcoPlus, and the EcoLite. The EcoPlus is a luxury version of the Eco and shares 95% of the same components. The EcoLite is a cheaper town car and uses only 70% of the components used in the Eco. The rest of the components are unique to the EcoLite. A comparison of an Eco with a similar petrol-fuelled car (Kyutia 215) is given in Figure 1. This table also gives a comparison with a hybrid car (Xdos-HybridC) where the petrol engine is supplemented by power from an electric motor. Hybrids are a popular way of reducing emissions and fuel consumption. Petrol currently costs $5 per litre in Erewhon. There are also experimental cars, not yet in production, which are fuelled by other low-emission alternatives to petrol such as hydrogen.

Model	Eco	Kyutia 215	Xdos-HybridC
Power source	Lithium-ion batteries, electric motor	Petrol	Petrol with assistance from an electric motor
Price	$9,999	$7,999	$9,500
Emissions (CO_2)	Zero	180 gram/kilometre	95 gram/kilometre
Economy	Approximately $1 per 20 kilometres (electricity charge)	8 litres/100km	5 litres/100km
Performance	0–100 kph: 18 seconds Max speed: 120kph	0–100kph: 10 seconds Max speed: 180kph	0–100kph: 12 seconds Max speed: 170kph
Range	160 kilometres until the battery needs re-charging	550 kilometres on a tank full of petrol	1,200 kilometres on a tank full of petrol

Figure 1 Comparison of the Eco with comparable conventional and hybrid cars

The Eco model range can be re-charged from a domestic electricity supply. However, to supplement this, the government has recently funded the development of 130 charging stations for electric cars spread throughout the country. It has also given businesses tax incentives to switch to electric cars and is heavily taxing cars with high CO_2 emissions because of the detrimental effect of excess CO_2 on the environment. It has also enacted a number of laws on car safety which EcoCar has to comply with. Erewhon itself remains a prosperous, developed country with a well-educated population. The government is committed to tackling social and economic problems in areas such as South Midshire. EcoCar still receives significant government grants to help keep the company financially viable.

The EcoCar model range is largely bought by 'green' consumers in Erewhon, who are prepared to pay a price premium for such a car. They are also popular in the Midshire region, where the residents are proud of their car making tradition and grateful to Professor Jacques and the government for ensuring its survival, albeit at a reduced level. Only 5% of EcoCar's production is exported.

Universal Motors

One year ago, EcoCar was bought by Universal Motors, the second largest car manufacturer in the world. Professor Jacques and his two colleagues remain as senior managers and board members of the company. Car production of electric cars is still very low (see Figure 2), but Universal Motors believes that demand for electric cars will be very significant in the future and purchased EcoCar as a way of entering this market. They believe that Lithium-ion batteries (the power source for the EcoCar range) will eventually become lighter, cheaper and give better performance and range.

Since purchasing the company Universal Motors have undertaken an external and internal analysis of EcoCar and invested further capital into the business.

Their internal analysis identified four main areas of weakness. These are given below:

(1)   **High cost of labour, skills shortage and production capacity problems**

Although EcoCar was established in an area where there already existed a pool of skilled car workers, the subsequent retirement of many of these workers has left a skills gap. Although unemployment remains high in the area, applicants for jobs appear to lack the skills and motivation of the older workers. EcoCar is finding it difficult to recruit skilled labour and this shortage is being reflected in increased wages and staff costs at the Lags Lane site. The urban location of the Lags Lane site also causes a problem. Inbound logistics are made expensive by the relative inaccessibility of the site and the general congestion on Midshire's main roads. Finally, there is insufficient production capacity at the Lags Lane site to meet the current demand for EcoCar's products. EcoCar attempts to produce the most profitable combination of its products within this constraint. However, it is unable to completely satisfy market demand.

(2)   **Lack of control and co-ordination**

The individual departments and functions of the company are poorly integrated. Although budgets are agreed annually, they are not properly co-ordinated or monitored. Recently, car production was halted by the shortage of an important sub-assembly. Components for this sub-assembly had to be purchased quickly at a cost 10% above the normal purchase price. Overtime also had to be paid to employees to minimise the delay in re-starting car production. A similar lack of co-ordination appears to exist within bought-in inventory items. A recent purchase order for superior quality car seats was agreed by senior management, despite the fact that few customers had ever specified this option on the EcoPlus model. The seats were delivered and stored, but the finance department was unable to pay for them within the supplier's agreed payment terms. This failure was leaked to a newspaper and a very public row took place between EcoCar and the supplier. Eventually short-term financing (at a premium interest rate) was agreed with one of the banks and the seat manufacturer was paid.

(3) Research & Development – succession and learning

In the initial growth of EcoCar, the technical capabilities of the three founding senior managers were very significant. However, these three managers are now aged 50 or over. There is concern that their technical expertise and thirst for innovation is diminishing. To some extent the senior managers recognised this themselves two years ago and instigated a graduate training scheme with the aim of 'bringing new thinking into the company and ensuring its future'. Four graduates were taken on and a graduate training scheme agreed. However, it was cut within a year because 'training costs got out of control' and all four graduates have subsequently left the firm. A resignation letter from one of the graduates criticised the 'poor management skills of senior managers'. Universal Motors is concerned that the research and management culture is inappropriate and outdated. As a result, the graduates were not properly managed or motivated and there is evidence that their contribution was not welcomed or recognised.

(4) The understanding of risk

Universal Motors is concerned that decisions are taken by the senior managers of EcoCar without a proper analysis of the associated risks. Although the three senior managers are individually quite risk averse, as a team they make quite risky decisions. At a recent meeting to discuss entering a car in an economy car rally (accompanied by a mobile charging system) various risks were discussed at length but not documented or analysed. After two hours of exhaustive discussion the three senior managers decided to vote on the decision. They all voted in favour. No further discussion was held about the risks they had just discussed. Furthermore, the risk of an employee leaving to join a competitor and taking valuable information with them is discussed at every board meeting. However, no action is taken to address the risk. There just seems to be a general expectation that it will not occur.

Outsourcing

To address the first internal weakness, Universal Motors is considering outsourcing the manufacture of the EcoLite model to an overseas company. Information relevant to this decision is presented in Figure 2. The potential manufacturer has quoted a production price to Universal Motors of $3,500 per car. The manufacturing plant is approximately 300 miles from Erewhon, which includes crossing the 40 mile wide Gulf of Berang.

There are 112 production hours available in total per week at the Lags Lane site (seven days per week, two eight hour shifts) which can be used for a combination of the three product lines.

The weekly overhead costs are $35,000 per week at Lags Lane. If the production of the EcoLite model is outsourced, it is forecast that overhead costs will fall by $1,250 per week. The transportation cost is estimated at $250 for each outsourced EcoLite produced.

	Eco	EcoPlus	EcoLite
Selling price per car ($)	9,999	12,999	6,999
Variable cost per car ($)	7,000	10,000	4,500
Weekly demand (cars)	6	5	6
Production time per car (hrs)	9	10	8

Figure 2: Information relevant to the outsourcing decision

(a) Universal Motors have explicitly recognised the need for analysing the external macro-environment and marketplace (industry) environment of EcoCar.

Required:

Analyse the external macro-environment and marketplace (industry) environment of EcoCar. **(16 marks)**

Professional marks will be awarded in part (a) for the inclusion of appropriate model(s) and the overall structure and clarity of the analysis. **(4 marks)**

(b) Universal Motors is considering outsourcing the EcoLite model to an overseas manufacturer, whilst retaining in-house production of the Eco and EcoPlus models.

Required:

Evaluate the financial and non-financial case for and against the outsourcing option. **(15 marks)**

(c) Three weaknesses identified by Universal Motors are (1) lack of control and co-ordination, (2) research and development – succession and learning and (3) the understanding of risk.

Required:

Analyse how each of these three weaknesses might be addressed at EcoCar.

(15 marks)

(Total: 50 marks)

83 2TEL

2Tel is one of the largest mobile network operators in the world. It has grown mainly through significant acquisitions and it has extensive experience in buying companies and integrating them into the group. 2Tel continually invests substantial funds in research into network technologies. Like all global mobile network operators, it is constantly looking for technical opportunities for making its networks quicker, more reliable and, if possible, cheaper to install and maintain.

A business opportunity has arisen in The Federated States (TFS) where network operator licences are about to be renewed. 2Tel is currently evaluating this opportunity and is considering either bidding directly for a licence (as 2Tel) or acquiring a current licensee and bidding through this company. 2Tel is interested in entering the highly regulated mobile network market in TFS, even though most of its acquisitions to date have been in countries where there is little or no government regulation of the mobile network operators.

The Federated States (TFS)

The Federated States is a densely populated country with a population of 70 million people. The country has experienced five years of economic decline, characterised by high unemployment, falling incomes, and rising personal and government debt. Crime rates are also increasing. A year ago, a new government was elected with a mandate to tackle the economic problems of the country. Its priority has been to reduce the national debt and to help achieve this aim, it has introduced higher taxes and cut welfare benefits. The removal of these welfare benefits provoked civil disturbance and rioting, where shops were looted and burnt and mass demonstrations, usually ending in violence, were held in the streets of major cities.

TFS is an increasingly socially fragmented country with vocal minority groups representing a wide range of pressure groups and communities. It has a comprehensive and complex legal system, presided over by senior judges who were largely appointed by the previous government. The current government has suggested that many recent judgements made by these judges are politically-motivated and are designed to hold back the government's reforms. The employment laws of TFS make it relatively expensive to employ people (there are minimum wages laws) and also difficult to dismiss them (employment protection laws). Legal proceedings are often time-consuming and expensive.

A report into the riots and demonstrations highlighted the role mobile phones and social networks played in co-ordinating attacks on shops and people. The report acknowledged that such communication devices had long been a widely used tool in organised crime in TFS, but that it had now also become a significant factor in organising mass disobedience. In an effort to prosecute offenders, the government asked mobile phone network operators to give it information about text messages and the timing and duration of phone calls which possible offenders had sent and received during the period of the riots. The information provided was used as supporting evidence in court, and helped convict a number of people.

The releasing of this information to the government has proved controversial. The network operators have been criticised by civil liberties organisations which believe that this is personal, confidential information and, under the terms of the Data Protection Act of TFS, should not have been released without the person's consent. On the other hand, the government has praised the network operators for their good citizenship and believes that the data provided is exempt from the Act as the Act allows data to be exempt if it is used 'for the detection and prevention of crime'. An influential newspaper, whilst recognising the contribution of the networks to the successful prosecution of offenders, felt that 'instead of helping catch offenders, the networks, by making their services unavailable might have prevented the offences in the first place'. One of the current network licensees, Z-Tel, is being sued for damages by people who claim that their confidential information has been illegally released to the government. The case has yet to be presented to a court, but lawyers for both sides are confident of success.

Licensing arrangements in TFS

Communication network licences are granted to mobile network operators for an eight-year period. Licences are allocated to bidding companies on the basis that the companies meet a certain number of criteria. This includes financial criteria, such as liquidity and gearing, and environmental criteria. Successive governments of TFS have enacted environmental regulations and set environmental targets (such as carbon emissions and recycling rates) which all companies operating in TFS have to achieve.

Beyond these minimum criteria, the licences are allocated to the highest bidders, the companies which offer the most money for a licence. There are four current licensees and these were the four highest bidders in 2009, the last time that the licences were granted. During the licence period, no new network operators can enter the market. All four licensees are of a similar size, although their profitability varies (see Table one). The government is keen to ensure that no one network provider dominates the market.

Table one: Comparative data (20X1) for the four licensees

All figures in $m	Z-Tel	T-Me	Tello	Co-nekt
Revenue	750	700	725	740
Gross profit	350	300	325	325
Net profit	125	80	100	125

The licences are due for renewal in three years' time. At present, the rules for licence granting are exactly the same as for the previous licence allocation – four licences given to the four applicants who fulfil the minimum criteria and make the four highest bids. However, some government ministers are unhappy about this and are lobbying for a change which favours bids from current licensees. The government has already stated that any of the current licensees which fail to be reallocated a licence will be paid a $100m exit fee to help the losing company adjust to the loss of its licence. This will be paid for by the company which is replacing them, and is in addition to the contract fee paid by the successful bidder to the government. Some government ministers feel this bias towards current licensees should go further. One government minister recently suggested that 'the help provided to us during the recent riots should be acknowledged in some way'. There has also been a suggestion that there should be more than four licensees. This would increase competition and would also raise more money for national debt repayments. However, except for introducing an exit fee, the government has not yet officially stated any changes to the rules on licence allocation.

The network operators are monitored by a regulator, Ofnet, appointed by the government. In general, Ofnet has been supportive of the four current mobile network operators and it has openly praised their attitude and service on a number of occasions. Ofnet's primary focus is on pricing, service availability and service transfer. All prices are agreed in a series of meetings between the regulator and the licensees. As a result, the prices set by the four operators are very similar and are slightly less than the operators would like them to be. The companies, therefore, have to compete on branding, service support and network quality. In many geographical locations, one of the networks often provides a better signal quality and network speed, and indeed poor signal coverage is the most often cited reason for customers changing service operators. It is already possible for subscribers to move to a different service provider, but Ofnet believes, that this should be made even easier, and so is bringing in regulations to enable this. Licensees who do not comply with these regulations will be fined. The licensees are unconvinced of the demand for moving provider. One commented 'most subscribers move due to poor network service, and they can already do this!'

Mobile devices in TFS

Despite the economic decline of the last five years, mobile devices are seen as essential to most people within TFS. The demand for mobile devices and the networks which support them has increased dramatically in the last five years. Furthermore, mobile devices are particularly prized by the young, who see having the latest up-to-date technology as an important status symbol. Consequently, the manufacturers of mobile devices continually update the features and functionality of their devices. This has had an important effect on the mobile networks. Demand for services has increased not only due to an increase in calls, messages and web browsing but also due to the increasing demand which improved services place on network availability, bandwidth and speed. Thus the network operators have to continually upgrade the technologies and configurations which support their service networks. Most people in TFS rent their phones as part of a contract with the network provider. The minimum contract period is for one year, although many people tie themselves in for longer periods to take advantage of lower prices. Most people upgrade their phones when they renew their contract, to ensure that they have the device with the latest features. Old phones are returned by customers to their network provider, who, in turn, sends them back to the original manufacturer. The environmentally-friendly disposal of these mobile phones is a continual problem for the mobile phone manufacturers.

Research into the tendering process

2Tel has commissioned research from Professor Tan of Midshire University, an acknowledged expert in probabilistic decision making, into the TFS bidding process. Here are some of his conclusions. He has determined probabilities using a bid price of $550m and the probabilities are based on four licences being available.

(1) If the bidding rules are not changed before the next licence allocation, then every bidder has a 0.4 probability of being granted a licence if their bid is for $550m.

(2) If the bidding rules are changed before the next licence allocation to favour current licence holders, then a current licence holder has a 0.6 probability of being granted a licence if they bid $550m for the licence. A new bidder has only a 0.2 chance of being allocated a licence if they bid $550m for the licence. These probabilities are based on research in other countries where bidding is biased towards the current licence holders.

(3) It will cost current licence holders $10m to prepare a bid for a licence. New bidders, because of their unfamiliarity with the bid process, will incur a cost of $20m to prepare their bid.

2Tel is particularly interested in acquiring T-Me, the smallest of the current licensees. Their research suggests that they can implement efficiency gains which will generate $100m net profit per annum for the final two years of the current contract. This compares with T-Me's current net profit levels of $80m per year. Further efficiency gains and increased usage will lead to $120m net profit per year for the eight years of the contract, should the offer for T-Me be successful. An initial approach to T-Me has suggested that an offer of $400m for T-Me would be accepted.

The same net profitability for the contract (eight years at $120m per annum) is also expected if 2Tel decides not to acquire T-Me and is successful in a direct bid for a licence.

Before entering any market (or industry), 2Tel commissions an independent briefing paper from a business analyst which considers both the external environment of that market or industry (the wider macro-environment which the market or industry works within) and the competitive environment of the market or industry itself (the market or industry the proposed company will work within). These briefing papers conclude with a brief summary of the opportunities and threats posed by the environment. These briefing papers are used by the board of 2Tel as part of its evaluation of whether a market is attractive to enter. In this case, whether it should attempt to enter the TFS mobile operator industry, and if it does attempt to enter, whether it should enter directly or through acquiring a current operator.

Required:

(a) Write the briefing paper required by 2Tel. The briefing paper should:

(i) Analyse the macro-environmental factors affecting the TFS mobile operator industry (14 marks)

(ii) Analyse competition within the TFS mobile operator industry (8 marks)

(iii) Conclude with a summary of the opportunities and threats identified in the analysis. (4 marks)

Professional marks are available in part (a) for the structure, coherence, style and clarity of the briefing paper. (4 marks)

(b)   2Tel also requires an evaluation of the relative advantages of bidding for a licence, either through acquiring T-Me, or through bidding directly. The evaluation should analyse four specific scenarios (acquire and not gain licence; acquire and gain licence; bid directly and gain licence; bid directly and not gain licence). The analysis of each scenario should include the financial implications of each scenario. The evaluation should conclude with your recommendation on the preferred entry strategy.

Required:

Produce the evaluation of each scenario as required by 2Tel.

Note: Construction of a decision tree is not required and ignore the time value of money in your evaluation.   **(20 marks)**

(Total: 50 marks)

84   QTS GROUP

A business architecture training market has developed in the last two decades in the continent of Eastaria to train business analysts in this important subject area. QTSBA and Aspire to Knowledge (A2K) are both specialist providers of business architecture training and compete in this market. QTSBA is part of the Quality Training Synergies (QTS) Group and it is the market leader in this niche market. QTS Group is currently considering the possible acquisition of A2K with the intention to merge it with QTSBA after acquisition.

QTS Group

QTS Group is a significant, publicly quoted, training and education provider in Eastaria. QTS Group controls a number of independent trading companies which serve niche training markets across Eastaria. Every day, companies across QTS Group deliver more than a thousand courses. To help establish a common delegate experience, QTS Group insists on a standard, centrally defined approach to training in an attempt to ensure that courses are delivered in a consistent way. Revenue and net profit for the group is shown in Table One.

	20X0	20X1	20X2	20X3	20X4	20X5
Revenue ($m)	600	605	610	710	800	875
Net profit ($m)	70	65	70	85	100	110

Table One: Revenue and net profit for QTS Group (20X0–20X5)

Much of the recent growth of QTS Group has been achieved through acquiring niche information technology training companies. QTS Group has a good reputation for managing such companies post acquisition. In the three companies acquired in the last two years, profitability (as measured by the ROCE and the net profit margin) has increased in all three companies post acquisition. QTS Group believes that it has core competencies in acquisition and strategic change implementation, and that these core competencies are demonstrated by the improved performance of these recently acquired companies.

However, shareholders of QTS Group remain concerned about the group's current high level of retained earnings. They perceive that recent acquisitions by QTS Group have delivered value to shareholders because there has been an increase in both the dividend payout ratio and in earnings per share. A vociferous minority of shareholders are lobbying the board to continue this policy of acquisitions, using the retained profit of the group to drive further growth, particularly in terms of revenue and profit. In acknowledgment of this, the QTS Group board has announced an 'acquisition fund' of $30m to further acquire companies and finance post-acquisition change. A2K is the first of a number of companies which QTS Group is looking to evaluate for possible acquisition.

Business strategy is decided at group level and then implemented by the individual companies. There is a formal reporting system from these companies to the group.

Although growth in the business architecture training market has slowed, QTS Group is committed to remaining in this market. It forecasts future world-wide growth in this market and it intends to look for opportunities outside of Eastaria in the future. Revenues and other relevant information from the business architecture training market in Eastaria are shown in Table Two.

	20X0	20X1	20X2	20X3	20X4	20X5
A2K revenue ($m)	12.0	14.0	16.0	17.0	17.0	16.5
QTSBA revenue ($m)	39.0	40.0	42.0	45.0	46.0	48.0
Total market revenue ($m)	175.0	190.0	196.0	200.0	202.0	202.0

Other information:

(1)   QTSBA is the market leader in this market sector

(2)   The second largest training provider, CompTrain, recorded revenue of $31.31m in 20X5

(3)   Independent research shows that companies operating in this market have an average return on capital employed (ROCE) of 25% and an average net profit margin of 10%

Table Two: Sales revenue and other relevant information in the business architecture training market in Eastaria (20X0–20X5)

QTSBA

In 20X2, QTSBA appointed an experienced senior management team to improve the company's performance in the business architecture training market. To attract capable managers, QTSBA offered remuneration packages which were linked directly to achieving sales revenue performance targets.

It is acknowledged within QTS Group that QTSBA has strong sales and marketing competencies and it has recently won two major government business architecture training contracts. However, it is having difficulties finding experienced trainers and it needs to quickly recruit these trainers as a number of training programmes it has successfully bid for are about to commence. It is also acknowledged in QTSBA that the sales and marketing department of QTSBA has spare capacity, 'we could sell more if we had more to sell' is a common complaint of the sales and marketing team.

QTSBA has attempted to produce e-learning products in the past. However, the project to develop these products was unsuccessful. A team of software developers was recruited and an e-learning development platform selected. However, the company found it difficult to control the programmers' work. As one senior manager commented, 'we are training course providers, not a software house.' It transpired that the purchased e-learning platform was slow and inflexible and the learning solutions produced by the team were not what customers wanted. After two years, the project was abandoned, the programming team disbanded and the investment written off.

Aspire to Knowledge (A2K)

A2K was established in 1986 by Lee Wan and Kim Cross. Around 15 years ago, up and coming business architecture guru Kath Goff joined the company. These three people are still the primary shareholders of the company. Lee owns 25% of the shares, Kim owns 35% of the shares and Kath owns 35% of the shares. The current marketing director and sales director of the company each own 2.5% of the shares. Lee and Kim are now retired and the board consists of Kath Goff (as chief executive officer – CEO), the marketing director and the sales director.

A2K's organisational structure is shown in Figure One. This chart only shows full-time business architecture trainers. The company also employs a number of sub-contracted trainers who are self-employed and who undertake training for A2K on an ad hoc basis.

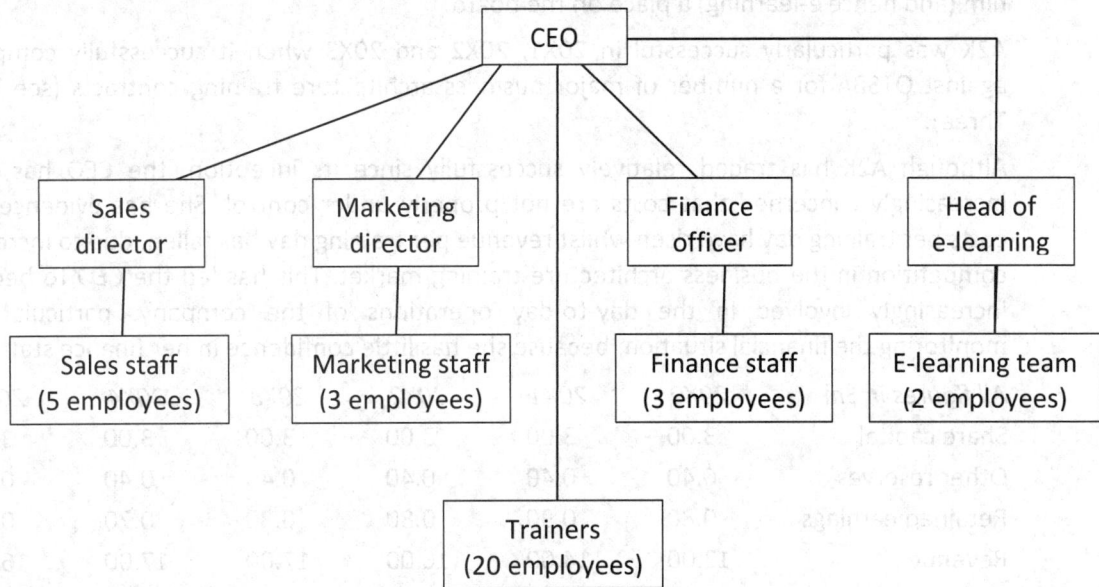

Figure One: A2K's organisational structure – 20X5

Kath Goff is an intelligent, charismatic individual with an in-depth knowledge of the business architecture training market. Although strategy is nominally the responsibility of the board, in practice the strategy reflects her vision. Indeed, she makes most of the significant decisions in the company. The marketing director has attempted to question her judgement in the past and has put forward alternative strategies. However, these have been quickly dismissed by Kath, claiming that he 'just doesn't understand the business architecture market'. Kath has also issued a number of public rebukes to other members of staff and employees who have found her direct approach unacceptable have quickly resigned and moved to other companies.

The early success of A2K was largely based on Lee and Kim's distinctive and innovative approach to training. The company soon became known as a company which did things slightly differently, with courses which were both challenging and humorous. To try and maintain this spirit, Kath still arranges regular company events, trying to recreate what she now considers to be the golden age of business architecture training. Indeed, Lee and Kim are always invited back to the annual 'celebration event' where Kath, Lee and Kim sit together all evening recounting tales from the old days. The current full-time trainers find such events tiresome and demotivating. They feel that customers now expect more professional, standard courses and that delegates' expectations have changed and are now more exacting. The full-time trainers employed by A2K are continually rated as 'excellent' by customers. However, these trainers are frustrated by their lack of input into company strategy and training decisions, as well as by the continued presence of Lee and Kim at company events. They find it hard to reconcile exciting tales of the past with the increasingly aging, fragile men sitting next to the CEO.

A2K has a small, but experienced e-learning software development team. A number of e-learning products have been produced over the last few years and are available for immediate purchase on the company's website. Sales are relatively strong and the unit profit margin, like all e-learning products, is significant as there is virtually no variable cost in delivering an e-learning course to a customer.

However, the e-learning team is demotivated. It is concerned at the company's apparent lack of commitment to e-learning (as against conventional face-to-face training) and the young head of e-learning, Ash Tag, is particularly angry at the company's reluctance to give him (and hence e-learning) a place on the board.

A2K was particularly successful in 20X1, 20X2 and 20X3 when it successfully competed against QTSBA for a number of major business architecture training contracts (see Table Three).

Although A2K has traded relatively successfully since its inception, the CEO has been increasingly concerned that costs are not properly under control. She has evidence that costs per training day have risen whilst revenue per training day has fallen, due to increased competition in the business architecture training market. This has led the CEO to become increasingly involved in the day-to-day operations of the company, particularly in monitoring the financial situation, because she has little confidence in her finance staff.

All figures in $m	20X0	20X1	20X2	20X3	20X4	20X5
Share capital	3.00	3.00	3.00	3.00	3.00	3.00
Other reserves	0.40	0.40	0.40	0.40	0.40	0.40
Retained earnings	0.80	0.90	0.80	0.80	0.70	0.60
Revenue	12.00	14.00	16.00	17.00	17.00	16.50
Net profit	1.75	1.65	1.65	1.60	1.45	1.40

Table Three: A2K – Figures extracted from financial statements: 20X0 to 20X5

Preparing for acquisition of A2K

The board of QTS Group is now preparing to approach A2K with an acquisition offer. Representatives of QTS Group have already met informally and independently with Lee and Kim (who both indicated their willingness to sell at the right price) and with the board of A2K (the CEO, sales director and marketing director). The latter meeting was quite strained, but the impression was formed that the acquisition would be considered favourably if the CEO, sales director and marketing director were employed, post-acquisition, in an autonomous company within QTS Group. This was put on the agenda, but no promises were made. Privately, the QTS Group board are sceptical whether these three senior managers could work in a more formal organisation or indeed, whether they are needed at all. They have no plans to make A2K an autonomous company within the group and indeed their intention is to merge the company with QTSBA.

Required:

The managing director of QTS Group has approached you as a business analyst and asked you to produce a briefing paper which addresses a number of key issues:

(a) Identify and discuss the benefits and advantages to QTS Group and QTSBA of acquiring A2K. The managing director stresses that he just wants the benefits and advantages considered. He wants you to focus on the positive factors which would emerge from this acquisition. **(19 marks)**

(b) QTS Group policy mandates that a strategic change evaluation should be undertaken before any possible acquisition is made. This looks at strategic change in terms of time, preservation, diversity, capability and readiness. These are five selected elements from the Balogun and Hope-Hailey model which considers the contextual features of strategic change.

Evaluate the strategic change required at A2K if the company is acquired and subsequently integrated with QTSBA. This evaluation should use the contextual features of time, preservation, diversity, capability and readiness. **(15 marks)**

(c) Finally, the managing director is interested in the organisational culture of A2K. He is concerned that it 'is just such a different company to us'. So, the final part of your briefing paper is to explain the principles of organisational culture and the concept and application of the 'cultural web' and Mintzberg's organisational configurations.

Explain the concepts of organisational culture, the cultural web and organisational configurations in the context of the possible acquisition of A2K and its post-acquisition integration with QTSBA. **(12 marks)**

Professional marks are available in question 1 for the tone, clarity, vocabulary and approach of your answer. **(4 marks)**

(Total: 50 marks)

85 POTS

Introduction

The EA Group has a portfolio of companies that currently specialise in alternative energy supply and associated products and services. It grew out of Power of the Sun (POTS) Co, one of the pioneers of solar heating, which still remains an autonomous company in the Group. The profits generated by POTS funded the initial development of the Group, which now comprises 12 companies. Only four of these companies are considered in this scenario.

Power of the Sun (POTS) Co

POTS Co was one of the first companies to realise the potential of solar powered energy solutions and it pioneered the use of the technology, particularly in government and city council (public sector) buildings. In the first 10 years of its existence, its net profit regularly exceeded 15%. Recent results for the company are shown in Figure 1. The approximate size of the overall market is also given (sector turnover).

All figures in $m	20X9	20X8	20X7	20X6
Sector turnover	357.00	357.00	356.00	355.00
POTS sales revenue	107.10	100.00	96.10	88.80
Gross profit	22.50	21.00	22.10	22.20
Net profit	7.50	7.00	8.70	9.80

Figure 1: Selected data for POTS Co

Although POTS was the main source of the profits which drove the expansion of the EA Group, many employees within POTS feel that it is now relatively neglected. Consumer surveys suggest that the brand is not as well recognised as it was and respondents who did recognise it saw it as a tired and traditional brand. Many of its most gifted managers have been promoted into the EA Group headquarters or other companies within the Group. It was expected that their expertise, gained with POTS, would help improve the performance of acquired companies. However, despite this loss of valuable resources, POTS still has recognised expertise and many valuable contacts and contracts in the public sector which the EA Group has been able to exploit. These contracts, particularly with city councils, have allowed the company to retain a significant presence in the solar powered energy market at a time when competitors have withdrawn from, or scaled down, their operations.

Neach Glass

The EA Group acquired Neach Glass in 20X3. Neach Glass was founded by Kevin Neach to provide high quality glass products. These were used in the original solar panels developed by POTS and a close relationship was built up between Kevin Neach and the managing director of POTS, Ken Nyg. Ken later became chief executive officer (CEO) of the EA Group. The glass panels continue to be used in POTS products. In 20X3, Kevin Neach informed Ken Nyg that Neach Glass was on the brink of going into administration. As a result, the EA Group acquired the company to help secure the supply of a vital component in the POTS product. Since that time, financial and management resources have been invested in Neach Glass in an attempt to improve market share and profitability. Some of POTS's best managers have been transferred to the company. Data for Neach Glass is shown in Figure 2. Again, the estimated size of the total market is shown as sector turnover.

All figures in $m	20X9	20X8	20X7	20X6
Sector turnover	88.20	89.00	89.50	90.00
Neach turnover	7.94	7.12	7.16	6.30
Gross profit	1.45	1.28	1.22	1.07
Net profit	0.72	0.57	0.57	0.45

Figure 2: Selected data for Neach Glass

ENCOS

In 2007, Ken Nyg recognised that other alternative energy sources other than solar power were becoming increasingly important. Council managers were increasingly requesting a combination of power sources with control systems that could be used to switch the power source to reflect the most economic combination of sources. As a result of this, the EA Group acquired ENergy COntrol Systems (ENCOS), a company with innovative control systems for monitoring power use and matching it to the most suitable and cheapest source of supply. ENCOS was acknowledged as a technical leader, but had little marketing expertise and few contracts in the public sector. ENCOS's control systems have sophisticated mathematical algorithms which are now used in many private sector applications. It has an excellent record in profitable delivery, with each contract carefully estimated and a detailed analysis of gross profit reported per contract. Financial data for ENCOS is shown in Figure 3. The market sector turnover is again given.

All figures in $m	20X9	20X8	20X7	20X6
Sector turnover	81.00	76.00	71.50	70.00
ENCOS turnover	21.00	17.00	14.30	13.30
Gross profit	5.00	4.00	2.75	2.55
Net profit	3.35	3.00	1.85	1.65

Figure 3: Selected data for ENCOS

Steeltown Information Technology

Steeltown City Council is the second largest city council in the country. Two years ago, responding to government initiatives to outsource non-core activities, it decided to outsource its information technology department to the private sector. The department developed and implemented bespoke in-house systems to support the departments of the council (housing, education, social services etc). Trade unions in the council mounted a vigorous campaign against the plan and employees were overwhelmingly against it. Many of the employees had worked for the council for many years and had experienced a stable work environment. However, this opposition hardened the council's resolve and they forced through the plan, citing the union's restricted working practices as a major problem.

The council invited private sector companies to tender for the work and resources of the department.

The EA Group were keen to broaden their technological services to the public sector and saw this as an opportunity to acquire an organisation that could spearhead its growth. As Ken Nyg said 'we must avoid being too narrow in focus. We started out in solar energy, before broadening out into other energy sources and services. We now wish to broaden again into information technology services in general and the acquisition of the Steeltown City Council's information technology department is a perfect vehicle for this. We see clear technology synergies with ENCOS who are technical leaders in control software design and development.'

Steeltown Information Technology, as the company is now called, has entered into a ten year exclusive contract with Steeltown City Council to supply information technology services. The contract price is based on current costs, plus inflation, plus a 5% gross profit margin. The contract will be renegotiated after five years, when it is expected that savings made by the company can be passed on to the council.

The IT director and his deputy, who both vigorously opposed privatisation, have not been transferred to the new company. They both took voluntary redundancy from the council. Other managers are philosophical, glad that the uncertainty of the last two years was behind them. One manager commented that although 'he was against outsourcing in principle, now the sale has been agreed, let's get on with it'. Very few new systems have been developed in the last two years whilst the future of the department was being discussed. There is now a backlog of applications to develop for a number of council departments. Users in these departments usually find it very difficult to specify system requirements in advance and there have been very few successfully implemented IT solutions.

Although the Steeltown City Council contract is on a cost plus basis, managers who have always been budget and service-driven will be expected to profitably deliver solutions to other potential customers in the public sector.

As part of preparing for strategic change at Steeltown Information Technology, the EA Group wishes to benchmark its performance. They have been provided with the information given in Figure 4.

	20X9	20X8	20X7	20X6
User satisfaction (1)	48%	46%	45%	44%
Faults reported (2)	200	250	375	425
User satisfaction (nationwide) (3)	45%	44%	44%	43%

Figure 4: Data for Steeltown City Council information technology department

(1)   measured by internally constructed and analysed user surveys at Steeltown City Council

(2)   measured by reported faults in software at Steeltown City Council

(3)   reported by city councils throughout the country

As another part of their preparation for strategic change at Steeltown Information Technology, the EA Group also wish to understand the contextual factors that will affect such change. They want to explore these factors before they firm up their proposed strategy for the newly acquired company.

Required:

(a) Analyse the performance of each of the four companies described in the scenario and assess each company's potential future contribution to the EA Group portfolio of businesses. **(24 marks)**

Professional marks will be awarded in part (a) for the clarity and structure of the answer. **(4 marks)**

(b) Time, scope, capability and readiness for change are four contextual factors that affect strategic change.

Evaluate the potential influence of these four factors at Steeltown Information Technology on any strategic change proposed by the EA Group. **(12 marks)**

(c) Discuss the principles, together with the advantages and the disadvantages, of benchmarking in the context of Steeltown Information Technology. **(10 marks)**

(Total: 50 marks)

86 **QTP**

QTP Co produces timber framed windows for builders' merchants, property builders and property maintenance companies. It does not sell windows directly to the general public. Members of the general public (and small building companies) can buy QTP windows through the builders' merchants supplied by QTP. These builders' merchants supply a wide range of products for property maintenance and improvement. They are usually located in large warehouse premises on the outskirts of towns and cities.

There are three primary raw materials (or components) for the windows which QTP makes.

– Timber (wood) which it orders from timber suppliers. Worldwide demand for timber is increasing and timber prices are relatively high and supply of some of the specialist timber which QTP requires is often in short supply.

– Glass which it orders from specialist glass manufacturers.

– Fittings, such as bolts, latches, handles, etc. which it sources from a number of small specialist producers.

QTP has a number of departments. This scenario considers just five of these departments and each of these departments is exactly aligned with activities of the value chain. They are:

– Inbound logistics and procurement

– Production

– Outbound logistics

– Marketing and sales

– Service

Production takes place on one dedicated production line where one machine (and supporting labour) undertakes all the tasks concerned with converting the components into the finished windows. There are no plans to buy a second machine or open up a second production line. Production takes place from 08.00 to 17.00 (nine hours). Although employees take breaks, these are organised so that the production line is always staffed. It is not possible, because of technical and environmental constraints, to extend the working day or organise a night shift. The company is effectively restricted to a nine-hour working day. Setting up and setting down of the machine has to take place within this nine-hour day.

Outbound logistics has a small fleet of vehicles which are used to deliver finished windows to the customer. Effective scheduling of this fleet is currently a problem and vehicle maintenance is becoming more expensive as the vehicles get older.

Standard and bespoke windows

The company offers both standard windows and bespoke windows.

Standard windows are made to a specification decided by QTP and they are produced to inventory. These windows are advertised in the company's catalogue and on its website. Customer orders for these windows are supplied from inventory and next day delivery is promised. The production of these windows is based on sales forecasts made by the marketing and sales department. These forecasts are used by the inbound logistics and procurement department to place orders for the raw materials for the windows. Because relatively large orders for components are placed in advance, QTP usually obtains significant discounts on published component prices.

Bespoke windows are produced to a specification required by the customer, usually resulting from consultation and negotiation between the marketing and sales department and the customer. They are made to exactly fit the customer's needs, in terms of timber type and quality, glass specification, window size and types of fitting. The marketing and sales department provides the customer with a proposed delivery date. A copy of the order, and the proposed delivery date, is also given to the production department, so that they can schedule the making of the windows and to inbound logistics and procurement so that they can order specific components for the windows.

At present, there is often a conflict between the production of standard and bespoke windows. It is essential that QTP achieves the promised delivery date for bespoke orders. To achieve this, it is often necessary for scheduled runs of standard windows to be postponed so that bespoke windows can be produced. This leads to less efficient use of the machine and labour (due to set up and set down time) and also to components for standard windows being held in inventory for longer than planned. Furthermore, component prices for bespoke orders are usually higher, reflecting smaller volumes and the need to fulfil tight deadlines. Bespoke window production and delivery to customers usually takes place as quickly as possible, to ensure that promised deadlines are met and inventory storage of finished windows minimised.

In the past, it was possible for bespoke orders to use common components bought in for standard windows. However, this led to continual disruption of the production of standard windows and now components for standard and bespoke orders are kept quite separate and are stored in different areas of the warehouse.

In general, the marketing and sales department prefers to make bespoke sales, rather than sales of the standard windows. They believe that bespoke windows provide exactly what the customer wants and this distinguishes QTP from its competitors who are more focused on selling standard windows. Unlike these competitors, the marketing and sales department at QTP contains staff who are experienced in window design and applications and customers value this. There is evidence that some important customers purchase their standard windows from QTP even though they could buy similar windows cheaper elsewhere, because they value QTP's flexibility in supplying them with bespoke windows. The marketing and sales director claims that, 'we have sales people who really understand windows and what customers want and need. We are not trying to sell them windows off-the-shelf, just because we have them in inventory.'

Furthermore marketing and sales staff claim that bespoke windows deliver higher revenue and higher profit to QTP than standard windows. However, this is challenged by the production manager who would prefer production to be focused on standard windows. Sales staff are currently rewarded on the basis of average revenue per window. At present, approximately 30% of QTP's sales volume is for bespoke windows, but this share is increasing annually.

Table One shows selected data for the production of standard and bespoke windows.

Revenue and costs per window ($)	Standard window	Bespoke window
Average revenue	85	110
Average inventory (storage) cost	15	5
Average raw material cost	20	40
Average transport cost (Note 1)	15	10
Average labour cost ($)	12	15
Average machine cost ($)	8	10
Production data		
Average number of windows produced per hour	12	10
Wastage rate for windows produced	2%	5%
Average set up time (Note 2)	10 minutes	15 minutes
Average set down time (Note 3)	20 minutes	45 minutes
Average production run (Note 4)	4 hours	2 hours
Other data		
Number of customer complaints per thousand windows	2	10

Table One: Selected QTP data: standard window and bespoke window production

Note (1) Transport costs concern distribution costs of finished goods to customers. Costs of inbound components are borne by the supplier.

Note (2) Time taken to set up the machine for a single production run of windows to one specification.

Note (3) Time taken to set down the machine (resetting parameters, cleaning, etc.) from a single production run of windows to one specification.

Note (4) Time of a single production run of windows to one specification.

Important: The machine is restricted to a nine-hour working day. Set up time and set down time must be within this nine-hour working day.

Management concerns

Senior management at QTP is exploring the possibility of moving the company to solely standard window production OR solely bespoke window production. They are also investigating issues in the five departments which are aligned to the activities of the value chain. They previously employed a business analyst who provided them with an analysis of the service department at QTP, documented in Appendix 1. Management has engaged you as her successor and they now require similar analyses for the remaining four departments.

Appendix 1: Analysis of service department in the value chain

---

Figure One: The service department at QTP: current analysis

Service

Service is concerned with activities which enhance or maintain the value of the window. This includes installation, repair, training, supply of parts and window adjustment. At QTP, service is primarily concerned with window replacement (repair).

Replacement of standard windows is usually required as a result of window deterioration. Evidence suggests that this is sometimes associated with windows or window components being held in inventory at QTP for too long and suffering some minor damage or imperfection, which has subsequently worsened. However, there is also evidence that some problems are a result of incorrect fitting. Standard window replacements are provided to the customer, usually for next day delivery. These are provided free-of-charge if the problem is due to faulty manufacture.

Problems with bespoke windows are usually associated with initial fitting and failure to meet specification. The window may be slightly too large, or the timber slightly the wrong colour. Because such windows are made to order, replacement can take some time, although the company attempts to 'rush through' such replacements, placing emergency component orders and interrupting scheduled production.

Figure Two: The service department at QTP: potential role after switch to standard windows production only OR bespoke windows production only

Switching completely to standard windows production

If production is switched completely to standard windows, then service will be primarily concerned with the replacement of defective windows. Better inventory management should lead to fewer problems with components and finished windows as both will remain in inventory for less time. Consideration could also be given to providing training on installation, so potentially reducing the number of defective windows caused by poor installation. This might involve formal certification for qualified installers. This should be attractive to customers, as it will reduce their wastage rates. QTP might also consider providing a guaranteed installation service itself. This might be particularly attractive to property builders who find it uneconomic to employ full-time window installers.

Switching completely to bespoke windows production

If production is switched completely to bespoke windows, then service will be primarily concerned with rectifying problems which arise as a result of the window failing to meet specification. Improved specification methods, using better computer aided design (CAD) software should reduce the need for service. The concept of providing a window installation service is particularly attractive for bespoke windows as slight failures in fit might be remedied on site, rather than returned to the factory. This eliminates delay and the cost of transporting the windows to and from the factory. Failures in appearance (such as timber colour) could be avoided by a pre-installation visit where a sample of the bespoke window (one window) could be confirmed with the customer.

Required:

QTP management would like you to prepare a briefing paper which:

(a) Analyses the current issues in the remaining four departments under consideration (inbound logistics and procurement, production, outbound logistics, marketing and sales), with appropriate reference to each department's role in the value chain. Appendix 1 Figure One is representative of the approach required. **(20 marks)**

(b) Evaluates the financial case for EITHER producing and selling standard windows only OR producing and selling bespoke windows only. The evaluation should include both options and could include any comments you have on the limitation of the data given in Table One. However, you should assume that the data given in this table accurately reflects the current situation. **(12 marks)**

(c) Analyses how the company could restructure elements of each of the remaining four departments (and hence the value chain) in the future for EITHER a switch to only standard windows production OR a switch to only bespoke windows production. Appendix 1 Figure Two is representative of the approach required and it clearly shows that you should include BOTH options in your analysis. **(14 marks)**

Professional marks will be awarded in question 1 for the structure, tone, coherence and clarity of your briefing paper. **(4 marks)**

(Total: 50 marks)

87   LING

Man Lal relaxed in business class as the aircraft skimmed across the Uril Mountains. Generally he considered himself a contented man. He had successfully built his company, Ling, to be the largest light bulb manufacturing company in the world, with global revenues of $750m. From its factories in Lindisztan it supplied a worldwide market for LED (light emitting diodes) light bulbs. Lal congratulated himself on the fact that he had quickly spotted the potential of LED light bulbs and had entered large-scale production whilst his rivals were still focusing their production on candescent and halogen bulbs. The world now realised that LED light bulbs provided a cheaper, more energy efficient, greener solution than all of its alternatives. To that end, many countries had passed legislation requiring domestic and business consumers to replace candescent light bulbs with greener equivalents. In fact, he was on his way right now to Skod, a country which had passed efficient lighting legislation which, from next year, banned the use of candescent bulbs in commercial premises and outlawed their production and importation after that date. Domestic consumers were expected to replace their candescent bulbs with newer technology as their bulbs failed. Man Lal confidently expected that LED would be, for many, the newer technology of choice.

The visit to Skod was of great significance to Man Lal because it was here that he did his business studies degree at Skodmore University. Indeed, he was due to give a lecture to the staff and students of the university the following day and he felt great personal pride in returning to describe the extent of his success and the fulfilment of his personal ambitions. He was also planning to visit a company called Flick which Ling was considering acquiring. This would be a new growth method for Ling. Up to now its worldwide expansion had been achieved by establishing wholly owned distribution companies in each targeted country. All production had remained in Lindisztan. However, for various reasons, Ling was now considering entering the Skod market by acquiring one of its light bulb producers, Flick.

In fact, remembering this brought a slight frown across Man Lal's face. To help fund his global expansion, he had sold 49% of Ling to institutional investors. These institutional investors required growth and high dividends and he was having difficulty meeting their demands. There was now very little growth in the domestic Lindisztan market and the distribution approach used to expand into foreign countries was taking a long time to mature. The investors were demanding quicker growth and acquisitions appeared to promise this. Despite paying high dividends over the last few years, the company still had significant retained profits and this was another issue for the institutional shareholders. They felt that this money should be used to promote growth and have agreed to a $400m acquisition fund. So, thought Man Lal, what better place to start those acquisitions than Skod, the place where I studied as a poor overseas student so many years ago. However, he had to admit to himself, he was still much happier with organic growth through setting up his own distribution companies. Ling had made a few acquisitions in Lindisztan, but had never bought a foreign company and he was worried about the risk of failure.

Turbulence buffeted the aircraft as it made its final descent into the capital of Skod. To distract himself, Man Lal picked up the latest copy of *Lighting Tomorrow*, the research magazine of the light bulb industry. He skim read an article on tubular daylight lighting which promised to reduce the need for electric lighting by introducing more daylight into a building. Effective daylighting (it said) is achieved through the strategic placement of skylights and windows, as well as lighting controls which monitor available daylight and respond as needed to decrease or increase electric lighting. Perhaps I need to look into this, thought Man Lal.

At the airport, Man Lal took a taxi to his hotel. He could not help but notice that Skod was not as neat and tidy as it used to be. A lot of shops and buildings had been closed down and there was graffiti across many buildings and bridges. 'Skod for Skodders', said one, 'Skod jobs for Skod people', said another. Man Lal remembered now that the Skod nationalist movement had become increasingly popular. He mentioned this to the taxi driver. 'Yes', he said, 'Most people are fed up with Skod being pushed around by the International Financing Consortium (IFC), we want prosperity and jobs for people who grew up here.'

Slightly unnerved, Man Lal, checked in at the hotel. He switched on the television. He watched with interest as Niklas Perch, the newly elected nationalist leader of the Skod government, outlined his plans for the future.

'We are committed to a return to prosperity', he said. 'To achieve this we have to make some short-term adjustments which may be unpopular with our trading partners. We are currently considering the imposition of import taxes as a way of protecting our home industry. We wish to create a protected commercial environment here in Skod in which our companies can prosper.

'We must also ask our citizens to continue with their energy saving measures. As you know, the government has agreed that all street lighting will be turned off from 2300 hours to 0500 hours. I have also decreed that all government offices must proactively embrace energy saving lighting and heating. In the same way, I expect our citizens to look at ways of saving money and energy.

'The government also recognises that the country continues to be in a recession, and that disposable income is falling for all people. However, I cannot condone the recent demonstrations against, and boycott of, foreign goods and food products. We must rebuild our country peacefully and legally. I would ask all citizens to support me in this.'

Just then, the air conditioning failed and the television went off. Another energy failure in Skod. There were three further failures that night. The hotel manager apologised to Man

Lal in the morning. 'I am sorry', he said 'but despite higher energy prices, this is an increasing feature of life in Skod.'

Skod electric light bulb industry

All electric light bulbs are largely made out of glass and metal and this is likely to remain the same in the foreseeable future. In Skod, 90% of glass is produced by three companies. However, for all of these three companies, light bulb manufacturers are unimportant customers. Most glass manufacture goes to the construction industry, light bulb manufacturers take less than 0.5% of the country's glass production. Metal manufacture in Skod is dominated by one company, OmniMetal. Most metal is sold to the automobile industry. Light bulb manufacturers take less than 0.1% of OmniMetal's production. However, the quality of glass and metal required by the light bulb manufacturers is quite standard, so switching between suppliers is, in theory, relatively easy. Light bulb manufacture takes place in factories which require substantial initial investment and have no obvious alternative use.

In Skod, light bulbs are low cost commodity products which are replaced infrequently by domestic consumers. Commercial consumers change their light bulbs a little more often and some businesses have recently switched all their bulbs to LED to save energy, reduce costs in the long term and to reflect their aspirations as 'green businesses'. There is very little brand awareness in the light bulb market and all the light bulbs have to fit the standard sockets used in the country.

Electric light bulb manufacture in Skod is dominated by the five companies listed in Table One. Two years ago a large American light bulb manufacturer, Krysal, attempted to enter the market. The five dominant companies in the industry reacted to this by cutting prices, running marketing campaigns which emphasised the benefits to the country of home-based production and lobbying supermarket groups to not stock products produced by the new entrant. Krysal withdrew from the market after six months. When not focused on fighting new entrants, the five main competitors are regularly involved in price cutting, disruption of competitors' distribution channels and aggressive marketing.

Company	Revenue (20X5)	Revenue (20X0)
Voltface	$85m	$80m
LiteWorld	$80m	$80m
Flick	$70m	$65m
ABC	$65m	$60m
L2L	$60m	$60m
Other companies	$140m	$145m
Total	$500m	$490m

Table One: Skod-based light bulb manufacturers

The products produced by the Skod light bulb industry are largely sold through supermarket groups (50%), household product superstores (30%) and large electrical chains (10%). The rest of the production is sold through small shops, except for a tiny percentage of production (less than 1%) which is sold directly to large organisations, such as government departments. However, light bulbs do not constitute a large sales item for any of these distribution channels. In fact, in a recent report, light bulb sales were one of the products which contributed less than 0.1% of a major supermarket's revenue.

The light bulb companies in Skod have largely focused on candescent (60% of production) and halogen (30% of production) technologies. Man Lal intends to fund the updating of the production facilities at Flick to allow the production of LED lights, alongside the continued production of candescent and halogen light bulbs. He wants to achieve this before domestic competitors in Skod gear up their own LED light bulb production. He believes that Ling's competencies in LED manufacture will give Flick a head start. Initial discussions with Flick suggest that the company is open to acquisition and a bid price has been agreed which is acceptable to both parties. Financial information for Flick and the Skod light bulb industry as a whole is shown in Appendix One.

Appendix One: Financial information for Flick and the Skod light bulb industry

Extract from financial statements

All figures in $millions

	Flick 20X5	Skod industry totals 20X5
Assets		
Non-current assets		
Property, plant, equipment	190	1,635
Goodwill	10	100
Total non-current assets	200	1,735
Current assets		
Inventory	45	200
Trade receivables	20	250
Cash and cash equivalents	35	115
Total current assets	100	565
Total assets	300	2,300
Equity and liabilities		
Share capital	150	1,000
Retained earnings	50	340
Non-current liabilities		
Long-term borrowings	70	750
Current liabilities		
Trade payables	29	200
Current tax payable	1	10
Total current liabilities	30	210
Total liabilities	100	960
Total equity and liabilities	300	2,300

Extract from financial statements

All figures in $millions

	Flick 20X5	Skod industry totals 20X5
Revenue	70.0	500.0
Cost of sales	(55.0)	(350.0)
Gross profit	15.0	150.0
Administrative expenses	(4.0)	(30.0)
Profit before tax and interest	11.0	120.0
Finance cost	(2.5)	(50.0)
Profit before tax	8.5	70.0
Tax expense	(1.0)	(12.0)
Profit for the period	7.5	58.0

Note: The Industry total column is for the Skod light bulb industry as a whole (including Flick).

Required:

(a) **Analyse the macro-environmental factors affecting the Skod light bulb industry using a PESTEL framework. Your analysis should reflect the fact that Ling might enter this industry directly by setting up a distribution company for its products or through the acquisition of Flick.** **(7 marks)**

(b) **Assess the attractiveness of the Skod light bulb industry using Porter's Five Forces framework.** **(13 marks)**

(c) Ling is considering entering the Skod light bulb industry by acquiring Flick.

Evaluate the potential acquisition of Flick by Ling from the perspectives of suitability and acceptability. **(18 marks)**

(d) The finance director of Ling is concerned that Ling has no expertise in acquiring foreign companies and he is advocating a strategic partnership with Flick instead.

Discuss the appropriateness of such an approach to facilitating Ling's proposed entry into the Skod light bulb market. **(8 marks)**

Professional marks are available in question 1 for the structure, coherence, style and clarity of your answer. **(4 marks)**

(Total: 50 marks)

Section 3

ANSWERS TO PRACTICE QUESTIONS

STRATEGIC ANALYSIS

1   CTC TELECOMMUNICATION

> 🔑
>
> **Key answer tips**
>
> This is a standard question on objectives and strategic planning. The key is to apply as much as possible to the specific circumstances of CTC.

(a)   The objectives of CTC will have to change for the reasons discussed below.

Shareholder wealth

Before privatisation CTC's main stakeholder was the government of C with the main objective of providing the best service the nation could afford. Income was set by the government to cover resources, so CTC was not expected to do more than breakeven financially.

Now the key stakeholders are shareholders and CTC's primary focus should be to maximise shareholder wealth and be profitable. Objectives will need to be set to support this over-riding objective.

Competition

Before privatisation CTC had the luxury of being a monopolist with the government setting service and price levels. Now the market in C has been opened up to allow foreign competition.

This will force CTC into ensuring that it adopts a marketing orientation and offers a quality service with value for money, or customers will switch to the competition. Objectives will need to be set by reference to market conditions and the actions of competitors.

Customer preferences

Before privatisation CTC had to deliver the best service the country could afford. Now, service levels are determined by what customers are willing to pay for. Some may be prepared to pay higher amounts for additional services, so CTC will need to develop a range of new services and tariffs to meet demand and set corresponding objectives.

CTC's whole approach needs to become more market driven rather than doing the best it could with the allocated resources.

Efficiency

Many state monopolies are inefficient. Given imminent competition and more demanding customers CTC will need to become much more efficient. Firms which have already made such a transition have usually found that radical changes are needed to improve cost control and change the culture of the organisation. Objectives will need to be set regarding cost and efficiency levels.

Resources

Prior to privatisation the level of resources was determined by the government. After privatisation the directors need to attract investors and other financiers and will set resources levels. As a consequence the directors need to consider the key issues for such investors – e.g. risk, growth prospects and so on – and set corporate objectives accordingly.

(b) Suitable strategic objectives for CTC could include the following:

Tutorial note

These objectives should be SMART (Specific, Relevant, Measurable, Achievable, Timescale).

Market share

e.g. 'CTC aims to retain 60% of its domestic market over the next 5 years'.

This is a suitable objective, as market share must be defended from new entrants to ensure that CTC can benefit from economies of scale to be competitive.

Market development

e.g. 'CTC aims to develop other markets so 25% of its revenue is derived from outside C within five years'.

This is a suitable objective, as CTC must look to other markets to ensure future growth and to reduce its risk exposure. These are necessary to increase shareholder value in the long run.

(c) The directors should adopt the rational planning model as a basic framework for future strategic planning. This involves the following steps:

Tutorial note

You should frame your answer around Johnson, Scholes and Whittington's rational model.

---

1 **Strategic analysis**

Strategic analysis essentially involves three aspects:

- CTC should perform external analysis to identify opportunities and threats. In particular, it should assess the risk of new entrants into the industry and perform detailed competitor analysis on potential rivals.

- CTC should also perform internal analysis to determine its own strengths and weaknesses. Weaknesses will need to be rectified in order to be competitive and CTC will need to develop core competences upon which to build strategy.

- and assessing their expectations and power. This should allow CTC to formulate a mission statement and to set strategic objectives for potential strategies.

2 **Strategic choice**

Strategic choice also involves three aspects:

- How to compete – CTC will need to decide whether to compete against new rivals as a cost leader, relying on economies of scale, or as a differentiator offering a higher quality product. The latter seems less likely so a detailed strategy focusing on costs needs to be formulated.

- Where to compete – as well as its domestic market, CTC needs to consider expansion into new markets. This stage will involve identifying the most attractive markets and deciding whether they are worth investing in.

- Choosing the method of expansion – once suitable foreign markets have been identified CTC will need to decide whether to expand via organic growth, acquisition or via a joint arrangement.

3 **Strategy implementation**

Strategy implementation involves the following:

- Translating long-term strategic objectives into detailed tactical and operational targets.

- Setting of detailed budgets and performance appraisal to control the business.

- Ongoing assessment as to whether the plans are on track and, if not, what action needs to be taken to rectify the situation.

- With all of this, CTC should ensure that planning is not a formal once-a-year exercise but an ongoing process where there is the flexibility to allow strategies to emerge in response to a changing market. This effectively blurs the distinction between steps 2 and 3 above, as they happen simultaneously.

2   3C PHARMACEUTICALS

> **Key answer tips**
>
> Part (a) asks for application of the product life cycle to 3C (many students completed a BCG analysis, which was not required!). It is vital that you comment on each product in terms of the overall portfolio and not just in isolation.
>
> In part (b) it is again vital that your comments concerning each option are put in the context of the impact on the portfolio as a whole.
>
> In part (c) ensure that you discuss each option, explain why there is an ethical issue and conclude.

(a)   The product life cycle model classifies products into four main phases:

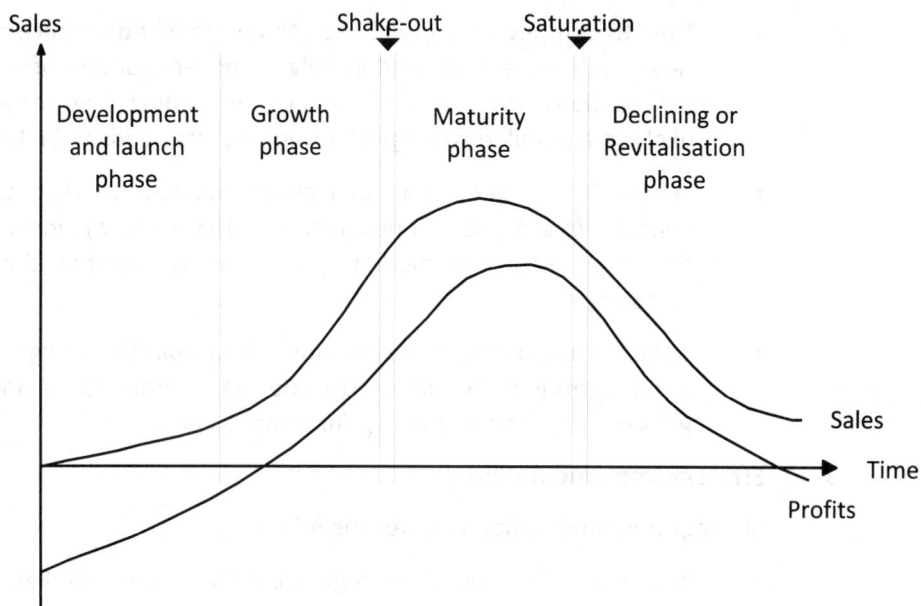

The model is normally used to assess the overall balance of the portfolio with respect to:

- Growth – e.g. new products replacing those at the end of the life cycle.

- Cash flow – e.g. positive cash flows from some products can help finance those that are currently cash negative.

- Other resource requirements.

- Risk – e.g. having some stable low risk products to compensate for other high risk ones.

The model can be applied to 3C as follows:

- The 240 drugs at various stages of development, either being tested or undergoing clinical trials, all of these fall into the 'development and launch' phase of the product life cycle. While being a significant drain on company resources, they are an essential part of the portfolio as they are needed to ensure the firm's future profitability by replacing older drugs that have come to the end of their life cycles.

- Epsilon is at the end of the 'growth' phase and is entering 'maturity', as high sales revenue growth has come to an end. As such it should be a net cash generator to help finance other products in the portfolio that are currently cash negative. However, it will not contribute to future growth.

- Beta is at the latter stages of the 'development and launch' phase as significant growth in sales revenue has yet to occur. As such it is unlikely to have reached breakeven sales revenue and is still a drain on the firm's resources.

- Alpha is coming to the end of the 'maturity' phase and will be entering 'decline' in 12 months' time when patent protection expires and generic copies flood the market. At present it is likely to be cash positive, helping to finance product development but will neither contribute to cash flow nor future growth beyond the next year.

Overall the portfolio is reasonably balanced in terms of future growth potential and cash flow. Beyond the next year it is vital that Beta becomes cash positive and further products move from development to launch.

(b) The three options will affect the portfolio as follows:

Alpha2

Alpha2 has already completed clinical trials so is ready to launch. This would effectively allow the patent protection for Alpha to be extended a further five years, preventing Alpha from entering the decline phase and lengthening the maturity phase.

This should prevent the portfolio from becoming unbalanced with respect to cash flow as the revised Alpha2 will generate cash to finance other products in the portfolio. It will also reduce the risk of the portfolio as sales revenue for Alpha2 will be more certain than estimated returns for other products currently in development.

Beta

Investing in a marketing campaign for Beta would move it into the growth phase and improve the immediate growth prospects of the portfolio.

However, the presence of a close substitute in the market increases the risks attached to Beta and may result in lower growth than expected and even delay Beta breaking even as extra funds would be required to establish Beta ahead of its rival. In the short term Beta may place greater demands on the portfolio cash flow rather than helping it.

Gamma

If Gamma completes the final clinical trials successfully, then it will quickly move from development and launch into the growth stage. Even if prices are set at a high level, expected demand should result in very high growth, improving the overall growth balance of the portfolio. However, there is no guarantee that Gamma will be successful and, on balance, this is the most risky option presented.

The impact on overall portfolio cash flow will depend, to some extent, on the price set and the sales volumes generated. If Gamma truly is a breakthrough product then a high price and a high sales volume might both be available, though there is a risk that some resource-limited countries might produce generic copies of the drug before the patent ends.

Recommendation

On balance, investing in Alpha2 appears to offer the safest way to balance the portfolio in terms of cash flow whereas Gamma offers the highest growth and profit potential. The final decision will depend on the risk aversion of the directors.

(c) Social responsibility is the idea that an organisation should behave responsibly in the interests of the society in which it operates.

The social responsibility implications of the three options given are as follows:

Alpha2

Extending the patent in the way described would delay competitors producing cheap generic copies. The ethical argument here is that, if 3C invests, then customers would not have access to cheaper pain killers so, in effect, 3C is increasing the pain of many sufferers.

However, there are many alternative pain killers on the market, including generic drugs, so the comparison is really between cheap pain relief and more expensive but better pain relief.

Beta

The ethical position with Beta is the other way round – one could argue that 3C has a moral duty to invest in Beta as this will increase the availability of drugs dealing with serious infection. However, if 3C does not invest in Beta, then there are equivalent drugs on the market for patients and hospitals are likely to prioritise such treatments anyway. What investment in Beta is likely to achieve is a fall in the price of such drugs due to extra competition. It could be argued that this should allow health trusts' funds to go further, thus treating more patients.

Gamma

The situation with Gamma is very different. Millions of people around the world are infected with HIV/AIDS and, although progress is being made with anti-retroviral drugs, Gamma would be a major step forward in treatment.

A separate ethical issue is the price that 3C should charge for Gamma. Selling Gamma at the lowest price possible would ensure greater access to sufferers, particularly in poorer countries in Africa where the situation is at its worst. A high price would effectively exclude such people from treatment.

There is thus a major ethical conflict between the higher profits that 3C could earn for its shareholders verses increased treatment for people in the developing world. While it could be argued that 'the business of business is business' and that it is up to governments to make funds available to pay for drugs, the ethical argument here is compelling.

Conclusion

On ethical grounds further investment should be put into Gamma. In fact, the key ethical argument against investing in Alpha2 or Beta is that they preclude investment in Gamma. The pricing issue is more complex.

3   ICOM

🔑

Key answer tips

This question is relatively short and straightforward and a lot more marks than usual could have been achieved for simple knowledge regurgitation rather than higher skilled application.

This question included what at the time was a new syllabus area of integrated reporting so candidates will have needed to be aware of the recent syllabus changes. However, it will have been difficult to apply this to the scenario and most of the marks would have been gained for a simple regurgitation of knowledge. The remainder of the question focused on goal setting (through the mission and CSFs) which relied on a simple knowledge of the link between areas such as CSFs and KPIs.

(a)   A mission statement defines the overriding direction and purpose of an organisation. Some organisations also have vision statements stating what the company aspires to. However, for the purpose of this answer, vision and mission are perceived as the same thing.

Most organisations have settled into an approach where a short snappy statement is supported by a much deeper description of what the organisation is about, its stakeholders and how it wishes to interact with those stakeholders.

The current mission statement of ICOM 'Simply the best in operations management' is a slogan and says nothing about who it is the best for. John Turvey's suggested replacement is much more specific, identifying the external stakeholders it is serving (members and student members) and, importantly, valuing the internal stakeholders (the staff) who will service and inspire the external stakeholders. This more specific statement should allow the organisation to tie the mission statement in with critical success factors. However, it could retain the current mission statement as a broad statement, using John Turvey's suggested replacement as a supplementary description of what the organisation is about.

Critical success factors (CSFs) are the things which the organisation must be good at to succeed. They are the few key areas where things must go right for the business to flourish. Some writers take a more limiting view. Johnson, Scholes and Whittington believe that CSFs are the product features which are particularly valued by a group of customers and, therefore, where the organisation must excel to outperform its competition.

John Turvey has identified 35 CSFs, which seems more than a few key areas and may lead to a lack of focus on the truly critical areas. He may need to reduce these in order to ensure success in a few key areas.

To satisfy our members seems a reasonable CSF, as it aligns directly with the mission statement.

To achieve a growth in membership by 5% year on year for the next five years is not necessarily something which the members themselves will value, unless it brings added benefits to them. Furthermore, CSFs should not have specific time-bound targets associated with them.

The need to maximise profits within acceptable risk is not acknowledged in the mission statement, but it is a given of most commercial organisations.

To ensure that the syllabus reflects the current operations environment is also aligned to the mission statement's desire to inspire student members

However, it is noticeable that there are no CSFs mentioned which are associated with staff and their motivation, despite the inclusion of this commitment in the mission statement.

Key performance indicators (KPIs) are the measurements used to monitor the achievement of the CSFs. They suggest how a CSF should be measured, but they do not include the measurement itself.

The only correctly expressed KPI is the third one (ROCE and the margin of safety). The ROCE will provide an indication of the efficient use of capital in generating profit. The risk taken is measured by the margin of safety which shows how far the current income would have to fall to result in a breakeven situation. Notice that neither the ROCE nor the margin of safety are given specific values. These specific values will be given in performance objectives which relate to defined timeframes. This allows the KPI to remain the same, but the performance objective can change.

The first suggested KPI can be improved by omitting the 95% target. At present, it is a mix between a KPI and a performance objective. An appropriate KPI would be 'the percentage of members rating us as excellent in an externally administered customer satisfaction survey'.

KPIs should be quantifiable, such that they can be compared to a standard or target, or an alternative performance, such as a prior year, or a competitor. There is no real quantifiable comparator for the other two suggested KPIs. For example, the KPI 'recruit an examinations manager to rewrite the syllabus' will either happen, or it will not. This KPI, and the KPI to implement a vigorous marketing campaign are really just actions, not KPIs.

Again, there is no key performance indicator associated with internal staff and their motivation.

(b)   Benchmarking is where one organisation compares its performance in a specific area to another organisation, the benchmark, to identify how much room there is for improvement. It then attempts to implement improved practices to narrow the gap between its own performance and the performance of the benchmark. In the context of the scenario, benchmarks might be used to improve the student recruitment process. Improving this process should help the company achieve CSFs and KPIs associated with student membership. For example, increasing the number of students registering with ICOM.

There are two main approaches to benchmarking which are relevant here:

- Competitive benchmarking within the same industry. In this case ICOM would benchmark itself against OMI. However, it may be that competitor information is not available or that competitors use different measurement techniques, providing an invalid comparison. Concerning student recruitment, comparative information is available. However, there is likely to be an absence of supporting information. ICOM cannot be sure how OMI has actually achieved a growth of 27% in student members. ICOM can benchmark its growth against OMI, but it has no insight into how OMI is achieving this growth, so it does not know what it needs to put in place to improve its student recruitment performance. The use of a percentage as a benchmark also needs comment. OMI's increase might be based on a much lower starting level and the percentage increase might not be a usable benchmark for ICOM.

- External functional benchmarking where a particular function (such as student recruitment) is compared with that function in the organisation which performs it best, regardless of what industry the company is in. Non-competing organisations are more likely to share data than competitors. For example, an accountancy institute might be prepared to share membership recruitment information with ICOM. However, given that the comparator will be in a different industry, the competitive situation might be quite different and this reduces the usefulness of the comparison. For example, competitors might act differently and rules for student membership may be dissimilar. However, with external functional benchmarking it is more likely that the comparator will not only share results, but also the process which has achieved these results. This will give important information to ICOM about what it needs to put in place to improve its performance.

(c) 'An integrated report is a concise communication about how an organisation's strategy, governance, performance and prospects lead to the creation of value over the short, medium and long term' (IIRC draft framework, April 2013).

Financial reports have long been part of business culture. The content, structure and rules for constructing these reports are still important. For most organisations, growth and profitability are still significant goals and this is reflected in the CSFs and KPIs of ICOM. Here, profitability will be measured by the ROCE and the ROCE will either be explicitly stated in the company's financial report or can be calculated from the provided financial data.

However, the development of approaches such as the balanced business scorecard has prompted companies to set performance measures in non-financial areas, such as customer satisfaction and process efficiency. However, within the normal financial reporting framework, there is no place for the company to report its progress (or lack of it) in these important non-financial areas.

The integrated report provides the opportunity for the organisation to restate its mission and how its strategy addresses this mission. Central to this will be a discussion of the CSFs and the KPIs which have been identified to measure business performance. KPIs will have associated performance objectives which can be reported in the integrated report.

Thus, the report not only restates the KPI and its associated performance objective, it also reports on whether that performance objective has been met and, if it has not, discusses reasons for failure and the actions which are being taken to ensure that this objective is met in the next reporting period. For example, it is in the integrated report where ICOM will report on its efforts to meet certain customer satisfaction targets and student recruitment targets. If it fails to meet these targets, then it will explain how this failure is being addressed.

However, an integrated report should be more than a summary of information from other communications; it should explicitly connect the information to communicate how value is created. Thus current and potential stakeholders should have better information about the future value of the organisation in which they are interested. Through a restatement of the mission statement, stakeholders will also have the direction and purpose of the organisation emphasised and re-affirmed.

ACCA Marking scheme		
		Marks
(a)	(a) Up to 1 mark for each appropriate point up to a maximum of	15
(b)	Up to 1 mark for each appropriate point up to a maximum of	5
(c)	Up to 1 mark for each appropriate point up to a maximum of	5
		—
Total		**20**
		—

Examiner's comments

In part (a) a number of candidates provided a good answer to this question, showing a clear understanding of what was required. The majority of candidates showed some knowledge of the qualities of a good mission statement and were able to apply this knowledge. Some candidates, however, drifted from the requirements of the question and went on to discuss how the CSFs could be achieved and the how to gather the data to measure the KPIs rather than respond to the question asked.

In part (b) the majority of candidates scored well on this question. Some candidates failed to obtain the marks for applying their knowledge to the scenario in question.

Part (c) was poorly answered and, indeed, not answered by a significant number of candidates. Integrated reporting has been embedded into the ACCA syllabus and candidates need to be aware of the principles and its application across the different areas of the qualification. There have also been a couple of articles in the Student Accountant on the subject, one specific to P3 and published shortly before the examination.

4   SWIFT   *Online question assistance*

Key answer tips

In part (a), when performing the analysis you should ensure that you include both financial measures *and* non-financial measures. Try to take a structured approach to your answer by using a strategic model – the answer uses the Johnson, Scholes and Whittington tests for evaluating a strategy, but other models such as the BCG matrix or Ashbridge portfolio display would also have been appropriate and scored marks.

In part (b) you need to have knowledge of Porter's diamond and be able to apply it to the scenario. This is not a commonly examined area, but this should reinforce the need for broad syllabus knowledge that is needed in order to pass this paper.

(a)   The acquisition of EVM can be analysed using the success criteria of *suitability, acceptability and feasibility.*

Suitability is concerned with whether a strategy addresses the issues identified when considering the strategic position of the company. In general terms the acquisition appears to make sense. The market is mature and competitive in Ambion, pushing down margins. These margins are further eroded by a government that is hostile to road transport resulting in high taxation on fuel, road taxes linked to carbon emission and restricted working practices.

The acquisition of EVM provides an opportunity for Swift to exploit their core competencies in a different geographical market where demand is rising, the national government is investing in road infrastructure and competition is immature. The increased size of the group will further allow Swift to exploit economies of scale when purchasing trucks and other equipment.

Concerns around suitability surround the potential clash of cultures between Swift and EVM. Swift has no experience of acquiring or running foreign companies. It has no experience of trading in Ecuria. Furthermore, although EVM is now in private hands, it may be possible that the work practices and expectations of employees may still reflect the time when they were working for the central government. Although altering these practices may give scope for even greater profitability, it may lead to labour disputes that harm the service and reputation of the company. Swift wishes to acquire this company and adopt the practices, principles and technology of the Ambion operation. This may lead to conflict that they may find hard to resolve.

Acceptability is concerned with the expected performance of a strategy in terms of return, risk and stakeholder reactions.

Return: EVM delivers a very similar (18%) Return on Capital Employed (ROCE) to Swift Transport. This appears to be a strong performance for the sector, and should certainly be acceptable to the Swift shareholders. The gross profit margin (20%) is higher than Swift, but the net profit margin (7.5%) is lower. This may support some of the concerns discussed under suitability. The company may still be carrying high costs from its days as a nationalised company. Swift presumably believes that it can improve the net profit margin by implementing competences gained in the Ambion market.

Risk: Both the current liquidity ratio (1.14%) and the acid test ratio (1.05%) are lower than the Swift equivalents and Swift will need to look at this. The introduction of Swift's practices may help reduce trade payables. The gearing ratio (30%) for EVM is much lower than Swift and perhaps reflects a more conservative approach to long-term lending and a reflection of the fledgling capital markets in the country. However, the interest cover ratio (5) is half that of Swift, perhaps reflecting lower profitability and higher business taxation.

Stakeholders: Joe Swift and his family are the major stakeholders in what is still a family-run private limited company. It is unlikely that there will be any opposition to the acquisition from shareholders. However, stakeholders such as drivers might be wary of this strategy and also the government, outspokenly criticised by Joe, may also respond in some way. For example, by imposing taxation on foreign investment.

Feasibility is about whether an organisation has the resources and competencies to deliver the strategy. It appears that Swift does, as funds are in place and the competences are what are partly driving the acquisition.

(b)   In his book *The Competitive Advantage of Nations,* Michael Porter suggests that there are inherent reasons why some nations are more competitive than others, and also why some industries within nations are more competitive than others. He suggests that the national home base of the organisation plays an important role in creating international advantage, something that will be very important to Joe Swift. He identifies four main determinants of national advantage and arranges these as a diamond, with each of these determinants interacting with and reinforcing each other. Two further determinants, chance and government, are discussed outside of the diamond in terms of how they influence and interact with the determinants inside the diamond. This model answer uses Porter's diamond as its basis. However, credit will also be given to candidates who use an alternative appropriate framework or model.

The four main determinants are:

The nation's position in *factor conditions,* such as skilled labour or infrastructure, necessary for firms to compete in a given industry. The acknowledged work ethic of the people and the investment in transport infrastructure by the government are significant factor conditions in Ecuria.

The nature of the home *demand conditions* for the industry's product or service. Home demand influences economies of scale, but it also shapes the rate and character of improvement and innovation. In Ecuria, the move to a market economy has stimulated a rapid growth in the transport of goods. The Ecurian people are traditionally demanding in their standards. They have a passion for precision and promptness and this has shaped the operations of EVM.

The presence or absence of *related and supporting industries* that are internationally competitive. Competitive advantage in certain industries confers potential advantages on firms in other industries. Porter suggests that the 'Swiss success in pharmaceuticals was closely connected to previous international success in the dye industry'. There is no evidence in the case study that Ecuria has internationally competitive industries related to logistics. Hence, it is the absence of these that is significant when considering this determinant.

The final determinant is *firm* strategy, *structure and rivalry.* This concerns the conditions in the nation governing how companies are created, organised and managed. It also considers the nature of domestic rivalry. EVM was created by nationalising the state-run haulage system. For the first few years of operation it had few competitors. The nature of the capital markets makes it very difficult to raise finance in Ecuria. Consequently, most of EVM's competitors are small, family-run companies who offer a local service. Porter suggests that there is a strong relationship between vigorous domestic rivalry and the creation and persistence of competitive advantage in an industry. There is little evidence of this emerging in Ecuria.

Porter also recognises the influence of chance and government. Chance events are developments outside the control of firms and the nation's government. Wars, external political developments and a reduction in foreign demand are all examples of chance factors. Government, in effect, helps shape the diamond by enacting policies that influence each of the determinants. In Ecuria, the government's approach to infrastructure investment and policies towards capital markets has affected factor conditions and impacted on firm structure and rivalry.

ACCA Marking scheme		
		Marks
(a)	1 mark for each relevant point up to a maximum of 15 marks.	15
(b)	1 mark for each relevant point up to a maximum of 10 marks.	10
		—
Total		**25**
		—

5   BOWLAND

Key answer tips

Part (a) of the question can be split into three parts – what are Bowland's existing competencies, what are the key success factors needed in retailing, and do these two things match up. So a good approach would be to split your time evenly between all three elements.

For part (b) an external analysis is normally a combination of both the PESTEL and 5 Forces models, but with only 15 marks available (and working on the basis of two marks per well explained point) you do not have to cover every element. So if, for example, you can't determine any relevant 'Technological' issues then just leave this factor out.

(a)   An organisation's **distinctive competences** are those things which an organisation does particularly well. They include the organisation's unique resources and capabilities as well as its strengths and its ability to overcome weaknesses. These competences can include aspects such as budgetary control, a strong technology base, a culture conducive to change and marketing skills.

Key success factors are those requirements which it is essential to have if one is to survive and prosper in a chosen industry/environment. These can include areas such as good service networks, up-to-date marketing intelligence and tight cost controls where margins are small.

It is not guaranteed that the distinctive competences and the key success factors are always in alignment. A company moving into the retail sector may have an excellent product research and development capability, but this alone will not help if it has no concept of service or poorly sited retail outlets. It is critical to ensure that what the company excels at is what is needed to be successful in that particular area.

The **strengths of Bowland Carpets** include **strong brand names** which maintain integrity within the different market segments where the company operates. The company has a **balanced portfolio of customers** and the **range of products is equally balanced**, ensuring that any sectorial decline can be compensated for by growth in other markets. Other strengths which the company currently has include a **good relationship with distributors and strong support from a powerful parent company**. Some of its distinctive competences, such as a strong brand and a reasonable range of products, are critical in the proposed new environment, as will be the financial support of the parent company. However there are some aspects which are cause for concern in the proposed new business environment.

The strength in the contract and industrial carpet segment will not be affected by the proposed vertical integration – sales tend to be through direct sales force. The strong **relationship with distributors** will however be **jeopardised by the opening up of retail outlets**. Other retail chains will be unwilling to permit a rival to operate so freely, and therefore there will be a reluctance to stock Bowland Carpets. Unless Bowland Carpets can obtain wide retail market coverage to compensate for this potential problem, sales revenue will be adversely affected. The **cost of developing extensive market coverage** will be enormous and whether it is in High Street outlets or specialist out-of-town centres the investment may be greater than the parent company has budgeted for. The company also has **no expertise in site appraisal and selection**. Although the newly-structured value chain will generate greater control there is an associated **lack of flexibility** along with an **increase in the fixed cost base** of the business.

Another key success factor is the **need for expertise in retailing**. It may be that the UK company can import this from the USA but the culture of marketing household durables may not be transferable internationally. Bowland Carpets as the domestic company has no experience in this field.

A critical factor in successful retailing is the ability to provide a **comprehensive range of products**. Does Bowland Carpets have one? It is unlikely that the competitive carpet manufacturers will provide such a supply to one of their rivals.

It would, therefore, appear that there is no close conformity between the distinctive competences of Bowland Carpets and the key success factors required in the carpet retailing sector.

(b) The **external environment** scan is an essential prerequisite prior to selecting a strategic option. It enables the company to identify and understand the key external and uncontrollable influences which will have an impact upon the company's strategy. The environment is increasingly turbulent and often hostile. Without this knowledge and appreciation the strategist will be operating in a mine-field. The acquisition of the external information is obtained by scanning the environment continuously and monitoring key indicators which should enable the company to position itself appropriately with respect to the external environment and the competition. The external scan should be structured around a SLEPT framework covering the following environments – social, legal, economic, political and technological. In addition it is also important to assess potential competitive reactions as part of the scanning process.

The environmental scan will influence the decision as to whether Bowland Carpets should concentrate on the UK or seek diversification elsewhere, either in products or markets. Possible factors are as follows:

- **Social issues**: Trends towards increasing car-centred shopping (superstores and out-of-town sites) or movements back to city centre shopping: trends in fashion and furnishing – will carpets become a fashion item and result in greater replacement sales? Other factors of importance to Bowland include the rate of growth or decline in populations and changes in the age distribution of the population. In the UK there will be an increasing proportion of the national population over retirement age. In developing countries there are very large numbers of young people. Rising standards of living lead to increased demand for certain types of goods. This is why developing countries are attractive to markets.

- **Legal issues**: Laws in the UK differ from the US. They come from common law, parliamentary legislation and government regulations derived from it, and obligations under EU membership and other treaties Legal factors that can influence decisions include aspects of employment law, e.g. minimum wage, laws to protect consumers and tax legislation. The monopoly/competition issues in this case are likely to be insignificant.

- **Economic issues**: An increased concentration for Bowland Carpets within the UK economy will depend upon future economic prospects, taxation policy (sales tax) and interest rates, income distribution and unemployment (influencing site location), trade barriers (cheap imports from Third World suppliers, or even low-cost tufted carpets from countries such as Belgium).

- **Political issues**: Government policy affects the whole economy and governments are responsible for enforcing and creating a stable framework in which business can be done. The quality of government policy is important in providing physical infrastructure, e.g. transport, social infrastructure, e.g. education and market infrastructure, e.g. planning and site development – town centre or out-of-town developments.

- **Technological issues**: is retailing technology evolutionary or revolutionary? Will it be costly or labour-saving? Will inventory control be facilitated so saving costs? Technology contributes to overall economic growth. It can increase total output with gains in productivity, reduced costs and new types of product. It influences the way in which markets are identified – database systems make it much easier to analyse the market place. Information technology encourages de-layering of organisational hierarchies and better communications.

- **Competitive issues**: It will be necessary to assess the likely responses of both carpet distributors and carpet manufacturers to the proposed incursion by Bowland Carpets. Will the reactions be benign or will they be aggressive?

6   MCGEORGE HOLDINGS PLC

Key answer tips

The question clearly states that you should use more than one model in part (a). Two of the most widely used models refer to the **product life cycle** and the **Boston Consulting Group (BCG) growth-share matrix**. It is on these two that this suggested answer will concentrate.

For part (b) you should aim to cover a range of benchmarking methods and remember that the question wants you to also cover the limitations of benchmarking.

(a)   It is obvious that McGeorge Holdings plc has allowed its range of products to grow without too much regard to the overall efficiency and effectiveness of the product spread. It is required that a more rational approach should be taken so as to rationalise the product portfolio.

The **product life cycle** can be used to assess where each of the products is located. Some products, in their *introductory stage*, may not be contributing well to overall profits because of initial research and market development costs, but they may, in the future, provide a regular stream of income to the company. Those in the *growth stage* should already be profit providers. It is in the later stages of the life cycle that close attention needs to be paid to products. In the *maturity/saturation stages* it may be prudent to assess whether there is any long-term future in the products. Would investment in alternative products be more sensible? This question is more critical when one investigates products in the *decline stage*. One has to decide if withdrawing these products might be wise. Products can still be profitable in the decline stage, particularly if competitors are exiting the market faster than market demand is falling. It is also important to assess how these products contribute to the overall performance of the company. Maybe withdrawing from a given line might alienate key customers. The products may also provide a complementary range and withdrawal from one area may adversely affect other product sales. If one withdraws certain products are there others which consumers can turn to or must they seek products from key competitors? It is also important to assess how costs such as marketing, distribution and even manufacturing have been allocated. The withdrawal of certain products could result in others having to share and carry higher costs, so making them price uncompetitive. One must not rush into product rationalisation programmes without considering the consequences of such an action.

The **BCG growth-share matrix** examines the inter-relationships between market share and market growth of given products. It assesses resource generation alongside resource needs. The '*cash-cow*' is described as such because products in this category (low growth and high market share) are usually very profitable and generate surplus funds, and so are often used to finance other developments. Such products are not recommended for deletion.

The '*stars*' generate high revenues because the products have high market shares, but because the market is growing fast such products need to be invested in heavily to maintain their position. These are unlikely to be highly profitable as yet, but decisions to withdraw such products should be rejected. It is likely that such products will become more profitable as market growth stabilises. Today's stars will usually become tomorrow's cash cows.

The *'problem child'* or *'question mark'* product is probably currently losing money. A prognosis needs to be made of future movements. Can the product achieve a significant share of the market? If the answer is 'Yes' then the product may proceed to become a 'star' and later a 'cash cow'. However if there are considerable doubts then the product may have to be withdrawn. It is often assumed that *'dogs'* – those products with low market share and low growth potential should be withdrawn from the market place. However some 'dogs' are known as 'cash dogs'. They occupy a niche position and are still capable of returning a profit. If this is the case, then they can be persevered with until they have little to offer the company. However true 'dogs' need to be eradicated. They consume too much management time and money. These need to be focused on present and future winners.

Adrian Reed needs to be careful which products to remove from the portfolio. Some rationalisation will be needed but this should be carried out carefully and not rushed into.

(b) **'Benchmarking'** the McGeorge organisation will enable Adrian Reed to assess in which areas the performance of his company falls short of that of his competitors and can help determine what action needs to be taken to correct any adverse findings.

There are several ways in which benchmarking can be carried out. **Internal benchmarking** can compare different units within McGeorge Holdings plc. Some centres may be more proficient than others and a transfer of knowledge and skills could be beneficial to the group as a whole. **Competitive benchmarking** attempts to compare products, processes and results and show where the company is failing with reference to those of competitors. The difficulty here is accessing confidential data of competitors. They are not going to make it easy for McGeorge by providing them with this information. **Customer benchmarking** attempts to compare corporate performance with the performance expected by customers. How far is there a gap between expected performance and actual? **Generic benchmarking** compares similar business functions between companies operating in different industries. For example how do financial results – gearing, liquidity, etc. compare in differing industrial sectors? **Process or activity benchmarking** attempts to identify the current best practice within an organisation (regardless of sector) for activities such as manufacturing, engineering or human resource management. Then this best practice can be imported into the McGeorge organisation, assuming compatibility.

There are a number of limitations associated with benchmarking. Can relevant data be obtained to make any comparison meaningful? Some of the comparisons may be meaningless. Circumstances between firms, environments and products all differ so making a comparison appear like comparing 'apples with oranges'. The process can appear to be an historical exercise. The world moves on and what was acceptable yesterday may be out of date tomorrow. Furthermore there is an implicit assumption that there is an optimum solution. A process can be efficient but does it add value – is it effective? It is possible that distribution costs can be reduced to almost zero by distributing nothing. Is this solution useful? If benchmarking concentrates on efficiency, ignoring effectiveness, then it is missing its purpose.

Reed could use benchmarking to assess the performance of the company, but this needs to be implemented carefully and results must be analysed critically without snap judgements being made.

7 NESTA

> **Key answer tips**
>
> Based on recent exam history, this is an area that students should perform well in. However, part (b) covers scenario planning – an area that students are likely to be less familiar with. The key to success is to identify the key influences in possible future scenarios (such as potential competitor responses to a new market entrant) and consider how this might impact on market attractiveness. But students are likely to need a strong mark in part (a) of this question in order to score well overall.

(a) NESTA has identified the growth of discount fixed-price stores in Eurobia and is considering entering the marketplace. The long economic recession in Eurobia has led to the increased popularity of these so-called 'dollar shops', where all goods and products are priced at $1·00. Most of these shops are on the high streets of towns and cities where there is particular financial hardship. NESTA has expertise in running such shops in Eyanke. The company is well-known within the retail trade of Eurobia, but it is largely unknown to the domestic consumers of the country. Only 5% of those polled recognised the NESTA brand.

The *bargaining power of NESTA* appears to be very strong. There are several factors that contribute to this:

- The products supplied by the supplier earn a relatively low profit margin for the buyer. Low profits provide a great incentive to buyers to pursue lower purchasing costs.

- Switching costs are relatively low as the products are largely unbranded commodity goods. The buyer should find it relatively easy to switch supplier.

- The purchased products are standard and undifferentiated. Buyers should always find it relatively easy to find alternative suppliers and can play companies off against each other in their search for better prices and other terms of supply.

- The products purchased from suppliers represent a significant fraction of the buyer's cost. Buying is price sensitive and the company is likely to spend a great deal of effort trying to ensure the best terms of supply.

- Purchasing companies are fewer and larger than potential suppliers. Suppliers may have alternative customers but their scope is limited. In contrast, the buying companies have many smaller supplying companies competing for their business.

Supplying companies are fragmented and the fixed-price discount channel represents a significant customer group. None of the suppliers appears to offer a credible threat of *forward integration* whereby they might become competitors of their current customers. From NESTA's perspective their high bargaining power is an attractive aspect of the discount fixed-price channel in Eurobia. Furthermore, effective purchasing systems, supplier selection and excellent logistics are perceived as core strengths of NESTA. There is a good match between the nature of the market and the core competencies of NESTA.

Within Eurobia there are currently three dominant competitors. The three fixed-price discount chains compete on profit margins (the target price is fixed at $1), on brand name and on expanding the number of outlets in the chain. The *intensity of the rivalry amongst existing competitors* is largely caused by their ambitious expansion plans. Apparently, few weeks go by without one of the companies announcing plans to extend their chain of shops. It is likely that a new arrival into the market will be *resisted,* particularly when it is a potential entrant as well-known (in the retail market) as NESTA. Resistance will probably be through tightened supplier contracts (better prices, agreement not to supply competitors), increased marketing and rapid store expansion. However, evidence from Table One also suggests that the market sector is continuing to grow. Year on year growth in the last two years has been around 13%, in an economy that is in recession. In such circumstances, companies competing in the market can continue to improve their results simply by keeping up with industry performance. It gives all competitors greater breathing space. Furthermore, perhaps the arrival of NESTA in the market may help grow the market (by giving it greater legitimacy) and by NESTA exploiting geographical areas not yet comprehensively served by existing competitors.

The main *barriers to entry* to any potential entrant is the capital required to rent, stock and staff the number of stores required to realise the required economies of scale and to establish a credible market presence. It appears that NESTA has both the capital and expertise, particularly as the economic recession has led to reduced shop rents and greater shop availability. Furthermore, possible *exit costs* have also been reduced by the willingness of landlords to consider short fixed-term leases. NESTA's main problem could be quickly establishing a brand name in a country where it is relatively unknown (5% awareness), and competing with three incumbents who are very well known. The survey showed that all three established brands were recognised by more than 90% of the consumers in Eurobia. Finally, there may also be barriers to entry erected by the government to prevent foreign companies opening.

The threat of *substitute products* is probably best considered in terms of alternative channels of supply. The scenario notes that the large supermarkets do supply ambient goods, but have so far resisted competing on price. They are differentiating through product (a wider range of branded goods) and through place (providing the convenience of purchasing a wide range of other goods, including food, in one location). Their sheer scale may mean that they have been willing to overlook the discount fixed-price market niche up to now. The largest discount fixed-price company has revenue of $330m, a fraction of the size of the largest supermarket group ($42,500m). However, the arrival of NESTA, an established global player, in the market may change the dynamic and cause the established supermarkets to take another look.

The supply of ambient goods is also well-suited to the internet and the growth of internet-based competitors has to be considered. The current market is firmly based around high street shopping. The internet might be a substitute channel, and indeed might be considered by NESTA as a way of differentiating itself on its entry into the market. The current internet home delivery service offered by the supermarkets is unlikely to be much of a threat as long as they continue to charge a significant fee for using it. It is clearly aimed at a different market segment.

(b) When the business environment is highly uncertain, it may be impossible to develop a single view of how environmental influences might impact on an organisation's strategy. Thus it might be useful for managers to envisage a number of alternative futures. These alternative futures are described in scenarios.

Scenarios are detailed and plausible views of how the business environment might develop in the future, based on different assumptions about key environmental influences and drivers for change within the industry or market itself. It is helpful if the number of influencing factors is *limited to a few significant ones,* so that the analysis does not become too complex. It is also preferable to focus on factors *which are largely out of the control of the organisation.* The organisation can influence its own behaviour and expertise. However, macroeconomic forces in a country are normally well beyond its scope of control. It can react to changes, but not influence them. Indeed, it has been recommended that managers should develop contingency plans (strategies) for each unfolding scenario. Johnson, Scholes and Whittington have also suggested that 'sharing and debating these scenarios improves organisational learning by making managers more perceptive about the forces in the business environment and what is really important'.

In NESTA, scenarios might be developed around four significant factors:

- The continued economic recession in Eurobia. The growth of discount fixed-price shops appears to depend upon continued economic problems. Recovery may lead to consumers shunning such shops. Scenarios might consider the economic situation remaining the same, improving and getting worse.

- The response of established companies in the market-place to NESTA's entry. The response of the incumbents is very difficult to predict. Scenarios might consider a neutral response. The current companies are, after all, relatively small (in retail terms) and inexperienced. A muted response might also be considered (increased marketing, tying in suppliers, more shops) and, alternatively, an aggressive response, perhaps leading to consolidation within the market sector due to takeovers or mergers.

- The attitude of the established supermarkets to the discount, fixed-price market. The conventional supermarkets are currently not competing on price against the discount fixed-price shops. They may continue to do this or they may wish to compete, perhaps by setting up specialised branded outlets or by acquiring one or more of the current significant players, and they have the relative size and economic power to do so.

- The implications of channel change, with customers preferring to shop via the internet. This has been a significant factor in many retail markets.

Scenarios would consider combinations of these factors. For example: economic recovery combined with a muted response from incumbents, together with established supermarkets continuing to ignore the discount, fixed-price niche. The attractiveness of entering the Eurobia market could be considered for each scenario, together with strategies for implementing any proposed entry in to the market.

Statistical information might be used to define and evaluate scenarios. For example, published economic data might assist the managers to define the likelihood of each of the three economic outcomes. Consumer data might help establish a statistical relationship between spending in the market sector and defined economic indicators.

This would help managers predict product demand in different scenarios. NESTA is experienced in the sector (although not in Eurobia) and so managers should have some understanding of the costs and margins of running such shops. This should give them some insight into the likelihood and effect of any responses of the firms currently competing in the Eurobia market.

Scenarios may be underpinned by models which predict the outcome of different scenarios. Random selection methods (Monte Carlo simulations) might be used to generate some of the input data to these models.

ACCA Marking scheme		
		Marks
(a)	1 mark for each relevant point up to a maximum of	15
(b)	1 mark for each relevant point up to a maximum of	10
Total		**25**

Examiner's comments

Candidates scored well in part (a), with some getting full marks. The only slight disappointment here was candidate's reluctance to use the financial data provided in Figure One of the scenario. This data was important because it revealed two things. Firstly, that the three companies in the industry were of a very similar size and, secondly, that the market they were participating in was growing. Both these factors are important when considering the competitive rivalry that exists within the industry and how incumbents are likely to react to the threat of new entrants. It was also clear that a significant number of candidates had not properly interpreted the revenue figures. NESTA is much larger than any of the companies operating in the market place (indeed it is bigger than the combined revenue of the companies). However, some candidates suggested that NESTA was much smaller, apparently confusing $120m with $120,000m. Again this relative size of NESTA and its potential competitors is important to the assessment of the market place and this misinterpretation led candidates astray.

For part (b), it can be argued that the term is commonly used in everyday language. For example; terms such as 'best-case' scenario and 'worst case scenario' are quite often used in television interviews and newspaper articles. However, it was clear that most candidates were unfamiliar with the concept of scenarios, producing answers using a variety of perspectives and frameworks. Porter's diamond, the suitability, feasibility and acceptability criteria and SWOT analysis were just three of the inappropriate approaches used, and all usually resulted in candidates scoring no marks for this part question.

8   ATD

> **Key answer tips**
>
> This question covers quantitative forecasting techniques. This type of question can throw many students who get bogged down in the numbers and in checking calculations rather than explaining them. Students who focus on the requirement and explain what the calculations mean and their relevance to the company in the scenario could score well in this question. Part (b) is much more straightforward and will probably be attempted first by students with better exam technique. Overall, though, success in the question overall is likely to depend on careful reading of the requirement in part (a).

(a)   ATD has been reliant on intuitive estimating, with the sales manager predicting sales from his experience. The company is now evaluating more formal techniques of estimating and a business analyst has produced initial spreadsheets using linear regression and time series analysis. The business analyst has now left the company, leaving his work unexplained.

Figure 1 is a least square analysis of the sales data, defining the equation of a straight line that 'best' fits the data by minimising the squares of deviations of actual values from the mean. In least squares analysis, one set of data is defined as the independent variable (x —— in this case, time) and the other set of data, sales, is defined as y – the dependent variable. From the data presented in Figure 1 the line of best fit is:

$y = 125.022 + 1.84x$

This equation can be used to predict a value for the next quarter (20X3 quarter 3):

$y = 125.022 + 1.84(15)$

$y = 152.62$

The positive value of b suggests that the overall sales trend is upwards.

The correlation coefficient 'r' shows the strength of the statistical relationship between the two variables. In Figure 1 the value of r is 0.253, which suggests that the two variables are weakly connected. The coefficient of determination (r^2) shows that 6.4% of the variation in sales (y) is due to the passage of time (x). Low coefficients of correlation (and determination) are usual when data is widely scattered around the mean and/or are related in a non-linear fashion. Both these factors might be applicable here, particularly due to the pattern caused by large seasonal variations.

At ATD, linear regression appears to be of little practical use. The predicted value for 20X3 quarter 3 appears too low (it is lower than all actual quarter 3 figures to date and much lower than the previous quarter 3 figure of 169). The technique might be more useful if the annual data was plotted (hence eliminating the seasonal variation) or to identify alternative variables which better explained the seasonal variation and to calculate a correlation coefficient between these and the sales data.

Time series analysis uses a moving average to define a trend. In Figure 2, the moving average has been calculated on a quarterly basis, which seems appropriate as this is how the data has been presented. The trend line is calculated from the average of the first two quarters (for example, quarters 1–4 and quarters 2–5) to allow the trend to be centralised against an actual sales value. The difference between the actual values and the trend line is also averaged to produce a seasonal variation. Any difference left between the actual sales value and the seasonally adjusted trend is defined as a residual variation. Figure 2 also shows the seasonally adjusted trend values.

Forecasting future values is achieved by extrapolating the trend line and then adding or subtracting the seasonal variation. There is no agreed way of extrapolating the trend. A scatter graph could be drawn and a trend line drawn by hand. Alternatively, a least square regression of the trend values could be performed to define a line of best fit. Using a 'best guess' approach, a trend value of 149 might be hypothesised for quarter 1 of 20X3, giving a predicted value of 134.3 (149 – 14.7), just below the actual recorded value of 137. Predicted values would also be calculated for subsequent quarters. For example, based on a (hand drawn) trend value of 151, the predicted value for quarter 3 of 20X3 would be 173.55 (151 + 22.55), which subjectively seems much more realistic than the 152.55 suggested by the least squares analysis.

The moving average method also explicitly defines the significant seasonal variations for this product and so reflects these in the predicted values, meaning that production capacity, inventory levels and resource purchase requirements are sensitive to the fluctuating demand. The high residual variation in 20X2 quarter 4 probably needs some investigation. It is possible that demand is falling faster than might be expected and this will have important consequences for estimated sales figures.

One of the problems of both techniques is that forecasts are based on past data. Sudden changes in the market will not be immediately reflected in the forecasts. Thus there may still be a role for the sales manager to use his experience, intuition and judgement to amend the forecasts produced by the statistical analysis.

Finally, of the two approaches presented here, time series analysis seems the most appropriate technique for sales forecasting at ATD.

(b)   A budget is essentially a short-term business plan. It is usually expressed in financial terms and it serves as a mechanism for converting the long-term plan and objectives of the company into an actionable blueprint for the near future, usually the next year. Most businesses have sales ambitions and it is the achievement of these that drive many budgets. At ATD, like in many organisations, the ability to sell sufficient products is the main problem. Setting and achieving sales targets, both in terms of volume and price, is a preoccupation, and in most organisations it is the limiting factor that the budgetary system is based around. In such circumstances, the sales budget is the first budget to be prepared as it determines the overall business activity for the forthcoming period. It is the level of sales that determines inventory requirements, production capacity, raw material purchases, etc. At ATD, the sales forecast not only determines the level of activity but also the pattern of that activity, with seasonal variations that will have to be taken into account in other activities. Such seasonal variations might reveal other limiting factors, such as production capacity or inventory storage space and these would have to be investigated and policies determined.

Budgets should allow proper, realistic targets to be set not only for sales but also for functions where there is clear accountability (such as production management and inventory management). Targets need to be rigorous and achievable. They also need to be connected to clear organisational demarcation where targets are under the control of a manager who has responsibility for that target. Thus budgeting should improve forecasting through requiring a rigorous and collectively responsible process. Flexing the budget would allow the performance of parts of the organisation to be assessed in the context of missed sales targets. For example, an analysis might reveal that the production manager has reduced target raw material costs even though lower sales volumes mean that overall revenue targets have not been met. At present, the production manager is frustrated because he feels that he is working 'tirelessly to keep costs down, but my only reward is that I cannot replace one of my best purchasing administrators who left last month'. However, we only have his assertion about his ability to keep costs down. With a flexed budget, the business can actually see if he has effectively controlled costs. Flexed budgets and their associated variances provide an important insight into how different functions or departments (and their managers) are actually performing.

There is also significant evidence to suggest that departmental managers will be motivated if they are required to strive to achieve targets that they themselves have helped set, fostering a sense of ownership and commitment. This would help address the managers' feelings of powerlessness and the sense that they are undervalued. Their morale should improve as they see their experience and opinions valued. Benefits should also accrue for the organisation as a whole. As knowledge from different departments is pooled, understanding, target setting and co-ordination should be improved due to the number of different departments involved in budget setting.

Because budgets include planning, feedback and control elements, they offer important insights into how an organisation should react to failed sales targets. The response of the CEO has been to take general measures which appear, on the face of it, to offer immediate savings, but have an unpredictable effect. Such indiscriminate measures as a ban on business travel, cancelled marketing initiatives and a complete freeze on recruitment may be legitimate responses, but without a budget, it is not really possible to assess their effectiveness. A proper variance analysis might suggest better reactions, and indeed if reduced sales targets are compensated for in some way by reduced raw material and labour costs, then the overall performance might not warrant, in the short term, such an extreme response. The organisation needs to respond to variances and exercise proper controls, revising plans (and budgets) if necessary. The suggested measures may be counter-productive. For example, banning business travel might prevent the production manager from travelling to a supplier where he would be able to negotiate reduced material costs. Cancelled marketing initiatives might further affect the capability of the organisation to meet sales targets and a complete freeze of recruitment may affect the organisation's effectiveness and its capacity to deliver products on time and to the required quality.

Thus a formal budgeting process would allow ATD to address three particular areas of concern. The ability of the organisation to make realistic forecasts, the poor morale of departmental managers and the appropriateness of the organisation's response to its failure to hit predicted sales targets.

	ACCA Marking scheme	
		Marks
(a)	1 mark for each relevant point up to a maximum of 5 marks for an explanation of the least squares regression data. This may include The expression of the equation (y = 125.022 + 1.84x) A predicted value using the equation The calculation of the coefficient of determination 1 mark for each relevant point up to a maximum of 5 marks for an explanation of the time series analysis data. This may include: – A predicted value using a reasonable assumption – Explanation of residual variation – Explanation of seasonally adjusted values 1 mark for each relevant point up to a maximum of 5 marks for relevance of the approaches to ATD.	15
(b)	1 mark for each relevant point up to a maximum of 10 marks.	10
	Total	**25**

Examiner's comments

In part (a) candidates did not score. Not enough points were made to get the marks on offer and many obvious points were missed. For example; most candidates did not explain the meaning of the correlation coefficient, calculate the coefficient of determination or explain the resulting value. Very few candidates were able to recognise that the least squares approach was inappropriate when applied to values which had such a marked seasonal variation. Overall, this was poorly answered.

In part (b) many candidates did not explain budgeting in the context of the scenario at all. Answers tended to be general and lacking in detail and again marks for this part question were relatively poor.

9 RETAIL WORLD

Key answer tips

This question involves dealing with lots of numbers and therefore should suit students who prefer numerical questions. A working knowledge of linear regression will be needed, though students simply had to explain and analyse it rather than perform calculations. But this may be an area that many students have avoided in their studies (particularly if they are weaker at calculations).

Part (b) covered big data which had featured in a recent exam article and students who had read this article would have been very well prepared for this requirement.

(a) Time series analysis

Time series analysis uses a moving average to define a trend. In Figure 1, the moving average is upwards in a year-on-year basis, with each quarterly result being greater than the equivalent quarter in the previous year. However, that trend does fluctuate on a seasonal basis within each year, with Q1 and Q4 showing positive seasonal fluctuations and Q2 and Q3 showing negative seasonal fluctuations. Given the seasonal nature of the business, it would seem appropriate to use this as a method of forecasting sales.

Although there is no single agreed method of extrapolating the trend, it could be suggested that it appears to be growing at about $2m per quarter over the last few quarters. If this were to continue, estimates for 2016 Q4 and 2017 Q1 would be as follows:

2016 quarter 4: 134.0 (2015 quarter 4 figure) + 8 (growth over the year) + 14.60 (seasonal adjustment) = **$156.60m**

2017 quarter 1: 136.0 (2016 quarter 1 figure) + 8 (growth over the year) + 25.02 (seasonal adjustment) = **$169.02m**

The relatively low residuals would suggest that the method of forecasting is reasonably accurate and that residual factors have little effect.

Although this method seems appropriate when accounting for the seasonal nature in forecasting, it does not take into account where the sales are growing. It is mentioned that business growth is through both expansion of existing stores and through the introduction of new stores. It would be worthwhile understanding which is having the greater effect. The analysis also does not take into account external trends such as overall industry growth as the data used is completely internal to the company.

The least squares regression has more varying results. Because of the highly seasonal nature of the data, the correlation between time and revenue does not seem particularly useful. For example, if the formula were to be used to predict 2016 Q4 revenue, it would suggest $138.08m ($110.93m + ($1.81m*15)) which is much lower than time series would suggest, which takes seasonal factors into account. The 2017 Q1 revenue would be predicted to be $139.89m using this method, again much lower than that predicted using the time series.

The correlation coefficient 'r', with a value of 0.33, suggests that the two variables are weakly connected. The coefficient of determination (r2) suggests that 11% of the variation in sales (y) is due to the passage of time (x). This would indicate a weak non-linear relationship, as suggested by the seasonal variations.

Therefore, this approach would not be considered an appropriate method of forecasting.

The least squares regression considering number of stores and revenue is more closely correlated. With a correlation coefficient of 0.94, there is a strongly positive relationship. Indeed, the coefficient of determination suggests that 88% of the variation in sales (y) is due to the variation in store numbers (x). This would seem to add further insight into the information provided in the time series analysis, suggesting the increase in store numbers is the greater driver for growth.

Using this method, the analyst could forecast average quarterly sales for 2017 and 2018 as $143.5m (69.50 + 0.02*3,700) and $149.5m (69.5 + 0.02*4,000) respectively, given the increase in store numbers predicted. However, this approach makes no attempt to take into account seasonal variations. Additionally, this method is using a very small data set, which does not provide trustworthy results.

Overall, therefore, given the seasonality of the industry, it would appear that time series would be the most appropriate approach for forecasting future sales. However, it may be that a combination of methods is used to extrapolate the general trend so as to maintain relevance for future periods.

There also remains the issue that the data presented for all three figures is somewhat limited in that it allows only a summary forecast of revenue for the entire organisation, rather than incorporating segmentation or external data, for example. Additionally, only limited, historical data has been used to determine relationships.

These may be partially resolved by the use of big data.

(b) **Big data**

Big data is a generic term used to describe the exponential growth of data, provided from numerous sources, available to organisations. The data is not useful in itself, it is the analysis of such data which provides valuable insights to an organisation. The finance director is right to be interested in this, as it can lead to an in-depth insight into trends and the driving forces behind those trends.

The three Vs of big data, volume, velocity and variety, can be examined to determine their contribution towards strategic development.

Volume can enhance the understanding of customer requirements and behaviour. The more data available, the greater the reliability of the trends and relationships discovered. In the analysis provided, there was a limited volume of data, spanning less than three years and incorporating only two variables. The use of big data would allow multivariate analysis over a greater time period or a greater number of shorter time periods to understand purchasing patterns better. This could help RW to create better strategies to capitalise on discovered trends.

Velocity refers to the speed of use of real-time data. As the majority of business transactions are now carried out using technology, these transactions can be captured and processed in real time if sufficient processing capacity is available. This ensures that strategies can be continually updated, in order to deliver competitive advantage. For example, as a new product is trending on social media, RW may then ensure they stock this product and aggressively market it in order to capture greater market share. Similarly, when customers are shopping online, RW could analyse their transactions in real time and use current and historic customer information to make recommendations for further purchases.

Variety refers to the different sources from which data is provided. As sources take different forms and include those not in RW's control, this is a challenging aspect of big data. However, if managed correctly, the variety provides the most detailed understanding of the market place, segmentation and individual customers. This could include competitor and industry information, sourced through key words online, to hashtags on social media and discussion forums.

There are many potential benefits which could be obtained through the analysis of big data. RW could use the results to determine where to locate their new stores. By accessing customers' shopping habits from credit and debit card records, they could determine which competing stores are used, and in which locations. This could help in the strategic planning of store locations, especially as RW is intending to continue to grow store numbers, at least over the next two years. This could help maximise the additional revenue to be gained from new stores.

RW are clearly trying to identify trends and maximise the use of them. The use of big data will provide more reliable and robust trend analysis and could lead to the discovery of previously unsuspected trends, allowing RW to capitalise on these before its industry competitors have even recognised the trend.

Further revenue streams are also available through the selling of data. Given the industry RW is in, there will be a number of branded items on offer to customers. Manufacturers of these brands are keen to carry out their own analysis and will pay for information to help with this. RW could capitalise on this new revenue stream.

Overall therefore, it would seem that the finance director is right to consider the use of big data. Indeed, RW may well find itself at a competitive disadvantage if it fails to do so. However, as with all decisions, the cost-benefit implications would need to be considered before implementation.

ACCA Marking scheme		Marks
(a)	Up to 1 mark for each relevant point up to a maximum of 15 marks. **Maximum**	**15**
	This may include marks for the accurate calculation of:	
	– Extrapolated values for the time series analysis (up to 2 marks)	
	– Predicted values for regression 1 (Figure 2) (up to 2 marks)	
	– Predicted values for regression 2 (Figure 3) (up to 2 marks)	
	– Coefficient of determination (regression 1 and regression 2) (up to 2 marks)	
(b)	Up to 1 mark for each relevant point up to a **Maximum**	**10**
Total		**25**

Examiner's comments

In general, candidates were more confident with the least squares analysis and produced correct forecasts and correct values and interpretation of the coefficient of determination. Most recognised that one of the data sets was much more useful for forecasting than the other. However, the seasonal nature of sales (quarter 1 and quarter 4 were much higher than the other two quarters) did suggest that time series analysis was likely to be appropriate. Candidates were less confident here, often producing forecasts which did not take the seasonal variations into account at all. Overall, this question was reasonably well answered.

In part (b) many candidates were unfamiliar with this area of the syllabus and produced very simplistic answers, such as 'variety refers to the variety of data' and many failed to apply their answer at all to the context of the scenario. Retail is a major user of big data, using it to continually update its buying, promotion and distribution tactics. This should have been recognised in candidates' answers. Overall, this part question was not particularly well answered.

9   MOOR FARM

Key answer tips

This is an unusual question in that it seems to cover a lot of ground such as external analysis, stakeholders, strategic capabilities and marketing. There may be a temptation for students to bring in a lot of models but students have to be careful with their time management and not to go overboard on one particular area. The areas themselves are relatively straightforward, but good, strong exam technique is needed to manage the requirements in this question. Part (b), on improving a website, would also need very specific suggestions rather than bland, generic answers.

(a)   Many issues will need to be considered in the formulation of a strategy for the estate. However, in the context of the scenario, special attention will have to be paid to the expectations of stakeholders, to external environmental factors beyond the control of the estate and to the strategic capabilities of the estate itself. These are now considered in turn.

Expectations of stakeholders

Any proposed strategy will have to take into account the expectations of many stakeholders, some of which have conflicting objectives. From an internal perspective, the strategy has to take into account the objectives of volunteers who make up 90% of the workforce. Any strategy that alienates volunteers may leave the charity unable to maintain the estate or meet its basic operational obligations. Volunteers have different objectives to a paid workforce and these needs have to be understood. Replacing volunteers is not as straightforward as replacing a paid workforce, where scarce labour can be attracted through improved pay and conditions.

Most organisations have relatively straightforward relationships with their customers. Providing a service or product to one customer rarely conflicts with offering a service or product to another. Where it does conflict, for example in providing audit and consultancy services, a supplier can usually elect not to supply the customer, who then looks elsewhere for a similar service. In the case of Moor Farm, potential customers do conflict. There are documented examples of cyclists clashing with walkers and dog walkers with farmers. Access to the land is free (a stipulation of the charitable bequest) and so it is difficult to exclude potential customers. Consequently, a strategy has to be developed that is sensitive to the conflicting needs of customers, within the constraints of the charitable bequest.

Finally, the Moor Farm estate also surrounds two villages where private homeowners are angry about the increasing number of visitors to certain parts of the estate. Attractions have been created, causing traffic problems. As well as having a moral responsibility to these homeowners, the estate also depends, to some extent, on rental income from some of the houses in these villages. Again, residents need to be considered in the definition of the estate's strategy.

External environmental issues

The estate needs to continually scan the external environment to identify issues that might affect its situation. Strategy may have to be developed to either exploit or reflect these external changes, most of which are outside the control of the estate. At best, it can only lobby those responsible for creating these influences.

In the scenario, mention is made of a changed political landscape where government funding is to be reduced on initiatives such as tree planting, protected pasture land and rural employment. This will affect the income of the estate. Changes in weather patterns are also causing problems for the mansion that is situated in the estate. Built originally to resist cold dry weather typical of the time, it has proved susceptible to the warmer, wetter winters now experienced in this part of the country. This is causing long-term maintenance issues as the fabric of the mansion deteriorates.

Finally, the population of the country is increasingly vocal about the 'rights' of individuals. The survey suggests that individuals believe that they have a 'right to roam' on private land, even when this violates the 'rights' of others, such as farmers and other land users. The estate has to take into account this social trend and potential stakeholder conflicts in its planned strategy.

Strategic capability

Finally, the strategy has to take into account the internal resources and competencies of the estate. The estate has significant tangible resources, such as land and property. It also has a unique resource, the only landscape garden developed by James Kent in the district. This is a unique resource which the strategy should aim to exploit. There are also other internal capabilities that should be recognised. A happy, motivated volunteer workforce must be properly utilised by any strategic change, not alienated. Amongst these are volunteers with exceptional skills in land management which could be used to exploit other opportunities on similar estates in the country. Leadership style also needs to be considered. The previous manager was well-liked and successful. Any sudden change in style may cause disruption and a fall in morale. The new leader has to be sensitive to her predecessor's leadership style, whilst building on the success of the previous leader by improving the visitor experience.

The estate has valuable and, in some cases, unique resources, which it needs to exploit with a varied set of stakeholders who sometimes come into conflict with each other. A stakeholder analysis, leading to appropriate stakeholder management policies, seems key here, and may provide some insights into how the website might be improved (part (b) of this question). One of these stakeholders, the government, needs to be particularly monitored, as their policies threaten the funding of the trust.

(b)   There is little point in having a well-designed website if it is difficult to find. The role of search engines is significant here. Moor Farm needs to be near the top of the search engine listings for search terms that are directly relevant. The estate needs to discuss what these terms might be. 'Moor Farm' is an obvious one, but searches such as 'walking in rural Cornaille' may bring in visitors who are not aware of the estate's existence. There is conflicting advice on how to structure a website to achieve a high position in a search engine listing. One fool-proof way is to buy sponsored links which are shown as such at the top of the displayed page. Some commercial organisations are dubious about the value of such links, but they seem completely appropriate in the context of a charitable estate.

Although the website is well regarded and well presented, it does not appear to have weather feeds that would avoid people coming on days when the weather was so poor that it might be dangerous, or, as in the quote, when it might spoil a family's enjoyment. The website may have a weather forecast, a feed on current conditions, and perhaps webcams showing the actual weather at a number of agreed locations. Of course, these feeds and webcams will also show good weather conditions as well, perhaps enticing people to the estate who were prevaricating about their visit.

The website currently shows information about events, but it does not allow customers to book these events. The *interactivity* of the site has to be improved, allowing customers to book and pay in advance, so that they can be sure that they will be able to attend the event and avoid the disappointment of the family who travelled 100 km only to find the event fully booked. Such a facility also has advantages for the estate. For example, it has some feel about the popularity of the event before it is run, so that the scale of the event can be altered to reflect the likely demand. Furthermore, payment is received in advance, thus improving cash flow.

Feedback from satisfied customers can be an important factor in attracting new customers. At present the site does not appear to allow visitors to post comments, photographs and recommendations. This means that an effective marketing tool, unsolicited recommendations, do not appear on the site. Comment has also been made about the enthusiasm and knowledge of the volunteers. This could be harnessed on the site by asking volunteers to write blogs, explaining what they are doing and what is going on. This could be linked through to Twitter and other social networking sites.

Finally, there is obviously a group of regular visitors to Moor Farm who wish to become more involved. As the quotation suggests 'we really want to know what is going on!'. The website can be used to develop a community that supports and promotes the estate. This could be achieved by asking users to register with their email address. They will then receive newsletters, special offers and information about forthcoming events. Special events can be offered to this community and part of the website can be set aside for members of this community. Not only will this provide the estate with valuable resource, it will also allow them to build up a marketing profile of likely visitors and, through surveys and questionnaires, continue to understand what different types of visitor want from the estate.

ACCA Marking scheme	
	Marks
1 mark for each appropriate point up to a maximum of	15
1 mark for each relevant point up to a maximum of	10
Total	**25**

Examiner's comments

In part (a) candidates tended to produce unstructured answers, due to one, or more, of the following reasons:

- Too much use of the Mendelow power/interest grid; leading to a consideration of stakeholder management, rather than the conflict caused by the different stakeholder perspectives and expectations.

- Overusing PESTLE, in a case study scenario where there was very little on, for example; technology, economy and environment. Technology was usually considered in the perspective of the website, which of course is an internal resource. Indeed it is an internal weakness.

- Attempting a SWOT analysis for which there was just insufficient information. This led to the consideration of weaknesses, which again resulted in an inappropriate in-depth analysis of the defects of the web site.

Overall, this part question was not well answered, and despite some very lengthy answers, relatively few candidates gained a pass mark on this part question.

Part (b) should have been relatively straightforward, and indeed many candidates did score well in this part question, cross-referencing their points to the comments made in the stakeholder survey. However, other candidates focused too much on the 6Is (interactivity etc...), introducing general points that they could not back up with a relevant example, because they were not appropriate in the context of the scenario.

Overall, although the question was popular, it was not answered as well as it should have been.

11   ONE ENERGY PLC   *Walk in the footsteps of a top tutor*

Tutor's top tips

(a)   *Financial analysis (13 marks)*

   Key to success:

   Include a broad range of measures

   Give opinions (not just calculations)

   Give equal weighting to non-ratio information (such as overdraft level, level of non-TFA etc.)

   Give an overall opinion which is consistent with the requirement

   Key dangers:

   Calculating too many ratios

   Too much detail in calculations

   Only doing ratios

   Lack of focus

(b)   *Software package evaluation*

   Key to success:

   Solid knowledge

   Relate answers to the scenario

   Key dangers:

   Lack of structure and knowledge

(a)   The judicious use of selected financial ratios should have indicated some cause for concern, leading to further investigation of the company and the industrial sector itself. It would have been very helpful to identify typical financial ratios in the sector that RiteSoftware is operating in. However, in the absence of such information, comparison between the two years will provide some evaluation and a basis for further investigation.

However, before calculating and commenting on the ratios, there are a number of things directly discernable from the financial figures provided by the company.

Firstly, goodwill is the most significant non-current asset. If the company is in the position that it needs further funding, then the extract suggests that there is little to secure this funding against. Most lenders prefer to lend against tangible assets, such as property. The value of goodwill has also increased substantially since 20X7, suggesting an acquisition. It would be useful to investigate this further.

Secondly, although trade receivables year on year have increased, in percentage terms, about the same as revenue, trade payables have increased significantly more. The efficiency ratios should cast more light on this; but it appears that the company may be using trade payables to finance cash flows. This hunch might be supported by the fact that the bank overdraft was actually reduced in 20X8.

Thirdly, although sales revenue increased by 10% in the period, cost of sales grew by a greater percentage, leading to a reduction in profit. It seems reasonable to assume that labour costs largely contributed to this cost of sales increase. The percentage increase in staff was almost 30%, a significant proportion for a small company to integrate and profitably utilise.

Finally, the extract from the accounts shows no retained profit, suggesting that this is being distributed to shareholders. This needs to be investigated.

Profitability

Two profitability ratios can be calculated from the extracted financial information. The ROCE (Return on Capital Employed) has almost halved. Although the actual profit remained the same, it was achieved with significantly higher borrowing.

The net profit margin has also almost halved. The absolute figures are also very low (less than 1% in 20X8) and this needs further investigation to see if such a figure is viable, or representative of the industry sector.

Efficiency

The general observation about trade payables made above appears to be borne out by the ratios. The average receivables settlement remains the same, suggesting good credit management in an expanding business. However, average payable days have increased significantly and are now beyond the 30 days normal for this business.

Sales revenue per employee has dropped from $33,500 in 20X7 to under $29,500 in 20X8.

Liquidity

Liquidity (measured through both the current and acid test ratios) has declined slightly during this period. Also, the values are rather low (approximately 0.76:1) and so this too would need investigation. Perhaps liquidity is traditionally low in this industry sector.

Financial gearing

The two gearing ratios discernable from the extracted information both give cause for concern. The gearing ratio itself has jumped from 25% to above 43%. The interest cover ratio has dropped to 2 from 7.5. Again, the sector needs investigation.

Conclusion

The financial figures of RiteSoftware do suggest that everything was not well and that further investigation was necessary. The figures suggest rising debt, cash flow problems, lowering efficiency and very poor profitability. Further investigation might have revealed that RiteSoftware was typical of the industry. However, it might have also identified the problems that led to the company's eventual demise.

(b) The lack of a formal evaluation of the financial figures of RiteSoftware is the subject of the first part of the question. However, the financial position is just part of the analysis required of the potential supplier. The question requires FOUR further ways in which OneEnergy failed to follow a proper evaluation procedure. In this model answer, the four suggestions are:

1   A failure to investigate the supplier's organisational structure and ownership

2   A failure to evaluate functional requirements

3   A failure to evaluate non-functional requirements

4   A failure to set proper evaluation criteria and follow a selection process

However, other appropriate suggestions made by the candidate will be given credit.

Organisational structure and ownership

The evaluation should have included an investigation into the structure of RiteSoftware, its shareholders and directors. A simple inquiry at Companies House (for example) would have revealed that the managing director of RiteSoftware had the same surname as the HR director of OneEnergy. The HR director could then have been asked directly if he was related to the managing director of RiteSoftware. Of course, there may have been no impropriety intended, but the fact would have come to light and been considered in the evaluation. Many organisations will either not procure from companies where directors and senior managers have relatives or will ask for that information to be disclosed by the supplier in order that it can be weighted in the evaluation of alternative suppliers.

Functional requirements of the software

The evaluation process did not formally define the functional requirements of the required system. The scenario mentions that three months ago, another set of amendments was requested from RiteSoftware to allow one of the divisions in OneEnergy to pay bonuses to lorry drivers in a certain way. This functional requirement should have been defined in advance in the process and it would have then been compared with the functions offered by the package. The gap between requirement and package could then be evaluated in advance. This allows two things. Firstly, the match of functionality and package will form part of the evaluation. It is not expected that every function requirement will be completely fulfilled but the degree of compromise has to be assessed in some way. Secondly, an understanding of the gap allows the compromise to be managed in advance. For example, in the context of the pay for lorry drivers it might have been possible to change the pay structure in such a way that rewarded the drivers but avoided the expense of commissioning and maintaining software amendments.

Non-functional requirements of the software

Many software packages do actually offer most of the functionality that the users require. However, how they deliver that functionality is very important and usability can be a great differentiator between competing packages. In the scenario, it seems clear that non-functional requirements such as user-friendliness have not been considered properly in the evaluation. If they had been then it would be unlikely that users would have problems understanding some of the terminology and structure of the software. Problems leading to comments such as 'it just does not work like we do' should have been identified in advance. Understanding user competencies and expectations would allow the gap between users' ability and the requirements of the package to be properly assessed. This measure would be part of the evaluation. Again, if the package is selected, the gap can be planned for in advance so that the extra training costs, alluded to in the scenario, are budgeted for at the outset.

Evaluation criteria and process

Finally, the scenario suggests that the board decided to purchase the RitePay software package without evaluating alternative solutions. It was felt that payroll rules and processes were relatively standard and so there was no need to look further than a package recommended by the HR director. Certainly, the discovery that the HR director is related to the managing director of RiteSoftware now puts his impartiality in doubt. Furthermore, subsequent requested amendments to the functionality of the package suggest that OneEnergy's payroll rules were not as standard as expected. However, the real problem with choosing one solution without evaluating alternatives is that there is no auditable evidence about how the supplier and the product were selected. At best this looks amateurish; at worst it might cause concern to the non-executive member of the board and its internal auditors. OneEnergy is a plc. The scenario suggests that the company does have a policy on competitive procurement. Avoiding it raises the chance of impropriety, reduces the opportunity of negotiating a good deal, and should attract the attention of non-executive directors and other significant stakeholders.

ACCA Marking scheme		Marks
(a)	Up to 1 mark for each non-ratio based observation up to a maximum of	5
	Up to 1 mark for each ratio based observation up to a maximum of	5
	Up to 3 marks for summary and integration of answer, giving a maximum of	13
(b)	Up to 1 mark for each relevant point up to a maximum of 3 marks for each failing. Four failings required, giving a maximum of	12
Total		**25**

Examiner's comments

In part (a) the data allowed candidates to calculate popular profitability, efficiency, liquidity and gearing ratios. There were also structural problems in the accounts concerning goodwill, retained profit and the financing of the company. It was clear that RiteSoftware was a company in trouble, run by directors that could see its imminent demise. Overall, candidates produced reasonable answers to this part question, many scoring pass marks on their analysis of a restricted set of ratios. However there was a wealth of information in the scenario that many candidates just did not use.

Part (b) should have resulted in answers that gave a relatively straightforward description of a rigorous evaluation process, comparing it to a company which had not used a process at all! The implication of each failing was signposted in the scenario. For example, the failure to define requirements in advance had led to the need to commission software amendments. Too many answers to this part question were disappointing and disorganised, failing to structure the answer in such a way to gain the marks on offer. In many instances this seemed to reflect unfamiliarity with this part of the syllabus.

12   INDEPENDENT LIVING

Key answer tips

In part (a) the key to success will be to combine knowledge with application. So there will be a mark firstly for explaining each element of the primary activities of the supply chain, and then another mark for explaining how it would apply to the scenario. Be careful to focus on primary activities and avoid the secondary/support activities. This will also be important in part (b). In this part there are 15 marks available spread over the 5 primary activities. So you should aim to make three suggestions for improvements in each of the five areas.

(a) IL supplies both manufactured products (crutches, walking frames) and bought-in products (mobility scooters, bath lifts). The value chain for these two sets of products is different and this is reflected in the following analysis.

The primary activities of the value chain are:

Inbound logistics

These are activities associated with receiving, storing and disseminating inputs to the product. Typical examples are materials handling, warehousing and inventory (stock) control.

For manufactured products this concerns collection of material from scrap merchants and the storage of that material prior to use. For bought-in products, inbound logistics is handled by the supplying manufacturers. Products are stored in the warehouse.

Operations

This is concerned with transforming inputs into the final product. This includes machining, assembly, testing and packaging. In the context of manufactured products this covers the production of crutches and walkers (and other simple aids), their testing and packaging. For bought-in products, operations is concerned with the careful opening of packaging, the addition of an IL transfer logo, the testing of the equipment and the re-packaging of the product into its original packaging.

Outbound logistics

These are activities associated with storing and then physically distributing the product to buyers. Finished goods warehousing, order processing and delivery is considered here.

At IL, both manufactured and bought-in products need to be stored prior to delivery. Distribution is undertaken by a national courier company. Orders are placed by telephone or through the website.

Marketing and sales

These are activities by which customers can learn of the existence of and then purchase the products. It includes advertising, promotion, sales and pricing. At IL this covers leaflets in hospitals and surgeries, a website catalogue and order taking and the giving of advice.

Service

These are activities associated with providing a service to enhance or maintain the value of the product. It includes installation, repair, training, parts supply and product adjustment. The simple nature of the manufactured products means that service is inappropriate. For bought-in product, service is undertaken by the original manufacturer.

(b) The value chain is used as a basis for answering the question. Many of the potential re-structuring suggestions produce cost reductions. However, it must be acknowledged that the charity also has the objective of providing jobs for severely disabled people. Suggestions for change have to reflect this fact. It is also clear from the scenario that some customers are prepared to pay price premiums for the goods by making donations to the charity as part of their purchase of these goods.

Inbound logistics

For bought in products, IL could explore the possibility of reducing scrap metal storage costs by requesting dealers to store the metal until it is required.

Furthermore, dealers may also be able to offer competitive delivery costs. This would remove the need for IL to maintain (and eventually replace) the lorry it uses for collection of this material. For bought in products, IL could explore the cost of using a specialist logistics company to carry out both its inbound and outbound logistics. This should produce economies of scale leading to reduced costs. Many of these logistics companies also offer storage facilities. However, IL already has storage at an airfield site and the employment of severely disabled labour is one of its objectives.

Operations

It seems vital that IL retains its manufacturing capability to help achieve its goal of providing work and income for severely disabled people. It could probably gain cost savings by outsourcing manufacture to cheaper countries (like its commercial competitors) but this would not meet its core objective. IL marketing could stress the location of the manufacture as an important differentiator. Customers might then perceive it as an ethical choice.

The operations part of the value chain for bought-in products is relatively labour intensive (see later notes) and could be simplified in two ways.

(1) Asking manufacturers to affix the IL logo and label prior to despatch to IL. The testing of the products could also be delegated to the manufacturer as they provide post-delivery support.

(2) Reducing inventory by arranging for bought in goods to be supplied to the customer directly by the manufacturer. Not only would this cut delivery costs but it would also reduce inventory costs, and eliminate the costly write-off of obsolete purchased inventory.

Employees in the warehouse could be reallocated to order processing and other administrative tasks.

Outbound logistics

The ordering of products through the website appears to be extremely effective. The site includes a product catalogue and a secure payment facility. However, although use of the website is growing, most orders are still placed by telephone. IL might consider ways of encouraging further use of the website, for example by offering discounts, cheaper prices and a wider range of products. It might also consider how it could make its website more available to potential consumers, perhaps by placing dedicated terminals in hospitals and surgeries.

The telephone ordering process is currently too complex because sales staff have to describe the products available and also provide purchasing advice and guidance. IL needs to consider ways of making details of their product range available to customers before they place the order (see below).

Marketing and sales

Relatively little sales and marketing takes place at IL which is probably due its charitable status. Charities are usually very keen to minimise their overhead costs. Traditional marketing appears to be very limited, restricted to leaflets in hospitals and surgeries. IL could consider replacing its current leaflets (which just give a phone number and a website) with a leaflet that effectively doubles as a catalogue, showing the products on offer. This should help improve the efficiency of the telephone ordering service. Display advertising in magazines and newspapers with coupons to request a catalogue would also increase the profile of the brand.

Many charities use Customer Relationship Management (CRM) systems to manage their donors. IL should explore the potential of this. It already has records of purchasers and also those purchasers that have made extra donations.

All sales and marketing material needs to stress the charitable status of the organisation. This effectively differentiates it from commercial competitors. There is already evidence that some customers are willing to reflect this by increasing the price they pay for goods by including a donation to support the charity.

Service

Because of the nature of the product, little direct support is required. However, IL could expand its website to give general support and advice on mobility problems and independent living.

ACCA Marking scheme		Marks
(a)	Up to 1 mark for identifying each primary activity (for example, inbound logistics) and up to 2 marks for discussing its application to IL in both contexts (metal scrap collection, supplier delivery) up to a maximum of 10 marks.	10
(b)	Up to 1 mark for each significant point (for example, arrange bought in products to be delivered directly to the customer from the manufacturer) up to a maximum of 15 marks.	15
Total		**25**

Examiner's comments

The first part of the question requested candidates to analyse the primary activities of the value chain for the product range at IL. Most candidates answered this fairly well, recognising that there were two value chains at IL, one concerned with manufactured goods and the other with 'bought in' products. However, it was also clear that a significant number of candidates were not familiar with the terminology and structure of the value chain. The 'Service' element of the value chain was also particularly misunderstood.

The second part of the question asked candidates to evaluate what changes IL might consider to the primary activities in the value chain to improve their competitiveness, whilst continuing to meet their charitable objectives. This part question was also answered fairly well although the inappropriateness of some solutions in the light of the charitable objectives was not sufficiently explored. Charities are an important part of the 'not-for-profit' sector of the economy and their structure and objectives should be understood by candidates. Question scenarios will not always be drawn from the private or public sectors of the economy.

However, overall the question was answered relatively well.

13   NOBLE PETS

> 🔑
>
> **Key answer tips**
>
> This question mixed together two very different topics. In part (a) it will be important that only primary activities are considered as no marks will be awarded for any discussion on the support activities. When discussing each activity students must bring in relevant information from the scenario rather than describe simple, generic activities. Part (b), on forecasting techniques, is much more challenging and includes a requirement to perform some calculations. This is an area that candidates have struggled with in the past but a review of the answer should highlight that the numbers were straightforward and involve nothing more than plugging numbers into a formula.

(a)   The value chain

There are five primary activities in the value chain: inbound logistics, operations, outbound logistics, sales and marketing and service. Each of these is now considered in turn.

Inbound logistics are activities associated with receiving and storing the inputs to the production process. In terms of the costs identified in the scenario, inbound logistics are concerned with raw foodstuff costs, the costs of cans and the transport costs (goods inward). In two of these areas (raw foodstuff costs and can costs) Noble Pets appears to be competitive. However, goods inward costs are higher than any of its competitors. The fact that raw foodstuff costs and can costs are competitive makes it seem unlikely that the high goods inward costs are due to procurement failings. What seems more likely is that the location of the factory makes transport costs higher. Travelling on relatively minor rural roads and negotiating the congested town centre and the growing suburbs of Milton will affect the fuel economy of the trucks which make deliveries to the plant. This will place Noble Pets at a disadvantage compared with competitors who may be located adjacent to major motorways. There is also some reputational damage caused by complaints from local residents kept awake by the trucks.

Operations are concerned with the production activities associated with turning inputs into their final form, outputs. Production at Noble Pets involves the processing of the raw materials, canning and labelling. In the context of the scenario, these are represented by production costs and direct labour costs. Direct labour costs are roughly in line with its competitors. However, production costs are higher. This is probably associated with the ageing technology of the plant itself. Although it was innovative when it was installed 40 years ago, technology changes have meant that there are more reliable and efficient alternatives available. The physical site is also constrained by housing developments which were built subsequent to the plant. Thus the original plant could not be expanded to obtain any further economies of scale.

Outbound logistics are the activities involved with distributing the product to the customer, in this instance the wholesalers and supermarkets. This area is represented by transport costs (goods outward) included in the table given in the scenario. Like inward logistics, these transport costs are higher than Noble Pets' competitors. This is again partly due to the nature of the roads which lead to the factory and to the congestion in Milton. It also seems very likely that most of the company's customers have relocated to locations which have good road links. Wholesaler and supermarket distribution centres are relatively flexible and footloose and most locate to easily accessible locations. A further problem with outbound logistics is the size of the trucks which can be used to carry the final product. The larger 44 tonne vehicles are banned from Milton town centre, so the company has to continue using the less cost-effective 36 tonne trucks. Again, it is likely that its competitors will be benefiting from the lower unit transport costs offered by the larger trucks.

Sales and marketing is concerned with the activities which make the buyer aware of the product (marketing) and also provide a means by which the buyer can purchase the product (sales). No details of the costs of sales and marketing are provided in the table. However, marketing is an acknowledged strength of the firm and has allowed the company to command a premium price for its products. The term 'noble' itself has positive connotations and appeals to the buyers' sense of duty to feed their pets with what appears to be a superior product. This is significant, because the firm is targeting the buyers of a product who are, in this case, not the consumers of that product.

In fact, the consumers' feedback is probably restricted to the pet's reluctance to eat the food. So advertising campaigns which stress the need for people to give their pets the best and that the best is provided by Noble Pets are very effective. Interestingly, the trend to move from moist foods to dry foods (discussed in part (b)) has been driven by buyers wanting more convenient foods rather than the preferences of the pets themselves.

Service activities are designed to support or enhance the product. Normally, these include services such as installation, repair, training and part supply. In the context of Noble Pets, this can be perceived as the factual information sheets and website designed to promote responsible and appropriate pet ownership. Although the advice is product neutral, its association with Noble Pets enhances the reputation of the company and makes it more likely that consumers will buy its products. The apparently unbiased advice which Noble Pets gives to the community is again an acknowledged strength of the company.

Summary

Noble Pets is a company trapped by its location and its technology. These have led to high transport costs and uncompetitive production costs. It may be possible to address the latter by installing new equipment which is more efficient and reliable, but the business case for replacing all the moist food production facilities depends on future trends in the relative popularity of dry and moist foods. However, it is difficult to see how the company can reduce its transport costs if it remains at the current site. Perhaps it has to continue relying on strong branding and praiseworthy service to allow it to charge a premium price for a product to buyers who are unaware that its content is really very much the same as its competitors' cheaper alternatives.

(b) **Quantitative analysis**

(i)   It is immediately clear from Table Two that the sales of moist pet foods are decreasing and the sales of dry pet foods are increasing. The decline in moist foods was particularly severe in the period 20X0–20X3. Since then, the downward curve has flattened out. The rate of increase for dry food sales has decreased in the last few years, but it is still showing healthy year-on-year growth. This change in pattern is due to the buyers of product requiring something which does not smell and can be left for longer in the pet's bowl.

The total sales of pet foods are worth closer examination.

Year	Moist food		Dry food		Total
	Production	Percentage	Production	Percentage	Production
	(000s tonnes)		(000s tonnes)		(000s tonnes)
20X0	370	55.89%	292	44.11%	662
20X1	350	53.27%	307	46.73%	657
20X2	331	50.77%	321	49.23%	652
20X3	325	49.69%	329	50.31%	654
20X4	315	48.02%	341	51.98%	656
20X5	310	46.90%	351	53.10%	661
20X6	310	46.34%	359	53.66%	669

This shows that, overall, pet food sales declined from 20X0 to 20X4 and only in 20X6 rose above the 20X0 level (and even then, by only just over 1%). Thus Noble Pets has been competing in, at best, a stagnant market dominated by four companies. The only way that any of these companies can grow is to take market share from each other and hence (in Porter's terms) competitive rivalry is high, compounded by low switching costs from one brand to another. It is probably these strains within the industry which has prompted Noble Pets management to ask the Milton plant to review its value chain.

The Milton plant has also suffered from a change in buying tastes. In 20X0, moist pet foods accounted for 55.89%. In 20X6, this figure had reduced to 46.34%. Although Noble Pets' share of this market remains the same (30%), this is a reduction in real terms of 18,000 tonnes of production (from 111,000 to 93,000 tonnes).

(ii)   The regression analysis for moist food sales suggests the following line of best fit.

$Y = a + bx$

$Y = 369.5714 - 9.86x$

The negative value of b shows that the slope of the curve is downwards. Substituting values for 20X7 (8), 20X8 (9) and 20X9 (10) into this equation gives the following (rounded) forecasts.

20X7: 291   20X8: 281   20X9: 271

These values do appear to be too low, given the flattening out of demand in 20X4, 20X5 and 20X6. The line of best fit is influenced by the rapid decline in the first four years of the analysis. Thus these forecasts appear too pessimistic when extrapolating the linear line of best fit.

The correlation coefficient r is negative (−0.94432), which is what would be expected given the production decline. The coefficient of determination of 0.89174 ($r2$), suggests that 89% of the variation can be explained by the passage of time or, more sensibly, by some factor or factors which have changed over this time – such as buyer behaviour. However, the correlation coefficient measures the strength of the linear relationship, and there does appear to be some obvious curve in the original data values.

Although the market for moist food has declined rapidly in the last few years, this decline appears to have been arrested. However, the steepness of this decline, in the early years of the analysis, has meant that the line of best fit produces estimates which appear too pessimistic. A free-hand extension of the curve joining the actual data points is likely to give estimates of over 300,000 tonnes for the next three years. This will have to be taken into account when deciding any further investment in the Milton plant. If Noble Pets retains its 30% share of the market, it still has a demand for 90,000 tonnes of moist pet foods. The other two factories producing moist pet food are relatively small, producing 40,000 tonnes between them. Thus a detailed financial analysis can reasonably be based on a demand of at least 50,000 tonnes in the period 20X7–20X9, even if the other plants work at full capacity.

ACCA Marking scheme			
			Marks
(a)		1 mark for each relevant point up to a maximum of 15 marks.	15
(b)	(i)	1 mark for each relevant point up to a maximum of 5 marks.	
	(ii)	1 mark for each relevant point up to a maximum of 5 marks. This may include 1 mark for arithmetically correct forecasts and 1 mark for explaining the coefficient of determination.	10
Total			**25**

STRATEGIC CHOICE

14   GRAFFOFF

> **Key answer tips**
>
> Although students are very comfortable with the areas covered in the question from a knowledge point of view, only very relevant and specific answers will score well here. The regurgitation of study notes is unlikely to score well and this is what may let many students down. Students need to apply their knowledge to the scenario and consider the problems that the company in the scenario are likely to experience.

(a)   Johnson and Scholes have identified franchising as a form of strategic alliance in their classification of methods of strategy development. In this approach, franchises are independently run businesses that would enter into a licence agreement with Graffoff to purchase training, equipment and materials in return for an exclusive geographical franchise area. The proposal is that the franchisee would buy or lease appropriate premises, not Graffoff as in Emile's organic expansion plan. Most franchises are required to make a large up-front payment, which would provide Emile with significant funds for investment or, indeed, for further dividend payments. There are also a number of avoided costs as franchisees usually pay for all the operating costs of the franchise.

Running their own business is usually sufficient to motivate the franchise owners and the motivation of any staff they employ is also their responsibility. Emile has already acknowledged that he is not a people person and so franchising neatly sub-contracts this issue. Thus, Emile could continue running Graffoff more or less as it is currently and he would avoid the problem of raising significant finance and managing a difficult period of expansion.

However, it is possible (but not inevitable) that the long-term returns to Graffoff might be lower than through directly owned or leased depots. Franchisees will take most of the profits and Graffoff will be dependent for income from materials supply and, usually, from a relatively small percentage of the franchise's annual sales specified in the licence contract. There are also important issues to consider in the appropriate selection and control of franchises. Although the initial fee will be received by Graffoff irrespective of the franchise's success, continuing income (and brand awareness) is dependent upon the success of the franchise. Graffoff has no experience in selecting appropriate franchisees, neither is there any evidence that it has systems in place to control quality and audit performance.

These would be needed to ensure that the product is being used correctly and that the correct percentage of sales is being paid to Graffoff. Such systems will need investment and development and need to be in place before the franchise scheme is launched.

Furthermore, the success of franchises is often determined by the visibility of the brand. Emile himself recognises that Graffoff has a very low profile and he acknowledges that he has very little expertise in this area. Also, it would be obvious to potential franchisees that it may be difficult to maintain sales volumes once the patent has expired. Thus, there may be problems in attracting franchisees, particularly those willing to invest a significant amount for a product which, they may consider, has a relatively short lifetime and whose brand awareness is low. Emile could address the first of these issues by employing marketing expertise and launching vigorous campaigns. He might also address the patent issue by looking at improving the product. Thus focusing on product development (what he is good at) and not business expansion, where he has little experience and interest.

Although franchising appears to reduce financial risk, it is unlikely to produce the financial returns as quickly as the internal growth option. Emile must not underestimate the time taken to draw up the licence agreement, develop systems to support the franchise and recruit and appoint franchisees. He must also accept that some franchises are likely to fail and that returns will be low in the early years of operation as the fledgling franchises seek to establish themselves as viable independent companies.

(b)

Strategic alliances take place where two or more organisations share resources and activities to pursue a strategy. Many organisations recognise that they need to acquire materials, skills, innovation, finance or access to markets, and increasingly recognise that these may be more readily obtained through cooperation rather than ownership. The franchising option is a type of alliance, and Emile sees it as a way of funding his expansion without incurring employee motivational and management issues that he is not confident in addressing.

In terms of Graffoff, the motivation for an alliance is likely to be *co-specialisation,* where each partner concentrates on activities that best match their capabilities. Graffoff specialises in product design and product development. Its weaknesses, in the context of the planned expansion, appear to lie in marketing, retail and finance. Franchising has already been considered as a type of alliance. Another type of alliance that Emile might consider is *a joint venture,* where a new organisation is set up jointly owned by its parents. It is often used by companies to enter a new geographical market where one of the companies provides the expertise and the other local knowledge and labour. This is not the case here, where expansion is within the country. Furthermore, there is no obvious candidate for a joint venture and, even if a partner could be found, it would take time to establish a contractual relationship. Emile, as an entrepreneur, might also find it difficult to work within a framework of a joint venture where he would need to cede a certain amount of control.

In *a network arrangement,* two or more organisations work in collaboration without a formal relationship. The Equipment Emporium already has 57 superstores in the country selling tools and machines. Emile rebuffed their initial advance offering to sell his product in the store, because of the need for mandatory product training. However, he might return to them and offer to set up small in-store outlets where his product could be demonstrated and its services sold. The Equipment Emporium would be paid a fee, but such an approach would, in essence, be the same as his organic growth plan but without the need for large scale capital investment. Furthermore, the locations already exist and are backed up by significant marketing expertise and high brand awareness. This kind of *opportunistic alliance* is a quick way of achieving the expansion that Emile requires and it draws on both partners' expertise. There is a concern in such a loose arrangement that one partner might steal the other's ideas or products, but that seems unlikely here. Graffoff is not interested in becoming a general machine superstore and The Equipment Emporium is primarily focused on products not services. From Emile's perspective, this *opportunistic alliance* provides a potential way of piloting his proposed organic growth expansion strategy before moving into dedicated premises or, indeed, offering the outlets to franchisees.

(c)   The consultant has suggested to Emile, that the company has internal sources of finance it can exploit to fully meet its required funding for organic growth. Typical sources of internal finance are retained profits, tighter credit control, reduced inventory and delayed payment to creditors. Given that Emile is committed to high dividend payments and that no information is given about inventory, two of these are relevant here.

Tightening up credit control makes it possible to release money for funding. The average settlement period for receivables can be calculated as (trade receivables/sales revenue) × 365. For the second year trading this is (260/1,600) × 365 = 59 (59.31) days. Thus, customers take, on average, 59 days to pay their debts, despite agreeing to a 30 day payment term.

Reducing this to the agreed 30 days would realise about $128,500, which could be used to invest in the business. Reducing it to 40 days (the sector-wide standard) would realise approximately $84,500.

However, these gains would only be achieved through implementing better procedures in accounts receivable. Emile realises that this section is poorly motivated and under-staffed. Thus some of the proposed savings may be offset by increased staffing costs. He is also very sensitive to upsetting his customers and so the need to strictly adhere to payment terms may create initial difficulties and strain customer relations. He will have to refrain, in future, from intervening in the debt collection process, and not offer the generous terms of payment that currently undermine the debt collection efforts of the accounts receivable department.

This approach might be allied to delaying payments to creditors. Given the limited information, a crude estimate of the average settlement period for payables (creditors) can be calculated by (trade payables/cost of sales) × 365. In this instance this is (75/1,375) × 365 = 20 (19.91) days. Thus Graffoff pays its creditors within 20 days, whilst 40 days is common in this sector. Bringing the company in line with this practice would realise up to a further $75,500 which again could be used for investment. There is no suggestion that this will cause a problem. The current fast payment of invoices seems to reflect the zeal of the administrator in accounts payable, rather than any policy of the company. If Graffoff elects to pay within 30 days (the normal credit terms for the country), this will still realise about $38,000.

This means that up to approximately $204,000 could be raised by Graffoff if customers adhered to payment terms and suppliers accepted sector-wide practice. This would result in a short-term, one-off acceleration of cash inflow.

Finally, the acknowledged problems with credit control might also cause Emile to consider factoring the company invoices. Debt factoring involves a third party taking over the businesses debt collection. Most factoring companies are willing to pay 80% of approved trade receivables in advance. At current values, this should lead to an immediate cash input of $208,000 and this might be an attractive alternative to trying to manage receivables internally. It might also address the problems of motivation and staffing in the accounts receivables section. Factoring might be very valuable in a period of expansion, improving cash flow and removing, from the company, responsibility for credit investigation and debt chasing.

Whichever options are chosen, internal finance resources cannot completely raise the $500,000 required for the organic growth plan and so the consultant is incorrect in his assertion. Emile would have to seek external sources of finance to make up the shortfall. However, the amount raised through internal sources may be sufficient to effectively finance either the franchising option or the building of an opportunistic alliance with The Equipment Emporium.

ACCA Marking scheme		
		Marks
(a)	1 mark for each appropriate point up to a maximum of	10
(b)	1 mark for each relevant point up to a maximum of	7
(c)	1 mark for each relevant point up to a maximum of	8
	The evaluation of the claim may include:	
	Receivables calculation:	1
	Value of reducing receivables to norm:	1
	Creditors calculation:	1
	Value of increasing this to norm:	1
Total		**25**

Examiner's comments

Part (a) was relatively well answered, using a structure suggested by the question; description, advantages, disadvantages, evaluation. Some candidates did try to use the Johnson, Scholes, Whittington framework of suitability, acceptability and feasibility but this framework did not really suit the information given in the scenario. Some candidates were confused about franchising, restricting their discussion to a franchise just offered to one company; the Equipment Emporium.

In part (b) many candidates were aware of joint ventures and licensing but really failed to suggest why these might be more appropriate or different to franchising. Candidates could have also made more of the potential link up with the Equipment Emporium. Some candidates suggested mergers, acquisitions and even selling the company. However, these are not strategic alliances.

Part (c) was poorly answered on three counts:

- Many answers were too general (reduce creditor days) and included no calculation at all, so the consultant's claim could not be properly evaluated.

- Too many candidates turned the question into a general question on the advantages and disadvantages of organic growth. There were some good answers to a totally different question. In the context of this examination, most of these answers scored zero.

- Finally, too many answers focused on external finance (share issues, more loans) and this was specifically excluded from the question.

Although question three was a popular question, many candidates scored poorly on parts (b) and (c).

15   ENVIRONMENT MANAGEMENT SOCIETY

Key answer tips

Try not to focus on simply regurgitating the pocket notes. Instead try to add as much relevance and specifics from the scenario as possible.

Context

The decline in the number of people taking the qualification appears to be a reflection of the maturity of the marketplace. The large pool of unqualified environmental managers and auditors that existed when the qualification was launched has now been exploited. There are now fewer candidates taking the examinations and fewer members joining the EMS. The organisation's response to this has been to look for international markets where it can promote the qualifications it currently offers. It hopes to find large pools of unqualified environmental managers and auditors in these markets.

The scenario suggests that EMS currently has relatively limited strategic ambitions. There is no evidence that EMS plans to develop new qualifications outside its current portfolio. Indeed, attempts to look at complementary qualifications (such as soil and water conservation) have been rejected by Council. Hence, expansion into new strategic business markets does not appear to be an option.

Strategy development

(a)   Internal development

Internal development takes place when strategies are developed by building on or developing the organisation's own capabilities. It is often termed organic growth. This is how EMS has operated up to now. The original certificates were developed by the founders of the Society. Since then, additional certificates have been added and the Diploma programme developed at the instigation of members and officers of the Society.

In many ways this type of organic growth is particularly suited to the configuration of the organisation, one where there is a risk-averse and cautious culture. The organic approach spreads cost and risk over time and growth is much easier to control and manage. However, growth can be slow and indeed, as in the case of EMS, may have ceased altogether. Growth is also restricted by the breadth of the organisation's capabilities. For example, EMS has not been able to develop (or indeed even consider developing) any products outside of its fairly restricted product range. Furthermore, although internal development may be a reasonable strategy for developing a home market it maybe an inappropriate strategy for breaking into new market places and territories. This is particularly true when, as it appears in the case of the EMS, internal resources have no previous experience of developing products in overseas markets.

In summary, internal growth has been the method of strategy development at EMS up to now, based on a strategic direction of consolidation and market penetration. There is no evidence that EMS is considering developing new products to arrest the fall in qualification numbers. However, the Board has suggested developing new markets for the current qualification range and India, China and Russia have been identified as potential targets. It seems unlikely that internal development will be an appropriate method of pursuing this strategic direction.

(b)   Mergers and acquisitions

A strategy of acquisition is one where one organisation (such as EMS) takes ownership of other existing organisations in the target countries. One of the most compelling reasons for acquisition is the speed it allows an organisation to enter a new product or market area. EMS might look to acquire organisations already offering certification in its target markets. These organisations would then become the mechanism for launching EMS qualifications into these markets. In addition, it is likely that these organisations will have qualifications that the EMS does not currently offer. These qualifications could then be offered, if appropriate, in EMS's home market. This arrangement would provide EMS with the opportunity to quickly offer its core competences into its target markets, as well as gaining new competencies which it could exploit at home.

However, acquisitions usually require considerable expenditure at some point in time and evidence suggests that there is a high risk that they will not deliver the returns that they promised. It is unlikely that the EMS will have enough money to fund such acquisitions and its status as a private limited entity means that it cannot currently access the markets to fund such growth. Any acquisitions will have to be funded from its cash reserves or from private equity investment groups. Furthermore, acquisitions also bring political and cultural issues which evidence suggests the organisation would have difficulty with. Under achievement in mergers and acquisitions often results from problems of cultural fit. This can be particularly problematic with international acquisitions, which is exactly the type of acquisition under consideration here. So, although acquisitions are a popular way of fuelling growth it is unlikely that EMS will have either the cash or the cultural will to pursue this method of strategy development. There is no evidence that EMS has any expertise in acquiring organisations in its home market and so such acquisitions overseas would be extremely risky.

(c) **Strategic alliances**

A strategic alliance takes place when two or more organisations share resources and activities to pursue a particular strategy. This approach has become increasingly popular for a number of reasons. In the context of EMS it would allow the organisation to enter into a marketplace without the large financial outlay of acquiring a local organisation. Furthermore, it would avoid the cultural dislocation of either acquiring or merging with another organisation. The motive for the alliance would be cospecialisation with each partner concentrating on the activities that best match their capabilities. Johnson, Scholes and Whittington suggest that co-specialisation alliances 'are used to enter new geographic markets where an organisation needs local knowledge and expertise'. This fits the EMS requirement exactly.

The exact nature of the alliance would require much thought and indeed different types of alliance might be forged in the three markets targeted by EMS. A joint venture is where a new organisation is set up jointly owned by the parents. This is a formal alliance and will obviously take some time to establish. EMS will have to contribute cost and resources to the newly established company, but such costs and resources should be much less than those incurred in an acquisition. However, joint ventures take time to establish and it may be not be an option if EMS wants to quickly move into a target marketplace to speedily arrest its falling numbers. A licence agreement could be an alternative where EMS licenses the use of its qualification in the target market. This could be organised in a number of ways. For example, a local organisation could market the EMS qualification as its own and pay EMS a fee for each issued certificate and diploma. Alternatively, the qualification may be marketed by the local organisation as an EMS qualification and EMS pays this organisation a licence fee for every certificate and diploma it issues in that country. This requires less commitment from EMS but it is likely to bring in less financial returns, with less control over how the qualification is marketed. Furthermore, if the qualification is successful, there is the risk that the local organisation will develop its own alternative so that it gains all the income from the transaction, not just a percentage of the transaction fee.

At first sight, the strategic alliance appears very appropriate to EMS's current situation. The licensing approach is particularly attractive because it seems to offer very quick access to new markets without any great financial commitment and without any cultural upheaval within EMS itself. However, the uptake of the qualification is unpredictable and the marketing and promotion of the qualification is outside the control of EMS. EMS may find this difficult to accept. Furthermore, the EMS will only be receiving a fraction of the income and so it must ensure that this fraction is sufficient to fuel growth expectations and service the newly qualified members in other countries. Finally, there is often a paradox in organisations where internal development has been the strategic method adopted so far. An organisation used to internal development and control often finds it difficult to trust partners in an alliance. Yet trust and cooperation is probably the most important ingredient of making such strategic alliances work.

ACCA Marking scheme	
	Marks
1 mark for each relevant point up to a maximum of 8 marks for internal development.	
There is a maximum of 4 marks for points relating to principles.	8
1 mark for each relevant point up to a maximum of 8 marks for acquisitions.	
There is a maximum of 4 marks for points relating to principles.	8
1 mark for each relevant point up to a maximum of 9 marks for strategic alliances.	
There is a maximum of 5 marks for points relating to principles.	9
Total	25

16 MMI 👣 *Walk in the footsteps of a top tutor*

Tutor's top tips

This was a strategic question that mixed financial analysis and acquisition assessment. This is the second time that the examiner has had strategic elements in the option questions and we can expect to see more of this in the future. It was the first time that financial analysis has featured in the option questions and this may have taken some students by surprise. But the same technique points apply as would have applied if this was part of the compulsory question.

Part (a)

This part of the question asked students to explain why two acquisitions had taken place and assess their post-acquisition performance.

Key to success:

Use a recognised model to assess why the acquisitions had taken place. The best one would be the Ashbridge matrix (used by the examiner) and well prepared students should be reasonably comfortable with this approach. But models such as Porter's acquisition tests could be used equally as well. The examiner even brings in the BCG matrix.

As is usual with financial analysis the key to getting the arks will be to explain why a ratio has changed and what the implications of such a change might be. There wasn't a lot of financial information provided so it is likely to be important to use as much of it as possible.

Dangers:

Not using the financial analysis

Not recognizing that the requirement had two elements (explain why the acquisitions had happened, and assessing their performance).

Part (b)

Having assessed two acquisitions that had already taken place, students were asked to assess a third proposed acquisition.

Key to success:

Apply the same techniques that were used in part (a). So use the same model and include financial analysis. Students could also have used the suitability, feasibility, and acceptability approach suggested by Johnson, Scholes and Whittington.

Make a recommendation as to whether the acquisition should proceed and justify it. It doesn't matter whether you think the acquisition should go ahead or not, as long as you have an opinion one way or the other and can back it up with sensible analysis.

Dangers:

The examiner complained that some students didn't include any financial analysis. This would have been a major error given the amount of financial information included in the question and the approach taken to part (a).

(a) **First Leisure**

The initial motivation for the acquisition of First Leisure was the need to diversify out of a declining market place (falling 5% over the recorded period) into an expanding one (increasing over 25% in the recorded period). The cash generated by the quarrying company was used to purchase a profitable, well-run company in an expanding market. Diversification was a direct response to environmental changes. Increased costs and falling reserves meant that there was little chance of finding new sites in its core market. MMI initially played no managerial role in First Leisure, allowing the managers who had made it successful to continue running the company. However, buying a company concerned with leisure appeared to be an example of unrelated diversification and there were some negative comments about the financial wisdom of this acquisition.

After a period of consolidation, certain unexpected synergies emerged that had not been clear at the time of acquisition. These came from the conversion of disused or unprofitable quarry sites into leisure parks. This conversion was doubly advantageous. In the first instance it reduced the operating costs of MMI, allowing it to shed costs associated with running unprofitable mines and maintaining security and safety at disused sites. Secondly, it allowed First Leisure to acquire sites relatively easily and cheaply in an environment where it was becoming more expensive and harder, because of planning restrictions, to purchase new sites. Johnson, Scholes and Whittington discuss the principles of economies of scope where an organisation has underutilised resources that it cannot effectively use or dispose of. It makes sense to switch these if possible to a new activity, in this instance leisure parks.

The turnover of First Leisure has doubled in six years. The figures summarised in table 1 suggest an expanding company in an expanding market and its market share continues to grow (up from 13% to 21% in the recorded period). Furthermore, gross profit margins have remained fairly constant but recent increases in the net profit margin suggests that costs appear to be under control, despite the recent issues concerning the supply of boats from Boatland. In corporate management terms MMI probably perceived that it would initially be playing a 'portfolio management' role at First Leisure.

However, the discovery of unexpected synergies has led to it adopting (and perhaps claiming in hindsight) a synergy manager role. In terms of the BCG matrix, First Leisure exhibits all the characteristics of a star business unit and so it should be retained in the portfolio. It has a high market share in a growing market and increasing margins means that even if it has spent heavily to gain this share (and there is no direct evidence of this in the scenario), costs are now beginning to fall.

Boatland

The synergies that emerged from acquiring First Leisure appear to have been unexpected. However, the acquisition of Boatland in 20X6 was largely justified on the grounds of synergy. Synergies were expected with First Leisure and with MMI itself. By this time the directors felt that they had built up significant managerial competencies that could be successfully applied to acquired companies. These managerial competencies could be used to drive extra value from underperforming companies and so deliver benefits to shareholders. In the case of Boatland the expected synergies with First Leisure were as follows:

- First Leisure had experienced difficulties in the supply and maintenance of boats for their leisure parks. Boatland seemed to offer a way out of this problem. First Leisure would become a preferred customer of Boatland, taking priority over other customers. MMI also perceived that cost savings could be found by bringing boat manufacture and maintenance into the Group. In this instance, MMI was pursuing a policy of backward integration, producing one of the inputs into First Leisure's current business activities.

- Secondly, Boatland itself appeared to be undervalued. The management team appeared to lack ambition, focusing on producing a limited number of craft to high specification. It was felt that the production of boats for First Leisure would help the company expand, allowing it to increase market share partly based on guaranteed orders from First Leisure.

In this instance MMI probably thought of itself as a synergy manager, helping Boatland develop strategic capabilities and exploiting synergies with both MMI and First Leisure. However, the acquisition has not brought the expected benefits. The boats provided for First Leisure have not been appropriately constructed for their purpose and, paradoxically, because of the way they are misused by holiday makers, maintenance costs and 'downtime' has increased. Furthermore, the status of First Leisure as a preferred customer has led to delays in boat manufacture and maintenance for established customers. Orders have fallen and so has the reputation of the company. This is reflected in the data provided in table 1. Revenue and market share has fallen in a static market place. More worrying is the significant fall in gross and net profit margins. The net profit margin has fallen from 13.04% in 2002 to just 4.29% in 20X8. Furthermore, difficulties also have been created for First Leisure, which are also disturbing its relationship with MMI. The problem at Boatland appears to be cultural and this is reflected not only on the results but in the loss of experienced boat building employees. When the company was bought it concentrated on building a small number of high quality boats to discerning customers who valued and cherished their boats. In contrast, First Leisure required a large number of simple, robust boats that could be used and abused by holiday makers. The products and markets are different and the perceived synergy was an illusion.

In BCG terms Boatland has a very small share of a static market. Although there is no evidence of it being a cash drain on MMI the conflict between the culture of Boatland and the cultures of MMI and First Leisure probably used up a disproportionate amount of company time and resources. In terms of the Ashridge Portfolio Display, Boatland appeared as a heartland business but it soon turned into a value trap business. It seems sensible to divest Boatland from the portfolio. However, the supply implications of this to First Leisure will have to be investigated and so divestment may have to wait until First Leisure has built up a relationship with an alternative supplier.

(b)   **Introduction**

Since 2002 MMI have built up a small portfolio of businesses that reflect different strategic directions. It has consolidated in its own market by shedding unprofitable or closed quarries and purchasing smaller competitors. This is reflected in the data given in table 1. During a period when the marketplace has declined by 5%, MMI has increased its market share from 20% to 28%. Gross profitability has remained fairly steady during the period, but the net profit margin has increased significantly since 2004. The increase in market share is probably due to the acquisition, in 2004, of two smaller competitors. The increase in the net profit margin can largely be traced to the disposal of redundant and unprofitable quarries to First Leisure. MMI's attempts at diversification have had mixed success. First Leisure, acquired in 2002, turned out to be an inspired acquisition as unexpected synergies emerged which assisted MMI's profitability. However, the expected synergies from the Boatland purchase have not materialised and MMI appear to have destroyed rather than created value in this acquisition.

In 2004 MMI acquired two of its smaller competitors, bringing five further mines or quarries into the group. MMI introduced its own managers into these companies resulting in a spectacular rise in revenues and profits that caused the CEO of MMI to claim that corporate management capabilities were now an important asset of MMI. So there appears to be evidence that MMI management can successfully improve the performance of an acquisition. However, Boatland is in a significantly different industry to these earlier acquisitions. MMI managers are familiar with the management of mines and quarries and probably found that the employees of these companies shared the culture of an industry they were familiar with. In contrast, at Boatland the sought after synergy was with First Leisure, not MMI, and so the MMI managers entered an industry and an environment they were unfamiliar with. Evidence from the First Leisure and Boatland acquisitions suggests that MMI is more successful when it employs a 'hands-off' approach to managing acquisitions which are not directly related to its core mining and quarrying operations. The incumbent management team are left to get on with the job with minimal interference from MMI.

InfoTech

The current financial position of InfoTech suggests that its management team may not be able to deliver the turnaround required. Market share and gross and net profit margins have fallen over the recorded period. Revenues have decreased by 16% at InfoTech in a period where the size of the market has increased by almost 25%. If MMI acquires InfoTech then the preferred 'hands-off' approach will be very risky, particularly considering the financial investment the company requires. MMI appears to have two alternatives if it goes ahead with the acquisition.

The first is to learn from its experience at Boatland and install managers who are more sensitive to the culture of the organisation and the industry as a whole. To do this, they will have to recognise that their perceived value adding managerial capabilities actually turned out to be value destroying at Boatland. MMI could recruit managers with established track records in the information technology industry. However, there is no evidence that MMI has successfully adopted this approach before.

The financial position alluded to above also needs to be considered. Boatland and First Leisure were both successful, profitable companies when they were acquired. In contrast, Infotech is making a loss and appears to require investment which it has failed to secure in its own right. This is a controversial reason for acquisition and in this context MMI is playing the role of a portfolio manager, one it has never played for a failing company. In terms of the BCG matrix, InfoTech is a business unit in a growing market but with a low market share. It would be defined as a question mark or problem child.

Suitability is one of the three success criteria Johnson, Scholes and Whittington use to judge strategic options. An approach which evaluates whether the acquisition addresses the situation in which MMI and InfoTech are operating would be a perfectly valid approach to answering this question.

ACCA Marking scheme		
		Marks
(a)	**First Leisure**	
	Up to 2 marks for recognising that this unrelated diversification was driven by environmental change; supported by appropriate data.	
	Up to 2 marks for issues concerning economies of scope	
	Up to 3 marks for interpreting the financial and market data.	
	Up to 2 marks for recognising the likely parenting role and for locating First Leisure on an appropriate analysis matrix.	
	Boatland	
	Up to 2 marks for recognising the synergies expected from Boatland.	
	Up to 2 marks for interpreting the financial and market data.	
	Up to 3 marks for explaining the failure of the acquisition.	15
	Up to 2 marks for recognising the likely parenting role and for locating Boatland in an appropriate analysis matrix.	
(b)	Up to 3 marks for interpreting the financial performance of MMI and summarising its acquisition strategy.	
	Up to 2 marks for recognising that a 'hands-off' approach has been more successful when MMI has pursued unrelated diversification	
	Up to 2 marks for recognising the difficulty of pursuing this approach at InfoTech	
	Up to 2 marks for interpreting the financial and market data	
	Up to 2 marks for recognising the likely parenting role and for locating InfoTech in an appropriate analysis matrix	10
Total		25

17 BLUESKY

(a)   BlueSky Analysis Ltd is now facing a new set of problems operating as a subsidiary of United Data Systems (UDS). It has lost its freedom to negotiate contracts but it would appear that the original difficulties that forced BlueSky into the hands of UDS still exist. In order to maintain the goodwill of the analysts/scientists at BlueSky, the subsidiary still permits the loose organisational structure to prevail. This culture of allowing analysts to operate independently, so reflecting the attitudes and beliefs of the senior management of BlueSky, has often resulted in personal interest superseding commercial wisdom. Working in isolation has been preferred to teamwork. This loose management control in the past led to cost overruns and delays in project completion. This situation has deteriorated since the acquisition. Table 1 demonstrates that in both of these areas performance is worse. There is an increase of about 20% in the number of projects not meeting the stated performance criteria it would also appear that the interface between clients and providers has also worsened. Managers are still not closely monitoring the operational situation.

Strategic analysis

Prior to the acquisition there was an implied criticism that the analysts were rarely in direct communication with the projects clients. They were shielded by the senior management of BlueSky who acted as a 'buffer'. It now is likely that the requirement to send contracts for vetting to the UDS financial centre will result in an even further separation of the analyst from the client.

Culture, structure and systems are all inextricably linked. Previously, BlueSky had innovation and project development as key objectives, but since the takeover the emphasis is focused more on efficiency. Although the 'big company' culture has not yet become invasive, a divisionalised configuration has also been an influence in that objectives are increasingly being determined by financial considerations. This switch in emphasis would inevitably affect the behavioural attitudes of the workforce. The most innovative and self-motivated type of analysts might find the current change in culture unacceptable and so might resign their positions.

With increasing competition the company cannot afford to lose its staff, but neither can it afford to lose contracts. Despite earlier criticisms of the cost over-runs and the delays, BlueSky has attempted to be responsive and flexible. Senior managers who had pursued and negotiated new business before the acquisition, understood the problems and issues. They could also relate to the clients better. Even so, their preference to be involved in the research themselves meant that they did not always pay due attention to their supervisory role. However, new contracts are now being determined at UDS headquarters. Although this might help to prevent contracts being accepted which could be unprofitable and/or have unacceptable lead times, it does mean that the ability to negotiate a contract quickly is lost, thus losing the BlueSky subsidiary the necessary speed of response which might be critical in these days when competition is becoming more threatening. Furthermore, the financial specialists may reject a contract because it is too small or does not provide the required level of profit.

This could prevent the company from getting follow-up contracts which may be bigger and more profitable, it is foolhardy to judge the viability of a contract solely in terms of the immediate profit on the one contract.

In addition to the cultural and organisational problems it is apparent that some longer-established clients are unhappy with the current situation. Quality and service are said to have deteriorated. It is not clear from the information provided whether this is an impression or a reality. It could be that they feel neglected by knowing that key contract issues were being decided within the USA but it is likely that speed of response and flexibility have worsened. It could also be the case that the original managers are now taking less interest in 'managing' their business and focusing more on the scientific work that they enjoy. This will not endear them to clients if their requests for information or help are being ignored or given low priority.

Quantitative analysis

The data in Table 1 demonstrates a deteriorating situation. Sales revenue has fallen slightly since the acquisition although the cost of sales has fallen by more. At first sight the improvement in gross profit would suggest that efficiency is improving. However, expenses rose disproportionately. Administration costs doubled, but there was a 20% fall in marketing costs. This was contrary to expectations. One of the purposes of any acquisition is to streamline administrative costs. The charges from the centre have risen by a substantial amount, whereas marketing, now so critical with increasing competition, is being neglected.

This is unwise, particularly when BlueSky's managers appear to be less involved than previously in finalising contracts. UDS has little experience in the fields of satellite surveillance, and data collection and interpretation. It needs to have increased marketing exposure, not a reduction in marketing expenditure. It also seems that order levels are falling. At the end of the final year as an independent company BlueSky had work in progress and an order book amounting to approximately 30% of the annual turnover. Currently the figure is only 17%. This could indicate that projects were now being more carefully managed but the percentage of contracts running over time suggests that this is not the case. The reality is that the order book is probably very low – another reason for more marketing.

The average value of the contract has doubled. This appears to have been an objective of UDS – 'big is beautiful'. This suggests that many smaller contracts, previously acceptable to BlueSky, are now being rejected. It is possible that UDS has not recognised that this market segment is totally different to that in which it is accustomed to operate in. Size may not be the critical factor. This could also explain why the order book level seems to be very low. This market might comprise many small contracts and in focusing only on large contracts, UDS is losing out on smaller but potentially profitable business. It is also important to recognise that with the increased size of contract, there are now too few contracts for most of the analysts to work alone. The emphasis will have to change to greater teamwork. Most of the analysts have previously enjoyed working in isolation. One of the key criticisms of the company has been a lack of co-ordination. It needs to be questioned whether the staff now have the appropriate skills to deal with this new mode of working. This could create problems for the future. Finally, there appears to be a reduction in non-current assets employed. The reason is for this is not clear. It could be that no investment in the subsidiary is now occurring, or even that the parent company is transferring assets to other parts of the company. It may even be the result of a revaluation of the assets. Whatever the reason is it does not suggest that UDS is currently prepared to invest heavily in the subsidiary. This is not a promising omen for the future.

(b)   (i)   The cultural web is a useful framework for discussing the cultural aspects of organisations. It believes that the central cultural paradigm is made up of a number of elements:

- power structure. Previously the scientists had a lot of power in terms which projects to pursue etc., now work had to be approved centrally.

- control systems. Previously scientists could concentrate solely on scientific work, whereas now financial criteria was imposed upon them.

- routines and rituals. Previously work was often carried out slowly with little management, now more interactivity and responsibility was expected.

- organisational structure. Responsibilities were confused previously, but UDS now tried to impose more roles, responsibilities and a wider span of control.

- symbols. The symbols are likely to change. UDS are likely to have stronger branding and focus, whereas analysts and scientist might feel they have lost the small company feel.

- stories and myths. It is likely that in the past stories would have revolved around scientific success, whereas going forward they are more likely to concern financial success.

(ii)   If BlueSky is to be incorporated within UDS as a division this will have to be carried out with care. A **change management programme** will have to be initiated so that employees understand the need for this re-structuring. Kotter and Schlesinger identified five generally acceptable strategies for managing change – those that might be relevant to BlueSky are explored below.

The first is **participation**. It is believed that people respond better to change if they have participated in the process and feel that they 'own' the change. This is particularly relevant with the type of intelligent staff employed by BlueSky. They should have the capacity to understand the reasons for the change. However, the danger with this process is that if the employees require certain features within the change and the company cannot deliver them then they become even more de-motivated. They feel that the concept of participation was nothing more than a sham. Furthermore, participation often is time consuming and BlueSky may not have the luxury to delay the process.

Education and communication is another recommended strategy and this is essential if staff are not to be 'left in the dark'. This is less attractive to an organisation such as BlueSky because it reduces the involvement of the employees and is a process of selling an already agreed on proposition. There is also the risk that the staff may not like the proposals and no amount of communication or education can alter that. **Power and coercion**, or even **manipulation** as strategies are unlikely to work in this scenario. The staff are too intelligent and too mobile to accept this. There may be the benefit of swiftness in decision-making but the probability of outcome is that staff will leave or, if they stay they will lack commitment and may even disrupt the change. A logical strategy is that negotiation should be attempted. There should be some means whereby the wishes of both parties could be accommodated. Although it is a time-consuming process, it is better to get it right than to risk future upheaval.

ORGANISATIONAL STRUCTURE

18 ALG TECHNOLOGY

> ### Key answer tips
>
> The scenario explicitly rejects a divisional structure so this would not score marks as a suggested structure in part (a).

(a) ALG Technology is a company operating in a number of fields of complex technologies and in several dynamic markets. Its current organisational structure based upon a functional division of work is not providing the necessary integration of activities, nor is it responding sufficiently to market needs. It is likely that a **matrix structure** or one **based on project teams** might work better but there will also be disadvantages associated with such a structure. The basis of such a structure is a multi-functional project team. The team is often small, flexible and temporary. It is often set up when management do not wish to set up separate divisions but are looking for increased co-operation among all their staff. It generally has two reporting lines – one to functional departments and one devoted to specialist products or teams. In the case of ALG Technology there will be a team focused around each specialist product group and each team will have representations from the various functional areas.

The **advantages** of a matrix or project team structure are as follows:

- The teams do not lose sight of their long-term objectives. They can remain more focused.

- There is more integration between the differing functional specialists – they become inter-disciplinary, resulting in greater co-operation and understand opposing or alternative opinions.

- Such a team is more responsive and flexible to environmental and technical change, so important for a company such as ALG. Because the team is now less bureaucratic and more focused, outcomes are much quicker as the bureaucracy is now replaced by a direct interplay between specialists – the interested parties.

- No one single functional area is likely to dominate. In a company such as ALG there is a danger that the views of scientists and engineers may triumph at the expense of prudent financial advice and market needs may also be ignored. There is a danger of the company becoming too product-orientated.

- Because staff are more directly involved in planning, control and decision making they become more motivated and committed – a key benefit for any company.

- Junior staff experience a wider range of inputs from a broad spectrum of areas. They lose their specialised isolation and become more valuable and 'rounded' employees. This provides a good training platform for future general managers.

- Experiences from one project team can easily and quickly be transmitted to other teams.

There are also **disadvantages**:

- Because of the dual representation within the teams there is a potential for conflict between project managers and functional heads.

- The two reporting lines can lead to confusion for members of the team. Where does their long-term future lie and where is it being determined?

- There is increased complexity in reporting, making such a structure costly to administer.

- Decision making can be slower and not be more responsive if every participant insists on full participation. This is a problem with all democratic and participatory organisations, as has been experienced by a number of Japanese companies.

- Because of dual reporting, there is a problem of allocating responsibilities. Who is in charge?

- This proposed new structure may lead to a dilution of priorities, particularly in resource allocation.

As a guideline for organising innovative project teams it is essential that structures should be flexible so as to encourage experts to break through conventional boundaries into new areas. There should also be leadership within the team of staff with a good technical background (**expert power**) and the team should not be dominated by superiors armed only with authority (**position power**).

(b) Organisational design can be influenced by many factors which can generally be divided into two categories – internal and external influences.

The **internal influences** comprise:

- Poor performance in the past. If a company has had difficulties such as are currently being experienced by ALG Technology then it is not surprising that it is considering a change in its organisational structure.

- If a company is now heavily influenced by entrepreneurs and innovators, a more flexible structure would be welcome. A 'machine bureaucracy', which might be what ALG Technology has become, would not be sympathetic to this type of employee. An adhocracy or an entrepreneurial structure might be more appropriate. (*Mintzberg*)

- A change in organisational ownership would inevitably have given the new shareholders a greater say on matters such as organisational design. Design will be more influenced by their management philosophy.

- There may have been a change in organisational goals. If quality of delivery is now given greater priority than product performance, as in the case of ALG, a structure more oriented to marketing might now be encouraged.

- A change in strategy will also help to influence the design of the organisation. If the company intends to compete with low prices then costs will now become critical. It is likely that there will be a more mechanistic approach to the structure with less focus on the individual. However with a differentiation strategy there is a potential for more informality, with more decision making being devoted to junior managers. This will be reflected in a less bureaucratic organisational structure.

The **external factors** that might influence organisational design are as follows:

- A **change in knowledge available** to a company. An increase in the availability and application of information technology (IT) now enables organisations to have greater control and communication within an organisation while having a smaller infrastructure to accomplish these functions.

- **Economic opportunities** may change: the globalisation of markets will necessitate a change in organisational structure to reflect and respond to these changes. In certain parts of the world barter has been re-introduced because of shortages of liquidity within the banking system. Organisations must build into their structures recognition of this 'problem'. Certain companies have had to create whole departments to respond to this condition.

- **Socio-demographic changes**: as organisations now operate in different parts of the world, each with different demographic and social regimes then differences such as attitudes to older people working, women in management, educational abilities matching requirements and labour force availability can all influence the design of organisational structures, resulting in more flexible and responsive organisations suiting local needs and cultures.

- **Ecological considerations**: 'Green' issues are becoming more significant in importance. Decisions on purchasing and distribution will be influenced by this and these, in turn, may affect the organisational structure. 'Just-in-time' supply techniques may be affected here (although just-in-time may be driven more by economic rather than ecological consideration).

- The **prevailing ideological beliefs** may also influence organisational design. In some countries planning may still be more dominant than a market culture. This could affect the organisational infrastructure with a greater reliance on planning departments than on a marketing and customer service. There has been much discussion on the differences between Japanese and Western-based companies. Concepts popular in Japan in the 1970s and 1980s such as jobs for life, promotion by seniority, job rotation have all affected the way in which organisations are configured. However it is also true to say that with the recent increased tendency towards globalisation these ideological differences are being reduced.

As can be noted from the above discussion, a number of these factors can be used to justify ALG Technology's need to change its organisational structure. Probably the most pressing reason for the change is its current poor performance. Resulting from this, there will probably be changes in both objectives and strategies. Although the environmental factors may have limited relevance here, the fact that ALG is now operating in a dynamic and global market place means that it has to be more responsive to market needs. With improved IT, it can now control its enterprises from a distance without sacrificing responsiveness. It can do so with a relatively flat organisation without the need for an extensive supportive infrastructure.

19 ICC ORGANISATION

Key answer tips

Focus on the use of the matrix organisational form as a way to manage the complexity of organisations with multiple structural interdependencies. The question was not popular in the examination, but when answered it attracted good marks. Organisation structure and design is a fundamental aspect of strategy implementation and should not be seen as a peripheral topic.

Part (a) is relatively straightforward provided you avoid irrelevant generalisations and keep to the facts of the company in question.

Summarise the benefits of the proposed structure to answer part (b).

For part (c) firstly explain what is meant by the quotation – it implies a degree of instability and dynamism in the matrix structure – and then explain how this can be managed.

(a) Complex organisations such as ICC contain multiple structural interdependencies such as geographic locations, product groups, market segments and functional specialisms (such as finance and R&D). Such organisations are unable to design a single structural form which adequately contains and optimises all the interdependencies. For example, a product-based structure focuses on product design and development but loses out on market responsiveness while a market or customer driven structure risks the failure to achieve product technical synergies.

Matrix structures have evolved from divisional structures as a response to this dilemma and as a means of meeting the structural needs of managing complex multinational organisations. Matrix structures are in themselves complex and require sophisticated management processes. A **matrix structure can be stable** (i.e. a permanent aspect of the structure, as is the case at ICC) **or transient**, i.e. a temporary multi-disciplinary team based structure as is frequently used to manage projects in high technology industries.

By choosing a matrix structure, the organisation does not choose one structure over another, but attempts to operate through two or more integrated structural forms by setting up dual or triple authority structures. In seeking to operate in this way, the organisation abandons the principle of unity of command in favour of the management of multiple interdependencies. ICC have adopted this principle for functional and geographic groupings. In other words functional managers based within a country report both to the country manager for local operational matters, but to their functional specialist at head office for technical direction.

(b)   Successfully adopted, designed, developed and operated, matrix forms can provide substantial advantages. A country-based matrix form combining S&M and SES would be based on two integrated dimensions – **product based and customer based**. The potential gains from the matrix form and how they could deal with the co-ordination problems can be summarised (**Johnson and Scholes**) under four main areas.

- **Improved decision-making** where there is potential conflict of interests such as 'product against market' or 'finance against sales'. The structure should assist in avoiding the danger of one element dominating the decision processes by combining interests at the point where the decision is made. The nature of the problem can be illustrated by reference to ICC, where SES and S&M operate as separate (non-matrix) divisions within each country. S&M are selling hardware that is not technically suitable and causing follow-on workload problems for the SES engineers.

- Within the matrix, **direct contact replaces the formalised reporting procedures** which may take place between independent divisions. Again we can see the consequences of a lack of co-ordination at ICC country level where SES staff are failing to pass on potential sales leads to the S&M staff.

- **Improved motivation**, due to closer involvement in the wider aspect of business strategy. For example, if ICC operated SES and S&M through a matrix, based on a customer account manager responsible for both product sales and customer support, then the motivation for achieving sales and selling the correct equipment would be achieved.

- **Improved management skills** with the ability to manage both customer/market and product decisions. The ensuing breadth of vision should create higher levels of flexibility and market responsiveness – a feature that ICC appear to have been missing at a customer level, where both product and market divisions were in part taken by surprise by the changes in the customers use of technology and changes in buying patterns.

(c)   The matrix form demands a great deal of the manager who must have the capability to deal with the tension that can arise between apparent conflicting objectives. A balancing of tension can only be achieved through a process of reconciliation and negotiation, a difficult position for the manager at the centre and what has been described as 'no place for managers seeking security and stability' (*Mintzberg*). In practice, as could be expected, managers appear to need considerable time and support to evolve skills in managing in matrix organisational forms (*Kanter*).

There are a number of specific challenges which organisational design must confront and solve if the matrix form is to work effectively. These can be summarised under four main areas:

- **Management of conflict** resulting from the removal of typical departmental boundaries and the introduction of conflicting objectives and accountability. The essence is collaboration within the matrix rather than internal competition which exists in some organisations.

- **Management of stress** arising from role conflict and role ambiguity leading to the potential for role overload. For example, it is not always clear in the matrix form exactly who is responsible for what. Care should be taken to ensure an even balance of workloads across the matrix, appropriate management development training and the use of mentoring systems by which a manager is given a clear point of access generally within a functional line (e.g. finance, marketing, personnel) to seek advice and assistance.

- **Management of the balance of power** arising from differing lines of authority. If the balance is upset and one authority line dominates then in effect the matrix breaks down and the organisation reverts to a hierarchical form. Note that a balance of power without co-operative decision making also leads to inertia as conflict is passed up the chains of command until a point is reached in the structure where a decision can be made.

- The **cost of management** arising from more time spent in meetings, discussions, information exchange and administrative support and potentially more managers to operate the organisation.

20 FRIGATE LIMITED

Key answer tips

In part (a), knowledge of the elements of the cultural web will be imperative. There are 7 elements so there are roughly two marks available for each one. Students should work on the principle that there will be 1 mark for explaining the element and 1 mark for relating it to the scenario.

For part (b) it will be important to use Mintzberg's terminology as this is flagged clearly in the question. It would appear that the existing structure is a simple or entrepreneurial one and students should illustrate the relevant elements of the scenario which provide this opinion. The new company accountant appears to have come from a machine bureaucracy and this structure should be explained. The final few marks are likely to be available for highlighting how it is difficult to combine this structures and how controls in each structure will be different.

(a) The cultural web is a representation of the taken for granted assumptions, or paradigm, of an organisation. The question specifically references the cultural web, but any framework that is appropriate for understanding the culture of an organisation can be used.

Symbols such as logos, offices, cars, titles, language and terminology are a shorthand representation of the nature of the organisation. At Frigate, the adoption of the term 'Commander' by its managing director, Ron Frew, and his use of naval terminology is indicative of how he wishes to be perceived and the way he wants the company to run. Indeed the name of the company itself reflects his naval obsession. The main symbol of his success is the motor cruiser that Frew owns and moors at the local port. The irony is that Frew actually has no naval experience. He is acting out a stereotype of how he perceives naval life to be.

Power structures are also likely to influence the key assumptions of an organisation. The most powerful groupings within the organisation are likely to be closely associated with core assumptions and beliefs. At Frigate, power is centred on one person. Leadership comes from a person who holds strongly held views, opinions and beliefs.

The organisational structure is likely to reflect power and show important roles and relationships. At Frigate, there is little formal structure and Ann Li's attempt to put one in place was opposed.

Control systems, measurements and reward systems emphasise what is important to monitor in the organisation. Frew is primarily concerned with cost control. Emphasis is on punishment (making deductions from wages for late arrival), rather than reward, which fits his naval stereotype. There appear to be few formal process controls and relationships with both customers and suppliers are confrontational. Ann Li's attempt to install formal controls throughout the organisation was resisted by Frew.

Routines and rituals define the 'way we do things around here'. For Frew there is a distinction between the routines of staff (must arrive on time, minimum holidays with no flexibility) and the rules that apply to himself — flexible working, long holidays, the expectation that employees will help him with his personal life.

The *stories* told by members of an organisation are usually concerned with success, disasters, heroes, villains and mavericks. It appears that Frew is the hero, seeing off lazy staff, unscrupulous suppliers (trying to sell me inferior quality goods for higher prices), problematic customers (moaning about prices and paying later and later) and bureaucratic officials (squandering my hard-earned money). These are identified as the villains. He even extends his stories to society as a whole, believing that a period working in the navy would do everyone good.

Finally, the company *paradigm* summarises and reinforces the other elements of the cultural web. Underpinning all of this is Frew's belief that the company is run for his own gratification and that of his immediate family. The benefits he receives and the lifestyle he enjoys is his reward for being a risk taker in a hostile environment which is always trying to limit him. He appears to see expenditure on his family (such as share gifts and holidays) as perfectly acceptable. Figure 1 summarises the cultural web for Frigate Ltd.

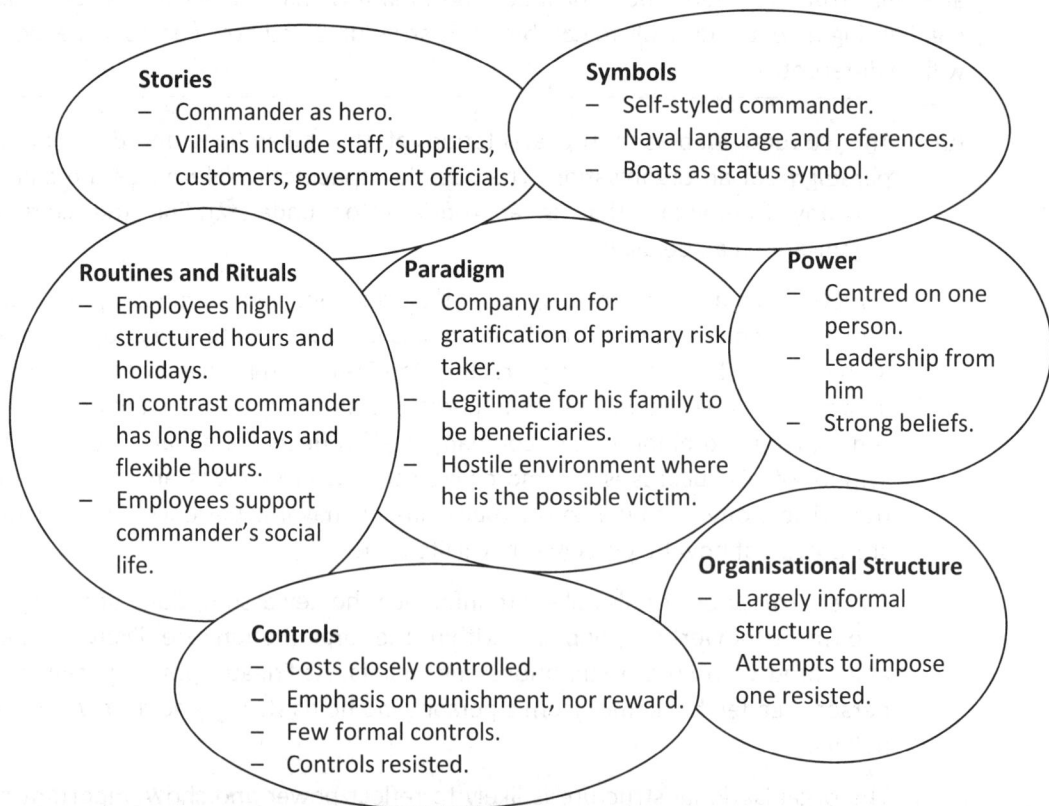

Figure 1: The cultural web at Frigate Limited

(b) An organisation's configuration considers how the structure, processes and relationships of an organisation work together. Henry Mintzberg has identified six configuration stereotypes. Each configuration is idealised, a simplification. Mintzberg is at pains to point out that no real organisation is exactly like any one of them. Some come close to a specific stereotype, others reflect combinations and yet others are in transition from one form to another.

In the context of Frigate, two configurations are of interest:

Firstly, the *entrepreneurial* organisational configuration has the following attributes relevant to Frigate.

Structure

- Simple, informal and flexible with few staff and no significant middle-line hierarchy.

- Activities revolve around the chief executive, who controls personally through direct supervision.

Context

- Simple and dynamic environment

- Strong leadership, autocratic

- Small organisation.

Power is focused on the chief executive, who personally exercises it. Formal controls are discouraged and seen as a threat to that person's authority. The typical owner (such as Ron Frew) exercises control through informal, direct (face-to-face) supervision. Employees may find such organisations highly restrictive. In Mintzberg's words they may not feel 'like the participants in an exciting journey, but like cattle being led to market for someone else's benefit'. Frigate Limited has many of the characteristics of an entrepreneurial organisation.

Secondly, in contrast Ann Li has joined from an organisation which is likely to have the attributes of a *machine bureaucracy* – another stereotype identified by Mintzberg. In structural terms these organisations are characterised by:

Structure

- Formal procedures

- Sharp division of labour

- Strict hierarchy.

Context

- Usually larger, mature organisation

- Rationalised, standardised processes

- Simple and stable environment.

In such organisations some operations are routine, many are rather simple and repetitive and as a result work processes are highly standardised. This is Ann Li's experience that she is trying to bring to Frigate.

An understanding of organisational configurations would have helped identify the likely failure of Ann Li's proposal. She is trying to introduce a functional organisational structure into a CEO-controlled environment and a formal set of processes into an environment where flexible processes are directed by the CEO. The key factor here is the mismatch between structure, processes and context. The failure of her proposals could have been predicted by someone who understood the need to correctly match organisational structure, controls and processes.

ACCA Marking scheme		Marks
(a)	1 mark for each relevant point up to a maximum of 15 marks for this part	15
(b)	1 mark for each relevant point up to a maximum of 10 marks for this part question.	10
Total		25

21 YVERN TRINKETS REGIONAL

> **Key answer tips**
>
> In part (a), on cost accounting, students often over-emphasise the calculations and spend too much time on these at the expense of a discussion of the decision involved. The discussion is likely to be both easier to attempt and worth more marks.
>
> In part (b) the four key generic strategies were clearly flagged by the examiner. A brief evaluation of each option was required where the key will have been making points which were relevant to the company in the scenario.

(a) Here is a monthly analysis of the data given in the scenario.

Product	A	B	C	D	Total
Production (units)	2,000	5,500	4,000	3,000	
Unit marginal costs					
Direct materials	3	5	2	4	
Direct labour	9	6	9	6	
Variable production overheads	2	3	1	2	
Variable cost per unit	14	14	12	12	
Total monthly variable cost	28,000	77,000	48,000	36,000	
Fixed monthly overheads	4,000	4,000	4,000	4,000	
Total in-house monthly cost	32,000	81,000	52,000	40,000	205,000
Buying costs per unit	11.5	16.5	12.5	13.5	
Total monthly buy in cost	23,000	90,750	50,000	40,500	204,250

The data suggest that only products A and C can be sourced more cheaply through outsourcing. Products B and D can be produced more cheaply in-house.

If products A and C are sub-contracted, the company would then have spare capacity. There is no evidence from the scenario that there is any demand for further production for B and D. More research has to be conducted to see if, in fact, production capacity is a limiting factor at the company and can be effectively utilised to produce more of B and D. If this is the case, then there would be a powerful argument for outsourcing A and C.

The reaction of the company's workforce also has to be taken into consideration. If production of B and D cannot be expanded to take up the spare capacity, then redundancies may be required and so strike action may take place as a result of an industrial dispute. Evidence also suggests that products A and C require more labour intensive processes. So even if spare capacity is used up, demand for labour would reduce. There are also likely to be costs associated with redundancies which do not appear to have been taken into consideration.

The company has no experience in managing an outsourced supplier and ensuring that supplied products are of the required quality. Contractual terms will have to be established for specifying the terms of supply and for specifying service level agreements and penalties for failing to supply. Quality acceptance criteria will have to be established and a process set up for formally accepting the products produced by the outsourcer. This management of the outsource supplier will require one-off and continuing costs which do not appear to have been factored into the proposal.

The company has always advertised itself as producing locally in the region. It is part of their marketing campaign and an attraction to local customers. Sourcing the products through geographically remote outsourcers invalidates the marketing message and may also lead to adverse customer reaction. The company needs to understand the reasons why customers buy its products in the first place before it makes such a decision.

The justification for outsourcing product C is purely made on the saving of fixed costs attributable to its manufacture. The variable production cost of C is actually less than the buy-in cost ($48,000 compared with $50,000), but the addition of the fixed overhead makes the outsourcing option cheaper. There are two issues here: the reliability of this estimate of fixed costs and the likelihood that these savings can be delivered by management when the production of the product is outsourced. It seems unlikely that all four products will have exactly the same direct effect on fixed costs; it looks more like an arbitrary figure. Furthermore, on many occasions, fixed costs savings do not actually materialise. Management fails to deliver.

Finally, the outsourcing prices offered may depend upon outsourcing the whole of production to Tinglia. If this is the case, then the outsourcing option is very slightly cheaper ($204,250 compared with $205,000) but this again depends upon the reliability of the fixed overhead data and the ability of management to save these fixed costs once production is outsourced. The cost of shutting the production capacity in Yvern and employee redundancy costs also have to be taken into consideration.

Summary

The decision to make or buy certain products should not be taken on cost savings alone. The company has considerable experience of making the products and the location they are produced in appears to be important to both the company (from its marketing message) and its customers. In contrast, the company has no experience in outsourcing and managing outsourced providers. In addition, the new managing director's assertion that 'all four products can be produced more cheaply by the supplier in Tinglia' is ambiguous. If he means that the products can be made more cheaply in Tinglia if all four products are outsourced, then he is just about correct, although data on overhead costs would have to be reconsidered and other costs associated with outsourcing investigated. However, if he means that all products can individually be produced more cheaply in Tinglia, then he is clearly incorrect. Products B and D can be produced more cheaply in-house. However, partial outsourcing may lead to spare labour and machine capacity issues in the factory in Yvern.

(b) The managing director states that he wishes to follow a generic strategy of cost leadership. However, it seems likely that he has misunderstood the term or that he is knowingly using it as a euphemism for cost reduction. His slide missed out important information.

Strategic advantage

Target	Low cost	Unique
All customers	Cost Leadership	Differentiation
Market segment	Cost Focus	Differentiation Focus

A generic strategy of cost leadership means being the lowest cost producer in the industry as a whole.

It seems unlikely that the company can pursue such a strategy. It has larger rivals (who will be able to obtain better economies of scale) both within the region and within the country as a whole. There is no evidence of technical advantage, and indeed the managing director has commented on outdated information technology. There is no suggestion, either, of other factors which would allow the company to achieve cost leadership, such as having favourable access to sources of supply, or raw materials or labour.

A differentiation strategy assumes that competitive advantage can be gained, in the industry as a whole, through particular characteristics of a company's product. Companies which pursue such a strategy worry less about costs and seek, instead, to be perceived in the industry as unique. For example, the product may be innovative or superior in some way. Again, this does not appear to apply to YTR, in the context of the industry.

Both cost leadership and differentiation require superior performance, which does not appear to be a characteristic of YTR.

A focused or niche strategy takes place when a firm concentrates its attention on one or more market segments or niches. In doing so it could aim to be a cost leader for a particular segment. This is the cost focus strategy identified in the managing director's slide. This is often associated with an environment where 'broader scope' companies exhibit an element of over-performance, offering a particular segment much more than it wants, at a price which reflects this. This may be a possible strategy for YTR if their products are largely indistinguishable from other producers in Yvern. However, outsourcing production does not appear to be the right way of pursuing this strategy.

Alternatively, a company might pursue differentiation for a particular segment; a differentiation focus strategy. This strategy seeks to provide a perceived high quality product to a selected market segment or niche. Such products may be heavily branded and sold at a substantial price premium. There is evidence to suggest that YTR has a strong brand and meets a demand for regional, locally produced products.

A better strategy for YTR is focus, where it can serve a particular niche where it can largely insulate itself from the competition. Porter suggests that a company must pursue one of these strategies. Both cost leadership and differentiation require superior performance and some form of focus strategy is easier, as it is simpler to dominate a niche market.

ACCA Marking scheme		
		Marks
(a)	1 mark for each appropriate point up to a maximum of 15 marks; this could include:	
(b)	– Up to 1 mark for analysis of data associated with each product, up to a maximum of 6 marks	
	– Up to 1 mark for quantitative analysis of sending complete production to Tinglia	
(b)	1 mark for each appropriate point up to a maximum of 10 marks	
Total		**25**

Examiner's comments

Part (a) was well answered by most candidates. The financial analysis (which revealed that the managing director's assertion was untrue) was correctly completed by most candidates and other issues, such as contradicting the marketing message, lack of experience in outsourcing etc. were also well covered. Indeed a significant number of candidates scored twelve marks or more on this part question.

Part (b), in general, was not answered particularly well. Many candidates did not make enough points about each generic strategy to get the marks on offer. Cost focus was also poorly dealt with. It is also very hard to make a case for the company following a cost leadership strategy. The signs in the case study are not encouraging (it is not big enough, it has outdated technology) and so a differentiation strategy, focused on a niche regional market, seems more acceptable. Many candidates acknowledged this and gained credit for this insight.

BUSINESS PROCESS CHANGE

22   COUNTRY CAR CLUB

Key answer tips

Although the question does not explicitly ask for it, the process-strategy matrix suggested by Paul Harmon would provide an appropriate context for the answer to this question.

However, other appropriate models or frameworks could be used by candidates to answer this part of the question.

(a)   Management of processes

The process-strategy matrix has two axes. The vertical axis is concerned with process complexity and dynamics. At the base of the vertical axis are simple processes often with simple procedures while at the top are complex processes which may require negotiation, discussion and complicated design. On the horizontal axis is the strategic value of these processes. Their importance increases from left to right with low value processes concerned with things that must be done but which add little value to products or services. On the extreme right of this axis are high value processes which are very important to success and add significant value to goods and services. From these two axes, Harmon categorises four quadrants and makes suggestions about how processes should be tackled in each quadrant.

Low strategic importance, low process complexity and dynamics

This quadrant contains relatively straightforward stable processes which add little business value. They are processes that must be carried out by the company but add nothing to the company's value proposition. These processes need to be automated in the most efficient way possible. They are often called 'commodity processes' and are suitable for standard software package solutions or outsourcing to organisations that specialise in that area. Payroll is a good example of this. Many standard software packages are available in the market place. Alternatively, a computer bureau can be used to process the payroll on behalf of the organisation.

Low strategic importance, high process complexity and dynamics

This quadrant is for relatively complex processes that need to be done but do not add significant value to the company's products or services. They are not at the heart of the company's core competencies. Harmon suggests that these should be outsourced to organisations which have them as their core business.

High strategic importance, low process complexity and dynamics

These processes lie in the lower right quadrant of the model. They tend to be relatively straightforward processes which, nevertheless, have a significant role in the organisation's activities. They are central to what the business does. The aim is to automate these, if possible, to gain cost reduction and improve quality and efficiency.

High strategic importance, high process complexity and dynamics

Finally, in the top right hand quadrant are high value, complex processes which often include human judgement and expertise and are often very difficult to automate. Harmon suggests that these might be the focus of major process redesign initiatives focusing on business process improvement through the improved performance of the people undertaking those processes.

In the context of 3C, the following recommendations are suggested. Clearly these are value judgements and credit will be given for coherently argued answers which do not match the examiner's conclusions.

(i)   Attendance at breakdowns

This appears to be of high strategic importance and, although some breakdowns are bound to be simple to fix, it requires the repairer to be knowledgeable, flexible and diplomatic. Consequently, it appears to be a candidate for the upper right quadrant of the process-strategy matrix. Hence it is suggested that the service should remain in-house and attention should be paid to improving the competency of the 'service patrol engineers'. Information technology should be harnessed to seek improvements in response time to breakdowns by improving the organisation and distribution of these engineers. Systems might also be developed to technically support engineers and to help them diagnose and fix roadside problems.

(ii)   Membership renewal

This should be a relatively straightforward process, so it sits in one of the two lower quadrants. It can be argued that it is a process that is core to the business and is not one (like payroll) which can be found across all businesses. It appears to be a candidate for the lower right quadrant. Hence it is a candidate for automation to gain efficiency. The organisation already has a bespoke system operated by in-house permanent employees. This seems an appropriate way of delivering this process. However, it might benefit from revisiting the way the bespoke system works. The scenario suggests that the current system sends out membership renewals on receipt of a confirmation from the member. The system might benefit from being built around a presumption of renewal, so that the member only contacts the organisation if he or she does not wish to renew.

(iii)   Vehicle insurance services

These appear to be a relatively complex process which is of little strategic importance to 3C. It appears to inhabit the top left hand quadrant of the matrix. Insurance is not only technically complex, it carries large risks and substantial regulatory requirements. It is likely that these regulatory requirements will undergo frequent changes. It would appear attractive to 3C to outsource this service to a specialist provider who would then badge it under 3C's name. This is relatively common practice and 3C's venture into insurance must have been very expensive. Outsourcing provides it with opportunities for providing a wider service with reduced in-house costs.

(iv)   Membership queries

Membership queries are of unpredictable complexity. They are also an important contact point between the company and their members. Failure to handle queries courteously and correctly could have important consequences for membership renewal. It is suggested that this is an upper right hand quadrant process – potentially complex and of high strategic importance to the company. Investment is required in people supported by innovative and speedy IT systems that allow the 3C staff to respond quickly and accurately to a wide range of questions. It is suggested that membership queries continue to remain in-house although the physical location of the call centre might reflect certain financial opportunities – such as low property rents and cheaper labour.

(v)   Vehicle history checks

Vehicle history checks appear to be of relatively low strategic importance to 3C. Automation should make such checks relatively straightforward, although the combination of accident damage, stolen vehicles, finance agreements and time when the vehicle was voluntarily taken off the road may make determining this history more complex then it first appears. Furthermore, the consequences of providing inaccurate or incomplete information may be quite severe. Someone who has unsuspectingly purchased a car which has been damaged and repaired might claim for damages against 3C when this was revealed. These damages might be extensive if someone died in the vehicle as a result of a botched repair. Consequently it is suggested that this is predominantly an upper left hand quadrant process which should be outsourced to an organisation which is already in this field.

Table 2.1 summarises the advice to the BAC.

Table 2.1

Attendance at repairs	Remains in-house. Improve competency of repair staff. Support them with IT systems
Membership renewal	Remains in-house and revisit basis of automation
Vehicle insurance	Outsource
Membership queries	Remains in-house. Improve competency of call centre staff. Support them with IT systems
Vehicle history	Outsource

(b) **Outsourcing**

In the question scenario the decision to outsource the purchase and maintenance of 3C vehicles is justified by its low strategic importance and its low to medium complexity. However, this only makes it a *candidate* for outsourcing and so tangible and intangible benefits would have to be attached to this suggestion in a subsequent detailed analysis. This part of the question asks candidates to analyse the advantages of outsourcing the process of the purchase and maintenance of 3C vehicles. It is suggested that advantages would include:

Purchasing benefits from economies of scale

AutoDirect purchase thousands of cars and vans for their customers each year. They should be able to negotiate substantial discounts from manufacturers, some of which can be passed on to their customers.

Predictable costs

The vehicle lease payments with AutoDirect are monthly and they include full maintenance of the car, including tyres and exhausts. Hence 3C will have predictable costs for budgeting purposes. Previously, costs would have been variable and unpredictable, depending upon the reliability of the vehicles.

Reduced overhead costs – garage and purchasing

The overhead costs associated with the garage and the garage and purchasing employees have been lost (except for the one manager retained to manage the contract with AutoDirect). There may also be an opportunity for realising income from the sale of the garage site. It is described as being in a residential area with no room for expansion and severe parking congestion. It may be possible to sell the garage for residential development.

Higher vehicle availability

The central garage itself is a bottleneck. Vehicles have to be driven or transported to this garage from all parts of the country and left there while they are serviced or repaired. They then have to be driven back to their operational area. AutoDirect has repair and servicing centres throughout the country and so it will be possible for vehicles to be taken locally for services and repairs – thus reducing vehicle downtime.

Freeing cash to use for other investments – from purchase to lease

The policy of purchasing vehicles meant that a considerable amount of cash has been tied up in fast depreciating assets. Switching to leasing will release this cash for investment elsewhere in the company.

Access to expertise and legislation

It is likely that vehicles will become increasingly subject to legislation designed to reduce carbon emissions. This, together with the increasing technical complexity of vehicles, will mean that vehicles will become increasingly difficult to maintain without specialist monitoring and repair equipment. It is unlikely that 3C can maintain such a level of investment and so outsourcing to a specialist makes good sense. AutoDirect will have to monitor legislation, advise on its implications and implement its requirements for its large customer base.

Concentration on core business

Although this issue is not explicitly considered in the scenario it is something that impacts on all organisations. The management of the garage does not appear to be a core strategic requirement. It must consume some elements of senior management time. Outsourcing frees up that time so it can be used to focus on issues directly relevant to the customer and the business as a whole.

	ACCA Marking scheme	
		Marks
(a)	Up to 3 marks for the recommendation and its justification in each of the process areas required by the question	
	Five process areas required giving a maximum of 15 marks	15
(b)	Up to 2 marks for each appropriate advantage identified by the candidate up to a maximum of 10 marks	10
Total		**25**

Examiner's comments

The scenario for this question concerned a car club that was reviewing its processes. It had already decided to outsource the purchase and maintenance of its own vehicles. The advantage this outsourcing offered the car club was the subject of the second part of this question. This was answered relatively well, although some candidates confused the vehicles of 3C with the vehicles of the club's members. Other candidates failed to make their points relevant to the scenario, using Information Technology examples instead.

The first part of the question listed five major process areas and asked candidates to suggest and justify recommendations for outsourcing or improvement in each of those areas. Many candidates provided excellent answers, often using Paul Harmon's framework as a reference point. The suggested answers have specific recommendations; for example, outsourcing of vehicle insurance services. However, there is no absolutely correct answer and so candidates who provided coherent justification for retaining such services in-house were also awarded appropriate marks.

23   STELLA ELECTRONICS

> **Key answer tips**
>
> For part (a), candidates should focus on identifying problems in the scenario and suggesting solutions for each one. In part (b), weaker candidates might focus on the textbook advantages and disadvantages of outsourcing rather than the make points that are relevant to this scenario (such as using some of the financial data that was provided).

(a)   **Issues with the current process**

- There are too many handoffs in the current process, particularly given the need to connect to each section by telephone. It seems likely that bottlenecks will form around these handoffs.

- The role of the supervisor is particularly redundant from the perspective of Stella Electronics (SE). Enquiries for other companies should not be part of their process and, from their perspective, the supervisor adds no value.

- The payment or service contract reference number and the password are requested relatively late in the process. The need to have these available could have been flagged earlier in the process, perhaps at first contact with the supervisor.

- On average, 153 people per day (600 calls × 0.85 × 30%) do not know their reference number. This means that SE is billed $153.00 per day for calls which are not resolved. It also wastes the end customer's time and money and is a potential source of complaint and dissatisfaction.

- On average, 18 people (17.85) per day ((600 − 90 − 153) × 5%) do not know their password. This means that SE is billed $18 per day for calls which are not resolved. It also wastes the end customer's time and money and is, again, a potential source of dissatisfaction and complaint.

- Although the split of staff across the sections seems reasonable at first sight (six people in technical support for 60% of queries, three people in Stella support for 25% refunds, and one person in the contracts section for 15% of queries), this masks two problems. Firstly, the contracts section is disproportionately understaffed (it should have 1.5 staff) and, secondly, and, more importantly, 100% of the calls have to pass though the three people in Stella support. This must be a bottleneck, and is likely to be the main reason for the poor service experienced by the end customer.

Potential solutions

> **Tutorial note**
>
> There are a range of potential solutions. Some ideas are presented below, but other legitimate answers will be given credit.

- A dedicated phone number could be given to SE customers to eradicate the need for a TCG supervisor.

- Different phone numbers could be given to SE customers for the three different types of query. Thus there will be a dedicated refund line, a dedicated contracts line and a dedicated technical support line.

- Staffing levels could be changed to reflect the frequency of calls. For example, an extra person could be provided in the contracts section, although this does not address the support bottleneck.

- The role of routing calls could be performed by an automated telephone system. For example, option 1 could be refunds, option 2 for technical queries and option 3 for service contracts. This would also provide a mechanism for handling other types of queries (option 4), which could be the responsibility of the supervisor if his or her role is retained.

- Customers requesting refunds or requiring technical support could be informed earlier in the process of the need to have their contract reference number and password ready. This could be given in the automated reply (see point above) to the initial phone call or menu choice selected or it could be requested by the supervisor, if this role is retained. The need for this could also be prominently displayed on their company's website.

- Multi-skilling staff so that they could effectively handle any part of the process would reduce handoffs. It may be difficult to include technical support in a multi-skilled role, but it certainly seems feasible to merge the refund and service contract roles. Reducing the number of swim lanes is an effective way of improving a business process.

(b) The financial case for outsourcing still remains very strong. At present, the cost to SE is $600 per day for a service provided by 10 people, giving a 24 hour service. SE has calculated that it will cost $50 to employ a person with similar competencies in Arborium for an eight hour shift. This produces a 24 hour cost of $150. If SE continues to employ 10 staff, then the total cost will be $1,500 per day. There would also be capital costs of re-establishing the infrastructure to provide the support service, including telephones, office furniture and training costs. There will also be operational costs, such as electricity and office rent and property charges.

So a like-to-like switch back to an in-house support unit seems impossible to justify on cost grounds. However, SE could consider alternative ways of dealing with calls. Technical queries could be addressed by improving support documentation (reducing the demand for queries) and by publishing frequently asked questions (FAQs) on its website. Email support could also be offered. The processing of refunds and the handling of service contracts could be provided by an online process. This seems particularly suited to refund processing. Contracts, which appears to require a dialogue between the customer and SE, seems less of a candidate for this. Improvements in query handling might also allow SE to reduce the number of people working in the centre to a level where the cost of the service would be roughly the same as the outsourced equivalent.

The cultural context of outsourcing needs consideration. Outsourcing, and particularly offshoring, appears to have a negative impact on customers who, as well as having difficulty in understanding the call centre staff based in different countries, increasingly view offshoring as a way of exporting employment. As the number of people out of work in Arborium continues to grow, so the pressure increases on companies to bring work back in-house. SE might be able to make some marketing or public relations capital out of bringing support back in-house and into the country.

Service is a primary activity on the value chain. It is a key point where customers interact with an organisation and form their opinions about it. At present, many customers have a negative view of SE informed by their contact with the TCG call centre. Queries take too long to process and there are problems in understanding the call centre staff. SE needs to consider whether it is wise to outsource such a customer-focused activity. Perhaps the support activities (information technology, procurement) of the value chain are better candidates for outsourcing.

However, it also has to be recognised that support is not a core activity of SE. It is primarily an electronics retailer. It might be reasonable to conclude that a company such as TCG, dedicated to providing call centre support, should give a better service, leaving SE time to focus on its core competencies and activity.

In the short term, it would seem sensible to introduce improvements at the TCG call centre. The service is already relatively cheap and could be made cheaper by reducing the number of calls (through improved documentation and website support) and by reducing the number of calls which are not resolved. In the longer term, SE might wish to re-consider the wisdom of outsourcing a customer-facing service and they may, on ethical grounds, wish to invest in jobs in the country where most of their customers are. Publicising this socially responsible decision might also boost sales.

ACCA Marking scheme		
		Marks
(a)	1 mark for each relevant point up to a maximum of 8 marks for evaluation of the problem. 1 mark for each relevant point up to a maximum of 8 marks for suggested improvements. A maximum of 15 marks for this part question.	15
(b)	1 mark for each relevant point up to a maximum of 10 marks. 1 mark will be allocated for the correct calculation of the daily cost of delivering the service in-house.	10
Total		**25**

24 TMP

Key answer tips

There are only 5 marks available for part (a) and the requirement asks you to 'identify' issues only. There is no need to evaluate or discuss them so a simple list should be sufficient. Try to split you points between drivers and barriers and have a target of around three of each.

In part (b), the examiner asks for the marketing mix but he is very explicit about which elements of the mix that you should consider. Therefore, you should limit your answer to these issues and not cover other elements of the 7P's model as no marks will be available for areas such as processes. There are 5 areas to cover for 20 marks so it is approximately 4 marks per area (which should give you a target of around 5 or 6 sentences in each area. Try to have a couple of specific recommendations in each area, explain them and justify them. The key will be to make them as specific as possible to TMP.

(a)   The main drivers for the adoption of e-business at TMP are:

- Cost reduction, specifically raw material costs (the cost of paper) and distribution costs to bookshops.

- Improved profit margin, perhaps achieved by removing the bookshop as an intermediary.

- Increased revenue, increasing sales (as well as profit margins) is an important objective.

- The desire to keep up-to-date (exemplified by the marketing director) and hence to avoid losing market share to businesses prepared to embrace e-business.

- Increased ecological concern about the use of timber for paper manufacture. The trees used to provide the timber are becoming increasingly scarce.

- People, in the shape of the marketing director and the graduate recruited to develop the website.

The main barriers to the adoption of e-business at TMP are:

- Concerns about the cost of developing the website, particularly when revenue and profits are decreasing. Marketing expenditure has been reduced and this is likely to continue.

- Concerns that it will destroy the relationship with bookshops and those sales will decrease overall as a result. Destroying existing channels is often a major barrier to change.

- Lack of technical ability within the company to develop and maintain the website and the impact this may have on its long-term viability.

- Concern about fraud and piracy. This may be within the context of the financial transactions of e-commerce. It may also reflect concerns about the pirating of books, leading to either cheap printed versions being produced and sold in local markets or to illegitimate copies being sold and distributed on the web.

- Other directors could be perceived as a barrier to the adoption of e-business.

(b)   **Product**

At present, TMP offer conventional physical books. E-business may provide opportunities for either replacing or augmenting this product. For example:

- Replacing the book with an electronic alternative that customers can read directly from the screen, view through an e-book reader or print off at their own cost. This may allow the range of products to be increased, introducing books that would be uneconomic to produce conventionally.

- Augmenting the product by providing supplementary services and features. For example, many text books now have an associated website that includes further case studies, exercises, solutions, simulations etc. This may be particularly applicable to management texts where readers often require further information.

Using e-business to change the nature of the product should help reinforce two of the drivers identified in the first part of this question. It should help reduce raw material costs as well as helping the company meet environmental targets. Augmenting the product should help deliver a better quality product to customers.

E-business also offers opportunities for extending the product range, perhaps offering (through intermediaries) management training, financial advice and other related services.

Price

At present TMP largely sells through bookshops and so the TMP price has to reflect a profit margin for the bookshop. If TMP exploits e-business to develop a channel that eliminates bookshops, then it should be able to simultaneously discount the price of the book and yet still improve their profit margin. E-business may also be an opportunity to experiment with differential pricing. The scenario notes that overseas sales are low because of the relatively high sales price of books. TMP may be able to combine differential pricing (in local currencies) with electronic alternatives to find a product that is saleable in these markets.

TMP has to be aware of any price-comparison websites and be prepared to monitor costs on these sites and react accordingly. They also have to be aware of large established channels, such as Amazon. Such sites will expect keen pricing, but will also pay commissions on books sold through the site.

Finally, TMP might seek an alternative price strategy, based for example on subscribing to the site, rather than selling books. A 'book' may become a continually updated web resource that customers pay to use on either a one-off or continuing basis. There is no need for them to actually own the book themselves. TMP therefore becomes a virtual library.

Direct pricing to customers also provides the opportunities for special offers, pre-publication prices and other deals. For example, special discount prices on related books can be offered to customers who have placed an order for a specific book.

Promotion

At present, promotion is restricted to a custom-built display case at bookshops and full-page display advertisements in magazines and journals. Such promotion reflects a conventional 'push' approach to marketing that focuses on the product rather than the customers. If the website records the details of visitors, then the company can identify potential customers for its products and target them in mail-shots and on-line suggestions. For example, customers who have bought certain titles may have others suggested to them when they next visit the site. Many sites also make buying suggestions based on the behaviour of other customers, for example displaying 'other titles which have been bought by customers who have bought this book'.

E-business will require the company to consider both its online and offline promotion. TMP may be able to reduce its offline expenditure, cutting back on advertising. In its place it might spend elsewhere, particularly in making sure that it figures prominently in search engine listings. Links to other sites should also be considered, allowing promotion of TMP books on related sites. For example, internet sites providing management advice, information and glossaries may have a link to the TMP site. TMP pays commission to the site on sales made through such links. Banner advertising might also be considered on such sites. A similar approach might be used with academic websites where a TMP book is recommended reading for a course.

Place

Bookshops have limited reach, although they do provide the facility for the potential buyer to handle the book (see physical evidence). The display advertising has unpredictable reach. Circulation figures are usually provided by journals and magazines but this does not give any information on how many people actually read the advertisements in question. The scenario suggests that both bookshops and journals appear to have declining reach, based on statistics about their closure. The internet has global reach. The relatively small percentage of books currently sold outside Arcadia is attributed to the cost of those books. However, it may be that the rest of the world is simply unfamiliar with TMP's booklist, a shortcoming that will be addressed by the internet site

In wider e-business terms, a consideration of place will also lead to TMP considering whether it is economic to continue printing in Arcadia which is a high-cost economy. The printing works were established 50 years ago and it seems likely that cost-savings could be gained by printing and distributing the books in lower labour cost economies.

Physical evidence

One of the problems in buying books is the ability to look inside those books before purchase. Often titles are insufficient to make a purchasing decision. One of the advantages of the bookshop is that the potential buyer can physically inspect the goods, looking at the content in detail to ensure that it meets their needs. In contrast, physical evidence is not possible at all through display advertising in a journal.

On the website, it would be possible to allow the potential buyer to view the contents of the book in detail and (usually) one physical chapter. This so-called 'look inside' facility allows them to base their buying decision on some (but not all) physical evidence. Further evidence can also be provided by unsolicited recommendations and reviews from other customers. Feedback, comments and rating systems are typical features on a website. These are rarely available through the bookshop. The bookshop employees have rarely read all the books they sell and, if they have read the book, are probably biased towards a sale. Sometimes, reviews have been placed in the book, often from a previous printing or edition. However, these are only the ones sanctioned by the publisher. Unsolicited references are one of the advantages of the website (as long as they are good!).

The problem of physical evidence can also be addressed by seeing the book as a website resource rather than a physical entity. If the reader pays for access, then very little expenditure is likely on a book that does not fulfil the reader's requirements and expectations.

ACCA Marking scheme		
		Marks
(a)	1 mark for each relevant point up to a maximum of 5 for this part question.	5
(b)	1 mark for each relevant point up to a maximum of 4 marks for each element of the marketing mix. There are five elements in the marketing mix specified in the question.	20
		___
Total		**25**
		___

25   INSTITUTE OF ANALYTICAL ACCOUNTANTS

> 🔑
>
> **Key answer tips**
>
> The examiner likes to give students a diagram to interpret and students need practise some past exam questions on this area before entering the exam hall. The process itself had more elements than in previous exams but this should have provided students with plenty of elements to discuss in their answer.
>
> Part (b) on software selection will rely on students' broad syllabus coverage. It is likely to have been an easy question for those students who had revised this area. Software has been a common exam area so students should have been prepared for it, but it is unlikely that students who had not learnt the pocket note lists would have generated enough points to score well in this area.

(a)   There is an acknowledged bottleneck in the task 'Enter question into Question Bank' (administration). The volume of questions received is too great for the number of administrators assigned to the task of entering them. This often means that questions received back from reviewers cannot be found on the database to have their outcome noted because they have not yet been entered into the system. This causes further frustration and delay. The simplification pattern assumes that most established processes have redundancies and duplication. It focuses on tackling bottlenecks and unnecessary tasks and unnecessary loops.

The backlog of question entering also seems to have had an effect on the quality of data entry. A recent check noted that one in ten questions had an error, making them unfit for purpose. The problem is accentuated by the fact that the administrators are not subject experts and so do not understand the content and context of the questions and answers they are inputting. Furthermore, the current process does not have any subsequent checks on the quality of the questions entered onto the system. This is potentially very serious, with students receiving questions which have spelling mistakes or answers where none of the solutions is correct.

One obvious solution is to increase the number of administrators entering questions into the question bank. However, this will be costly and the quality problems are likely to remain.

One of the potential ways of reducing the bottleneck is to delay question entry until the question has been accepted. Currently, 20% of questions are immediately rejected by the reviewer and a further 15% are sent back to the author for revision. Of these, 30% are rejected on the second review. This approach would also mean that the administrators would not have to enter the suggested amendments (Update Question), where further errors are almost certainly made.

Reducing the number of swim lanes is often advocated by proponents of business process change. It is a central tenant of the gaps and disconnects redesign pattern. Handoffs between departments are often a source of problems and bottlenecks. One possibility is to move the tasks currently performed in the administration department into the education department where the employees have a greater understanding of the question subject matter and so are unlikely to make as many errors in data entry.

This could be combined with the suggestion outlined in the previous paragraph. However, it seems unlikely that the education department would welcome the suggestion and there seems likely to be staff issues and changes, reducing the number of people in administration and employing higher-cost employees in education.

Changing the sequence of tasks may also bring benefits. For example, the Select Reviewer process (Education) could be performed before the questions are submitted. Therefore all questions from a particular author are automatically sent to a specific reviewer. The need for anonymity would seem to preclude the direct despatch of questions from the author to the reviewer and this could reduce the efficiency of the proposal. However, the time taken to forward the proposed questions to reviewers would probably be reduced by this pre-selection approach.

The inclusion of the finance department as a swim lane also raises certain possibilities. This may be due to some agreed separation of duties between administration/education and the processing of payments. However, the inclusion of 'raise a reject notification' on this swim lane seems a poor fit. It is essentially an administrative process (as it has no apparent financial implications) and so should be performed by either administration or education. So, this task needs to be relocated in the proposed business process.

The re-engineering pattern essentially starts with a blank sheet of paper and the process is re-designed from the beginning focusing on its goals. At the IAA, the goal might be 'to have reviewed questions accurately entered into a computer system at the cheapest cost possible'.

Whether or not it qualifies for the term 're-engineering', a radical solution is to implement a workflow-type system where the author enters the question into a computer system and the question is routed automatically (through anonymously preassigning reviewers to authors) to the specified reviewer. If the author enters the question, he or she is unlikely to make many errors in data entry. Furthermore, if they do, these can be corrected by the reviewer. From the perspective of the IAA, the cost of entering the questions is transferred to the author and so the bottleneck is removed and administrative costs are reduced at one stroke.

The indication of the acceptability of the question is now the responsibility of the reviewer. Accepted responses can lead to the automatic raising of a payment notification which is sent to Finance. Rejection would lead to the automatic raising of a reject notification which is sent electronically to the author. Questions that need revising would also automatically be returned to the author to make amendments prior to re-submission to the second review process.

This re-engineered solution potentially removes IAA departments from the process completely, except for payment by Finance and even this could be automated. The need for administrative staff would be greatly reduced and it is difficult to see how this would not lead to redundancies. There may also have to be fewer employees in Education, although they could perhaps be redeployed on more strategic issues.

The implications for IAA staff of such a solution may mean that it is internally unpopular and difficult to implement, despite the financial and time benefits it will bring to the organisation.

(b)   The advantages to the IAA of purchasing a software package include the following:

Speed of implementation: The software package is already available in the market. It has a number of significant users. The IAA only has to configure it for its environment and populate it with data. This must be quicker than the alternative of building a bespoke solution which would require specifying requirements in detail, developing a design, building the solution and testing its functionality and reliability. Thus, as speed to market is an important issue for IAA, the software package solution has significant implementation advantages over the bespoke build.

Quality of the software: A bespoke build will require significant testing. Faults will be found that will need fixing and this will delay the availability of the package. It is impossible to find all faults in testing and so problems are likely to occur with the implemented solution which could cause operational problems and costs. The software package is already implemented at a number of sites and it can reasonably be assumed that most faults will have been found and fixed. The package is, in comparison to the bespoke build, a tried and tested solution.

Try before buy: The requirements for a bespoke build are specified in text and in appropriate models. Although prototypes may be built during system construction, it is not until the end of the build that users get the opportunity to experience the system that they have specified. At this stage it is usual to find misunderstandings that need to be rectified. In contrast, the software package is already available and users can experiment with it before buying it. Any failure to fulfil requirements can be identified prior to the package being purchased and presumably this was part of the evaluation of competing software solutions undertaken by IAA. Any compromises that IAA needs to make to accommodate the package should have been taken into account in the selection process.

Predicted maintenance costs: With a bespoke software build it is difficult to predict future maintenance costs. Much will depend upon future requirements and the design quality of the software. However, with software packages, maintenance fees are agreed in advance. Such fees will include further fault fixes (which would be an unpredictable cost in a bespoke build) and new features requested by the user community and with costs shared across all users. It is likely that IAA will be able to contribute requests and might reasonably expect to have some of these requests agreed by the software supplier and implemented in a release. Furthermore, although less appropriate in the IAA scenario, the software supplier will also build in legislative changes or requirements. The scenario mentions that the package offers invoicing and there may be changes in product taxes made by the government.

Access to expertise: It might also be expected that the software provider will have built up a considerable amount of domain expertise in implementing software at a number of examination boards. The company may have ideas and the software features that have not been envisaged by IAA but would bring unforeseen benefits to the organisation. It is difficult for many companies to frame requirements outside their normal ways of business and hence many bespoke systems are restricted to the requirements envisaged by people whose horizons are restricted by their experience of the organisation they are currently working in. A software package may bring in new ideas and possibilities.

Initial cost: No information is provided about the price of the software package solution. However, it seems likely that it will be cheaper than a bespoke build. Because the software is already built, its contribution to overheads (or profit) of the software producer is likely to be very significant. This should give IAA greater potential for negotiating a favourable price. It is also increasingly popular to pay for packages on a 'fee-for-use' basis with the software provided through a browser application. This means that the IAA can tailor the price paid to the number of students that they have attempting their examinations. In contrast, most bespoke builds have to be paid for in full as soon as the software is delivered.

How the software operates will help determine the pattern of how the IAA will work in the future. Although it is possible to tailor packages to fit requirements, this is not good practice. The cost of tailoring and the subsequent cost and difficulty of implementing new releases mean that any benefits of competitive advantage are soon eroded by the cost of maintaining the software solution. The users must be advised that they may not be getting the system they required in the initial requirements gathering stage. The difference between what they wanted and what the package offers should have been part of the software package evaluation. Users may have to change the way they work, re-assess how they want to work and adjust to how the software package actually allows them to work.

ACCA Marking scheme		Marks
(a)	Up to 1 mark for each appropriate point up to a maximum of	15
(b)	1 mark for each appropriate point up to a maximum of	10
Total		**25**

Examiner's comments

Part (a) was satisfactorily answered by some candidates. They applied themselves to the scenario and generally came up with solutions that addressed the problem. However, a significant number of candidates did not relate their answer to the scenario at all. They described general re-design principles and patterns and made, at best, fleeting reference to how these could be applied to the scenario. Such answers, many of which went on for several pages, could be given little credit. What is the point of the examiner developing a scenario, if the question can be answered with abstract textbook descriptions?

In part (b) too many candidates answered this part of the question with long answers giving the general disadvantages of a package solution (erosion of competitive edge, problem of long-term lock-in) which were irrelevant to the actual question asked. Consequently marks on this part question (and indeed for the question as a whole) were relatively low.

26 FLEXIPIPE

(a) A critical evaluation of using the software package approach at Flexipipe could be structured around three factors. The first concerns the wisdom of using a package solution for a process where the company enjoys a competitive edge over its competitors. The second factor focuses on the difficulties of selecting an appropriate package in an environment where requirements are difficult to define and are still subject to change. The final factor revolves around the problem of successfully procuring a software package in an organisation which lacks both experience and a process for selecting and procuring a nonstandard software application. Each of these factors is now considered in turn. Other appropriate factors and relevant approaches will be given credit.

Competitive edge

It is generally accepted that software package solutions cannot provide organisations with a competitive edge. By definition such packages are available to all companies in a sector or market and so any commercial advantages offered by the package are available to all organisations competing in that market.

It is recognised that the control of the production process at Flexipipe was very innovative. It provided the company with significant competitive edge over their competitors. For this reason, it seemed unlikely from the start that Flexipipe would find a package that fulfilled its exact requirements and that any selected package would constrain the production process. Indeed, this is what happened, with the new system unable to replicate the flexibility and efficiency of the existing one.

Initially, the company would have been advised to consider the location of the process on the Harmon process/strategy grid. The process is strategically important and relatively complex. Software package solutions should primarily be considered for reasonably straightforward commodity processes which have low strategic importance to the company, such as payroll and accounts. Thus, in the context of Flexipipe, a bespoke software solution would, from the outset, appear to have been more appropriate.

Complexity and nature of requirements

It was recognised from the start that it was relatively difficult to specify all the requirements of the production process in advance because many decisions were intuitively taken by experienced managers and supervisors on the factory floor. It was often difficult for them to explain why they had taken certain effective decisions. It is very risky to select a software package against incomplete or unarticulated requirements. If significant requirements are missed or misunderstood then it is difficult to address the problems this might cause.

There are at least three potential approaches to addressing the problem of the software failing to fulfil requirements, but each of these has disadvantages. The first approach is to ask the software vendor to integrate these requirements into the next release of the package. However, even if the software vendor agrees, it may be a costly solution as well as allowing such innovations to become available to all users of the package. The second approach is to ask the software vendor to build a tailored version of the application to fulfil specific requirements. This is likely to be expensive (so reducing the cost advantages of buying a package) and cause long-term maintenance problems and costs as the tailored version has to be integrated with new releases of the standard software package. The final approach is to seek a manual work-around for the missing requirements. However, this may also be costly as well as reducing the business benefits which should have been obtained. Whichever approach is taken, it is likely to either reduce the benefits or increase the costs of adopting a software package solution.

It was also recognised that requirements are likely to change in the long term. There is no guarantee that the software vendor will develop the package to fit newly emerging requirements and so the issues of tailoring and work-around will again have to be considered. Most package selection takes place against current requirements and so this approach is well-suited to circumstances where requirements rarely change and, if they do, they are specified by legislative bodies and the software vendors must make the changes to keep their product compliant. Payroll and integrated accounts applications are typical of this. Applications that are subject to long-term changes (such as the production process at Flexipipe) and do not require legislative compliance, are less appropriate to this approach.

Absence of mature procurement process and management expertise

It was recognised from the outset that Flexipipe did not have an established process for software package selection and implementation. This was a very risky project in which to try and establish a process and select an appropriate package. Lack of procurement expertise in general has been a problem in the past for the company when a key supplier of raw materials for the pipes went out of business. This caused short-term production problems, although an alternative supplier had eventually been found. However, procurement still only employs two people full-time and they are relatively junior and overworked. The company appears to have a very immature procurement process.

The long-term commitment to an external supplier is very problematic in software supply, where moving formerly in-house applications to a new supplier can be technically difficult, expensive and disruptive. In general, there are significant risks associated with the long-term viability of software suppliers and the maintenance of software applications that are critical to the company. Companies go out of business, as in the case study scenario, and companies are sold. It is feasible that a software supplier might be bought by a competitor of Flexipipe, threatening long-term supply. These problems are largely absent in bespoke development, particularly if this development is undertaken in-house. The software program code belongs to the company (not the supplier) and its long-term development is under its control.

(b) In the context of the Flexipipe project, here are some of the issues that could have been addressed by a formal software package evaluation process. It is important that candidates identify elements of the process relevant to the Flexipipe scenario. A generic evaluation process is insufficient.

The business case for all software procurement projects should be assessed *to see if a package is an appropriate solution.* In some instances a bespoke IT development may be better suited. As mentioned in the answer to the first part of this question, the Harmon grid considers process complexity and strategic importance and it could have been used as a guide to assessing the appropriateness of the software package solution approach. If it had been used at Flexipipe then it seems likely that the software package approach would have been abandoned at an early stage of the project.

The requirements must be carefully and comprehensively specified before embarking on a procurement exercise. Difficulties with specifying requirements may again lead to a re-consideration of the bespoke approach. In the case study scenario, mention is made of the system failing to fulfil a number of functional requirements, such as monitoring process variance. The inference is that these requirements were either not specified or were incorrectly specified in advance and so were not part of the package assessment. Similarly, problems with 'usability' may be due to the failure of defining specific usability requirements in advance and so these were not considered when the package was evaluated.

The tendering method has to be made more formal and competitive. A post-project review has shown that there were at least three other packages which should have been considered in the evaluation process. A more formal process would have had a mechanism for finding these potential suppliers. The openness of the tendering process would also have been assisted by advertising in trade magazines and internet tendering sites, which may have also brought forward other potential suppliers. This is an important step because it allows a transparency in the process, and avoids selecting a supplier purely on the recommendation of one internal employee: as in the case of Flexipipe. It would have avoided the situation of a package being selected solely on the basis of a visit to an exhibition.

Suppliers who submit tenders must be evaluated against criteria agreed in advance. Buying a software package leads to a long-term relationship between the supplier and the customer, so the latter must be comfortable with the supplier's credentials. In the context of Flexipipe this would involve setting standard measures and minimum values for liquidity, gearing and profitability. There also has to be some way of off-setting the supplier's suitability with the suitability of the product. That is, how a package with limited functionality from a well-established, financially sound supplier is evaluated against a more functional, usable package from a newly established company with high financial gearing and low turnover. The balance between such factors has to be established in advance, often using a high-level weighted matrix. In the context of the scenario, appropriate financial checks should have identified the high gearing and poor liquidity of the supplier that eventually led to its collapse.

A proper process also needs to be in place to evaluate the potential solution against the specified requirements. It is important to establish the 'fit' between the requirements and the potential solution and to use this 'fit' in the final selection. It has been stated elsewhere that it is unlikely that a package solution will exactly fulfil all requirements. However, if the 'fit' is known and understood in advance then negotiation with users may lead to them dropping, modifying or finding workaround for these gaps. Perhaps some of the functional shortcomings identified by users might have been tolerated, if they had been known and understood in advance.

Finally, *a planned implementation is an important part of the process.* Perhaps the lack of usability of the software was down to the absence of training and the belief that users could 'to pick up the software as they go along'. This is a risky approach, even in circumstances even with experienced users and in a situation where the software product is a good fit with their requirements.

ACCA Marking scheme		
		Marks
(a)	1 mark for each appropriate point up to a maximum of	12
(b)	1 mark for each appropriate point up to a maximum of	13
Total		**25**

Examiner's comments

Unfortunately, in part (a) too many candidates just read the first few words critically evaluate the decision and so the focus of their answer was on the decision itself (made without consultation, made without understanding requirements), rather than on the decision to follow the software package approach as a whole. It was agreed that credit should be given for this alternative interpretation of the question, but it must be stressed that candidates must carefully read the whole of the question and determine what is required in the context of the scenario. As one marker commented, 'it is as if they have read the first few words of the question and then dived into an answer'.

Part (b) was relatively straightforward, asking candidates to analyse how a formal process for software procurement, evaluation and implementation would have addressed the problems experienced in the production process project. However, as in question three (see later notes), too much focus was on describing a process for software package procurement as opposed to how it would address the problems experienced by the company.

INFORMATION TECHNOLOGY

27   PERFECT SHOPPER 👣 *Walk in the footsteps of a top tutor*

👣

Tutor's top tips

Approach to the question

*If, as always, you start by reading **the first paragraph only** the following can be determined:*

- *the key competitors will be supermarkets*
- *it is a franchised network of local shops, with Perfect Shopper selling to the shops, who then in turn sell on to the public*
- *it is competing at the low end part of the market and aiming for economies of scale*
- *it uses large central warehouses*
- *suppliers deliver directly to these warehouses*
- *there are no own-branded goods.*

*Now look at the requirements **before** reading the rest of the question. This will ensure that you*

- *read the question in the correct manner,*
- *do not need to read the question more than once,*
- *save time and can begin planning.*

Requirement

(a)   the primary activities of the value chain

> *This should be an easy start to the question that is a simple test of knowledge.*

(b)   restructuring the upstream supply chain

> *They key here will be to focus on suppliers (and even the suppliers of suppliers). Set up a planning page that will record information on inbound logistics and procurement. A lot of the key points needed have already been read in the first paragraph of the question.*

(c)   restructuring the downstream supply chain

> *The key here will be to focus on outbound logistics and to consider the relationship with both the neighbourhood shops as well as the end consumer.*

Reading the question

*Now **actively** read the question i.e. as you read it you should add all relevant points to your planning page(s).*

- *The key issues to pick out from the question as are as follows:*
- *Perfect Shopper (PS) use haulage contractors to deliver good to the franchisees*
- *franchisees purchasing costs are reduced by around 10% by using PS*
- *PS also manage their downstream chain by providing promotional material, signage and display units*
- *The next two paragraphs of the question give more details on the downstream supply chain and the problems should become evident at this point (e.g. sales representatives only have an input once every three months)*

Answering the question

Part (a) Primary activities of the value chain

As the examiner's comments point out, the key issue to remember here is that there are only five marks available for describing the five primary activities. So you should only need one sentence on each activity – ideally related to the scenario.

Part (b) Upstream supply chain management

This may be the toughest part of the question as we are told very little about PS's upstream chain after the first paragraph in the question. What we are told is:

- PS use centralised warehousing

- PS buy in bulk in order to get price discounts

- Suppliers control the delivery of products to warehouses

- PS only purchase pre-branded products

In order to score marks in this question you could therefore examine how PS might change/improve each of these four areas. The examiner suggests that there are 3 marks available for each valid point made.

Part (c) Downstream supply chain management

The question provides much more information on the relationship with franchisees such as:

- PS provide some marketing material

- franchisees are not exclusive

- deliveries are made every two weeks

- sales reps only meet every three months

- prices need reviewing

- there is low brand recognition

- the ordering system is inflexible (and orders cannot be revised downwards)

- order variations can only be made by phone

So there are many areas to consider for improvement. You should choose three or four of these and create a paragraph which explains what you would change and how it would help the business.

(a)   Inbound logistics: Handling and storing bulk orders delivered by suppliers and stored on large pallets in regional warehouses. All inbound logistics currently undertaken by the food suppliers or by contractors appointed by these suppliers.

Operations: Splitting bulk pallets into smaller packages, packing, sealing and storing these packages.

Outbound logistics: Delivery to neighbourhood shops using locally contracted distribution companies.

Marketing and Sales: Specially commissioned signs and personalised sales literature. Promotions and special offers.

Service: Specialist in-store display units for certain goods, three monthly meeting between franchisee and representative.

(b) Perfect Shopper currently has a relatively short upstream supply chain. They are bulk purchasers from established suppliers of branded goods. Their main strength at the moment is to offer these branded goods at discounted prices to neighbourhood shops that would normally have to pay premium prices for these goods.

In the upstream supply chain, the issue of branding is a significant one. At present, Perfect Shopper only provides branded goods from established names to its customers. As far as the suppliers are concerned, Perfect Shopper is the customer and the company's regional warehouses are supplied as if they were the warehouses of conventional supermarkets. Perfect Shopper might look at the following restructuring opportunities within this context:

- Examining the arrangements for the delivery of products from suppliers to the regional warehouses. At present this is in the hands of the suppliers or contractors appointed by suppliers. It appears that when Perfect Shopper was established it decided not to contract its own distribution. This must now be open to review. It is likely that competitors have established contractual arrangements with logistics companies to collect products from suppliers. Perfect Shopper must examine this, accompanied by an investigation into downstream distribution. A significant distribution contract would probably include the branding of lorries and vans and this would provide an opportunity to increase brand visibility and so tackle this issue at the same time.

- Contracting the supply and distribution of goods also offers other opportunities. Many integrated logistics contractors also supply storage and warehousing solutions and it would be useful for Perfect Shopper to evaluate the costs of these. Essentially, distribution, warehousing and packaging could be outsourced to an integrated logistics company and Perfect Shopper could re-position itself as a primarily sales and marketing operation.

- Finally, Perfect Shopper must review how it communicates orders and ordering requirements with its suppliers. Their reliance on supplier deliveries suggests that the relationship is a relatively straightforward one. There may be opportunities for sharing information and allowing suppliers access to forecasted demand. There are many examples where organisations have allowed suppliers access to their information to reduce costs and to improve the efficiency of the supply chain as a whole.

The suggestions listed above assume that Perfect Shopper continues to only supply branded goods. Moving further upstream in the supply chain potentially moves the company into the manufacture and supply of goods. This will raise a number of significant issues about the franchise itself.

At present Perfect Shopper has, by necessity, concentrated on branded goods. It has not really had to understand how these goods sell in specific locations because it has not been able to offer alternatives. The content of the standing order reflects how the neighbourhood shop wishes to compete in its locality. However, if Perfect Shopper decides to commission its own brand then the breadth of products is increased. Neighbourhood shops would be able to offer 'own brand' products to compete with supermarkets who also focus on own brand products. It would also increase the visibility of the brand. However, Perfect Shopper must be sure that this approach is appropriate as a whole. It could easily produce an own brand that reduces the overall image of the company and hence devalues the franchise. Much more research is needed to assess the viability of producing 'own brand' goods.

(c)   A number of opportunities appear to exist in the downstream supply chain.

As already mentioned above, Perfect Shopper can revisit its contract distribution arrangements. At present, distribution to neighbourhood shops is in the hands of locally appointed contract distributors. As already suggested, it may be possible to contract one integrated logistics company to carry out both inbound and outbound logistics, so gaining economies of scale and opportunities for branding.

One of the problems identified in the independent report was the inflexibility of the ordering and delivering system. The ordering system appears to be built around a fixed standard delivery made every two weeks, agreed in advance for a three month period. Variations can be made to this standard order, but only increases – not decreases. Presumably, this arrangement is required to allow Perfect Shopper to forecast demand over a three month period and to place bulk orders to reflect these commitments. However, this may cause at least two problems. The first is that participating shops place a relatively low standard order and rely on variations to fulfil demand. This causes problems for Perfect Shopper. Secondly, any unpredictable fall in demand during the three month period leads to the shop having storage problems and unsold stock. This potentially creates problems for the shop owner, who may also begin to question the value of the franchise. Hence Perfect Shopper might wish to consider a much more flexible system where orders can be made to match demand and deliveries can be made as required. This would also remove the requirement for a three monthly meeting between the franchisee and the sales representative from Perfect Shopper. Investments in IT systems will be required to support this, with participating shops placing orders over the Internet to reflect their requirements. This move towards a more flexible purchasing arrangement may also make the outsourcing of warehousing and distribution even more appealing.

Perfect Shopper may also wish to investigate whether they can also provide value added services to customers, which not only simplify the ordering system but also allow the shop managers to better understand their customers and fulfil their requirements. The supply chain may legitimately include the customer's customers, particularly for franchisers. This is already acknowledged because Perfect Shopper produces tailored marketing material aimed at the end-consumer. Point of Sales (PoS) devices feeding information back to Perfect Shopper would allow sales information to be analysed and fed back to the shopkeeper as well as allowing automatic replenishment based on purchasing trends. However, this may be culturally difficult for independent neighbourhood shopkeepers to accept. Furthermore, it would potentially include information outside the products offered by Perfect Shopper and the implications of this would have to be considered. However, a whole shop sales analysis might be a useful service to offer existing and potential franchisees.

Customers are increasingly willing to order products over the Internet. It seems unlikely that individual shopkeepers would be able to establish and maintain their own Internet-based service. It would be useful for Perfect Shopper to explore the potential of establishing a central website with customers placing orders from local shops. Again there are issues about scope, because Perfect Shopper does not offer a whole-shop service. However, Michael de Kare-Silver has identified groceries as a product area that has good potential for Internet purchase. In his electronic shopping potential test any product scoring over 20 has good potential. Groceries scored 27.

ACCA Marking scheme			
			Marks
(a)	Up to 1 mark for each part of the value chain up		5
(b)	Up to 3 marks for each relevant point relating to the scenario		10
	Up to 3 marks for each relevant point relating to the scenario		10
			—
Total			**25**
			—

Examiner's comments

This question began by asking the candidate to identify the primary activities of the company's value chain. This was generally well answered by candidates. The next two parts of the question asked candidates to explain how the company might re-structure its upstream and downstream supply chain to address the problems identified in the case study scenario.

This question was the most popular of the optional questions and it was answered well by most candidates. In contrast to question two, most candidates explicitly referenced the case study scenario and some excellent answers were produced. The only criticism that could be made was that too many candidates wrote too much about the primary activities of the value chain. Some candidates wrote two or three pages on this, to gain the five marks on offer, when perhaps ten lines might have been sufficient. Such lengthy answers may have caused candidates time problems and meant that they did not complete the paper.

28   JAYNE COX DIRECT

Key answer tips

Value chains are a favourite topic of the examiner's and mixing them with elements of information technology is a common theme. The examiner has made the point that students 'will only be given credit for suggestions that use technology (rather than organisational changes) and that are clearly relevant to the case study scenario and the products it concerns'. So the key to success will be to focus on getting the relevance correct and to concentrate on IT issues.

(a)   The value chain was introduced by Michael Porter as a way of examining all the activities a firm performs and how these activities interact. By understanding the value chain the analyst can understand costs and identify existing and potential sources of differentiation. The value chain of the organisation is concerned with creating value for customers. A firm is profitable if the value it commands from the customer exceeds the costs involved in creating the product or service that delivers that value.

The primary activities of the value chain are the activities required to physically produce the product, get it to the customer and provide that customer with after-sales service and assistance. Support activities provide organisation-wide functions (such as procurement and technology) to support the primary activities. In general, they support the whole value chain.

In the context of Jayne Cox Direct, the primary activities and their problems are:

Inbound logistics – activities associated with receiving, storing and distributing inputs to the product. This includes warehousing, inventory control and raw materials. At Jayne Cox Direct this concerns wood, upholstery, textiles and other raw materials. It concerns the storage of these raw materials before they are used in production. At Jayne Cox Direct there are documented problems with the e-mail purchase ordering system, which has led to the non-delivery of an expected order. High inventory levels are also commented on in the scenario and these need further investigation.

Operations – activities concerned with transforming the inputs into their final form; machining, packaging, assembly and testing. At Jayne Cox Direct this is the production process of furniture manufacture. Despite high inventory levels and a relatively slow production process, almost half of the promised delivery dates are not achieved. The reasons for this again need further investigation. Perhaps the method for estimating the delivery date is too optimistic. Alternatively, there may be inefficiencies in the production process which need addressing. As well as disappointing customers, failure to meet the proposed delivery date causes increased administrative costs, as a member of the sales team has to contact the customer and rearrange the delivery date.

Outbound logistics – activities associated with storing finished goods and physically distributing these to the customer. At Jayne Cox Direct this is the storage of completed furniture and the delivery of furniture, using their vans, to customers. The cost of storing of finished goods is exacerbated by the need to store them longer than is necessary. There are two reasons for this. The first is concerned with customers not being able to meet revised delivery dates and so deferring delivery. The second reason is the return and storage of goods where delivery cannot be made because the customer is not at home to sign for them. Storage of finished goods increases inventory holding costs. Failed deliveries increase administrative costs (a member of the sales team has to telephone customers to re-arrange the delivery) and distribution costs (the delivery has to be made again).

Marketing and sales – activities that allow a buyer to become aware of a product, induces them to purchase this product and supports the actual purchase of the product. At Jayne Cox Direct this is achieved largely by display advertising in quality magazines and through a web-based ordering system. The sequence of the web-based ordering system may repay investigation and amendment. The estimated delivery time is given after the order has been placed and this causes some customers to immediately cancel their orders. It is perhaps unlikely that such customers will return to place orders with Jayne Cox Direct.

Servicing – activities that enhance or maintain the value of the product, including repair, parts supply and product adjustment. At Jayne Cox Direct this would concern replacement of faulty or spoilt goods, complaints handling and product care information. Customers are critical of after-sales service at Jayne Cox Direct and the managing director believes that this contributes to low customer retention.

The value chain also considers a number of secondary or support activities. Only one of these is specifically relevant in the context of the Jayne Cox Direct scenario.

Procurement refers to the function of purchasing inputs used in the organisation's value chain. It does not refer to the purchase inputs themselves. The cost of the procurement function may be relatively small, but their practices greatly affect the quality and cost of the final product. At Jayne Cox Direct, the cost of wood, upholstery and textiles will be an important determinant of the product cost. The long-term arrangement with suppliers needs investigating. Three timber suppliers provide 95% of the wood. Such arrangements may lead to suppliers becoming comfortable and progressively uncompetitive.

(b)   This question is primarily concerned with re-examining the upstream and downstream supply chains to explore opportunities for reducing cost, improving order-to-delivery time, improving delivery practices and enhancing customer service. Clearly there are many possibilities. Candidates, however, will only be given credit for suggestions that use technology (rather than organisational changes) and that are clearly relevant to the case study scenario and the products it concerns.

Upstream supply chain solutions

The upstream activities concern selecting suppliers (procurement), placing orders (procurement) and storing raw material inventory (inbound logistics). Dave Chaffey identifies six main challenges in the supply chain. Three of these six are relevant to Jayne Cox Direct.

*   Reduce order-to-delivery time

*   Manage inventory more effectively

*   Improve demand forecasting.

Suggestions for improvement might include:

As mentioned in the answer to the first part of this question, procurement continually uses the same long-established suppliers (for example, 95% of timber comes from three established suppliers). These suppliers may have become complacent and uncompetitive. The company might consider using e-procurement websites to identify a wider range of suppliers and then select between these suppliers on the basis of cost and quality when placing individual orders. Such an approach should help drive down raw material costs and re-focus the costs and service offered by the established suppliers.

Although the purchase orders are placed through email, the ordering process is relatively cumbersome with suppliers occasionally failing to respond to emails or, when an expected delivery is not received, claiming they did not receive them in the first place. The payment system (operated by accounts) sometimes fails to match purchase orders with supplier invoices, leading to delayed supplier payment and discontent. The company might consider a new system to administer purchasing and payment, linked electronically (through EDI) to the suppliers, so that orders are automatically entered into the supplier's system and all invoice reconciliation and payment is performed electronically. This may require the company to continue to trade with a selected number of small suppliers, but it should help avoid non-delivery, reduce administrative costs and improve supplier relationships.

To avoid delays through inventory shortages, linkage with supplier systems might be increased by allowing suppliers to see the demand for certain products so that suppliers can, to some extent, anticipate demand and so should be able to supply more quickly. This would require further investigation and it seems likely that it would work better for certain raw materials than others. For example, the textile suppliers would be able to see the relative demand for different patterns and adjust their production accordingly. This should lead to Jayne Cox Direct achieving a higher percentage of planned customer order dates, as well as reducing delivery lead time.

Increased integration also brings the promise of better inventory management, with the opportunity of suppliers effectively producing to order rather than to stock, which is, in effect, an extension of what Jayne Cox Direct is doing. Closer integration of customer and supplier systems also provides the opportunity for 'just in time' manufacture where raw materials arrive just before they are needed in the production process. Although this transfers inventory costs to suppliers, more understanding of demand should mean that suppliers' inventory management is also more effective. Reduced inventory costs for the supplier might also be passed on to Jayne Cox Direct, resulting in lower input costs. An understanding of demand and the relative costs of storage and ordering should also allow Jayne Cox Direct to implement systems that optimise order quantities (the EOQ model).

Downstream supply chain solutions

Downstream supply to customers is relatively simple as there are no intermediaries, as the company supplies directly to the consumer. However, evidence suggests that some consumers are relatively disaffected. A further challenge cited by Dave Chaffey is relevant here, the need to improve aftersales/post-sales operations (service on the value chain). The company also needs to consider the costs of finished goods storage (outbound logistics), distribution to customers (outbound logistics). Furthermore, although processing orders is relatively effective, customers feel uninformed in the period between order placement and order fulfilment.

Some technological solutions here might include:

To introduce technology to support the planning and co-ordinating of deliveries so that delivery vans are used more efficiently and effectively. This might simultaneously increase the likelihood of customers being at home to receive deliveries. The products being delivered are bulky and valuable and so it is vital that someone is available at the delivery address to receive them. Failed deliveries are running at 30%, and this leads to increased inventory holding costs associated with storing the returned item at the warehouse, higher administrative costs of arranging a re-delivery and extra costs of actually making that re-delivery. Technology could be used to improve van utilisation (route planning software) as well as increasing the chance of a customer being at home (automated emails to the customer, automated text messages confirming delivery that day, perhaps confirming likely delivery time).

Part of the delivery problem is caused by the failure to continually inform customers about the progress of their order. The processing and payment for the goods appears to go quite smoothly and an estimated delivery date is given to the customer at the time of order. However, the customer receives no further information until an actual delivery date is confirmed by telephone less than one week before the planned delivery.

Many actual delivery dates are not the same as the original estimated delivery date because of procurement issues. Some customers cannot make this new date (often after keeping the original date free) and so a new date has to be negotiated (an administration cost) and this often leads to the finished product being stored for longer (increasing inventory cost). An IT system that allows the customer to track their orders; updates likely delivery dates as they become available and gives the customer some feeling of progress and involvement would increase customer satisfaction and, by increasing the chance of achieving target delivery dates, reduce inventory cost and other expenses.

Customers have also complained about the absence of after-sales service. Using technology to provide answers to frequently asked questions (how do I get stains out of the upholstery), make and handle complaints and order replacement materials (particularly textiles) would appear to be beneficial. Service should help retain customers. Newsletters, special offers for established customers and targeted emails should also boost customer retention.

ACCA Marking scheme		
		Marks
(a)	1 mark for each appropriate point up to a maximum of.	12
(b)	1 mark for each appropriate point up to a maximum of	13
		—
Total		**25**
		—

Examiner's comments

Part (a) was relatively well done, although many candidates started to suggest ways of overcoming these weaknesses, which was the really the focus of the second part of the question. This meant that candidates wasted time by covering the same ground twice.

Part (b) was relatively well answered, although too many candidates forgot to focus their answer on technology and strayed into organisational responses (outsourcing, restructuring) which were not part of the requirement.

29 PROTECH-PUBLIC

Key answer tips

In this scenario, the organisation has yet to start trading on the Internet. However, the issue is not necessarily when to start trading using this medium, but whether or not to start trading. You will therefore need to review the scenario information to obtain information about OOB, and then think of the strategic issues involved with trading on the Internet. Many of the points that are relevant to the IT strategy of an organisation such as cost and support of core business will also be relevant in this situation. So, make a list of the strategic issues and provide relevant scenario information before writing out the answer in full. As a rough guide, you should have about six topics to discuss in order to achieve a good pass standard.

(a)   The scenario suggests a number of reasons why outsourcing should be beneficial to the city authority.

Firstly, over the last decade there have been fluctuations in demand for IT staff. The authority has recruited to meet short-term demand but, because of the problems of shedding labour, the IT department has not proportionally contracted once that demand has passed. The implication is that, as a result, IT staff costs are higher than they should be. The outsourcing model provides a way of matching supply to demand. Employees are only brought in when there is a specific project for them to work on.

There has been a history of conflict between managers in the IT department and managers in the Finance Department. The Chief Executive Officer (CEO) has spent a significant amount of time trying to resolve this conflict. Employee surveys by the HR department have reported that morale is low in the IT department, despite above average pay and relatively secure employment. Outsourcing IT would appear to offer the following advantages to the authority.

The chief executive and his team would be able to focus on delivering services to the city, rather than spending time and energy on resolving internal problems. The chief executive has recently been criticised for failing to tackle the housing problems of the city. Outsourcing IT would give him more time to address external issues and services, which are the primary objectives and responsibilities of the authority.

Although the problems of low morale may be in part due to management problems, it must also be recognised that promotion opportunities and recognition will probably be lower in an organisation where IT is a relatively small support, rather than core activity. This is reflected in the ingratitude of users towards IT staff ('we are always being told that we are overhead, not core to the business of the authority'). It can be argued that IT staff might be better motivated in an organisation where IT is the core activity and where there should be greater scope for learning new skills and gaining promotion.

Finally, the dispute between IT managers and finance managers has still not been resolved. Outsourcing the IT department will, at best, eliminate the problem and, at worst, make this someone else's problem. In reality, the inability to resolve internal political problems is often given as an important reason for outsourcing.

The director of IT is keen to exploit the opportunities of web services and cloud computing but has not been able to recruit someone of sufficient calibre. As he says, 'there are probably other technologies that I have not even heard of that we should be exploring and exploiting'. An outsourced IT supplier should have a much greater range of knowledge and skills that it can then make available to its customers. It will be keen to be at the leading edge of technologies, because these technologies offer it possible competitive advantage, and so it will bear the cost of recruiting and retaining specialist employees.

Finally, the chief executive recognises that outsourcing IT is likely to be a model followed by other authorities. The formation of a separate company in which the city authority has a significant stake might provide an appropriate vehicle for gaining contracts with other authorities. They might be particularly attracted to working with a company which has significant public sector expertise and ownership. Profits made by the company may be distributed by dividend to the authority, bringing in income that can be used to reduce taxes or improve services.

(b)   In the past, business analysts have been employed within the IT department. It is proposed that these analysts will now move to a new BA department reporting directly to the chief executive. Their brief is 'to deliver solutions that demonstrably offer benefits to the organisation and to the people of the city, using information technology where appropriate'. They will be responsible for liaising between users and the new, outsourced IT company. The business analysts will have to establish credibility with the user departments, demonstrating the role and contribution of the business analyst role. The question focuses on new or enhanced competencies they will need, rather than generic skills such as 'good communication skills' and 'team working' which they would have needed when they were sited in the IT department.

Competencies they will require might include:

Strategy analysis They will have to develop an external business focus which, at the very least, looks for opportunities in the wider environment. The CEO expects them to be 'outward looking and unconstrained by current process and technology'. Techniques such as SWOT analysis might be useful here.

Business case development The absence of cross-charging suggests that business cases were relatively simple in the authority and it appears that business analysts were not involved in the process. In the new arrangement, agreeing the business case becomes their responsibility and so they will have to liaise with users to ensure that benefits are properly defined. If the solution requires an IT element then there are now very tangible costs which will be charged by an external supplier. This is particularly significant if software is involved. The supplier will need well specified requirements to estimate from. Costs and benefits will have to be compared using an appropriate approach. The business analyst will also have to participate in benefits realisation, assessing whether the promised benefits had actually been delivered at the cost envisaged in the original proposal.

Business process modelling The business analysts must be prepared to come up with solutions that do not include information technology. For example, they might suggest a small change to a clerical business process that delivers significant benefits. It is unlikely that they would have formulated such solutions when they were part of the IT department. Business process modelling and redesign skills will be needed to facilitate this.

Requirements definition Requirements definition would have been an important part of the business analysts' job when they were in the IT department. However, the scenario suggests a relatively flexible relationship with users, with changes to requirements being accommodated right up until software release. Although the outsourced IT supplier may take a similar approach, changes will be charged for. Hence in the outsourced arrangement there will be a need for business analysts to define requirements more completely and also to manage changes to those requirements. The detailed definition should also allow them to resolve issues where there is debate over whether the change is actually a change or is what was specified in the first place. The business analyst may also be involved in *testing* the solution received from the supplier.

Procurement The relationship between the city authority and the IT provider is now a supplier–customer relationship. The business analysts will have to gain supplier and contract management skills, allowing them to successfully manage this relationship.

ACCA Marking scheme		
		Marks
(a)	1 mark for each relevant point up to a maximum of 12 marks.	12
(b)	1 mark for each relevant point up to a maximum of 7 marks.	7
		——
Total		**19**
		——

Examiner's comments

In Part (a), most candidates answered this relatively well, although many did not recognise that the formation of a joint company might itself bring significant advantages to the city authority. The formation of a separate company in which the city authority has a significant stake might provide an appropriate vehicle for gaining contracts with other public authorities. They might be particularly attracted to working with a company which has significant public sector expertise and ownership. Profits made by the company may be distributed by dividend to the authority, bringing in income that can be used to reduce taxes or improve services.

In part (b), many candidates failed to identify any relevant competencies (falling back on generalisations such as 'good communication skills') and hence did not score well in this part question.

30   GOOD SPORTS

Key answer tips

The key in this question is to split up your points between parts (a) and (b). Part (a) wants you to discuss fairly generic advantages and disadvantages of e-business (the resource audit model would be a useful one to use here). Part (b) then wants an application of these benefits and problems to Good Sports. A key issue to pick up on in part (b) will be the loss of competitive advantage that Good Sports gets from its personal contact with customers.

(a)   **To:**   Good Sports Limited

From: xxxxx

E – Business strategy

Clearly, the markets that Good Sports operates in are being affected by the development of e-business and its experiences to date are mixed to say the least. In many ways the advantages and disadvantages of e-business are best related to the benefit the customer gets from the activity.

- First, through integrating and accelerating business processes, e-business technologies enable response and delivery times to be speeded up.

- Second, there are new business opportunities for information-based products and services.

- Third, websites can be linked with customer databases and provide much greater insights into customer buying behaviour and needs.

- Fourth, there is far greater ability for interaction with the customer, which enables customisation and a dialogue to be developed.

- Finally, customers may themselves form communities able to contact one another.

There is considerable evidence to show how small operators like Good Sports are able to base their whole strategy on e-business and achieve high rates of growth. The key to Good Sport's survival is customer service – in strategic terms they are very much niche marketers supplying specialist service and advice to a small section of the local market. The nature of the business means that face-to-face contact is crucial in moving customers from awareness to action (AIDA – awareness, interest, desire and action). There are therefore limits to the ability of e-business to replace such contact.

Yours,

(b)   Good Sports has pursued a conscious niche or focus differentiation strategy, seeking to serve a local market in a way that isolates it from the competition of the large national sports good retailers competing on the basis of supplying famous brands at highly competitive prices. Does it make strategic sense for Good Sports to make the heavy investment necessary to supply goods online? Will this enhance its ability to supply their chosen market?

In terms of price, e-business is bringing much greater price transparency – the problem for companies like Good Sports is that customers may use their expertise to research into a particular type and brand of sports equipment and then simply search the Internet for the cheapest supply. Porter in an article examining the impact of the Internet argues that rather than making strategy obsolete it has in fact made it more important. The Internet has tended to weaken industry profitability and made it more difficult to hold onto operational advantages. Choosing which customers you serve and how are even more critical decisions.

However the personal advice and performance side of the business could be linked to new ways of promoting the product and communicating with the customer. The development of customer communities referred to above could be a real way of increasing customer loyalty. The partners are anxious to avoid head-on competition with the national retailers. One way of increasing the size and strength of the niche they occupy is to use the Internet as a means of targeting their particular customers and providing insights into the use and performance of certain types of equipment by local clubs and users. There is considerable scope for innovation that enhances the service offered to their customers. As always there is a need to balance the costs and benefits of time spent. The Internet can provide a relatively cost effective way of providing greater service to their customers. There is little in the scenario to suggest they have reached saturation point in their chosen niche market. Overall there is a need for Good Sports to decide what and where its market is and how this can be improved by the use of e-business.

31   CRONIN AUTO RETAIL

> **Key answer tips**
>
> The requirements were very clear, but, to score well in this area, students would have had to make their points as relevant as possible to the scenario. Weaker students may have simply regurgitated their study notes and explained the approaches rather than applying them to the scenario and this is unlikely to have scored well.

(a)   This question uses four of the '6 Is' developed by McDonald and Wilson to explore the differences between traditional and e-marketing. Candidate answers do not have to be strictly classified within each of the factors identified below. In reality, suggestions will cross the boundaries of these factors.

Interactivity concerns the development of a two-way relationship between the customer and the supplier. The traditional display advertising and mail-shots used by CAR are examples of 'push media' where the marketing message is broadcast to current and potential customers. Their current website continues this approach, with the stock listing essentially representing a continually updated, but widely accessible, display advertisement. Supplementing mail-shots with e-mails could be immediately considered by CAR and would be a cheaper alternative to mail-shots. However, it still remains a 'push technique' with little dialogue with the customer.

Here are three ideas that CAR could consider to improve the interactivity of its site. Other legitimate suggestions will also be given credit.

(1)   Encouraging potential buyers on their website to ask questions about any car that they are interested in. Both questions and answers are published. This may provide someone with the vital information that clinches the sale. It also creates a great enthusiasm around the car. Buyers may move quickly so that they do not lose the opportunity to buy the car.

On e-bay, customers are encouraged to 'ask a question' of the seller and this often leads to long threads where the supplier and potential buyers interact.

(2)   Many buyers would like to test drive a car before they purchase it. CAR could provide the opportunity for customers to book a test drive over the Internet.

(3)   Once a purchase had been complete, CAR might encourage feedback which could be published on the website. In this instance, customers are actually providing information that is commercially useful to buyers. This may be in the form of testimonials, or in the form of more structured feedback that e-bay encourages. Suppliers who have 100% positive feedback backed up by testimonials from previous buyers are powerfully reinforcing their marketing message.

Intelligence is about identifying and understanding the needs of potential customers and how they wish to be communicated with. It is traditionally the area of market research and marketing research. Currently CAR does very little research. It relies on a database that only consists of people who have actually bought cars from the company. Collecting email addresses through promotions and interactivity initiatives (see above) provides a much greater pool of potential customers who can be kept up-to-date through email.

It can also give CAR significant intelligence about the type of cars that they are interested in and at what price. At present, the buyers for CAR use their experience when buying cars at auction and there is some concern that they buy what they would like to drive, not what the customers want to drive. It would be useful to support this experience with quantitative information about the type of cars potential buyers are really interested in. This may lead to a change in buying policy.

Individualisation concerns the tailoring of marketing information to each individual, unlike traditional media where the same message tends to be sent to everyone. Personalisation is a key element in building an effective relationship with the customer. In the context of CAR, individuals who have shown interest in a certain model or type of car may be selectively emailed when a similar car becomes available. This approach may also be used for current customers. For example, someone who purchased a particular car two or three years ago might be e-mailed about an opportunity to upgrade to an updated model. For individualisation to be successful, sufficient details must be collected through the intelligence and interactive facets of the '6 Is'.

Individualisation will also be key in offering relevant after-sales service. This may concern inviting customers to return their cars for servicing at the correct dates or offering services only appropriate to that type of car. For example, circulating details of air-conditioning renewal only to customers with air conditioned cars.

Independence of location concerns the geographical location of the company. Electronic media increases the geographical reach of a company. For many companies this gives opportunities to sell into international markets which had previously been inaccessible to them.

This facet of the new media is unlikely to be appropriate to CAR. Most sales are to customers who are within two hours' drive of the CAR premises. The commodity nature of the cars that CAR are selling means that similar cars will be available throughout the country, often from garages that offer local service and support. Independence of location would be more significant if CAR was selling collectors or classic cars where each car is relatively rare and people are prepared to travel long distances to view the car they are interested in. Furthermore, the long term lease on CAR's current premises makes it unlikely that they will be able to locate to a cheaper site and hence exploit the independence of location offered by the new media.

(b) Procurement is concerned with purchasing goods or services for the organisation. It is concerned with sourcing items at the right price, delivered at the right time, to the right quality, in the right quantity and from the right source. Many contemporary definitions of procurement also include the inbound logistics required to get the product from the supplier to the customer.

E-procurement looks at the opportunities presented by automating aspects of procurement to improve the performance of the five 'rights' identified above. There is a wide range of potential answers to this part of the question depending on the scope and focus of e-procurement selected by the candidate. Solutions may vary from the simple automation of part of the system, to re-thinking the way the company does business.

In the context of CAR, two distinct types of procurement can be identified. The first is production-related procurement and is directly related to the core activities of the organisation. This relates to the purchase of cars for sale and the purchase of parts required for servicing or repairing vehicles. The second is non-production procurement.

CAR has always purchased its vehicles through experienced buyers attending auctions. On average this attendance costs the company $500 per day, leading to the purchase (on average) of five cars. This purchasing cost of $100 per car represents 5% of the average profit margin on each car. This cost could be eliminated if cars were purchased through e-auctions, with bids made on-line. The risk here is that the cars bought were not of the right quality. CAR prides itself in the personal selection of its cars. However, it could be argued that cars which are less than two years old with a full service history are unlikely to have much wrong with them.

The parts needed for servicing and mechanical repairs are ordered from motor factors or manufacturers. A number of regular suppliers are retained, many in long-term relationships with CAR. This is known as systematic sourcing. Most of the problems here are caused by the need to pass requisitions for parts through a procurement manager. The first problem is the delay in the purchasing cycle. There is a backlog of requisitions that have to be reviewed, agreed and sourced by the procurement manager. This is particularly problematic when a customer's car is in the garage awaiting a part. The customer is likely to be frustrated and annoyed by the delay, whilst the car is occupying garage space that could have been profitably used for a fee-paying job. The second problem is the cost of the paperwork and the processing time of the procurement manager associated with the purchase. The final problem is that purchases can only be made between 10.00 and 16.00 when the procurement manager is at work. Mechanics work 07.00 to 19.00 and are frustrated that they cannot make orders outside the times the procurement manager is at work. Giving the mechanics the systems and authorisation to order parts (up to a certain value limit) from specified suppliers over the Internet should deliver cost savings and speed up repairs and services. A direct ordering system should also reduce administrative errors and enhance customer goodwill. CAR might also use e-procurement to open up competitive bidding between potential suppliers; posting their requirements on their website and inviting competing bids. Parts could be sourced from a number of suppliers, taking advantage of the lowest prices for each part. This could be combined with just-in-time supply, reducing the cost of stock holding at CAR.

Non-production procurement is concerned with ordering things such as stationery, paper, ink toner and other office supplies. Christa Degnan (quoted in Chaffney, E-Business and E-Commerce Management) suggested that for 'every dollar a company earns in revenue, 50 cents to 55 cents is spent on indirect goods and services – things like office supplies and computer equipment. That half dollar represents an opportunity. By driving costs out of the purchasing process, companies can increase profits without having to sell more goods'. CAR is in this situation. It uses the same process for office supplies as it does for car parts. However, most office supplies are cheap, commodity products where sometimes the cost of ordering the product exceeds the value of the purchased product, particularly where a cumbersome purchasing process is in place. With little differentiation between products, it is the availability and cost of the product that become the most significant aspects in the procurement process. E-procurement should provide better information, identifying alternative suppliers and allowing spot sourcing of office products to fulfil immediate need.

Overall, e-procurement should reduce the administrative burden on the procurement manager, giving him or her the opportunity to concentrate on negotiating terms, agreements and product standardisation; more strategic tasks in the procurement process.

ACCA Marking scheme		
		Marks
(a)	Up to 1 mark for describing the meaning of each of the four as defined in the question. Up to 1 mark for appropriate point that applies them to the scenario up to a maximum of	16
(b)	Up to 1 mark for each appropriate point up to a maximum of	9
Total		**25**

Examiner's comments

Part (b)(worth nine marks) was particularly well answered although many candidates focussed on the problems of procuring stationery and motor parts, rather than the actual cars themselves – the company's primary procurement activity. However, despite this narrow focus, many candidates scored 7 marks or more for this part question. The first part of the question was also relatively well answered, although the independence of location was something of a red herring. The scenario paints a picture of a company that stresses its physical location (café, children's play facility) and its commitment to it (long lease) in a commercial environment where the physical proximity of customer and supplier is important. The better answers identified that the principle of independence of location was NOT particularly relevant to the case study organisation. This is an important point. Just as you must not assume that case study characters are correct or virtuous, you must also not assume that all academic assertions and principles are always relevant to the case study environment. However, overall, this was a popular and relatively well-answered question.

32 SRO

Key answer tips

The key in part (a) will be to recognise that there are four components needed in an answer – problems in both application and general controls, as well as necessary improvements for both. Given 15 marks for all four elements only 2 or 3 problems in each area will have needed to have been identified.

Part (b) concerning corporate governance and ethics is examined in a strategic manner rather than the more technical manner that students who have sat P1 may be accustomed to.

(a) SRO has recognised the importance of the need for functioning systems at all times, and so have ensured that a backup is available. This is key, as any loss of functionality will affect its ability to operate, given that the entire operations are carried out online. However, there are some problems with its general controls, which could severely disrupt business.

General controls

These are controls which relate to the computer environment and, hence, could affect any or all applications in use. These may be policies with regards to the treatment of hardware or procurement, for example, or could be specific security procedures which are in place. SRO appears to recognise the need for general controls by having a separate computer centre, with secure access, a firewall and a password system to protect against unauthorised access. However, despite this recognition, there are a number of areas where the general controls are inadequate.

The computer centre is not secured despite the capability to do so. The reason given is not sufficient to risk security controls for. Although the 'majority of staff' at headquarters are IT support personnel, there are still some staff who should not have access to the computer centre. Indeed, not all IT staff need access to the main servers. Temporary staff should not fulfil roles which are strategically important and so, to risk the entire operations by providing them with unrestricted access, SRO is not showing adequate control. Similarly, the use of a general user id and simple password means that they have access not just to the hardware, but to the entire system too. The user id and password would be simple to guess should anyone be attempting to hack into the system. SRO must immediately revert to the fingerprint access system, and must ensure that all staff are aware of the importance of preventing unauthorised access. The 'administrator' user should be removed immediately, and only those with administrator rights should be afforded them in conjunction with their unique user ID. Temporary staff should be issued with unique user ids so that SRO can ascertain who has carried out any transactions on the system. In addition, users should be reminded of the necessity of changing passwords regularly and not writing them down anywhere. This could be enforced in training and by the provision of a procedures document.

The firewall has been turned off to allow the intelligent software to upload its finding onto SRO's system. Unfortunately, turning off the firewall not only allows this to happen, it also opens the systems to the threat of hackers. The firewall should be immediately re-installed. If it is finding difficulties with the application, it may be that there is a security risk with that. This should be thoroughly investigated and corrected.

SRO has taken precautions to have a backup system in place as contingency against disasters. However, the system should be in a remote location, rather than in the same location as the main servers. If there were a fire, for example, both the main servers and the backup servers would be affected. Similarly, by having a direct link between the servers, any data corruption or unauthorised access would affect both the servers and their backups. There should be a slight time delay in the connection to prevent this from happening, so immediately a problem is detected the link could be terminated, allowing the backup to be unaffected.

The controls mentioned above would affect all systems. There are some controls which affect only specific applications used by the organisation. These are known as application controls and help ensure that transactions are authorised, and are completely and accurately recorded, processed and reported.

Application controls

There are some issues with the application controls on the review system, which form a threat to the accuracy and reliability of the information provided on the system.

The intelligent software itself appears to provide out-of-date information and there is, currently, no way of assessing whether this is the case. A verification check may be necessary to ascertain the date of the initial posting of information and whether this is earlier or later than the date of information already held.

The reviews posted by users may, or may not, be a fair representation of the service offered. SRO does not verify that the information is correct, nor do they verify whether the users are who they claim to be. Indeed, the ability for users to post anonymously means that they could post whatever they like. There is a possibility that the users may be employed by the stores being reviewed, and giving positive reviews in order to benefit from them. Alternatively, they may be posting negative reviews about their competitors, again compromising the reliability and independence of the reviews. If this were happening, and were to be discovered, it could threaten the entire existence of SRO. It may be that a control needs to be included whereby reviewers can only submit a review if there has been an actual transaction with the store. Similarly, the stores should have the opportunity to respond to a review, made simpler if there is a transaction identifier available.

Overall, it appears that, despite having many of the tools in place, SRO is not using them adequately. Procedures should be clearly defined and adhered to in order to protect from such risks.

(b) There are two areas of concern identified by SRO:

Commercial conflicts of interest

SRO's business objective is to 'provide an unbiased review of online stores to ensure the customer has all available information'. So, to meet this objective they should focus on both the terms 'unbiased' and 'all available information'. The fact that SRO provides some reviews itself, which, although honest, seek to show certain stores in a positive light, goes against this objective.

The dilemma for SRO is that the online stores themselves provide both sets of revenue streams for SRO. It is in SRO's interest that the reviews are accurate, otherwise they will lose its users who rely on SRO for an honest and truthful review. Should they use another comparison site, or shop around themselves, SRO will no longer gain commission or advertising revenue. However, if the reviews are negative, it is also unlikely that the store in question will advertise in future on SRO's site and commission sales will also fall, as users of SRO's site will not follow links towards a store with negative reviews.

SRO either needs to change its business objective to remove the terms 'unbiased' and 'all available information', or they need to consider how to do this whilst maintaining their revenue streams. Ideally, the provision of honest reviews should encourage the stores to provide a good service at all times and then this would no longer be an issue.

Relocating company operations

SRO is considering moving its operations to an overseas country with tax and cost benefits. Whilst this may seem to be an attractive option from a financial perspective, there are other elements which should be considered.

The dilemma is that the benefits obtained financially may be counteracted by operational problems. The country they are considering relocating to is poorly regulated and does not have legislative controls with regards to the quality of information systems or security of data contained within them, even for personal data. This could lead to the risk of loss of personal data of the registered users, which could cause great reputational damage, should it occur. SRO has already recognised some control issues with its systems and it is likely that these would be worsened in a poorly regulated country.

It is mentioned that the country's culture is such that accepting unauthorised payments is considered acceptable, even if it is not publicly acknowledged. SRO would have the dilemma of whether to behave within the culture of the country, even though such business behaviour may be seen as illegal or considered unethical in its home nation, or whether to take a stance against it, and thus put themselves at a competitive disadvantage. The latter would be in line with their current code of conduct, but it may be difficult to convince locally sourced staff of this.

Given that Amy created the company quite recently, in 2010, with the aim of overcoming the unethical behaviour she perceived to exist in the online retail industry, it would appear that both of the dilemmas considered above would risk the entire paradigm of the company, its reason for existence.

ACCA Marking scheme		
		Marks
(a)	Up to 1 mark for each appropriate point up to a maximum of 15 marks	
(b)	Up to 1 mark for each appropriate point up to a maximum of 10 marks	
Total		**25**

Examiner's comments

Part (a) was well answered. Some candidates could have benefited from suggesting why each specific control problem was important e.g. what could be the effect of this breach of control, rather than simply quoting the information from the scenario.

For part (b) some candidates would have benefitted from an ability to apply the concepts to the information provided in the scenario.

33 BRIDGE CO

Key answer tips

Software selection is a common exam area and one that relies as much on knowledge as it does on application. In this area students often lack the detailed knowledge required to score well as well as failing to have specifics in their suggestions and arguments. But if these problems are avoided, and students have the requisite knowledge, this is a question where some students can score very highly.

(a)

Tutorial note

The structure of this answer is just one way which Bridge Co could have procured the software package in a structured way. Other answers with an appropriate approach will be given credit.

Stage One: Evaluation

This is concerned with establishing whether a commercial off-the-shelf software package would be an appropriate way of automating the CRM requirements. A framework such as the Harmon process – strategy matrix could be used. There is no evidence in the scenario that any alternative (outsourcing, bespoke software development) to the software package approach was considered. Generally, CRM applications are likely to be relatively complex and of medium strategic importance. Consequently, by chance, a software package approach does appear a reasonable response, although it would have been beneficial for that decision to stem from a proper evaluation, rather than the whim and the will of the new sales and marketing executive.

Stage Two: Business case

This stage would require the definition of a formal business case, including a financial evaluation of the proposed investment. This was avoided by negotiating the price down to below the capex threshold at Bridge Co. If this had not been done, then a business case would have been required. The failure to produce a business case has two consequences. First, it meant that no other likely costs associated with the software purchase were ever considered. These were either avoided (such as the training costs) or had to be funded out of the operational budget (the cost of data migration). Second, and more importantly, there was no attempt to establish what benefits the Custcare CRM package offered the organisation. These could have been financial benefits (so could be compared with costs using an appropriate investment appraisal technique) or they could have been intangible benefits (such as improved customer satisfaction). Both tangible and intangible benefits could have been subject to a benefits realisation review at the end of the project, to see whether the anticipated benefits had materialised. The failure to document the anticipated benefits in advance means that although the software is being used, there is an air of disappointment and deflation about the project outcome.

Stage Three: Requirements definition

This stage is concerned with defining the requirements which the software package is to be evaluated against. No formal requirements definition was performed at Bridge Co. Teri was enthusiastic about the product, based on her experience at her previous company. She felt that the requirements would be very similar at Bridge Co. In fact, she was proved correct, as far as the functional requirements were concerned. The sales and marketing staff appear to be quite happy with the features of the software and, indeed, it has provided valuable functionality which they did not anticipate. However, important non-functional and technical requirements were missed. These concerned the technical interface with the order processing system and the overall slow performance of the software. Performance and interface requirements should have been part of the requirements specification which the package was evaluated against. More thought could also have been given to supplier requirements: what Bridge Co would like from the supplying company. This would have prompted thoughts about support requirements and also the geographical location of the supplier. At the end of the interview Mick says, 'I just wish we had chosen a product produced by a company here in Deeland.' This could have been one of the evaluation criteria.

Stage 4: Evaluation of competing products

The need to compile and issue a formal Invitation to Tender (ITT) would have required Bridge Co to consider alternative products and suppliers. Even just following the capex requirements at Bridge Co would have forced the sales and marketing department to consider three competitive responses to their requirements. This was not done, no alternatives were considered. It may have been possible to find a solution which did fulfil the technical interface requirements and achieved the required performance. However, even if this were not possible, and Custcare remained the best solution, the formality of the ITT process would have allowed Teri to demonstrate that the package had been selected after proper consideration of alternatives. It would have introduced an element of due diligence and transparency which is missing from the project.

Stage 5: Contract negotiation

Once a potential solution is identified, a detailed investigation of the contract is required to remove or amend clauses which the customer is unhappy about. Contracts are usually framed in favour of the software supplier. It is at this stage that Bridge Co would have identified two issues which subsequently caused problems. First, the legal jurisdiction of the contract; this could have been changed, through negotiation, from Solland to Deeland. Second, the restriction on who can be employed as contract staff on Custcare projects. Again, this would probably have been removed after negotiation (or a preferential contract rate agreed). Contractual arrangements are very difficult to change retrospectively. They need to be reviewed before the purchase is completed. If insurmountable problems occur (for example, a reluctance to vary a clause), then the customer can legitimately withdraw at this stage, citing the unacceptable risk the clause exposes them to.

Stage 6: Implementation

Effective training, appropriate documentation and successful data migration are central to the success of the project. Proper consideration of them also contributes to the business case (stage 2). Omitting training has been a false economy at Bridge Co, leading to too much use of an inadequate support agreement. Data migration had to be separately funded and turned out to be disproportionally expensive.

(b) The Custcare solution did provide a quick solution to the CRM requirement at Bridge Co. *Speed of implementation* is a claimed advantage of commercial off-the-shelf software packages and this is valid in this scenario. It would be at least 18 months before the IT department could even start to look at the sales and marketing department's requirement. In contrast, the Custcare solution was up and running within three months.

The Custcare solution did provide comprehensive functionality. The sales and marketing department were impressed with the package. It did all the things they wanted it to do and it also gave them ideas and possibilities which they would never have thought of. Software packages have the advantage of incorporating *industry best practice* within a broad, comprehensive functionality. Custcare allows an organisation without a CRM, such as Bridge Co, to quickly get up to speed and to offer services as least as good as some of its competitors.

Despite the extra costs of data migration, the software package does appear to offer a relatively cheap solution. In general, software packages, where the cost of development and maintenance is shared amongst many customers, are *usually much cheaper* than bespoke alternatives. The Custcare solution has still cost less than $30,000. The internal IT department has quoted a price of $18,000 just for requirements analysis. Given that they still have to develop and test the solution, this suggests that the overall cost will be much greater than the money spent on the Custcare solution.

There have been no complaints about the robustness of the Custcare solution. The only difficulties concern its failure to meet certain requirements, and the problems of support and training. In general, software packages are of *better quality* than bespoke alternatives. The package has been extensively used by many users in a range of organisations and problems will have been progressively identified and solved. It is impossible to exhaustively test bespoke solutions, so they are often beset with robustness and reliability problems, particularly in the period just after implementation.

The two problems reported by Mick are relatively easy to solve. A piece of bespoke software could be developed as a *bridge* between the CRM and the order processing system. This bridge would import files from the CRM system in one format and then convert them into the format required by the order processing system, and vice versa. The performance of the software could be addressed by improving the specification of hardware at Bridge Co, or by scheduling jobs so that complex reports and queries are run when the system is not busy, for example, overnight. These solutions are not ideal, but provide a reasonable way forward. Overall, the software package approach still seems a reasonable way forward.

ACCA Marking scheme		
		Marks
(a)	1 mark for each relevant point about stages in the process of software procurement up to a maximum of 15 marks.	15
(b)	1 mark for each relevant point made for discussing the relative advantages of a software package over a bespoke solution up to a maximum of 10 marks.	10
Total		**25**

Examiner's comments

In part (a) very few candidates focused on a process that encompassed evaluation, selection and implementation. Too many answers identified a problem in the scenario and then suggested how this might have been avoided. Such an approach did gain credit, but it tended to lead to long disjointed answers, with much repetition (with similar problems addressed through similar solutions repeated at length) and no overall coherent process.

Part (b) should have been a relatively straightforward part question. All approved study material contains sufficient information for a well-prepared candidate to easily score eight marks or more. Many candidates did get good marks on this part question, but far too many quickly gave the advantages and then, at similar length, described the disadvantages of the software package solution, which was not required. Other candidates gave the advantages of a bespoke approach (also not required) and the disadvantages of the bespoke approach (for which some credit could be given if information was provided that had not already been included in the advantages of the package approach). Some candidates wasted a lot of time by inappropriately answering this question. Candidates are advised to read the questions very carefully.

E-MARKETING

34   AEC   *Walk in the footsteps of a top tutor*

Tutor's top tips

Approach to the question

*If, as always, you start by reading the **first paragraph only** the following can be determined:*

the business runs accountancy courses

it is a worldwide business

it also targets the CPD market (though this is underperforming)

*Now look at the requirements **before** reading the rest of the question. This will ensure that you read the question in the correct manner, do not need to read the question more than once, save time and can begin planning.*

Requirement

(a)   The characteristics of electronic marketing

*The key to most requirements is to choose the most appropriate model – in this case the best model is McDonald and Wilson's 6I's model (as suggested in the official exam text). It is important to distinguish that in this section you are not being asked to create an e-marketing plan (that is required in part b) of the question), you are merely asked to **explain the differences that e-marketing** has to traditional marketing media. The 6I's model best achieves this .You could set up a planning page with the 6I's listed out and then add points to this plan as you read the question.*

(b)   Marketing mix

*In this part of the question you are asked **to use e-marketing**. You should be able to distinguish this clearly from part a) of the question and not mix your answers together – part a) wants you to explain e-marketing (this will focus on its differences and benefits), part b) then wants you to use it (this will focus on practical suggestions for AEC). The most appropriate model will be the 7P's model and you could approach this in the same way as part a) – set could set up a planning page with the 7P's listed out and then add points to this plan as you read the question.*

Reading the question

*Now **actively** read the question i.e. as you read it you should add all relevant points to your planning page(s).*

The key issues to pick out from the question as are as follows:

- *AEC provide three products – training for professional examinations, material for these courses, and CPD courses. So part b) of your answer should explain how to market each of these courses/products.*

- *AEC have recently won a large, new customer. The impact on this customer should be considered in both parts of your answer.*

- *The company are planning to switch from traditional marketing to e-marketing but won't do both – there is only a 3% overall increase in marketing forecasted. Therefore you need to make clear in part a) that the e-marketing benefits will have to outweigh the loss of the traditional marketing channels.*

Answering the question

Part (a) 6I's

As stated, if you have fully understood the impact of the final paragraph of the question, then there will be a mark or two for explaining that the e-marketing benefits will have to outweigh the loss of the traditional marketing channels. But there are plenty of other marks available if this point is missed.

There are 10 marks available and if you work to the normal rule of 2 marks per well explained point then you only have to cover 4 or 5 of the 6I's. The key issue will be to relate the model to the scenario (for example, by referencing the win of the new, large client).

For example, using independence of location, traditional marketing can be used to target customers in all parts of the world. But AEC could expand this through e-marketing by allowing these customers to also book courses online – something that isn't happening at the moment. So e-marketing should make it easier and therefore more attractive to customers to choose AEC as their training provider. It should also reduce administrative burdens for larger clients and might allow AEC to attract more multi-national customers.

Part (b) 7P's

As this is e-marketing it will probably be best to extend the traditional 4P's of the marketing mix to the 7P's i.e. we should include a discussion of processes, physical evidence and people. The key will be to make the points relevant to AEC (something that examiner suggested some students failed to do) and to perhaps explain the impact on all the company's products.

Using physical evidence for example, the website could stand out if it had useful links to other websites. For accountancy training courses these could be links to the relevant accounting bodies. For CPD courses, these could be links to relevant legislative bodies, standards, tax authorities etc. This might make the website more useful and encourage repeat visits.

(a)   A key characteristic of traditional marketing media such as advertising and direct mail is that it is predominantly a 'push' technology where the media is distributed to customers and potential customers. There is limited interaction with the customer and indeed, in the case of advertising and to a lesser degree direct mail, there is no certainty that the intended recipient actually received the message. In contrast, the new media, particularly the Internet, is predominantly a 'pull' technology – the customer having initiated the visit to the web site. This may lead to subsequent push activities, such as sending e-mails to people who have registered their interest on the site, but the initial communication is a pull event. The marketing manager must be careful that, by switching so much of her budget to pull technologies, she does not forego opportunities to find new customers – or reinforce her message – through established push technologies. She must ensure that the company's web site is established in such a way that sufficient people find it, and that when they do, they are prepared to record enough details to allow subsequent push activities.

Dave Chaffey examines the difference between traditional and new marketing media in the context of six 'I's; interactivity, intelligence, individualisation, integration, industry restructuring and independence of location. Four of these are used in this answer.

Interactivity is a significant feature of the new media, allowing a long-term dialogue to develop between the customer and the supplier. In the context of the web site, this is likely to be through e-mails, providing the customer with information and special offers for their areas of specific interest. To initiate this dialogue the web site must capture information such as e-mail address, name, age, gender and areas of interest. The AEC site only collects such information for people who wish to view downloadable study material. This is too restrictive and it will probably exclude all the potential CPD customers. AEC needs to consider ways of making it easier and worthwhile for visitors to the site to register their details. There is no evidence of AEC contemplating the potential use of interactive digital TV or mobile phones to establish long-term dialogues with their customers.

Intelligence has also been a key feature of the new media – allowing the relatively cheap collection of marketing research data about customers' requirements. This is routinely available from web logs and these logs need to be viewed and analysed using appropriate software. This type of analysis is rarely available in the traditional media. For example, AEC does not know how often their training course catalogue is accessed and which pages are looked at. It only knows which training courses are eventually bought. With the new media the company is able to see which services and products are accessed and also to measure how many of these are turned into actual sales. This conversion rate may be an important source of information – for example, why are certain web pages often visited but few sales result – is it a problem with the web page? – is it a problem with the product? An understanding of visit patterns allows the organisation to focus on particular products and services. This analysis should already be available to AEC but there is no evidence that it uses it or is even aware of it.

The new media also permit the marketing to be *individualised*, geared to a particular market segment, company or individual person. In the context of AEC this individualisation could be achieved in at least two ways to reflect clear market segmentation. AEC has recently won a contract to supply professional accountancy training to a global accounting company. All students working for this company will now be trained by AEC in one of its worldwide centres. At present this company and its students will be served through a generic web site. However, the flexibility of the new media means that a site could be developed specifically for this requirement. The whole site would be geared, and branded, towards the requirements of the global accounting company. Information that is irrelevant to that customer, such as CPD, would not appear on the site. This individualised approach should strengthen the relationship with the customer. Similarly, individuals may have their own access customised as a result of the profile that they have entered. So, for example, if they have already stated that they are currently sitting the professional stage of an examination scheme then only information relevant to that stage will be presented to them when they log in. This is an example of the principle of mass customisation that was only available in a limited form in the traditional media. AEC does not exploit this at present, but uses a generic web site that looks and feels the same, whoever the user is.

Finally, the new media provide *independence* of location allowing the company to move into geographical areas that would have been unreachable before. The Internet effectively provides a worldwide market that is open 24 hours per day, seven days per week. It is difficult to think of any traditional media which would have permitted this global reach so cheaply. Furthermore, the web site might also omit the actual physical location of the company because there is no requirement for information to be physically sent to an address. It should also be impossible for the potential customer to gauge the size of the supplying company. AEC has exploited this to some extent as it serves a world-wide market from no clear geographical centre. However, the absence of on-line course booking means that certain physical contact details have to be provided and these might undermine the global perspective.

(b) The marketing mix has traditionally consisted of four major components: product, place (distribution), promotion and price. More recently, three further elements have been added, particularly for the marketing of services – people, process and physical evidence. Some authors, however, contend that these new elements are really only sub-sets of the original four components.

In the context of this question, the Ps, whether there are 4 or 7, provide a good framework for the answer, although such a framework is not mandated. The model answer below actually uses '5Ps', relating them to both technology and the situation at AEC.

Product

The product is a fundamental element of the marketing mix. If the product is not 'right' it is unlikely that the marketers will be able to persuade customers to buy the product or, if they do buy it, to convince them to become repeat buyers. In the context of the new technology, an organisation may seek opportunities for developing the product or service. These opportunities emerge from re-considering the core product or identifying options for extending it.

In the context of AEC the consideration of the product is complicated by there being at least three products promoted on their web site; training courses and training manuals for students studying for professional qualifications and training courses for qualified accountants undertaking continuing professional development (CPD). The course training manual is a tangible physical product that can be handled before purchase. Potential customers can try before they buy because a sub-section of a manual is available for inspection. This is an admirable policy. Potential customers do not have to believe that the manuals are comprehensive and well-written; they can make their own judgement based on a sample. In contrast, the training courses are services, bought on the promise of satisfaction.

AEC might profitably consider delivering elements of both student and CPD training courses through web casts and pod casts. Such courses might be fully on-line or the new technologies might be integrated with older ones, such as workshops and offline assignments, to provide a blended approach to learning. This may be particularly appropriate for student tuition where competence is assessed by a formal examination, not by attendance at a course. AEC is already distributing course catalogues and course schedules through the Internet. However, there is no physical evidence to support the customer's evaluation of such courses. AEC might consider having sample videoed sessions available on the web so that prospective customers can assess the content and approach to training.

Although training documentation is currently available through the web site it could benefit from re-focusing. At present students pay a fixed fee which gives them access to the whole set of manuals. However, manuals for modules at the end of the scheme will only be relevant if the student passes the earlier modules. Lack of confidence may deter the student from committing to the whole manual set at the beginning of his or her studies. Similarly, candidates who become aware of AEC products only after they have passed the first few modules are unlikely to pay a fee for a manual set which includes manuals for modules that they have already passed or for which they are exempted. Consequently, it would appear more sensible to allow candidates to select the manuals they require and pay a fee per manual, with a discounted fee for buying the whole set.

AEC might also wish to consider *product bundling* where it offers further products and services to complement its core products. For example, travel booking, accommodation services and entertainment bookings might be offered to qualified accountants attending CPD courses. AEC is also in a market place where the product needs to be continually updated and developed to reflect changing or clarified requirements. For example, new training manuals may need releasing every year.

Price

The Internet has allowed pricing to be much more transparent to potential customers. They can easily visit the sites of competing companies and compare prices for similar products and services. Such accessibility may deter AEC from using the web site to offer *differential pricing*. The Internet makes products available worldwide but candidates in poorer countries are often unable to afford prices set in richer parts of the world. Consequently, AEC should consider the potential of differential pricing, making prices reflect local currencies and conditions. There is a risk of alienating people in richer countries but it may be a risk worth taking and it is possible that candidates in these richer countries may perceive differential pricing as ethical practice. Web sites produced in national languages using domain names registered in that country might not be discovered or accessed by candidates in the developed world and so differential pricing is never uncovered. However, there is still a risk that customers buying at a lower price will then sell to buyers in the segments that are charged a higher price – so AEC will have to monitor this.

The ability to continually update information on the Internet makes the dynamic pricing of products and services attractive. It is extensively used by airlines (booking early attracts large discounts) and hotels (auctioning off rooms they cannot fill that night). It appears that AEC should also consider differential pricing, particularly using early booking discounts to get the CPD courses up and running. It may also be possible to provide cheap 'late booking' offers to fill the last few places on a course. However, there is the possibility that this will alienate people who have already booked and paid the standard fee. Hence, this will also have to be given more detailed consideration.

AEC might also wish to consider an alternative pricing structure for the documentation. At present manuals are purchased and this might still be the case if it adopts the more modular approach suggested in the previous section. However, there may be large areas of the manual that the student is familiar with. An alternative approach is to charge the student only when they access the material. Hence, students pay for a web service on demand – rather than through purchased download. This 'on demand' payment for actual use is becoming an increasingly popular model of delivering products.

Finally, because off-line booking incurs administrative costs and overheads it is usual to offer on-line customers a significant discount. Hence the pricing structure must recognise this. People booking through an on-line channel now expect to get a discounted price.

Place

It has been argued that the Internet has the greatest implications for place in the marketing mix because, as a distribution channel, it has a global reach, available 24 hours per day, seven days per week. AEC is already exploiting this global reach, although it has to ensure that its products make sense in a global perspective. The training manuals are easy to exploit globally as they are downloaded products which can be printed off throughout the world. The dates and locations of training courses, in their current format, is also globally accessible but is only really relevant to people living in the geographical regions near to the eight training centres. This is particularly true of CPD courses which are only run in three centres worldwide. The global reach of the Internet can only be exploited in the context of the courses if they use the technology discussed in the *product* section of this answer, perhaps exploiting the *price* differentials discussed in the previous section.

Promotion

Although AEC has an established web site it has not actively promoted it. The promotion of the web site may involve both technology and established marketing media. From the technology perspective, AEC might consider the following to increase its web site visibility.

1   Search Engine registration. This remains the primary method of users finding products and services. Over 80% of web users state that they use search engines to find information. There are five main parameters on which search engines base the order of their ranking.

  –   Title – keywords in the title of a web page

  –   Meta tags

  –   Frequency of keyword in the text

  –   Hidden graphic text

  –   Links from other sites.

  AEC must ensure that their web site is constructed in such a way that it has a good chance of appearing on the first page of search engine listings.

2   Building links with other web sites should increase traffic to the site as well as improving search engine ranking. The current AEC site does not appear to link (or be linked) to any other sites.

3   Viral marketing is the term used when e-mail is used to transmit a promotional message to another potential customer. It enables a customer browsing the site to forward a page to a colleague. There is no evidence that the AEC site supports this.

4   On-line advertising includes *banner advertising*. As well as potentially driving customers to the site, the banner advert also builds brand awareness and reminds the customer about the company and its services. AEC must consider this.

Off-line marketing should also be concerned with promoting the web site in established media such as print, TV and radio. Key issues to communicate are the URL and the online value proposition. It may also be used for special sales promotions and offers to attract visitors to the site. 50% of the marketing manager's budget is being spent on off-line marketing media. She must consider how to integrate the web site into this part of the promotional mix.

Process

This concerns the processes used to support the customer's interaction with AEC. At present the training course part of the web site is predominantly an information site. It provides information about the product and the location and cost of the product. However, it is not used for either purchase or post-sales support. Hence if a student or a qualified accountant wishes to book on a course they have to physically contact a person who then takes booking and payment details. There is no evidence that post-sales support such as sending joining instructions, answering queries and receiving course feedback is supported by the web site. It would be useful for AEC to consider whether training purchase and post-sales processes could be integrated into its web site. After all, a payment process has already been set up for the training manual part of the site. The automation of routine processes and answers to common questions might help free up the company's administrative resources as well as providing a better service to customers and exploiting the Internet's *independence of location.*

	ACCA Marking scheme	
		Marks
(a)	Up to 2 marks for recognising the distinction between push and pull technologies in the context of the scenario	2
	Up to 2 marks for issues concerned with interactivity	2
	Up to 2 marks for issues concerned with intelligence	2
	Up to 2 marks for issues concerned with individualisation	2
	Up to 2 marks for issues concerned with independence	2
	Credit will also be given for candidates who focus on Chaffey's other 'I's – industry restructuring and integration	
(b)	Up to 4 marks for issues concerned with product	4
	Up to 3 marks for issues concerned with price	3
	Up to 2 marks for issues concerned with place	2
	Up to 4 marks for issues concerned with promotion	4
	Up to 2 marks for issues concerned with process	2
	Credit will also be given for candidates who focus on other 'p's' – physical evidence and people	
Total		**25**

35   THE HOLIDAY COMPANY

Key answer tips

This question is similar in style and requirement to questions that have been set in the past. In part (a) the elements of the 6I's model are clearly flagged and in part (b) an understanding of how prices are set is required. The key is to focus more on application rather than a regurgitation of knowledge.

(a)   Dilip is justified in his decision to attempt to exploit the principles of electronic marketing, as companies can benefit greatly from this approach. The five principles referred to in the question requirement may be exploited as follows:

   (i)   **Intelligence**

   The internet can be used as a low cost option of gathering intelligence about customers and potential customers. The website could use cookies to track the customers' mouse clicks, and see what has been of interest to them, and at what point they leave an area of the site. For example, do they get as far as looking at availability of a holiday and then leave the site when the price is displayed, or do they move on to another area on reading details about the hotel being offered? This can help to determine new product lines and other elements of the marketing mix.

   If customers register on the site, then the company can also track their individual preferences over time, and this can help to exploit individualisation. As Dilip says, the company currently has no idea whether customers even read their brochure. The use of e-marketing will allow analysis of who visited which part of the site, how long they stayed there, whether they went on to get more information and how many times they re-visit the same page.

(ii) **Individualisation**

The current approach of sending the same marketing, covering all holidays, to every client is not appropriate for the luxury, bespoke service which Inspirations wishes to offer.

Inspirations should ensure it makes use of the features of promotion which offer individualisation, given that they are offering a bespoke service, which is, by its nature, individual. This is only possible if the company also exploits the use of intelligence, as previously mentioned. For example, if a customer has shown interest in gourmet food holidays, information relating to these can be shown on the home page. It may then offer a personalised home page when that customer visits again, with specific suggestions for them.

Customers should be able to save information on holidays which they are interested in and return to these. Inspirations could send emails if there is anything similar which may be of interest to those customers. Or, if a customer has booked a specific holiday in the past, such as a river cruise, the company may send them an email in the future with similar holidays.

(iii) **Interactivity**

This principle works on the idea of a 'pull' marketing approach, whereby the customers are driving the marketing and selling process, rather than the company 'pushing' its holidays at them. Given that the company wishes to sell bespoke holidays, this element is crucial.

The interactivity should begin with the use of search engines, such that when a potential customer types 'luxury holidays' or 'bespoke holidays', for example, Inspirations is one of the first to appear in the search results. Once on the website, the customer should be able to search from easy menus, such as 'destination' or 'holiday type'. The customer should then be shown a range of options, and further action on their part may lead them to further details regarding the holiday being viewed. In this way, the customer will only view holidays and further information which is of interest to them.

Further interactivity may be provided in the form of a two-way dialogue with a holiday adviser, through an online chat function. This could work well with HC's new business unit if the adviser is knowledgeable and able to offer enhanced services, such as managing the overall booking. This could be a valued differentiator for Inspirations: offering a personalised service, as if in-store, without the customer having to be inconvenienced by visiting the store.

(iv) **Integration**

Holiday companies could make great use of integration, which is about sharing knowledge and marketing activity between different parts of the company. For example, if customers switch to Inspirations holidays, having previously been a customer of HC, this information could be shared such that there is already some knowledge of the customers' preferences.

Inspirations could also integrate the different elements of the holiday experience and the databases of different companies supplying the services. For example, it may be possible for the customer to book hotels, flights, car hire and excursions. Inspirations could integrate the information, such that once a customer has booked a holiday, marketing information could be sent for the elements which have not been included. Once a holiday has been booked, the website may offer suggestions for upgrades and further options. If, for example, a holiday is booked at a particular destination, then trips available at that destination may be marketed. Depending upon the holiday purpose, different add-ons could be offered. For example, the gourmet trips for food lovers could forward details of excursions to food production facilities, with booking offers if combined with an existing holiday.

(v) Independence of location

Independence of location allows the possibility of selling into global markets. Provided Inspirations has access to flights departing from different countries, there is nothing to stop it operating as a global travel provider. It is intending to make more use of online sales, with the internet being the main source of marketing this new business, therefore high street branches are not necessary in this instance.

In order to exploit the global market, Inspirations must ensure that it offers the ability to view holiday prices, and pay, in foreign currencies. It should also ensure that it considers the current trends of holiday destinations for different markets worldwide.

(b) There are a number of influences which must be considered when determining a pricing strategy which will deliver the business and corporate objectives of an organisation.

Mission and objectives

Clearly, the objectives which are to be achieved should form a key element when determining the pricing strategy. HC's new business unit has the mission of 'delivering a high quality service for discerning travellers', and aims to 'achieve revenue of $100m by 2018'. If the business unit is aiming for high quality, then its pricing strategy should be in line with this, in order that customer perception is in line with what the company hopes to deliver. This may lead to a premium pricing strategy for Inspirations to maintain the suggestion of a difference between the standard holidays offered and the new range of holidays. Prices should be higher to reflect the quality offered. HC must also consider the desired revenue, 25% of total company revenue but only 5% of volume; this suggests that the pricing must be set at a higher level than current offerings in order to achieve this. Price is a key element in differentiating its product.

Whilst organisations may use discounting as an aid to getting market share, a clear objective of HC, the use of discounting, in this market segment, would contradict the desired message of premium quality.

Cost

If a price fails to take cost into consideration, then the organisation may not be profitable and difficulties may arise in the long term. Although organisations have been known to sell products as a loss leader in order to attract other purchases, it does not seem as if this would be an appropriate strategy for Inspirations. It must cover its costs when deciding its prices.

The premium holidays offered will make use of the best hotels, with high ratings and quality features, and intend to use premium airlines and seat options only. These will be costly to the company and should be incorporated into the price. Inspirations could choose to price each individual option on a 'cost plus margin' basis, or simply ensure that the overall cost is covered when deciding the final price using some other basis.

Competition

There are a number of competitors already operating in the luxury holiday market, and Inspirations must consider what it is charging for equivalent services. Given the transparency of information available over the internet, customers will easily be able to compare holidays and prices. Inspirations does not own the hotels it intends to use for the holidays offered, and will not have exclusive use of them. Therefore, the price should either match those offered by similar competitors, or they should differentiate in some way and therefore be able to charge a justifiably higher price.

Customers

Customers will have a limit regarding what they are prepared to pay for a particular offering. Inspirations must ensure that its pricing is within that limit for its target customer group. Given that these are luxury holidays, Inspirations are targeting higher income customers. Whilst price competition may not be the main focus for these customers, they will still want perceived value for money. This will determine the upper price they are prepared to pay.

Controls

There are a number of external influences affecting the travel industry. Although it is often the airline or the hotel company which is subjected to these influences, such as local passenger taxes and visa requirements, the holiday company must consider these when determining its pricing strategy. For example, should these be incorporated into the price of the holiday or shown separately? Also, can the airline or hotel companies impose controls on the holiday company, such as a legal requirement not to discount their prices in any way?

Overall, therefore, Inspirations should consider a combination of the above influences to ensure that it sets a price which delivers a profitable product which meets the corporate objectives.

ACCA Marking scheme		Marks
(a)	Up to 3 marks per heading discussed, up to a maximum of 15 marks	
(b)	Up to 2 marks per heading discussed, up to a maximum of 10 marks	
Total		**25**

Examiner's comments

Candidates answered part (a) reasonably well, although some were clearly unaware of what these principles actually were. Intelligence is NOT to do with the intelligence of employees in the company, integration is NOT to do with tuning web sites to reflect cultural and language requirements.

In part (b), answers based around costs, competition, customers and controls scored well. However, too many answers were unfocussed and instead concentrated on Porter's basis of competition, which led to a few relevant points (and marks) but such answers seldom gained enough marks to pass this part question.

36 HGT

Key answer tips

Part (a) of this question asks students to quantify the cost savings and revenue increases. This should open the door for the need to perform some calculations. The bulk of the marks where for these calculations and the fact the business was making a loss and that a contribution figure was given should have been the trigger that pointed students towards break even calculations. Students who failed to spot these triggers are likely to have scored poorly. Part (b) required the use of the marketing mix and was very broad in scope. This should have allowed students to score well but some students are likely to have been confused by the unusual wording of the requirement.

This question is more straightforward than it will have appeared to students. The requirements seem a little confusing and students are likely to have struggled with the difference between short term and long term solutions to the business problems. Hopefully, the use of the word 'marketing' in part (b) will point students towards the marketing mix, but students then may struggle for time as they try to cover as many of the 7 elements of the marketing mix as possible. Part (a) was equally open-ended and there is scope here for students to tie themselves up in knots by finding it difficult to determine the level and detail that will be required for their calculations and suggestions.

(a)   Short term changes

Tutorial note

Any short-term strategy which produces reasonably justifiable income increases or cost savings (in the context of the scenario) is acceptable.

A simple analysis of the financial data shows why the trust is currently running at a loss.

The annual fixed costs are $60,000. Monthly visitor figures are 1,000 per month. The gardens are only open for eight months per year. So, as a result, 8,000 visits generate $40,000 direct income. The contribution from café sales is estimated at $1.25 per visitor. Only 60% of visitors use the café, generating an annual contribution of $6,000. This leaves an annual financial shortfall of $14,000 per year, which explains why the trust is gradually using up the legacy left by Clive Popper.

Immediate actions that might be considered include:

Reduce the admission fee to the price consumers are willing to pay. Surveys have suggested that the price that consumers are willing to pay is $3.25. Reducing the admission price to this level would mean that a breakeven visitor volume would be 15,000, assuming that 60% of these visitors still use the café and the contribution from café sales remains $1.25. This assumes that the contribution from each admission would be $3.25, as the scenario does not identify any variable cost associated with each visit.

Here are the workings, where n is the required number of visitors:

0.6n × 1.25 + 3.25n = 60,000 0.75n + 3.25n = 60,000

4n = 60,000, so n = 15,000

15,000 visits × 3.25 = $48,750 admittance revenue

15,000 visits × 0.6 × 1.25 = $11,250 profit from café sales, giving a total revenue of $60,000

Obviously the trust will have to consider the likelihood of such a dramatic increase in visitor numbers (from the current 8,000 per year). If visitor numbers do not increase as significantly as a result of reducing the price to $3.25, then overall contribution towards fixed costs may actually fall. In fact, reducing the price to $3.25 would require an increase in visitors of (4n = 14,000) 3,500 from the previous level not to make the financial performance of HGT any worse than it is currently.

Introduce a season's membership card. Evidence suggests that 20% of visitors would consider purchasing an annual membership card, if it were priced at $9. This would have the advantage of providing a short-term boost to cash flow. However, the actual income is difficult to estimate. There are 8,000 visits per year, but the scenario does not specify how many individual visitors there are. It seems likely that some people are likely to make more than one visit in a year. However, if an estimate of 6,000 individual visitors is used, then this would give a relatively immediate income of 6,000 × 0.2 × 9 = $10,800 which could be used to meet short-term cash flow problems. Obviously, income from future visits will be lost, but it could be argued that the promise of subsequent free admission will encourage people to visit more, leading to more use of, and income from, the café.

Short-term actions that might be considered include:

Relocate the café. The café was much more popular when it was located in the gatehouse, where café users were not required to pay an admission fee for the garden. Moving the café inside the garden may have seemed like a good idea at the time, but takings have reduced considerably. It should be relatively easy to relocate the café to the gatehouse because the site it previously occupied is still empty. There will be some costs associated with removal and refurbishment, but if the café returns to its previous levels of use, then profit from this source should be $625 per month (500 visitors × $1.25 contribution), or $5,000 over the eight-month season (8 × $625).

Increase revenues from the café. There have been some criticisms that the café menu is limited in scope and does not offer substantial lunches. Perhaps the limited nature of its menu means that revenue is unnecessarily low and that better, more appealing drinks and food may be offered at a higher contribution. There may also be scope for reducing supply costs. A more attractive menu may also lead to an improvement in the take up of customers. Currently, only 60% of garden visitors actually use the café. For example, an increase in contribution to $1.75 per visit and an increase to a 75% take up of customers would lead to an increase of $4,500 in revenue ((8,000 × 0.75 × 1.75) – 6,000) over the eight-month season, based on current visitor numbers.

Reduce display advertising.

Note: Although the savings from cancelling the subscription is long term (greater than three months), the action to cancel has to be implemented immediately. However, credit will be given to the candidate whether this is included in part (a) or part (b).

There is always concern that reducing advertising expenditure is an inappropriate instinctive response to financial problems. However, evidence from the consumer survey suggests that the display advertisements are not effective and although six months of advertisements have been booked, three of these can be cancelled without penalty. The survey suggests that 5% of visitors heard about the garden through the Heritage Gardens magazine. Even if all visits represented individual visitors, this would only lead to 50 visits per month (1,000 × 0.05), producing an income of $287.50 per month ($250.00 (admittance fee: 50 × $5) and $37.50 spent at the café (50 × 0.6 × 1.25)). So, the monthly cost of $500 per advert is only generating $287.50 in income. Furthermore, it has to be recalled that the survey only asked respondents for one choice about how they heard about the gardens. Respondents who heard about the garden through the Heritage Gardens magazine might have also heard about it through other media.

(b)   Long term changes

Tutorial note

There is considerable scope around all the 'p's of the marketing mix in the question and candidates may well interpret the applicability of some of these as either short or long-term strategies. For example, although reducing the price to the target price could be made immediately, it is understandable if some candidates would wish to consider it as a longer-term strategy. Furthermore, the effect of cancelling the subscriptions might also be included in this section as its effect will not be felt until three months' time This model answer focuses on product and promotion. However, answers centred, for example, on physical evidence and price will be given as much credit as long as they are relevant to the scenario.

In the long term, HGT needs to reflect more on what product it actually offers to the consumer. Most of the marketing is currently focused on the historical importance of the garden and the efforts that have been made to restore it. HGT stresses the restoration effort and the importance of William Wessex as a garden designer. This is very much the trust's perception of what is important, with a focus on history and restoration.

However, whether this is the focus of visitors is open to question. To them, the garden offers *an experience*, and HGT needs to understand what that experience is. Perhaps it is the opportunity to wander around in a peaceful, safe, attractive environment, enjoying the plants and flowers. Certainly, the consumer survey suggests that this is the motivation of 85% of visitors. Perhaps this should be the main basis of the marketing message.

In understanding this experience, HGT might also be able to augment the product to help visitors enjoy the gardens and to increase visitor numbers. For example, more visitors with young children might be attracted if a supervised play area were provided well away from the garden. HGT might also consider selling appropriate supporting products in the café. HGT needs to think more widely about the product: what it is from a customer's perspective and what can be done to improve their experience of the product. For example, it might consider selling plants.

HGT has also just focused on the private visitor. Businesses might also benefit from running events in the garden environment, particularly those with products aimed at well-being or gardening. The definition of the customer may also require re-definition.

Finally, the product is constrained by its opening season – eight months. HGT has assumed that there will be fewer visitors in the four months when the weather is colder. However, this assumption has never been tested and it could be argued that the garden offers walking 'in a peaceful, beautiful, safe environment' the whole of the year. Indeed, the reason given by 65% of the respondents for visiting the garden arguably remains relevant in the colder period. Perhaps special events can be organised to compensate for the relative scarcity of flowering plants in this season. The effect of extending the opening season on fixed costs will also have to be evaluated.

Promotion has focused on display advertising. Perhaps these display advertisements have the wrong message (heritage and restoration) and are placed in the wrong magazine (Heritage Gardens). Evidence from the survey supports this. Only 5% of visits were prompted by the expensive advertisements in the Heritage Gardens magazine. Again, focusing on heritage rather than a peaceful garden experience might be the fundamental issue here. HGT needs to reconsider its message and how it can be effectively communicated.

Publicity and public relations have been particularly poor. The work in the garden has not been recorded in the local press. Consequently, many of the people in the local area are not aware of the garden. HGT needs to actively engage with local newspapers, local radio and tourist agencies to raise its profile. The recent articles written by the trust's administrator have been one of the main reasons prompting visits to the garden. However, it has taken a crisis within the trust to prompt it to use this relatively simple form of promotion.

The internet also has many possibilities. At present the site is relatively static, concentrating again on the restoration of the gardens and stressing their historical importance. There is no interaction with the user. HGT should reconsider the design and content of the site. Again it needs to ensure that the message about the experience is relevant. There is also an opportunity to use the internet to build a community to support the gardens and perhaps this can be part of the service offered to those taking up annual membership, introduced in the short-term suggestions. The internet also provides an opportunity to:

Reconsider the pricing structure. Perhaps discounts could be given for pre-booking. Pricing may also be differentiated by age. Currently there is one price per visit. However, lower prices could be offered to the elderly, children and those on state support benefits.

Providing *physical evidence* – showing visitors through webcams and videos the type of experience that they will get by visiting the garden.

Improving the *process* of purchasing tickets, particularly in applying for an annual membership.

ACCA Marking scheme		
		Marks
(a)	1 mark for each relevant point up to a maximum of 15 marks. The answer might include certain calculations, which will be marked as follows:	
	– Calculation of direct income	0.5
	– Calculation of café income	0.5
	– Calculation of financial shortfall	1
	– Breakeven analysis for consumer price	2
	– Calculation of income from annual subscriptions	1
	– Income if café returns to previous level of use	1
	– Calculations associated with increased café revenue	1
	– Cost saving associated with display advert cancellation	2
	Maximum	15
(b)	1 mark for each relevant point up to a	
	Maximum	10
Total		25

Examiner's comments

In part (a) candidates were relatively adept at identifying short-term changes (such as changing the admission price, moving the café) but were less prepared to attempt quantifying these in any way. A number of expected values could be calculated from the scenario (based on percentage take up) but very, very few candidates used this information. Many answers were too general and did not include the quantitative support required to get the marks on offer.

In part (b) many candidates seem to quickly run out of ideas, yet the five other facets of the marketing mix; promotion, place, process, physical evidence and product could all have provided the basis for potential strategies and helped candidates easily gain most of the ten marks on offer for this part question.

37 BA TIMES

Key answer tips

Part (a) of this question should be familiar to well prepared students. Part (b) is very open ended. Guidance was given to students in the form of specific issues that the editor was concerned about and these should hopefully give students some focus to their answer.

(a) Victor urgently needs to revisit his business model to look at the opportunities presented by new technology and new media. Revenues from his current business are falling due to reduced advertising spend and fewer subscribers. On the other hand, production, distribution and office costs are increasing. These problems are not unique to the *BA Times*. The sales of printed magazines and the profits of publishers are falling dramatically throughout Umboria.

Perhaps because of his conventional publishing background, Victor still perceives his core business as the publishing of a printed magazine. The *BA Times* does have a website, but it is designed to provide tempting tasters for the magazine, running extracts of stories that can only be read in full by people who subsequently buy a printed copy of the magazine. Thus the website is seen as a way of marketing the magazine and, in itself, provides far fewer services and information than the magazine. Emerging technology provides Victor with the opportunity to revisit this business model in the context of four of the '6Is' of e-marketing: individualisation, interactivity, intelligence and independence of location.

Individualisation

A survey of people who had not renewed their subscription revealed that some subscribers believe that the magazine includes too much information which is irrelevant to them. One respondent commented that, 'I am studying the ABC syllabus and so in-depth articles on ICFC topics and examinations are not relevant to me. I quite enjoy reading the news parts, but not the in-depth analysis of examinations that I am not taking.' One ABC candidate remarked that, 'I have reached the final stage of my examinations. I do not want to read articles about the stages I have already passed. I reckon only about 15% of *BA Times* is relevant to me now.'

A key feature of the new technology and media is the opportunity to *individualise* or tailor the product to meet specific requirements and for that tailoring to be driven and performed by the customer. So, for example, if all the resources are made available on a website, the customer only needs to access those resources that he or she wants. This can be achieved by him or her just ignoring menu options for other institutes or examinations or, more innovatively, by configuring the website so that it just reflects an individual's interest (*myBATImes*). Furthermore, through registering interests either directly on the website, or through linked social and business networking sites, the candidate can be kept informed of articles, news, comments and blogs relevant to their interests, institute and examination stage. A centralised website resource would allow Victor to expand the number of relevant resources available (which he is under pressure to do) without making his printed magazine any larger or more expensive. He can also supplement conventional text articles with webcasts and podcasts. If the candidate wants a hard copy of any article, then he or she can locate it and print it out, thus transferring printed costs to the subscriber. The website should be considered as a comprehensive knowledge centre where all relevant resources are stored.

Interactivity

A key characteristic of the internet is the opportunity it provides for interactivity. Traditional printed media, such as magazines, are predominantly *push media* where the message is broadcast from the company to the customer. There is limited interaction with the customer. Evidence of this is provided in the scenario, where, although there are readers' letters, the monthly gap between issues means that many topics just lose their currency, or are made irrelevant by changed circumstances. The only person who can immediately comment on topics raised in a reader's letter is the editor of the magazine. One of survey respondents commented on this. 'Some of the readers' letters are really irritating or just plain wrong, but the editor seldom makes a comment! It really annoys me!' A key characteristic of the internet is *interactivity*. Issues raised on a website can be commented on immediately and threads developed. In general, the internet is a *pull media* where the customer initiates contact and is seeking information on a website.

Communities of interest are important features of the internet. The *BA Times* largely fails to exploit its unique position of being independent of the two large professional associations. It could provide writers with an opportunity for controversy and speculation, generating feedback which would unlikely to be acceptable to the official websites of the professional associations. The site itself can become a natural host to communities of interest, discussing and documenting topics relevant to that community and making resources available to new members. Feedback can also be provided on written articles, asking for clarification or providing extra information.

The interactivity of the website is also enhanced by the ability to continually update it. Reference has already been made to the time gap between issues. Significant events may take place the day after a print deadline. The website can be updated immediately to report on emerging issues and concerns. This should again increase the use of the website, ensuring that users see the *BA Times* as a valuable source of information.

Intelligence

The Internet can be used as a relatively low cost method of collecting information from and about customers. Online questionnaires can be used to help understand how users rate the website and to understand what products and services they are looking for. Website analytics can be used to identify which pages are looked at and what browsers and search terms are used to arrive at such pages. Both questionnaires and analytics will help Victor tailor the content to his potential customers.

By exploiting editorial independence and interactivity, the site can become the one-stop resource for all aspiring business analysts. If this becomes the case, then capturing information about visitors will allow Victor to build up a very significant resource which cannot only be used to improve the website but also (as long as permission is given) to provide intelligence to other companies which wish to exploit this market, for example, learning providers and, indeed, the professional associations themselves.

Independence of location

Finally, a further clear benefit of contemporary technology is its ability to provide an organisation with independence of location. Although this answer has focused on the central role of a website resource, Victor could exploit opportunities for independence of location within the current printed magazine model. Production currently takes place in an expensive area of Umboria, a country where wage rates are also high. Production could be moved to a country where wages, equipment and operational costs are cheaper and then shipped to customers from there. Similarly, the Head Office could be moved to a cheaper area, offering the company potential savings on overhead costs.

(b) Victor himself is a potential barrier to the extensive use of new technology and media. His background is in printed magazines and this is a product that he feels comfortable with. He likes the physical, tactile feel of magazines and evidence suggests that his product is well liked and respected in the industry. But, increasing costs and changing reading habits mean that the future of the printed magazine industry looks bleak. However, even if Victor can overcome his preference for printed media, he has a further problem in understanding how new technology is going to turn round the fortunes of the *BA Times* and return it to profit.

A simple option is to *just employ new technology to reduce costs*. This might give him some breathing space in which to develop a future business strategy or plan his retirement. Alternatively, he could consider an option to embrace the new technology more extensively and re-position the printed *BA Times* as just one channel to his target market. It is possible that the introduction of a comprehensive web resource may lead to a further fall in the circulation of a printed copy version of the *BA Times*. However, this would have to be researched. Perhaps his readership contains people like himself who would still want to receive a physical copy of a magazine.

If a more radical shift to new technology and new media is to be justified, then Victor would have to be convinced of the possibility of generating income from at least three sources. These would offset a fall in income from the printed magazine and also address the issue of the financial viability of the company.

Increased advertising: The very breadth of the *BA Times* (news, articles, three associations, many examinations) probably makes display advertising only attractive to the larger learning providers which provide courses at all levels across all qualifications. Targeted advertising is much easier on the web and so the new resource may attract advertising from a wider range of learning providers. An extended product range (for example, recruitment resources) made available on the website should also bring in new advertisers from different sectors. If Victor can establish the *BA Times* website as the premier one-stop resource for business analysts, then attracting significant advertising should be no problem.

Subscription services within the website: Many websites contain both free and subscription resources. High quality free services can be a taster for attracting customers to the resources which are only available for a subscription. This is an established approach in web-based services and is particularly relevant in a competitive environment like examinations. Candidates may believe that investing relatively small amounts of money in extra services might give them an edge in preparing for examinations.

Income from selling intelligence: The facility of websites to capture information about visitors and their interests has already been discussed in the answer to the first part of this question. This will be of potential use to other organisations and with the person's consent can be forwarded and sold.

Victor is also concerned about the reaction of advertisers to any proposal to adopt new technology within the *BA Times*. However, it is likely that Victor will receive a positive response from advertisers. At present, advertising revenue is falling. In general, there is a growing disenchantment with push marketing technologies, where advertisers cannot be sure that their message has reached the intended market. Advertising on a comprehensive website has many of the advantages that have already been discussed. Advertisements can be made specific and individualised, they can be quickly and easily updated, and the effectiveness of an advertisement or a campaign can be relatively easily analysed through the responses received from the website.

Finally, Victor is concerned about the effect on subscribers who cannot access a website or, like him, value a printed copy and wish to still receive one. At this stage, there is no reason why a smaller run of the printed version cannot be maintained by exploiting technology to reduce printing, distribution and office costs. Contribution to overheads will be reduced, but income from other sources (see above) should compensate for this. Some advertisers may also wish to continue advertising in the printed edition to supplement their web-based marketing.

The nature of the web resource also allows Victor to reconsider the range of products he has to offer. At present the magazine is focused on news and preparing candidates for examinations. Income is derived from learning providers advertising in the pages of the magazine. Victor might consider moving into related business areas that would appeal to his readership. From the feedback given, the most obvious candidate is probably recruitment. One of the respondents to the survey commented that, 'I became a business analyst to get a job, not just to sit examinations and read about examining bodies.' Victor might have lost focus here. For many candidates, taking examinations is a means to an end, not an end in itself, and job opportunities and careers do not seem to be considered in the *BA Times* at present. Articles about certain job roles and interview advice might be provided and a potential new income stream should open up for Victor from recruitment agencies placing advertisements for jobs which they have been contracted to fill.

ACCA Marking scheme		
		Marks
(a)	1 mark for each relevant point up to a maximum of 15 marks, with a maximum of 5 marks for each individual 'i'.	15
(b)	1 mark for each relevant point up to a maximum of 10 marks.	10
Total		**25**

Examiner's comments

Part (a) was fairly well answered by candidates, although very few developed their answer to get the marks on offer. There was also significant repetition; with the same point being made in two or more 'I's. The independence of location was particularly poorly answered, with relatively few candidates recognising the fact that the company was based in a high cost area.

In part (b) many answers were not well structured. Most candidates did score some marks, but few really got to the heart of this question and score significant marks (eight or more) for this part question. Many answers were short and superficial and did not really address the specific requirements of the question.

38 CHEMICAL TRANSPORT

Key answer tips

In part (a), Harmon's process strategy matrix should be used. In part (b), covering CRM, many different points will have scored marks so there is a little scope here for the use of some business awareness as well as the knowledge contained in the study text.

(a) Paul Harmon has proposed a process-strategy matrix that considers the strategic importance of the process on one axis and the complexity of the process on the other. This leads to four quadrants for which Harmon suggests different generic process solutions. For example, for relatively simple processes of low strategic importance he suggests standard software package solutions or outsourcing. The location of each of the three processes defined in the question is considered in the following text, together with potential solution options in the context of CT.

Payroll is usually of relatively *low complexity and low strategic importance.* It is normally fulfilled by a commercial off-the-shelf software package. At CT the payroll requirements are relatively complex because of the combination of bonuses and deductions which have been developed and enhanced over the last few years. Consequently, payroll has been developed as a bespoke application by the in-house IT team. However, there is no evidence that the pay arrangements are effective. Drivers find them confusing and they certainly do not find them motivating. It could be suggested that CT should simplify its pay arrangements and adopt a commercial off-the-shelf package solution. Adopting such a solution would also address long-term costs and problems. Payroll is subject to continual and unpredictable legislative changes. With a standard package these changes are part of a fixed maintenance fee. Bespoke changes are unpredictable in both occurrence and duration and so are potentially time-consuming and expensive. Indeed, recent changes in legislation led to the IT team being fully occupied for three months, developing and testing the required modifications to the payroll system. There is also the chance that the IT team could make a mistake or miss something important in the legislation. IT savings could be recycled into the drivers' pay system. A simplified payment system could lead to drivers being offered better pay deals without costing the company any more overall. It could also help motivate the drivers more effectively, which the scenario indicates is not happening with the existing system.

The legal advice process is currently outsourced to a legal consultancy, although the cost of such advice is causing the company to consider appointing a full-time, employed expert. CT is operating in an environment that is continually subject to legislation. Chemical transport and handling is dangerous and appropriate legislation is inevitable. Drivers and driving hours and the maintenance of trucks and trailers are also likely to be subject to both national and international legislation. Legislation is time-consuming to monitor and the potential cost of non-compliance is very high. It could result in substantial damages or fines. CT recognises that the current legal experts deliver an excellent service. It seems unlikely that it will be easy to find a full-time expert with such a wide range of knowledge, so employment is risky and also likely to be relatively expensive. The person will be the sole expert and so, as well as the problems of verifying advice, it also seems likely that there will be problems in motivating and keeping such an employee in a job role where there is no onward career path. In Paul Harmon's terms, the legal advice process appears to be a *complex process with little strategic significance.* The advice for this type of process is to continue to outsource and maintain the service of the legal consultancy.

The extension of the website to allow the chemical wholesalers to place and track orders is strategically very important to CT. It recognises that failure to implement such functions will jeopardise future contracts. The chemical wholesalers may begin to look for an alternative distributor. CT probably recognises that such a feature might also help them sign up more wholesalers and so the extended website can be part of their business strategy. Whether the process is complex or not is a matter of judgement. There will be clear security issues and it will be important to partition the system so that competitors' details are kept securely and separately. It is also likely that requirements are not yet extensively defined and will change as the details of the wholesalers' requirements become clear. The company has an IT capability with some expertise in web-based systems. If a commercial off-the-shelf software solution is used to fulfil the payroll requirements, then this IT team is potentially freed up to work on the enhanced website system. Consequently it is suggested that this application is a *relatively complex process with strategic importance* and so is best developed in-house as a bespoke system.

(b) The provision of delivery placement and tracking is, at the moment, an important element of customer retention. However, in a wider sense the company's website has to be reviewed to see if it can be harnessed to acquire further customers, to enhance the service it offers (above and beyond placing and tracking deliveries) and also to assist in the long-term retention of customers. It must be recalled that the present website is only used for information purposes. It only contains information about the company: its structures, history, key contacts and case studies. However, it must also be recalled that CT only deals with a relatively small business market. In B2B applications there tends to be far fewer but larger buyers (Chaffey, 2007).

Customer acquisition

The scenario suggests that chemical wholesalers are CT's current customers. The site should be constructed with their interests and requirements in mind. Evidence suggests that CT has recognised expertise in the difficult and dangerous task of chemical distribution where there is a need for compliance with stringent and emerging legislation. The website needs to provide examples of this and also constant updates which tempt people to return to the site to view the latest information. CT does not have to reveal its complete expertise. However, regular, selected updates on new legislative requirements and new chemical distribution challenges may prompt return visits and so increasingly suggest to potential customers that this is a business avenue that is worth exploring. The case studies already on the website will strengthen the message of expertise and also demonstrate to potential customers that outsourcing to CT will have both business and financial benefits. Testimonials from established customers will help support this message. It has to be recognised that it is a B2B website and that no contract or purchase will be entered into as a result of the website alone. It is about building up confidence and information that may lead to contact being made between CT and a potential customer. Overall, the website should look professional and business-like and appropriately discreet. Existing customers may not wish certain information to be given out and CT itself must not give too much valuable information to competitors about its pricing or its range of current customers.

It is also important that potential customers find the CT website when they are looking for information or for a potential haulier. Although it is less important than in a B2C website, it is still helpful if CT ensures that the website is optimised so that it appears high up in website searches. This is not easy to reliably achieve and so purchasing sponsored links can also be very valuable. The website address also has to be promoted in any offline marketing undertaken by the company. Again, it must be recalled that CT must have a relatively finite set of potential customers. These should be relatively easy to target with marketing information and sales calls that will include the website details.

CT may also benefit from collecting details about the people who are visiting its site. This may again be achieved through offering selected information only to visitors who leave their email address. So, although some technical information might be offered for free, other information – such as important changes in international legislation – might only be available to visitors who have provided their email details. These email details may just be used as part of an analysis (which companies are looking at us) or they might be used to target future promotional campaign.

Customer retention

Customer retention refers to marketing activities taken by an organisation to keep its existing customers. The scenario has already identified the placement and tracking of orders. Customers might be offered a service which helps them plan deliveries to help minimise distribution costs. This is potentially even more valuable if it can assist in distributing chemicals directly to the end customer, hence avoiding wholesaler storage costs. Payment for the delivery might also be organised through the website, with inducements made for fast on-line payment. Customer retention is improved by integrating the systems of the supplier and the customer. Not only does this provide a better and cheaper service, it also effectively makes it more difficult for the customer to move to an alternative supplier. Thus, as well as extending its web service, CT should consider establishing links to the front end of the process (ordering, planning) and to the back end (payment and reconciliation). Customers also value relevant management information. CT needs to identify what information it can offer its customers to help them run their company more effectively or keep down costs. For example, making an earlier delivery may enable the wholesaler to use the customer's storage facility rather than their own.

Tutorial note

It is likely that candidates' answers will vary in scope and credit will be given as appropriate. However, answers must recognise that CT will require a B2B website and that purchase transactions are unlikely to take place on the strength of the website alone. The website will just be the potential start of a selling process.

ACCA Marking scheme		
		Marks
(a)	1 mark for each relevant point up to a maximum of 5 marks for each process area. Three process areas required, giving a maximum of	15
(b)	1 mark for each relevant point up to a maximum of 5 marks for principles and 1 mark for each relevant point up to a maximum of 5 marks for the evaluation.	10
Total		25

Examiner's comments

In general part (a) was very well answered, with a significant number of candidates scoring thirteen marks or more. Alternate recommendations to those in the model answers (for example; whether to in-source rather than outsource legal advice) were permitted if they were well justified.

Part (b) was not answered particularly well and too many candidates seemed to be unfamiliar with this application. There was too much reliance in the answers on e-marketing and the 6Is, which were only partly relevant to the situation described in the scenario. This approach also led to many suggestions which were inappropriate to a Business to Business (B2B) company such as CT, where it is very unlikely that products will be ordered via the internet. Candidates are reminded of the importance of targeting their answer to the scenario and avoiding inappropriate theoretical considerations. Too many answers reflected a Business to Consumer (B2C) situation and so little credit could be given.

39   ITTRAIN

Key answer tips

This question concerns pricing and the marketing mix – areas where students have traditionally performed poorly in past examinations. Part (a) includes both a calculation and a discussion and it is likely that weaker students will spend more time on one of these areas at the expense of the other. In terms of format for the discussion elements, an article on pricing on the ACCA website will have helped greatly and those students who had read this article will have scored well here. The marketing mix focuses on three areas and it will be important to focus on application to the scenario rather than simple regurgitation of knowledge. These are syllabus areas that are always popular with students but is one in which they typically perform less well than they have expected. This question is likely to follow that pattern.

Tutorial note

A number of different legitimate approaches could be used to answer this question. The structure used here is based on the one produced by Ken Garrett in his article on Business Strategy and Pricing, published in the February 2011 Student Accountant. However, alternative frameworks are acceptable as long as appropriate points are made.

(a)   **Mission and marketing objectives**

Pricing is ultimately part of an organisation's strategy. It should reflect the organisation's self-perception and its feeling about its position in the market. Marco wants to position iTTrain as a quality provider to the business market. Does his suggested price of $750 per delegate reflect this? It could be argued that this is a reasonable price as long as other factors support it.

He is not providing a 'no frills' service to self-financed candidates, so his price can reflect this. His main benchmark is AQT, and he is suggesting a price which undercuts their list price ($900), and their discounted price ($810), so his company theoretically offers the same (or better) quality at a more competitive price.

Pricing objectives

In the short term, there can be a variety of pricing objectives. Sometimes, irrespective of long-term objectives, the need to survive and increase short-term cash flows will dictate price cuts. At present, Marco is not in this position. He wishes to establish iTTrain in the market place, and he is looking for short-term modest profitability. His price should reflect this.

Costing and financial analysis

> #### Tutorial note
>
> *The financial analysis may be undertaken in a variety of ways and appropriate credit will be given to alternatives. In the following analysis, Marco's suggested price of $750 per delegate is used as a basis of the analysis.*
>
> *Expected contribution is calculated by using the values from AQT.*

Figure 1 shows the contribution for class sizes of three to nine delegates on a course. iTTrain will not run courses with fewer than three delegates, and the training rooms at CityCentre have a maximum capacity of nine delegates.

The expected contribution per course has been calculated using the probabilities derived from courses at AQT. The delegate fee is $750.

Course length: 3 days. All financial figures in $.

Probability	Delegates	Lecturer	Room	Manual*	Lunch	Total cost	Income	Contrib	Exp contrib
0.15	3	450	250	60	30	2,250	2,250	0	0
0.21	4	450	250	80	40	2,300	3,000	700	147
0.25	5	450	250	100	50	2,350	3,750	1,400	350
0.19	6	450	250	120	60	2,400	4,500	2,100	399
0.07	7	450	250	140	70	2,450	5,250	2,800	196
0.08	8	450	250	160	80	2,500	6,000	3,500	280
0.05	9	450	250	180	90	2,550	6,750	4,200	210
							Total expected contribution		1,582

*Manual cost is per delegate per course

Figure 1: Contribution for class sizes of three to nine delegates

The expected contribution per course is $1,582.

Thus the breakeven on a course basis is $65,000/1,582 = 41.09 courses.

The company plans to offer 40 courses per year. If the contribution per course is $1,582, then iTTrain will make a small operating loss (40 × $1,582 = $63,280 – $65,000) = ($1,720).

A consideration of the profitability at different delegate volume levels is also instructive, showing that an average attendance of six delegates per course is required to achieve operating profitability assuming that 40 courses a year actually do run. In other words, classes have to operate at a minimum of two-thirds capacity, on average, for the company to be profitable if only 40 courses actually run during the first year.

All financial figures are in $

Number of delegates	Contribution	Fixed overheads	Operating profit (loss)
3	0	65,000	(65,000)
4	28,000	65,000	(37,000)
5	56,000	65,000	(9,000)
6	84,000	65,000	19,000
7	112,000	65,000	47,000
8	140,000	65,000	75,000
9	168,000	65,000	103,000

A number of options might be considered:

- To increase the price towards their nearest competitor. For example, assuming the same attendance pattern as above, increasing the price towards that of their nearest competitor (AQT), at just under $800 per delegate, would maintain their competitive price advantage while potentially increasing the expected value, realising a modest profit. (Note that sensitivity analysis could be undertaken to verify this using the same method used to calculate the expected value based on a delegate price of $750.)

- Decreasing costs: The lecturer and training room rates are standard rates. It may be possible to agree bulk booking discounts. A 5% discount on lecturing and room booking rates increases the expected contribution per course to $1,687.00 (assuming a course fee of $750). On 40 courses, this gives an expected income of $67,480, producing an operating profit $2,480, returning a modest operating margin of 3.68% (2,480/67,840).

- An exploration of other scenarios which combine increasing the price and decreasing the costs.

- Revisiting overheads, although little information is given in the scenario about this. Marco might be prepared to take less income from the firm in its formative years.

The financial analysis suggests that the $750 delegate fee suggested by Marco appears to be too low to produce the modest profit he would like. It also has to be recalled that the analysis is based on statistical probabilities which are from a well-established training company. Marco has to consider the likelihood of a newly formed training company initially having the same attendance pattern as an established company such as AQT.

Importantly, he has also assumed that all 40 scheduled courses will run. This assumption has to be examined and the sensitivity of profitability to only a certain proportion of courses running has to be explored. Consideration might also be given to the likely proportion of under-subscribed courses at the price actually set. At first sight it appears that a course which does not attract enough delegates will not incur any cost, because all training provision costs are variable. However, there may be cancellation costs associated with the training venue and the freelance lecturer.

Competition

It appears that price is not the only determinant of consumer selection, otherwise the cheaper training providers would dominate the market. Consumers are clearly also affected by non-price factors such as quality of the training and the quality of the place (where the training is provided). Consequently, Marco can price the training at the price he has suggested because there is considerable evidence that consumers (particularly corporate buyers) are willing to pay that price (or more) to get a service which they are satisfied or delighted with.

Consumers

Suppliers have to keep in mind how much consumers are willing to pay. Evidence from AQT suggests that corporate customers (iTTrain's target market) are able to pay the price which Marco has suggested. In contrast, the cheaper 'no frills' training providers appear to appeal to self-financed customers for whom price is an issue. The existence of training brokers as intermediaries in the supply chain does complicate the situation. If Marco wishes to offer them a margin as great as AQT, then he has to reduce his price (to training brokers) to $675 per delegate, which will obviously affect contribution.

Controls

The market is not subject to any legislative pricing controls.

Setting prices

As stated before, Marco wishes to set prices to show a short-term modest profit.

Strategic approaches (tactics or ploys)

A number of tactics or ploys can be used within the pricing strategy, for example: price skimming, penetration pricing, product-line pricing, etc. None of these appear to be particularly appropriate to iTTrain. However, many training companies (like airlines) provide 'early-bird' (early booking) discounts in an attempt to quickly reach a critical mass. Early-bird payments also improve cash flow. iTTrain might also wish to consider 'late booking' discounts, perhaps through training brokers, to provide extra contribution in courses which they are already committed to run.

Summary

Taking all factors into consideration, the suggested price of $750 per delegate appears to be broadly acceptable, except for its likely impact on the financial performance of the company as a whole, specifically the achievement of Marco's modest profit objective. He should consider raising the price to just under $800 per delegate, which gives him some margin of safety, particularly if costs can be reduced through bulk discounts. It also provides more leeway with the discounts he will have to give to training brokers. To some extent, Marco can experiment with the price level. It is the most flexible part of the marketing mix. In business nothing will remain constant. The economy, taste, innovation and competitor actions will change constantly, forcing prices to be continually reappraised. In reality most companies are price-takers, rather than price makers and Marco's pricing approach will have to reflect this.

(b)   The **physical environment** in which the service is offered is often central to the consumer's understanding of the service and to their satisfaction or enjoyment of the service. It must reflect customer expectations and the overall brand positioning. Marco has taken this into consideration in the selection of the CityCentre training centre as his course venue. As a result, delegates should experience a physical environment which reflects the quality of the teaching and course documentation. Marco also has the opportunity to give prospective buyers a feel for the physical environment by providing a virtual tour of the location on iTTrain's website. Physical evidence of good quality documentation and teaching can be provided through sample hand-outs and a sample teaching presentation. In the niche which Marco is trying to position iTTrain, physical evidence of the quality of the company is very important.

Most services require direct interaction between the consumer and the **people** who represent the service provider's organisation. In conventional terms, employee selection, training and motivation are significant considerations. Most successful businesses devote time and resources to managing their customer-facing staff. In the context of iTTrain, this is particularly significant. One of the most important people in the process, the lecturers, are not employees of iTTrain, they are self-employed contractors. Marco must ensure that lecturers are properly briefed, conduct themselves correctly and act in such a way that is consistent with the quality branding. Formal audits (observation of courses, feedback questionnaires) will be both a source of control and of marketing material (delegate testimonies). Marco also has to recognise that although he might make the initial sale, many subsequent sales may be down to the customer's enjoyment of the course and pass rates, and central to this will be the performance of the lecturers.

The **process** which surrounds the service is often perceived, by the customer, as part of that service. There is a significant difference between purchasing a product and a service. The service is often consumed only once (course attendance) whilst a product (such as a computer) might be used many times. The service often requires direct interaction between the person ordering and consuming the service and the service provider (the lecturer). In contrast, the producer of a computer seldom meets the customer. Service is often abstract and transitory and this can accentuate the consumer's expectations and their reflections on the success of the experience. They often perceive that the ordering process, the ease of payment and the accuracy of joining instructions are part of the service and include them in their assessment. Thus Marco must ensure that all the processes which precede and follow the actual teaching process are effective and customer focused.

	ACCA Marking scheme	
		Marks
(a)	For the non-financial analysis: 1 mark for an appropriate point up to a maximum of 9 marks. For the financial analysis, up to a maximum of 10 marks. There is a maximum of 16 marks for the complete part question.	
	– Table of figures showing values for different class sizes (2 marks)	
	– Expected contribution per course (2 marks)	
	– Breakeven analysis (2 marks)	
	– Course running value and implication (1 mark)	
	– Options for flexing (2 marks)	
	– Assumptions (2 marks)	16
(b)	1 mark for each appropriate point up to a maximum of 3 marks for each part of the marketing mix. Three parts are specified (physical evidence, people and process), so there is a maximum of 9 marks.	9
	Total	25

Examiner's comments

In Part (a) financial analysis was often very limited, with little use of expected values. The non-financial analysis was often very poorly structured and was not well integrated with the financial analysis. It was possible to easily calculate the breakeven number of courses or breakeven course price from the data provided. Such an analysis would have shown that the proposed $750 delegate fee was slightly too low. Good candidates recognised this and suggested a higher price that not only allowed the company to potentially make the required modest profit but was also more in line with the quality image that it wished to convey, so aligning financial and non-financial considerations. Very few candidates commented on the likelihood of the start-up IT training company achieving the course sizes of an established training provider, thus undermining the legitimacy of the expected values.

Part (b) was poorly answered despite clear signposts in the scenario; the importance of the lecturers (people), the significance of course material (course manuals), the need for an easy transaction process. Candidates could have used their own experience of education providers in the ACCA market to help them answer this part question. For example; it is possible to go on-line and watch presentations (allowing the possible candidate to view the lecturer and experience the teaching style), many web sites allow the download of sample course material and most make it very easy for candidates to register and pay their money. Candidates should not be afraid to using relevant practical experience when answering such questions.

40 MARATEC

Key answer tips

This question focused on e-marketing and e-procurement. Lots of help is provided by the examiner and the areas for students to consider are clearly flagged. The scenario is relatively brief so there is less scope for poor time management. This should therefore have been a straightforward question for students. However, past experience has shown that often weaker students focus too much on knowledge in these topics rather than application and this is unlikely to score well in this type of question.

(a)   **E-marketing**

Currently, Maratec is using a traditional model of marketing, which is not fully supporting the needs of the company as it strives for growth. By adopting e-marketing, further growth would be made possible and the issues identified would be addressed.

Price – Maratec uses cost plus pricing, which may cause some lost sales, as the cost is unknown at the time of agreement with the customer. The use of the external procurement company and the procurement of small orders of specific materials is likely to increase the costs and therefore lead to higher prices. Whilst high prices are not necessarily a problem, the inability to set the price when negotiating with the customer is not ideal.

The use of e-marketing will require Maratec to be more specific with regards to pricing. Although it may display a 'contact us for price' instruction online, it would need to be able to provide a price within a reasonable time. Should it introduce e-procurement (see part b), then price links could be introduced to make this quicker.

E-marketing could be used to offer special discounts on large orders, or on pricing for a subsequent item of furniture, following a previous order.

Promotion – Maratec's current promotion model may work for a small company, but if the company wants to grow, then this is a crucial area for change. The current method of promotion is limited. The use of expensive brochures means that all potential customers see the same products, and the company only produces a new brochure very year. E-marketing allows individualisation, or personalised marketing. The website could record visitors' click patterns and use targeted promotion based on the patterns detected. For example, if a potential customer browses tables and chairs, then Maratec could send them an email focused on these products.

The reach of promotion is also limited, either to those who have an acquaintance with an owner of a Maratec piece of furniture, or those who attend certain exhibitions. Whilst Maratec has a focused differentiation strategy, this may be appropriate. However, Maratec is looking to increase its sales, including an expansion of segments, to reach corporate clients. Online promotion may be a good way to make initial contact with these potential customers.

Place – As Maratec produces bespoke furniture, it does not make sense to have many showrooms as each piece of furniture displayed only exhibits the style of Maratec and is not for sale. To open further stores would lead to high additional costs. However, by using e-marketing, the market reach is as wide as Maratec choose to make it; global clients could purchase products, on the condition that Maratec will support transactions from that country and will provide shipping to that destination.

Processes – Many of the processes, excluding the actual production of the furniture, could benefit from the use of e-marketing techniques. The clients' designs could be uploaded and progress shown when the client logs in to their own account. This would make the update process much smoother and overcome the difficulties of a client visiting the manufacturing plant. Maratec could post videos of the production process if required.

Details of the materials sourced and the expected date of completion could be stored and updated as appropriate. Corporate clients could have access to re-order screens, allowing them to place orders for duplicates of its previously produced products.

Physical evidence – This is critical to Maratec's success. As items are bespoke, there is no finished product to view before purchase. Therefore evidence of previous successes is important. Images of items may be placed on the website. This will help with visualisation for clients, as more images can be uploaded than in a traditional brochure. Maratec could also post evidence of the quality, in the form of quality standards awarded, and supplier quality statuses. Additionally, the word-of-mouth promotion may be extended through physical evidence, with customer reviews posted on the site.

If Maratec uses advanced manufacturing techniques such as computer aided design and manufacturing, the clients' designs could be transformed into 3-D images, which again would assist with visualisation and ensure that enquiries are converted into actual orders.

(b)   E-procurement

Procurement involves the sourcing of suppliers and forming of agreements with them, enabling purchasing of the right quality materials, whilst ensuring that the time and price are right for the company. This is not currently carried out by Maratec, who chooses to use a specialist procurement company instead.

Principles of e-procurement

E-procurement makes use of electronic forms of communication to simplify the entire production process. It relies upon connections between suppliers' and purchasers' systems, enabling automated transactions.

The focus is on getting the entire procurement process right: materials are delivered in the right quantity and quality, at the right price, from the right seller and at the right time.

Most e-procurement systems require registration and login so that both supplier and buyer details are stored and both administrative (address, etc.) and historical data are available.

E-procurement can be approached in a number of different ways. For example, in a B2B marketplace, suppliers and buyers trade through a third party site. The relationship, and contractual relationship, is with the third party, although buyers and suppliers may enter into regular trades. The third party sites usually focus on one industry, e.g. providing materials for the furniture trade. This would give Maratec access to many suppliers as needed for the growth of its business. This would be the closest to their current model, with the third party taking some of the procurement responsibility by providing appropriate suppliers in the marketplace.

An alternative approach suitable for Maratec could be buyer centric. Using this model, Maratec would have relationships with a number of individual suppliers. Systems would be integrated, and a procurement management system managed by Maratec allowing the selection of the best supplier for each requirement. This would also simplify management reporting, as the system would integrate with internal transactional systems, e.g. production control and accounting as well as internal reporting systems.

Benefits – There are many benefits of e-procurement, although not all would be applicable to Maratec. This would certainly pass the control of the procurement process to Maratec, who currently relies on a third party service. As Maratec uses specific materials for their products, it is important to have access to a wide choice of suppliers, as a specific piece may be difficult to find. Simultaneously, however, Maratec may build a relationship with a certain supplier, who may suggest certain raw materials as they become available.

There should be obvious cost reductions, as this would cut out the middle-man and enable Maratec to shop around for the best price, regardless of location. It should also speed up the process as there will be no need for communication with the procurement company, and Maratec could select suppliers who are able to deliver within a specified date range, or who are pre-approved on the system as they meet quality and reliability standards.

Risks – It is suggested that a procurement manager will only be recruited should the decision to use e-procurement go ahead. This may be risky as the e-procurement decision could be made without expert advice of a procurement manager. The model and method of implementation may be flawed and the system unusable for Maratec's purposes.

It is not known what agreement Maratec has with the procurement company currently being used. There may be a need to compensate the company for the cessation of the contract.

If implementation is successful, there are still risks. Maratec's strategy requires quality materials in order to succeed. There is a danger that quality may be compromised if purchases can be made from any source, anywhere in the world. There is also the danger that deliveries may not be made on time. These two risks alone could eradicate all the benefits of e-procurement.

E-procurement should reduce the administrative burden of purchasing, but cannot replace the strategic requirements such as sourcing and negotiating with appropriate suppliers, to help meet Maratec's strategic objectives.

Maratec will also need to consider data security. By making transactions online, it is possible that competitors may obtain access to their data, providing information about their strategy, products and customers.

ACCA Marking scheme			Marks
(a)	Up to 1 mark for each relevant point up to a maximum of 3 marks for each aspect of the marketing mix. Five aspects required giving a maximum of 15 marks.		
		Maximum	15
(b)	Up to 1 mark for each relevant point up to a maximum of 10 marks.		
		Maximum	10
Total			25

Examiner's comments

Part (a) was relatively well answered by most candidates and most related their answers to the scenario.

In part (b), although there was evidence that some candidates were unfamiliar with this part of the syllabus, most candidates answered this part question well, making appropriate references to the question scenario. They also correctly followed the requirements of the question, focusing on benefits and risks and making the distinction clear to the marker.

PROJECT MANAGEMENT

41   HOMEDELIVER

> 🔑
>
> **Key answer tips**
>
> The easiest part of the question was part (c) so it will have been important to either do this part first or to ensure that enough time was left to attempt this section. With the other elements, it is important to remember that application will be worth more marks than knowledge.

(a)   A post-project review takes place once the project has been completed. In fact, it can often be the last stage of the project, with the review culminating in the sign-off of the project and the formal dissolution of the project team. The focus of the post-project review is on the conduct of the project itself, not the product it has delivered. The aim is to identify and understand what went well and what went badly in the project and to feed lessons learned back into the project management standards with the aim of improving subsequent project management in the organisation.

A post-implementation review focuses on the product delivered by the project. It usually takes place a specified time after the product has been delivered. This allows the actual users of the product an opportunity to use and experience the product or service and to feedback their observations into a formal review. The post-implementation review will focus on the product's fitness for purpose. The review will not only discuss strategies for fixing or addressing identified faults, but it will also make recommendations on how to avoid these faults in the future. In this instance these lessons learned are fed back into the product production process.

A benefits realisation review also takes place after the product has been delivered. It is primarily concerned with revisiting the business case to see if the costs predicted at the initiation of the project were accurate and that the predicted benefits have actually accrued. In effect, it is a review of the initial cost/benefit analysis and any subsequent updates made to this analysis during the conduct of the project. It may be part of a post-implementation review, although the long-term nature of most benefits means that the post-implementation review is often held too soon to properly conduct benefits realisation. In fact, it can be argued that benefits realisation is actually a series of reviews where the predicted long-term costs and benefits of the business case are monitored. Again, one of the objectives is to identify lessons learned and in this case to feed these back into the benefits management process of the organisation.

(b) **Post-project review at HomeDeliver**

The following issues could have been raised at the HomeDeliver post-project review. They are presented here with lessons learned that should be fed back into the project management process.

- The late allocation of HomeDeliver order administrators full-time to the project. Initially, employees were allocated part-time to the project. However this hampered project progress as these administrators also needed to undertake their normal operational duties. Consequently, the project began to significantly slip. Even though selected order administrators were added full-time to the project it was too late and the software was delivered two months behind schedule.

  Lessons learned: it is likely that deadlines will slip if appropriate employees are not allocated full-time to the project.

- The failure to consult catalogue supervisors and agents. There is evidence in the scenario that internal stakeholders were identified and consulted throughout the project. However, external stakeholders, such as the catalogue supervisors and agents, were not consulted at all. This meant that they had little understanding of the software prior to its implementation. It also meant that their requirements were not taken into consideration when developing the software. Hence the need to amend an order was not included in the software solution.

  Lessons learned: ensure that stakeholder analysis includes both external and internal stakeholders and make sure that external stakeholders are included in the requirements gathering process where appropriate.

- The scope of implementation, implementing all supervisors and agents immediately. In retrospect, implementing all supervisors (and their agents) was too ambitious and risky. It would have been wiser to establish a pilot project where only selected supervisors and agents used the new system. Experience from this pilot could have been used to modify the software and fix faults and omissions before rolling out to the rest of the organisation. The scope should have been defined in the project initiation document and this should have been risk assessed.

  Lessons learned: the risk assessment of the scope of projects is important and project managers should look to mitigate risk by reducing scope.

Post implementation review at HomeDeliver

The following issues could have been raised at the HomeDeliver post-implementation review. They are presented here with recommendations that should be fed back into the software development process.

- Faults and omissions in the computer software. The omission of the order amendment facility has already been considered. However, the failure of the software to work with a popular browser needs investigating. Testing should consider a range of browsers. The post-implementation review should also consider why these faults were not found before the software was released. A possible reason is that the software was tested by full-time employees of HomeDeliver in a controlled office environment. It was not acceptance tested by the part-time, home-based agents who were actually going to use the software. These people were likely to be less familiar with computer applications and were also likely to use a wide variety of hardware and software.

Lessons learned: acceptance testing should be undertaken by real business users in the hardware and software environment they are actually working in. Testing across multiple browsers must be considered.

- Faults in the documentation. The documentation supporting the implementation was both inappropriate and inappropriately distributed. Distributing the user manual as a PDF file raises at least two issues. Firstly, whether the email, and its attached file, had actually been received by the agent. A significant number of them claim that they did not receive the email. Secondly, it seems unreasonable to expect self-employed agents to print out a large, colour manual at their own cost. A failure to print out and study the manual probably contributed to agents being unable to use the software to enter multiple orders for one household. Spelling and functionality faults in the manual undermine confidence in both the documentation and the software it supports.

    Lessons learned: documentation must be carefully inspected before software release and its physical distribution should be carefully considered. Distributing documentation electronically may seem easy and cheap, but it may have important unanticipated consequences.

- Training of employees. It was perceived that the software was easy to use and so no formal training was given to agents. However, this missed the opportunity to find early faults (for example, not running under a certain browser). The inability of many agents to claim that the system could not support multiple orders from one household also suggests that the software was not as easy to use as its developers claimed.

    Lessons learned: As well as imparting skills, training provides an opportunity to build rapport with users and to identify possible issues and faults with the software at an earlier stage.

(c) The potential benefits to HomeDeliver of the new electronic ordering system might include:

- Staff savings from the reduction or elimination of order administrators at HomeDeliver. This benefit should be relatively easy to quantify.

- Staff savings from reduced catalogue supervisor costs. In the new system, supervisors appear to have significantly less work and so each supervisor should be able to co-ordinate more agents. However, supervisors are currently rewarded on the basis of how many agents they administer. So savings could only be made if this contractual arrangement was changed.

- Improved cash flow, because money is now sent daily rather than at the end of the week. Improved cash flow will reduce borrowing costs or increase investment income. This benefit should be relatively easy to quantify.

- The system should lead to the customer receiving their goods more quickly. Orders are entered at the end of the day, not in the week after the order has been placed. This is a benefit for the customer, not HomeDeliver. However, it could be argued that improved customer service may lead to more customers and, because there is less elapsed time between order and delivery, to fewer cancelled orders. It would be relatively difficult to quantitatively predict both of these benefits in advance.

ACCA Marking scheme		
		Marks
(a)	1 mark for each relevant point up to a maximum of 2 marks for each type of review and up to a maximum of 6 marks for this part question.	6
(b)	1 mark for each relevant point up to a maximum of 6 marks for each type of review. Two types of review, giving a maximum of 12 marks for this part question.	12
(c)	1 mark for each relevant point up to a maximum of 7 marks.	7
Total		**25**

42 ASW   Walk in the footsteps of a top tutor

Tutor's top tips

This question was unusual in that it had three parts to it (rather than the normal two). It covered project management, quality and systems development. The question included a diagram of a project plan.

Part (b)

Students were asked to suggest some options for solving project slippage that was occurring in the question.

Key to success:

Suggest a range of options rather than focusing on just one

Try to give as much specifics as possible to give an answer which is relevant to the scenario rather than simple regurgitation or bookwork

Dangers:

Determining which option was best was the final requirement and therefore shouldn't have been considered in this part of a student's answer

Simple regurgitation of the textbook is unlikely to get enough marks to pass the requirement

Part (c)

The final part of the requirement asked students to suggest which of the proposed options would be the best solution.

Key to success:

Justifying your suggestions

Avoid repetition of the points made in the previous part of the question

Dangers:

Not spotting the link to the previous part of the requirement. This part of the requirement clearly started with 'As a result of your evaluation....' making it quite clear that your answer to part (c) must be based on what you argued in part (b)

(b)   The project manager could request an extension to the deadline. The case study scenario suggests that early delays in the project were caused by the absence of key CaetInsure staff and changes in user requirements in the re-insurance module. These delays meant that the full system specification was signed off three weeks later than initially agreed. Unfortunately, the delivery date of the whole project was not re-negotiated at this point as it was suggested that 'time could be made up' during the programming stage. Furthermore, the marketing department of CaetInsure had already announced the launch of a new product to coincide with the implementation of the software and they did not want to change these dates. However, the project manager could now return to CaetInsure and inform them that it had not been possible to catch up with the proposed schedule and to remind them that the initial slippage had been caused by them. Although the deadline date is associated with a product launch it is unlikely that this is crucial. It is not a matter of life and death. It might be irksome to delay the launch by a few weeks, but it is unlikely that many people will notice or indeed care about it. There are many significant successful products which have been released long after their intended release date. In many ways it is an artificial deadline.

However, there are at least three problems associated with this suggestion. The first is that the delay is now longer than the three weeks incurred at the specification stage. Consequently, the project manager will have to explain that there have been further delays to the project. Secondly, the project manager will have to be very confident about his revised delivery date. The project plan does not explicitly contain any time for programmers fixing faults found in system and acceptance testing and it seems very likely that faults will be found in this testing. Finally, some negotiation will have to take place on the late delivery penalty clause charges the sales account manager agreed in the initial contract. If some (or all) of these clauses are enacted then the profitability of the project will be significantly affected.

The project manager could consider a functional reduction in the scope of the software solution

The scenario suggests that the re-insurance functionality has been a problem throughout the project. There may also be unresolved issues in other parts of the software. However, it must be remembered that the ASW product is a proven software solution, bespoke development is only concerned with customising the basic product to fulfil certain customer requirements. Therefore it is likely that there are large areas of the software that can be successfully delivered to the customer. The key issue here is whether this reduced functionality will fulfil the requirements associated with the proposed new product which CaetInsure intends to launch. If it does then the delivery of a partial solution does not have a significant business impact and the product launch can go ahead as planned. The project manager needs to discuss this with the customer as quickly as possible. He has to be sure that the reduced scope does indeed fulfil these requirements and, if it does, to focus testing, migration and document production on these parts of the software. He will also have to estimate the delivery time of the second phase of the software that fulfils the complete user requirement.

There are three elements of this suggestion that the project manager should bear in mind. Firstly, the impact of reduced scope on the penalty clauses of the contract. It would appear harsh to deliver a part solution but to still be fully penalised for not delivering the total solution. Consequently some contract renegotiation is necessary. Secondly, there will be an unexpected overhead associated with delivering a second phase which contains the full product.

This is the overhead of *regression testing*, making sure that changes made to the product in the second release do not unintentionally affect the software solution that has already been delivered. Finally, the specification of data migration programs will have to be reviewed to see if they need to be changed in the light of the reduced functionality. Any changes will affect data migration programs which are currently being written or tested.

The project manager could consider taking steps which might reduce the quality of the product

A number of options might be considered around the testing of the software. One option is to considerably reduce system testing and hand over the software to acceptance testing ahead of the proposed schedule. The point has already been made that the software is essentially a package that has to be tailored for specific functions. Consequently, large areas of the software have been tested before, much of it by actual users out in the businesses that are using this solution. Programs for the CaetInsure version will have been unit tested by programmers before they have been released to system testers and so no area of the system is *untested*, although there will be areas that have not been *independently tested*. Another option is to reduce the scope of system testing, focusing it on testing functionality rather than usability (which will be one focus of acceptance testing) and performance (which can be difficult to perform effectively in a software house environment where the user's actual hardware configuration cannot be easily mimicked). A further option is to execute system and acceptance testing in parallel.

There are a number of issues with this approach which the project manager needs to consider. The first is that the acceptance testers are likely to find significantly more faults than they would if full system testing had preceded acceptance testing. This can lead to a reduction in customer confidence which could jeopardise the whole project. Secondly, faults identified by both system and user acceptance testers have to be carefully managed. Configuration management becomes a very significant issue and appropriate version control of the software is an essential overhead. Confidence is undermined by the constant releases of new versions of the software, some of which, due to poor configuration management, contain faults which have already been reported and fixed in earlier versions of the software.

The project manager might consider requesting more resources

Finally the project manager may request further resources for the project. The current project plan is at a high level of detail. It does not show how many system testers are actually working on the system or how many technical authors are writing the documentation. It may be possible to add more resources and so reduce the elapsed time of the activity. Resources might also be asked to work smarter or work longer. For example, testing might be prioritised so that the most important areas of the software from the user's perspective are tested first. It may also be possible to automate certain areas of testing or to outsource it to specialist testing companies. Programmers might be asked to focus more on static testing (which is particularly effective at finding faults) and to work overtime to beat their deadlines.

However, the project manager must be aware that adding resources to a late running project often slows the project down as established members of the project team explain requirements, standards and procedures to any newcomers. A key factor here will be the precision of the requirements. If these are well specified then it should be possible to add testing staff reasonably effectively, or indeed to outsource testing to countries where it can be conducted relatively cheaply.

It may also be possible to bring in technical authors and automated testing tools specialists who can speed up these activities. Programming is more of an issue. It will be very difficult to bring new programmers up to speed. However, it may be possible to transfer resources from other projects and to support the established programmers by providing appropriate hardware and software.

Finally, the addition of resources to the project will have an impact on project profitability. The project estimate will have assumed a certain commitment of resources. Adding resources will reduce the profit margin and indeed, in the extreme, may make the project itself unprofitable.

(c)   There is no correct answer for this part of the question. However, it is suggested that a combination of the above strategies would be appropriate. The deadline is not crucial in the wider scheme of things and there is no statutory requirement to deliver on time. However the deadline is significant to the customer and a failure to meet this deadline may cause internal problems and a 'loss of face'. This is particularly significant in this context because ASW is an external supplier. It might have been easier to negotiate an extended deadline if the software were being supplied by an internal IT department. Hence, it might be suggested that, in these circumstances, the deadline should not be extended for an initial release. However, it may be possible to negotiate the scope of this release, making sure that the key functions are in place and tested when the software is delivered. The customer might accept this reduction in scope as recognition of the delays caused earlier in the project when, due to the absence of key personnel, the full system specification was signed off three weeks late.

It could be argued that the current tasks of ASW, system testing and writing the user manual, could be shortened by adding further resources to the project. Effective testing will depend upon the quality of the specifications but it may be possible to add more resources and back this up with reduced test coverage. The amount of testing performed is driven by risk. There has to be a balance between the cost and time of more testing and the consequences of failure. Although the insurance system appears to be mission-critical to CaetInsure, there is a robust current system that could be reverted to during the planned parallel running.

It would also appear that more resources could be added to writing the user manual. There is already slack between the scheduled completion of the user manual and its use in the training course.

ASW might also consider starting writing the data migration programs before week 22. It appears from the project plan that ASW are waiting for system testing to be complete before writing these programs. It may be possible to start beforehand, writing migration routines for the parts of the system that have already passed system testing.

The acceptance testing is outside the control of ASW. It is being performed by CaetInsure. However, again CaetInsure might consider reducing the time taken for acceptance testing by adding more resources to the task and by accepting a greater risk of failure during parallel running.

On balance, it might be suggested that further resources are quickly added to the project and that the test coverage is reduced. Hence the solution is largely concerned with adding resources and potentially reducing quality. If the customer is happy to slightly reduce the scope of the initial release to reflect past delays then this is a bonus. However, it is suggested that in this project the delivery date should remain fixed. Relaxing this is not an appropriate strategy in this instance.

ACCA Marking Scheme

		Marks
(b)	Up to 1 mark for each relevant point up to a maximum of 3 marks for each strategy	10
(c)	Up to 2 marks for each relevant point up to a maximum of 6 marks for this part of the question.	6
Total		**16**

Examiner's comments

Part (b) was answered relatively well, with many candidates giving a range of options.

For part (c) there was often some overlap in answers between this and the previous part question. The distinction was that part (b) was really looking for the range of options available to the project manager, while part c required the candidate to select from that range, probably suggesting a mixed strategy. Many candidates did not adequately justify their answer in the context of the scenario.

43   LDB   ![key icon] ***Online question assistance***

Key answer tips

The key to success in this question is to be as relevant and specific as possible. Do not simply regurgitate your notes. Instead only include areas of the project management syllabus area that are relevant to the question being asked, and add as much detail as possible to your suggestions.

(a)   The elements of good project management that helped make the branch rationalisation project successful might include:

(1)   A sponsor (Len Peters) was appointed to own the project. A sponsor is required to make important and decisive decisions about project scope, conduct and approach. In the case study scenario, the precise terms of the voluntary redundancy arrangements were quickly specified. Without a sponsor projects tend to drift and to stall when important decisions have to be made.

(2)   The objectives of the project were clearly defined. The target was to cut the number of branch banks by at least 20% and branch employment costs by at least 10%. Quantification makes these specific objectives measurable. It should be clear at the end of the project if the project has successfully met its objectives. Projects that have general objectives, such as 'improve management information' are less focused and more difficult to evaluate.

(3)   Constraints were specified at the outset of the project. For example, a time constraint was defined (two years) and an operational constraint (no compulsory staff redundancies) agreed. This latter restriction meant that the project team was clear at the onset about the scope of the changes they could implement. If constraints are not defined in advance then project teams might suggest inappropriate solutions.

(4)   An experienced full-time project manager was appointed. The project team was also made up of full-time staff seconded to the project. This meant that they could focus completely on the project and not be distracted by their usual jobs. Part-time secondments to projects rarely work because the team members still have to undertake elements of their day job and the urgency of these often takes precedence over project work.

(5)   Potential slippage in the project and its cause was identified and dealt with relatively early in the project's life. This meant that early re-scheduling could be carried out and an extension to the deadline agreed. It helps the management of expectations and helps avoid unexpected last-minute changes in scope.

(6)   The project team formally conducted benefits realisation, reporting on the actual performance of the project. This confirmed that the original objectives had been met. A formal post-project meeting was also held to review lessons learnt on the project. This led to a change in estimating assumptions which had led to the original optimistic values. Lessons are learnt on many projects which are not fed back into the project management system. Consequently, another team commits the same mistake or operates under the same false assumption.

(b)   (i)   LDB could assess the priority of the three initiatives on the process-strategy matrix suggested by Paul Harmon. The matrix has two axes. The vertical axis is concerned with process complexity and dynamics. At the base of the vertical axis are simple procedures often with simple algorithms while at the top are complex processes which may require negotiation, discussion and complicated design. On the horizontal axis is the strategic value of these processes. Their importance increases from left to right with low value processes concerned with things that must be done but which add little value to products or services. On the extreme right of this axis are high value processes which are very important to success and add significant value to goods and services. From these two axes, Harmon categorises four quadrants and makes suggestions about how processes should be tackled in each quadrant.

Low strategic importance, low process complexity and dynamics

This quadrant contains relatively straightforward stable processes which add little business value. They are processes that must be done in the company but add nothing to the company's value proposition. These processes need to be automated in the most efficient way possible. They are often called 'commodity processes' and are suitable for standard software package solutions and/or outsourcing to organisations that specialise in that area.

Low strategic importance, high process complexity and dynamics

This quadrant is for relatively complex processes that need to be done but do not add significant value to the company's products or services. They are not at the heart of the company's core competencies. Harmon suggests that these should be outsourced to organisations which have them as their core business.

High strategic importance, low process complexity and dynamics

These processes lie in the lower right quadrant of the model. They tend to be relatively straightforward processes which, nevertheless, have a significant role on the organisation's activities. They are central to what the business does. The aim is to automate these, if possible, to gain cost reduction and improve quality and efficiency.

High strategic importance, high process complexity and dynamics

Finally, in the top right hand quadrant are high value, complex processes which often include human judgement and expertise and are often very difficult to automate. Harmon suggests that these might be the focus of major process redesign initiatives focusing on business process improvement through the improved performance of the people undertaking those processes.

(ii) In the context of LDB, the following is suggested. Clearly these are value judgements and credit will be given for coherently argued answers which do not match the examiner's conclusions.

- *The integration of the two bespoke payroll systems currently operated by the two banks into one consolidated payroll system.* Payroll has to be produced but does not add significant value to the end-customer. It is unlikely that the recipients of the system (the bank staff) will notice any difference if a new system is implemented. The bank is considering re-developing this process because of the high cost of updating and maintaining two separate systems. This appears to be of low strategic importance. From the case study it is not clear how complex the payroll requirements are or how difficult it will be to transfer data from the current systems to a new solution. The most obvious approach is to suggest that a standardised software package is bought and data transferred to this solution. It appears sensible to undertake this work using the in-house IT departments who will be familiar with the current systems and so should be able to undertake accurate data mapping and successful data transfer to the new system. However, if this is difficult and time-consuming, there might be some benefit in outsourcing the solution and data transfer problems to a specialist software provider, allowing internal IT to concentrate on more strategic applications.

- *The updating of all personal computer hardware and software to reflect contemporary technologies and the subsequent maintenance of that hardware.* The bank is perhaps looking for efficiency savings through the standardisation of the desktop. Again, this does not appear to directly give value to the bank's customers. Consequently, this also appears to be of low strategic importance. However, it could be of relatively high complexity, particularly when considering the maintenance of hardware. There seems a clear case for outsourcing this process to a specialist technology company who can bring all hardware and software up to date and then maintain it at that level.

- *The development of processes, systems and software to support private banking.* This appears to be of high strategic importance and high complexity. It delivers services to end-customers who the bank has identified as a source of business growth. Elements of human judgement and interaction will be required when providing this service. The fulfilment of personal requirements for the wealthy customer will bring variety, risk and reward. The development of processes, systems and software to support private banking should have high priority and should be developed in-house. The success of such an operation should deliver handsome profits to LDB. This may mean that, given resources are finite, the development of the new payroll system should be outsourced to a specialist in that functional area.

ACCA Marking scheme			
			Marks
(a)		Up to 1 mark for identifying an element of good project management (for example; the allocation of a sponsor). Up to 2 marks for describing the significance of each of these elements within the context of the scenario up to a total of 12 marks.	12
(b)	(i)	Up to 1 mark for each significant point (for example, describing the implications of a quadrant) up to a maximum of 4 marks.	4
	(ii)	Up to 1 mark for each recommendation and up to 2 marks for the justification of each recommendation up to a maximum of 3 marks for each process initiative. Three process initiatives gives a maximum of 9 marks.	9
Total			**25**

Examiner's comments

This first part question was poorly answered in two ways. Firstly, too many candidates developed answers that discussed project management in general and did not apply them to the scenario, although these links were relatively easy to make. Unsuccessful candidates are encouraged to read the model answer to see how this part question should have been structured.

Secondly, a significant number of candidates constructed theoretical answers around aspects of project management which were irrelevant or inappropriate to the case study scenario. Such answers seemed to be answering a different question – identify the principles of good project management – to the one set in the examination. Project management appears to be a significant area of weakness despite its relevance to accountants and real-world business.

Candidates need to understand the principles of project management and, more importantly, apply them to a case study scenario. The link between theory and application was very poor.

The second part of the question was answered slightly better, although the suggested solutions were often unjustified and many marks could not be given for very brief answers. There were three marks on offer for each solution. Answers such as 'buy a software package' or 'outsource to a specialist' are clearly insufficient to gain such marks. Answers need to be expanded and clearly justified.

Overall, answers were poor and insufficient for the marks on offer.

44   8-HATS PROMOTIONS

🔑

Key answer tips

Part (a) is on investment appraisal is a key management accounting area that all students should be comfortable with. Time management would have been critical as there were 5 elements to discuss in 15 marks and weaker students may overrun on some or all of these parts at the detriment of part (b). Part (b) is on matrix structures, which has not been a common exam area. The biggest problem for students is likely to be in leaving enough time for this section.

(a)   In the scenario, Barry Blunt commented on simple payback (and its supposed advantage over discounted cash flow), the selection of the discount rate, the role of the IRR, the importance of intangible benefits and the realisation of benefits. Each of these five themes is elaborated on below:

Simple payback calculation (time to payback)

Job One All figures in $000

C/F	0	−110	−60	−45	−5
	Year 0	Year 1	Year 2	Year 3	Year 4
Total costs	110	10	10	10	10
Total savings	0	60	25	50	70
Cumulative	−110	−60	−45	−5	55
C/F	0	−90	−50	−35	−5

Job Two all figures in $000

C/F	0	−90	−50	−35	−5
	Year 0	Year 1	Year 2	Year 3	Year 4
Total costs	90	20	20	10	10
Total savings	0	60	35	40	35
Cumulative	−90	−50	−35	−5	20

Figure 1: Payback calculations for 8-Hats

The calculations (Figure 1) show that Barry Blunt's assertion is not true, both jobs payback early in year 4. If payback (time to payback) had been used, Job One would probably still have been selected because it pays back more in Year 4 than Job 2.

Barry also seems to misunderstand the limitations of payback. It ignores all cash flows beyond the payback period, which in longer projects can be very significant. In this example, payback ignores the fact that Job 1 has a significantly higher net cash flow inflow on year 4 than Job 2.

The discount rate

Inflation is taken into account in setting the discount rate. However, interest forgone, the cost of capital (if money is being borrowed to fund the investment) and risk will also have an influence. Interest forgone is concerned with the opportunity cost of investing the money in a bank deposit account and earning interest. The cost of capital is concerned with the cost of borrowing money to fund investment. A risk premium would reflect the perceived risk associated with these two internal projects. The discount rate used will incorporate an allowance for risk which will determine the required rate of return or 'hurdle rate' that a project must exceed for it to be viable. Information about risk-free interest rates during the period, the risk profile of the company and the company's cost of capital (using the Capital Asset Pricing Model) would also have been of relevance.

Even if there was an economic logic to changing the discount rate to 3% or 4% this would have no overall effect on the selection of the projects. In fact it is likely to have made Job 1 even more attractive than Job 2, as the cash flows in year 3 and 4 would have been discounted less. In fact, if a discount rate of 4% is used (and this calculation is not expected of the candidate) then the gap in NPV between Jobs 1 and 2 increases.

The Internal Rate of return (IRR)

The IRR is basically the discount rate that produces an NPV of zero for net project cash flows. If the selection is between two projects with the same scale of investment (which is the case here), then it has no effect on which project is selected. The project with the greatest NPV will usually produce the higher IRR. However, the IRR does become important when any project selected has to achieve a pre-specified company rate, or where projects with different scales of investment are being compared. This is not the case at 8-Hats.

Tangible and intangible benefits

The fundamental problem with investment appraisal generally is the reliability of cash flow estimates made for future cash inflows and outflows. For both jobs there seems to be an inclusion of specific monetary values for what appear to be intangible benefits – better information and improved staff morale. As Barry Blunt says, these are important, but it is very unlikely that either of these could be predicted with any certainty, particularly at the start of the project. Estimating for later time periods in the project is also very difficult and it is significant that these benefits increase as the project progresses. These intangible benefits amount to $110,000 for Job One and $50,000 for Job Two. If these intangible benefits are deducted from the analysis then, in fact, Job Two has a higher NPV than Job One. However, both are negative, suggesting that neither project should be attempted.

Benefits realisation

Finally, Barry has a fundamental misunderstanding of benefits realisation. The feasibility study is concerned with establishing the business case of a project and it should identify the project's benefits and costs. Benefits realisation is concerned with establishing whether the predicted benefits in the business case have been realised once the product or service delivered by the project has been in place for some time. It compares actual costs and benefits with those predicted in the business case. It cannot take place after the feasibility study of the project because at that point the project has not been completed and so any predicted benefits could not, at that stage, have been realised.

(b)   8-Hats Promotions are currently structured in functional departments, with each function representing activities of the company that have either been acquired (for example travel) or organically developed. Each job is passed between functions, with each function focusing on optimising its part of the transaction. Thus the sales department concentrates on winning the job by fiercely reducing prices because the sales managers are rewarded on turnover, not profit. The events department focuses on providing the most rewarding client experience and the travel department on selling travel options with the best profit margin. The focus of the travel department can cause conflict with the sales and marketing department and the operations department has the problem of trying to profitably deliver an event at a price agreed by sales and marketing department but with the functionality promised by the events department. The finance department has responsibility for managing the cash flow of the job and the payment of invoices and collection of money owing. There have been occasions where a job has been jeopardised by the failure of the company to pay key suppliers on time.

The problems described above are typical of a functional structure and the 'silo effect' caused by departments sub-optimising based on their own objectives and interests. The job, which is effectively being passed across the silos, suffers due to lack of co-ordination. Conflicts between two silos can often only be dealt with by managers who are above the silos. There is an example in the scenario where Barry Blunt has to intervene to arrange extra funding to pay supplier invoices when those suppliers threaten to boycott a folk music festival.

The matrix structure is an attempt to manage key elements of the company across the functional departments. This might be a product, project or a clearly defined client sector. In the context of 8-Hats it is jobs, which are effectively projects, and potentially, key accounts (such as Kuizan) that need to be managed across the functional silos.

Each job has the characteristics of a project. It has an established start, it runs for a few months, and then has a specified finish which is often the event itself (such as the folk festival or a Kuizan customer experience event). A multi-disciplinary project team drawn from all of the functional sections would allow continuity and focus on delivering a successful and profitable project. Because much of the company is project-based, a set of profitable projects should lead to a profitable company. Decisions within the project will, to some extent, reflect a consensus view of all concerned. The sales manager responsible for agreeing the deal would still be involved at event realisation and would also contribute to the management of cash flow through the complete project. This commitment to the project goal should lead to a more rewarding client experience. The need to keep clients satisfied is another potential element to the matrix, with account managers being appointed to key accounts with the responsibility of managing clients across both silos and projects.

The need for project teams to reflect a consensus view often means that decisions may take longer in a matrix structure and tension within the multi-disciplinary team may lead to a large amount of conflict. This conflict is more likely when cost and profit responsibilities are either unclear or counter-productive. At 8-Hats, the practice of rewarding sales managers on a turnover basis will have to be reviewed, otherwise there will be significant tension between the line (function) and the project. It has also been claimed that job and task responsibilities are unclear in a matrix structure and so the company will have to address this. Johnson, Scholes and Whittington make the point that 'one arm of the matrix has to lead in the sense that it dictates some key parameters within which the other arm must work'. In the context of the case study scenario it seems reasonable to devolve profit responsibility and work allocation to the project, leaving the functions to provide technical support and (perhaps) appraisal and competence definition responsibilities. The line manager becomes primarily responsible for the person and the project manager for the project. Such a change would require key cultural changes at 8-Hats.

ACCA Marking scheme		Marks
(a)	Up to 1 mark for each appropriate point up to a maximum of	15
(b)	1 mark for each appropriate point up to a maximum of	10
Total		**25**

Examiner's comments

This question was relatively unpopular and was not particularly well answered. Perhaps its unpopularity was due to the second part of the question which asked candidates to discuss the principles, benefits and problems of introducing a matrix management structure into the company (8-Hats) described in the scenario. This required the application of knowledge first introduced in paper F1. However, many candidates seemed unfamiliar with the term often claiming that the approach currently used at 8-Hats (functional, distinct organisational silos) with all its attendant problems was, in fact, an example of matrix management. Perhaps the problem with the first part of the question was that most of Barry Blunt's comments were wrong, borne out of ignorance and folly. The point has been made before; case study scenario characters are not always correct or virtuous. Some candidates tried to defend Barry's incorrect assumptions and conclusions and so scored few of the marks on offer. In general, the first part of this question was not well answered, with many candidates only offering definitions of the terms on offer, with a review of their general advantages and disadvantages. There was little attempt to apply answers to the tone and slant of Barry's comments.

45   INSTITUTE OF INDEPENDENT ANALYSTS

> 🔑
>
> **Key answer tips**
>
> In part (a) weaker students may spend time checking or performing unnecessary calculations. Instead, better answers will focus on whether the information used in the calculation should have been there and they will apply the Ward and Daniel benefits scale to the numbers.
>
> Part (b) requires a mixture of knowledge and application, but, as a key exam area, these should be areas that students have spent time on during their studies and should not cause too many issues (assuming that students do not become too bogged down in part (a) of the question and leave enough time for this part of the question).

(a)   **Overview**

The table presented in the scenario suggests that the project is currently financially viable. It returns a net present value of $10,925. However, the basis of the discount rate selection could be questioned. Although there is little information in the scenario about this, it might be felt that it has been set artificially low to produce a positive NPV. Also, the duration of the investment appraisal is quite long (seven years). Three and five year appraisals are more common. So again, the basis of this could be questioned. Perhaps seven-year investment periods are common at the IIA, but this needs to be investigated and confirmed.

It would also be beneficial to perform a sensitivity analysis on the data. A relatively small change in the initial cost of the software makes the NPV negative.

Costs

Software costs

Although the software package has a fixed cost, the IIA wishes to make a number of significant bespoke amendments. The actual detail of these amendments is still under discussion. They are currently estimated at $25,000 and this cost is part of the year 1 payment. However, this estimate may change once the detail of the requirement is agreed. The IIA must keep bespoke requirements under review to ensure that costs do not rise substantially, invalidating the financial business case for the investment. The scenario also suggests that there are problems in defining the detail of the requirement and these may lead to project delays, meaning that benefits may not begin to accrue until year 3 (or beyond), which will seriously affect the financial viability of the project. The final delivered cost of the project will also determine the maintenance cost, as it is calculated at 10% of the final delivered software cost. So, an increase in the initial cost of the software will also have long-term implications which may again affect the overall viability of the project.

Question bank costs

External consultants are to be paid a fixed fee for each question they successfully deliver to the question bank. The current estimate is for the initial delivery of 2,000 questions (with payments spread over year 0 and year 1) and then the subsequent update and amendment of 100 questions per year. These costs are within the control of the IIA and so appear reasonably definite. However, it is unclear why a question bank cost of $50,000 would be incurred immediately (year 0) as question setters are only paid on the acceptance of their question. This demands further investigation. If it is incorrect and the costs are actually incurred in years 1 and 2, then the NPV of the project will be increased.

Security costs

This is a definite cost; a fixed price has been agreed with a security firm who have guaranteed it for the duration of the project.

Disruption costs

The IIA believes that implementing the new assessment system will lead to a temporary reduction in productivity and staff morale in the examinations department. They have estimated that this will cost them $15,000 in year 1 and 2 of the project. However, this is really an intangible cost and is impossible to accurately predict in advance.

Benefits

Reduced marker costs

The reduction in marker costs can be accurately predicted. Manual marking will not be required once the new assessment method is in place. In Ward and Daniel's terms this is a *financial benefit*, and it can be accurately predicted in advance. The only issue may be the timing of the benefits, given the current problems in specifying the bespoke system requirements.

Reduced administrative costs

The reduction in administrative costs is difficult to predict accurately in advance because the undefined bespoke software amendments will affect the administration of the assessment process. However, by simulating the new work process, it should be relatively easy to forecast how many administrative posts will be lost and at what cost. Thus, using Ward and Daniel's classification, this is either a *financial* (at best) or *quantifiable* (at worst) benefit. The IIA should revisit their cost saving estimates as soon as the bespoke element of the software is agreed.

Increased student numbers

The final benefit is extra income from increased student numbers attracted by the convenience of computer-based assessment. It is difficult to put a credible value on this in advance of the project. At best, using Ward and Daniel's classification, this is a *measurable* benefit. It concerns an aspect of performance which is currently being measured (student numbers), but it is not possible to estimate how much performance will improve when the computer-based assessment system has been implemented. It may be possible to get credible evidence from other professional bodies which have implemented computer-based assessment to support this, but there is no evidence that this has been done. It is the IIA's best guess.

Summary

There is a strong argument for taking disruption costs and increased student numbers out of the financial appraisal of the project. It is difficult to put credible values on these in advance of the project. The effect of doing this (for information) is shown below.

> **Tutorial note**
>
> The answer provides a revised NPV calculation but this is there to aid the understanding of some of the points made in the answer. It was not expected that students would do this, and no marks are awarded for it.

All figures in $000s

Year	0	1	2	3	4	5	6	7
Costs								
Initial software	200	200						
Software maintenance			40	40	40	40	40	40
Question bank	50	50	5	5	5	5	5	5
Security			20	20	20	20	20	20
Total costs	250	250	65	65	65	65	65	65
Income/Savings								
Marker fees	0	0	125	125	125	125	125	125
Admin saving	0	20	30	30	30	30	30	30
Total benefits	0	20	155	155	155	155	155	155
Benefits – costs	(250)	(230)	90	90	90	90	90	90
Discount factor	1	0.926	0.857	0.794	0.735	0.681	0.630	0.583
Present value	(250)	(212.98)	77.13	71.46	66.15	61.29	56.70	52.47

Net present value (77.78)

The net present value is now less than zero, so there is no financial case for the project. However, this does not mean that the project should not go ahead. IIA management may feel that intangible benefits make the investment worthwhile and so the project may be progressed.

(b) A *benefit owner* is someone who has responsibility for defining, agreeing and delivering a benefit defined in the business case. Without benefit owners, benefits are unlikely to happen. It is very unlikely that the project manager responsible for a change project (as alluded to by the IIA director) would be the benefit owner. Their responsibility is to deliver the project, not to operationally run the outcome of the project. This must be the responsibility of the business and so the benefit owner should be a person who has authority to make business decisions which help deliver the benefits. Many projects which have promised cost savings have not delivered them because no-one had responsibility for making those savings. It is very important that the IIA appoints a benefit owner for the administrative cost reductions. First, because the extent of those savings cannot be reliably estimated due to problems in requirements definition and, second, because someone has to actually make these staff cuts when the new system is in place to deliver the benefits promised in the initial business case.

A *benefits map* helps the benefit owner determine what has to be put in place to deliver the promised benefit. The map can also be used to show how the benefits relate to the objectives of the organisation. For example, increased student numbers may be part of improving the accessibility of the qualification. Benefits may require business changes and *enabling changes* which have to be put in place to deliver the benefit. For example, the eventual elimination of marker costs (a benefit) will only be achieved once a question bank has been defined (an identified cost). A process will have to be put in place to define how questions will be commissioned, how they will be evaluated and how they will be entered and maintained in the question bank. These business and enabling changes require tasks which will have to be estimated and scheduled in a project plan. They form the link between the IT enabler (the software solution) and actually delivering the benefit. The benefits map shows exactly what has to be done to actually deliver the promised benefit.

Benefits realisation is a post-implementation activity which actually compares the delivered benefits with the promised benefits (and costs) forecast in the business case. This is another key role for benefit owners. Also, because of the nature of the financial case (where benefits are delivered annually), it is useful if benefits realisation is a series of reviews. The primary objective is to establish which benefits have been delivered and which have not. Undelivered benefits are investigated and remedial action may be taken. Unanticipated benefits may have also emerged and these are also considered in the reviews. Lessons learnt are fed back into the *benefits management process*. It is often very difficult to disaggregate benefits as time passes. For example; an increase in student numbers may be due as much to the improvement of marketing, to the decline of competing institutes or to demographic change, as it is to computer-based assessment. However, benefits realisation remains worthwhile, if only to stress that someone has to have continuing responsibility for realising the promised benefits which justified the financial investment made by the organisation.

	ACCA Marking Scheme	
		Marks
(a)	1 mark for each appropriate point up to a maximum of 6 marks for issues concerning costs. 1 mark for each appropriate point up to a maximum of 6 marks for issues concerning benefits (including benefit classification). 1 mark for each appropriate point in the overall evaluation, up to a maximum of 3 marks.	15
(b)	1 mark for each appropriate point up to a maximum of 4 marks for each concept (benefit owner, benefits map, benefits realisation). Up to a maximum of 10 marks.	10
Total		**25**

46   TKP

(a)   The first stages of risk management are the identification, descriptions and assessment of the risk. This assessment is primarily concerned with the *likelihood* of them occurring and the *severity of impact* on the organisation or project should they occur. Sometimes the likelihood is a subjective probability, the opinions of experienced managers or experts in the field. On other occasions, there is some statistical evidence on which to base the assessment. For example, in project 1, TKP identified that 20 IT software companies with annual revenues between $3m and $10m went out of business last year. This represented 10% of the total number of software companies reporting such revenues. Its report to the client suggested that there was a 10% chance of the current preferred supplier (who had a turnover of $5m) ceasing business and this would have a significant short-term support implication. This compared to a business failure rate of 1% for software companies with an annual revenue exceeding $100m. The client felt that the probability of supplier failure was too high, so eventually bought a software solution from a much larger, well-known, software supplier. In this case, the likelihood of the risk led the client to changing its procurement decision. The risk itself does not go away, large companies also fail, but the probability of the risk occurring is reduced.

The *avoidance (or prevention) of a risk* is a legitimate risk response. In project 1, the client could avoid the risk 'failure of the supplier' by commissioning an in-house bespoke solution. Similarly, TKP itself avoids the risks associated with trading in different cultures, by restricting its projects to clients based in Zeeland.

There are three further responses to risks.

Risk mitigation (or risk contingency) actions are what the organisation will do to counter the risk, should the risk take place. Mitigation actions are designed to lessen the impact on the organisation of the risk occurring. In project 2, TKP recommends that the producers of the iProjector should establish an escrow agreement with the company which produces the chip which enhances the quality of the projected image. It was agreed that design details of this chip should be lodged with a third party who would make them available to the producers of the iProjector should the company which owned the enhanced image technology cease trading. This is a mitigation approach to the risk 'failure of the supplier'. The supplier is relatively high risk (less than three years of trading, inexperienced management team), and the product (the iProjector) is completely dependent upon the supply of the image enhancing chip. The failure of the business supplying the chips would have significant impact on iProjector production. If the escrow agreement had to be enacted, then it would take the producers of the iProjector some time to establish alternative production. Consequently (and TKP have suggested this), it might be prudent to hold significant stocks of the chips to ensure continued production. In such circumstances, the need to mitigate risk is more important than implementing contemporary just-in-time supply practices. In some instances a mitigation action can be put in place immediately. In other instances risk mitigation actions are only enacted should the risk occur. The risk has been recognised and the organisation has a rehearsed or planned response. For example, in project 1, TKP has identified 'poor quality of current data' as a risk associated with the migration of data from the current systems to the proposed software package solution. It has established a strategy for data cleansing if that risk actually materialises. Importantly, the client knows in advance how to respond to a risk. It avoids making a hasty, ill-thought out response to an unforeseen event.

Risk transfer actions are concerned with transferring the risk and the assessment and consequences of that risk to another party. This can be done in a number of ways. TKP itself has liability insurance which potentially protects the company from the financial consequences of being sued by clients for giving poor advice. TKP has identified this as a risk, but is unlikely to be able to assess either the probability of that risk occurring or establishing meaningful mitigation measures to minimise the effect of that risk. Consequently, the responsibility for both of these is transferred to an insurance company. They establish the risk, through a series of questions, and compute a premium which reflects the risk and the compensation maximum which will have to be paid if that risk occurs. TKP pays the insurance premiums. TKP itself also transfers risks in project 2. It is unsure about how to establish patents and so it refers the client to another company. Transferring avoids the risk associated with 'establishing the patent incorrectly' and the financial consequences of this.

Finally, risk may be identified but just accepted as part of doing business. *Risk acceptance* is particularly appropriate when the probability of the risk is low or the impact of that risk is relatively insignificant. Risks may also be accepted when there are no realistic mitigation or transfer actions. In project 2, the producers of the iProjector are concerned that there is 'a risk that a major telephone producer will launch a product with features and functionality similar to ours'. This is a risk, but there is little that can be done about it. Risks of competition are often best accepted.

The discussion above is primarily concerned with deciding what action to take for each risk. Once these actions are agreed, then a plan may be required to put them into place. For example, establishing an escrow agreement will require certain activities to be done.

Risks must also be monitored. For example, in project 2, the risk of supplier failure can be monitored through a company checking agency. Many of these companies offer a continuous monitoring service which evaluates financial results, share prices and other significant business movements. Reports are produced, highlighting factors which may be of particular concern. Risks will also disappear once certain stages of the project have been completed and, similarly, new ones will appear, often due to changes in the business environment. Many organisations use a risk register or risk log to document and monitor risks and such logs often specify a risk owner, a person responsible for adequate management of the risk.

(b) Every project is constrained in some way by its scope, time and cost. These limitations are often called the **triple constraint**. The scope concerns what has to be delivered by the project, time is when the project should deliver by, and cost is concerned with how much can be spent on achieving the deliverable (the budget). Quality is also an important feature of projects. Some authors include quality in their triple constraint (instead of scope), others add it as a further constraint (quadruple constraint), whilst others believe that quality considerations are inherent in setting the scope, time and cost goals of a project. How a particular project is managed depends greatly on the pressures in the triple constraint.

In project 1, the reluctance of the company to re-visit the business case means that the budget (or cost) of the solution is fixed. The implementation date might be desirable, but it does not seem to be business critical. It is an internal system and so any delays in implementation will not affect customers. It will also be a relatively seamless transition for most employees in the company. They already record the time record details which the new system will collect and so all they will see is a changed user interface. Only the direct users of the output (account managers and the project office) will be affected by any delay. The scope of the software package is also pre-defined. If it fails to meet requirements, then the users will have to adjust their expectations or business methods. There is no money to finance customisation or add-on systems, so in this sense the scope of the solution is also fixed. The quality of the software, in terms of its reliability and robustness, should also be good, as it is a popular software solution used in many large companies.

In project 2, the launch date is fixed. It has been heavily publicised, the venue is booked and over 400 attendees are expected, including newspaper journalists. Thus the time of the project is fixed. However, although orders will be taken at the launch, the product is not expected to ship until a month after launch. Thus the scope of the product shown at the launch date might be restricted and inherent quality problems might not yet be solved. Any defects can be explained away (this is a pre-production model) or, more effectively, they may be avoided by ensuring that the product is demonstrated to attendees, not used by them. The project manager must ensure that key functionality of the product is available on launch date (such as producing an image of a certain quality), but other functionality, not central to the presentation (for example, promised support for all image file formats) could be delayed until after the presentation. The company should make extra funds available to ensure that the launch date is successful.

ACCA Marking scheme		
		Marks
(a)	1 mark for each relevant point up to 15 marks.	15
(b)	1 mark for each relevant point up to 2 marks for principles. 1 mark for each relevant point up to a maximum of 4 marks for each project. Maximum of 10 marks in total.	10
Total		**25**

47 A CLOTHING COMPANY

Key answer tips

It is important that you recognise that each part of the question concerns different parts of this chapter – part (a) is on project initiation (and the PID in particular), whilst part (b) is on project management and how a manager can attribute to this. Don't mix the parts up and ensure that you put the right elements in the right part (your pocket notes should help here). After that you have to remember to apply your knowledge to the scenario.

(a) The production of initial documentation concerning the business case and initiation of the project would have addressed many of the issues that subsequently arose in the website re-design. This documentation would typically include:

- A summary of the business justification of the project. These are the business objectives that have been defined in the business case to justify the project.

- The scope of the project, defined in terms of project objectives and ultimate deliverables.

- Constraints and targets that apply to the project.

- Project roles and responsibilities, for example; the definition of the project sponsor and the project manager. It is useful if this part of the document specifies the level up to which named individuals (or roles) can authorise:

- The commitment of resources

- The sign-off of deliverables

- Changes to project objectives and deliverables

- Changes to constraints

- Resources committed to the project

- Risks and assumptions associated with the project. These are considered below in the context of the clothing company's website re-design project.

The business justification of the project

The MM does specify business objectives such as 'increase sales revenue' and 'improve market visibility' (see meeting 1) but these are poorly defined objectives in that they are not quantified. A formal cost-benefit analysis undertaken at the start of the project would have forced the MM to quantify how much sales would increase and by when. The MM would also have been required to document the assumptions behind these predictions and to demonstrate a causal link between the functionality of the website and sales volume. The other suggested objective, improve market visibility, also requires further specification and quantification. The MM provides no evidence of current market visibility (and what this actually means) and how its improvement will be measured. Some research is needed to quantify market visibility and to set realistic targets for its improvement. The statement of the project's business benefits is an important issue in contemporary project management. It is suggested that these benefits are kept constantly under review to ensure that the project has not strayed from its original justification. Furthermore, at the end of the project, the business benefits have to be reviewed to assess whether they have been realised. Because the MM has not specified measurable objectives in advance, the success of the project is impossible to assess. There is no benchmark to assess it against.

The scope of the project

On at least two occasions there appears to be confusion about the scope of the project. The TD originally produces a design that is too like the current site, 'We expected it to do much more' (meeting 2). However, the most significant misunderstanding about scope is between the board and the MM. It concerns the interpretation of the scope of the word 're-design'. The board appears to perceive that re-design does not include the development and implementation of the software, while the MM holds the opposite view. The scope of the re-design would have been clarified in a project initiation document.

Constraints that apply to the project

Constraints are often defined in terms of cost and time. The absence of a formal cost-benefit analysis for this project has already been recognised, so costs (and budget) were not formally agreed at the start of the project. There is also no evidence that a projected delivery time for the project was agreed at the start of the project. Indeed, it was the elapsed time, as well as the escalating cost, that first caused the board to be alarmed about the website re-design project. It also appears that the TD had technical constraints in mind which were also not articulated. These emerged in meeting 4 and caused delays documented in meetings 5 and 6. Again, technical constraints should have been documented in the project initiation document.

Project roles and responsibilities

Although it is not clearly stated, it appears that the sponsor of the project is the MM. However, at one critical point of the project the RP makes a decision to accept a design (meeting 4) which is subsequently overturned by the MM. This confusion of responsibility causes both cost and delay. If project roles and responsibilities had been properly defined, then it would have been recognised that the RP did not have sufficient authority to sign-off deliverables. Furthermore, the formal allocating of roles would have also meant that a project manager would have been nominated with the responsibility of delivering the project. In the scenario there is never any clear indication of who is playing the role of project manager and this is a major flaw.

Resources committed to the project

There is no evidence that the resources available to the project had been identified and documented at the start of the project. Problems only begin to emerge late in the project when the Board's decision to launch on 1 March prompts the TD to express concern that there are not enough developers to deliver the system on time.

Risks and assumptions associated with the project

Most project management methods suggest that risks should be formally documented and managed. Each risk is identified and its potential effect quantified. For each significant risk, avoidance actions are suggested which are steps that can be taken to prevent the risk from occurring. Mitigation actions are also defined for each risk. These are steps that can be taken to reduce the impact of the risks if they occur. Again there is no evidence to show that this has been done. As problems emerged in the project they were dealt with on an ad hoc basis. A consideration of risk at the outset of the project can lead to changes in how the project is conducted. For example, the risk of poor scoping of requirements could have prompted a more formal definition of requirements scope (an avoidance action).

Initial project structure and arrangements for management control

This is an initial project structure describing how the project will be broken down into stages with an associated list of project milestones. It is a very high-level plan which provides a context for the detailed plans that will follow. There is no evidence of such a structure in the website re-design project and so the absence of detailed planning (see below) goes unnoticed. The project initiation document might also include management control information concerning, for example, progress reporting and monitoring arrangements. If these had been defined in advance then their absence (see below) would have been clear in the actual project.

(b) Effective project management could have improved the conduct of the website re-design project in the following ways:

Detailed planning

During the delivery of the project the lack of a formal detailed plan means that there is no baseline for review and control. The absence of monitoring progress against that plan is also very evident. The meetings are events where, although progress appears to have been made, it is unclear how much progress has been made towards the delivery of the final re-designed website. Effective project management would have mandated the production of a detailed plan. There is no mention of a project plan, a critical path analysis, a Gantt chart or supporting project management software.

Effective monitoring and control

The board were not kept up to date about progress and were only alerted to potential issue when the finance director became concerned about spiralling costs. This is a failure of monitoring and control, aggravated by the fact that there is no project plan to monitor against. Effective project management would have required formal progress to the sponsor (in this case the board). Such monitoring should lead to project control, where suggested actions are considered and implemented to deal with project slippage. The planning, monitoring and controlling aspects of project management are completely absent from the scenario and so none of the usual project management monitoring and reporting structures were in place to alert the board.

Mandating of substitutes

Initial progress is hampered by the absence of key personnel at meetings 3 and 4 and the inappropriate sign-off by the RP (already discussed above) of the technical design. The requirement for the TD to produce a technical report also slows progress. These problems could have been addressed by ensuring that substitutes were available for these meetings who understood their role and the scope of their authority. Effective project management would have ensured that progress would not have been delayed by the absence of key personnel from the progress meetings.

Standards for cost-benefit analysis

The cost-benefit analysis provided by the MM is flawed in two ways. Firstly, the assumptions underpinning the benefits are not explained. There is no supporting documentation and it appears, at face value, that year four and five benefits have been greatly inflated to justify the project. Secondly, it would be usual to discount future costs and benefits using an agreed discount rate. This has not been done, so the time value of money has not been taken into account. Effective project management would have defined standards for the cost-benefit analysis based on accepted practice.

Estimating, risks and quality

The reaction of the board to the cost-benefit analysis also appears unrealistic. They appear to have suggested a budget and a timescale which does not take into account the complexity of the remaining work or the resources available to undertake it. The estimating part of the project management framework appears to be lacking. It is clear at the final meeting that the website will not be ready for launch. However, the MM decides to take the risk and achieve the imposed deadline and take a chance on the quality of the software. This decision is made against the advice of his TD and without any information about the quality of the software. Effective project management would have mandated a framework for considering the balance between risk and quality.

The MM does not inform the board of the TD's advice. The MM, like many project managers (because the MM now appears to have adopted this role) finds it politically more acceptable to deliver a poor quality product on time than a better quality product late. Unfortunately the product quality is so poor that the decision proves to be the wrong one and the removal of the software (and the resignation of the MM) ends the project scenario.

ACCA Marking scheme		
		Marks
(a)	Up to 2 marks for each relevant point relating to the scenario	15
(b)	Up to 2 marks for each relevant point relating to the scenario	10
		——
Total		**25**
		——

Examiner's comments

This question was the least popular of the optional questions and it was also very poorly answered. Some candidates did appear to have a theoretical understanding of this part of the syllabus, but they failed to apply such knowledge to the circumstances described in the scenario. Most answers were general descriptions of the contents of a business case and a project initiation document. Such answers gained few marks, because this was not the focus of the question. The question concerned how such things would have helped prevent some of the problems documented in the scenario.

Part (b) was an opportunity to discuss issues of the conduct and conclusion of a project. The scenario gave plenty of opportunity for the basis of a good answer, but most candidates again opted for a restricted, theoretical answer which did not use the context of the scenario. Some candidates also repeated some points from the first part of the question (concerning project initiation), failing to note that this part of the question specifically asked for further improvements.

48 PAA

Key answer tips

For part (a) it will be important to apply knowledge to the scenario rather than simply regurgitating the pocket notes. Benefits management is a key part of the syllabus and students who were aware of the benefits scale suggested by Ward and Daniel should have scored very well in part (b).

(a) Meetings were held throughout the design and construction of the centre. These meetings focused on the building of the centre, monitoring progress and resolving minor issues that arose during construction. The successful completion of the centre on budget and ahead of schedule suggests that these meetings were effective. However, the absence of a wider **project initiation document** or **terms of reference** created problems that could have been resolved or better understood. An analysis of how a standard document could have helped address some of the issues that affected the construction and subsequent evaluation of the centre is given below.

There was confusion about the **objectives** of the project. The local authority is unable to recognise the distinction between *project objectives* and *business objectives*. The business objective of the project was to deliver payback in four years as required by the Private/Public investment policy. In contrast, the project objective was to build the centre by June 2011 for $600,000. By their very nature, the business objectives are not within the control of the project manager from the construction company responsible for building the centre. The achievement of the business objectives will involve much more than just delivering a building.

They will concern marketing, sales and the successful operation of the centre. Evidence seems to suggest that the project manager was not (as the second project sponsor claimed) a failure. He delivered the building within budget and ahead of schedule. The problem was the failure of the local authority to distinguish between the project objectives (constructing the building) and the wider business objectives which the building was to help satisfy. It appears that nobody was either aware of, or willing to take responsibility for these wider objectives. It is recommended that future projects should clearly distinguish between project and business objectives and assign responsibilities to each.

The **scope** of the project was well-defined by the standard architectural drawings agreed between the construction company and the project sponsor. The only significant problem concerned the quality of the internal painting. There is no way (post project) of reconciling this misunderstanding. The construction company felt that it had come to an arrangement about this with the initial sponsor, but no documentation could be found to irrevocably support this. The letter confirming the intended finish produced by the construction company was not counter-signed by the project sponsor. This is an important lesson for the construction company in future projects. Changes or clarifications to the specification must be counter-signed by both parties. This is also appropriate to the local authority's project management methods, continuing to demand that all changes must be counter-signed by both parties.

The **constraints** of the project were relatively well-defined in terms of time and cost, as these were defined in the original business case. However, tension was caused within the project when it became clear that certain labour and sourcing requirements of the Private/Public policy were not being adhered to. Specifically, these concerned the use of sub-contracted labour (not to be used without the commissioning agency's permission) and sourcing at least 80% of timber on the project from sustainable forests. The generic terms of the Private/Public investment policy were not made available to the construction company. It is suggested that the local authority should, in future, integrate such objectives explicitly into the project terms of reference.

The **authority** of the project is the sponsor responsible for making decisions about the project, providing resources, considering and agreeing changes. They should also promote the project within the local authority and accept the project once it has been completed. The original sponsor on the local authority was very supportive of the centre's design but their successor seemed unsure of her responsibilities and focused on obtaining concessions from the suppliers under the pretext of 'value for money' rather than considering the wider issues, such as defining who had responsibility for delivering the business objectives. She also failed to promote the project to her fellow employees and tried to blame the builders for the failure. The role of the project sponsor should be formally defined within the local authority. Their responsibilities should be clear and failure to adhere to those responsibilities should be addressed.

The **resources** available to the project were relatively well defined, although the lack of local authority staff able and willing to discuss disability access meant that the contractors had to use their own initiative in this area. Fortunately for them, they interpreted legal requirements correctly and the delivered centre was deemed to be compliant with legislation. However, this is a risky approach and is not recommended for the future. Local authority resources and support required by projects should be specifically defined in advance. If they are unavailable during the project then substitutes must be provided.

(b) This part of the question evaluates the four sets of benefits identified in the payback calculation. It requires the categorisation and critical evaluation of each benefit.

Ward and Daniel use the term 'observable benefits' to describe the least explicit benefits such as *increased staff morale* in the case of the community centre. They suggest that such benefits should be assessed against clear criteria by someone who is qualified to make such an assessment. So, for example, current staff morale and motivation might be assessed in an independent survey and compared to results from a similar survey conducted once the centre has been built and occupied.

In the context of the centre it might seem reasonable to assume that improved staff morale and motivation will have a positive effect on the success of the centre. For example, it may lead to better customer service, which may, in turn, lead to customers returning more often or using more facilities whilst they are there. It may also lead to reduced staff turnover, so decreasing costs associated with recruitment, induction and training.

However, from a benefits perspective, two issues have to be specifically addressed.

Firstly, the relatively significant estimated benefits attributed to improved staff morale in the original payback calculation must be questioned. In terms of increased benefits it is difficult to disentangle benefits due to this from other factors which might lead to increased customer use. In terms of reduced recruitment costs, there is little to suggest that staff turnover is high at the moment. 80% of the staff has been with the centre for over five years and there is an economic recession in the country, with unprecedented unemployment.

Secondly, and perhaps more fundamentally, the whole basis of the benefit needs further consideration. It is unclear why moving to the new centre would necessarily improve staff morale and motivation in the first place. There may be some intellectual support for the view that a pleasant working environment contributes towards motivation, but, in the initial stages the centre is likely to have temporary teething problems leading to (at least in the short term) a more stressful work environment. Similarly, even if a survey found that morale and motivation had increased it would be hazardous to attribute this to the investment in the centre as it may be largely due to external factors affecting each individual.

A **measurable benefit** is one where an aspect of performance is currently being measured or could be measured. However, it is not possible to estimate with any certainty, in advance, how much performance will improve when the changes are completed. In the context of the centre, *increased income* seems a reasonable measurable benefit. It seems reasonable to expect that current income is measured and that similar measures may be collected in the future.

The estimates on the payback calculation need further scrutiny, particularly the large increases predicted for years three and four. It should be acknowledged that few benefits are instantaneous and that use will only increase as the reputation of the centre grows. However, this growth in customer use is not associated with any increased costs which would seem unlikely. Hence, the basis of these benefits requires further investigation.

A **quantifiable benefit** is one where there is sufficient evidence to forecast how much improvement or benefit should result from the proposed changes. In such circumstances the level of performance prior to the change is known and the improvement can be specifically attributed to the investment, rather than to other changes. *Energy savings* appears to fit into this category. Energy use could be established for the current building. The Private/Public investment policy requires buildings constructed under this arrangement to meet specified target energy levels. The construction methods and design of the building should reflect the need to meet this target. Thus there is a good basis for predicting energy savings, although, of course, the actual savings will not be known until after implementation.

Finally, a **financial benefit** is one where a financial value can be obtained by applying a cost, price or any other valid financial formula to a quantifiable benefit. Thus we might re-classify the quantifiable benefit of *energy savings* as a financial benefit, assuming that the new building meets the minimum level required by the initiative. There are still important assumptions here, and the real performance can only be assessed after the building has been used for a while. There is still an element of estimation, and indeed the new building may surpass the minimum levels assumed in the cost/benefit analysis. In contrast *rental savings* on the current properties are both definite and immediate and are correctly recorded in the payback calculation.

In summary, the benefits in the payback calculation should probably have been initially restricted to financial and quantifiable benefits. The other benefits are important and should have been documented in the business case, but it seems inappropriate to artificially quantify these benefits to satisfy the need to achieve a payback target. However, if the measurable benefits are included in the business case, their underlying assumptions and probability should be communicated to the decision-maker. Furthermore, efforts might also be made to better estimate the likely benefits, perhaps through looking at performance in similar centres, and using this as a benchmark to elevate the benefits to being, at least, quantifiable.

ACCA Marking scheme		
		Marks
(a)	1 mark for each appropriate point up to a maximum of	13
(b)	1 mark for each appropriate point up to a maximum of	12
		——
Total		**25**
		——

> **Examiner's comments**
>
> In part (a) most candidates were able to describe the structure and contents of a project initiation document, and many did so at length; but this was not the question requirement. Indeed some answers contained only theory and made no reference to the scenario at all. Thus many candidates did not score highly in this part of the question, although they may have written a lot. Candidates need to carefully consider their approach to such questions. It might be better to start with the problem or issue from the scenario and then to reflect on how (in this case) a project initiation document would have addressed this problem. For example, in the scenario it emerges that '80% of the timber used in the building must come from sustainable forests'. The construction company did not know this at the start of the project. It seems likely that a project initiation document that forces the definition of constraints on the project would have unearthed and documented this. It might also be recommended that these general terms of the private/public investment policy should be explicitly integrated into all future project initiation documents created by the local authority under this initiative. The focus of the answer should be on the scenario, not the theory.
>
> Part (b) was not answered particularly well. Candidates need to ensure that they are familiar with contemporary benefits management. Benefits management is increasingly important in organisations and candidates would gain from understanding its principles and the issues it is attempting to address.

49 BRIGHTTOWN

> 🔑
>
> **Key answer tips**
>
> Part (a) may appear difficult and distract students from easier marks available later on in the question. But it is only worth 5 marks and focused on a core syllabus area. In part (b) the examiner explains the types of benefits that may exist, making this part a lot more manageable for students. Part (c) requires the use of Mendelow's matrix, and students who used this model will score well here.

(a)   **Objectives and scope**

From the perspective of the 'traffic lite' project, the change in mayor has led to an immediate change in the objectives driving the project. This illustrates how public sector projects are susceptible to sudden external environmental changes outside their control. The project initially proposed to reduce traffic congestion by making traffic lights sensitive to traffic flow. It was suggested that this would improve journey times for all vehicles using the roads of Brighttown. However, the incoming mayor now wishes to reduce traffic congestion by attracting car users onto public transport. Consequently she wants to develop a traffic light system which will give priority to buses. This should ensure that buses run on time. The project is no longer concerned with reducing journey times for all users. Indeed, congestion for private cars may get worse and this could further encourage car users to switch to public transport.

An important first step would be to confirm that the new mayor wishes to be the **project sponsor** for the project, because the project has lost its sponsor, the former mayor. The **project scope** also needs to be reviewed. The initial project was essentially a self-contained technical project aimed at producing a system which reduced queuing traffic. The revised proposal has much wider political scope and is concerned with discouraging car use and improving public bus services. Thus there are also proposals to increase car parking charges, to reduce the number of car park spaces (by selling off certain car parks for housing development) and to increase the frequency, quality and punctuality of buses. The project scope appears to have been widened considerably, although this will have to be confirmed with the new project sponsor.

Only once the scope of the revised project been agreed can revised **project objectives** be agreed and a new **project plan** developed, allocating the resources available to the project to the tasks required to complete the project. It is at this stage that the project manager will be able to work out if the proposed delivery date (a **project constraint**) is still manageable. If it is not, then some kind of agreement will have to be forged with the project sponsor. This may be to reduce the scope of the project, add more resources, or some combination of the two.

(b)   **Cost benefit**

The re-defined project will have much more tangible effects than its predecessor and these could be classified using the standard approach suggested in the scenario. Benefits would include:

–   One-off financial benefit from selling certain car parks – this appears to be a predictable *financial benefit* of $325,000 which can be confidently included in a cost/benefit analysis.

–   Increased income from public bus use – this appears to be a *measurable benefit*, in that it is an aspect of performance which can be measured (for example, bus fares collected per day), but it is not possible to estimate how much income will actually increase until the project is completed.

–   Increased income from car parks – this appears to be a *quantifiable benefit* if the assumption is made that usage of the car parks will stay at 95%. There may indeed be sufficient confidence to define it as a financial benefit. Car park places will be reduced from 1,000 to 800, but the increase in fees will compensate for this reduction in capacity. Current expected daily income is $1,000 \times \$3 \times 0.95 = \$2,850$. Future expected income will be $800 \times \$4 \times 0.95 = \$3,040$.

–   Improved punctuality of buses – this will again be a measurable benefit. It will be defined in terms of a Service Level promised to the residents of Brighttown. Improved punctuality might also help tempt a number of vehicle users to use public transport instead.

–   Reduced emissions – buses are more energy efficient and emit less carbon dioxide than the conventional vehicles used by most of the inhabitants of Brighttown. This benefit should again be measurable (but non-financial) and should benefit the whole of the town, not just areas around traffic lights.

–   Improved perception of the town – the incoming mayor believes that her policy will help attract green consumers and green companies to the town. Difficulties in classifying what is meant by these terms makes this likely to be an observable benefit, where a group, such as the Go Green team, established by the council itself can decide (based on their judgement) whether the benefit has been realised or not.

The costs of implementing the project will also have to be re-assessed. These costs will now include:

– The cost of purchasing more buses to meet the increased demand and frequency of service.

– The operational costs of running more buses, including salary costs of more bus drivers.

– Costs associated with the disposal of car parks.

– Costs associated with slowing down drivers (both economic and emotional).

The technical implementation requirements of the project will also change and this is almost certain to have cost implications because a solution will have to be developed which allows buses to be prioritised. A feasibility study will have to be commissioned to examine whether such a solution is technically feasible and, if it is, the costs of the solution will have to be estimated and entered into the cost-benefit analysis.

(c) A stakeholder grid (Mendelow) provides a framework for understanding how project team members should communicate with each stakeholder or stakeholder group. The grid itself has two axes. One axis is concerned with the power or influence of the stakeholder in this particular project. The other axis is concerned with the stakeholder's interest in the project.

The incoming mayor: High power and high interest. The mayor is a key player in the project and should be carefully and actively managed throughout. The mayor is currently enthusiastic about the project and this enthusiasm has to be sustained. As the likely project sponsor, it will be the mayor's responsibility to promote the project internally and to make resources available to it. It will also be up to her to ensure that the promised business benefits are actually delivered. However, she is also the person who can cancel the project at any time.

OfRoad – a government agency: OfRoad were critical of the previous mayor's justification for the project. They felt that the business case was solely based on intangible benefits and lacked credibility. It is likely that they will be more supportive of the revised proposals for two reasons. Firstly, the proposal uses the classification of benefits which it has suggested. Secondly, the proposal includes tangible benefits which can confidently be included in a cost-benefit analysis. OfRoad is likely to have high power (because it can intervene in local transport decisions) but relatively low interest in this particular project as the town appears to be following its guidelines. An appropriate management strategy would be to keep watch and monitor the situation, making sure that nothing happens on the project which would cause the agency to take a sudden interest in it.

The private motorist of Brighttown: Most of these motorists will have a high interest in the project, because it impacts them directly; but, individually, they have very little power. Their chance to influence policy has just passed, and mayoral elections are not due for another five years. The suggested stakeholder management approach here is to keep them informed. However, their response will have to be monitored. If they organise themselves and band together as a group, they might be able to stage disruptive actions which might raise their power and have an impact on the project. This makes the point that stakeholder management is a continual process, as stakeholders may take up different positions in the grid as they organise themselves or as the project progresses.

ACCA Marking scheme

		Marks
(a)	1 mark for each appropriate point up to a maximum of 5 marks	
(b)	1 mark for each appropriate point up to a maximum of 14 marks; this could include:	
	– Up to 1 mark for values for each quantitative or financial benefit	
	– Up to 0.5 mark for classifying each benefit correctly up to a maximum of 3 marks	
(c)	1 mark for each appropriate point up to a maximum of 2 marks for each stakeholder. Three stakeholders leading to a maximum of 6 marks for this part question	
Total		**25**

Examiner's comments

Part (a) was relatively well answered, although many answers were not well structured and some strayed outside of what might be expected within a terms of reference.

Part (b) was answered rather well. The most common mistakes were

- To not clearly identify the benefit. Benefits need action words; such as reduce carbon emissions, improve the punctuality of buses. It was unclear in many answers what the actual benefit was.

- To not include costs or to try and classify costs using the benefits classification. Many answers were so focused on benefits that obvious costs (and marks), such as the cost of buses, the cost of new bus crews, were omitted completely.

In part (c), generally answers were stronger on locating stakeholders within the grid, than suggesting an appropriate management strategy; high interest / high power stakeholders expect more than just being informed!

FINANCING

50 WOODS EDUCATIONAL INSTITUTION

Key answer tips

You are not given very much detail about the institution in the question, so it is important you make the most of what little information there is in order to make your answer as relevant as possible.

(a) Financial objectives

In its current position, a financial objective is unlikely to be the major objective of the educational institution. However, as the institution develops its business of offering private sector courses and seminars, such that these account for perhaps 50% of total income, financial objectives will become a more significant element in strategic planning and control.

The institution should first consider what its mission should be. The current mission is relevant to its research and academic programmes. It must decide whether private sector courses are intended simply to provide profits to finance research and academic programmes, or whether there is a new objective in the delivery of these courses. If there is, the mission statement would have to be amended.

If the purpose of private sector courses is primarily to generate profits to help finance research and academic programmes, there should be financial objectives for sales income and profitability from these courses. The objective might be expressed in terms of achieving sufficient profits from private sector courses to finance a target percentage of research and academic courses. Alternatively, since profitability might be an arbitrary measurement (since many costs of academic programmes and private sector courses, particularly teaching staff costs, are common costs), the objective could be expressed in terms of achieving sales income targets. The aim of the Head of Education that 50% of its income should come from private sector courses within five years could well be adopted as a strategic financial target.

Income from the government will remain important. There are two financial objectives that could be relevant to the institution with regard to its cash limits. First, it should aim to remain within the cash limits it is set, plus the net cash income from its private sector training. Second, on the assumption that government policy on cash limits will remain consistent, targets could be set for maintaining or increasing the cash limits each year. This will only happen if the institution's staff produce sufficient research publications and achieve appropriate ratings for teaching quality. A target for cash limits would therefore be a supporting target, subsidiary to the more important objective of achieving the targeted standards of excellence in research and teaching.

Although the institution is a not-for-profit organisation, it has to operate within its income. The institution appears to want to increase its income, or at least diversify its sources of income, in order to develop. Objectives relating to income and controlling spending within income limits therefore seem essential.

(b)   **Performance measures**

> **Tutorial note**
>
> *You are asked to choose two from each type of measure. The answer that follows discusses all the measures listed, in order to assist you with your studies.*

The measures considered below could be applied primarily to the private sector training activities, and not so much to research or academic education.

Value added

*   Value added is calculated as sales income less external purchase costs, such as the cost of materials and external services. Total value added can then be shared between the various stakeholder beneficiaries, which in the case of the institution would be staff salaries, non-current asset depreciation, new non-current asset purchases and so on. (For a company, beneficiaries of value added would also include payments of taxation to the government, payments of interest to lenders and payments of dividends to shareholders.)

- Private sector courses should generate extra value added, which can then be used to pay for more staff and equipment.

- The value added by research activities could be measured by looking at the number of articles that the institution's staff have had published in academic journals.

- Targets can be set for the value added to be achieved each year, and actual value added compared with the target.

Profitability

- The profitability of private sector courses can be measured. The usefulness of profit measures will depend on the extent to which costs can be directly attributed to private sector courses. If large amounts of cost are apportionments of shared costs, such as costs of administration and teaching staff and establishment running costs, then profit measures might be of limited value.

- The non-current assets of the institution may have been provided by the government many years ago, perhaps for free. It would assist the calculation of genuine profitability if fair values could be assigned to these assets for this purpose, for example to estimate a fair depreciation charge.

- It is important that private sector training does earn extra money for the institution, and measures of contribution earned from these activities and directly attributable profit would certainly be useful.

- As the institution develops its private sector training programmes, targets for profitability should rise year by year.

Return on investment

- Return on investment is commonly measured in accounting terms as profit divided by capital employed. The advantage of ROI as a performance measure, compared with profit, is that the amount of profit earned is related to the size of investment required to obtain the profit.

- Capital employed is measured as the book value of net assets, so again it would be useful if all the net assets could be revalued to fair value.

- In the context of the educational institution, it will be important to make sure that private sector training courses are not just profitable, but that they earn a sufficiently large profit to justify the effort and resources committed to them. Measuring ROI could be useful in this respect, although the measurement of profit and the assignment of assets employed to the private sector programmes is likely to be somewhat arbitrary.

- The current wording of the mission statement is entirely qualitative. It would be useful to introduce some quantitative measures such as ROI.

Customer satisfaction

- The purpose of measuring customer satisfaction is to test customer reaction to the organisation's services, which in this case would be the training courses and seminars. Low levels of satisfaction would indicate a need to improve course content or quality of delivery. High levels of satisfaction are necessary to sustain growth in the 'business'. It is widely accepted that setting targets for customer satisfaction (and monitoring actual performance against target) can help with the management of service quality, which in turn should help to achieve long-term growth.

- Unfortunately, the institution is unlikely to be able to afford expensive methods of measuring customer satisfaction, such as an externally-provided quality audit. It is likely to rely on the completion of course questionnaires by delegates at the end of their course. Responses in course questionnaires can be used to monitor the content and delivery of the course, the course materials, the venue, the catering arrangements, and so on – all factors that could influence decisions by customers to return again for more courses in the future.

- In the final analysis, customer satisfaction can be measured indirectly by the number of delegates returning to the institution. If they were unhappy with the course, they would not choose to come again for another course.

Competitive position

- Measurements of competitive position are generally qualitative rather than quantitative. They assess the position of the organisation in its market. In the case of the educational institution, competitive position could be measured in terms of being a high-price or low-price training provider, or a provider of general training programmes or specialist courses, or a provider of business courses or technical courses. The institution should decide what position it wants to establish in the training market, and what position it is currently in. It can then plan to move from its current position to its target position, and monitor progress towards the target over time.

- The major problem in assessing competitive position is to gain reliable information about competitors. You will know all the details about your own business, but you cannot identify your position in the market unless you can gather information about all the market participants.

Market share

- Market share is a measurement of the proportion of the total market that an organisation has captured. It is usually measured as a quantified percentage, such as a 25% market share. Targets can be set for the market share the institution would like to achieve, and actual market share monitored at regular intervals over time.

- However, the private sector training market is very fragmented, and there are no reliable measurements. Even within specific segments of the market, such as business studies training, or engineering training, it is difficult to measure the total market size.

- Targets for market share might therefore have to be qualitative rather than quantitative, such as a target of being the main provider of specific types of course to businesses in a specified geographical area.

- Market share is linked to customer satisfaction in the sense that, if customers are unhappy, they will leave and market share will fall. Therefore market share cannot be pursued as a target in isolation. Market share should be targeted together with a commitment to ensuring customer satisfaction.

(c) **Integrated reporting**

Integrated reporting provides an opportunity for re-emphasising mission and values as well as providing an insight into progress made towards strategic goals. WEI needs to recognise that the nature of what it does will undergo significant changes. Private sector courses will become a major part of its activities, and this will affect the institution's staff. In view of this major change in the character of the institution and its activities, it is important that all stakeholders are fully aware of the nature of the changes in the institutions objectives and strategic direction.

For example, it would be sensible to make public a financial objective for increasing the percentage of total income of the institution from private sector training, to a target percentage within a stated period of time (e.g. to 50% of total income within five years).

Integrated reporting provides an opportunity for the organisation to communicate or reinforce its strategy to its stakeholders, including any changes made to that strategy. It also provides a vehicle for illustrating progress through relevant measures of strategic performance. Failure to meet set targets can be commented upon and remedial actions, if appropriate, can be outlined. An integrated report for WEI could combine some of its traditional reporting to a review of its progress towards some of the targets identified in part (b).

51 POTATO-TO-GO INC

Key answer tips

For part (a) of the question, in the appendix, where you calculate the key ratios that you want to discuss in your financial analysis, there would be no need to calculate the ratios for every year. You should only need to compare this year's results to last year's results. In part (b) you might find it useful to bring in Porter's diamond (which is specifically designed to examine overseas expansion). In part (c), don't just list out possible sources of finance – make sure instead that you relate them to the scenario.

(a) **Financial performance**

Recent performance indicators of the company are shown in the appendix. These show the following trends.

- Turnover has been falling for two years

- Profits have been falling for three years

- Net profit percentages have fallen from 34% in 2003 to 11% in 20X6

- There is now no significant growth in outlets

- Turnover per outlet has been falling for several years.

- In addition, dividend cover is currently very low. If profits continue to fall, then it will not be possible to maintain the current dividend, let alone supply future growth.

The relatively low P/E ratio may be the result of poor growth prospects and/or worries about the company's viability due to the $80m repayment of loan stock.

Appendix – Performance indicators

	20X2	20X3	20X4	20X5	20X6
% growth/(decline)	N/a	19%	2%	(7)%	(5)%
Net profit margin	32%	34%	24%	16%	11%
Turnover per outlet	0.54	0.59	0.58	0.53	0.50

(b)   Overseas expansion

Fast food companies such as McDonalds and Pizza Hut have been very successful on a global basis, enjoying marketing and purchasing economies of scale and developing brand strength. However, it is unclear whether the overseas operation that is planned will allow great economies of scale. To obtain those it may be necessary to expand rapidly once the operation has proved itself in the New England market.

North America shares the closest tastes in fast food to Europe, so the product should be well-received. On the other hand, existing types of fast food outlet (burger, pizza, taco, etc.) are much more established so PTG will face intense competition.

Apart from the problem of raising finance (which is discussed below) particular problems and risks could arise from managing at a distance, misjudging the market and currency fluctuations.

Local professional advice will have to be sought on location, interior layout and decor, opening hours, prices, wage rates, types of employee and legal responsibilities.

Exit from the venture will be made easier if a separate operating subsidiary is set up with its own management. This would facilitate sale of the undertaking, and might insulate the parent company from some of the financing risks, although the parent company may be required to give guarantees.

(c)   Financing the overseas expansion

The lack of internally generated funds means that additional finance must first be raised to redeem the loan stock before considering how to finance the expansion. In total 80 + 130 = $210 million of new funds are required.

Equity

Equity does not appear to be a feasible solution:

- Rights issue: at the end of 20X6 the market capitalisation of PTG was

  PAT × P/E = 28 × 9 = $252 million.

  It is highly unlikely that shareholders would be willing to invest a further $210 million via a rights issue. Furthermore, the Edwards family (51% stake) have indicated that they would be unwilling to take up rights, in which case their holding would be diluted.

- Public issue: the Edwards family own 51% of the shares, giving them control. Any significant public issue of shares would dilute their stake to below 50%, a situation they are unlikely to find acceptable.

- In any case the poor dividend cover and low P/E ratio mean that it is not a good time to issue equity.

Debt

Debt looks more attractive:

- If PTG can convince lenders that the decline in profits will not continue, then a replacement loan for the debentures might be available. The gearing level is not excessive and there appears to be plenty of security (non-current assets $180m, net current assets $60m) that could be provided by fixed or floating charges.

- Mortgages could be taken out to cover the bulk of the cost of acquiring overseas premises, though this still leaves fitting out the restaurants and working capital requirements.

Franchising

Global fast food firms often operate on a franchise system.

Franchising has two main advantages in this context:

- The franchisees themselves inject a substantial amount of capital, so helping to fund the enterprise.

- The franchisees have local expertise and experience, thus reducing cultural risks.

Joint ventures

To supply additional finance, PTG could consider a joint venture with a US company which could give further assistance in an unknown market and if it is with an organisation that already has suitable sites there could be considerable advantages.

- The joint venture approach was adopted when Burger King entered the Japanese market.

52   DAVID SILVESTER

Key answer tips

In part (b) of this question you may find it useful to split the critical success factors between those that come from the company's resources and those which come from its competencies (as is shown in the pocket notes).

(a)   **To**:   David Silvester

From:

Funding strategy for Gift Designs Ltd

Clearly, you have identified a real business opportunity and face both business and financial risks in turning the opportunity into reality. One possible model you can use is that of the product life cycle which as a one-product firm is effectively the life cycle for the company. Linking business risk to financial risk is important – in the early stages of the business the business risk is high and the high death rate among new start-ups is well publicised; consequently, there is a need to go for low financial risk.

Funding the business is essentially deciding the balance between debt and equity finance, and equity offers the low risk that you should be looking for. As the firm grows and develops so the balance between debt and equity will change. A new business venture like this could, in Boston Consulting Group analysis terms, be seen as a problem child with a non-existent market share but high growth potential. The business risks are very high, and consequently the financial risks taken should be very low and so the financing method should avoid taking on large amounts of debt with a commitment to service the debt.

You need to take advantage of investors who are willing to accept the risks associated with a business start-up – venture capitalists and business angels accept the risks associated with putting equity capital in but may expect a significant share in the ownership of the business. This they will seek to realise once the business is successfully established. As the business moves into growth and then maturity so the business risks will reduce and access to debt finance becomes feasible and cost effective. In maturity the business should be able to generate significant retained earnings to finance further development. Dividend policy will also be affected by the stage in the life cycle that the business has reached.

Yours,

(b)   David even at this early stage needs to identify the critical success factors and related performance indicators that will show that the concept is turning into a business reality. Many of the success factors will be linked to customer needs and expectations and therefore where David's business must excel in order to outperform the competition. As an innovator one of the critical success factors will be the time taken to develop and launch the new vase. Being first-to-market will be critical for success. His ability to generate sales revenue from demanding corporate customers will be a real indicator of that success.

David will need to ensure that he has adequate patent protection for the product and recognise that it will have a product life cycle.

There look to be a number of alternative markets and the ability to customise the product may be a CSF. Greiner indicates the different stages a growing business goes through and the different problems associated with each stage. One of David's key problems will be to decide what type of business he wants to be. From the scenario it looks as if he is aiming to carry out most of the functions himself and there is a need to decide what he does and what he gets others to do for him. Indeed the skills he has may be as an innovator rather than as someone who carries out manufacture, distribution, etc. Gift Designs may develop most quickly as a firm that creates new products and then licences them to larger firms with the skills to penetrate the many market opportunities that are present. It is important for David to recognise that turning the product concept into a viable and growing business may result in a business and a business model very different to what he anticipated. Gift Designs needs to have the flexibility and agility to take advantage of the opportunities that will emerge over time.

53 SATELLITE NAVIGATION SYSTEMS

(a) **Report on performance**

Production and sales

Production and sales were 1,100 units in September and October, 950 units in November and 900 units in December. There has thus been a marked decline over the four-month period. This good performance in the first two months and poor performance in the latter two months may be due to a seasonal variation. If this is the case, it would be good for the budget to reflect the expected seasonal variation, rather than just being a flat 1,000 units per month.

Tutorial note

The output was calculated by taking the standard cost of actual output and dividing by the standard cost per system, i.e. $1,276,000/$1,160 = 1,100 units, $1,102,000/$1,160 = 950 units and $1,044,000/$1,160 = 900 units.

Materials

The material price variance was favourable for the first two months, and then very adverse for November and December. This was possibly due to the exchange rate movement if the systems are imported. The effect of the exchange rate variations should be quantified. Any remaining adverse variances may be due to inefficient purchasing by the purchasing manager. It should be investigated as to whether there are alternative suppliers for the systems.

The material usage variance was adverse in every month, but was particularly bad in October and even worse in December. In October the variance was $7,200 A and as the material cost was $400 per unit, this meant that an extra $7,200/$400 = 18 units were used on a production of 1,100 units. In December, the variance was $16,000/$400 = 40 extra units on production of 900 units. This variance could possibly be due to the large batch of systems which did not have the correct adaptors.

Labour

The labour rate variance was adverse in September and October and substantially adverse in November and December. Expressing the variances as percentages, for September the standard labour cost was $320 × 1,100 units = $352,000 and thus the variance was $4,200 A/$352,000 = 1.1% A. In November the variance was $5,500 A/$352,000 = 1.6% A. These minor variances could be explained by more overtime than expected being worked, especially as production was high in the first two months. Then things were much worse in the latter two months, for November the variance was $23,100 A/($320 per unit × 950 units) = 7.6% A and in December the variance was $24,000 A/($320 per unit × 900 units) = 8.3%. These substantial variances are almost certainly due to higher wage rates being offered in order to retain the staff and lower the labour turnover.

The labour efficiency variance was $16,000 favourable in September ($16,000/$352,000 = 4.5% F), zero in October and $32,000 adverse in November and December ($32,000 A/$320 per unit × 950 units) = 10.5% A, and $32,000 A/$320 per unit × 900 units) = 11.1% A). It would be expected that some of this variance was due to the large batch of systems which did not have the correct adaptors. This problem was not apparent until fitting was attempted, thus involving the fitters in extra work. If this were the case then we would expect the labour efficiency variance to tie up with the material usage variance, but it does not. We are also told that there is a fluctuation of ± 25% in the fitting times, so even the substantial variances for November and December fall within this range and thus might not represent inefficiency, but simply the fitting of a higher proportion of more labour intensive systems.

It would be very useful to have information on the number of staff leaving the business. Overtime is unlikely to be the cause for the labour variances in November and December as production was lower than budget.

Variable overheads

The variable overhead efficiency variance is based on labour hours and thus simply moves in line with the labour efficiency variance.

The expenditure variance was $7,000 A in September, improved to $2,000 A in October and then $2,000 F in November. It was zero in December. For this variance to have any meaning it must be sub-analysed into its different components in order to determine which ones are being overspent and which ones underspent.

Taking the variable overheads as a whole, the variance gets worse as production levels fall, perhaps indicating that the variable overheads are not entirely variable but may include a fixed element.

Fixed overheads

The fixed overhead volume variance simply reflects the better than expected production in the first two months and the worse than expected production in the latter two months. The fixed overhead volume variance has no significance as it does not represent a cash flow (if we make more or less units than expected then the fixed overheads do not change), but is simply a mathematical device to reconcile budgeted profit with actual profit in an absorption costing system.

The fixed overhead expenditure variance is $5,000 A, $10,000 A, $20,000 A and $20,000 A over the four months and thus shows a worsening pattern, but again in order to understand where things are going wrong we need to sub-analyse the fixed overhead into their different components. We have been told that rent, rates insurance and computing costs have risen in price noticeably; these costs may be regarded as uncontrollable. Managers' attention should be devoted to investigating the controllable costs and reducing any overspend.

Conclusion

Overall the actual cost was 4.4% worse than expected (($4,906,201 − $4,698,000)/ $4,698,000). Whilst this variance might not be regarded as significant, the individual variances in many cases are much bigger and should be investigated. There is a marked decline in performance in November and December. It is important that the individual variances are investigated and their causes understood so that future performance improves.

(b) The finance function

The finance department's role has moved beyond simply providing information on performance and results. Increasingly the finance function plays a core role in the support and implementation of strategic decision making.

Decision support

The first role it can offer is in decision support. For example, the finance department could attempt to quantify the effect of the exchange rate variations on material. This may be supplemented by qualitative information of expectations of future changes in exchange rates. This could support a change in purchasing strategy to one that considers overseas purchasing and this might ultimately lead to a change in competitive strategy if SNS believes that it could achieve a low cost strategy from such a position.

The material variance needs careful investigation in order to find out where the excess units were used, which systems and which teams of fitters were involved. This could change operational strategies and plans.

Strategy development

The finance function might even play a key role in the development of new strategic choices not consider by SNS. For example, it could investigate whether material variances are instead due to inefficient purchasing by the purchasing manager. This could lead to a change in the supply chain of the system, with either alternative suppliers users or even a switch towards e-procurement. The finance function could perform cost-benefit analysis on each of the opportunities.

Strategy implementation

The finance function could consider whether the use of different systems, the training and recruitment of new staff, and the job design of existing staff is adequate. It would be useful to have information on the standard times for different systems and the numbers of the different systems, instead of treating all systems alike. The high labour turnover also means that experienced workers are leaving and that new workers are constantly having to be trained. The efficiency of the new workers would be lower than existing staff and this could be harming the implantation of many of SNS's plans.

Performance measurement

As can be seen in part (a), the finance function can play a role in the assessment of performance within an organisation. But this role has been expanded upon by organisations to include the development of new performance measures and associated KPI's and targets for these measures. For example, staff morale, SNS's competitiveness, levels of innovation etc., might be measures that the finance function suggest should be measured within SNS. It should also be noted that many of these measures will be non-financial in nature and yet the finance function will still be responsible for their creation and measurement.

Conclusion

The role of the finance function is expanding and it is playing a much more fundamental role in the development of the business. Accountants need to be skilled in working on a wide range of decision support and strategic initiatives.

54   X PLC

Key answer tips

In part (a), the budget for the next four quarters is required. However, closing stock values are determined by the following quarter's sales demand and material usage, so the budget for Q5 will also need to be prepared.

(a)

Units	Q1	Q2	Q3	Q4	Q5
Sales demand	2,250	2,050	1,650	2,050	1,250
Add closing inventory (W1)	615	495	615	375	616
Less opening inventory (W2)	(675)	(615)	(495)	(615)	(375)
Production budget	2,190	1,930	1,770	1,810	1,490
Raw material usage (× 3 kg)	6,570	5,790	5,310	5,430	4,470
Closing inventory (W3)	2,605.5	2,389.5	2,443.5	2,011.5	
Opening inventory (W4)	(2,956.5)	(2,605.5)	(2,389.5)	(2,443.5)	
Purchases budget for B in kgs	6,219	5,574	5,364	4,998	
Purchases budget for B in $	43,533	39,018	37,548	34,986	

Total purchases budget for material B for Quarters 1–4 = $155,085

Workings

(W1) Q1 0.3 × 2,050

(W2) The opening inventory for any quarter is the same as the closing inventory of the previous quarter. The opening inventory for Q1 is 0.3 × 2,250 = 675

(W3) Q1 0.45 × 5,790

(W4) The opening inventory for any quarter is the same as the closing inventory of the previous quarter. The opening inventory for Q1 is 0.45 × 6,570 = 2,956.5

(b)   From a budget preparation perspective, if Material A is in short supply then this becomes the principal budget factor. This will affect budget preparation because the first step in the budgetary process will be to determine the optimum mix of products according to their contribution per kg of Material A. The optimum production plan can then be determined and the sales budget can be derived from the production plan. Once the production plan has been determined then Material B, labour and overhead budgets can be derived.

However, the change may also have an impact from a strategic and decision making perspective. New strategic decisions may have to be taken on competitive strategy, the viability of Product W overall, inventory holding strategy and even supply chain management.

The limit on the level of production may mean that there is spare capacity in the factory and the fixed overhead absorption rate will increase. This will increase the cost per unit of products and lower profitability. It appears from the scenario that rivals will be experiencing similar problems, but X Plc might be able to gain a competitive advantage if it can somehow negate this problem (for example, by finding cheaper suppliers, buying the material overseas or changing the product design). Alternatively, the creation of the budget may support a decision to abandon Product W altogether (it might be seen as a 'dog' in a BCG box) and to support investment elsewhere in the organisation's portfolio of products.

There may be knock on effects on other products; if lower production levels mean that there are spare labour resources it could mean that output of products which do not use Material A could be increased. Preparing the budgets for Product W would support strategic decisions to change or alter the production plans and sales strategies of other products, both now and in the future.

But it will be important that new information and revised budget is not the only driver of these strategic and operational decisions. X Plc should continue to carry out qualitative analysis of its environment to ensure that these changes are long-term and that market trends and threats are identified and planned for. Relying solely on the budgets may give a solely financial perspective that is often short-term, can be driven by any bias of the preparer and is overly focused on internal business capabilities and changes rather than external environmental changes.

It may be, for example, that the shortage of the material has been caused by a temporary change in supplier production strategies rather than any weakening of X's competitive strategy or that rivals have plans to leave the market and that X's market share will rise in the future (and the cost of the material subsequently fall as economies of scales are once again attained).Therefore, budgets can play a useful part in supporting organisational strategy, but they cannot be used in isolation and must be supplement by qualitative analysis.

(c)   (i)   The net present value of a project is the sum of the present values of the future cash flows which have been discounted at a rate which takes account of the time value of money.

The expected net present value takes into account the uncertainty or risk associated with the campaigns by weighting each possible outcome by its probability and finding the sum of the results.

The expected value alone gives no indication of the range of possible outcomes. The standard deviation provides a measure of the spread of the possible outcomes; a higher standard deviation indicates a wide range of possible outcomes and therefore a higher level of risk.

(ii)   The company needs to assess the expected outcome of the different campaigns alongside the level of risk in order to decide which campaign to go ahead with. Campaigns J and L have the same expected outcome but L has a higher standard deviation, indicating a higher risk. Campaign J is therefore preferable to campaign L. Campaign K has the same level of risk as L but a higher expected value. K is therefore preferable to L. Campaign K has a higher expected value than J but also has a higher standard deviation and is therefore more risky. The choice between J and K will depend on the risk appetite of the company and how risk averse it is.

55   WORLD ENGINES

Key answer tips

In creating the decision tree for part (a) it will be important to present it well so that it is clearly labelled and easily understood. But, equally, it must be discussed – there are as many marks for this as there are for the calculations. Part (b) requires practical suggestions on risk reduction which will test students' wider business sense rather than their syllabus knowledge.

(a)   A decision tree for the information in the scenario is given below.

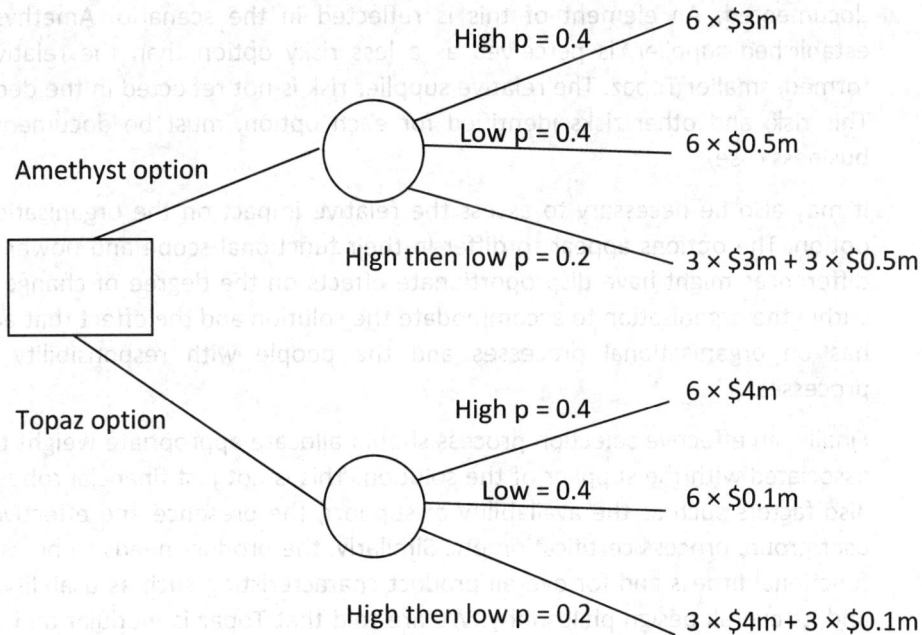

The expected value of Amethyst is:

($18m × 0.4) + ($3m × 0.4) + ($10.5m × 0.2) = $10.5m MINUS cost of $7m = $3.5m

The expected value of Topaz is:

($24m × 0.4) + ($0.6m × 0.4) + ($12.3m × 0.2) = $12.3 MINUS cost of $8m = $4.3m

The analysis suggests that the Topaz option should be chosen.

This decision tree is based on the information available at this point in time. The probabilities set in the workshop are subjective and are not based on an analysis of past statistical data. As the divisional director recalls in the scenario, 'it was relatively hard to get everyone to agree and debate at the workshop became a little heated.' The sensitivity of the outcome to slight alterations in probability assessments should be undertaken. It is also unlikely that the predicted returns will be completely accurate. The basis of these estimates is not given, but a further sensitivity analysis, this time focusing on returns, would be valuable. The predicted annual return of Topaz ($4m per annum) under conditions of high demand needs particular attention. This value (and its associated probability) contributes about 78% of the total expected value of this option. If the annual returns are overestimated by 10% (say $3.6m per annum not $4.0m), then this ceases to be the best option.

Software prices may also be negotiable, and changes in prices and structure may also need to be experimented with. The decision tree will have been just one input into the procurement decision.

(b)   As highlighted in the first part of the answer, the decision tree is only one input to the procurement decision. The scenario states that the returns used in the decision tree analysis were based on tangible benefits. The business case for each option would also have to state *intangible benefits* offered by each option. For example, the Topaz option offers a more contemporary user interface and this may provide intangible benefits associated with a better user experience. Intangible benefits need to be identified and listed for each option.

Importantly, the risk associated with each option will also have to be considered and documented. An element of this is reflected in the scenario. Amethyst, a well-established supplier, is perceived as a less risky option than the relatively newly formed, smaller Topaz. The relative supplier risk is not reflected in the decision tree. This risk, and other risks identified for each option, must be documented in the business case.

It may also be necessary to assess the relative impact on the organisation of each option. The options appear to differ in their functional scope and power and these differences might have disproportionate effects on the degree of change necessary within the organisation to accommodate the solution and the effect that each option has on organisational processes and the people with responsibility for those processes.

Finally, an effective selection process should allocate appropriate weight to features associated with the supplier of the solution. This is not just financial robustness, but also factors such as the availability of support, the presence and effectiveness of a user group, process certification etc. Similarly, the product needs to be assessed for functional fitness and for overall product characteristics, such as usability, flexibility and its overall design philosophy. We are told that Topaz is modular and up-to-date and this may be in its favour, but it will not be reflected in the decision tree analysis.

(c)   The risk assessment for Topaz has documented concerns about the long-term viability and stability of the supplier. Current financial analysis reveals a profitable, liquid and lowly geared company. However, the company is relatively young and it has a very small turnover compared to WE. It also has to be recognised that WE intends to enter a long-term relationship with this supplier. Hence the continuing success and viability of Topaz is important to WE. *A risk avoidance strategy* would be to avoid purchasing from small, newly-established companies. Hence Topaz would not be considered.

Should this risk actually take place, and Topaz goes out of business, then its impact may be mitigated by the following:

- The software used in the product is perceived to be innovative, modular and up-to-date. WE should ensure that this software is lodged in an escrow agreement. In such an agreement the source code is stored with an independent third party. If Topaz goes out of business, then their customers (including WE) have access to the software source code which should allow them, or their appointed agents, to maintain and support it.

- WE should also consider establishing in-house expertise in the programming language used by the Topaz product. This could have two objectives:

  (1) As a basis for developing a long-term in-house software application that could be used to replace the software elements of the product offered by Topaz. The team could also be used to develop other significant applications required by the company. The software is contemporary and powerful and so other applications within WE should not be difficult to find.

  (2) To provide a basis for enacting the escrow agreement if Topaz goes out of business. Access to the source code is particularly appropriate if an in-house team is able to pick up the software, maintain it and develop it.

- WE is a very significant company, with considerable assets. It should be relatively easy for it to maintain funds which could be used for purchasing Topaz should it run into difficulties. Many large companies take this approach as it secures software supply and potentially severs the supply, in this case, of the software to competitors.

WE need to maintain a contingency plan for moving to an alternative supplier or an in-house team. This contingency plan could be linked to monitoring the financial performance of Topaz. Many financial organisations offer a continuous monitoring facility to ensure that suppliers are not just evaluated at the point of purchase, but throughout the subsequent business relationship. This is particularly important when the supplier's application is business-critical to the customer and any interruption in supply would have significant implications.

The key lessons learned from the fatal air crash should result in WE developing risk avoidance or mitigation actions to make sure that such catastrophic events do not happen again, or, if they do happen, that they have less impact on the organisation. Potential actions include:

(1) Not permitting teams to travel together – the complete evaluation team was in the aircraft. Many organisations insist that key employees do not travel together to conferences and meetings.

(2) Looking for safer transport alternatives – the fatal journey was on a small commuter plane travelling a distance which might have been undertaken by car or train. The riskiness of different ways of travelling needs to be considered. Small commuter airlines and aircraft may have less stringent safety procedures than larger, mainstream airlines. Again, this would have to be investigated.

(3) Eliminating unnecessary travel – was the journey necessary? Encouraging employees to work from the home or the office reduces the risk of travel accidents by avoiding travel in the first place. The company might not only consider electronic meetings as a way of cutting costs, but also as a way of reducing the chance of fatal travel accidents.

(4) Finally, ensuring that all documentation is up-to-date and self-explanatory, so that it can be picked up easily by other employees of the organisation, hence avoiding the situation described in the scenario where the divisional director has to piece together fragments of documentation left by the unfortunate team.

ACCA Marking scheme		Marks
(a)	Up to 5 marks for the decision tree analysis and decision tree diagram Typically this will include (up to a maximum of 5 marks)	
	Diagram of the decision tree: 1 mark	1
	Expected income from Amethyst: 1 mark	1
	Expected value of Amethyst: 1 mark	1
	Expected income from Topaz: 1 mark	1
	Expected value of Topaz: 1 mark	1
	Conclusion (Topaz): 1 mark	1
	Other marks (up to 4 marks) including subjective nature of probabilities, sensitivity analysis, only part of the procurement decision	4
	Maximum	9
(b)	1 mark for each relevant point up to a maximum of	6
(c)	1 mark for each appropriate point up to a maximum of 5 marks for software vendor issues, 1 mark for each appropriate point up to a maximum of 5 marks for employee travel issues – maximum of 10 marks for this sub-question	15
Total		**25**

Examiner's comments

In part (a) many candidates showed that they were very familiar with constructing and interpreting decision trees and so scored reasonably well on this part question. The most common error was to forget to subtract the cost of the investment. However, it also has to be said, that some answers were very poor and it was unclear why the candidate chose to answer this optional question.

In part (b), candidates who knew this topic well, produced good answers, centred on risk, supplier viability and software functionality. In contrast, some answers were very poor and rambling; not answering the specific question at all.

In part (c) there were some very good answers. However, there were also some very poor answers, lacking in content or generally describing risk management without any context at all.

Overall, this question was unpopular. Candidate performance tended to be good, with candidates confident in the application and limitations of decision tree analysis and able to properly discuss risk in context, or poor, with candidates unable to properly undertake decision tree analysis or discuss the concept of risk in the context of the scenario.

56   COOLFREEZE

🔑 **Key answer tips**

These are new areas to the syllabus but not to the qualification. These are areas that have been covered at lower level papers. However, notice that at this level the emphasis is on the analysis of the numbers in terms of what they tell us and what their limitations might be, rather than on performing lots of detailed calculations.

(a)   Spreadsheet analysis

I have had the opportunity to analyse the spreadsheet that you provided. My analysis suggests that the forecasting team used moving averages to help them analyse past sales and forecast the future. This is a well-established technique of analysing a time series and you are incorrect in your assumption that it is 'not based on a well-accepted approach'.

Explanation of the spreadsheet construction

The technique is based on averaging figures in the time series. For example, column D is calculated by adding up the first four figures (56, 70, 74, 60) and then adding this total to the total moved on by one quarter (70, 74, 60, 60). This value is than divided by 8 (the number of values in the total calculation) to give the average value in column E. This represents the trend of the time series.

The figures in column F are the variation of the trend from the actual sales figures. These variations are analysed in part 2 where a seasonal variation is calculated.

This seasonal variation is then subtracted from the total variation of each quarter to determine the random or residual variation (column H).

The author of the spreadsheet has checked that the total of the trend plus seasonal plus random variation comes to the original sales figure (column I).

It is difficult to identify where the forecast figures come from. They are roughly in line with the observed trends and represent a very modest increase on the previous year (less than 1% growth). The forecasting group probably thought they were being very realistic.

Analysis

Time series analysis is based on past data. It cannot be used to predict sudden changes in the marketplace. The sales manager had expressed reservations when the forecasts were agreed. His sales staff had already reported that customers were less optimistic about the future because of a weakening economy and the availability of cheap foreign imports. In retrospect, a greater consideration of the external environment should have been included in the overall forecasting approach. Perhaps a number of scenarios should have been considered that took into account changes in the external marketplace.

However, even without such consideration it is clear from the trend figures that growth had been weakening. The growth from 2006 to 2007 (based on the quarter 3 trend figure) was about 11%. In contrast the growth from quarter 2 of 2008 to quarter 2 of 2009 (again based on the trend values) was less than 1%. The final two actual sales figures for 2009 were, in total, exactly the same as the previous year (150 units). This weakening was reflected in the cautious forecasts put forward by the forecasting team. However, there appears very little in the statistical data that suggests that the rapid decline in sales experienced in quarter 2 of 2010 could have been anticipated from the data alone.

The forecasting team might have given further consideration to the sudden increase in random variations in the last three analysed quarters. These might have suggested that the external environment was changing and that other factors were beginning to influence the marketplace. The absolute random variation reported in the last three quarters is greater than that reported in total in the preceding six quarters.

One of the weaknesses of the approach used by the forecasting team is that data from four years ago is given as much weight as much more recent data. This could have been addressed by using exponential smoothing that uses a smoothing constant to reduce the influence of early data considered in the time series. This method uses a series of weights with higher weights given to the most recent data.

(b) **Performance analysis**

The budgeted sales volume for the second quarter of 2010 was 83 units. Except for warnings from the sales manager, there was no evidence that this would not be achieved. The actual sales for the previous three quarters had been in-line with the forecast and so there was no clear case for the budgeting committee to change its sales forecast.

Flexing the budget allows us to look at the consequences if the planned level of output had been 50 (actual sales) rather than 83 (planned sales).

This flexed budget is presented below.

Output (sales)	50 units
Sales revenue	$50,000
Raw materials	($17,500)
Labour	($16,250)
Fixed overheads	($18,000)
Operating profit (loss)	($1,750)

The table below compares budget, actual and the flexed budget.

	Budget	Actual	Flexed budget
Units	83	50	50
Price	$1,000.00	$900.00	$100.00
Revenue	$83,000.00	$45,000.00	$50,000.00
Raw materials	($29,050.00)	($15,000.00)	($17,500.00)
Labour	($26,975.00)	($15,750.00)	($16,250.00)
Fixed overheads	($18,000.00)	($18,000.00)	($18,000.00)
Operating profit	$8,975.00	($3,750.00)	($1,750.00)

A number of conclusions can be drawn.

Sales volume

The sales volume variance for quarter 1 is an adverse variance. The sales manager should be held accountable for this.

However, in fairness to him, he had warned of weakening demand at the meeting of the planning committee that set the targets for the four quarters. The reasons appear to be associated with changes in the external environment. Customers are reluctant to invest in new machines or replace old machinery in times of difficult trading conditions. Cheaper foreign imports have also been identified.

Sales price variance

The sales price variance for quarter 1 is also an adverse variance. This is due to lower prices being charged. The sales manager is again accountable for this. He has probably discounted prices to compete with cheaper foreign imports. He warned in the scenario of cheaper foreign imports undercutting prices by about 10%. It appears that the sales manager has had to match these prices, as the sales unit price fell to $900 in this quarter.

Materials variance

The materials variance is a favourable variance because actual costs ($15,000) are less than the flexed budget $17,500.

There may be at least two reasons for this. On the one hand the production manager may have been able to reduce the amount of raw material used in the manufacture of the equipment. This may be possible, although with such a well-established product this seems unlikely. It is more likely that the procurement manger has been able to negotiate lower prices for raw materials.

CoolFreeze has had to reduce its prices (reflected in the sales price variance) but this has been partly offset by obtaining lower prices from suppliers.

Labour variance

The labour variance is again favourable because actual labour costs were less than the flexed budget. The variance is relatively small; $500. There may, again, be two possible reasons for this. Firstly, that labour costs have been reduced by paying lower rates. This would be the responsibility of the personnel department. This may be possible; perhaps some employees have left and have been replaced by cheaper employees. Alternatively, perhaps the number of hours required to produce each unit has been reduced. This would be the responsibility of the production manager. Further information is needed to come to a firm conclusion.

Overhead costs

Fixed overheads have remained as per the original budget.

Summary

Your assertion that 'we have all made mistakes' seems rather sweeping. The main problems to be addressed appear to be in sales volume and sales price. These are the responsibility of the sales manager. In contrast, raw materials and labour costs have been well controlled with positive variances achieved by the production and procurement managers. Similarly, overheads have been maintained at their budgeted value.

57 MANTIS & GEAR

(a) Performance analysis

The sales manager is correct in that the sales volume has outperformed budgeted sales volume by 27,000 units, or 11.1% over budget. This is a positive sign in a situation where there is increased competition and more demanding customers.

However, profitability is much lower than budgeted at 4.5% rather than the 24.7% budgeted, or the 27% expected if the budget was flexed to represent actual sales volume. This could have a serious impact on the future sustainability of the business. The flexed budget can be analysed to determine where performance has been worse than expected. Differences between expected and actual performance can then be investigated. The flexed budget and variances are as follows:

	Budget units	Actual units	Flexed budget	Variance to flexed
Sales volume	243,000	270,000	270,000	
	Budget	Actual		
	$000	$000		$000
Sales revenue	36,450	36,450	40,500	4,050 Adverse
Direct materials	15,795	18,630	17,550	1,080 Adverse
Direct labour	3,402	4,725	3,780	945 Adverse
Overheads	8,250	11,450	8,250	3,200 Adverse
Operating profit	9,003	1,645	10,920	

From the above, it can be seen that all calculated variances are adverse when considered against the flexed budget. Although the actual sales revenue is the same as budgeted, this is from a much higher sales volume. The average selling price per unit was budgeted at $150, but the average actual selling price per unit was $135, a decrease of 10%. It may be that this was reduced in order for the sales team to hit targets, especially if their commission is based on sales volume rather than revenue. Alternatively, it could be that the price was necessarily reduced in order to cope with increased competition.

Direct materials should have cost $17.55m for the actual units produced. However, they cost $18.63m, an adverse materials variance of $1.08m. This may either be due to the price or quality of materials used, but further information would be required to determine which. It is possible that price may be an important factor, as the sales manager mentioned fulfilling orders with a short lead time. This may have meant that higher prices were paid if materials were sourced at short notice, or not using economic order techniques. Furthermore, it was stated that customers wanted 'more attractive' products, which may have led to more advanced component parts, thus increasing costs. In addition, the industry is a dynamic industry with rapidly developing technology; the cost of new technology may be higher than the standard costs budgeted for. This is one of the difficulties of using standard costing in an environment where products are frequently enhanced or new products developed.

Direct labour has also shown an adverse variance of $3.2m. This may be due to either the rate paid, or the hours worked on products. If orders were satisfied at short notice, this may have required overtime, which could affect the labour rate variance causing it to be higher due to enhanced overtime payments. In addition, special and customer-specific orders may require longer than standard hours as they may not yet have benefitted from the learning curve effect associated with standard, repeat orders.

Fixed overheads show a $3.2m adverse variance, which is 39% higher than budgeted. This is clearly a major problem and suggests that either the standard absorption rate of overheads is incorrect, or that overheads have not been controlled throughout the year. The focus on meeting increased orders may have distracted management attention from overhead control, thus leading to inefficiencies related to these costs. Overheads include those indirect elements of cost which are not specifically attributed to a product, such as cleaning materials, machine maintenance, supervisor salaries and factory rent and rates, heating and lighting. By treating them as fixed overheads, the suggestion is that they should not change with a variation in activity volumes. It is vital that the company analyses the overhead spend urgently, as this has had a major impact on profitability.

Overall, M&G should have made a budgeted profit of $10.92m on the actual sales, but instead made a profit of $1.645m, a difference of $9.275m.

One of the problems of using a standard costing system is that standard costs are based on historical information, and in a changing environment these are unlikely to remain accurate for long. It may be that the standards used in the budget are simply no longer realistic, and these need analysing before the blame is placed upon any particular department within the organisation. The suggestion of activity based costing could certainly assist with this in terms of understanding the overheads, although it will have no impact on the labour or material standards used; these would need separate analysis.

(b) Activity based costing

Activity based costing attempts to discover what drives costs to be incurred. Cost pools are established which include all of the costs caused by one cost driver. These cost pools are then absorbed into products based on the driver activity related to each product. For example, M&G may recognise the cost driver 'machine set ups' which would occur every time the manufacturing line is set up to produce a different product or model. Following the initial recognition of costs, drivers and activities, overhead costs can then be allocated to products or customers accordingly.

Activity based costing was developed to improve the accuracy of costing in an environment where methods of production were becoming more automated and less labour intensive. The introduction of greater product ranges also demanded enhanced costing methods in order to both understand how costs were driven (and hence determine how to successfully reduce costs) and also to enhance product pricing in an increasingly competitive environment. For M&G, given the falling profitability and the increasing competition, it is important that the company determines how to reduce costs and become competitive on price without affecting profitability.

Although activity based costing should prove to be beneficial in the long term, the initial implementation of the method is a time-consuming and complex task which requires the identification of numerous activities and their cost drivers. In reality, these may number in their hundreds or even thousands. Given the volume of products in M&G's portfolio, this is likely to be an especially complex task. In addition, as new products and methods are introduced, the analysis of activities and drivers needs to be updated. The introduction of activity based costing may take up to a year and will require the participation of managers and staff in all departments. Given the growth of the company, it may be that departmental managers are feeling under pressure of enhanced activity volume and may not give sufficient thought to the identification of activities and their drivers, which would make the results irrelevant.

Additionally, some managers may be resistant to the idea of change. Although this does not appear to be a problem in M&G, the pressure of work mentioned above may contribute to resistance. The impact of the change on their roles would also be a contributory factor. The sales manager, specifically, feels that performance is good and may see the introduction of new costing and pricing methods as something which will make it more difficult for him to hit targets. His participation is important as he will need to determine the cost drivers relevant to sales activities. This participation is essential to determine the profitability of customers, a key feature of activity based costing, and this itself may lead to resistance as he may see it as a route to losing some of his more 'lucrative' contracts.

The majority of M&G's customers are repeat business customers and, even if activity based costing were to be successfully introduced, they may not accept changes in pricing. For example, analysis might suggest that a product incurs greater costs than expected and so its price is increased as a result. The customer for this product may refuse to pay this price and so seek an alternative supplier for the product. This may, however, be beneficial to M&G to focus on more profitable customers or products, providing market share does not fall substantially.

Despite the limitations, in a period of increasing overheads (M&G's overheads are 39% greater than budgeted) and falling profitability, the use of activity based costing to determine cost behaviour can lead to increased efficiency as cost drivers are recognised and a focus placed on reducing the main cost drivers. Therefore the implementation of this method could bring future cost advantages to M&G, and help to regain the previous levels of profitability.

	ACCA Marking scheme	
		Marks
(a)	Up to 1 mark for each item of quantitative analysis, including variances and profitability ratios. Up to 1 mark for each appropriate qualitative point, specifically reasons for variances and how the variances contribute to the current situation. Up to 1 mark for all other qualitative points not related to variances but relevant to the question. Up to a maximum of 15 marks for this part of the question.	15
(b)	Up to 2 marks for discussing the principles of activity based costing. Up to 2 marks for explaining the reason for its development (either theoretical or within the context of the scenario). Up to 6 marks for the evaluation of activity based costing in the context of M&G.	10
Total		**25**

Examiner's comments

In part (a) a minority of candidates scored very highly, showing a clear understanding of variances. Some candidates did not calculate variances, and therefore were unable to obtain marks for doing so, simply calculating profit margins instead. Although there were marks to be obtained for this, it would be impossible to obtain the full 15 marks available by discussing this element alone. Other candidates failed to flex the budget, showing a lack of understanding of this area. However, these candidates were often able to obtain some marks for discussing the reasons, if they had done so. An acceptable alternative was for candidates to break down the figures into budget and actual figures per unit, rather than to flex the budget, as this would lead to equivalent analysis.

Part (b) required the discussion of a specific costing technique. The majority of candidates were able to describe this, but as with previous questions, many failed to get the marks for applying their answer to the scenario provided.

STRATEGY AND PEOPLE

58   ROCK BOTTOM   *Walk in the footsteps of a top tutor*

Tutor's top tips

Part (a) Life cycle and management style

Key to success:

Allocate time equally between 3 phases. There are 3 phases x 2 elements = 6 parts to the question. So with 18 marks available in total that gives you around 3 marks per part. So you cannot spend too much time on any element of any phase of the requirement (in fact, you have time to make a maximum of two issues per element).

Answer both elements i.e. the reasons for success and failure, and the contribution of Rick Hein's leadership style.

Understand the scenario. The examiner suggested some students misunderstood that whilst franchising was considered, other opportunities were pursued.

You could use a model to generate ideas. Even something as simple as a SWOT – reasons for success could come from strengths and opportunities, whilst the reasons for failure could come from the weaknesses and threats. The answer uses PLC to distinguish stages and you might also have found this useful.

Recognising that each stage was very different – stage 1: mainly successful, stage 2: some success and some failures, stage 3: mainly failures.

Key dangers:

*   *Lack of structure*

*   *Mixing stages together*

*   *Too much time spent on one stage*

Simply regurgitating the scenario (not adding value). For example, regurgitation would state that at stage 2 the company listed on stock exchange. But to gain marks in the exam you would have to develop this further, for example, by explaining that this would mean that the company would need to be more transparent and have strong corporate governance.

In part (b) it is important that you have the correct focus on the answer requirements rather than simply explaining franchising. This means explaining that in 1988 franchising was feasible (because the business would have been too attractive to franchisees), but that by 20X7 it was unattractive to franchisees and franchising would not have been feasible. So we focus on the feasibility of franchising rather than its advantages and disadvantages.

(a)   The product life cycle model suggests that a product passes through six stages: introduction, development, growth, shakeout, maturity and decline. The first Rock Bottom phase appears to coincide with the introduction, development and growth periods of the products offered by the company. These highly specified, high quality products were new to the country and were quickly adopted by a certain consumer segment (see below). The life cycle concept also applies to services, and the innovative way in which Rock Bottom sold and marketed the products distinguished the company from potential competitors. Not only were these competitors still selling inferior and older products but their retail methods looked outdated compared with Rock.

Bottom's bright, specialist shops. Rock Bottom's entry into the market-place also exploited two important changes in the external environment. The first was the technological advance of the Japanese consumer electronics industry. The second was the growing economic power of young people, who wished to spend their increasing disposable income on products that allowed them to enjoy popular music. Early entrants into an industry gain experience of that industry sooner than others. This may not only be translated into cost advantages but also into customer loyalty that helps them through subsequent stages of the product's life cycle. Rock Bottom enjoyed the advantages of a first mover in this industry.

Hein's leadership style appears to have been consistent with contemporary society and more than acceptable to his young target market. As an entrepreneur, his charismatic leadership was concerned with building a vision for the organisation and then energising people to achieve it. The latter he achieved through appointing branch managers who reflected, to some degree, his own style and approach. His willingness to delegate considerable responsibility to these leaders, and to reward them well, was also relatively innovative. The shops were also staffed by young people who understood the capabilities of the products they were selling. It was an early recognition that intangible resources of skills and knowledge were important to the organisation.

In summary, in the first phase Rock Bottom's organisation and Hein's leadership style appear to have been aligned with contemporary society, the customer base, employees and Rock Bottom's position in the product/service life cycle.

The second phase of the Rock Bottom story appears to reflect the shakeout and maturity phases of the product life cycle. The entry of competitors into the market is a feature of the growth stage. However, it is in the shakeout stage that the market becomes saturated with competitors. The Rock Bottom product and service approach is easily imitated. Hein initially reacted to these new challenges by a growing maturity, recognising that outrageous behaviour might deter the banks from lending to him. However, the need to raise money to fund expansion and a latent need to realise (and enjoy) his investment led to the company being floated on the country's stock exchange. This, eventually, created two problems.

The first was the need for the company to provide acceptable returns to shareholders. This would have been a new challenge for Hein. He would have to not only maintain dividends to external shareholders, but he would also have to monitor and improve the publicly quoted share price. In an attempt to establish an organisation that could deliver such value, changes were made in the organisational structure and style. Most of the phase 1 entrepreneur-style managers left.

This may have been inevitable anyway as Rock Bottom would have had problems continuing with such high individual reward packages in a maturing market. However, the new public limited organisation also demanded managers who were more transactional leaders, focusing on designing systems and controlling performance. This style of management was alien to Rick's approach. The second problem was the need for the organisation to become more transparent. The publishing of Hein's financial details was embarrassing, particularly as his income fuelled a life-style that was becoming less acceptable to society. What had once appeared innovative and amusing now looked like an indulgence. The challenge now was for Hein to change his leadership style to suit the new situation. However, he ultimately failed to do this. Like many leaders who have risen to their position through entrepreneurial ability and a dominant spirit, the concept of serving stakeholders rather than ordering them around proved too difficult to grasp. The sensible thing would have been to leave Rock Bottom and start afresh. However, like many entrepreneurs he was emotionally attached to the company and so he persuaded a group of private equity financiers to help him buy it back. Combining the roles of Chairman and Chief Executive Officer (CEO) is also controversial and likely to attract criticism concerning corporate governance.

In summary, in the second phase of Hein's leadership he failed to change his approach to reflect changing social values, a maturing product/service market-place and the need to serve new and important stakeholders in the organisation. He clearly saw the public limited company as a 'shackle' on his ambition and its obligations an infringement of his personal privacy.

It can be argued that Hein took Rock Bottom back into private ownership just as the product life cycle moved into its decline stage. The product life cycle is a timely reminder that any product or service has a finite life. Forty years earlier, as a young man, Hein was in touch with the technological and social changes that created a demand for his product and service. However, he had now lost touch with the forces shaping the external environment. Products have now moved on. Music is increasingly delivered through downloaded files that are then played through computers (for home use) or MP3s (for portable use). Even where consumers use traditional electronic equipment, the reliability of this equipment means that it is seldom replaced. The delivery method, through specialised shops, which once seemed so innovative is now widely imitated and increasingly, due to the Internet, less cost-effective. Consumers of these products are knowledgeable buyers and are only willing to purchase, after careful cost and delivery comparisons, through the Internet. Hence, Hein is in a situation where he faces more competition to supply products which are used and replaced less frequently, using a sales channel that is increasingly uncompetitive. Consequently, Hein's attempt to re-vitalise the shops by using the approach he adopted in phase 1 of the company was always doomed to failure. This failure was also guaranteed by the continued presence of the managers appointed in phase 2 of the company. These were managers used to tight controls and targets set by centralised management. To suddenly be let loose was not what they wanted and Hein appears to have reacted to their inability to act entrepreneurially with anger and abuse. Hein's final acts of reinvention concerned the return to a hedonistic, conspicuous life style that he had enjoyed in the early days of the company. He probably felt that this was possible now that he did not have the reporting requirements of the public limited company. However, he had failed to recognise significant changes in society. He celebrated the freeing of 'Rock Bottom from its shackles' by throwing a large celebration party.

Celebrities were flown in from all over the world to attend. It seems inevitable that the cost and carbon footprint of such an event would now attract criticism.

Finally, in summary, Hein's approach and leadership style in phase 3 became increasingly out of step with society's expectations, customers' requirements and employees' expectations. However, unlike phase 2, Hein was now free of the responsibilities and controls of professional management in a public limited company. This led him to conspicuous activities that further devalued the brand, meaning that its demise was inevitable.

(b) At the end of the first phase Hein still had managers who were entrepreneurial in their outlook. It might have been attractive for them to become franchisees, particularly as this might be a way of protecting their income through the more challenging stages of the product and service life cycle that lay ahead. However, by the time Hein came to look at franchising again (phase 3), the managers were unlikely to be of the type that would take up the challenge of running a franchise. These were managers used to meeting targets within the context of centrally determined policies and budgets within a public limited company. Hein would have to make these employees redundant (at significant cost) and with no certainty that he could find franchisees to replace them.

At the end of phase 1, Rock Bottom was a strong brand, associated with youth and innovation. First movers often retain customer loyalty even when their products and approach have been imitated by new aggressive entrants to the market. A strong brand is essential for a successful franchise as it is a significant part of what the franchisee is buying. However, by the time Hein came to look at franchising again in phase 3, the brand was devalued by his behaviour and incongruent with customer expectations and sales channels. For example, it had no Internet sales channel. If Hein had developed Rock Bottom as a franchise it would have given him the opportunity to focus on building the brand, rather than financing the expansion of the business through the issue of shares.

At the end of phase 1, Rock Bottom was still a financially successful company. If it had been franchised at this point, then Hein could have realised some of his investment (through franchise fees) and used some of this to reward himself, and the rest of the money could have been used to consolidate the brand. Much of the future financial risk would have been passed to the franchisees. There would have been no need to take Rock Bottom public and so suffer the scrutiny associated with a public limited company. However, by the time Hein came to look at franchising again in phase 3, most of the shops were trading at a loss. He saw franchising as a way of disposing of the company in what he hoped was a sufficiently well-structured way. In effect, it was to minimise losses. It seems highly unlikely that franchisees would have been attracted by investing in something that was actually making a loss. Even if they were, it is unlikely that the franchise fees (and hence the money immediately realised) would be very high.

ACCA Marking scheme		
		Marks
(a)	Up to 1 mark for each relevant point up to a maximum of 6 marks for each phase.	
	Three phases required, giving a maximum of	18
(b)	Up to 1 mark for each relevant point up to a maximum of	7
Total		**25**

59 ARC

Key answer tips

This question builds on knowledge acquired in Paper F1 and therefore may be more attractive to students who have sat that paper most recently. For those with the requisite knowledge the question is very straightforward. But it is likely that many students will have not studied this area recently and therefore may lack enough knowledge to tackle this question confidently.

(a) Prior to attending the course, Sully Truin appeared to have, in McGregor's terms, many elements of a Theory X manager about him. He felt that it was necessary to closely control and direct staff in order to get them to do what was needed. He perceived that, in general, employees wished to avoid responsibility and so wanted to be closely directed and controlled. This belief was reflected in work design in the company where employees were increasingly restricted to relatively simple repetitive tasks, for which he had defined well-established procedures. While he was attending the course, Sully still had relatively trivial control issues referred to him and he was exasperated by his employees' inability to take actions to resolve these issues. His initial diagnosis of this reluctance was that this was due to their personal inadequacies rather than the result of the work situation that he had created. In terms of the Tannenbaum and Schmidt model, Sully originally displayed a manager-centred leadership, whereby he made a decision and then announced it. Finally, in terms of the Blake and Mouton managerial grid, Sully's style is primarily that of authority/obedience. His main concern is task completion, with a leadership style which dictates what should be done and how it should be done.

The course questioned Sully's tough-minded management approach, promoting a more democratic style where leadership responsibilities are shared with subordinates, who are also involved in the planning of tasks, not just their execution.

The course essentially suggested that Sully changed his style of leadership, moving to the right on the Tannenbaum and Schmidt model and towards a stereotypical Theory Y manager. The course was run by a company who promoted the benefits of a democratic style of management.

However, contingency or situational theorists have argued that there is no one 'best leadership style' and that style has to be contingent, at least, on the nature of the work to be done and the needs of the people doing that work. Within the context of the case study scenario, the choice of leadership style probably depends on three factors:

- *The characteristics of the leader.* As already discussed, Sully tends towards a Theory X style. However, his willingness to change style as a result of the course might suggest that his approach may be due to a lack of confidence in his subordinates rather than the reflection of deeply held values about leadership.

- *The characteristics of those led.* It could be argued that Sully's style has necessarily led to him employing people who are comfortable with his style, and demand a work environment which is routine, well-specified and tightly controlled. When Sully changes his style after the course, they are unable to contribute effectively and are left confused and anxious. It is their suggestion that Sully returns to his old style of leadership.

- *The situation itself, the nature of the task.* In the case study scenario, the task has been increasingly constrained, so that it can be closely defined and controlled by Sully. It is relatively simple but decisions on problems have to be taken quickly. This is why they are referred to Sully. He is good at making an instant decision and has the authority to back it up. When subordinates were asked to take responsibility for these decisions, they felt that they did not have sufficient authority or experience and so they consulted their colleagues, which took time, before arriving at a decision.

Contingency or situational theorists would probably be critical of a training course that appeared to encourage a management style that would be unlikely to be appropriate for all situations. Even the most democratic of managers has to adopt an authoritarian style at some point to get certain things done or problems resolved.

From a contingency perspective, it could be argued that before going on the course, ARC had a relatively good fit between leadership, subordinates and the task. Sully Truin was relatively well-liked, he was trusted by his employees to make decisions, and his power was high. As owner of the company he has the power to reward and punish employees. The tasks required of employees were clearly laid down and were well defined.

Reversion to Sully's old style of management might make employees feel more comfortable but it does not solve the fundamental problems. The company is still over-reliant on Sully and, as well as causing him personal health problems, this also severely restricts the company's ability to expand. The company could look more closely at the definition of the task and the competencies required of employees. The speed of change may have also been an important factor in the failure of Sully's new democratic approach. His sudden conversion from Theory X to Theory Y manager was too much, too soon and left employees anxious and confused.

> **Tutorial note**
>
> This part question on leadership may be answered in a number of ways. The main focus of the answer should be on Sully Truin's leadership style both before and after the management training course and the effect these styles have on his employees. It is expected that candidates will also comment on the speed of change and its consequences, as well as the principles of a training company offering a course which promotes a particular style as the 'best approach to leadership'. The model answer includes reference to underpinning theories first encountered in F1, The Accountant in Business.

(b)   In general, business systems have five types of business activity: *planning, enabling, doing, monitoring and control.* In the scenario, employees are primarily responsible for doing and monitoring. However, the control activity, taking action when the monitoring shows that some action is required, is undertaken by Sully Truin. This manifested itself in the emails and phone calls he received whilst he was on the management training course.

The term *job enrichment* refers to a number of different processes including job rotation, enlarging and aggregating tasks. However, the term has become specifically used to refer to a policy of vertical task amalgamation. It is roughly analogous to merging the swim-lanes of a current business process model. An enriched job often contains responsibility for *planning* the job and for taking *control* actions when they are required.

There are five core characteristics of enriched jobs.

- *Skill variety:* The job requires the use of a range of skills and talents.

- *Task identity:* (sometimes called closure): the job includes all the tasks needed to complete an identifiable product or process.

- *Task significance:* the degree to which the job has an impact on other people's lives or work.

- *Autonomy:* employees have a degree of freedom, independence and discretion in scheduling and organising the work.

- *Feedback:* the degree to which employees possess information of the actual results of their performance.

In the context of these characteristics, giving employees responsibility for responding to problems (a controlling activity) was a first step towards job enrichment, particularly as it would lead to task closure (completing the solution of an operational problem) and emphasise the task significance (the impact of the decision on the field crews).

However, Sully's sudden change of style caused two problems.

Firstly, it exposed gaps in the knowledge and skills of the employees. These might be addressed through coaching from Sully. Secondly, it identified that the employees were happier following well-established routines and were quite content to be led. Asking them to take responsibility for decision-making led to anxiety and procrastination, culminating in their request for Sully to return to his old style of leadership.

The strength of the employee's need for growth in the job is an important moderator. Such moderators explain why jobs which have considerable potential to motivate will not automatically generate a high level of motivation and satisfaction for all employees. Evidence suggests that the employees at ARC are naturally content within their job. People who have found the job too restrictive have left the company.

If Sully pursues his ideas for job enrichment, then he will have to carefully assess his current staff to see which, if any, are willing to pursue this wider role. Evidence suggests that 'employees with low growth needs are less likely to experience a positive outcome when their job is enriched' (Bratton and Gold). Consequently, Sully may have to bring new people in from outside if he wants to pursue his job enrichment policy.

His assessment of the skills, competencies and desires of his employees has to be even more comprehensive if he wishes to extend jobs to include planning and enabling tasks. However, such an extension would allow them to assist him finding and establishing contracts, helping grow the company.

ACCA Marking scheme		
		Marks
(a)	1 mark for each relevant point up to a maximum of 15 marks.	15
(b)	1 mark for each relevant point up to a maximum of 5 marks for the principles of job enrichment and up to 5 marks for its application at ARC.	10
Total		**25**

Examiner's comments

This question was not very popular, but candidates who chose to do it often adopted a good answer structure to part (a) based on the requirement; before, after and reasons for failure. Many candidates recognised that the manager had moved from a stereotypical Theory X manager to a stereotypical Theory Y manager. Many answers made appropriate reference to management theory, and those citing contingency theory were particularly insightful, because the characteristics of the 'led' were significant in the context of the second part of this question. Overall, this part of the question was answered relatively well, with many candidates gaining a pass mark on this part question.

Part (b) was worth ten marks. This part question was answered less well. Many candidates struggled to provide enough relevant information on job enrichment and also failed to apply it to the case study situation. It seems likely that its potential application was reduced at ARC by the fact that many of the people who it may have attracted have left the company. The characteristics of the led may make it very difficult for the manager to implement a job enrichment scheme. Remember, although a particular concept may generally be perceived as a good thing (job enrichment in this question), it may not necessarily be so within the described case study scenario. Candidates must always reflect the context of the scenario in their answers.

60   TMZ

(a)   Performance analysis

There is considerable evidence to suggest that strategic drift particularly affects organisations which have experienced a long period of relative continuity during which strategy has either remained unchanged or changed incrementally to react to relatively minor changes in the external environment or industry. This appears to be the case at TMZ. It had enjoyed 35 years of success and growth based on contracting musical artists to its record label and recording and distributing their songs and music through an appropriate physical media. Table one shows that revenues increased continuously in the period 1965–2000. Profit margins fell during the period, reflecting problems in cost control as established musical acts took longer to produce albums and senior staff of TMZ adopted a more relaxed and indulgent approach to their artists. However, even at the end of the period, TMZ remained a profitable company.

Table one: gross and net profit margin – 1965–2000

	1965	1970	1980	1990	2000
Revenue ($million)	10	70	120	150	170
Gross profit margin	40.00%	42.86%	37.50%	33.33%	29.41%
Net profit margin	30.00%	31.43%	25.00%	20.00%	14.71%

During this period, the company had reacted positively to significant changes in its environment. Sociocultural changes, represented by musical fashion and technology changes (from vinyl, through tape cassette to compact disc (CD)) had been successfully surmounted. However, such success can often lead to complacency, with the organisation continuing to pursue a strategy which progressively fails to address the changing strategic position of the organisation and this failure leads to deterioration in organisational performance. This is known as *strategic drift*.

Evidence for this strategic drift starts to emerge in 2003, four years after the launch of the first file sharing company. People within TMZ warned about the possible implications of digital downloading of music. However, senior management at TMZ had rejected this warning and believed that the drop in revenue was due to 'the wrong music, promoted to the wrong people at the wrong price'. They adopted a policy of signing new artists, increasing advertising spend and cutting CD prices. In the policy, 2003–2007, revenues dropped significantly and the company made significant losses (see table two).

$million	2003	2004	2005	2006	2007
Revenue	165	150	130	100	80
Gross profit	45	30	10	0	(10)
Net profit	20	5	(15)	(20)	(30)
Gross profit margin	27.27%	20.00%	7.69%	0.00%	(12.50%)
Net profit margin	12.12%	3.33%	(11.54%)	(20.00%)	(37.50%)

Table two: gross and net profit margin – 2003 – 2007

Johnson, Scholes and Whittington suggest that it is important to realise why strategic drift occurs. They suggest that managers, faced with the complexities of steering an organisation, tend to look for solutions based on the *current ways of doing and seeing things*, grounded in the *existing organisational culture*. So, for example, when revenues from compact discs (CDs) started to decline, the senior managers at TMZ instigated relatively conventional responses to falling sales (increased advertising, reduced prices) and also adopted approaches which had worked before (signing new artists). These may have worked if the environmental change had not been so significant. However, what they failed to realise was that the way people were consuming music was fundamentally changing.

The realisation of performance problems is often followed by a period of flux where no clear direction is pursued. When conventional strategies failed, TMZ resorted to litigation, suing the companies who downloaded music to consumers. In effect, TMZ was attempting to preserve the status quo, trying to ensure that the market remained the same as the one they had operated in so successfully for 40 years. However, not only did this not arrest the decline of the company, it also led to problems with both performers and music fans. In 2010, with the very existence of the company threatened, management was able to define a strategy which worked with the digital download and music-sharing community, to establish a completely different business model based on licensing and ring tones.

This illustrates that a period of flux may itself be followed by *transformational change*, in which there is a fundamental change in strategic direction. TMZ re-defined its business model in 2010. It was fortunate that it had enough stakeholder investment to see it through a difficult period. In many organisations transformational change takes place too late and the organisation fails.

Johnson, Scholes and Whittington suggest that the challenge for managers is to stand apart from their own experience and organisational culture so that they are able to recognise the emerging strategic issues which they face. They also suggest that a second challenge relates to the management of strategic change. New strategies might require actions outside the scope of the existing culture. Thus people within the organisation are required to substantially change their core assumptions and their ways of doing things. The senior management at TMZ were warned about the possible effect of digital downloading, but they were unable to change their basic assumptions about how the music industry worked.

(b) The learning organisation

The point has already been made that strategic drift will take place when changes in an organisation's environment take place at a greater rate than the rate of strategic change within the organisation itself. In such circumstances, the organisation begins to be increasingly misaligned with the environment it is operating in. The challenge is to try to ensure that misalignment does not occur in the first place, but if it does, to tackle it quickly.

The likelihood of strategic drift suggests that the strategy development process in an organisation needs to encourage people to have the capacity and willingness to challenge and change their core assumptions and 'ways of doing things'. This is one of the commonly claimed principles of a 'learning organisation'.

Traditionally, organisations have been organised and structured around order and control. They were built for stability and continuity, rather than change. However, influential writers have increasingly claimed that this is unsuitable for the dynamic conditions of trading in the 21st century. They have suggested that modern society and all of its institutions are in a continuous process of transformation and to react to this we all must become adept at learning. 'We must become able not only to transform our institutions, in response to changing situations and requirements; we must invent and develop institutions which are 'learning systems', that is to say, systems capable of bringing about their own continuing transformation.' (Donald Schon)

The learning organisation is an 'ideal' towards which organisations should evolve in order to respond to contemporary pressures. It is characterised by a view that both collective and individual learning is key to organisational success. A learning organisation is one which is capable of continual regeneration based on the knowledge, experience and skills of individuals working in an organisational culture which encourages mutual questioning and challenge. It emphasises the potential capability of an organisation to regenerate from within.

Advocates of the learning organisation suggest that the collective knowledge of all the individuals within an organisation greatly exceeds what the organisation 'knows' in its formal documentation, filing and information systems. They suggest that it is the responsibility of management to encourage processes which reveal the knowledge of individuals and encourage the sharing of this knowledge. Hence the learning organisation is closely connected with the principles of knowledge management, the other strand in the CEO's policy statement. As a result of free-flowing knowledge, individuals within an organisation become more sensitive to the changes happening around them and this helps them contribute to identifying opportunities and threats in the external environment and also to them developing strategies to tackle these threats or to exploit the opportunities.

In such an approach managers play a less directive and a more facilitative role. It is easy to see the attraction of this to TMZ where the impact of digital downloading was already being discussed in 2003, but was dismissed by complacent senior management. In contrast, in a learning organisation, ideas which do not fit in with current norms are not dismissed or ignored, but acted upon. Questioning and challenging the 'taken-for-granted' is essential if an organisation is to avoid strategic drift. It helps build a resilient organisation which does not take success for granted and reinvents itself using internal capabilities to build a new business model. A new business model was eventually adopted by TMZ, but only when it was close to extinction and radical change was needed to ensure survival.

(c) **Knowledge management**

Johnson, Scholes and Whittington define organisational knowledge as the 'collective and shared experience accumulated through systems, routines and activities of sharing across an organisation'. Managing organisational knowledge is important because as organisations get larger, it becomes more difficult to share what people know. The organisation increasingly does not 'know what it knows' and so it makes unnecessary mistakes, duplicates activity and misses opportunities as a result of this. Furthermore, it is also increasingly likely that organisations, particularly in countries such as Artazia, will have to achieve competitive advantage through accumulated experience (their knowledge), rather than through conventional assets such as physical resources. Fearghal McHugh writing in the Student Accountant (issue 07/2010) suggested that 'having knowledge can be regarded as more important than possessing the other means of production – land, building, labour and capital – because all the other sources are readily available in an advanced global society'.

Knowledge management itself has been facilitated by the increasing functionality of computerised information systems. In this context an important distinction is made between data, information and knowledge. Knowledge is primarily associated with the discovery of trends or patterns of behaviour. Discovering such patterns would have helped TMZ realise that consumers were moving away from purchasing physical music media to downloading its digital equivalent. In the market which TMZ currently finds itself in, discovering patterns and trends remains extremely important as consumer behaviour is still unpredictable and is affected by new technologies, emerging legislation and changes in values.

Conventional knowledge management systems are often based around an intranet application where all explicit knowledge about processes, procedures, standards, products, customers and policies are stored. Such repositories are convenient places to locate explicit organisational knowledge and they have practical benefits, such as eliminating the costs of storage, printing and distribution. Data warehouses can store vast amounts of information and provide the basis of reports, comparisons and responses to queries posed at different levels of summation. Data mining software may be used to discover previously unknown relationships between data and these can be used to guide decision-making and predict future behaviour.

However, although technology has provided many opportunities to analyse the formal data captured by an organisation, the social aspects of knowledge sharing remain important. Employees need opportunities to develop, discuss and share information which they feel would be mutually beneficial. Not only might this require physical facilities (coffee areas, restrooms, social and sports clubs), it also requires a culture of trust in the organisation supported by a leadership approach which values learning and an organisational structure which supports communication and information sharing. Thus there is a clear link between knowledge management and the principles of the learning organisation. Social networks can also be used to support this facet of knowledge sharing and indeed might be the natural preference of the younger employees of the organisation. It is in the social aspects of knowledge sharing that many employees reveal their tacit knowledge (knowledge which they do not know they know, as opposed to explicit knowledge) which can be vital for the effective performance of a particular task.

	ACCA Marking scheme	
		Marks
(a)	1 mark for each appropriate point up to a maximum of 15 marks; this could include:	
	– Up to 1 mark for correct GP margin and appropriate comment 1965–2000	
	– Up to 1 mark for correct NP margin and appropriate comment 1965–2000	
	– Up to 1 mark for GP margin and appropriate comment 2003–2007	
	– Up to 1 mark for NP margin and appropriate comment 2003–2007	
(b)	1 mark for each appropriate point up to a maximum of 5 marks	
(c)	1 mark for each appropriate point up to a maximum of 5 marks	
Total		**25**

Examiner's comments

Part (a) was not particularly well answered by candidates. Too many answers simply consisted of re-iterated facts from the case study, not presented in any context of analysis. The most useful analysis context would have been the principles of strategic drift. However, many answers made no reference to this at all, despite the question specifically asking for it. As a result, very few candidates scored eight marks or more in this question.

In part (b) it was clear that many candidates knew very little about the learning organisation concept and were unable to score more than one or two marks. Often answers were just along the lines of 'a learning organisation is an organisation where people learn'. This was very disappointing.

For part (c) it was clear that many candidates knew very little about this concept and were unable to score more than one or two marks. Often answers were along the lines of 'knowledge management concerns the management of knowledge' and, overall, answers were very disappointing.

61   NATIONAL COLLEGE

Key answer tips

You will need knowledge on competency frameworks. Without this knowledge it will be difficult to score a high mark. The ACCA qualification is built on a competency framework and you should use that as a foundation for your knowledge.

Competencies define what is expected from an individual in an organisation, both in terms of content and levels of performance. They should provide a map of the behaviours that will be valued, recognised and, in some organisations, rewarded. Employees have a set of objectives to work towards and are clear about how they are expected to perform their jobs. This would have been very useful at National College because the inappropriateness of some of the performance measures would have become clearer at a much earlier stage.

Originally, many competency frameworks concentrated on behavioural elements, for example, developing softer skills such as problem-solving. However, competency frameworks are increasingly becoming more ambitious and including technical competencies that in many ways are more specific and easier to assess than behaviours. Many examination syllabuses are cross-referenced to national competency frameworks and the Institute of Managerial Finance might consider this for their examinations. Competencies are normally expressed at a number of levels; reflecting increasing demands in those competences. For example, in the Skills Framework for the Information Age (SFIA), which has four levels (3–7), level 3 is apply, level 4 is enable, level 5 advise and level 6 initiate or influence.

The competency framework usually defines competencies for each *role* within the organisation. There are typically ten or less competencies for each role. The detail for each competence has to be carefully balanced. If it is too general then employees are unsure of what is required and managers will have a problem in assessing staff against the defined competency. On the other hand, if the definition of each competence is too detailed, it can be excessively time-consuming to develop, administer and maintain. In reality, defining the appropriate level of detail is one of the key challenges of defining an effective competency framework. Performance against current competencies and the development of desired competencies becomes one of the focuses of the appraisal. Adopting an appropriate competency framework should lead to a fairer appraisal system at the National College. It should also improve the fairness of the recruitment process.

Competency frameworks may be developed internally, usually using HR consultants. KPMG developed theirs in partnership with Saville & Holdsworth Ltd (ACCA Case Study). Alternatively, the organisation can use a framework published by an external organisation – usually a trade association or a government body. The best solution is often a compromise between the two, using externally proven frameworks but tuning them so that they are relevant to the organisation. This has the added promise of providing a link between organisational and personal objectives. SFIA is published in two variants; SFIA, which is intended as a basis for tailoring to an organisation's needs, and SFIAplus which should be treated as a standard and should not be customised.

Competency frameworks were originally focused on performance management and development. However, contemporary advocates now see competency frameworks as a significant contributor to organisational performance through focusing and reviewing an individual's capability and potential. The competency framework might also be an important element in change management. The CIPD Change Agenda Focus on the Learner concluded that 'competencies have been a feature of progressive human resources development for more than a decade. What is new is their central importance as a means of providing a framework for the learner to take responsibility for their own learning'. Gold (referencing Holbeche, 1999) suggests that advocates of competencies perceive them as a mechanism for aligning organisational objectives with 'the various HR activities of recruitment, selection, appraisal, training and reward'.

ACCA Marking scheme	
	Marks
(b) 1 mark for each relevant point up to a maximum of 10 marks	10
	—
Total	**10**
	—

62 COOPER UNIVERSITY

Key answer tips

Part (a), on process redesign, is an area that candidates can often struggle with. It is regularly examined and those candidates who have practiced some similar past exam questions should have found many similarities to past requirements.

Part (b) requires a knowledge of job design and the ability to apply this knowledge to the scenario.

(a) Process redesign

Tutorial note

There are more than four problem areas to discuss. Candidates are only expected to discuss four.

The current process has a number of problems which may be causing the student comments in the student experience report.

- **Timing of coursework deadlines**

  The course appears to be badly coordinated in that similar deadlines are set for different subjects. This causes periods of high activity for students, followed by periods of low activity. It would be preferable if the workload was evened out over the duration of the programme. This would address one of the student comments:

  'We always have about four pieces of coursework to submit at the same time, and then weeks where nothing is required. I wish the university would manage our programme better'

  A solution would be to coordinate this at the start of the course. The head of department could play a more proactive role and communicate with the lecturers after coursework deadlines have been submitted, to organise a more balanced schedule across all subjects.

- **Timing of the coursework requirements publication**

The lecturer releases the coursework requirements on the VLE at the beginning of the course, and so requirements are available before the work has been covered in class. This means that students may complete the work without having all of the relevant information to help them. As one student commented:

'I completed and submitted my coursework early in order to manage my workload better, but then the lecturer gave an additional lecture to help us with our coursework. This contained very useful information, which we had not previously covered. I was not allowed to resubmit my work and so suffered from being efficient'

A solution may be to issue a timed release on the VLE, which will release the coursework details as soon as the lectures relating to that topic are complete. This could also assist with students feeling that too many pieces of coursework need completing simultaneously, as it will stagger their release.

- **Release of marks**

It appears there are three different records of student marks, and all are input manually, which could lead to errors. The student who commented that their end of year results gave a different mark would be rightly concerned that the incorrect mark had been allocated to their degree classification.

'I received one mark from the VLE system, but when my end-of-year results were released the mark was different'

As a solution, the data should be input only once, by the lecturer marking the work, and a summary of the marks should be available for download by the head of department and the administrator, should they still need to do this. The VLE system could also be linked to other systems within the university, automatically feeding marks directly into these systems, so avoiding input errors.

- **Accuracy of coursework requirements**

It appears that there are problems with the accuracy of coursework requirements, and that adjustments have been made after they have been published. As one student commented, this meant that time was wasted on work which was not necessary.

'There were errors in the initial coursework requirements, which were subsequently significantly changed. I had already started the assignment so this time was wasted'

An additional step could be added into the process, whereby another lecturer proof reads the requirements and checks them for accuracy, relevance and validity. Although this would add time to the overall process, it does not appear that time is an issue at the start of the process.

- **Marking and feedback activities**

The guideline relating to the timing of marking is a little vague, *'within two teaching weeks of the submitted coursework being collected from the course administration office by the lecturer'*, and allows the lecturer to delay collection of the scripts in order to delay the marking. This could be one of the reasons why students complain about the time taken to mark their coursework.

'It takes weeks to receive my marks, by which time I've forgotten what the coursework was about'

Additionally, there appears to be no communication to the lecturer when coursework is ready to mark. The VLE or the administration office should inform the lecturer that scripts are available.

It would appear that the lecturer marks the hard copy and types their feedback onto a new word processed document which is then uploaded on to the VLE. This appears to lead to the feedback being difficult to understand, as the feedback is on a separate document. As one student commented:

'My feedback was on a separate document so I found it difficult to relate to the coursework submitted'

There are a number of possible solutions to these problems. The hard copy seems to be redundant if the VLE system is used for feedback. One possibility is to drop the hard copy submission to the administrator so that the student makes just a single submission on the VLE. The system could send an automated email to the lecturer once a submission has been made, or the lecturer could periodically log on to the system to view submissions.

The VLE system could be upgraded to allow online marking, with the online annotation of scripts, and automatic addition of marks awarded. This would align the feedback to the coursework and would ensure that the lecturer marks the correct, up-to-date version of the work submitted. This should help eradicate the following problems.

'The lecturer said he did not receive the hard copy of my coursework but I know I handed it in. This was counted as a non-submission'

'I accidentally submitted an unfinished piece of coursework to the administration office but submitted the correct one to the system. The lecturer marked the unfinished piece'

The university guideline should be amended to suggest that marking should be completed within a set number of weeks of the coursework submission date, not the date that the lecturer collects the scripts from the administration office.

It may be possible for the administrator to be removed entirely from the process; guidelines could be issued by the head of department, and it has already been suggested that marks could be automatically fed into the administrative systems, eliminating the need for manual input.

- **System deficiencies**

The system does not appear to allow for the re-submission of completed coursework. This means that if an upload does not occur correctly, or the student uploads the wrong document, they may be assessed unfairly.

'I completed and submitted my coursework early in order to manage my workload better... I was not allowed to resubmit my work and so suffered from being efficient'

It should be possible to submit coursework more than once, with a new receipt given each time, until the final submission deadline. To ensure that the correct file is uploaded, there should be an additional process whereby the system opens the uploaded file and asks the student to verify that it is the correct, up-to-date version.

(b) **Job design**

Any changes in processes, in this case driven by customer (student) expectations, can lead to changes in job design. Both the changing process and the changing requirements of the student will lead to a number of new responsibilities and capabilities required of different staff.

There are a number of different approaches to job design, including scientific management, job enrichment, Japanese management and re-engineering. The current approach seems to be quite close to that of scientific management, but the suggestion of 'one best way' associated with this approach may be less relevant in the changing environment.

Re-engineering requires a fundamental rethink in how processes are carried out and often leads to the automation of roles. Whilst some automation may be required in this instance, it is unlikely at this stage that lecturers will be completely replaced by technology.

The Japanese model focuses on lean methods and minimisation of waste. Whilst still relevant to service industries, it is more commonly used in a manufacturing environment and is less common in an academic environment. However, some elements may be introduced here, such as a reduction in overlap of taught subjects, but is unlikely to have a major influence on changing the current job design of lecturers.

Job enrichment would seem to be a more appropriate approach to job design in this scenario, given lecturer concerns and the need to move away from the current scientific management model. This should satisfy the needs of the lecturer, the student and the university. Elements of job enrichment may arise as a result of process changes discussed in the first part of this answer.

For example, the suggested process change creates a requirement for the head of department to become more engaged with the lecturers, who would need to work with them to coordinate the assessments to meet the needs of the students. This may enrich their role as they become more involved in planning and decision-making. From the feedback, it would suggest that this coordination would also need to extend to the course content to ensure a lack of repetition and a rational continuation of studies. In addition to providing job enrichment to the lecturers, this would address the following student's concern:

'My course didn't seem well coordinated. Some topics were repeated and others failed to cover the syllabus, making it difficult to move up from one year to the next'

Lecturers, who traditionally appear to work alone, will be required to cooperate with each other, and play a much closer role in the development and well-being of students. This means that they will need to develop social and pastoral skills. They are used to working to strict guidelines and processes and it is likely that this will need to change to meet the individual requirements of students.

It would seem that job enrichment would assist in retaining lecturers, who do not seem to be stimulated by their roles. Job enrichment would allow them to be challenged as it brings in some responsibility for planning and control. Perhaps an opportunity to manage a subject, as part of the programme team, may allow for some planning and control activities in addition to planning of coursework. The analysis of student performance and feedback and lecturer involvement in determining improvements would also enrich their roles.

Job rotation, with lecturers teaching different subjects each year, may make jobs more challenging, but this in turn should make the job more interesting as it does not become routine.

Hackman and Oldham suggest that job enrichment involves five key characteristics, one of which is task identity, or the inclusion of all tasks needed to complete a process. So, if lecturers were to be responsible for the entire outcome of a subject, from the creation of the syllabus content, the writing and marking of coursework, the planning of lessons and the analysis of results, this would suggest an enriched role. Another of the five suggested characteristics is autonomy, whereby the lecturers should have discretion in the organisation of their work. A removal or reduction in the strict guidelines would help in achieving this.

Job redesign should also exploit the use of technology, even if not using it to fully re-engineer processes, and this needs to be considered in the university. Even though a VLE system exists, it is not fully utilised and manual processes still dominate.

University lecturers are knowledge workers and therefore the organisation should carefully consider how they treat them. Knowledge is a vital asset to universities and should be acquired, managed and exploited to make the most of it. The turnover of lecturers means that knowledge is being lost to the university and this needs to be controlled. If the university were to introduce activities which further develop the knowledge of lecturers, such as research seminars and attendance at conferences, this may stimulate learning and creativity and encourage lecturers to remain and to stay motivated.

In order to ensure that job redesign fully meet the needs of the university and the students, the new roles should be carefully analysed. This can be done through the use of a competency framework. The university should list all the competences required as an institute and further narrow these down to departmental and individual competences. This framework can then be used to assess any further staff development requirements.

'My lecturer wasn't very supportive when I had personal problems'

It may be that the lecturer appeared unsupportive to the student quoted in the feedback because they simply did not know how to react to that student. A competency framework for lecturers may include the addition of a section on pastoral care. The university may choose to run internal courses to ensure that staff has the acquired necessary competences in this area. There may be an existing requirement for communication skills, but this may be emphasised in relation to internal communication within the course team. Meetings may be scheduled to enable this.

The competency framework may assist in succession planning, which seems essential in a university hoping to improve its student experience, but subject to a high turnover of lecturing staff.

ACCA Marking scheme		
		Marks
(a)	Up to 2 marks for correctly diagnosing and explaining a problem with the current process. Up to 2 marks for suggesting an appropriate solution.	
	Four process problems are required giving a total of	16
(b)	1 mark for each relevant point up to a maximum of	9
Total		**25**

63   WPHA

> 🔑
>
> **Key answer tips**
>
> In part (a) the examiner has clearly set out the approach and criteria required and students need to apply this to the scenario. Part (b) required knowledge of a relatively new exam area but the model and criteria are clearly flagged in the requirement and these need to be applied to the scenario.

(a)   The head of the authority has not fully learned from the prior mistakes of WPHA's software projects. Had the four-stage process been followed, the authority might not have implemented systems which did not fulfil their needs, and caused operational difficulties.

The content of each of the stages, and their significance to this project and to WPHA, may be summarised as follows:

Stage one – Evaluate whether a COTS solution is an appropriate approach

The business case for the system should be assessed to determine whether a COTS solution is appropriate, or whether a bespoke system would be better suited to the needs of the organisation. The head of the authority seems fairly clear that a COTS would be most appropriate, although the decision appears to be mainly on cost grounds. It is likely that this would be important, given that the majority of funding is from taxation, but it should not be the only deciding factor. Complexity of a process often has an impact on whether a COTS package is appropriate, as does the availability of suitable packages. It does not seem in this scenario that the process to be automated is particularly complex and it also seems relatively routine in nature. This would need to be verified, but if it were true, then the COTS approach is probably the more appropriate.

If this stage were omitted, it is possible that the authority would make the wrong choices on the basis of cost alone. This could make the entire project a waste of time and funding as it may lead to another failure.

Stage two – Define the requirements for the new software

It is quite clear from the scenario that WPHA has suffered in the past from a failure to define requirements correctly. Hence, this is not a good reason for omitting this step entirely. The head of the authority suggests they 'go straight to stage three and look at competing packages to see which provides the best features', but it would be impossible to ascertain which was most suited if the requirements had not been defined. Indeed, if they omit this step, then it is likely that this system will also require workarounds as the previous systems have done.

Requirements defined within this step will encompass various functional and non-functional requirements. Functional requirements should include the operational processes which must be possible using this system, such as the ability to adjust payroll for one-off events. It is important to consider potential future requirements, such that the system will continue to be valuable into the future.

Non-functional requirements may include requirements from the supplier, such as support mechanisms. It would appear that WPHA is limited in its IT support provision, so this may be considered an important requirement.

There may also be technical requirements. It is likely that the authority will not wish to spend more than necessary and therefore it could be essential that the software is able to operate on the existing hardware.

Stage three – Evaluate competing packages

Given the responsibility towards the public in providing a value for money service, it is important that WPHA gets the best package in terms of meeting their needs within budgetary constraints. By evaluating competing packages, rather than simply considering one, the value for money should be greater as the best package will be selected.

The evaluation process could follow a 'tender' approach, whereby suppliers bid to supply the software required, giving feedback to them on which requirements are met (or not) and to what extent. The process should certainly be formalised, and this could help to provide accountability to the public that the best system has been selected. The tenders should be evaluated against the requirements given at stage two, in addition to any other criteria, such as implementation deadlines, overall budget, etc. The comparison may use a weighted ranking basis to ensure the decision is not based on a single factor, but gives the best option overall. Without this, a public organisation may be tempted to simply choose the cheapest option, given their budgetary limitations.

Stage four – Implement the selected package

There should be a planned implementation which includes testing, training, installation and data transfer. This is a key part of the process which connects strongly with the overall reliability of the system. A system which is not tested adequately by users (in addition to the software developers) may not meet the needs of the organisation, or may be found to be lacking user-friendliness. A failure to train staff could lead to resistance and problems in data transfer could invalidate the entire output of the software.

(b) The HR director is concerned that the focus is simply on the information technology rather than the people, processes and organisational structure. The POPIT model recognises the equal importance of each when enhancing a business process. This has been developed to take a more holistic view of process change, considering those elements which could affect the success of the project.

Processes seem to be a key area which should be considered. One process which is particularly important is the level of IT support available within the organisation. Organisations with poor IT support in place are likely to need to address this, as part of process improvement. WPHA has been subjected to system workarounds, having to 'fiddle' data to achieve the desired output in the payroll and HRM systems, for example. This is probably due to the very limited IT support available.

Manual processes should be identified to determine whether there is scope to eliminate these. It would appear that this has already been done to an extent by considering the need for an ERPS to assist in organisation-wide reporting, currently a labour-intensive process. WPHA should take the opportunity to see whether there are other such processes which could be eliminated. Given the few processes described, none of which seem to run efficiently, it is likely that there may be others.

The organisation aspect of the POPIT model considers elements of structure, management configuration and support and roles and responsibilities, for example. The board seems to support this change in the organisation, but it is likely to also impact upon the management in the individual hospitals. It needs to be considered whether the management in the separate areas of the organisation will support this change. If not, it could have an impact on the success of the change project. The board may need to convince them that the new system will make life easier for all, rather than be introduced to 'spy' on their budgeting and management control systems.

Roles and responsibilities should also be considered, specifically within the change process itself. Who will be involved in the change project and how will it affect their day-to-day roles? They will need to be given clear guidance of what is expected as well as the resources needed. For example, it seems that the head of the authority is keen to keep costs low; those involved would need to be assured that the project would be given sufficient resources to succeed.

People can be a key reason for failure of a project. If there is resistance, then it may impede the progress of the project, impact upon the end result, or even halt a project completely. Staff morale and motivation should be taken into consideration and the authority should ensure that any possible negative impact is mitigated. It may be that reward systems need to be introduced which align with the new process and ultimately the goals of the authority.

The skills also need to be considered. It would appear that the authority does not currently run a high level of information systems. Therefore, personnel may not be in possession of adequate skills for the new system. This is itself can be a cause for resistance. Training should be considered as part of the change process.

Although IT skills may not be fully present, the staff should be skilled in their individual area of work. For this reason, they should be encouraged to participate in the design of the new system. Had this happened in the past, the systems might have been designed to fully meet departmental needs, rather than finding workarounds.

Overall, therefore, the HR director is right to consider the other elements of the POPIT model, as to do so should positively affect the outcome of this project.

ACCA Marking scheme	
	Marks
(a) Up to 4 marks per heading. Up to a maximum of 16 marks overall	
(b) Up to 3 marks per heading. Up to a maximum of 9 marks overall	
Total	25

Examiner's comments

Part (a) was very similar to previous questions of its type and should have provided little difficulty to the well-prepared candidate. Some candidates scored very highly for this reason, although there were a number of candidates who could not apply their knowledge to the scenario, providing a very generic response and thus missing out on some of the available marks.

Part (b) was less well answered, requiring the discussion of other elements of the POPIT model. This was not the first time this had been examined, but it did not seem familiar to the majority of candidates. A number of candidates omitted this part question

MANAGING STRATEGIC CHANGE

64 PSI

Key answer tips

(a) The first part of the question asked candidates to analyse the nature, scope and type of strategic change at PSI. This should have been straightforward if students were aware of the different categories in the text – evolution v revolution, adaptation v reconstruction.

(b) The second part of the question asked candidates to identify and analyse the internal contextual features that could influence the success or failure of the chief executive's proposed strategic change at PSI. The terms used pointed to the Balogun and Hope Hailey model. However, even if students were not aware of this model, there were many easy points that could have been made form issues identified in the question.

(a) The proposal to develop and sell a software package for the general retail industry represents a major strategic decision for PSI. Up till now it has been relatively successful in identifying and servicing the software needs of a specialist niche market – the retail pharmacy market. In Michael Porter's terms it is currently a focused differentiator. Its proposed entry into the general retail market represents both a new product and a new market and so, using the perspective of Ansoff's growth matrix, it is a diversification strategy with high levels of risk. The proposal would lead to significant strategic change and, perhaps not surprisingly, is meeting resistance from the software development director who is responsible for a key activity in this change.

Johnson, Scholes and Whittington (JSW) argue that there is a danger in believing that there is 'only one way, or one best way, to change organisational strategies'. They believe that most strategies are profoundly influenced by earlier strategies and their success or failure. Consequently, strategies are often incremental in nature, adding to or adapting, previous or existing strategy. Rarely is the proposed change so fundamental that it challenges the existing business model and the processes and activities that support it.

JSW make use of a model developed by Balogun and Hope Hailey, which identifies four types of change which have very different degrees of impact. It is suggested that there are two key measures of change. Firstly, the *nature of change* – how big is it? *Incremental* or 'step-by-step' change does not challenge the existing way of doing things and may indeed reinforce the organisation's processes and culture. It is therefore likely to meet less resistance than *Big Bang* or quantum change, which represents significant change to most or all the organisation. Often this *Big Bang* change is necessary to respond to a crisis facing the firm, such as a major fall in profitability, and/or the appointment of a new chief executive.

Secondly, the *scope* of change process is important – how much of the firm's activities are to be changed? If the change does not alter the basic business model (or 'paradigm' in JSW's terms) then it is regarded as 'a *realignment of strategy* rather than a fundamental change in strategic direction' (JSW). However, if the proposed change is a radical challenge to the existing business model or paradigm then it is regarded as a *transformational* change.

The consideration of the two key measures of change enables the identification of four types of change. These four types are used in this answer but other models and approaches would be acceptable.

	Scope of change	
Nature of change	Realignment	Transformation
Incremental	**Adaptation**	**Evolution**
Big Bang	**Reconstruction**	**Revolution**

- *Adaptation* is a change that can be made within the current business model (realignment) and it occurs incrementally. JSW argue this is the most common form of change in organisations.

- *Reconstruction* represents significant change in the organisation, often prompted by a crisis, such as an unwelcome takeover bid, but it does not require a fundamental change to the business model. Turnaround strategies where the aim is to rapidly reduce costs or increase revenues to ensure business survival may affect the whole organisation, but not change the basic business model.

- *Evolution* is a change in strategy, which requires the business model to be significantly changed over a period of time. The perceived need for 'transformation' may be as result of careful business analysis leading to a planned evolutionary change. Alternatively, change may take place through an emergent process where the scope of change only becomes apparent once it is completed.

- *Revolution* affects the whole of the organisation and the scope of change requires a fundamental shift in the business model – the way the firm chooses to compete.

Viewed dispassionately, it appears that PSI's proposed move into the general retail market represents an evolutionary change. It is incremental because it will build on the skills, routines and beliefs of those in the organisation. However, it is transformational because the proposed move away from the current market niche to a market which requires a generic solution is a fundamental change in strategic direction. It is likely that internal processes and activities will need to significantly change for the company to successfully develop and sell the new packages. In PSI's case, the evolution is driven top-down, by the chief executive's desire to create a company which is an attractive acquisition, at which point he can realise some or all of his investment in the company.

Interestingly, the three directors may not all perceive the change as evolutionary. The entrepreneurial chief executive and the sales and marketing director may see the proposal as adaptive change, realigning the company to take advantage of a business opportunity which will lead to realising their personal goals. Indeed they may see the current product as just the specific implementation of a generic retail software solution. In contrast, the software development director is more likely to agree with our assessment of the change as evolutionary.

(b) JSW argue that successfully managing change depends on context. This context is made up of a number of factors or contingencies peculiar to the organisation under consideration. How change is managed in a relatively small privately owned firm like PSI is very different to how it might be managed in a large international firm of accountants with hundreds of partners.

Tutorial note

Balogun and Hope Hailey's contextual features are a key model in the management of strategic change.

JSW again use the work of Balogun and Hope Hailey to consider the contextual features that need to be taken into account in deciding how a strategic change programme should be managed. These features are shown in the diagram below and are used in the model answer. However candidates could adopt other models and approaches.

Contextual features and their influence on strategic change programmes

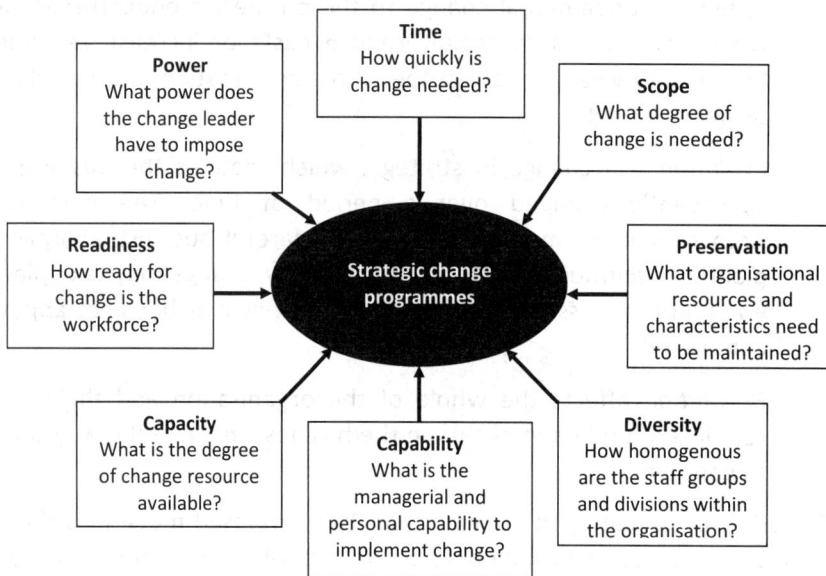

Source: Johnson, Scholes and Whittington

In the context of PSI, the following observations could be made.

- *Time* – the company is not facing any immediate financial or business problems and so there is no apparent need for rapid change. Figure 1 suggests a company that is slowly consolidating in its market place. There is no evidence of a crisis that requires urgent remedial action. It is likely that it will take a relatively long time to develop the new generic software package, particularly when the current pressures on the software development team are taken into account. They are already having problems meeting deadlines for the current product. The only urgency is that injected by the impatience of the chief executive who may want to quickly introduce change to achieve the objectives of realising his investment in the company.

The natural inclination of the software team and their director will be to use any available time to consolidate the current product and to improve its quality. In contrast, the chief executive will want to use available time to produce the new generic product. This will almost certainly lead to conflict, both within the organisation and with customers pressurising the software team for fault rectification and new requirements. The increased concentration of pharmacies into nationwide chains may also increase the power of certain customers.

- *Scope* – the degree of change should not be underestimated in a relatively small firm like PSI. Supplying a clearly defined segment supported by a vertical marketing strategy is very different to the horizontal marketing strategy required for the proposed move into the general retail market. The company has built up expertise in a niche market. It is unlikely that it will have comparable expertise in the generic retail market as well as in the other niche retail markets that it intends to target with its configurable software package.

- *Preservation* – clearly software development skills are a crucial resource and capability and must be preserved to enable the proposed strategic change. The retention of the software team's expertise and motivation is essential. If they are upset by the proposed change and disturbed by the further pressures it is likely to create then it is unlikely that they will support it. The agreement of the software development director to the change is also vital and some way of securing this must be explored. Although the proposed change is largely based on the competency of current personnel, it is likely that they will be disturbed by the increased pressure imposed on them and so there is a high probability that key employees will leave the company.

- *Diversity* – Change may be helped if there is a diversity of experience. However, change may be hampered if the organisation has followed a particular strategy for a number of years. The relative stability of the last three years and the company's stated objective to be a 'highly skilled professional company providing quality software services to the retail pharmacy industry' seem at odds with the chief executive's vision of expansion. There is also evidence to suggest that the goals of the sales force and those of the software developers are already conflicting and there seems even more opportunity for this to occur in the context of a generic retail software package. Change will be hampered by the current conflict between sales and development.

- *Capability* – The chief executive and sales and marketing director are entrepreneurial in outlook and want change to fuel growth and their personal aspirations. The software development director is much less enthusiastic as he can clearly see the implications of the proposed change in strategic direction. Furthermore, over the last three years the workforce has been relatively settled and has not been subject to much significant change. In some ways the small size of the business may make change easy to facilitate (see power), but there may also be significant barriers to change. The software development director and his staff control and implement the key activity of the new strategy. It may be difficult to overcome their lack of enthusiasm for the proposed change.

- *Capacity* is concerned with resources such as people, finance and information. More detailed analysis will be necessary to see if PSI has the necessary resources to implement the proposed change. However, evidence from the scenario is not encouraging. For example, the company has recently been criticised at a user group conference for failing to meet its proposed release deadlines. The acquisition of necessary resources will take both time and money. There is no evidence that the company has the finances to support the acquisition of new resources. It is a private company and so it will not be able to raise money through the stock market. It will rely on further investments from the current shareholders (and the software development director may be reluctant to participate in this) or on bank finance. Furthermore, it usually takes a long time to integrate software developers into a business. There is a long learning curve during which they have to learn not only how the product works, but how it is designed. Hence they are unlikely to be productive until several months after appointment and this lack of progress might again clash with the impatience of the chief executive.

- *Readiness* – There is no evidence that the organisation is ready for the type of change proposed by the chief executive. In fact the current pressure on the software development team suggests that they may not welcome the proposed new strategy. What they might be ready for is a strategy that leads to a consolidation of the pharmaceutical product so that faults are fixed and new requirements released on time.

- *Power* – the chief executive has the ultimate power in this organisation, reinforced by (through combining with the sales and marketing director) ownership of the majority of the shares. However he must secure the co-operation of the software development director to make progress. The fact that he has power may lead to him forcing through a strategy which is essentially wrong for the organisation.

Overall, an analysis of the context for change at PSI should provide warning signs to the chief executive. Although the chief executive has the power to impose change, there are concerns about the scope and capacity for change which may make it very difficult for the company to preserve its current resources and competencies. There is a real concern that these will actually be destroyed by the proposed change and this will lead to major difficulties in their current market. There is already evidence of this from the scenario. The company has been criticised at a user group conference for quality failures and there are doubts about whether planned new features will be released on time. The product is fundamental to the efficient purchasing and stock control required in contemporary pharmacies. Customers may switch to a competitor if they feel that their emerging requirements are not met with sufficient promptness and quality.

The workforce is neither ready for change nor diverse enough to welcome change. There are current conflicts between sales and development which are likely to be escalated by the proposed strategic change. Finally, there are also grave doubts about the capacity of the company to deliver the proposed change within the likely time scale required by the chief executive.

There is a concern that the chief executive will rely on managing change through coercion, which 'is the imposition of change or the issuing of edicts about change'. This is not unusual in small firms where the chief executive also has a large ownership stake in the business. It is most appropriate in crisis situations where time is of the essence and clear direction is imperative. However, PSI does not appear to be in a crisis situation. Unfortunately, however, it looks like the chief executive is about to create one!

	ACCA Marking scheme	
		Marks
(a)	Up to 2 marks for recognising that PSI is pursuing a diversification strategy	2
	Up to 2 marks for explaining the nature of change	2
	Up to 2 marks for explaining the scope of change	2
	Up to 4 marks for exploring the types of change with particular reference to the situation at PSI	4
(b)	Up to 3 marks for an analysis of each feature that could influence the success or failure of the proposed strategic change at PSI up to a maximum of 15 marks	15
	Eight possible features are described in detail in the model answer	
	A possible mark allocation (1 mark per point up to a maximum of 3 marks) for one of these features (time) is given below.	
	– Explanation of possible effect of time	
	– Recognition that time is not an issue at PSI – there is no evidence of a crisis that requires remedial action	
	– Relatively long time to develop a new product given current time pressures	
	– Impatience of the chief executive imposes arbitrary urgency	
	– Conflict between chief executive and software development director over time allocation.	
Total		**25**

Examiner's comments

This question concerned strategic change. It was the least popular of the optional questions. Candidates who attempted this question seldom scored more than half marks. The question relates to section C2 of the syllabus and it was clear that candidates, by and large, were unfamiliar with this area of the syllabus. The suggested answer is based around two models. The first part of the question asked candidates to analyse the nature, scope and type of strategic change at PSI (the company considered in the scenario). The suggested answer uses the Balogun and Hope Hailey model which specifically addresses these issues and uses these terms. Some candidates were familiar with this model and scored well as a result. The second part of the question asked candidates to identify and analyse the internal contextual features that could influence the success or failure of the chief executive's proposed strategic change at PSI. The suggested answer again uses a model attributable to Balogun and Hope Hailey. The cultural web would also have been an appropriate basis for answering this question.

However, notwithstanding a lack of familiarity with this part of the syllabus, there were plenty of clues in the case study scenario that could have provided the basis of an answer. For example:

Issues concerned with moving from supplying a specialist niche market (retail pharmacies) to a general retail market. This is quite a substantial change for a company of this size operating in a marketplace which they are currently struggling to service.

Issues concerned with the clash between the chief executive and sales director on one hand and the software development director on the other. The software development director (and his staff) are key to the success of the new strategy but are unenthusiastic about proposed changes.

Issues concerned with leadership style of the chief executive, particularly in the context of a relatively small private limited company. The chief executive has significant power and can impose change, even though this change may be wrong for the organisation. As a private company it is unclear how the organisation will finance the software product development.

Issues concerned with the problems currently experienced with the software product and the demands of existing retail pharmacy customers for new features and facilities. The company is failing to satisfy customers even in its established niche market.

Issues concerning the conflicting goals between the sales force and the software developers. There is increased pressure on the software development team which is bound to intensify if the generic software package is developed and delivered.

Issues around the need for change. The company is not facing any immediate financial or business problems and there is no evidence of a crisis requiring immediate remedial action. The exit strategy of the chief executive appears to be driving the strategy.

Even if the candidate was unfamiliar with this syllabus area, an answer to this question (particularly part b) could probably have been crafted out of the general points listed above, without resorting to any specific published model.

65   ICOMPUTE

Key answer tips

The models needed were the cultural web and Harmon's process-strategy matrix. These are common exam models which students should practice before sitting the exam. Good knowledge of these models will provide a solid foundation for a pass in this question. The key will be to use the scenario to ensure that the models are made as relevant as possible.

(a)   The culture of an organisation can be explored from a variety of perspectives and through a number of frameworks and models. No specific model or framework is required by the question so a variety of appropriate approaches are acceptable. This model answer uses selected elements of the cultural web.

Stories are told by employees in an organisation. These often concern events from the history of the organisation and highlight significant issues and personalities. In the context of iCompute, there is evidence of stories that celebrate the earlier years of the organisation when founder Ron Yeates had an important role. 'Ron used to debate responsibility for requirements changes with the customer.' In contrast modern management is perceived as weak, giving in too easily in negotiations with customers. Not only is this perceived weakness affecting morale, but it also appears to be affecting profit margins and this is an important consequence for the organisation.

Symbols include logos, offices, cars, titles and the type of language and terminology commonly used within the organisation. The language and symbols of technology appear to dominate at iCompute. Software developers constantly scan the horizon for new technological opportunities. They embrace these technologies and solutions and, as a result, continually distract the organisation. As soon as a technical direction or solution is agreed, or almost agreed, a new alternative is suggested causing doubt and delay. One of the managers claimed that the company was 'in a state of constant technical paralysis'. This paralysis has implications. Furthermore, technological objectives can quickly outweigh business and financial objectives, to the detriment of the company as a whole.

The perceived inability of managers to effectively participate in technological discussions is derided by software developers who suggest that they are technically out of touch. Ownership and understanding of up-to-date mobile phones is perceived to be important, particularly by the software developers who are an important and powerful group within the organisation.

Finally, the language of the manager who suggested that support should be outsourced is very illuminating. Support calls are not from customers but from 'incompetent end users, too lazy to read user guides'. Re-focusing managers on customers appears to be long overdue.

Routines and rituals concern the 'way we do things around here'. At iCompute this involves long working hours and after-work social activities such as football, socialising and playing computer games. The latter of these reinforces the technical focus (discussed in symbols) of employees. The routines and rituals of the organisation are largely male-oriented (football, computer games) and would probably exclude most females. This would almost certainly contribute to the company's inability to recruit and retain women employees. Furthermore, long working hours and after-work activities will also alienate employees who have to get home to undertake family commitments or simply do not wish to be 'one of the lads'. This must contribute to almost one-third of all employees leaving within their first year at the company. The consequence of this culture is an expensive recruitment and training process.

The control systems of the organisation include measurement and reward systems. Within iCompute technical expertise is only rewarded to a certain organisational level. To earn more, technically adept employees have to become managers. Evidence appears to suggest that many are unsuited to management, unable to deal appropriately with their former peers. These managers also seem anxious to show that their technical expertise is not diminishing, emphasising the importance of technology as a symbol within the organisation. Consequently, they often try to demonstrate this expertise (for example, through programming) but are unaware that this brings derision rather than respect. The absence of measurement systems has recently been recognised by management within the company. This has led to the initiation of an in-house project to improve time recording. However, software developers within the company see this as an unwelcome initiative.

Paradigm and discussion

Initially, iCompute was an entrepreneurial organisation with a significant work ethic based on long hours, technical innovation and competitive management. Although the organisation has superficially matured, the stories told by employees and the recruitment and retention of similarly minded people, has led to the continuation of a male-oriented, technologically focused workforce managed by unprepared and unsuitable managers. Managers' reaction to conflict is to avoid it (agreeing with customers over requirements), outsource it (software support) or put in formal computer systems to control it (the implementation of a time recording system). The failure to recruit and retain female staff appears to be a direct consequence of the organisational culture of iCompute. The 'work hard, play hard work ethic' is only suitable for employees with certain objectives, characteristics and minimal childcare responsibilities. This culture needs to change if the company is to employ a more balanced and representative workforce that is focused on business rather than technological objectives.

(b)   The question does not suggest an appropriate framework to use in the candidate's answer. This model answer uses the Harmon process-strategy grid as its reference point. However, credit would be given for any appropriate alternative framework.

The primary purpose of the Harmon process-strategy matrix is to ensure that organisations focus their process redesign efforts in the most appropriate areas. The grid has two axes. One is concerned with process complexity and the other with strategic importance. For each quadrant of the grid Harmon suggests appropriate solution options. For example, straightforward commodity processes with low process complexity and low strategic importance should be either outsourced or automated, using a commercial off-the-shelf software package. Elements of this grid can be applied to the three high level process applications identified at iCompute.

Advice on legal issues Bespoke systems development is risky. There is evidence in the scenario of litigation between iCompute and two of its customers. Contracts have to be carefully worded and advice taken to head off or manage legal disputes. Although iCompute is considering moving this process in-house, it seems unlikely that it will be able to afford, attract or motivate an internal legal team. Advice on legal issues could be classified as a process of high complexity and low strategic importance on the process/strategy matrix. Consequently, it seems that continuing the outsourcing arrangement should be the preferred option. The current supplier employs experts who keep up-to-date in an increasingly complex field. They can also advise on employee legislation.

Software support is provided by the company to support both its bespoke and package solutions. This used to be organised in-house, but was outsourced a year ago. Subsequent customer feedback has been poor, but even without this feedback, it could be argued that outsourcing was a poor decision. Service is one of the primary activities of Porter's value chain. It directly influences the customer's perception of the supplier and the likelihood of a repeat purchase. In the context of iCompute, feedback from end users to their managers is likely to influence future software purchasing decisions. Consequently, not only is support relatively complex (as acknowledged by the manager who made the outsourcing decision) but it is also of strategic importance to iCompute. This suggests that iCompute should bring support back in-house, perhaps by the use of an automated system.

Time recording The management of iCompute requires much more detailed time recording information, showing how long employees have worked on certain tasks and projects. Some contracts are on a time and materials basis and time recording data is required for accurate and prompt billing. However, most contracts are on a fixed price basis and better internal information is required on which to build quotes for this type of work. The company has decided to develop software in-house to support this high level process. This appears to be a questionable decision for at least three reasons. Firstly, it uses resources which could be employed on external fee-earning contracts. Secondly, accurate time recording is a key requirement in many professions (lawyers, accountants, etc.) and it seems highly likely that a range of off-the-shelf packages would be available to fulfil their needs. Finally, it could be argued that the application is a relatively simple low-value process in the process-strategy matrix and so should be carried out either through a software package or an outsourced solution.

ACCA Marking scheme	
	Marks
(a) 1 mark for each appropriate point up to a maximum of 13 marks.	13
(b) Up to 1 mark for the suggested framework.	
Up to 4 marks for each high level process.	
Up to a maximum of 12 marks for this part question.	12
Total	**25**

Examiner's comments

In part (a) most candidates appeared to be familiar with the cultural web, but they seemed happier to describe its constituent parts, rather than use it as a basis for analysis. Thus many questions were long on description but short on analysis. For example, many candidates identified long working hours and certain social activities (computer games, football) as issues, but did not suggest that these were likely to discriminate against people with families and other interests and commitments. They failed to recognise that this young, male oriented, environment was likely to lead to the high labour turnover that the company experiences, as well as the problem of recruiting and retaining female staff. High labour turnover leads to increased recruitment and training costs which affects the overall profitability of the enterprise. Other problems are also likely to arise from an unbalanced work force engaged in vacuous technical one-upmanship with their managers. The question asked for analysis and implications, not the classification of information given in the scenario into the constituent parts of the cultural web.

In part (b) most candidates used Harmon's process-strategy grid in their answer and they used it very well, leading to some excellent marks. The only significant issue in some answers was the unnecessary descriptive detail of the grid itself. The question does not ask the candidate to describe an appropriate framework, but to use it. A brief introduction to the framework would have sufficed. Again, too much description may have led to some candidates experiencing time pressure later in the paper. Some candidates tried to apply the suitability, acceptability and feasibility framework to this part question but the approach did not really work, leading to long theoretical answers that scored few points.

66   ZOOMBA

(a)   Type of change

JSW make use of a model developed by Balogun and Hope Hailey, which identifies four types of change based on two key measures of change. Firstly, the *nature of change* – how big is it? *Incremental* or 'step-by-step' change does not challenge the existing way of doing things and may indeed reinforce the organisation's processes and culture. It is therefore likely to meet less resistance than *Big Bang* or quantum change, which represents significant change to most or all the organisation. Often this *Big Bang* change is necessary to respond to a crisis facing the firm, such as a major fall in profitability, and/or the appointment of a new chief executive.

Secondly, the *scope* of change process is important – how much of the firm's activities are to be changed? If the change does not alter the basic business model (or 'paradigm' in JSW's terms) then it is regarded as 'a *realignment of strategy* rather than a fundamental change in strategic direction' (JSW). However, if the proposed change is a radical challenge to the existing business model or paradigm then it is regarded as a *transformational* change.

The consideration of the two key measures of change enables the identification of four types of change:

	Scope of change	
Nature of change	Realignment	Transformation
Incremental	**Adaptation**	**Evolution**
Big Bang	**Reconstruction**	**Revolution**

It appears that Zoomba's attempt to enter the pop up market represents an adaptation. Adaptation is a change that can be made within the current business model (realignment) and it occurs incrementally. JSW argue this is the most common form of change in organisations.

It is incremental because it will build on the existing skills, routines and beliefs of those in the organisation. There may be some changed processes, but these are likely to be small in nature. Zoomba is seeking to realign itself with the social changes that are happening in the market and take part in an emerging opportunity. There is unlikely to be a need for a complete business transformation as Zoomba continues to perform well despite increased market competition and a downturn in the economy. There will be no need for a radical redesign of the business model and, ideally, the pop ups should look and feel exactly like the product and service provided at the permanent locations.

(b)   Business change lifecycle

It can be seen that the need for the strategic change is being driven by the need to align strategy with the changes that are happening in Zoomba's environment. However, this will only be the first stage in the change management process. The business change lifecycle defines five stages in the successful realisation of change:

–   **Alignment**

This is explained in part (a) and it can be seen that Zoomba is trying to align itself with the emerging opportunity for pop up restaurants. Zoomba will also require some internal alignment and Elise Hazelwood is trying to achieve this through the creation of new business processes, improved IT systems and the management of specialist teams of staff to work within the pop ups.

–   **Definition**

At this stage the aim will be to define goals for the project and build the business case for the pop up restaurants. The project appears to have been well defined by both Grace Grove and Elise Hazelwood.

From a change management perspective it is at this stage that the potential resistance to change from staff should have been considered. Elise Hazelwood should have created plans for overcoming staff resistance by considering contextual features such as the fact that staff seemed to be taken by surprise by the change, that there is no evidence of previous such changes for staff and that little support seems to have been in place for staff in coping with the change. These elements are considered further in part (c).

–   **Design**

At the design stage, plans for new processes, systems and work methods will be made. Elise Hazelwood has clearly designed changes to elements such as the business processes and IT systems, though part (c) will suggest that further consideration should have been given to staff changes. It will also have been important to establish patterns for dealing with the resistance expected at the definition stage. A style of leadership should have been determined and as well as a consideration of changes in staff routines and controls.

–   **Implementation**

The detailed designs will then be put into place. Change and business owners will play their part and a communication plan will be necessary for all key stakeholders.

Change management will now become vital. Whether a participative, coercive or alternative approach is necessary (which will be determined at the definition and design stages), it will be important that the change is achieved. It can be seen that the change in Zoomba failed because of poor implementation and this is explored further in the next part of the answer.

–   **Realisation**

This is the stage that Zoomba now finds itself in. The aim is to ensure that the alignment has taken place but that does not appear to be the case for Zoomba. It is likely that further changes will be required as the alignment continues. In the next part of the answer it will be argued that these changes will be directed more at staff than at other areas of the business system.

(c)   **Reasons for the project failure**

A useful model for explaining the failures in the system is the POPIT model. The POPIT model provides four views of a business system that must be considered for the successful implementation of business change. These elements must work together and be aligned for successful change to be realised. A failure in one area can lead to a failure across the entire business system. The areas to be considered are as follows:

Processes must be well defined, efficient, documented and understood. Zoomba appears to have done this. Elise Hazelwood appears to have sought efficiency in areas such as venue location, food production, material supplies, etc. The lessons learnt review appears to highlight that these areas have worked well in the project.

Information Technology needs to support the changes that are taking place within the system. It needs to provide the relevant information at the point that it is needed. Elise Hazelwood's previous IT experience appears to have helped here. The IT system worked well and controls were considered to ensure that risks were reduced.

There was some attempt made on the *organisation* for success. Project team staff were appointed as managers at the pop ups and arrangements were put in place for the secondment of staff. But this could have been much better organised. Job roles were unclear, visitors observed disorganised service and staff appeared to be unaware of potential secondments to the pop ups. This is related to the final view on the business system – its people.

People in the organisation need to have the right skills and motivation to carry out the tasks. This is an area that Elise Hazelwood appears to have ignored almost entirely. She has put managers in place at the pop ups but hasn't really considered the people that they will be managing. There is evidence of poor motivation in the poor service provided to customers and some of that may be down to a lack of consideration of job design. Seconding staff into pop ups without prior notice or explanation needs to be better planned and organised.

There also appears to be evidence of a lack of staff training (service was slower than usual and staff complained of spending too much time learning new, temporary processes) as well as a failure to consider staff development (one staff member complained of a lost development opportunity rather than an enhanced experience).

These are problems that can be rectified for future pop ups. But they highlight that a business system is made up of many components, and a failure to consider one of these views can harm the successes made in other areas.

67   STRATEGIES

> 🔑
>
> **Key answer tips**
>
> Marks would be available in this question for bringing in the Johnson, Scholes and Whittington approach to strategic planning.

(a)   Strategy formulation is a continuous process of refinement based on past trends, current conditions and estimates of the future, resulting in a clear expression of strategic direction, the implementation of which is also planned in terms of resource allocation and structure. The strategy then comes about or is realised in actuality. This process is shown in the diagram below as the planned intended strategy (also known as the deliberate strategy). In Honda's case the plan was to compete with the larger European and American bikes of 250ccs and over. However, the actual strategy pursued by a company over a three- to five-year period may diverge from the deliberate strategy for many reasons, as outlined below:

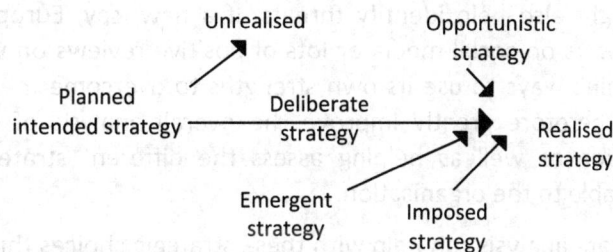

The obvious reason is that an intended strategy is not implemented because its underlying assumptions turn out to be invalid or because the pace of developments overtakes it. Factors affecting the strategy realisation will include changes in the organisation's external environment e.g. changes in the market for the goods and services that the firm produces and in the nature of the competition facing the company, and also its internal environment. Honda had problems with their large machines and resorted to selling the small 50cc bikes just to raise money.

Mintzberg argues that strategies can emerge, perhaps as a result of the processes of negotiation, bargaining and compromise, rather than be due to a deliberate planning process. This emergent strategy would be one that arises from an external stimulus not envisaged in the planned strategy. For example, if a supplier, pursuing modern ideas on supplier/customer relationships, encouraged a partnership approach to sourcing.

It is easy to imagine that buyers in the customer organisation might see benefits in this, and could pursue the idea to the point where sourcing strategy took on an aspect, not at all contemplated when planned strategic developments were laid down.

Sometimes changes from the intended strategy come about in opportunistic or entrepreneurial ways, e.g. an enterprise can find a new process or resource that enables dramatic cost reductions. Finally, strategy may be imposed. For example, recession and threat of a takeover may force a strategy of cost cutting and retrenchment. Technological developments may cause an organisation to develop new products to replace the ones that have become obsolescent.

(b)   **Big data**

Big data is a term that is commonly used to describe the large amount of data that exists, often in digital form, about human behaviour, tastes and interactions. For example, social network users will often have a list of interests in their profile or pages that they like, mobile phone users will download lots of similar apps, website users will recommend products to others or leave reviews of products that they use, or customers might provide feedback on the service that they have received (good or bad). Organisations are now making large IT investments towards managing and maintain big data with a view to revealing patterns and trends.

It is these trends and patterns that businesses are hoping to exploit from a strategic perspective. Environmental analysis using models such as PESTLE or Porter's 5 forces has always been based on a great degree of subjectivity. Analysis of big data could help reduce this subjectivity. Honda could, for example, examine customer data to consider changes in demographics or trends towards bikes with better fuel economy or with larger engines. It does not need to be limited to just customer data, the analysis could be broadened to examine the data of non-customers or non-motorcyclists. This is likely to create new strategic opportunities for the business and could help in the development of new products or new markets.

It might also help identify threats. If a new, say, European bike is gaining lots of followers on social media or lots of positive reviews on websites, then Honda could examine ways to use its own strengths to overcome these. The analysis of big data will therefore greatly improve the overall analysis of the organisations strategic position as well as helping assess the different strategic choices that might be available to the organisation.

Big data analysis can help with these strategic choices through the use of techniques such as predictive modelling. This will provide predictions on future behaviour based on past behaviour and interactions. Again, this might not even have to come from the behaviour of existing or past customers. Honda could analyse how customers of rivals have behaved when a new type of engine was launched or a new marketing initiative trialled. It might be possible to determine what type of product designs are popular with different demographics and this will influence what new products or markets are targeted by the organisation.

Big data analysis will then influence how the strategic choices are implemented. The analysis can be used to shape the content and channel(s) used for marketing, for example. Honda might determine that a new target audience is better targeted via peer-to-peer recommendations that through traditionally bus advertising, say. Big data will also play a key role and new metrics used to monitor and assess the success of strategic implementation. Analysis will help answer questions such whether positive responses are being created by customers etc.

Analysis of big data is not without its costs and risks. But the strategic rewards can be immense. This is why many organisations now have deliberate investments aimed at getting the most from the big data that is out there.

68 WEBFILMS

🔑

Key answer tips

In part (a) the examiner is very clear on which features should be assessed and this should help students who are less familiar with the model. As long as students focus on applying the model rather than explaining it then they should score well in this part of the question. Part (b) concerned organisational structures and, whilst not difficult, it is a rarely examined syllabus area. This reinforces the examiner's view that a wide syllabus coverage is required in order to be confident of success in this paper.

(a) Contextual features

The Balogun and Hope Hailey model is used to explore the contextual features of change which need to be considered if that change is to be successful. Five of those contextual features were explored in this question.

Time – This looks at how quickly change is needed. There does not appear to be an immediate need for change as the business is doing well, but is looking at how to successfully compete in the future. Therefore there should be sufficient time to adequately plan the change, leading to a greater chance of success. Indeed, the actions leading towards the change are likely to be incremental, at least internally. However, the CEO has suggested that the entire switchover to the new strategy needs to take place in a single event. From an external perspective, this may be viewed as a 'Big Bang' change, which may lead to greater resistance from those external stakeholders affected by the change. However, if the marketing campaign is well-planned, then change may appear incremental, as customers will have time to get used to the changes which will be implemented.

Scope – This refers to the degree of change required. This may be considered a realignment of existing processes, or a transformational strategic change. Webfilms is planning to move from being a focused differentiator to a hybrid company operating with a broader customer base and a greater focus on cost efficiencies. This is a leap in strategy which needs to be very well planned in order for it to be successful. It is not impossible for a company to move around the strategy clock, but it may take time to gain acceptance from its customers. The continuing focus on quality, which may also be considered under preservation, should help with the success of the strategic change.

Scope also considers the type of business being carried out. This is being expanded to include services which have not previously been offered (e.g. broadband provision). The way in which business is to be carried out (boundary-less working) is also changing. These are areas unfamiliar to Webfilms and may influence the success of the change unless appropriate expertise is acquired.

Readiness – This examines how ready the workforce is for change. Webfilms has successfully undergone transformational change in the past and so its workforce may be well prepared for it to happen again. However, it appears there is resistance from a key player in this strategy. The creative director and his team are important to the success of the change and their resistance could jeopardise the strategy. The CEO will need to bring them on board for it to be successful.

Preservation – This looks at the organisational resources and characteristics which will be maintained throughout the change. The main business of the company will stay the same: offering programmes through the internet. This should ensure that the existing customer base remains, as long as it is still done successfully. However, the failure to preserve the advertisement-free approach may alienate existing customers.

Power – This looks at the power the change leader has to impose the change on the organisation. The CEO is the person driving the change and has the power to do so by virtue of her position in the organisation. She also has the experience, as she transformed the company from a postal-based to internet-based provider. However, it appears she plans to do this using force rather than consensus ('this is going to happen. It's up to you whether you want to be involved...'). This use of power may initially deter resistance, but it may have the opposite effect in the long term, demotivating the critically important creative development team.

There seems little doubt that the CEO is again suggesting transformational change as the company reinvents itself. Whether it is incremental or big bang depends on perspective. As mentioned before, internally it could be perceived as incremental and so the change would be classified as evolution. However, to external stakeholders it might appear as big bang, and hence represents revolutionary change.

(b)   **Boundary-less organisation**

Boundary-less organisation structures increase flexibility of organisations in dynamic environments and require collaboration with external parties to work. The lack of traditional structures and use of external relationships is becoming common in organisation, particularly those in a hi-tech environment. Boundary-less organisations are frequently dispersed over geographical borders and so require good communications technology and integrated systems to succeed.

Three forms of boundary-less working are mentioned in the scenario, as options for change in Webfilms.

Hollow organisation structure – where non-core processes are outsourced to external providers. This does not seem to be far-reaching enough for Webfilms. It would assist with cost efficiencies but would probably prevent them from being able to implement the full new strategy as it lacks the resources to achieve this. However, if it considers some of the new services to be incremental and non-core, such as the online gaming service, then these could be outsourced to a company with expertise in this area. Similarly, advertising might be defined as non-core and sub-contracted to an organisation which has experience in this area. There may also be administrative services within the company, such as information technology, payroll, accounts, which could be outsourced.

Modular organisation structure – a hollow organisation which further outsources some elements of the production process. This would assist Webfilms in carrying out their new strategy. It could outsource some of the production processes for programmes, making use of external expertise to deliver those programmes with which it has little or no experience, such as documentaries and current affairs programmes. It could also outsource the translation of programmes into different languages. This would allow Webfilms' own creative staff to continue to provide programmes which they are familiar with and might ally some of the fears and concerns of the creative director.

Virtual organisation structure – an organisation with no formal geographical structure, but operates through a series of linked IT systems, partnerships and collaborative agreements. This appears to be most appropriate to Webfilms. It would incorporate the modular structure described above but further extend this to incorporate a range of agreements with external parties together with a more flexible approach to internal working. For example, agreements would be needed with providers of previously screened programmes, with advertisers and with local technical support services for broadband provision. Relationships may have to be developed with competitors and Webfilms may need to be willing to make compromises, for example, by offering competitors access to original Webfilms programmes and films. Internally, Webfilms could operate flexibly over geographical boundaries, allowing them to have local personnel in place to better understand the viewing preferences of the different geographical locations which it serves.

Overall, it seems that boundary-less working is necessary if the new strategy is to be successful. It will not only increase the flexibility of operations, but will also contribute towards cost efficiencies.

ACCA Marking scheme		
		Marks
(a)	Up to 1 mark for each relevant point up to a maximum of 3 marks for each contextual factor. Five contextual factors giving a maximum of 15 marks plus 1 mark in classifying the change as per the Balogun and Hope Hailey model. Total of 16 marks.	
	Total	**16**
(b)	Up to 1 mark for each relevant point up to a maximum of 3 marks for each configuration. Three configurations giving a maximum of 9 marks.	
	Maximum	**9**
Total		**25**

Examiner's comments

In part (a) some candidates scored highly on this question and showed a clear ability to apply the model and to use it to assess how each element would affect the likely success of the strategy. However some candidate responses developed outside of the scope of the question, covering all elements of the change model, rather than just those specified. Those candidates did not lose marks for this, but did not gain marks for those elements of their response and put themselves under unnecessary time pressure.

Part (b) was less well answered, despite the provision of definitions of each approach. Better candidates recognised that simply re-writing the scenario (in this case the definitions provided) would not gain marks and added value by applying the concepts to the information provided in the scenario.

Section 4

ANSWERS TO SCENARIO-BASED QUESTIONS

69   OCEANIA NATIONAL AIRLINES (ONA)   Walk in the footsteps of a top tutor

Tutor's top tips

Approach to the question

*Always start the large, compulsory question by reading the **first paragraph only** so that information on the company, its market etc. can be determined.*

From the first paragraph in this question you can discover:

- *there are 2 distinct markets – tourists and business users*

- *the company runs an airline business*

- *they aim to exploit the growth in business and leisure travel*

*Now look at the requirements **before** reading the rest of the question. This will ensure that you read the question in the correct manner, do not need to read the question more than once, save time and can begin planning.*

Requirement

(a)   *Evaluation of strengths and weaknesses*

The key to most requirements is to choose the most appropriate model. The examiner suggests that more than one model can score marks, but that does not mean that you have to use a lot of models. The key will be to choose the most appropriate model, build an answer around that model, and then, if you have time, to briefly show how other models could have been useful.

The examiner clearly states that opportunities and threats are not required, so the SWOT model would be inappropriate. However, the first part of the model (SW) could have been used – this is what the official answer does. An assessment of strengths and weaknesses is an internal assessment and therefore an internal tool such as the resource audit or the value chain would have been most appropriate.

It is important to choose the model with which you are most comfortable. For the purpose of this walkthrough the resource audit (sometimes called the 'M's model') is chosen. A brief plan of the resource audit should be set up on a blank page with space for each of the key areas (i.e. manpower, machinery, markets, money etc.). This can be used to record key information in the question as you read it, and also it should ensure that you do not miss anything important from your answer.

(b)   Strategy evaluation

The question asks for an explanation and evaluation of a 'no frills' strategy. The official text for the syllabus suggests that strategies are best evaluated using three criteria: feasibility, suitability and acceptability. So again, these headings can be recorded on a planning page and you can add points to them as you read the question.

(c)   Strategic choice

The key again will be to determine which model will be most appropriate. There are 3 choices: Porter's generics, the strategic clock or Ansoff. The first two models will be important if ONA want to improve their position, the second would be most appropriate if ONA are looking for new ways to grow. It is not entirely clear which goal is most relevant at this stage, so part of the task when reading the question should be to determine which model is most relevant.

Reading the question

*Now **actively** read the question i.e. as you read it you should add all relevant points to your planning page(s).*

The key issues to pick out from the question as are as follows:

- *ONA serve two markets – the regional and international sectors. Therefore, when choosing strategies in part c), you should choose a strategy for each sector.*
- *The company's strengths seem to be laid out clearly in the section on image, service and employment. Weaknesses are less apparent and it is therefore very likely that they will arise from numerical analysis of the three sets of data that have been provided.*
- *The market is very competitive and there have been lots of new entrants (especially at the 'no frills' part of the market).*
- *Sales channels appear to be a critical success factor and it will be important that answers discuss the issues between using website sales and travel agent sales.*
- *In the section on future strategy it appears that ONA want to solve their existing problems rather than try new markets or diversify, so for part c) of the question Porter's generics or the strategic clock may be more important than the Ansoff matrix.*

Answering the question

Part (a) Strengths and weaknesses

This is the analysis part of the question and therefore one of the most important things to remember will be to include an analysis of the numbers that have been provided in the question. There are no marks for illustrating, explaining or calculating ratios so don't get bogged down on these. Also, you should only need to calculate the ratios for 20X4 and 20X6 rather than doing the calculations for all three years which would add little to your answer. Instead, allocate around half of the total marks for quantitative analysis (therefore 10 marks) and work on the basis of around 2 marks for each well explained point. This means that you should choose 5 or 6 key ratios and explain why they might have changed and whether they create a strength or weakness for the company.

For example, there has been a 2.5% fall in net profit margin which could be down to poor control of overheads (e.g. wages and salaries) and this indicates a weakness of the business.

For other strengths and weaknesses, go through as many of the 'M's' in the resource audit as possible. Remember for each one that you should explain why it is a strength or weakness. If we take 'manpower' as an example; the service provided and motivation of staff can be seen as a strength of ONA. But on the other hand, the fact that salaries are above industry average and have attached expensive benefits will create a weakness for the company.

This is just one part of the resource audit, but all of the elements can be considered in the same manner in order to create a complete answer to this part of the question when combined with the quantitative analysis.

Part (b) Strategy evaluation

The examiner explains that the first part of this section on the features of a 'no frills' approach was well answered.

For the second part it is very important to reach the same conclusion as the company – that this is an inappropriate strategy for ONA. The 3 professional marks available are likely to be available for justifying this position.

If you use the feasibility, suitability and acceptability model suggested by Johnson, Scholes and Whittington you should achieve a good, well balanced answer. Some of the key issues might be as follows:

(i)   Feasibility

This examines whether a strategy is possible based on a company's current resources and position. Therefore it will be important to link it back to some of the issues discovered in part a).

The key issues to discuss might be:

- ONA have higher wage rates than rivals

- because ONA have older aircraft their maintenance costs are likely to be higher

- it would be easier to achieve if the sales channels were changed so that more sales were made via a website than through the travel agents

- ONA may need to seek out alternative airports with lower landing fees and baggage handling costs etc.

- it should be possible to copy the ideas of successful 'no frills' airlines and avoid their past mistakes

(ii) Suitability

This examines whether the strategy is appropriate for the company's environment and whether it will solve the businesses problems.

The key issues to discuss might be:

- there is already significant competition in this part of the market who will have lower cost bases and more experience at offering a no frill service

- these rivals may also react aggressively to any attempt by ONA to enter the market

- in order for ONA to achieve this strategy greater economies of scale would be necessary. This would mean an investment in more aircraft, more destinations etc. but it is likely that ONA would still be behind the scale of rivals

(iii) Acceptability

This area examines whether the strategy will be acceptable to the key stakeholders of the business.

The key issues to discuss might be:

- this is likely to require a reduction in customer service – something that ONA prides itself on. This may be unacceptable to both customers and shareholders

- moving to alternative/cheaper destinations may not be acceptable to business users

- a change of selling channels may not be acceptable to the citizens of Oceania who have a culture of using travel agents to make their bookings.

Overall, there are 13 marks available (excluding the professional marks) which allows for about 4 marks for each of the three evaluation criteria. So you should aim to cover 2 issues under each of the headings above and finish with an overall conclusion that this is an inappropriate strategy.

Part (c) Strategic choice

As already stated it will probably be more relevant in this section to use a competitive strategy model, such as Porter's generics or the strategic clock, than to use the Ansoff matrix. Also, as there are 2 market segments (regional and international) then the answer can choose strategies for each segment. There are around 4/5 marks available for each segment so you should only have to make 2 points for each one. The key will be to make the points relevant to the company in the question and to avoid suggesting a no frills approach that has already been discarded in part b).

Overall

The key points to take away from this question and apply to other compulsory, strategic questions are:

- find the requirements before reading the full question

- for each part of the question, choose one key model and apply it to the scenario

- include quantitative analysis in all analysis answers

- allocate your time appropriately between all sections of the requirement.

(a) **Strengths**

(1) Strong brand identity particularly with the citizens of Oceania. A quoted recent survey suggested that 90% of people preferred to travel ONA for regional flights and 70% preferred to travel ONA for international flights. 85% of respondents were proud of their airline and felt that it projected a positive image of Oceania.

(2) ONA have an exemplary safety record. There have been no fatal accidents since its formation in 1997.

(3) Excellent customer service recognised by the Regional Airline of the Year award and the Golden Bowl as provider of the best airline food in the world.

(4) High business class load factors, particularly in the regional sector. This appears to suggest that ONA are particularly strong in the business market.

(5) Relatively strong cargo performance. In the period 20X4–20X6 when passenger air travel revenue had increased by 12% (and air travel to Oceania by 15%) and cargo revenue by 10%, ONA increased cargo revenue by 11%, just above the industry average.

(6) Financially, although the net profit margin has fallen (see weaknesses), the gross profit margin remains relatively stable. Hence the cost of sales (excluding wages, salaries and financing) has moved roughly in line with revenue. The gross profit margin for 20X4 is 37.04% and for 20X6 it is 36.98%, very little change.

(7) The settlement of debt is an important issue for an organisation. The average settlement period for receivables is concerned with how long it takes for customers to pay the amounts owing. This is low at ONA (29 days) and reducing, suggesting effective credit control and an industry where many customers pay before they are able to use the service. It is likely that much of the debt is tied-up with commission sales and cargo services.

(8) The gearing ratio measures the contribution of long-term lenders to the long-term capital structure of the business. Gearing for ONA remained relatively stable during the period 20X4–20X6. It stood at 71.13% in 20X6, a marginal increase on the 20X4 figure of 71.05%.

(9) Conveniently scheduled flights to business travel for the regional sector. Allows business to be conducted in one day, with a flight out in the morning and a flight back in the evening. Most cities in this sector also receive an extra flight in the middle of the day.

(10) Highly motivated, courteous employees.

Weaknesses

(1) High cost base. The most tangible evidence of this is the average pilot salary given in Table 1. Pilot salary costs appear to be over 10% higher than their competitors. The scenario also suggests that ONA pay above industry average salaries, offer excellent benefits (such as free health care) and have a generous non-contributory pension scheme. Other hints of high costs (insourced non-core activities such as catering, highly unionised) are also mentioned in the scenario. High costs are also hinted at in Tables 1 and 2, with ONA having relatively older aircraft, presumably requiring more maintenance, and lower utilisation hours than their competitors. The average wage of an employee rose by about 7% during the period under consideration.

(2) Poor growth rate. The scenario makes the point that in the period 20X4–20X6, passenger air travel revenue has increased world-wide by 12% (and revenue from air travel to Oceania by 15%). However, ONA only recorded a 4.6% increase in passenger revenue in this period.

(3) Low frequency of flights in the international sector, where there is on average only one flight per day to each destination. This makes it very difficult for the airline to gain any operational economies of scale in this sector.

(4) The mixed airliner fleet is largely a result of the merger of the two airlines that formed ONA. The airframes for the bulk of the fleet are from two competing manufacturers (Boeing and Airbus). The information given in Table 1 suggests that the two aircraft types (Boeing 737 and A320) are very similar. The need to service and maintain two aircraft types creates an unnecessary cost.

(5) Although the airline offers on-line booking, it does not currently offer on-line check-in. Hence overheads still remain in the embarkation process. Business travellers particularly favour on-line check-in as it means they can leave their homes and meetings later. In 20X6 the New Straits Times reported a recent global survey that showed that air travellers spend an average of four days in a year in queues at airline check-in counters.

(6) Table 2 shows below average load factors in standard class seating. This is particularly significant on international sector flights.

(7) Return on capital employed (ROCE) and return on ordinary shareholders' funds (ROSF) are important measures of profitability. Both of these ratios show a significant fall in 20X6. The fall can be largely attributed to a decline in net profit due to increases in costs outstripping increases in revenue.

(8) The reduction in profitability is also revealed by the net profit margin which has reduced from 12.10% in 20X4 to 9.66% in 20X6. However, the gross profit percentage remains relatively stable and so it appears that it is the increased cost of wages, salaries and borrowing that has caused ONA profitability problems.

(9) Efficiency ratios are used to examine how well the resources of the business are managed. The sales revenue per employee has reduced during the period, perhaps suggesting a reduction in productivity that needs to be investigated. In contrast, the average settlement period for payables shows a marginal rise.

Trade payables provide a free source of finance, but extending the average settlement period too far can lead to loss of goodwill with suppliers. ONA already have a high settlement period for payables, although this may be typical in this industry.

(10) Liquidity (both current and acid test ratios) fell significantly in 20X6. This may affect the ability of the company to meet its short-term obligations.

(11) Finally, the interest cover ratio has declined considerably during the period covered in Table 1. In 20X4, it was 5.44, but by 20X6 it had declined to 3.73. The lower the level of profit coverage, the greater the risk to lenders that interest payments will not be met.

Credit will also be given to points which are discernable from the scenario but have not been covered above. The extent of unionisation and the percentage of sales made through commission sales might be thought of as strengths or weaknesses depending upon perspective.

(b)   (i)   A 'no frills' strategy combines low price with low perceived benefits of the product or service. It is primarily associated with commodity goods and services where customers do not discern or value differences in the products or services offered by competing suppliers. In some circumstances the customer cannot afford the better quality product or service of a particular supplier. 'No frills' strategies are particularly attractive in price-sensitive markets. Within the airline sector, the term 'no frills' is associated with a low cost pricing strategy. In Europe, at the time of writing, easyJet and Ryanair are the two dominant 'no frills' low-cost budget airlines. In Asia, AirAsia and Tiger Airways are examples of 'no frills' low-cost budget carriers. 'No frills' strategies usually exist in markets where buyers have high power coupled with low switching costs and so there is little brand loyalty. It is also prevalent in markets where there are few providers with similar market shares. As a result of this the cost structure of each provider is similar and new product and service initiatives are quickly copied. Finally a 'no frills' strategy might be pursued by a company entering the market, using this as a strategy to gain market share before progressing to alternative strategies.

(ii)   'No frills' low-cost budget airlines are usually associated with the following characteristics. Each of these characteristics is considered in the context of Oceania National Airlines (ONA).

- Operational economies of scale

  Increased flight frequency brings operational economies and is attractive to both business and leisure travellers. In the international sector where ONA is currently experiencing competition from established 'no frills' low-cost budget airlines ONA has, on average, one flight per day to each city. It would have to greatly extend its flight network, flight frequency and the size of its aircraft fleet if it planned to become a 'no frills' carrier in this sector. This fleet expansion appears counter to the culture of an organisation that has expanded very gradually since its formation. Table 1 shows only three aircraft added to the fleet in the period 20X4–20X6. It is likely that the fleet size would have to double for ONA to become a serious 'no frills' operator in the international sector. In the regional sector, the flight density, an average of three flights per day, is more characteristic of a 'no frills' airline. However, ONA would have to address the relatively low utilisation of its aircraft (see Tables 1 and 2) and the cost of maintenance associated with a relatively old fleet of aircraft.

- Reduced costs through direct sales

  On-line booking is primarily aimed at eliminating commission sales (usually made through travel agents). 'No frills' low-cost budget airlines typically achieve over 80% of their sales on-line. The comparative figure for ONA (see Table 2) is 40% for regional sales and 60% for international sales, compared with an average of 84% for their competitors. Clearly a major change in selling channels would have to take place for ONA to become a 'no frills' low-cost budget airline. It is difficult to know whether this is possible. The low percentage of regional on-line sales seems to suggest that the citizens of Oceania may be more comfortable buying through third parties such as travel agents.

- Reduced customer service

  'No frills' low-cost budget airlines usually do not offer customer services such as free meals, free drinks and the allocation of passengers to specific seats. ONA prides itself on its in-flight customer service and this was one of the major factors that led to its accolade as Regional Airline of the Year. To move to a 'no frills' strategy, ONA would have to abandon a long held tradition of excellent customer service. This would require a major cultural change within the organisation. It would also probably lead to disbanding the award winning (Golden Bowl) catering department and the redundancies of catering staff could prove difficult to implement in a heavily unionised organisation.

Johnson, Scholes and Whittington have suggested that if an organisation is to 'achieve competitive advantage through a low price strategy then it has two basic choices. The first is to try and identify a market segment which is unattractive (or inaccessible) to competitors and in this way avoid competitive pressures to erode price.' It is not possible for ONA to pursue this policy in the international sector because of significant competition from established continental 'no frills' low-cost budget airlines. It may be a candidate strategy for the regional sector, but the emergence of small 'no frills' low-cost budget airlines in these countries threaten this. Many of these airlines enter the market with very low overheads and use the 'no frills' approach as a strategy to gain market share before progressing to alternative strategies.

Secondly, a 'no frills' strategy depends for its success on margin. Johnson, Scholes and Whittington suggest that 'in the long run, a low price strategy cannot be pursued without a low-cost base'. Evidence from the scenario suggests that ONA does not have a low cost base. It continues to maintain overheads (such as a catering department) that its competitors have either disbanded or outsourced. More fundamentally (from Table 2), its flight crew enjoy above average wages and the whole company is heavily unionised. The scenario acknowledges that the company pays above industry salaries and offers excellent benefits such as a generous non-contributory pension. Aircraft utilisation and aircraft age also suggest a relatively high cost base. The aircraft are older than their competitors and presumably incur greater maintenance costs. ONA's utilisation of its aircraft is also lower than its competitors. It seems highly unlikely that ONA can achieve the changes required in culture, cost base and operations required for it to become a 'no frills' low-cost budget airline. Other factors serve to reinforce this. For example:

- Many 'no frills' low-cost budget airlines fly into airports that offer cheaper taking off and landing fees. Many of these airports are relatively remote from the cities they serve. This may be acceptable to leisure travellers, but not to business travellers – ONA's primary market in the regional sector.

- Most 'no frills' low-cost budget airlines have a standardised fleet leading to commonality and familiarity in maintenance. Although ONA has a relatively small fleet it is split between three aircraft types. This is due to historical reasons. The Boeing 737s and Airbus A320s appear to be very similar aircraft. However, the Boeings were inherited from OceaniaAir and the Airbuses from Transport Oceania.

In conclusion, the CEO's decision to reject a 'no frills' strategy for ONA appears to be justifiable. It would require major changes in structure, cost and culture that would be difficult to justify given ONA's current position. Revolution is the term used by Balogun and Hope to describe a major rapid strategic change. It is associated with a sudden transformation required to react to extreme pressures on the organisation. Such an approach is often required when the company is facing a crisis and needs to quickly change direction. There is no evidence to support the need for a radical transformation. This is why the CEO brands the change to a 'no frills' low-cost budget airline as 'unnecessary'. The financial situation (Table 3) is still relatively healthy and there is no evidence of corporate predators. It can be argued that a more incremental approach to change would be beneficial, building on the strengths of the organisation and the competencies of its employees. Moving ONA to a 'no frills' model would require seismic changes in cost and culture. If ONA really wanted to move into this sector then they would be better advised to start afresh with a separate brand and airline and to concentrate on the regional sector where it has a head start over many of its competitors.

(c)   Within the strategy clock, ONA might consider both differentiation and focus. A differentiation strategy seeks to provide products or services that offer different benefits from those offered by competitors. These benefits are valued by customers and so can lead to increased market share and, in the context of ONA, higher seat utilisation. Differentiation is particularly attractive when it provides the opportunity of providing a price premium. In other words, margins are enhanced through differentiation. Air travellers may be willing to pay more to travel with an airline that offers seat allocation and free in-flight food and drinks.

However, such a broad-based differentiation strategy may be inappropriate for ONA because of the need to service both business and leisure travellers. Consequently, the potential strategy also has to be considered in the context of the two sectors that the company perceives that it services. In the regional sector a focused differentiation strategy looks particularly attractive. Here, the strategy focuses on a selected niche or market segment. The most obvious focus is on business travel and building the company's strengths in this sector. This focus on the business traveller might be achieved through:

- Ensuring that flight times are appropriate for the business working day. This is already a perceived strength of the company. This needs to be built on.

- Providing more space in the aircraft by changing the seating configuration – and the balance between business and standard class. ONA currently has a low seat occupancy rate and a reduction in seat capacity could be borne.

- Fewer passengers in the aircraft may also lead to improved throughput times. Loading and unloading aircraft is quicker, minimising the delays encountered by the traveller.

- Providing supporting business services – lounges with fax and internet facilities.

- Speeding the process of booking and embarkation (through electronic check-in), so making the process of booking and embarkation easier and faster.

- Providing loyalty schemes that are aimed at the business traveller.

Although this focused differentiation is aimed at the business customer it is also likely that particular aspects of it will be valued by certain leisure travellers. Given the strong regional brand (people from Oceania are likely to travel ONA) and the nature of the leisure travel in this sector (families visiting relatives) it seems unlikely that there will be a significant fall off in leisure travel in the regional sector.

In the international sector, the strategic customer is less clear. This sector is serving both the leisure and business market and is also competing with strong 'no frills' competitors. The nature of customer and competition is different. A strategy of differentiation could still be pursued, although perhaps general differentiation (without a price premium) may be more effective with the aim of increasing seat occupancy rate. This sector would also benefit from most of the suggested improvements of the regional sector – providing more space in aircraft, faster passenger throughput, electronic check-in etc. However, these small changes will not address the relatively low flight frequency in this sector. This could be addressed through seeking alliances with established airlines in the continental countries that it services. Simple code share agreements could double ONA's frequencies overnight. Obviously, ONA would be seeking a good cultural fit – the 'no frills' low-cost budget airlines would not be candidates for code shares.

ONA's perception of market segmentation, reflected in splitting regional from international travel and distinguishing leisure from business appears to be a sensible understanding of the marketplace. However, it might also be useful for them to consider on-line customers and commission customers (travel agents) as different segments. Perceiving travel agents as the strategic customer would lead to a different strategic focus, one in which the amount and structure of commission played an important part.

Finally, whichever strategy ONA adopts, it must continue to review its operational efficiency. An important strategic capability in any organisation is to ensure that attention is paid to cost-efficiency. It can be argued that a continual reduction in costs is necessary for any organisation in a competitive market. Management of costs is a threshold competence for survival. ONA needs to address some of the weaknesses identified earlier in the question. Specific points, not covered elsewhere, include:

- Improved employee productivity to address the downward decline in efficiency ratios.

- Progressive standardisation of the fleet to produce economies of scale in maintenance and training. This should reduce the cost base.

- Careful monitoring of expenditure, particularly on wages and salaries, to ensure that these do not exceed revenue increases.

Candidates may address this question in a number of ways. In the model answer given above, the strategy clock is used – as it uses the term 'no frills' in its definition and so it seems appropriate to look at other options within this structure. However, answers that use other frameworks (such as Ansoff's product/market matrix) are perfectly acceptable. Furthermore, answers which focus on the suitability, acceptability and feasibility of certain options are also acceptable.

ACCA Marking scheme		Marks
(a)	Up to 2 marks for each identified strength up to a maximum of 10 marks for strengths	
	Up to 2 marks for each identified weakness up to a maximum of 10 marks for weaknesses	20
(b) (i)	Up to 1 mark for each relevant point up to a maximum of 4 marks	
(ii)	Up to 2 marks for each relevant point concerning the inappropriateness of a no-frills solution, up to a maximum of 13 marks	
	Professional presentation of coherent argument: up to 3 marks	20
(c)	Explanation of alternative strategies: Up to 2 marks for each significant point up to a maximum of 8 marks.	
	2 marks also available for professional presentation and coherence of the complete answer.	10
Total		**50**

Examiner's comments

The first part of this question asked candidates to evaluate the strengths and weaknesses of ONA and to explore how these impacted on the company's performance. Many of these strengths and weaknesses were signposted in the text and others were readily discernable from the tabular and financial data. Most candidates answered this part of the question reasonably well. However, three points need to be made;

1   Not enough use was made of the financial data. Relatively easy marks were available for calculating and interpreting standard financial ratios. One marker commented that the 'analysis of the financial information was often weak. Use of this information often went no further than extracting superficial data that was immediately obvious from the tables, for example that net profit after tax had fallen'.

2   Some candidates adopted over-elaborate frameworks and models to answer the question. On one hand this was good to see, but on the other it did mean that many of the answers were very long. Valuable time was taken up in explaining the model, rather than the strengths and weaknesses of ONA. This was a particular problem when inappropriate models were used (such as PESTEL), leading candidates to discuss opportunities and threats which were explicitly excluded from the question.

3   One marker commented that 'candidates frequently started this question with a paragraph describing SWOT analysis and then noting that only strengths and weaknesses were required for the answer. This was a complete waste of time'.

The second part of the compulsory question asked candidates to explain the key features of a 'no-frills' low-cost strategy. Credit was given for both generic answers and for answers which specifically referenced the airline industry. This was answered relatively well.

The question then asked candidates to explain why moving to a 'no-frills' low-cost strategy would be inappropriate for ONA. This part of the question was not answered particularly well. The question asked candidates to adopt and support a particular position. Overall, candidates did not give sufficient ideas to get the marks on offer. The better answers actually adopted the suitability, acceptability and feasibility success criteria suggested by Johnson, Scholes and Whittingham.

Not only did this give plenty of scope for a good answer, it also allowed candidates to score well on the professional marks available for this question. Professional marks were given to answers that strongly supported the specified position – the inappropriateness of a move to a 'no-frills' low cost airline. Too many answers were neutral in tone and did not carry sufficient conviction. Answers were diluted by offering alternatives (the focus of the next part of the question) or by suggestions about how a 'no-frills' approach might be made to work. Although some of these ideas were interesting, they were not the intended focus of the question.

Finally, candidates were asked to evaluate other strategic options ONA could consider to address the airline's current financial and operational weaknesses. There are two key parts of this requirement. The word 'other', meaning other than 'no frills' and so marks could not be awarded for an option which had been specifically rejected by the organisation. Secondly, the question was particularly looking for strategic options, encouraging candidates to explore the strategy clock or any other appropriate framework. Indeed the better answers adopted the strategy clock, Ansoff's matrix or further applied the suitability, acceptability and feasibility success criteria. Answers that used these approaches tended to score well and gained the professional marks on offer. Unfortunately, some candidates did not pitch their answers at a strategic level, focusing more on piecemeal operational improvements. Credit was given for such suggestions, but such answers tended to be quite limited and were not awarded the professional marks, as they did not address strategic options in an appropriate framework.

Three further aspects also need stressing;

1   Financial and quantitative information is provided in scenarios for a reason. Please use it appropriately. Many candidates ignored this information completely.

2   The information in the scenario is very important. Many answers were too general and lacked appropriate context. Candidates must also make sure that they answer the question set, not the question they would like to have been set.

3   Do not use theories inappropriately in a scatter-gun approach. Trying to reference too many theories led to some answers becoming too complicated, too long and too irrelevant. Candidates must make sure that answers are focussed and contain enough relevant points to get the marks on offer.

70   THE NATIONAL MUSEUM   *Walk in the footsteps of a top tutor*

Tutor's top tips

Part (a)

This part of the requirement explicitly asked for a PESTEL analysis. This should have given students the correct focus and avoided doubt about which model should be used in answers.

Key to success:

Apply the model to the scenario.

Try to cover all areas of the PESTEL (the examiner complained that some students failed to cover the 'legal' issues.

Dangers:

Using alternative models. When the examiner is explicit in which model should be used then no other models are deemed necessary.

Straying into internal issues (e.g. strengths and weaknesses of the museum). A PESTEL model is an examination of the external influences on an organisation (the examiner highlights this by referring to it in the question as a 'macro-environmental' analysis).

Poor time management. The examiner suggested that the majority of students found this to be a straightforward section of the exam but that weaker students often spent too long on it at the expense of other parts of the exam. Certainly spending more than five minutes per section of the PESTEL would not be time efficient.

Part (b)

This part of the requirement wanted students to assess the organisational cultural issues that caused the failure of the museums strategy.

Key to success:

Use an appropriate model. There are a range of cultural models that can be used (Handy, Peters & Waterman, the cultural web) and generally the examiner expects students to choose one model and apply it to the scenario. The cultural web plays a big part in the syllabus and is covered in two different chapters of the textbook so it should be seen as the most easily assessable and familiar model for students. The examiner used this model in his answer.

Apply the model to the scenario. Don't simply explain what the model is. Instead use examples from the case of stories, structure, symbols etc. to explain why the problems arose. Show a link between the parts of the cultural web (e.g. there are clear status symbols for some staff in the museum) and the failure of the strategy (the Director General proposed removing these).

Dangers:

Not focusing on culture. Some students strayed into change management (perhaps because this had featured in the June 20X8 exam?). The examiner's opinion was that there was not enough material given in the case to 20 marks worth of material on change management. The requirement also clearly stated it wanted the focus to be on cultural issues.

Part (c)

Key to success:

Note the two parts of this requirement – there will be marks available for explaining the lenses and then applying the lenses to the scenario. So start with the explanation of what they are (but recognise that this is only likely to be worth a couple of marks and should be done briefly/quickly).

Show how each lense would apply to the museum and why/how the one that was used caused the problems that occurred.

Dangers:

The examiner specifically highlighted this area as one of the parts of the paper that a significant minority of students exhibited a lack of knowledge. It is important for the exam that you cover all the main areas of the syllabus – and Johnson, Scholes and Whittington are seen by the examiner as being key to the design of the whole syllabus

(a)   The PESTEL framework may be used to explore the macro-environmental influences that might affect an organisation. There are six main influences in the framework: political, economic, social, technological, environmental and legal. However, these influences are inter-linked and so, for example, political developments and environmental requirements are often implemented through enacting legislation. Candidates will be given credit for identifying the main macro-environmental influences that affect the NM, whether or not they are classified under the same influences as the examiner's model answer.

Political

Monitoring, understanding and adapting to the political environment is absolutely essential for the National Museum. It is currently very reliant on government funding and so is significantly affected by the recently elected government's decision to gradually reduce that funding. The implications of this were recognised by the Board of Trustees and led to the appointment of a new Director General. Unfortunately, senior staff at the museum did not share this perception of the significance of the funding changes. Their opposition to change, which culminated in the Director General's resignation, has led to further political ramifications. The government is now threatening heavier funding cuts and further political trustee appointments. Furthermore, it does appear that the political context has changed for the foreseeable future. The government has only just been elected and the opposition also agrees that the reliance of museums on government funding has to be reduced.

The political appointment of two (and possibly more) trustees is also important to the National Museum. It was significant that it was the two trustees appointed by the government who supported the Director General and his proposed changes. Finally, the continued funding of the government will now largely depend on performance measures – such as accessibility – which have been determined by a political agenda. The museum must strive to meet these objectives even if they are not shared by senior staff. The old ways – built around an assessment of Heritage Collections – appear to have gone forever and senior staff members need to recognise this.

Economic

Up to now the National Museum has been largely sheltered from the economic environment. It has been funded by the government, not the marketplace, and that funding has been largely determined by stable internal factors, such as artefacts in the Heritage Collection. Evidence from the scenario and Figure 1, suggests that this funding is stable, increasing on an annual basis to reflect inflation. However, the progressive reduction of government funding will mean that the museum will be exposed to economic realities. It will have to set realistic admission charges. Resources will also have to be used effectively and new opportunities identified and exploited for increasing income. The Director General included a number of these ideas in his proposals. However, it will be difficult to set a charge that will attract sufficient customers to cover the museum's costs, particularly as visitors have been used to paying only a nominal entry charge.

Social

The social environment is important to the museum from at least two different perspectives. The first is that social inclusion is an important part of the government's targets. The government is committed to increasing museum attendance by both lower social classes and by younger people who they feel need to be made more aware of their heritage. The visitor information shown in Figure 3 suggests that not only are visitor numbers declining in total, but the average age of these visitors is increasing. The percentage of visitors aged 22 and under visiting the NM has decreased from 19% of the total visitors (in 20X4) to just over 12% in 20X7. The museum needs to identify what it needs to do to attract such groups to the museum. The Director General had suggested free admission. This could be combined with popular exhibitions (perhaps tied in with television programmes or films) and 'hands-on' opportunities. It appears that the immediate neighbourhood of the museum now houses many of the people the government would like as visitors and so, from this angle, the location of the museum is an advantage. However, the comment of the Director of Art and Architecture about popularity and historical significance hardly bodes well for the future.

The decay of the neighbourhood and the increased crime rate may also deter fee-paying visitors. The museum is becoming increasingly isolated in its environment, with many of its traditional middle-class customers moving away from the area and reluctant to visit. The extensive reporting of a recent assault on a visitor is also likely to deter visitors. The museum needs to react to these issues by ensuring that good and safe transport links are maintained to the museum and by improving security both in the museum and in its immediate vicinity. Visitors need to feel safe and secure. If the museum believes this to be unachievable, then it might consider moving to a new site.

Technological

It is estimated that only 10% of the museum's collection is on view to visitors. Technology provides opportunities for displaying and viewing artefacts on-line. It provides an opportunity for the museum to become a virtual museum – allowing visitors from all over the world access to images and information about its collections. Indeed, such an approach should also help the museum achieve some of its technology and accessibility targets set by the government. Technology can also be used to increase marketing activity, providing on-line access to products and allowing these products to be bought through a secure payment facility. The appropriate use of technology frees the museum from its physical space constraints and also overcomes issues associated with its physical location.

Environmental

It can be argued that all contemporary organisations have to be aware of environmental issues and the impact their activities have on the environment. These are likely to be exacerbated by the museum being located in an old building which itself requires regular maintenance and upgrading to reflect government requirements. It is also very unlikely that such an old building will be energy efficient and so heating costs are likely to be high and to continue to increase. The museum needs to adopt appropriate policies on recycling and energy conservation, but it may be difficult to achieve these targets in the context of an old building. Consequently, environmental issues may combine with social issues to encourage the consideration of the possible relocation of the museum to a modern building in a more appropriate location. However, the museum building is also of architectural importance, and so some acceptable alternative use for the building might also have to be suggested.

Legal

Legal issues affect the museum in at least two ways. Firstly, there is already evidence that the museum has had to adapt to legal requirements for disability access and to reflect health and safety requirements. Some of these requirements appear to have required changes in the building which have been met with disapproval. It is likely that modifications will be expensive and relatively awkward, leading again to unsightly and aesthetically unpleasing modifications to the building. Further tightening of legislation might be expected from a government with a mandate for social inclusion. For example, it might specify that all documentation should be available in Braille or in different languages. Legislation concerning fire safety, heating, cooking and food preparation might also exist or be expected.

Secondly, the museum is run by a Board of Trustees. There are legal requirements about the behaviour of such trustees. The museum must be aware of these and ensure that their work is properly scoped and monitored. Trustees have, and must accept, ultimate responsibility for directing the affairs of the museum, ensuring that it is solvent, well-run, and meeting the needs for which it has been set up. The museum is a charity and it is the responsibility of the trustees to ensure that its operation complies with the charity law of the country.

(b) The underlying cultural issues that would explain the failure of the Director General's strategy at the National Museum can be explored using the cultural web. It can be used to understand the behaviours of an organisation – the day-to-day way in which the organisation operates – and the taken-for-granted assumptions that lie at the core of an organisation's culture. The question suggests that it was a lack of understanding of the National Museum's culture that lay at the heart of the Director General's failure. In this suggested answer the cultural web is used as a way of exploring the failure of the Director General's strategy from a cultural perspective. However, other appropriate models and frameworks that explore the cultural perspective will also be given credit.

A cultural web for the National Museum is suggested in Figure 1. The cultural web is made up of a set of factors that overlap and reinforce each other. The symbols explore the logos, offices, titles and terminology of the organisation. The large offices, the special dining room and the dedicated personal assistants are clear symbols of hierarchy and power in the museum. Furthermore, the language used by directors in their stories (see below) suggests a certain amount of disdain for both customers and managers. The status of professor conferred on section heads with Heritage Collections also provides relative status within the heads of collection sections themselves. The proposal of the Director General to close the heads' dining room and to remove their dedicated personal assistants would take away two important symbols of status and is likely to be an unpopular suggestion.

The *power* structures of the organisation are significant. Power can be seen as the ability of certain groups to persuade or coerce others to follow a certain course of action. At present, power is vested in the heads of collection sections, reflected by their dominance on the Board of Directors. Three of the five directors represent collection sections. Similarly the Board of Trustees is dominated by people who are well-known and respected in academic fields relevant to the museum's collections. The power of external stakeholders (such as the government) has, until the election of the new government, been relatively weak. They have merely handed over funding for the trustees to distribute. The Director General of the museum has been a part-time post.

The appointment of an external, full-time Director General with private sector experience threatens this power base and his suggestion for the new organisation structure takes away the dominance of the collection heads. On his proposed board, only one of six directors represents the collection sections.

The *organisational* structure is likely to reflect and reinforce the power structure. This appears to be the case at the museum. However, it is interesting to note that the collections themselves are not evenly represented. Both the Director of Industrial Art and the Director of Media and Contemporary Art represent five collection sections. However, only two collection areas are represented by the Director of Art and Architecture. This imbalance, reinforced by different symbols (professorships) and reflected in stories (see later) might suggest a certain amount of disharmony between the collection heads, which the Director General might have been able to exploit. Management at the museum are largely seen as administrators facilitating the museum's activities. This is reinforced by the title of the director concerned; Director of Administration.

The *controls* of the organisation relate to the measurements and reward systems which emphasise what is important to the organisation. At the National Museum the relative budget of each section has been heavily influenced by the Heritage Collections. These collections help determine how much the museum receives as a whole and it appears (from the budget figures) that the Board of Trustees also use this as a guide when allocating the finance internally. Certainly, the sections with the Heritage Collections appear to receive the largest budgets. Once this division has been established the principle of allocating increases based on last year's allocation, plus a percentage, perpetuates the division and indeed accentuates it in real financial terms. Hence, smaller sections remain small and their chance of obtaining artefacts for them to be defined a Heritage Collection becomes slimmer every year. Again, this may suggest a potential conflict between the larger and smaller collection sections of the museum. Finally, up until the election of the new government, there appears to have been no required measures of outputs (visitor numbers, accessibility etc.). The museum was given a budget to maintain the collections, not to attract visitors. The proposal of the Director General to allocate budgets on visitor popularity disturbs the well-established way of distributing budgets in a way that reinforced the current power base.

The *routines and rituals* are the way members of the organisation go about their daily work and the special events or particular activities that reinforce the 'way we do things around here'. It is clear from the scenario that it is not thought unacceptable for directors to directly lobby the Board of Trustees and to write letters to the press and appear on television programmes to promote their views. In many organisations issues within the boardroom remain confidential and are resolved there. However, this is clearly not now the case at the National Museum. The scenario suggests that there are certain *rites of challenge* (exemplified by the new Director General's proposals) but equally there are strong *rites of counter-challenge*, resistance to the new ways of doing things. Often such rites are limited to grumbling or working-to-rule, but at the National Museum they extend to lobbying powerful external forces in the hope that these forces can be combined to resist the suggested changes.

Stories are used by members of the organisation to tell people what is important in the organisation. The quotes included in the scenario are illuminating both in content and language. The Director of Art and Architecture believes that Heritage Collections have a value that transcends popularity with the 'undiscerning public'. He also alludes to the relative importance of collections.

He suggests that fashion may not be a suitable subject for a collection, unlike art and architecture. Similarly, the anonymous quote about lack of consultation, that includes a reference to the new Director General as 'an ex-grocer', attempts to belittle both management and commerce.

In the centre of the cultural web is the paradigm of the National Museum. This is the set of assumptions that are largely held in common and are taken for granted in the organisation. These might be:

- The museum exists for the good of the nation
- It is a guardian of the continuity of the nation's heritage and culture
- What constitutes heritage and culture is determined by experts
- The government funds the purchase and maintenance of artefacts that represent this heritage and culture.

There are two important elements of the Director General's proposals that are missing from this paradigm; visitors and customers. Changing the current paradigm may take considerable time and effort.

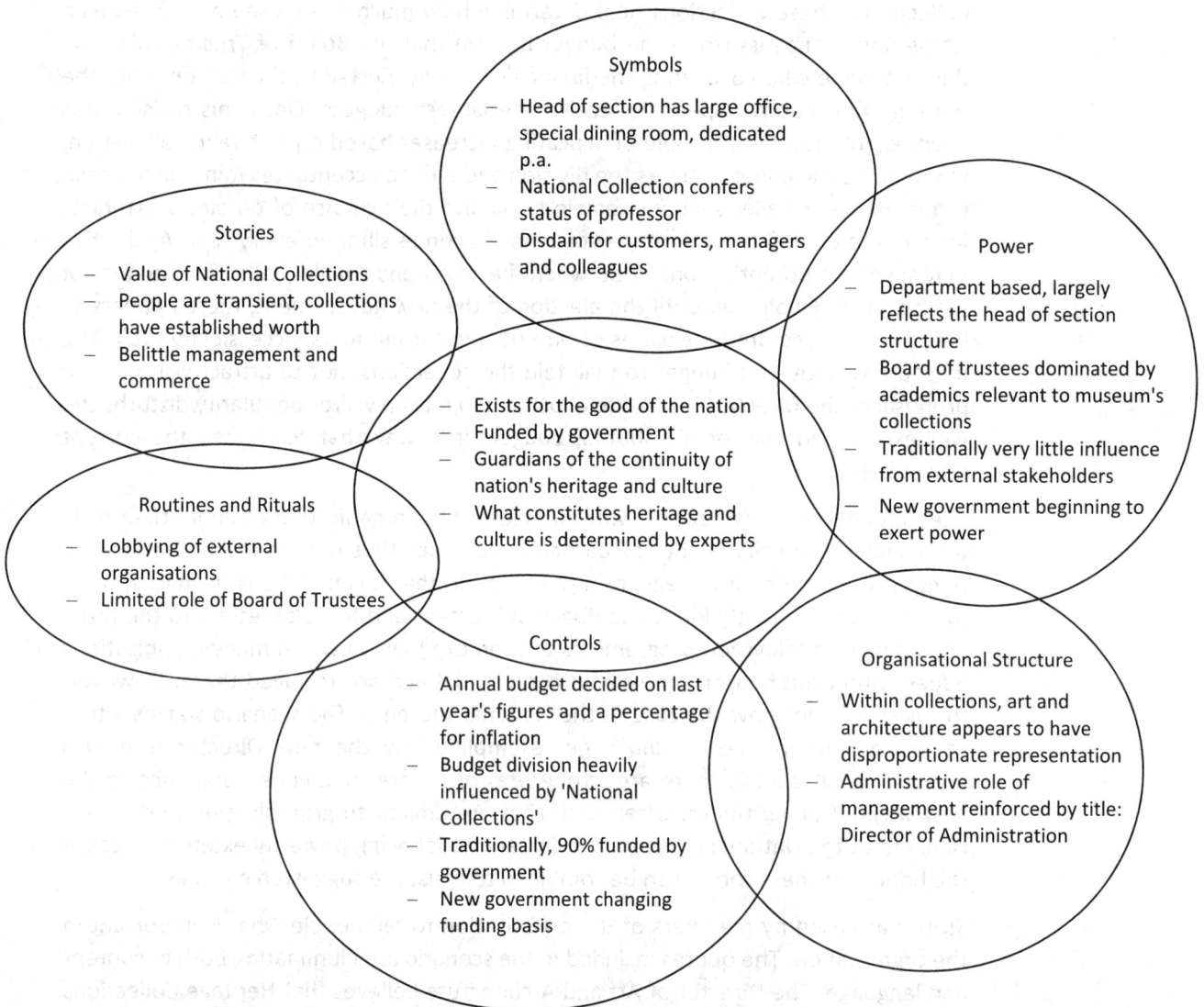

Symbols
- Head of section has large office, special dining room, dedicated p.a.
- National Collection confers status of professor
- Disdain for customers, managers and colleagues

Stories
- Value of National Collections
- People are transient, collections have established worth
- Belittle management and commerce

Power
- Department based, largely reflects the head of section structure
- Board of trustees dominated by academics relevant to museum's collections
- Traditionally very little influence from external stakeholders
- New government beginning to exert power

(centre)
- Exists for the good of the nation
- Funded by government
- Guardians of the continuity of nation's heritage and culture
- What constitutes heritage and culture is determined by experts

Routines and Rituals
- Lobbying of external organisations
- Limited role of Board of Trustees

Controls
- Annual budget decided on last year's figures and a percentage for inflation
- Budget division heavily influenced by 'National Collections'
- Traditionally, 90% funded by government
- New government changing funding basis

Organisational Structure
- Within collections, art and architecture appears to have disproportionate representation
- Administrative role of management reinforced by title: Director of Administration

Figure 1: Possible cultural web for the National Museum

Candidate answers which considered the cultural web from a perspective of how it might have helped the Director General develop and implement proposals are also acceptable. For example:

- He may have considered deferring one or both of the proposals to remove the head of collection sections' dining room and their dedicated personal assistants. These are important symbols of their status and the financial gains from removing them seem unlikely to outweigh the consequences of their removal.

- He might have considered simply adding directors to the organisational structure, rather than inviting conflict by removing two of the collection directors. For example, replacing the current Director of Administration with the four new directors of his proposed structure (Finance, Visitor Services, Resources, Information Systems) might then have been more acceptable. The actual number of collection related directors remains the same (three), but their relative power in the board would have been decreased.

- An analysis of the cultural web identifies a possible conflict between the collection section heads that could have been exploited. A significant number of sections are not designated as Heritage Collections and so are not headed by professors. These sections are also less well represented on the board and they receive less money, which is allocated in a way that accentuates and perpetuates the relative wealth of the powerful sections. Published stories and deriding fashion, reinforces this division. The Director General could have identified proposals that could have brought the heads of certain sections 'on side' and so destroy the apparently harmonious position of the collection heads.

- He also needed to recognise the structure of the Board of Trustees. Their current composition meant that there was little chance that they would support his proposals.

- Finally, he would have benefited from understanding the paradigm of the National Museum and how at odds this paradigm is with his own vision and with the vision of the incoming government. In this context the cultural web has important implications for the heads of collection sections. Both the *power and controls* elements of the cultural web are undergoing significant change. The new government is exploiting its position as a major stakeholder and insisting on new controls and measures that reflect their paradigm. Although the heads of collection sections have successfully lobbied for the removal of the Director General, they are very unlikely to change the government's policy. Indeed the sacking of the Director General has strengthened the government's action and resolve. The sacking of the Director General may have been a *pyrrhic victory* and a much worse defeat now awaits the heads of collection sections.

(c)   The *design* lens views strategy as the deliberate positioning of an organisation as the result of some 'rational, analytical, structured and directive process'. Through the design lens it is the responsibility of top management to plan the destiny of the organisation. Lower levels of management carry out the operational actions required by the strategy. The design lens is associated with objective setting and a plan for moving the organisation towards these objectives. In the context of the scenario, the government is now significantly involved in objective setting and tying funding to those objectives. The Director General has responsibility for defining and delivering a strategy within these objectives. There is evidence that he has gone about this in a 'top-down' way and not sought advice from current employees. On the television programme, employees were particularly critical of a lack of consultation; 'these proposals have been produced with no input from museum staff. They have been handed down from on-high'. In many ways, the approach taken at the National Museum under the new Director General represents the design lens view of strategy. Such an approach is not unusual in public sector organisations, where elements of strategy are dictated by government manifestos.

Strategy as *experience* provides a more adaptive approach to strategy, building on and changing the existing strategy. Changes are incremental as the organisation adapts to new opportunities and threats in the environment. The experience lens views strategy development as the combination of individual and collective experience together with the taken-for-granted assumptions of cultural influences. However, it has to be recognised that the assumptions and practices of the organisation may become so ingrained that it is difficult for people to question or change them. This certainly appears to be true for the heads of collection sections at the National Museum. The museum is now facing a fundamental change in the way it will be funded and the increased influence of the government suggests a change in the paradigm of the organisation. It seems unlikely that people with a vested interest in the current arrangement and perpetuating that current arrangement will come up with the change in strategy that is now required. The 'taken-for-granted' behaviour of people in organisations is one of the major barriers to developing innovative strategies. Strategy as experience seems innately conservative. It could work well when a small incremental change is required within a stable environment. However, this does not appear to be the situation at the National Museum and so developing strategy as experience may not seem a possible way forward and perhaps this is why the Director General explicitly rejected this approach.

Strategy as *ideas* has a central role for innovation and new ideas. It sees strategy as emerging from the variety and diversity in an organisation. It is as likely to come from the bottom of the organisation as from the top. Consequently, the organisation should foster conditions that allow ideas to emerge and to be considered for inclusion in a 'mainstream strategy'. Certain conditions, such as a changing and unpredictable environment foster ideas and innovation. It could be argued that the macro-environmental conditions for adopting this lens are present at the National Museum. Political, social and environmental influences might lead to new ideas – for example, the relocation of the museum and the exploitation of on-line access to resources creating a virtual museum. The museum is undergoing a fundamental change in priorities and funding and the consequences of these changes is unpredictable. On the other hand, the museum is a long-established conservative organisation with many symbols of hierarchy and deference. There is no evidence in the scenario of a group of people generating conflicting ideas and encouraged to compete with each other in an open and supportive environment.

The National Museum seems to be dominated by powerful individuals protecting their own interests. Finally, a key factor in the selection of ideas is the marketplace. The National Museum is currently operating in a protected economic environment, although this is set to change.

There is plenty of evidence to suggest that it is difficult to change strategies in a hierarchical or deferential structure. At the National Museum the Director General decided to pursue a designed strategy. In many ways this appeared to be the natural lens to adopt given the objectives set by the newly elected government that was beginning to exert its power. This strategy may have worked if he had been more sensitive to the cultural web and, also, if he had not asked for the backing of the Board of Trustees. This was always unlikely to be forthcoming given its composition. The paradigm change means that it is unlikely that the experience lens would have proved fruitful. However, it may have been possible to exploit strategy as ideas if the Director General had carefully selected heads of collection sections who were relative losers under the current system.

ACCA Marking scheme		
		Marks
(a)	Up to 2 marks for identifying appropriate macro-environmental influences in each of the six PESTEL areas – even if it is justifying the lack of influence. A further 8 marks are available for giving credit to candidates who have extended their argument in selected areas of the framework. It must be accepted that each area of the PESTEL will have a differential effect.	20
(b)	Up to 2 marks for each significant cultural factor identified by the candidate up to a maximum of 8 marks. Up to 2 marks for an explanation of how each factor contributed to the rejection of the Director General's proposals, up to a maximum of 10 marks. This includes any ethical issues raised within the cultural analysis. Up to 2 professional marks are available for the overall clarity and coherence of the analysis	20
(c)	Up to 8 marks for the insights offered by the lenses into the case study scenario. Up to 2 professional marks are available for the overall clarity and coherence of the analysis.	10
Total		**50**

Examiner's comments

The first part of this question asked candidates to analyse the macro-environment of the National Museum. This was a straight forward question and, by specifically asking for a PESTEL analysis, it mimicked the same question part of the pilot paper. There were plenty of clues in the case study, most of which featured in candidate's answers. The only area that did not get much coverage was the legal responsibilities of the Board of Trustees.

PESTEL is concerned with the external environment and so points made about internal budget allocations could not be given marks. Overall, straying on to internal issues (such as strengths and weaknesses) was the only mistake made by candidates answering this part question. In general, it was answered very well.

The second part of this question asked candidates to assess the underlying organisational cultural issues that would explain the failure of the Director General's proposed strategy at the National Museum. Unlike the previous part of the question, no specific model or framework was suggested for this part of the question. A quote from one of the trustees was given to help candidates understand what was meant by organisational culture.

This guidance appeared to be successful as the vast majority of answers did focus on organisational culture and not cultural forces concerned with nationality, history, arts or religion.

The model answer to this question uses the cultural web as a way of exploring cultural influences at the National Museum and considering how they would be affected by the Director General's proposed strategy. The case study scenario is rich with material to support this approach. For example, there are clear symbols of status which the Director General proposes to withdraw. There are important stories in the case study scenario which demonstrate how certain staff members view the public and management. There are well established financial controls which will be disturbed by the proposed new budgetary allocation method. There are important clues in the current and proposed organisation structure about how the Director General wished to redistribute power in the organisation.

Candidates could also have used the cultural web to reflect upon the acceptability of staff lobbying external organisations (television and press) and publically criticising the Director General. By failing to consider these factors (and indeed in some instances, failing to exploit divisions that a cultural web analysis would have exposed) the Director General's proposed strategy was doomed to failure. It is clear that the organisation's current culture is not compatible with the strategy that the Director General wishes to develop. Candidates who used the cultural web, if only in part, in their answers generally scored reasonably well in this part question. However, despite the explicit reference to cultural issues, many candidates focussed their answers on the scope and nature of change, accusing the Director General of proposing big bang change when incremental change would be more appropriate and pursuing revolution to evolution. These answers did gain marks, but only significant marks if they were related to the focus of the question; *the underlying organisational cultural issues.* Without such references such answers were light on detail, because the case study did not have enough information to support such an approach to the analysis. Consequently, answers tended to focus solely on blaming the Director General for not consulting staff when formulating his proposed strategy. This may be a legitimate point, but was insufficient to gain the twenty marks on offer for this part question. The final part of this question asked candidates to explain the three strategy lenses; design, experience and ideas and explain how each of these lenses could help our understanding of the process of strategy development at the National Museum. Understanding these lenses is not only a defined objective in the study guide, but also underpins the whole of the Business Analysis syllabus. Some candidates were very well prepared for this part question, showed great understanding and gained full marks. Others showed very little knowledge and so only scored two or three marks.

71   SHOAL PLC

Key answer tips

In part (a), the key issue for students is likely to be time management. There are 3 business units to discuss for a total of 15 marks (so 5 marks for each SBU). For each SBU there are 3 things to do – assess its market growth (probably using a very brief PESTEL), assess its market share (and include a commentary on its financial performance) and place it in the Boston box (or alternatively a model such as the Ashridge display might have been used).

Each of these elements will have to be done succinctly and include an analysis of the financial data available. It would be inappropriate, for example, to perform a full PESTEL on each SBU, but one or two key points should be pulled out.

In part (b) (i), it is clear that the professional skills marks are available for identifying and justifying an appropriate model and students should start with this. Contextual features are part of the Balogun and Hope Hailey model and this is the model that should be suggested. The model identifies 8 potential contextual features and students should aim to discuss 6 or 7 of these in order to get full marks. Each feature should be explained and made relevant to the scenario to gain around 2 marks per feature.

In part (b) (ii), no particular model is required. Students should focus on coming up with specific and relevant ideas on the changes needed within Shoal plc. With 8 marks available (and a further 2 for professional skills), it may be a good target to come up with around 8 suggestions for change.

In part (c), the bulk of the marks will be available for simple bookwork. There are three rationales to be explained for approximately 3 marks each. Shoal appears to be a synergy manager, but any justified conclusion is likely to be allowed by the examiner for the final mark or two.

(a)   Portfolio analysis

A PESTEL analysis of ShoalFish would focus on the fact that it is fishing in an area where fish stocks are rapidly declining (environmental) and it is increasingly exposed to government intervention and restrictions (political). It is a relatively small player (12% market share) in a large, but declining market place (5% over two years). Profits are declining, although ShoalFish appear to have arrested the decline in the profit margin. The 20X9 gross profit margin (4.9%) shows an increase over the 20X8 figure (4.7%). This may mean that the company has been able to bring operating costs in line with the declining turnover.

In terms of the Boston Box, it has the characteristics of a dog, a company with a small market share in a declining market. However, Shoal plc perceives that there are important synergies between ShoalFish and the other companies in the Shoal plc portfolio. For example, it helps secure a significant proportion of the raw materials required by ShoalPro. ShoalPro is also ShoalFish's main customer, accounting for 40% of the company's catch. ShoalFish also has an intended role following the purchase of the Captain Haddock group of restaurants. Shoal plc would like ShoalFish to directly supply the Captain Haddock restaurants and so potentially reduce raw material costs at Captain Haddock.

Shoal plc needs to look carefully at the viability of maintaining this fleet. They are operating in an area where owner-skippers are very common (almost half of the boats in the western oceans are owned and operated by the boat's captain). There may be an opportunity for ShoalFish to sell, lease or rent their ships, perhaps to individual owners, with the promise of guaranteed sales to ShoalPro (and potentially Captain Haddock). Alternatively, they could tolerate declining performance from this part of the portfolio, in the knowledge that it forms an important part of the supply chain for other companies in the portfolio.

ShoalPro

ShoalPro is a profitable and expanding organisation. A significant percentage of its raw fish supply is currently provided by ShoalFish, but this percentage is declining as it increasingly processes fish for other companies. It is in a mature, but still expanding (+2% from 20X7 to 20X9) market-place where it holds a significant (40%) and slightly increasing market share. Gross profit margins are improving slightly (from 10% in 20X7 to 10.6% in 20X9), suggesting that costs are increasing at a slower rate than revenues.

Its consistent profitability would classify this business, using Boston Box terminology, as a cash cow. A company with a significant market share in a low growth market.

A PESTEL analysis would focus on the fact that ShoalPro factories are in a region which attracts national grants due to high local unemployment (political and economic). This reduces operating costs and the persistence of high unemployment suggests that a local skilled workforce is still accessible to ShoalPro (socio-cultural). Analysis suggests that ShoalPro is an important part of the Shoal plc portfolio and should be retained and maintained.

ShoalFarm

ShoalFarm is a relatively new acquisition. It currently has a relatively low market share (10%) in an expanding market-place. ShoalFarm is itself growing (+12% from 20X7 to 20X9), but not as fast as its market (+20% in the same period). A PESTEL analysis would reveal a market-place that is perceived as ethically acceptable, stressing the conservation of fish supplies (socio-cultural). It seems likely that this will increase in importance in the future although the difficulty of finding potential sites (environmental) may be a significant factor. Gross profit is high (14% in 20X7, comfortably out-performing ShoalFish and ShoalPro) but declined in 20X8 (12.7%), recovering slightly in 20X9 (13.3%).

ShoalFarm may also have a significant role to play in providing raw materials for both ShoalPro and the potential acquisition – Captain Haddock restaurants. In terms of the Boston Box classification, ShoalFarm is probably a question mark or problem child. It needs increasing investment to ensure that it becomes a key player in a significant market-place. If Shoal plc is prepared to do this, then the recommendation is that they should expand and develop. If they do not – and the potential synergies with Captain Haddock are not realised – they may wish to divest.

Overall, the three companies can be seen as integrated parts in a comprehensive value chain. Conflicting environmental forces are at work, on the one hand reducing the level of dependency between the companies and, on the other hand, reinforcing the competitive advantages (synergies) of being in a vertically integrated group. The potential acquisition of Captain Haddock could further enhance these advantages but only if the correct inter-firm trading relationships are established.

(b) **Change management**

(i) **Contextual features**

Shoal plc recognises that there is no 'one right way' to manage change. The success of any planned change programme will depend upon an understanding of the context in which the change will take place. Balogun and Hope Hailey have highlighted a number of important contextual features that need to be taken into account when designing change programmes. These features are used as a basis for this model answer. However, other frameworks that recognise the context that changes takes place within could be used by the candidate and appropriate credit will be given.

Shoal plc has little *time* to complete the acquisition and effect the strategic change necessary. The decline in Captain Haddock's turnover and profits is increasing dramatically. The resignation of the chairman and managing director of the company was triggered by concerns about breaking bank covenants. If Shoal plc does acquire Captain Haddock then strategic change will have to be implemented quickly.

Shoal plc will need to put into place policies that help them *preserve* the aspects of Captain Haddock that need to be retained for future success. It is recognised that the employees and the training they receive are first rate. Steps need to be put in place to ensure that these employees remain within the company. Similarly, the Captain Haddock brand is strong and needs to be re-affirmed.

Change is usually easier if there is *a diversity* of experience, views and opinions within the organisation. This is not discernable at Captain Haddock. The suggestion is that most employees are recruited directly from school or university and then remain within the Captain Haddock training programme as they progress through the company. There is very much a policy of 'recruit from below'. In such circumstances it is unlikely that norms and practices will be challenged. A homogenous internally shared view was developed that Captain Haddock did things the right way, whatever was changing in the world outside. Shoal plc will have to be sensitive to this, as well as recognising that it will need to bring the required diversity of thinking to the company.

Capability is concerned with the extent or experience of managing change in the organisation. Within Captain Haddock there appears to be little experience of such change. Indeed the preservation of established norms and practices was the focus of management and the supporting training. In contrast, Shoal plc have experience of managing change and this is a major capability that it should bring to Captain Haddock. However, it has to be recognised that this capability has not been tested in the restaurant sector and Shoal plc will have to be sure that their capability is applicable to this sector.

The *capacity* of an organisation for change considers the resources available to support change. Change may be costly, both in real financial terms and management time. Captain Haddock has little capacity for change from its own resources. So, this is again something that Shoal plc will bring to the company. Substantial investment will not only be required to improve Captain Haddock's financial position, in terms of fulfilling bank covenants, but also to finance the change programme necessary within the company.

There appears to be little doubt that Captain Haddock is *ready* for change. Two senior members of management who could have been the focus for some resistance to change have left the company and employee representatives are keen for someone to come in and 'effectively lead employees who have become increasingly demoralised by the decline of the company'. Shoal plc should acquire an organisation that is receptive to appropriate change.

It is necessary to identify people in the organisation who have the *power* to effect change. Again, this will be a key responsibility of Shoal plc if they acquire Captain Haddock. They must give the appointed management sufficient power to implement the required changes.

So, in summary, Shoal plc will be faced with ensuring that many of the contextual requirements for successful change are put in place. They will need to provide management with appropriate capability and diversity and then give them the power and capacity to effect required changes. They will have to move quickly to preserve Captain Haddock's strengths, but they will find a workforce that is receptive for change.

The final contextual feature that needs consideration is the *scope* of change. The type of change required at Captain Haddock can be viewed in the context of the following model.

	Scope of change	
Nature of change	**Realignment**	**Transformation**
Incremental	Adaptation	Evolution
Big Bang	Reconstruction	Revolution

Adaptation is change that can be accommodated within the current paradigm and can be introduced incrementally in the organisation.

Reconstruction is change that may be rapid and create upheaval in the organisation but which does not fundamentally change the underlying paradigm.

Evolution is a change that does require a paradigm change but one that can be introduced over time *Revolution* is a change that requires rapid change associated with a change in paradigm. *Reconstruction* appears to fit the situation at Captain Haddock.

(ii) **Elements of strategic change**

This part of the question can be answered in a number of ways and all legitimate approaches will be given credit. However, it is suggested that the answer should consider:

- Focusing on profitable and/or core activities

- Divesting non-profitable and/or ill-fitting activities

- Changing senior management

- Effective stakeholder management

- Financial restructuring.

This model answer uses the structure suggested by Johnson, Scholes and Whittington for implementing a *turnaround* strategy. Change is required quickly but there is no need to radically change what the organisation is doing.

There is a need for a *realignment* of strategy rather than a fundamental change of strategic direction. It has already been recognised in the previous answer that Captain Haddock requires reconstruction. This is often associated with a *turnaround* situation where there is a need for structural changes to deal with a decline in financial performance and changing market conditions. In *a turnaround* situation the emphasis should be on rapid change and rapid cost reduction and/or revenue generation. Thus Shoal plc should be aware of some of the main elements of a turnaround strategy as they will need these if they acquire Captain Haddock. These main elements could form the basis of a strategy for change to return the company to profitability.

(1) The change strategy might commence with crisis stabilisation with a short-term focus on cost reduction and revenue increase. One of the synergies identified by Shoal plc (the provision of fish directly to Captain Haddock restaurants) should aid cost reduction. There is evidence that focusing on reducing operational costs is a significant factor in a successful turnaround strategy.

(2) Implementing management changes at the top level. The resignation of the chairman and managing director of Captain Haddock has already facilitated this. Their resignation will also support the reduction of costs. The reduction of the costs of senior management is a further characteristic of a successful turnaround strategy.

(3) Gaining stakeholder support. It is vital that key stakeholders are kept informed during the change process. A clear assessment of the power of different stakeholders will be vitally important. Evidence from the scenario suggests that employees are supportive of change. The banks should also welcome the acquisition by a large and well-established company such as Shoal plc.

(4) Shoal plc will have to clarify target markets and re-establish the Captain Haddock brand. There is evidence that the company has unsuccessfully diversified into new market-places which did not deliver profits. The company has to get 'back to basics' and re-establish itself in its traditional market-place.

(5) Captain Haddock will need to be re-focused on core activities and products. It may be possible to dispose of the land bought for investment. Clarifying the target markets provides the opportunity to discontinue products or services that are not focused on those markets.

(6) Financial restructuring of Captain Haddock is necessary and is part of the capability that Shoal plc will bring to the company. Evidence suggests that Captain Haddock should be delivering gross profits of about $11 million per year, so making the $15 million investment a relatively modest outlay.

(7) Shoal plc will need to prioritise critical improvement areas, delivering quick and significant improvements.

Finally, Shoal plc need to be aware that a successful turnaround strategy should focus on getting the existing business right, rather than quickly diversifying into new markets and businesses.

(c)   **Corporate Parenting Rationales**

Portfolio managers, synergy managers and parental developers represent three corporate rationales for value creation in a multi-business organisation as suggested by Johnson, Scholes and Whittington. The distinction between the three is considered here.

Portfolio managers act as an agent on behalf of financial markets and shareholders. They seek to increase the value of the companies in their portfolio more efficiently and effectively than financial markets could achieve. They seek to acquire under-performing or under-valued companies and to improve their performance so that they can later be sold at a premium. In many instances, poorly performing parts or businesses of the acquired company are sold off as part of performance improvement. The key issue for most portfolio managers is the opportunity to extract value from a business. The nature of that business, the market it is operating in and its relationship to other businesses in the portfolio is relatively unimportant. Portfolio managers manage businesses with a low cost centre and do not intervene significantly in the running of each business in the portfolio. Instead, they set financial targets for the senior executives of those companies, with high rewards for those executives who achieve their targets. The value-added activities of a portfolio manager are usually restricted to investment, setting expectations and standards and for monitoring performance. The profile of a portfolio manager does not fit the philosophy of Shoal plc.

Johnson, Scholes and Whittington claim that synergy is often seen as the *raison d'etre* of the corporate parent, with value being enhanced across the business units in a number of ways. Underpinning this approach is the belief that the whole is worth more than the constituent parts. Johnson, Scholes and Whittington particularly identify the sharing of resources or activities; for example, a common brand name (as in the case of Shoal plc) may provide value to different products within different businesses. There may also be common skills or competencies across businesses. For example, expertise built up in the politics of fishing is likely to be transferable throughout the Shoal plc businesses.

Shoal plc also sees the synergy in terms of one business being a customer of another. For example, guaranteeing a supply of raw material or as a guaranteed customer of a product. This may be problematic because it could lead to inefficiencies and confused objectives within each company. The 'supplying' company may not control costs or ensure quality sufficiently because it knows it has a guaranteed customer for some of its products. Similarly, the 'purchasing' company might not be able to meet profit objectives because of the cost and quantity of the raw material it has to purchase from its related supplier. Business managers are usually rewarded on the performance of their business unit, but under this strategy they are being asked to co-operate in something that could compromise the performance of their business unit. As Johnson, Scholes and Whittington suggest, the manager of the business unit might respond by asking 'what's in it for me? and they may conclude that there is very little'. There is also a concern that Shoal plc knows a lot about sourcing and processing fish, but not much about the restaurant industry. It may be that Captain Haddock is quite different to other companies in the portfolio and so the hoped for synergies may not appear. However, despite these reservations, it is clear that Shoal plc's overall corporate philosophy is that of a synergy manager.

Finally, the parental developer uses the competencies *of the parent* to add value to businesses in the portfolio. So, in this instance, the parent company is confident about its resources and capabilities and wishes to use these to enhance the value of the businesses in the portfolio. For example, the parental developer may have a brand name that is recognisable throughout the world and is associated with value and quality. Such a company needs to identify businesses which are not currently fulfilling their potential but could if they were associated with a well-known brand. In effect, their brand name brings these companies to a wider audience who automatically assign the values of the parent to those of the acquired company. For parental developers, achieving synergies between companies in the portfolio is not a priority. The focus is on providing the companies in the portfolio with the competencies of the parent. This is not really the approach of Shoal plc. Developing strategic capabilities, achieving synergies and transferring managerial capabilities are not value-adding activities of a parental developer.

ACCA Marking scheme		
		Marks
(a)	1 mark for each relevant point up to a maximum of 5 marks for each company. There are three companies in the analysis, giving a maximum of 15 marks for this part of the question.	
		15
(b) (i)	1 mark for each relevant point up to a maximum of 13 marks for this part question. In addition there are 2 professional marks allocated as follows: 1 mark for the identification of an appropriate model, 1 mark for the justification of an appropriate model.	
	Maximum	15
(ii)	1 mark for each relevant point up to a maximum of 8 marks for this part question.	
	Maximum	8
	In addition, there are 2 professional marks allocated as follows: 1 mark for the cogency of the analysis and 1 mark for overall application to the case study environment.	?
(c)	1 mark for each relevant point up to a maximum of 3 marks for each corporate rationale. There are three corporate rationales giving a maximum of 9 marks. 1 mark for recognising that Shoal plc is a synergy developer, giving a maximum of 10 marks for this part of the question	
	Maximum	10
Total		50

Examiner's comments

In the first part of the question, most candidates answered well, correctly interpreting the textual and financial information given in the scenario. However, surprisingly few candidates actually used portfolio analysis, despite the fact that the financial information was aligned to the data needed to classify the companies within the Boston Box. Furthermore, some candidates analysed the data as if these three companies were the only companies in the portfolio. In reality, there are eleven more companies for which data is not given. It is important to carefully read the scenario. However, overall, this was a popular and well-answered part of the question.

The second part of the question suggested that candidates should use an appropriate model, but no specific model was mandated. Performance was very patchy in this part of the question. Some candidates wrote very little, others described the change process (required in (b) (ii)), whilst others did identify an appropriate model (the Balogun and Hope Hailey kaleidoscope or the cultural web) but failed to us it in the context of the case study scenario. The best answers used an appropriate model and provided relevant cross-reference to the case study scenario for each facet of their selected model.

Part (b) (ii) was reasonably well answered with some candidates being aware of an approach specifically geared to a turnaround situation. However, even those who were not familiar with this approach, were able to give a sensible answer gaining pass marks, often using Lewin's unfreeze- transition (change) – freeze framework as an overall structure to their answer.

The final part of this question was relatively theoretical. It asked candidates to explain three corporate rationales; portfolio managers, synergy managers and parental developers and to assess their relevance to the overall corporate rationale of Shoal plc. As mentioned in the introduction, this was very poorly attempted with many candidates scoring three marks or less. This appears to have been due to a lack of knowledge in this area of the syllabus.

72   AUTOFONE

Key answer tips

There can be confusion for some students in part (a), when asked for a competitive analysis, as to which model to use. The examiner will be looking for Porter's Five Forces analysis. But the examiner has stated that, in future, where he believes such confusion might arise, he will be more explicit as to which model to use.

(a)   One possible approach to answering this part of the question is provided by using Michael Porter's five forces framework. The framework is designed to analyse 'the structure of an industry and its competitors' (Porter, 20X4). There are five inter-connecting forces in the framework; potential entrants (the threat of entry), the bargaining power of suppliers, the bargaining power of buyers, the threat of substitutes and the competitive rivalry that exists amongst existing organisations in the industry. Each of these is now considered in turn in the context of AutoFone, focusing on those factors that have a significant effect on their industry. It must be recognised that other models might have been used in framing this answer and credit will be given for using appropriate models in the context of the AutoFone retail shops division.

Potential entrants (the threat of entry)

New entrants into an industry bring new capacity and resources with which they aim to gain market share. Their entry may lead to price reductions, increased costs and reduced profitability for organisations already in that market. Potential entrants may be deterred by high barriers to entry and by the threat of aggressive retaliation from existing competitors in the industry.

In the context of AutoFone's retail sales business, the following barriers appear to be the most significant:

Access to supply channels

The retail outlets of AutoFone were established before the network providers developed their own retail outlets. At the time, the network providers were sceptical that mobile phones could be sold through shops. Consequently, AutoFone was able to negotiate favourable long-term supply deals. It now seems unlikely that the network providers would sign such deals (because the new entrant will be a competitor of their own retail business) and, if they did, any deals would be at less favourable terms. As the managing director of one of the networks suggested, 'AutoFone had got away with incredible profit margins' when they signed the original deals in 1990. Improved supply terms would be attractive to the network provider and phone manufacturers (who would increase their profitability on each unit sold) but it would also cause profitability problems for the new entrant. Furthermore, the provision of networks is currently highly regulated, with licences still having thirteen years to run. It seems unlikely that public policy restricting the number of network providers allowed to provide services will change in the foreseeable future and so access to supply channels will remain a very significant barrier to entry.

Economies of scale deter entry by forcing the new entrant to come in at such a large scale that they risk strong reaction from existing firms in the marketplace. In the context of AutoFone, these economies of scale are associated with purchasing, service and distribution of products through a large scale retail network of 415 shops. Any new entrant would have to enter at a scale that would incur relatively significant capital investment. Furthermore, evidence suggests that the AutoFone brand is well known in the market place, with consumers identifying it, in 20X5, as one of the 'top 20' brands in the country. New entrants would not only have to fund a large number of retail outlets, they would also have to support their entry by investing heavily in 'un-recoverable up-front advertising' (Porter, 20X4). Capital will also be required for establishing significant inventories in the large number of retail shops required to achieve the required economies of scale.

Bargaining power of suppliers

Suppliers exert bargaining power over participants in an industry by raising prices or reducing the quality of their goods and services. Suppliers tend to be powerful when the industry is dominated by a few companies. This is the case with the mobile phone industry where the supply of networks is dominated by relatively few suppliers. The potential role of suppliers restricting the supply channel has already been recognised as a barrier to entry. However, when supplier power is high, there is a possibility that the suppliers themselves will seek forward integration, with 'suppliers competing directly with their buyers if they do not obtain the prices, and hence the margins that they seek' (Johnson, Scholes and Whittington, 20X5). This is exactly the situation affecting AutoFone, with network suppliers now running their own retail outlets.

There are two further elements of the retail phone market which encourage the supplier group to exert significant power. These are:

- The supplier group does not have to contend with other substitute products for sale to the industry. There are few direct substitutes for the mobile phone (see below).

- The supplier's product is an important input to the buyer's business. In AutoFone's situation it is a vital input into the business.

Hence the bargaining power of suppliers is extremely high in AutoFone's retail industry, although this is reduced by AutoFone's long-term supply contracts.

Bargaining power of buyers

Buyers attempt to obtain lower prices or seek to get increased or better quality services or products. They do this by playing competitors off against each other. Under certain conditions a buyer group can have considerable influence. Many of these conditions only arise when the buyer itself is an organisation, not an individual consumer. For example, Porter suggests that buyer power is high when there is a credible threat of the buyer integrating backwards into the market place and so becoming a competitor. Such conditions do not appear to apply to the retail phone industry which is largely aimed at individual consumers.

However, some of the circumstances of significant buyer bargaining power do appear to exist in the industry. For example: *the products buyers purchase are standard or undifferentiated*. Buyers are always sure that they can find an alternative supplier and so they can play one supplier off against another. This is the case for sale of mobile phones as a whole, not just the retail sector. Furthermore, *buyers face few switching costs*. The only real lock-in is the term of the contract, currently twelve months long, after which buyers can switch to a competitor without penalty.

Threat of substitutes

Substitute products are usually products that can perform the same *function* as the product of the industry under consideration. The threat to the mobile phone industry is largely from other products that support mobile communication, such as Personal Digital Assistants (PDAs). However, the trend has been to integrate this technology into the offerings of the industry. The products offered by AutoFone include phones that are also mp3 players, radios, cameras and allow email and web access. Hence the industry appears to be relatively free of potential substitutes.

Competitive rivalry in the industry

Rivalry normally always takes place within an industry. Rivals jockey for position by reducing prices, launching advertising campaigns and improving customer service or product warranty. In the context of the retail mobile phone industry, the intensity of the rivalry is fuelled by:

Equally balanced competitors. The information in Table 2 suggests that the retail sales market is relatively equally divided between the five main suppliers. Evidence suggests this creates instability in the market because the companies are 'prone to fight each other and have the resources for sustained and vigorous retaliation'. (Porter, 20X4)

Lack of differentiation or switching costs. Mobile phones are largely perceived by customers as commodities. In such circumstances buyer choice is based on price and service, and this results in intense pressure for price and service competition.

Slowing industry growth. Evidence from Table 2 also suggests that industry growth is slowing considerably. There was less than 1% growth in 20X7. This means that competitors will increasingly pursue growth by increasing market share. This will intensify the rivalry between the competitors.

(b)   The two longest serving directors of AutoFone have suggested that the retail business should be divested and that AutoFone should re-position itself as an on-line retailer of phones. They argue that an organisation concentrating solely on Internet sales and insurance would be a 'smaller but more profitable' organisation. The CEO is vehemently opposed to such a strategy because it was the shop-based approach to selling mobile phones that formed the original basis of the company. He has strong emotional attachment to the retail business. The two directors claim that this attachment is clouding his judgement and hence he is unable to see the logic of an 'economically justifiable exit from the retail business'.

This question asks the candidate to draft a supporting case for the CEO's position, so that his response is not just seen to be based upon emotional attachment. The briefing paper should challenge the suggestion of the two directors and provide a reasoned case for opposing the divestment of the retail sales business. Of course, divestment might be the best option. The four network providers might pay a handsome price to remove AutoFone from the market. However, this is not the focus of the question!

Briefing paper

Introduction

This paper begins by looking at the basis of the directors' suggestion and claims that they have not interpreted the business situation correctly. It then goes on to examine the exit barriers that AutoFone must consider if they are to seriously consider moving out of the retail sales market.

Product and industry life cycles

It has to be recognised that industries and products move through life-cycles. The slowdown in market growth documented in table 2 suggests that, in the context of the product life-cycle model, the mobile phone market appears to be in either the shake-out or maturity stage. This means that buyers will be increasingly selective and that for many buyers the purchase will be a repeat event affected by previous experience. Companies in the market will have to fight to gain market share and the emphasis will increasingly be on efficiency and low cost. Similarly, industries pass from rapid growth into the more modest growth associated with industry maturity. Like most infant industries the mobile phone industry experienced rapid growth as it developed. However, evidence from table 2 and table 3 suggests that both growth and profits are now reducing as the industry matures. Slowing growth in the industry means that there is more competition for market share as companies seek to maintain their own growth at the expense of others. The transition to maturity usually means that the old 'way of life' of the company has to change. It is significant that the idea for divestment has come from the two longest serving directors. They can recall the excitement associated with rapid growth and, in the case of AutoFone, the pioneering of a business idea. In many ways the current expansion of AFDirect recalls the early period of AutoFone and so operating in the growing Internet market appeals to them.

Financial analysis

An analysis of Table 3 shows how profitability has fallen. The ROCE has steadily declined from over 18% in 20X3 to just over 5% in 20X7. Net profit margin has fallen from just over 12% in 20X3 to just over 3% in 20X7. Gross profit margins have not fallen quite as much as this. However, liquidity has remained almost constant during this period and so the ability of the company to meet its short term financial obligations has not been impaired by the fall in profitability. Gearing has risen during the period, from just over 21% to just over 32% and this reflects increased dependence on borrowed money. However, the absolute level of gearing should probably not be a cause for concern.

Porter suggests that one of the issues of the transition to a mature market is that directors have to scale down their expectations of financial performance. 'If managers try to meet the old standards, they may take actions that are extremely dysfunctional for the long-term health of the company.' The concern is that the two directors are pursuing such a policy, giving up too quickly and sacrificing a market and market share in favour of a course of action that they believe will deliver short-term profits. Divestment means that they are avoiding the challenges of taking a business like AutoFone into its mature stage.

Industry structure

Evidence from the analysis of AutoFone's competitive position (part a) suggests that AutoFone is in a retail industry dominated by powerful suppliers. Customer bargaining power is also relatively strong and reduced growth in the industry has led to relatively fierce competition. However, there is little threat from substitutes or new entrants because of the high entry barriers. Consequently, AutoFone is in a unique position based on its early entry into the market before the network providers became aware of the potential of retail sales. Furthermore, the company's uniqueness is enhanced by the fact that it is the only retail outlet to offer genuinely independent advice. The two directors appear to wish to carry on in the old way rather than changing strategy and expectations to reflect the maturing of the product and the industry. The real challenge for the board is to exploit AutoFone's unique market position in this changing landscape.

Exit barriers

Exit barriers are economic, strategic and emotional factors that keep companies competing in industries in which they are earning low or even negative returns. These are the barriers concerned with preventing the company from leaving the industry. In the context of AutoFone there are at least two potential non-emotional exit barriers which need to be considered.

Costs associated with leaving the industry

- The high cost of terminating shop leases. AutoFone achieved low start up costs by taking on very long leases. These leases are often in areas just outside the main shopping areas and so may be difficult to re-let.

- The high cost of staff redundancies and the liquidation of stock. There are currently 1,400 employees in the retail shops division.

Loss of strategic interrelationship with other parts of the company

The divestment of the retail shops business is likely to have an important effect on the two remaining divisions (AFDirect and AFInsure) in at least two ways

Reduced brand perception. Research has shown that AutoFone is a well recognised brand. However, most of this brand awareness was built by the retail shops division. The brand is also being constantly reinforced by consumers seeing and visiting these shops. Removing these will lose this reinforcement. Indeed if shops lie empty (because of the difficulty of reletting shops with long leases) it could harm the brand. Customers may perceive that AutoFone is a company in trouble (or indeed has ceased trading altogether) and so the Internet and insurance arms suffer as a result.

Reduced sell-on into related businesses. Evidence (from table 2) suggests that most insurance sales are in the age bands which predominantly purchase from the retail shops. Hence it seems likely that most insurance sales result from the sales of mobile phones in the retail sales operation. There are probably two reasons for this. Firstly, retail sales are mainly to customers in a certain age group. These customers are less confident in their purchase (which is why they are visiting the shop) and as a result can be guided in the purchase of insurance. Secondly, sales assistants giving this advice are given commission incentives to sell insurance. Consequently, the closing of the shops may have a major effect on the income of the insurance business.

There is also the issue of the cross-selling benefits between the retail sales and Internet sales business. There is evidence to suggest that some customers visit a retail branch to physically see the phones and to get advice before ordering on the Internet. This is currently an issue for staff in the shops who spend time explaining the features of a particular phone only to see the potential customer leave and order the same item on the Internet. Of course not all of these Internet orders are made through AFDirect because customers may take advantage of better offers from rival suppliers. However, a percentage of those sales must be as a result of a shop visit and the company potentially loses the benefit of these goodwill sales as a result of closing their shops. There is also evidence that Internet customers value the option of visiting a shop to get after-sales service for a product bought from AFDirect over the Internet. Although sales staff currently dislike offering this service, removing it may again hit Internet sales.

Conclusion

The company needs to recognise that the mobile phone market has matured and this has implications for both growth and profits. However, AutoFone remains in good shape to exploit the opportunities, such as repeat buying, of a maturing market place. Although profitability has declined, liquidity has remained constant. Gearing has increased but it has not risen to a figure which would cause concern. There are significant exit barriers to leaving the market place. The most significant of these is the loss of a strategic interrelationship with other parts of the company. The Internet division could suffer significantly if AutoFone closed its retail shops division.

ACCA Marking scheme		Marks
(a)	Up to 5 marks are available for recognising issues concerned with the difficulties facing potential new entrants into this industry.	5
	Up to 4 marks for recognising the very powerful bargaining position of suppliers in this industry.	4
	Up to 3 marks for identifying the bargaining power of customers.	3
	Up to 2 marks for identifying the threat of substitutes to the products offered in the industry.	2
	Up to 4 marks for identifying how competitors in the industry compete with each other.	4
	Up to 2 professional marks for the logical structure and clarity of information in the context of the case study scenario.	2
(b)	Up to 3 marks for recognising the brand recognition implications of moving out of retail sales.	3
	Up to 3 marks for recognising the likely impact on AFDirect and AFInsure	3
	Up to 2 marks for recognising cost implications of exit on leases, staff, stock	2
	Up to 2 marks for recognising that the financial position is not as poor as suggested by the two directors	2
	Up to 2 marks for interpreting the structural changes in the industry	2
	Up to 3 professional marks for using an appropriate style for the report and for the strength of argument and for appropriately utilising evidence from within the context of the case study	3
Total		**35**

Examiner's comments

The only general point I wish to make concerns the use of case study scenarios. Many candidates had a problem applying the theoretical knowledge they had learned to the context of the scenario. At this level, there are relatively few marks available for describing a model such as Porter's five competitive forces. The vast majority of the marks are for recognising the presence and effect of these forces in the context of the case study scenario. Many of the answers seemed to suggest that candidates had very little practice in the application of models. If this is the case, candidates should integrate such practice into their preparation for the examination.

It is important that the fifteen minute reading time at the start of the examination is used effectively. One of the ways of making it more effective is to read the questions before reading the case study! This allows the candidate to put the case study into the context of the questions.

As in other papers, there is no irrelevant information in the case study scenarios. Candidates must concentrate on linking the scenario information to questions and (where applicable) to appropriate models. For example, the case study for section A stressed the value of the brand. This was relevant to part a (as an entry barrier to potential suppliers) and part b (as a reason for not leaving the retail market).

This question was based on a scenario of a mobile telephone company – AutoFone. There were three parts to this question. The first part asked candidates to analyse the competitive environment of AutoFone's retail sales division. This was worth twenty marks which included two professional marks. Two of the directors of AutoFone had suggested that this division should be sold off and that AutoFone should reposition itself as an on-line retailer of phones. The second part of the question asked candidates to write a briefing paper to the CEO to support the strategy of retaining the retail shops division. This was worth fifteen marks including three professional marks.

The first part of the question asked candidates to use an appropriate model or models to analyse the competitive environment. As expected, most candidates chose to use Porter's five competitive forces as a framework for answering this question. The scenario itself was constructed to encourage this approach. For example, there are very clear barriers to entry signposted in the scenario and the data summarised in table 2 provided information about industry competitors. Some candidates chose to use PESTEL and SWOT. PESTEL is concerned primarily with the macro environment and SWOT considers internal factors as well as external ones. However, candidates who used these two models could gain marks as they do identify relevant issues in the scenario. For example, the political perspective of PESTEL helps identify the issue of the government control of network licences and the long-term implications of this. Unfortunately many candidates penalised themselves by actually describing and using all three models (five forces, PESTEL and SWOT), leading to long answers with significant repetition. There is little to be gained by using different models to make the same points. It was also apparent that this repetition led to some candidates having time problems later on in the examination. This part of the question was only worth 20 marks and time should have been allocated accordingly. In general, this part of the question was answered relatively well with many candidates making appropriate use of the model they had selected.

The second part of the question asked candidates to draft a briefing paper to support a particular strategy. The CEO is strongly opposed to the suggestion of the two directors to sell off the retail shops division and to reposition the company as an on-line retailer of phones. The three professional marks associated with this part of the question reflect the fact that candidates are given extra credit for a well-argued, coherent case for retaining the retail shops division. Candidates needed to extract the information in the scenario that could be marshalled to support the case for retention. This part of the question was not answered well by many candidates. Consequently, I thought it would be useful to look at this part of the question in some depth and to identify how marks might have been gained by using information from the scenario.

The scenario explicitly defines two financial exit barriers. The first is the long shop leases that AutoFone have agreed in order to secure low initial rentals. It seems unlikely that these will all be immediately reassigned, particularly given their location on the edge of main shopping areas. The second is the cost of making the employees of the retail shops redundant. The scenario also makes it clear that brand image is a significant strength of AutoFone. Indeed it is has been 'rated by consumers as one of the top 20 brands in the country'. Closing retail branches sends the wrong message. The visibility of the brand is reduced as consumers no longer see the retail shops that serve to reinforce the brand image.

Furthermore, if the shops are closed down and perhaps some lie empty for a while, the brand can be tarnished and AutoFone would be seen as a company in difficulties or, perhaps, as one that has ceased trading altogether. Many candidates recognised that the closure of the branches removed the possibility of cross-selling that exists at the moment. It can be argued that internet sales will be affected by removing the pre-sales discussion and post-sales service and support provided by the shops. A further significant point is that table 1 shows that insurance is sold primarily to the age groups that purchase from the retail shops. 54% of retail shop sales are to people aged 41 and over. 71% of insurance sales are made to this age category. This compares with 22% of internet sales (AFDirect) made to people aged 41 and over. The inference is that AFInsure will suffer from closing the retail shops division. Many candidates also stated that people aged 41 and over had more disposable income than younger people and so were a more attractive market. This fact was not explicitly stated in the scenario, but it seems a reasonable assumption and credit was given for this observation.

The financial information that supported this case study primarily showed that the retail shops division is still in reasonably good shape. Nothing in the figures suggests that a radical change in strategic direction is necessary. The company is still profitable and indeed profit margins have improved in 20X7, compared to 20X6. Liquidity has remained fairly constant since 20X3, and although gearing has increased it is not significantly geared given the type of retail operation it is running. Some candidates did recognise this, suggesting that the two directors were panicking to think of closing a division that produced 85% of the company's revenue. They suggested that the two directors should just recognise that the product/market has reached a mature stage (table 2 and the financial figures support this) and so should scale down their expectations and adjust to new circumstances.

So, here in point form, are the main issues raised above. Each point (in suitably expanded form) would be worth one or two marks. It is not an exhaustive list, but it shows how marks can be gained by using the information in the scenario. There is a maximum of twelve marks for this question (remember the three other marks are for style, format and approach). However, more significantly, a candidate had to only make some of the following points to guarantee a pass mark on this question. Unfortunately many failed to do so.

- Cost of continuing leases, re-assignment costs

- Cost of making staff redundant

- Visibility of the brand

- Damage to the brand (closure, empty shops)

- Effect on internet sales of removal of pre-sales and post-sales support

- Effect on insurance sales and that division

- Age group analysis of retail and insurance sales (wealthy consumers)

- Financial figures do not support case for radical change

- Profitability has improved in 20X7 compared with 20X6 (corner turned?)

- Liquidity constant since 20X3

- Gearing slightly increased but not significant

- Retail division generates 85% of the revenue

- Recognition of mature stage of product/market (table 2 supports this)

- Directors over-reacting, need to recognise change and manage accordingly

73 WET

(a) This first part of the question asks the candidate to analyse the strategic position at WET. Johnson, Scholes and Whittington describe the strategic position in terms of three aspects; the environment, strategic capability and expectations and purpose. All three aspects are appropriate in the analysis of the strategic position of WET and this classification forms the basis of the model answer. However, candidates could have adopted a number of approaches to this question, perhaps choosing to focus on certain models (such as the value chain) or exploring the organisation through an analysis of the cultural web. All such answers will be given credit as long as they are within the context of WET and consider the external environment, internal resources and capabilities, and the expectations of various stakeholders. In the context of the ACCA *Business Analysis* syllabus, the strategic position is defined within section A of the detailed syllabus.

The environment

The PESTEL framework can be used to analyse the macro-environment. A number of influences are discernable from the case study scenario.

90% of WET's income is from members and donors (see Figure 1) who live in Arcadia, a country which has had ten years of sustained economic growth but which is now experiencing economic problems. The scenario reports a decline in Gross Domestic Product (GDP) for three successive quarters, increasing unemployment, stagnant wages and a fall in retail sales. There are also increasing problems with servicing both personal and business debt leading to business bankruptcy and homelessness. These are classic symptoms of a recession and this will have an effect on both individual and business donations and also on membership renewal. WET is 20% funded by donations (see Figure 1). In general, people give more when they earn more and lower earnings will almost inevitably mean lower donations. Furthermore, it could reasonably be expected that a recession places greater demand on certain charities, such as those dealing with social care (for example, homelessness). WET is not one of those charities (and so should not experience an increase in demand), so there must also be a concern that donors will switch donations to social care charities in times of recession. Similarly, current members may not renew their membership for financial reasons.

The pressures in the economy also appear to have stimulated the government to change the rules on charity taxation in an effort to raise government revenues. Previously, charities received an income from the government of 20% of the total value of donations and membership fees to reflect the income tax the donor would have paid on the amount paid to the charity. However, the government has declared that this is unfair as not all donations or membership fees are from Arcadian taxpayers or from people in Arcadia who actually pay tax. Consequently, in the future, charities will have to prove that the donation or membership fee was from an Arcadian tax payer. Collecting the donor's details will place an increased administrative strain on the charity, incurring more costs. The changes are also likely to lead to a fall in income. There are two reasons for this. Firstly, some of the donations were actually from non-Arcadian taxpayers (see Figure 1) and also research and evidence from elsewhere suggests that 30% of donors will not give the GiftHelp details required and so the charity will not be able to reclaim tax.

Although the recession in Arcadia has brought economic and political issues to the fore, the wider environment remains very significant to WET. The wetlands that they depend upon are likely to be drying out in a country where rainfall has dropped significantly. This will lead to the loss of the habitat that the charity wishes to protect. The charity must continue to monitor the situation and to support initiatives that should reduce climate change and perhaps increase rainfall.

The five forces framework proposed by Porter is usually applied to private profit-making organisations. However, the framework could also be useful in a not-for-profit organisation, considering the services provided by a sector (however that sector is defined). In such sectors, competitiveness may be about gaining advantage through demonstrable excellence. From WET's perspective, it needs to consider two overlapping sectors. Figure 1 suggests that 55% of members and 85% of donors give money (through donations or membership) to other charities. In such circumstances, WET is competing for the 'charity dollar'. However, 45% of members and 15% of donors gave no money to other charities, suggesting that these people are focused on the wetlands cause.

If charities as a whole are considered as a sector, then there appears to be a constant threat to WET of new entrants into this sector. The *barriers to entry* appear to be quite low. The ease with which a charity can be established has been widely criticised, but suggested reforms to the Commission of Charities have been rejected by the Government. However, if wetland preservation is perceived as a sector then the barriers to entry are quite considerable. WET already owns all of the significant wetland sites in Arcadia and, because of climate change, new sites would have to be artificially created at great expense. The scenario mentions a charity that has been formed to raise money to create a new wetland. The amount of money pledged so far ($90,000) is not only well below their target but also represents money that may have been donated to WET if this new charity had not been permitted.

The threat of substitutes is ever-present. WET competes for disposable income and so is exposed to *generic substitution* where donors and members decide to 'do without' or to spend their money elsewhere, including other charitable causes such as social care, particularly in a recession. If donors are giving to increase their own well-being and to feel good about themselves ('warm glow') then perhaps any charity will do, as *switching costs* are very low. The point has already been made that certain charities will experience higher demand during a recession and so WET will be vulnerable to such competition. However, if donors are committed to the wetland cause then supplier power is high because WET is the only significant wetland charity in Arcadia.

The competitive rivalry again depends upon the perception of the sector WET is competing in. In the charity sector as a whole, WET is a small player. Figure 2 illustrates that most money is given to health charities, followed by social care and international causes. However, in the wetland sector, WET is the dominant charity, led by a recognised and charismatic public figure.

Strategic capability

The strategic capability of an organisation is made up of resources and competences. Considering this capability leads to a consideration of *strengths and weaknesses,* with the aim of forming a view of the internal influences on future strategic choices.

WET have significant tangible resources in terms of the wetlands that they own. They also have experienced and knowledgeable human resources, many of whom give their services for free. They also have a strong brand, associated with a well-known public figure. However, although these resources are significant and represent important strengths, the way they have been deployed needs examination. This analysis concerns the competences of the organisation; the activities and processes through which an organisation deploys its resources. The wetlands are uninviting to members, with poor access and poor facilities. The volunteers are disillusioned by poor management and feel that they are not valued. These significant weaknesses appear to be contributing to the organisation's inability to maintain the *threshold capabilities* required to retain members.

However, it also has to be recognised that WET does have unique resources (the wetlands) that competitors would find it almost impossible to obtain. It also has, in Zohail Abbas, a well recognised public figure that potential competitors in the wetlands sector would find hard to imitate. However, these *unique resources,* do need to be better exploited.

A cursory examination of the value chain reinforces some of the weaknesses identified above and identifies others. Within the primary activities, service is weak and this is contributing to a decline in membership. Marketing and sales is also an acknowledged weakness of the organisation. Within the support activities, human resource management (particularly of volunteers) has already been identified as a problem. Technology development (in terms of IT technology) is also a problem with restricted and cumbersome systems causing problems in the primary activities.

Summary of strengths and weaknesses

Strengths	Weaknesses
Ownership of wetlands	Management of volunteers
Experienced volunteer work force	Wetland access and facilities
Strong brand	Marketing and sales
High profile leader	Information systems

Expectations and purposes

The two previous sections have considered the influence of the environment and the resources available to the organisation. This section looks at what people expect from the organisation. This is particularly significant in WET because it has undergone a significant change in what Johnson, Scholes and Whittington term 'its ethical stance'. Under Zohail Abbas, the organisation was shaped by ideology and was 'mission-driven', demonstrating a single-minded zeal that charities usually require to achieve their aims. However, charities still have to be financially and operationally viable and WET relies on two important stakeholders; members and volunteers.

In his speech at the 20X9 AGM Dr Abbas admitted that he had failed to sufficiently take into account the needs of members (leading to a decline in membership) and of volunteers (leading to a large turnover and scarcity of volunteers). WET now needs to recognise that 'stakeholder interests and expectations should be more explicitly incorporated in the organisation's purposes and strategies' (Johnson, Scholes and Whittington). Any strategy devised by the CEO needs to recognise this shift in ethical stance.

Understanding stakeholder perspectives and expectations is an important part of analysing the organisation's strategic position. Members require better access to wetland sites and more feedback on the activities of the organisation. Volunteers wish to be valued more, treated professionally and be given the chance to participate in decision-making. Having sufficient, knowledgeable volunteers appears to be necessary if some of the members' expectations are to be fulfilled. The contribution of volunteers becomes even more significant in a recession, when an organisation might have to reduce paid staff. WET also have to be aware of the potential effects of the recession on individual volunteers. For example, it appears that the failure to pay travelling expenses may have caused unnecessary hardship and led to the loss of volunteers. The CEO must also be aware that the consultation exercise with both members and volunteers will have fostered the expectations of a more open and democratic leadership culture, contrasting with Dr Abbas's autocratic style.

The original mission statement of WET was to preserve, restore and manage wetlands in Arcadia. It might be an appropriate time to revisit this mission statement, to explicitly recognise stakeholder concerns. For example, many members and volunteers are concerned with observing and saving wildlife, not wetlands. This could be explicitly recognised in the mission statement 'to save wetlands and their wildlife' or perhaps to 'preserve, restore and manage wetlands for wildlife and those who wish to observe them'. This would be a mission statement to which most of the stakeholders in WET could subscribe.

(b) A number of problems have been explicitly identified in the scenario. However, the swim lane flowchart helps identify two further problems, which may themselves explain some of the other documented difficulties.

1 Firstly, the flowchart clearly shows that sales and marketing receive renewal confirmations before payment is cleared. This means that membership cards and booklets are being sent to members whose payments have not yet cleared. The receipt of this documentation probably suggests to these members that payment has cleared, so response to the payment request is not necessary. They probably see it as an administrative mistake and ignore the reminder. This would help explain the very low rates of people who pay when they receive their payment request. It is not, as the finance manager said 'an unethical response from supposedly ethical people', but a problem caused by their own system. Perhaps those that do subsequently pay have taken the trouble of checking whether money has been debited to WET from their bank or credit card account. The consequence of this faulty process is that a significant number of members unwittingly receive a free year's membership. It may also help explain why a number of members do not receive a renewal invoice at the end of their membership year. These renewal invoices are only sent to members who have been updated on the system after their payments have cleared. If the payment never cleared, then the membership will have lapsed on the system and a renewal invoice will not be raised the following year.

2   Secondly, the receipt of a cleared renewal payment is only recorded when the membership details are updated on the Membership computer system by the Membership Department. Consequently, renewal reminders will be sent out to members whose payment is still awaiting clearance. It currently takes the Finance Department an average of five days from the receipt of the renewal to notifying the Membership Department of the cleared payment. There is also a backlog of cleared notifications in this department, awaiting entry into the computer system. These members may also receive unwanted renewal reminders. Finally, members who have received a membership card and booklet through the process described in the previous paragraph will also receive a renewal reminder letter. Presumably most members ignore this letter (after all, they have received the new card and booklet) and believe that the charity is inefficient and is wasting money on producing renewal reminders for those who have already renewed their membership. Charities have to be careful about spending money on wasteful administrative processes. It might be these renewal reminders that led to the accusations about the charity wasting money.

A number of options can be considered for redesigning the membership renewal process. Some are given below. They range from simple changes, remedying the faults identified in the previous answer, to significant changes in the way WET will accept payment. Credit will be given for answers that suggest feasible amendments and also specify the likely consequences of the change to WET as an organisation, to employees in affected departments and to the systems they use.

- Remedy the fault identified in the previous part of the question 1(b) by only notifying sales and marketing of membership renewal once payment has been cleared, not just received. The consequence of this is that a membership card and booklet will only be sent to members who have paid their subscriptions. This should lead to an increase in subscription income because a percentage of members whose payment did not clear first time will now make sure that their payment clears. No changes are required to the membership computer system or departmental responsibilities.

- Remedy the second fault identified above, so that renewal reminders are only sent to members who have not responded to the renewal invoice, not to members who have responded but whose payment is still awaiting clearance. This could be achieved by initially updating the membership system when a payment is received. The consequence of this is that renewal reminder letters will not be sent to members who have renewed, but not yet had their payment cleared. This will reduce waste and improve member's perception of the efficiency of the organisation. However, it will require a change to the computer system and will also lead to more work for the Membership Department and another handoff between the Finance and Membership Departments. This handoff will introduce the chance of error and delay. The Membership Department already has a backlog in entering the details of members' renewals where payments have successfully cleared.

- A suggested generic process improvement is to reduce the number of handoffs between parts of the organisation by reducing the number of swim lanes. It is perceived that handoffs have the potential for introducing delay, cost and error. A number of options are possible, but perhaps the most obvious is to merge (for the purpose of this process) the functions of the Finance and the Membership Departments. This is because at one point (and perhaps two, if the previous suggestion is adopted) Finance are simply notifying the Membership Department of an event (payment cleared and, potentially, payment received), which the Membership Department has to then enter into the computer system. The case study scenario suggests that there is a backlog of membership details to enter. This probably results in renewal reminders being sent to members who have already renewed and whose payment has cleared. Merging the swim lanes will require all staff to have access to the computer system, sufficient competency in using it and sufficient numbers to clear the backlog. The likely consequence of the change is that renewal reminder letters will not be sent to members who have already renewed and paid. This will reduce waste and improve members' perception of the efficiency of the organisation. Another likely consequence is that staff may need re-training, their jobs redefined and any political problems caused by merging two departments will have to be identified and addressed.

- Another generic process improvement approach is to make sure that validation takes place as soon as possible. It should be part of the primary activity, not a separate activity as it is at the moment. This approach is particularly appropriate in the checking of payment details in the renew membership process. The early validation of payment could be achieved by giving the member the option of renewing by credit card over the Internet. 60% of the payments are made through credit cards. About 5% of these payments are completed incorrectly and the Finance Department have to raise a finance request to ask for the correct details. If a member was able to make a credit card payment over the internet then all errors should be eliminated, as the validation of details will be made straight away by the credit card provider. WET should receive the money sooner (improving the cash flow position) and there should be a reduction in finance requests. This should reduce costs and perhaps allow a reduction in head count in the Finance Department. However, the internet site would have to be extended to include an e-commerce solution and this will cost money. As well as the initial cost, the provider of the financial solution will also charge a fee for each transaction.

- The final option presented here is a more radical solution that is currently used by many subscription organisations. The principle is that renewal will happen automatically unless the member specifically asks for it not to. They have to 'opt out', rather than 'opt in' as under the present solution. Automatic renewals could initially charge the credit card used for the previous year's membership. Renewals that required a positive response would only be sent out to those who paid by cheque. Renewals to credit card customers would remind them that the card would be debited on a certain date, but that no action was necessary to secure another year's membership. This should help address the retained membership issue discussed in the scenario, based on the fact that opting out is much harder than opting in.

WET might also consider offering payment by direct debit, using similar process logic to that used for credit cards. In a bid to reduce members who pay by cheque, discounts may be offered for paying by direct debit or automatically triggered credit card transactions. As well as increasing subscription income from higher member retention, the solution should lead to improved cash flow and reduced administrative costs. Changes to the membership computer system will have to be specified, implemented and tested.

(c)   The incoming CEO of WET has identified the better acquisition and management of members, volunteers and donors as an important objective. She has identified them all as important *customers of WET* and she sees e-mail and website technology as facilitating the acquisition, retention and exploitation of these customers. In discussing customer relationship management, Dave Chaffey (see syllabus Reading List) considers customer acquisition, customer retention and what he terms customer extension. This classification is used in this model answer. However answers that still make the same points, but do not use this classification, are perfectly acceptable.

Customer acquisition

Customer acquisition is concerned with two things. The first is using the website to acquire new customers (donors, members and volunteers). The second is to convert customers acquired through conventional means into on-line customers.

When people visit the WET website they may already be committed to becoming a member, a volunteer or giving a donation. For these people, the process of enrolment or donation must be completely clear and complete. There must be no break in the process which might allow doubt or hesitation and lead the participant to withdrawing. The final two options suggested in the answer to question 1(b), would provide such a complete solution. Customers enrolling or donating on the website might also be given inducements, such as a reduced membership rate or a free book.

People who visit the website and are still uncertain about joining or donating might be induced to take part in an offer, which requires them to enter basic details (such as name and e-mail address) in return for some service or product. For example, free tickets for an open day or discounted prices on selected books. These e-mail details are essentially sales leads and become the basis of selected future e-mails encouraging recipients to join or donate. They might also be used (if a phone number is requested) for telephone sales calls.

Incentives may also be required to convert current customers to the web site. A typical approach is to define a members' area where members have access to various resources and offers. For example, a webcam showing live action from selected wetlands. Existing members would also be encouraged to renew membership on-line, as discussed in the previous part question.

Customer retention

Customer profiling is a key area of both acquisition and retention. WET needs to understand the needs and interests of individuals and target them accordingly. At the broader level, customers can be differentiated into segments, such as prospects, members, volunteers and donors. These segments will be communicated to in different ways and this can be reflected in the website, for example, by establishing different areas for volunteers and members. However, profiling can also take place at the individual level, reflected in personalised e-mails to individuals that reference known interests and so encourage continued participation in WET.

On-line communities are a key feature of e-business and may be created to reflect purpose, position, interest or profession. Two of these communities are particularly relevant to WET. The primary one is of *interest,* creating a community for people who share the same interest or passion for wetlands and the wildlife they support. This could be created as an extension of the current WET website or as an independent site, where criticisms of WET itself could be posted. WET should either sponsor or co-brand such a site. Communities provide an opportunity for members and volunteers to actively contribute to WET and build up loyalty, making continued membership more likely. They also provide WET with important feedback and ideas for improving their service to both members and volunteers. WET themselves might also wish to get involved in communities of *purpose* where people are going through the same process or trying to achieve a particular objective. For example, there are websites dedicated to providing a one-stop-shop for those wishing to make donation to charity.

Customer extension

This has the aim of increasing the lifetime value of the customer by encouraging cross-sales. This may be within the scope of WET itself, for example, by selling WET branded goods. However, it is also likely to include links and advertising on the WET site for associated products. WET will receive income from direct advertising fees or from a commission in the sales generated from the site. For example, book purchases may be handled through a specialist book site (leading to commission payments) or binoculars purchased from a manufacturer (payment for advertising space). Direct e-mail is also an effective way of telling customers about the products of other companies and can also be used to publicise promotions and new features and so encourage visits to the website.

	ACCA Marking scheme	Marks
(a)	1 mark for each relevant point up to a maximum of 25 marks. This includes a professional mark for appropriate tone, a professional mark for appropriate structure and two professional marks for the scope of the answer (4 marks in total).	25
(b)	1 mark for each relevant point up to a maximum of 15 marks.	15
(c)	1 mark for each relevant point up to a maximum of 10 marks.	10
Total		**50**

Examiner's comments

In general, the first part question was answered well by candidates, using a wide range of appropriate models and frameworks. PESTEL analysis was widely used, and although this was appropriate, there was insufficient information in the case study scenario to completely answer the question using this framework. For example, there was little about technology and socio-cultural issues. Consequently, many candidates discussed the restricted web site technology of WET under this heading, which is strictly an internal weakness. In this instance, we were prepared to give credit, as this weakness was part of the wider understanding of the strategic position. However, candidates must be careful in the future to stick to external issues if a PESTEL analysis is specified in the question.

Relatively few candidates used the five forces framework, although valuable points could have been made using this approach. For example, the low barriers to entry were a particular issue raised by the Commission of Charities reluctance to tighten up on charity registration. Similarly, the threat of substitutes is ever present, with WET competing for the 'charity dollar' in an environment where 'doing without' is also likely. A discussion of low switching costs would also have brought credit.

Finally, some candidates did not restrict themselves to assessing the strategic position. They began to suggest strategic solutions and options which were not required by the question and so no credit was no given. This reinforces the need for the candidate to carefully read the question and to answer within its scope.

However, overall this part question was answered well, if a little narrowly, with many answers well-written and well-structured, so gaining most of the professional marks on offer.

The case study scenario included a description of the process for membership renewal. This textual description was supported by a swim lane flowchart. Candidates were asked to analyse faults in the renewal process and to suggest solutions. This part of the question was worth 15 marks. It required an analysis of the business situation and the formulation of appropriate solutions. It did not require long theoretical descriptions of process redesign patterns, although these could have been usefully applied to the scenario.

This was a practical analysis question and it is disappointing that many candidates were unable to answer it effectively. Too many answers simply suggested that the computer system was at fault and should be fixed. Candidates failed to spot glaring errors in the process (sales and marketing received renewal confirmations before payment was cleared, delayed acknowledgement of payments led to renewal notifications being sent to members who had paid) and so many answers were too general and did not gain the marks on offer. Good answers needed to identify the fault, describe its consequences and suggest solutions, which could have been quite simple, and did not require any cross-reference to theoretical concepts.

Effective customer relationship management is essential to charities. Sheila Jenkins wishes to use email and website technology to facilitate the acquisition and retention of WET's customers and support WET's aim to gain increased revenues from members and donors. This part question was about effective customer relationship management; acquiring, retaining and exploiting customers. It was not a general question about the principles and benefits of web site and email technology. Too many answers were not in the context of the question. For example, independence of location (place) may be an attribute of the new media, but how can this be harnessed (if it can) in the context of customer relationship management? Many candidates probably thought they had answered this question relatively well (talking about 7Ps and 6Is) but in reality many answers did not score well and overall, this part question was disappointedly answered. In many cases, candidates provided good answers to a very different question.

74 REINK CO

(a) Introduction

This first section of the required report analyses the internal competencies of ReInk (in terms of its strengths and weaknesses) and the external environment which the company currently operates in. This environment creates opportunities for, and threats to, the organisation.

Strengths

Technological expertise is a significant strength of the company. It has successfully developed an innovative process for cheaply and successfully refilling ink cartridges. The technical elements of this process have been patented, which gives the company a further six years protection. The technical expertise of Dexter Black is acknowledged by his staff and his competitors. Many of the senior technical employees have been attracted to ReInk by the opportunity to work with an acknowledged expert in the field. Most of the skilled, experienced staff still remain at ReInk, although many are now seeking job opportunities elsewhere (see weaknesses).

The long-term contract with the government Department of Revenue Collections (DoRC) is an important asset. As well as providing 20% of the company's revenues, it also helps promote the legitimacy of ReInk as a significant and reliable supplier. Selling into other government departments may be a significant opportunity (see opportunities)

Location: Although ReInk is a high technology company, its operations are in a declining industrial town and are relatively cheap. Indeed, Dexter was originally attracted to the town by government grants and a rent-free period. Although this has now expired, the rent remains low. Furthermore, property prices in the area are also cheap, and the area offers a good standard of living. This means that staff can be attracted by relatively modest salaries, as one commented, 'I took a pay cut to come here. But I can now afford a bigger house and my children can breathe fresh country air.' In a market place where companies primarily compete on price, low production costs are important.

Weaknesses

The major weakness which has to be immediately addressed is the *financial state of the company*. Although ReInk is making a small operating profit, it is undermined by the need to service a considerable debt. The recent decision by Firmsure bank to reduce the company's overdraft facility has created a cash flow crisis which threatens the continued existence of the company. Capital needs to be injected into the company so that it can meet next month's payroll obligations.

Weak management team: The technological expertise of Dexter has been acknowledged. However, he has little commercial expertise or experience and the directors he has appointed to address this weakness have failed to deliver. The technologists at the company also have little faith in their management team, claiming that the sales director 'does not really understand the product' and the HR director 'clearly has no experience in dealing with professional staff'. The overall competence of the management team can be classified as a company weakness.

Demotivated staff: The employees are proud of their achievements and respect the technological expertise of Dexter. However, the attitude of senior management and the obvious financial problems of the company have combined to demotivate and demoralise them. A poorly thought out programme of cost cutting and staff regrading has compounded this attitude, and many are resigned to the company failing and are actively looking for other jobs.

The final weakness concerns *poor brand awareness*. Although ReInk is a technological leader, the public has little knowledge of its services and capabilities. Marketing has focused on the website, to the detriment of all other channels, where the company is up against competitors who appear to offer similar services and also have very similar trading names.

Opportunities

The continued decline of the economy provides a significant opportunity for ReInk. Both domestic and commercial users will be looking to reduce their printing costs and so the market place should be growing. Indeed, ReInk will have to monitor the economy to detect any upturn which could adversely affect the demand for its product.

Increased awareness of the need to reuse and recycle products should also provide the company with significant sales opportunities. The number of 'green consumers' is growing within the country. These consumers may have particular concerns about using printer cartridges which can only be used once, or which are expensive to recycle.

Government contracts: The economic problems in the country have accentuated the need for government departments to show value-for-money, as well as demonstrating excellent reuse and recycling practices.

Threats

Legal threats: It is important for the organisation to continually scan the legal environment to identify potential threats. Original Equipment Manufacturers (OEMs) have failed in their attempts to make refilling their products illegal. However, they continue to lobby political parties to change the law, citing their need for income from printer consumables to fund their investment in advances in printer technology. The company also has to be aware of threats to their patented process, or indeed to patents which might threaten their competitive edge.

Technical threats: Threats will continue to emerge from new technology. These threats might be to produce reusable ink services at a lower cost, or indeed to remove the need for ink replacement all together. The printer industry is very technology driven and ReInk will have to continuously monitor new innovations and product announcements to see if its services and products are threatened.

Competitive rivalry: The print consumables industry is very competitive. Entry costs into the industry are relatively low, and companies largely compete on price. This is partly why OEMs, with their higher costs, find it difficult to compete in this market. Consequently, they largely compete on quality and the generation of fear amongst consumers that unauthorised products could damage their printers, and, if they do, their printer warranty will be invalid. Thus it is an extremely competitive environment, with relatively low brand loyalty. If the potential damage to printers is overlooked, then there are no switching costs in moving to a different consumables supplier.

Finally, *the government is considering privatising the DoRC.* This could jeopardise the continuation of the contract to supply this department with reusable ink products and services, on which ReInk is highly dependent as it contributes 20% of its revenue.

In summary, the company is operating in a very competitive industry where OEMs also compete aggressively on non-price criteria. However, economic and environmental issues provide ReInk with opportunities for growth if they can properly harness their strengths and address the financial and management weaknesses of the company.

(b) **Introduction**

The second part of this report looks at the contextual features which will have to be taken into consideration if strategic change is to be successfully implemented at ReInk.

Time: refers to the amount of time available to implement change. An organisation which faces immediate problems has a quite different context for change than one which is stable enough to be able to plan carefully for incremental change over a number of years. ReInk has pressing financial problems and so Vi Ventures (VV) will have to move quickly to make their investment. However, once that investment is made, VV will then have some time to make the changes necessary to address the financial performance of ReInk. For example, investing in initiatives to increase brand awareness and increase sales which will increase the company's operating profit.

Preservation: In most change situations there is a need to preserve some elements of the current organisation. In particular, the change will have to safeguard the competencies which are vital if the change is to succeed. In the case of ReInk, these are the skills and experience of the technologists. These employees are key to the success of the company, but have become demotivated and restless, and some are actively looking for other jobs. If VV makes their proposed investment in ReInk, then they must move swiftly to reassure the senior technical staff and dissuade them from leaving the company.

Diversity: Diversity refers to *diversity of experience.* Change can be assisted by a significant degree of diversity of experience, views and opinions within the organisation. It is hampered by a homogenous view, formed from pursuing the same strategy for years. The latter seems more likely at ReInk. The focus has been on technical excellence and innovation. There are no clear groups offering a different perspective. If the proposed investment does take place, then VV can expect some resistance to change as they bring in new ideas and directions.

Capability: Capability concerns the experience the organisation has in managing change. Some organisations have experience of effectively managing change and also have a workforce which has readily accepted and implemented these changes. At ReInk, the opposite appears to apply. The management team has been unable to formulate any changes which have improved the financial performance of the company. Moreover, the changes they have implemented have not been accepted by the workforce and indeed have led to a fall in staff motivation. VV's experience of implementing change will be an important capability which they will bring to ReInk.

Capacity: Change programmes require management and financial resources. Capacity for change is concerned with whether the organisation has sufficient resources to effect the required change. In some circumstances, the organisation might have the capability to undertake the change, but they do not have the resources *(capacity)* to carry it out. At ReInk, the current management do not have the capability or the capacity. VV will have to invest financial and management resources to successfully implement strategic change.

Readiness: Readiness for change refers to how changes will be welcomed in the organisation. There may be certain employee groups who are resistant to change and will hamper the progress of change programmes. This appears unlikely at ReInk. The technologists are likely to positively embrace change as they are very disillusioned with the expertise of the current management team. VV should have little problem in convincing this group about the need for change, particularly as VV will be anxious that their competencies are *preserved* within the company. The most difficult group might be the current management team. Except for Dexter, it seems unlikely that they will have a role in the future. VV should be aware of this and ensure that the acquisition takes place in a way which does not alienate this group. Otherwise, the investment may not go ahead, as the management team protect their position, even if this is at the long-term detriment of the company.

Power: For change to be successful there has to be someone in the organisation who has the power to effect the desired changes. This again will influence the terms associated with VV's proposed investment. Given the situation, they need to be in a position in ReInk where they have such power, unencumbered by the current managing director or current members of the management team. They have to have an appropriate shareholder structure in place as part of the investment agreement, otherwise they may not be in a position to bring in the changes which their competencies and finances should allow.

Scope: A proposed change may just need to realign the organisation within the current organisational beliefs or assumptions. Alternatively, it may require fundamental transformational change. *Transformational change* is usually associated with an elemental change in strategic direction. The scope of change is often associated with the nature of change. *Incremental change* takes place over a longer period of time, *'big bang'* takes place very quickly, and is typically needed when the organisation is facing crisis or needs to change direction very quickly. The scope and nature of change can be represented in the following table:

		Scope of the change	
		Realignment	Transformation
Nature of the change	Incremental	Adaptation	Evolution
	Big Bang	Reconstruction	Revolution

VV probably needs to implement **Reconstruction** change at ReInk. This type of change is rapid and usually brings about a great deal of upheaval, but it does not fundamentally change the paradigm of the organisation. It is typical of a turnaround situation where there is a need for major structural changes to deal with a decline in financial performance.

In summary, VV needs to be aware of the context of change at ReInk before it finalises its investment and the terms of that investment. It needs to ensure that it has the *power* to speedily implement the required changes and *preserve* the competencies of the company. It will bring important *capabilities, capacity and diversity* of experience to a company which lacks them. In return, it will find a company which generally is ready for change and should welcome it, although vested interests in the current management team will have to be carefully considered during negotiations on the terms of the proposed investment. Finally, it will need to *reconstruct* ReInk, quickly implementing the required changes, but not fundamentally changing the nature and direction of the business.

(c)   **Introduction**

This final section of the report uses a TOWS matrix to generate strategic options. Each quadrant of the matrix is used to identify options which address a different combination of internal factors (strengths and weaknesses) and external factors (opportunities and threats).

		Internal factors	
		Strengths (S)	Weaknesses (W)
External factors	Opportunities (O)	SO	WO
	Threats (T)	ST	WT

TOWS analysis of ReInk:

SO – this quadrant is used to generate options which use the strengths of the business to take advantage of identified opportunities. The government of the country is committed to environmental policies and demonstrating value-for-money. ReInk has a product which fulfils both of these criteria and it also has a track record in the sector, through its contract with the DoRC. A strategy of focusing on a market niche of government and public sector organisations may be very lucrative and generate good short-term results. It will take time to address the weakness of brand awareness (see WO), but focusing sales and marketing on a well-defined business-to-business sector should be much easier.

WO – is concerned with options which take advantage of opportunities by overcoming weaknesses in the organisation. The growth of the green consumer has been recognised as an opportunity. In general, individual consumers are increasingly keen to recycle products, particularly if it also brings economic benefits, as they are likely to be affected by living in a country which is experiencing continuing economic decline. ReInk can offer reusability and cost savings. However, its brand awareness is low. Addressing this weakness should allow it to take advantage of the opportunities offered by the green consumer movement. Like many WO options, this is a medium-term initiative.

ST – this quadrant is used to generate options which use strengths to avoid or counter threats. One of the threats which affect ReInk is the continual technology development from an industry which is committed to deliver better and cheaper technology. Continual research of the technical environment, combined with internal innovation, reinforces the need for a strategy which is committed to continual product development. It particularly needs to ensure that new patented processes are in place when its current patent runs out. Like many ST options, this is a medium-term initiative.

WT – is concerned with generating options which minimise weaknesses or avoid threats. These are primarily defensive, aiming to avoid threats and the impact of weaknesses. To a large extent, the weaknesses identified in the SWOT analysis are being addressed by inviting investment and participation from Vi Ventures. However, it is unlikely that the company will ever have the financial strength and brand awareness of the large OEMs which it is competing with. One of these companies (Landy) is aggressive in its statements about warranty and is litigious. Avoiding this company in the marketplace, by not offering refills for its products, could be a reasonable defensive strategy.

In summary, there are viable strategic options in all quadrants of the TOWS matrix. In many respects, the investment of money and expertise by VV represents a reasonable initial strategy in the WT quadrant. The WO and ST quadrants seem to both offer medium-term initiatives. However, the analysis of the SO quadrant, focusing sales and marketing on a well-defined business sector (government and public sector organisations), appears to offer achievable short-term success which would help address the profitability of the company and offer VV early rewards for its investment in ReInk.

ACCA Marking scheme		
		Marks
(a)	1 mark for each relevant point. Up to 6 marks for each heading under the SWOT analysis up to a maximum of 20 marks.	20
(b)	1 mark for each relevant point up to a maximum of 14 marks.	14
(c)	1 mark for each relevant point up to a maximum of 3 marks for each quadrant of the matrix, up to a maximum of 12 marks.	12
Up to 4 professional marks for the complete assessment required by Vi Ventures; up to 1 mark for appropriate quality, up to 1 mark for fluency and up to 1 mark for appropriate report tone and up to 1 mark for the professionalism of the complete answer.		4
Total		50

Examiner's comments

This first part of the question was worth twenty marks. Candidates answered this part question relatively well. The main problem was misclassification. For example; classifying the financial situation of the company as a threat (presumably because it is a threat to the firm's existence), rather than as an internal weakness. Misclassified answers were given some credit, but in SWOT analysis classification is important, otherwise the analysis is just an unstructured list. Furthermore, some candidates gave relevant points, extracted from the case study, in their answer but actually did not actually classify them at all. This really is just copying parts of the scenario into an answer. Little credit could be given for such answers.

For part (b), candidates did not have to recall the model; but they had to apply it. Part of this application was an understanding of the meaning of the contextual factor itself. For example; time is concerned with how much time is available to execute the change. Is there a need for rapid strategic change? It is not concerned with 'it is time that this organisation changed'. Although this model has been used in a number of past examinations, many candidates still seemed unfamiliar with it. They were forced to guess what each of the contextual factors is (although some are indeed easy to guess) and many answers made little reference to the scenario. Importantly, the model (and the question) is about strategic change; it is not about the organisation as a whole. So scope is about the scope of change; not about the scope of marketing or the scope of the organisation's operations as a whole. Many candidates did not focus their answers on strategic change and consequently candidates did not score too well on this part question.

For part (c) It was possible to define a potentially feasible option for each quadrant of the matrix, although the SO quadrant probably contained the most valuable options in terms of the scenario. This part question was worth twelve marks. This was not particularly well answered by candidates, with some candidates getting the quadrants wrong (trying to find strengths to overcome weaknesses) and very few focusing on strategic options; preferring to describe a limited tactical response. Many candidates seemed to be familiar with the matrix but not with its application.

The whole of this question was based on an assessment report required by Vi Ventures and candidates were given professional marks for the overall quality, construction, fluency and professionalism of their report-based answer to this question. Issues considered here include vocabulary (is it appropriate to a professional report?), tone and approach (reflecting Vi Ventures as the recipient), fluency of argument and structure; and, finally, are there appropriate introductions and summaries? Overall, presentation was fairly good. However, the context of the report was often forgotten. It was for Vi Ventures; and this should have driven the tone and content of report, particularly in part (b), where Vi Ventures need to be aware of their possible input into the strategic change process at ReInk.

75   ROAM GROUP CO

Key answer tips

There are two key elements needed in order to score well in part (a) (i) of this question:

*   the question asked for an appraisal of a number of business units and this should have pointed students towards the use of the BCG matrix. Although the model is not asked for by name (and this is usually the case in the exam), this model is likely to provide the best framework for the analysis that was required.

*   Given the presence of the financial data in Table 1, this should provide students with an indicator that financial analysis of the three business units would also be required.

In part (a) (ii) the use of the Johnson, Scholes and Whittington strategy evaluation tests was needed – a examined area that candidates should be expecting to see in the exam.

Part (b) is tougher as it is not a syllabus area that appears regularly in examinations, but it is only worth 10 marks and sensible analysis will score some reasonable marks here.

(a) **(i)** **Introduction**

The Roam Group currently consists of three operating companies: Stuart Roam Road Transport, Stuart Roam Warehousing and Stuart Roam Rail. Roam Group Co (The Roam Group) is a corporate holding company which facilitates the acquisition of operating companies in the Group. This first part of the report evaluates the performance and contribution of each of the three current operating companies and assesses their relative significance in The Roam Group's future business strategy. The portfolio analysis references two significant models: the Boston Box (or BCG matrix), suggested by the Boston Consulting Group, which uses a classification based upon a company's market growth and market share, and the parenting matrix of the Ashridge Portfolio Display which focuses on the fit between the company and its parent.

Stuart Roam Road Transport

Stuart Roam Road Transport (SRRT) is a central part of The Roam Group. Not only does it reflect the original business purpose of the Group, but it is also a fundamental part of its current business strategy, linking customers to rail, warehouse and, potentially, airports. It is also the largest revenue generating part of the Group, contributing 57.39% of the Group's revenues in 20X5 and 54.83% of its operating profit. The company has extensive experience in road freight and it is now the dominant company in this business sector. There is also a clear emotional attachment to the industry, with the managing director taking time out once a month to return to everyday trucking. It has an outstanding brand image, promoted partly through significant non-corporate initiatives (the New-Roamantics), which give it free high-profile promotion. The brand image is supported by a clever catch phrase painted on every truck and by the ownership of a modern, reliable, efficient fleet of trucks. In terms of the Ashridge portfolio model, partly because of the historical development of the group, SRRT is definitely a heartland business.

The road freight market has experienced relatively little growth over the last four years (2.50% growth). SRRT has increased its market share over this time (from 25.00% to 28.05%), with a 15% increase in revenues. In Boston Box terms it is a cash cow, although fairly low margins reduce the amount of money it can produce for investment in itself or in other companies in the Group. These relatively low operating profits appear to be typical for the industry sector, with SRRT consistently performing slightly better than industry averages.

Stuart Roam Warehousing

Stuart Roam Warehousing operates a number of efficient, automated warehouses around the country. The physical size of these warehouses provides another opportunity for promoting the brand image and colours of The Roam Group. There is clear synergy with the road transport operation. Indeed, the Group probably had little hesitation in entering this sector of the market. Powerful external forces (including the growth of outsourcing, the growth of internet shopping and retailers requiring an integrated logistics solution) meant that the business case would have been overwhelming.

As a whole, the sector is expanding. The market has grown from revenues of $2,850m to $3,200m dollars in four years – a growth of 12.28%. Stuart Roam Warehousing has experienced a 26.00% growth in this time period, although their market share is still less than 10% (9.84%). Operating margins are slightly higher than the road transport sector and the ROCE is also higher. Stuart Roam Warehousing contributes over 40% (40.47%) of the operating profit of the whole Group. In the Boston Box analysis, there is a practical problem in defining what is meant by 'high', so the company is either a question mark or a star depending on the assessment of its market share. However it is classified, it needs further nurturing and investment. In the context of the Ashridge portfolio model, the company appears to be a heartland business. The Group has a good feel for the business and there seems to be a good fit between the business opportunities and the characteristics and capabilities of the Group as a whole. Overall, its financial performance is largely in line with industry averages.

Stuart Roam Rail

The rail freight market appears to be expanding rapidly. There is a 26.00% rise in industry revenue between 20X1 and 20X5. Perhaps this reflects the increasing cost of road transport, increasing road congestion and fears about the environmental impact of road transport. However, Stuart Roam Rail is a very small player in this market. It has failed to match growth (only 6.6% growth over this period) and its market share has fallen (from 4.20% to 3.56%). Its financial performance is relatively poor, reporting lower operating margins and ROCE than the industry averages. Importantly, the acquisition of FDRC by the Group does not seem to have made a positive impact. In fact, despite an increase in revenues, overall financial performance appears to be worse. In 20X2 (the last year the company traded as FDRC), the company reported an operating profit of 4.95% (4.75% in 20X5) and a ROCE of 3.85% (3.50% in 20X5). This decline in performance is important to bear in mind when considering the possible acquisition of Godiva airport.

In Boston Box terms, Stuart Roam Rail is definitely a question mark (problem child, wildcat). The Group needs to investigate why the company is failing to grab an increasing market share of a rapidly expanding industry. There are at least three possibilities contained within the scenario. Firstly, the company is small and will find it difficult to match the economies of scale enjoyed by the two large rail freight companies. This probably contributes to high operating costs. Secondly, the company has no expertise in the bulk freight contracts (coal, iron ore, oil) which dominate the Meeland economy. This will make it difficult to take these contracts from the current incumbents. Finally, it is unclear whether the transport of consumer food and drink is really suitable for rail transport. The company is distributing to supermarkets, many of which are unlikely to be directly accessible to the rail network. Road transport is a much more flexible alternative.

There are also cultural problems within The Roam Group. The company is used to dealing with a transport method where the medium (roads) is free and drivers are relatively unskilled. In the rail network the transport medium (rails) is charged on a usage basis by a monopoly supplier. Train drivers have to undergo extensive training and are constrained in their route selection. Road and rail are both methods of transport, but they have quite different characteristics.

In the context of the Ashridge portfolio model, this cultural problem might suggest that the company is a value trap business. It is typical of a company which initially appears attractive because there appears to be opportunities for the parent to add value. Value trap businesses should only be included in the strategy if they can be moved into the heartland. This will probably only be possible if new skills, competencies or resources are gained by The Roam Group.

However, on the upside, the company has developed an innovative mini-container system for transferring goods from road to rail and for storage in the warehouse. Also, the supermarkets, aware of the demands of the green consumer, are attracted to rail alternatives and perhaps see this as the primary way of distributing in the future, particularly if loads can be quickly transferred onto road vehicles for the last part of the journey from the railhead to supermarket.

Conclusion

In summary, SRRT and Stuart Roam Warehousing are both heartland businesses. However, the similarities between rail transport and distribution and road transport and distribution may have been misjudged. The rail company is potentially a value trap business and the Group will have to reconsider how to move it into the heartland. In Boston Box terms, it is also a problem child (question mark, wildcat) and so their strategy for moving it into the heartland must also address the underlying reasons why market share is falling in a rapidly expanding business sector.

(ii) **Introduction**

This section of the report considers the proposed acquisition of Godiva airport in the context of its suitability, acceptability and feasibility.

Suitability

The suitability of a strategy addresses the circumstances in which the organisation is operating –— its strategic position. Here we have to ask the question, does the acquisition of Godiva airport by The Roam Group make sense? It does appear to be appropriate at a very superficial level – provided by Sir John Watt in his press release. Road, rail and air are all means of transport with different strengths and weaknesses. However, analysis has already revealed (part (i)) that the similarities between road and rail are much less than might be expected. This is particularly true from a customer perspective. Supermarkets tend to have many individual sites, convenient for road transport but not for rail. There are still doubts whether rail can be used as a significant way of distributing consumer food and drink from the warehouse to the supermarket. The integrated mini-containers represent a possible solution, but the cost of unloading and loading at the rail terminal might make their extensive use unlikely on cost grounds. Even if the mini-container system can be extended to aircraft, airports are relatively few and far between, making distance to supermarket sites even more of an issue. Furthermore, air freighting consumer goods is unlikely to deliver the economies of scale associated with rail freight, or to appeal to the eco-sensibilities of the supermarkets.

However, this broad consideration of the complementary nature of transport alternatives hides another, more fundamental issue. The Roam Group is considering buying an airport, not an airline. This is roughly analogous to buying a station (or set of stations) for Stuart Roam Rail or a portfolio of toll roads for Stuart Roam Road Transport. Sir John Watt's statement does appear to imply the purchase, use or formation of an airline sometime in the future, but that is all. The Roam Group has no experience in running airports and although they intend to offer the opportunity to 'no-frills' airlines to offer scheduled passenger services from the airport, there is no evidence that any airline is currently interested in this option. Indeed, the relatively sparsely populated hinterland of the airport makes it difficult to imagine that there would be much demand for such services. If 'no-frills' airlines were to fly out of Godiva, it seems likely that they would have done so by now.

Acceptability

The acceptability of the strategy is concerned with expected outcomes in terms of return, risk and shareholder reaction. Returns are the benefits which stakeholders would expect to get from the strategy, both in financial and non-financial terms.

The financial performance of the airport can only be assessed from the snapshot of its 20X5 performance. It would have been useful to have been given access to data for previous years. However, the industry average performance figures given by the aviation industry consultant can give some measure of the airport's relative performance. Unsurprisingly, the primary asset of the company is the airport site itself which is valued at $6m.

Trading profitability appears quite reasonable. The gross profit margin is 28.21% and an operating profit margin 15.38% (compared to a 17.50% industry average). Indeed, the operating profit compares favourably with the companies currently in The Roam Group. It is much better than, for example, Stuart Roam Rail. However, it has taken significant investment to generate these returns and the Return on Capital Employed (ROCE) is much lower than the industry average. Even if the ROCE calculation excludes interest costs in its calculation (as in Atrill and McLaney), it is still only 2.19%, a very low return. In contrast, liquidity is relatively good (a current ratio of 2.50 – average 2.25), although there appears to be a disproportionally high inventory value. When this is excluded, the acid test ratio is only 1.125, compared to an industry average of 1.50. Gearing is higher than the industry average (59.12% compared to 40%). Finally, in a country where the normal payment period is 30 days, the airport is achieving this for receivables, but is paying in over 60 days (62.57 days). This needs to be investigated further. It might be due to administrative incompetence or to cash flow constraints, with suppliers providing free credit.

Overall, the financial situation is mixed. The airport is trading quite reasonably, but its performance is affected by long-term debts which contribute to a high gearing and a low ROCE. The acid test ratio is of some concern, particularly as customers are paying on time, but payments to suppliers are over twice the accepted payment norm in Meeland.

Risk concerns the probability and consequences of the failure of the acquisition. From the perspective of the resources of the Group, the cost of the acquisition is relatively small and any operating losses could easily be absorbed. A failed acquisition would not be catastrophic for the Group. However, the case has already been made for further investment in Stuart Roam Rail and Stuart Roam Warehousing (two potential problem children) and these may be partially starved of funds due to money being invested in the airport. Managers and employees in other companies may become demotivated by investment in, what might appear to them, an ego-driven vanity project.

The shareholders might also be ambivalent towards the purchase. The Roam family still own the majority of the shares. Their hearts appear to be in road freight, and an investment in an airport might be a step too far.

Feasibility

Finally, feasibility is concerned with whether an organisation has the resources and competencies to deliver a strategy. The issue of financial resources has been considered in the previous section. However, a consideration of competencies is particularly relevant here.

There seems little doubt that the company has significant competencies in road transport and it has been able to adapt these to warehousing. However, these competencies have not proved useful in the rail transport industry. Indeed, since the acquisition of FDRC, the performance of the company has deteriorated. This makes it doubtful that The Roam Group will be able to turn round the performance of an airport – an organisation which is not directly involved in transport. The appropriate competencies are just not in place.

Conclusion

It is the final point about competencies which reinforces the view that the purchase of Godiva airport is an inappropriate strategy and a poor investment for the Group. The company can clearly afford the purchase price of the airport, and absorb any subsequent operating losses, but this will be at the cost of reducing shareholder value and reduced investment and performance in other companies in the Group. Money and management focus would be much better spent on improving the market share of Stuart Roam Warehousing and the overall performance of Stuart Roam Rail. From a suitability perspective, the acquisition does not make sense because it does not appear to address the requirements of customers. It is surprising that someone as experienced as Sir John Watt is advocating this acquisition.

However, one final point must be raised. Perhaps the acquisition is not about airport and 'no-frills' airlines; or indeed, about air freight at all. In a country where land for warehousing is getting scarcer and more expensive, Godiva airport offers 450 hectares of land. At commercial warehousing costs, this would cost $9m to buy. At the offer price of $7m, The Roam Group is getting a discount of about 22% on normal land values. Perhaps land is at the heart of the purchase, particularly as the airport site is next to a motorway and a town where SRRT has three depots and warehouses. The declared strategy might not be the real motive. Getting cheaper land for warehouse development might be the real reason for this acquisition, and from that perspective, it makes a lot more sense, particularly if it frees up existing Roam sites within the town which can be sold for housing or office development.

(b) Johnson, Scholes and Whittington identify four ways of sustaining a price-based strategy: to accept reduced margins, to win a price war, to reduce costs or to focus on specific segments of the market. Elements of all of these might be discerned from the case study scenario. Indeed, the company's focus on consumer food and drink for supermarkets is a continuing example of the last of these strategies. However, this model answer focuses on possibilities offered by reduced margins and a price war.

An organisation pursuing elements of a low price strategy may be prepared to accept a reduced margin, either because it can sell more volume than its competitors or because it can cross-subsidise that business from other business units in the portfolio. The Roam Group can pursue both these options within the context of Stuart Roam Road Transport. It is a dominant player in the road transport market place (generating high volume and revenue) and it is generating good returns in the warehousing business which could be used to cross-subsidise the transport section. It is generally accepted that margins are relatively low in road transport, so reducing operational margins still further might force rivals to exit the business. Market growth is relatively static (2.5% over the last five years), so continued growth requires SRRT to take market share from its rivals. A price war might also achieve this aim. The company is financially sound and evidence suggests that it has greater financial resources than many of its competitors. If it chose to, SRRT should be able to initiate, sustain and win a price war with short or medium-term losses in contribution driving competitors out of the market.

With respect to differentiation, Johnson, Scholes and Whittington offer three ways of sustaining differentiation: creating difficulty of imitation, pursuing imperfect mobility and the re-investment of margin. Two of these are considered here. Imperfect mobility of resources or competencies can be achieved in a number of ways. Two approaches might be applicable at SRRT. It can attempt to increase the difficulty and cost to the customer of switching its supplier. The integration of road transport, warehousing and rail transport using the mini-containers developed by the company might be a key feature here. Nobody can match this flexibility at present (particularly with the eco-friendliness of rail travel which is especially attractive to supermarkets). It may be possible to imitate it, but it will require considerable investment. However, what is virtually impossible to imitate is the contribution of the New-Roamantics. This is not a carefully crafted management initiative but a group which has spontaneously developed through a shared interest in the Stuart Roam trucks. It is a unique way of promoting the brand. It is unlikely that customers will buy solely because of it, but it does ensure that Stuart Roam is always in their consciousness and there is a certain aspect of fame by association. Subtly encouraging and rewarding this club will maintain an important differentiator between the Stuart Roam Road Transport company and its rivals.

ACCA Marking scheme			
			Marks
(a)	(i)	1 mark for each relevant point up to a maximum of 7 marks for each company in the Group, up to a maximum of 21 marks for the answer. Within the analysis, marks may be given for the correct calculation of market share change (1 mark), market size change (1 mark) and appropriate classification using a portfolio analysis model (1 mark).	21
	(ii)	1 mark for each relevant point up to a maximum of 15 marks. Within the analysis, it is possible for the candidate to calculate and interpret a number of financial ratios. Marks will be allocated for the correct calculation and interpretation of gross profit margin, net profit margin, ROCE, liquidity, gearing, payables and receivables, up to a maximum of 6 marks.	15
		Professional marks: Up to 1 mark each for the clarity, structure, logical flow and appropriate tone of the answer.	4
(b)		1 mark for each relevant point up to a maximum of 10 marks.	10
Total			50

76 HAMMOND SHOES

Key answer tips

The format of this question is a little unusual and may catch out some students. Students were presented with a SWOT as part of the scenario rather than having to create one for themselves. On the positive side, this should have stopped students from going off on tangents and confusing weaknesses with threats etc. and ensured that everyone was starting with the same analysis base. Students had to then perform financial analysis on some numbers for a fairly generous 14 marks and all students should have scored well here. A TOWS matrix was required for part (b), but other techniques such as the Ansoff matrix combined with strategy evaluation tests would also have scored well here. The final section covered the communication of vision and mission were there would have been a reasonable amount of marks for simple knowledge regurgitation (though a pass mark would only then be achievable in this section if that knowledge was then applied to the scenario.

(a)   The following financial analysis focuses on the profitability and gearing of Hammond Shoes manufacturing division.

Profitability: The effect of cheap imports appears to be reflected in the profitability of the company. Revenues and gross profit have both fallen significantly in the four years of data given in Figure 1. In 20X1 the company reported a gross profit margin of 23.5% and a net profit margin of 8.2%. This has declined steadily over the period under consideration. The figures for 20X3 were 20.0% and 4.7% and for 20X5, 17.9% and 2.9% respectively. There has been a general failure to keep costs under control over this period. Sales have fallen by $150m in four years – almost an 18% decrease. In contrast the cost of sales has decreased by only $75m, a decrease of about 11.5%. This probably reflects the problem of reducing labour to react to lower demand, particularly in a country where generous redundancy payments are enforced by law and in an organisation which sees the employment of local labour as one of its objectives. The Return on Capital Employed (ROCE) has dropped substantially, from 24.14% in 20X1 to 6.45% in 20X5.

Gearing: The capital structure of the company has changed significantly in the last four years and this is probably of great concern to the family who are averse to risk and borrowing. Long-term borrowings have increased dramatically and retained earnings are falling, reflecting higher dividends being taken by the family. Traditionally, the company has been very low geared, reflecting the social values of the family. The gearing ratio was only 6.9% in 20X1, but has risen to over 22.5% in 20X5. During this period, retained profit has fallen and an increasing number of long-term loans have been taken out to finance activities. Overall, gearing may still appear quite low and indeed this is probably the view of the senior management of the company. However, the speed of these funding changes is a concern, particularly when trade receivables and trade payables are considered.

One of the values held by the family is the importance of paying suppliers on time. In Arnland, goods are normally supplied on 30 days credit. In 20X1, Hammond Shoes, on average, exceeded this target, paying on 28 days. However by 20X3 this value had risen to 43 days and by 20X5 to 63 days. During the same period, trade receivables, from the selected data provided, appear to have come down (from 50.54 days in 20X1 to 44.43 days in 20X5). It is difficult to escape the conclusion that Hammond Shoes is increasingly using suppliers as a source of free credit on top of the loans they have taken from the banks. Financing costs have risen significantly over the last four years, affecting profits and also causing the interest cover ratio to fall dramatically from 14 to 1.33

Tutorial note

These are the original answers as provided by the ACCA. However, there may be different ways to calculate these numbers (for example, it would be normal to calculate the receivables days based on revenue rather than on cost of sales). However this will not change the analysis and the accuracy of the numbers is not important for the answer.

Gearing % = long term liabilities/(share capital + reserves + long term liabilities) = 2000/2660 = 75%. The financial analysis essentially supports the descriptive analysis provided by the business analysts. Profits are falling, with the firm unable to cut costs sufficiently quickly. The company is increasingly dependent on external finance which is likely to cause disquiet amongst the owning family (on ethical grounds) and may concern suppliers.

Investment analysis:

The two scenarios developed by the senior managers also reflect the pessimism of the company. There seems to be universal acceptance that in the next three years the company will still experience low sales even after the company invests in the new production facilities. Beyond that, managers only see a 30% chance of higher sales resulting and this depends upon favourable changes in the business environment.

For both scenarios, the net benefits of the first three years are $5m per year, giving a total of $15m.

For the next three years, managers suggest that there is a 0.7 chance of continuing low demand, leading to net benefits staying at $5m per year, giving a further benefit of $15m total, with an expected value of $10.5 ($15m × 0.7). Higher demand would lead to net benefits of $10m per year, providing a total of $30m, but with an expected value of only $9m ($30m × 0.3).

Thus the expected benefits of the project are only $34.5 ($15m + $10.5m + $9m), which is below the proposed investment of $37.5m. Only if the second scenario materialises after three years will the investment (in broad terms) have been justified. This scenario would return $45m.

However, it has to be recognised that the projection only covers the first six years of the new production facilities. The factory was last updated twenty years ago and so it seems reasonable to expect net profits to continue for many years after the six years explicitly considered in the scenario, but it must be recognised that predicting net benefits beyond that horizon becomes increasingly unreliable and subjective.

(b)   This question does not require the candidate to use a specific framework for generating strategic options. A number of possibilities exist. The TOWS matrix, the strategy clock and the Ansoff matrix all come to mind. Each of these frameworks has sufficient facets to generate the number of options or directions required to gain the marks on offer. For the purpose of this answer, the TOWS matrix is used, because it fits so well with the SWOT analysis produced by the consultants. However, the focus is on the options generated, not the framework itself and so other frameworks may be as appropriate.

The TOWS matrix is a way of generating directions from an understanding of the organisation's strategic position. It builds directly on the work of the SWOT with each quadrant identifying options that address a different combination of the internal factors (strengths and weaknesses) and external factors (opportunities and threats).

	Internal factors	
	Strengths	**Weaknesses**
Opportunities	SO – options that use strengths to take advantage of opportunities	WO – options that take advantage of opportunities by overcoming weaknesses
External factors Threats	ST – options that use strengths to avoid threats	WT – options that minimise weaknesses and avoid threats

Taking each quadrant in turn:

SO – using strengths to take advantage of opportunities. A number of possible options might be considered here. Hammond Shoes' retail expertise is an acknowledged strength of the company, and it may be possible to use it to take advantage of the opportunities provided by increased consumer spending and consumerism in Arnland. Two possible options come to mind. Firstly, the company could consider selling competing products or complementary goods in its retail shops. This would give consumers a greater choice of products and allow Hammond Shoes to reap some of the profit margins enjoyed by its competitors. Given the company's acknowledged retail expertise, this option should help preserve the long-term future of the shops.

Secondly, the increasing appetite of the public for safe, car-free shopping from a variety of shops might suggest the development of retail 'villages' on the land that Hammond Shoes have, both in Petatown and in the, now disused, factory in the north of the country. This option would combine the twin strengths of retail experience and the availability of land owned by the company, to provide consumers with an experience they increasingly seek and value. The fact that only two sites are available in towns where there are currently no Hammond Shoes retail shops means that there is no apparent reason why the creation of the retail villages should not be combined with the diversification of the products offered in the retail stores.

The software expertise of the company's information systems department can also be used to fulfil consumer's desire for increased purchases over the Internet. Up to now this software expertise has been mainly used to develop in-house production and retail systems which are acknowledged as being amongst the best in the industry. This expertise might be used to develop an innovative e-commerce site. This, of course, also opens up the possibility of sales outside Arnland, something that is unlikely at the moment, given that all the retail shops are within the country.

WO – options that take advantage of opportunities by overcoming weaknesses. To some extent this option contains the approach suggested by the Board, upgrading production machinery. This is addressing a known weakness (out-dated production facilities), simultaneously tackling another weakness, the cost of production. Here the approach is to reduce unit cost by improving productivity and reducing energy costs through the use of modern production equipment. The Board perceives that overcoming these weaknesses will allow the company to continue to compete in the market they are familiar with.

Reducing energy costs might also be used to appeal to the increasing number of green consumers of Arnland who take into account ethical issues when making purchasing decisions. The business analysts have identified these savings as an opportunity in their SWOT analysis. They should be attracted to a product that has been produced using an energy efficient process, and has not travelled thousands of kilometres (using energy consuming boats, road transport and trains). At the time of writing, there is an increased interest in measuring product miles or kilometres, a term used to assess the environmental impact of delivering a product from its point of production to its point of sale. Although the measures are controversial, this need not necessarily concern the messages put out by Hammond Shoes' marketing department.

Hammond Shoes might also use the negative impact of television programmes showing the use of cheap and exploited labour in the production of goods in Orietaria as part of their marketing message. Although the consultants have suggested that the production of shoes in Arnland is a weakness (because of high costs) it could be turned into a strength if the country of origin becomes an important part of the buying decision for people who are willing to pay a premium for ethically sourced products. This might be supported by political initiatives, for example, the support of one of the political parties in Arnland for environmentally responsible purchasing. Their manifesto suggests that 'shorter shipping distances reduce energy use and pollution. Purchasing locally supports communities and local jobs'.

ST – options that use strengths to avoid threats. The company is an acknowledged leader in shoe design and distribution software. It also has significant retail competencies. The company might consider reviewing these to see whether innovative production and retail systems could not be combined and extended to provide economies of supply that partly compensate for the relative high cost of production. So, although production costs cannot easily be reduced, supply and storage costs might be.

The extensive property ownership of the organisation is also perceived as a significant strength. In the short term there may be an opportunity to buy time whilst the cost of producing overseas increases due to rising fuel costs and demands for better pay in the producing countries. Thus, cheaper competition might be seen as a short-term threat, which will eventually disappear. The property portfolio could be used to help finance Hammond Shoes through this period. It might do this by disposing of property, or perhaps more innovatively, by selling all of its property and leasing it back. This would provide liquidity which could be used to ease the company through the next few years.

WT – *options that minimise weaknesses and avoid threats.* The high cost of labour (weakness) and the continued provision of cheap imports (threat) may mean that Hammond Shoes should consider diversifying into areas of the footwear market where there is either less demand for raw materials or where a premium can be charged, either due to the quality of the product or due to appropriate branding. For example, focusing on shoes for children, which requires greater precision and less raw material, might be a possibility. The attraction of this is that it is a product which needs regular renewal (as feet grow) and because parents are conscious of getting exactly the right fit to avoid permanent damage to their children's feet. The acknowledged strengths of the retail experience, where employees have extensive product knowledge and excellent customer care, might also be harnessed to support this approach. Branding can reinforce the message, focusing on Hammond Shoes as primarily a supplier of children's shoes. Adult shoes may be given a lower marketing profile, but are available for cross-selling when parents are visiting for measuring and fitting shoes for their children.

Other niche areas might include high quality fashion shoes and boots, where customers are willing to pay a premium for the product. This might demand a certain amount of exclusivity, reinforced through appropriate marketing. Again, one of the attractions of the fashion market is the relatively short shelf-life of the product. Many consumers wish to renew their shoes each season as a fashion statement, not due to any desire to keep their feet dry and clean.

(c)   A mission statement defines the overriding direction and purpose of an organisation. Some organisations also have *vision* statements stating what the company aspires to. However, for the purpose of this answer, vision and mission are perceived as largely the same thing. Mission statements have their critics, with many believing that they are bland and too wide-ranging. There may be some truth in this view; after all there are only a limited number of ways that the words customer, quality and leader can be re-arranged. However, most organisations appear to have settled into an approach where a short snappy slogan or strap line is supported by a much deeper description of what the organisation is about, its stakeholders and how it wishes to interact with those stakeholders. It defines how the organisation wants to do business. At the time of writing Virgin Atlantic has three elements to its mission statement, all expanded into specific objectives on its website. *To grow a profitable airline, where people love to fly and where people love to work.* Part of ACCA's mission is to *provide opportunity and access to people of ability around the world and to support our members throughout their careers in accounting, business and finance.*

If there is substantial disagreement within the organisation about its overall mission then there may be significant problems in determining the strategic direction of the organisation. Defining a mission statement also provides an opportunity for the organisation to communicate its core corporate values. These may be explicitly defined within the mission itself or they may be in subsidiary statements, corporate reports or web resources. These values tell customers and suppliers how the organisation wishes to operate. They represent the core values and principles that guide the organisations' actions. These could, for example, concern aspects of corporate social responsibility. The ACCA has core values of opportunity, diversity, *innovation, accountability and integrity.*

One of the problems at Hammond Shoes appears to be that the core values of the organisation are implied, but not explicitly stated. Originally, these were provided by the beliefs of the founding brothers – provision of education and housing for employees, secure jobs and good working conditions. Privately, the family still have these principles but they have largely failed to communicate and promote them. Commercial organisations with important core social values are increasingly rare. The extent of this communication failure at Hammond Shoes even extends to the senior management of the company. Their promotion of the potential benefits of outsourcing of production indicated a failure to understand that this would effectively remove a significant part of the company's reason for existence. Its core values include the provision of fair employment opportunities for the people of Petatown and the reaction of the family to removing this central mission illustrates that this value remains core to the continued existence of the company.

Thus the Hammond family should explicitly state their core values, perhaps as a detailed expansion of a short, clear mission statement. This would allow the family to articulate its beliefs and communicate these to customers, suppliers and employees.

A number of writers on organisations use a MOST analysis to help understand the internal environment of an organisation. MOST stands for Mission, Objectives, Strategy and Tactics. The aim of this analysis is to see whether the four facets actually exist (checking for omission) and, if they do, whether they align. Objectives are statements of specific outcomes that the organisation wishes to achieve. They are often expressed in financial terms, such as profit levels, turnover or dividend distribution to shareholders. Marketing objectives are also very common; such as a target market share and customer service provision. Johnson, Scholes and Whittington also believe that general, unquantifiable objectives are acceptable. They recognise that objectives such as 'being a leader in technology' is important to state, but could be difficult to quantify and may indeed encourage spurious quantification. In the context of Hammond Shoes, the company does appear to have certain objectives, such as keeping production in Petatown and providing educational opportunities for employees. As Johnson, Scholes and Whittington point out, 'there are times when specific objectives are required'. This is when urgent action is necessary, as at Hammond Shoes, when it becomes important for the management to focus on a limited number of quantified, priority requirements and not waste their energies pursuing vaguely stated ones.

Furthermore, the existence of such objectives provides an opportunity for managers and employees throughout the organisation to align their own work with stated objectives and so see how what they do contributes to objectives that, in turn, serve the corporate mission. The company clearly fails to cascade objectives down through the organisation and, again, at a period of crisis, this may be a significant weakness. For example, the core value of treating suppliers fairly could have been enshrined within an objective of paying all suppliers within 30 days. The absence of this specific objective and hence the impossibility of cascading it down to those responsible for cash flow management and payment has meant that this section has imposed its own objective of extending payment terms as much as possible. Evidence suggests that they now stand at over 60 days, so the company is failing to meet one of its core values – fairness to suppliers.

Hence, Hammond Shoes does not have a clearly defined mission or explicitly stated values. Its objectives are restricted and rarely quantified. Its strategy is now under review, although it has made certain tactical decisions such as resisting outsourcing and commissioning updated production facilities in Petatown. Thus in the MOST analysis, there are some elements omitted and hence alignment is impossible. This needs to be addressed.

ACCA Marking scheme		Marks
(a)	1 mark for each appropriate point up to a maximum of.	14
(b)	1 mark for each appropriate point up to a maximum of.	20
	Up to 4 further marks are available for the style, structure and clarity of the answer.	4
(c)	1 mark for each appropriate point up to a maximum of	12
Total		**50**

Examiner's comments

In part (a) most candidates recognised this and, as well as calculating appropriate ratios, provided a good textual analysis of their results. However, the quantitative analysis of the proposed investment was less well tackled. Some candidates ignored the returns given in the scenario completely, confining their analysis to the figures presented in the financial statements and trying to apply the suitability, acceptability and feasibility criteria to the proposed investment. Other candidates were aware that the analysis should be based on the cost, income and probabilities described in the scenario, but surprisingly few were able to properly calculate expected values and so gain the marks on offer. However, despite this weakness, candidates still performed reasonably well on the first part of this question.

For part (b) no specific framework was given, although the inclusion of a SWOT analysis in the case study scenario might have suggested a TOWS analysis to candidates. However, the strategy clock, Ansoff matrix and Porter's generic strategies could all be successfully applied to the case study situation. There was no need for answers to include all these frameworks as their application often suggests the same strategic option. The examiner's advice is to only use more than one framework where a further framework gives an insight or provides a suggestion that the initial framework has failed to provide. People who describe three or four frameworks in such questions rarely score better than a candidate who has restricted themselves to a proper analysis based on one appropriate framework. A considerable number of candidates did use appropriate frameworks in this question but often failed to apply them sufficiently to the case study scenario to gain many marks.

Unfortunately, too many candidates also tried to apply PESTEL and Porter's Five Forces to the case study scenario. Both of these frameworks are more appropriate for defining strategic position, rather than strategic options and so candidates struggled to score significant marks. In fact, their PESTEL analysis was often little more than a re-iteration of information from the case study scenario and no strategic options were generated at all. This is unsurprising, as the PESTEL analysis usually precedes the SWOT and indeed feeds into it to define the opportunities and threats facing the organisation. As a result, many candidates wrote long answers using inappropriate frameworks that did not address the requirements of the question. Consequently, many candidates scored disappointingly on this question and this greatly affected their ability to pass the whole paper.

Part (c) was satisfactorily answered, although a surprising number of candidates failed to answer this part question at all. Some candidates believed that values were about the value to the customer and so found themselves in an inappropriate cul-de-sac of describing value propositions, value chains and value networks. This was surprising given the emphasis on business values in the case study.

77 ABC LEARNING

Key answer tips

It is clear in the scenario and the requirement that the company uses Porter's Five Forces to analyse its environment. Therefore it is important to focus on this model in part (a) and there is no need to use any other model in order to score full marks. In part (b) the company has made a decision to enter a new market. Therefore do not discuss the validity of this decision. Instead focus on what the requirement wants – is the particular target company they are considering the right one to buy? The key to any question on stakeholders – as was required in part (c) – is to use Mendelow's matrix. Applying this model to the scenario would help you score high marks in this part of the question.

(a)   This question asks candidates to analyse the business analysis certification training industry (BACTI) in Erewhon using Porter's five forces framework. This is the preferred approach of Xenon, the company commissioned to undertake the study. In this context it seems a reasonable model to use. The forces ultimately determine the profit potential of the industry and ABCL will be keen to invest in an industry where there is long-term return on its investment. The framework also helps identify how a potential new entrant (such as ABCL) might position itself in the industry. The five forces driving industry competition are the threat of entrants, the threat of substitute products or services, the bargaining power of suppliers, the bargaining power of buyers and the competitive rivalry between existing firms in the industry. Looking at each of these in turn:

The threat of entry

New entrants to an industry bring new capacity. Existing suppliers stand to lose market share and have their profitability eroded. In the context of ABCL, the threat of entry is a particularly significant issue because they are, themselves, threatening to enter the industry. Consequently they need to understand the barriers to entry to see if they are sufficient to deter or delay their potential entrance. Furthermore, an understanding of these barriers will give them an understanding of how likely it is that other companies will consider entering the industry. If barriers are high then the threat of entry is low.

In the context of the scenario, the main barriers appear to be:

- Access to supply channels. The industry is dominated by three established providers who know the industry very well and have established relationships with key suppliers of expertise; the lecturing staff. In two instances, CATalyst and Batrain, lecturers are full-time employees with attractive salary packages, share options and generous benefits. In the case of Ecoba Ltd, the company promotes the images and expertise of the high-profile presenters that it uses. Although these presenters are on sub-contract, they feel secure about the arrangement. As one of them commented 'students are attracted to the company because they know I will be teaching a certain module. I suppose I could be substituted by a cheaper resource, but the students would soon complain that they had been misled.'

- The fees of 60% of all students are paid for by their employer. The three established suppliers have good relationships with the major corporate customers and, in some cases, have set up infrastructure (dedicated training sessions, personalised websites) to support these contracts. Although corporate customers do switch provider (see later), it might be difficult, in the short term, for ABCL to gain corporate clients.

- Expected retaliation is an accepted barrier to entry. The industry in Erewhon has a history of vigorous retaliation to entrants. The scenario mentions that ABCL has commissioned the study from Xenon because of the well documented experience of another Arcadian company, Megatrain. Megatrain's proposed entry into this market place was met by price-cutting and promotional campaigns from the established suppliers. This was supported by a campaign to discredit the CEO of Megatrain and to highlight its foreign ownership. Porter makes the point that there is a strong likelihood of retaliation where there are established firms with great commitment to the industry and who are relatively illiquid. This is supported by evidence from Ecoba's balance sheet where goodwill and property are both significant assets.

- The cost and time taken to achieve gold level certification may also deter ABCL from entering the industry. All three main providers currently have EloBA's gold standard. To be a creditable alternative, ABCL has to achieve this level of certification. Evidence from the case study suggests that it takes at least one year to achieve this certification. In the meantime ABCL will be trading at a disadvantage.

- The three providers dominating the industry have well-established brands, supported by extensive marketing. ABCL will have to invest heavily to overcome existing customer loyalties and to build up a brand that appears to be a credible player in the industry. This will require time, and investment in building a brand name is particularly risky since, as nPorter explicitly recognised 'it has no salvage value if entry fails'. However, there are only 15 major corporate customers. ABCL could target these to gain market share. It is possible that ABCL already works with these customers in Arcadia, and they may also be attracted by ABCL's e-learning expertise.

Threat of substitutes

The threat of substitutes is again important to ABCL because it would not want to invest in an industry where the product or service is under threat. Substitution reduces demand and might, in extreme cases, lead to the product or service becoming obsolete.

The threat of substitutes appears to be constant in this industry. There is no legislative or certification requirement to study for the examinations with an accredited provider. Evidence from the case study suggests that a large proportion of students do not attend formal classes but prefer to study on their own.

The case study also mentions that one of the smaller providers has gained some success by providing 'blended' learning solutions where tutors provide some support, but students are expected to complete e-learning modules. In effect, these students are substituting face-to-face tuition with e-learning. The case study scenario mentions that the three established providers, whilst acknowledging the possibilities of e-learning, are retaining their classroom-based model. Not only is it profitable, but it allows the companies to employ their investments in specially-designed classrooms, buildings and staff.

ABCL might consider the threat of substitutes as a business opportunity. They do have expertise in providing e-learning materials and it might be a way of entering the market place with products that are significantly differentiated from their competitors.

Bargaining power of buyers

The power of buyers concerns the ability of buyers to force down prices, bargaining for higher quality or more services by playing providers off against each other. In the scenario it appears that:

(1) The power of the corporate buyers is relatively high. The scenario mentions that 60% of all students are paid for by their employer. There is a history of these corporate buyers regularly changing providers to gain better prices. For example, the scenario states that a large insurance company had recently placed all its training with Ecoba after several years of using CATalyst as its sole provider.

(2) The cost of switching providers is relatively low. This applies to both corporate buyers and individual students.

(3) In general, the products purchased are standard and undifferentiated. The three main providers all deliver training through face-to-face classroom training. Buyers are always sure that they can find alternative providers.

(4)   There is some threat of the supplier (provider) being bought by a buyer (customer). The case study scenario provides an example where WAC, a major supplier of business analysis consultancy services, has itself bought one of the smaller providers and now delivers all of its business analysis training in-house. Hence there is a credible threat of backward integration.

All of the above suggest that the bargaining power of buyers is high in this industry.

Bargaining power of suppliers

Suppliers exert bargaining powers by threatening to raise prices or reduce the quality of their services. The conditions that make suppliers powerful tend to mirror those that make a buyer powerful. Very few of the conditions that would lead to high supplier (provider) power appear to exist in the case study scenario. The only circumstances that might apply are:

- The supplier (provider) industry is dominated by a few companies and is certainly more concentrated than the industries it sells to. Suppliers selling to more fragmented buyers will normally be able to influence prices, acceptable quality and supply terms.

- Porter also recognises that labour is a supplier. The case study scenario suggests that it is difficult to find competent, committed lecturing staff. This, of course, poses another problem for the providers. Lecturers on flexible contracts can threaten to either move to work with competitors or set up their own business to compete in the market.

Competitive rivalry between existing firms

The rivalry amongst existing firms needs to be understood. Are rivals bitter and aggressive or do they appear to exhibit a large degree of mutual tolerance? In the case study scenario the three companies that dominate the industry seem to co-exist on relatively good terms and indeed appeared to co-operate to provide a co-ordinated response to Megatrain's potential entry into the industry. They also appear to tolerate the existence of a relatively large number of smaller providers. Industry growth is still strong and this means that firms can expand and improve their performance by just keeping up with industry growth.

However, the products are relatively undifferentiated, particularly once gold level certification has been achieved. They are all providing training services for certification examinations using classroom-based tuition. As already recognised there is little to stop customers switching between competitors, and this will increase competitive rivalry.

The preoccupation of the three main providers seems to be the protection of their marketplace from large new entrants. Hence ABCL can expect a vigorous response to their proposed entry into the industry.

(b) **Report Title:** An evaluation of the attractiveness of Ecoba Ltd as an acquisition target for ABCL

Author: A business analyst, Xenon Ltd

Date: March 20X9

Executive summary

In January 20X9, Xenon Ltd (referred to from this point as we or us) produced an interim report analysing the business analysis certification training industry (BACTI) in Erewhon. As a result of this report, ABCL asked us to evaluate the attractiveness of Ecoba Ltd as an acquisition target. This report examines the ownership, business model and performance of the three main suppliers in the industry. Ecoba Ltd has a dominant shareholder who is approaching retirement and so is likely to be amenable to realising her investment in the company. In contrast, the other two main suppliers have relatively complex ownership structures which, in our experience, lead to immediate rebuttal or protracted negotiation. Ecoba's business model currently minimises training and administrative overheads and could be retained or, in the longer term, remodelled to reflect the operating preferences of the acquiring company. Ecoba's financial performance is acceptable. It is not as profitable as its competitors, but it is very lightly geared, while other ratios are roughly in line with industry competitors. Our conclusion is that Ecoba Ltd is a viable and attractive acquisition proposition for ABCL.

Introduction

In January 20X9, Xenon Ltd (referred to from this point as we) produced an interim report analysing the business analysis certification training industry (BACTI) in Erewhon. As a result of this report, ABCL asked us to evaluate the attractiveness of Ecoba Ltd as an acquisition target. This report examines the ownership, business model and performance of the three main suppliers in the industry. This short report analyses the current operational and financial position of Ecoba. It also explains why we believe that Ecoba is, between the three main suppliers in the industry, the most appropriate target for acquisition.

Analysis

Ecoba is a private limited company, almost wholly owned by its founder Gillian Vari. It is the smallest of the three providers that dominate the BACTI marketplace. CATalyst is a wholly owned subsidiary of the Tuition Group, a training and education provider quoted on the Erewhon stock market. In their latest annual report, Tuition Group identified CATalyst as core to their strategy and a source of significant growth. We do not believe that they would be interested in selling CATalyst, except at a premium price. Batrain is a private limited company, with shares equally divided between the eight founding directors. Given this share distribution, and the age profile of the directors, we feel that it is likely that any proposed acquisition of Batrain would either be immediately rebuffed or it would lead to a complex and drawn out negotiation given the number of stakeholders involved. In contrast, Gillian Vari is approaching retirement. She holds 95% of Ecoba's shares and we feel that she might be amenable to realising her investment in Ecoba.

Ecoba itself does not employ any full-time teaching staff (except Gillian herself). Their strategy is to employ well-known industry 'names' on sub-contract and to publicise these names in their advertisements, website and other publicity. They also publish the name of the lecturer on their class timetables. Gillian is averse to employing full-time lecturing staff because 'they have to be paid if courses do not run and during the long vacations'. It is perhaps this reliance on sub-contract staff that leads to the cost of sales running at about 80% of revenue. This figure is significantly higher than their two main competitors (65% and 63%) and this needs further investigation. We suspect that the competitors classify full-time staff as overheads (rather than cost of sales) but we need to investigate this.

Overall, sub-contract lecturers appear quite happy with this arrangement as they believe that there is little chance of being replaced by lesser 'names' or, as happens at the other two companies, by full-time staff at too short notice to arrange alternative work bookings. However, they do complain about how long it takes Ecoba to pay their invoices. This is supported by the financial data. The average payables settlement period is 144 days in 20X8, up from 130 days in 20X7. Comparing these with the two rivals suggests that this is not the industry norm. It will be important, in the short-term at least, to retain these lecturers. Any concerns they might have about working for new management might be partly offset by the goodwill generated by paying their invoices much more quickly.

The inefficiency that leads to a high number of settlement days for payables is also reflected in the average receivables settlement days. In 20X8 this was up to 71 days, compared to 64 days the previous year. Again, comparisons suggest that this is not the norm for the industry. Gillian has always been careful to keep administrative overheads relatively low. However, this suggests that they are finding it increasingly difficult to manage the payment of suppliers and the chasing of customer payments. Increased efficiencies in this area appear to be on offer to any company that acquires Ecoba. The sales revenue to capital employed (another efficiency or activity ratio) has increased from 3.16 to 3.76 in the past year. This improvement now means that it outperforms its rivals (3.36 and 3.19).

Before considering any further financial ratios, the extracted financial information suggests the following:

- Significant increases in trade payables (40%) and trade receivables (43%)

- Significant rise in revenue (almost 30% from 20X7 to 20X8)

- Significant rise in cash and cash equivalents (40%)

- Increase in retained earnings

- Increase in valuation of intangible assets. This would need investigation

Ecoba is not as profitable as its two main rivals. Gross profit is much lower (at about 20%, compared with 35% and 37%) although this probably reflects the large scale employment of sub-contract staff. Net profit is also lower, but not substantially so (at 4.55%, compared with 6% and 8%). However, all profitability ratios at Ecoba (ROCE, gross profit margin and net profit margin) showed slight improvements in 20X8 compared with 20X7.

Liquidity at Ecoba appears to be relatively stable. Inventories are relatively low in this industry and so the current and the acid test ratios are almost exactly the same. Although the absolute value of these ratios is relatively low (0.91 – 0.93), similar figures are returned by their competitors and so there does not seem to be any particular cause for concern.

Ecoba is very lightly geared, with gearing ratios much lower than their competitors. In 20X7 the gearing ratio was 4.2% with an interest cover ratio of 37.5 times. This had reduced in 20X8 to 3.8% and the interest cover ratio had increased to 50.

Conclusion

The picture that emerges is of a company that is relatively risk averse. This is reflected in their employment of sub-contract lecturing staff rather than full-time staff (allowing Gillian to balance supply with demand) and the minimisation of overhead administrative staffing costs. This latter appears to have been a false economy as it has led to poor credit control and complaints from suppliers about late payment. Financial gearing is very low and any buyer of the company has the opportunity to use the company's unused borrowing capacity. Gillian has also been prepared to live with lower profitability figures than her rivals and this may be a reflection of the fact that she has fewer shareholders to consider.

Any company that acquires Ecoba gets a company where changes can be quickly made to improve efficiency. We suggest that Gillian's business model should be retained in the short term, but in the long term it would be possible to change the model to potentially improve profitability. In conclusion, we believe that acquiring Ecoba will provide ABCL with a cost-effective entry into the BACTI market in Erewhon.

(c)   Transfer in ownership of a company creates anxieties amongst customers, suppliers and employees. ABCL are right to consider stakeholder management during this transition, particularly now that Gillian Vari has left the company. However, there is insufficient time to manage everyone to the same degree. Also, it is not necessary. There may be stakeholders who are indifferent to the change and involving them may be difficult to achieve, unsettling and time-consuming.

Stakeholder analysis usually involves some mapping of power against interest. This can be used to determine how they should be managed. The following represent the most likely stakeholders that the management of ABCL will need to manage. The suggested categorisation is arguable, so students do not have to agree completely with this analysis to gain the marks on offer.

Corporate customers: the scenario mentions that two corporate customers have recently switched their training contracts to Ecoba. They may be unsettled by the change, particularly as the person who negotiated those contracts (Gillian Vari) has now left the company. One of the customers specifically changed provider because they were impressed by the 'named' lecturers that Ecoba could provide. They would need to be reassured that these lecturers will remain under new ownership. In stakeholder mapping terms it could be argued that corporate customers have high power (because they can move their contracts elsewhere) and high interest. It is advisable for ABCL to actively manage these key players during the transition period, perhaps by appointing account managers with specific responsibility for each corporate customer.

Lecturers: these are the named 'suppliers' on contract to Ecoba. It is likely that these stakeholders will be anxious about the acquisition as they know that the two main competitors employ full-time lecturers. ABCL also employ full-time tutors in its operations in Arcadia. Lecturers will be worried that the business model of Ecoba will be changed by the new management. On the other hand, Ecoba will, at least in the short term, wish to retain these names to allow business continuity and to fulfil the expectations of at least one corporate client. This group of stakeholders might be classified as having high power (because they can work for established competitors) and some interest. A reasonable stakeholder strategy might be to keep these lecturers satisfied. An early move to prompt invoice payment may help keep them onside.

Full-time administrative staff employed by Ecoba. There is evidence in the case study scenario that administration is under pressure and this will have to be investigated. Failure to pay suppliers on time or chase up debts might be due to time pressure or incompetence. In stakeholder management terms this group can probably be defined as having high interest but very little power. They are best managed by keeping them informed about proposed changes. At most, they should be kept onside.

Individual students. This is a large, diverse group. As customers they are focused on passing examinations. Individually, they have relatively low power, and, in the context of the transition, they probably have very little interest. The size and diversity of the group make it difficult to agree a stakeholder management strategy. There could be an argument for ignoring this group completely. As long as lecturers and, to some extent, administrative staff, are properly managed then this group should see little tangible change. Minimal effort should be put into managing individual students.

EIoBA. The EIoBA run the certification scheme. They will wish to be assured that ABCL will maintain the standards achieved by Ecoba. The EIoBA is a powerful stakeholder as it could potentially withdraw accreditation. Hence it has high power. It is difficult to gauge its interest as the scenario gives little information about it. However, at worst it should be kept satisfied throughout the transition process, so that it does not become excessively interested and hence a key player in the success of the transition.

ACCA Marking scheme		
		Marks
(a)	1 mark for each significant point (for example, access to supply channels) up to a maximum of 20 marks.	20
(b)	1 mark for each significant point (for example, issue of poor credit control) and up to 1 mark for each supporting calculation (for example, accounts receivable – 71 days and rising) up to a maximum of 16 marks Up to 4 additional professional marks for structure, persuasiveness and a coherent conclusion supporting the acquisition of Ecoba.	
	Maximum	**20**
(c)	1 mark for each significant point (e.g. classification of stakeholders) up to a maximum of 10 marks.	10
Total		**50**

Examiner's comments

This compulsory question was answered relatively well, with good use of the case study material.

The first part of the question asked candidates to use Porter's framework to analyse the business analysis certification industry (BACTI) in Erewhon and to assess whether it was an attractive market for ABCL to enter. Most candidates answered this question relatively well, showing an understanding of Porter's framework and an ability to apply it to the case study scenario. The scenario explicitly stated that Xenon analyses an industry by using Porter's five forces framework. It was expected that candidates would use this in their analysis. However, some candidates elected to use his 'diamond' analysis instead. The two frameworks overlap to some extent and so candidates using this approach were able to gain some marks, although there was probably insufficient information in the case study scenario to get a pass mark using this approach.

The second part of the compulsory question assumed that Xenon had decided to enter the BACTI market by acquiring one of the three big companies currently dominating the marketplace. Ecoba Ltd had been identified as the most appropriate target and candidates were required to write a short report evaluating Ecoba Ltd, analysing whether it was the most appropriate and attractive of the three possible acquisition targets of ABCL. Overall, candidates answered this part question relatively well, calculating and using financial information that had been signposted in the scenario. Some candidates took the suitability, feasibility, acceptability approach which sometimes led to answers with little reference to the case study scenario. A straightforward financial evaluation would have been more appropriate. Furthermore, some candidates questioned the attractiveness of the marketplace as a whole. This was not the point of this part question, it had already been considered in the first part of the question. ABCL have already decided to enter this marketplace, it is now just a question of which company to acquire.

The final part of the compulsory question asked candidates to identify and analyse the stakeholders in Ecoba Ltd and analyse how ABCL could successfully manage them during the ownership transition. Markers were instructed to interpret stakeholders quite widely and to include some that are not identified in the model answer. Most candidates answered this part question relatively well, with appropriate use of the Mendelow matrix often leading to high marks for this part question.

78   GREENTECH   *Walk in the footsteps of a top tutor*

Tutor's top tips

Approach to the question

(a)   SWOT Analysis

The examiner seen this as a way of giving students some easy marks to start off

Key to success:

Stick to this model – the examiner plans to be more explicit in terms of which models to use in these sorts of exam scenarios. There will be no need for other models and use of other models will achieve nothing except wasting your time.

Manage your time well – a common mistake is to read the requirement and then allow yourself 1.8 minutes/mark. But this ignores the fact that it will have taken you around 25/30 minutes to read the requirement leaving you with only around 60 minutes for 50 marks. So you need to allocate 1.2 minutes per mark which means that you can spend no longer than 15 minutes on this part of the requirement.

Cover all 4 areas – in 15 minutes you only have enough time to cover around two factors in each area of the SWOT. Any more than this will waste time and gain you few extra marks.

Key dangers:

Using other models

Spending too long on this section

Not using full sentences. For example, when discussing strengths a weaker student might simply write that 'The company is in a good financial position'. But the better student will write a more specific answer such as 'The company has a good financial position and has built up $17m of surplus cash.

(b)   Strategy evaluation

Key to success:

Recognise the technique to use: 'evaluate.....the strategy options' is a very common exam requirement. The examiner normally uses the Johnson, Scholes and Whittington criteria of suitability, feasibility and acceptability to assess strategies and answer these requirements.

Evaluate all three proposals

Link back to part (a)

Answer the question: justify the selection. Don't take other views and don't suggest alternatives. You will only get the 2 professional marks if you take the correct 'slant'. That is, all 3 likely to be feasible, but Ang's is MOST suitable, and only one that's likely to be acceptable.

Use P3 terminology – such as 'product development', 'market development' etc.

Expand points by answering 'so what?'

Good time management. There are 3 strategies and we need to assess 3 criteria for each (9 things to do), and then provide a justification for the strategy that was followed. So overall there are 10 things to do for 20 marks. This means that each 'element' is only worth 2 marks each so you can't afford to spend too long on any single element.

Key dangers:

Spending too much time on one strategy

Incorrect focus

No/incorrect model

(c) **(i)** **Process redesign**

Key to success:

Be prepared for the topic – process redesign is seen as a key topic by the current examiner and it forms a link to many other areas within the syllabus.

Be comfortable with interpreting diagrams – again, the new examiner likes to provide diagrams for you to interpret. You will never have to draw them, but you need to be able to look at one and spot the problems.

Link problems and solutions. For example we discover a problem: 20% of orders are rejected late in the process; therefore we need to develop a solution to this problem: move credit checks to earlier in the process.

Key dangers:

Drawing diagrams

Explaining 'process', 'redesign' etc. The examiner is not testing your knowledge here. This is a test of how you can apply this knowledge to a scenario.

(ii) **Strategic planning**

Key to success:

Try to use a recognised model. For example, the answer uses the strategy lenses, but you could just as easily have used JSW's approach, Harmon's process strategy matrix (both words are used in the requirement) or compared the rational approach (strategy leads process redesign) to the incremental/ emergent approach (process redesigns lead strategy).

Key dangers:

Lack of focus

Answers which are too general

(a) The current strategic position of *greenTech* could be summarised in a brief SWOT analysis. Credit will also be given to candidates who have used appropriate alternative models or frameworks.

Strengths

The company has a good financial position, with, by April 20X8, a cash surplus of $17 million.

The company has explicitly positioned itself as a focused differentiator in a very competitive market place.

The company has a stable, successful management team that has been in place since 1990.

The company has important core competencies in the production of green technology. It was the development of these competencies that formed the basis of Professor Ag Wan's suggestion.

Weaknesses

Despite recent increases, marketing as a whole is under-funded. It currently stands at about 0.3% of turnover.

None of the marketing budget is specifically aimed at the sale of fully assembled green computers. This was recognized by Lewis-Read, who believed that the company should invest in marketing these computers to both home and corporate customers.

The current process for ordering and configuring computers has a number of efficiency problems. This leads to low conversion of enquiries into accepted orders.

Opportunities

The Lewis-Read proposal points out that the government has just agreed a preferential procurement policy for energy efficient computers with high recyclable content.

The general public is increasingly conscious of the need to conserve the environment. 'Green consumers' are increasing both in numbers and visibility.

Other industrial sectors are looking for opportunities to provide products that are quiet, recyclable and have low emissions.

Web-based technology now exists that allows customers to construct virtual prototypes of machines and equipment.

Threats

Although sales are increasing, the company is still relatively small in global terms and so it is unlikely to be able to compete with the established global suppliers of fully assembled computers. There are significant barriers to entry to this market.

Lack of manufacturing capability is a threat as it makes the company vulnerable to problems in the supply chain. The acquisition of a manufacturing company to address this is part of Fenix's proposal.

(b)   The team from the accountants Lewis-Read has suggested a strategy that protects and builds on the company's current position. Johnson, Scholes and Whittington identify two broad options within this approach. The first concerns *consolidation* which may include downsizing or withdrawal from certain activities. The second is *market penetration* where an organisation gains market share, usually by increasing marketing activity. This seems to be what Lewis-Read has in mind.

However, their proposal appears to envisage market penetration in only one of the three specific sectors served by *greenTech*, the provision of fully assembled green computers. This focus is probably based on a perception of high potential demand coupled with low current marketing investment in this area. Trends suggest that the overall market for this type of computer should be growing rapidly. Domestic customers and companies are increasingly aware of their carbon footprint and wish to reduce consumption both on ethical and economic grounds. The scenario also states that the government is promoting energy efficient computers with high recyclable content in their procurement policy. Consequently, demand should be growing. On the other hand, *greenTech*'s marketing spend suggests that not only is the overall budget relatively small, but that none of it appears to be specifically aimed at the green consumer. In contrast, over half of the budget is currently specifically targeted at the electronics industry or home buyers of components. This lack of marketing investment may explain the relatively small growth in sales in the fully assembled green computer's revenue stream. Thus it appears that the company is failing to address a growing market because its marketing spend is too small, with none of it specifically focused on that sector.

It is possible that *greenTech*'s reluctance to market their computers directly to domestic and commercial companies is due to their perception that they will be seen to be competing with two of their commercial customers. This will require careful consideration. However, withdrawal from some activities is a legitimate tactic within a 'protect and build' strategy. Perhaps the loss of some commercial customers will be more than compensated for by direct computer sales to customers.

The second proposal, from the team representing the corporate recovery specialists, Fenix, is to develop products to offer a more comprehensive service to the electronics industry. This is a strategic direction of *product development*, where organisations deliver modified or new products to existing markets. Fenix's suggestion is primarily focused on adding new products (expanded product range) and services (special requirements) beyond current capabilities. The scenario suggests that 70% of the electronics industry currently use *greenTech* components somewhere in their products. However, there may be scope for supplying more products and services to these established customers as well as supplying to those who do not currently use *greenTech's* products.

Fenix also makes the point that buying a manufacturing capability will protect the supply chain. greenTech currently has no manufacturing capability of their own and so they are at the mercy of their suppliers. These suppliers might raise prices, supply competitors, fail to meet demand or go out of business. A manufacturing facility could avoid all of these as well as perhaps providing an opportunity to cut supply costs. Furthermore, it could be argued that supplying a more comprehensive range of products to established customers may help protect current business with these customers.

However, Fenix recognise that manufacturing is beyond *greenTech's* current capabilities. Consequently, there is the issue of how these capabilities will be acquired. Their proposal is for the company to spend its cash surplus acquiring companies that already have these capabilities. It would be costly, risky and time-consuming to develop these capabilities organically. So, although *greenTech* has no experience of making acquisitions and making them work, Fenix's suggestion of acquisition seems very sensible.

The final proposal from Professor Ag Wan from MidShire University is for *greenTech* to look for opportunities where the company could use its core competencies with green technology within other industries and products. This is the strategic direction of *finding new* uses *for existing products and knowledge.* Johnson, Scholes and Whittington provide an example: 'manufacturers of stainless steel have progressively found new applications for existing products, which were originally used for cutlery and tableware. Nowadays the uses include aerospace, automobile exhausts, beer barrels and many applications in the chemical manufacturing industry.' For the company itself, this is probably quite a radical way of looking at itself. Instead of being seen as essentially a components supplier it becomes a supplier of ideas and technology. Professor Ag Wan's suggestion makes *greenTech* re-consider what industry they are in and this reflection should allow them to see a potentially much bigger market (green technology) in which they have already demonstrated capabilities in one sector (electronics).

Contemporary social trends also support Professor Ag Wan's suggestion. All industries will have to find greener ways of working if they are to satisfy three important forces. The first is the 'green consumers' who wish to purchase from companies with demonstrable sustainability policies. The second is governments who are increasingly likely to pass laws on emissions and responsibility for waste disposal. The third force is the increasing cost of disposal as the number of potential disposal sites decreases. Thus the market *for greenTech's* products, know-how and testing should be large and increasing.

The problem facing *greenTech* is how they will find these markets and exploit them. Professor Ag Wan's suggestion is that the surplus cash should be spent on finding these markets using market research.

The scenario states that *greenTech* opted for the third option (from Professor Ag Wan) and put it into operation. This briefing paper suggests why this option was selected by the company. Although all three of the suggestions are feasible it argues that Ag Wan's proposal is a more suitable fit.

The first suggestion, from Lewis-Read, appears to address the imbalance between a large potential market (green computers) and an under-promoted and under-sold product (fully assembled green computers). However, the supply of computers is a very competitive market and the money that greenTech has to spend on marketing is probably insufficient for it to make a serious impact. There are already global brands supplying computers at highly competitive prices. It must be recognised that *greenTech's* products could be sold initially at a premium price to reflect its niche position. However, if the market-place demands it, the major suppliers will have little difficulty in producing machines that directly compete with *greenTech.* The product can easily be imitated. Indeed the scenario reveals that *greenTech* already supplies two medium-sized computer manufacturers with components for green products in their range.

These manufacturers might feel uneasy about greenTech becoming a significant competitor and consequently withdraw their business, so weakening this revenue stream. greenTech may be better advised to position their fully assembled computers as a complete kit, just as kit car manufacturers are prepared to provide assembled cars to customers without the time or expertise to assemble them.

Overall, Lewis-Read's proposal does not appear to be a particularly *feasible* strategy. Johnson, Scholes and Whittington suggest that an assessment has to be made about the extent to which the organisation's current capabilities (resources and competences) have to change to reach the *threshold* requirements for a strategy. In the case of *greenTech,* major investment would be required to overcome entry barriers and maintain market share. It is unlikely that the cash available would be sufficient to cope with the global players who already supply fully assembled computers.

The second suggestion, from Fenix, has many good points. *greenTech* is currently reliant on its suppliers because it lacks a manufacturing capability. It appears to make sense to move upstream in the supply chain to secure supply. Flexibility in the products supplied and reduced costs are also attractive bonuses. However, the company has grown organically and it is still run by the management team that formed it in 1990. It has no experience in acquiring companies, integrating them and running them successfully. All evidence suggests that many acquisitions do not deliver the benefits that had been claimed for them, even when they are acquired by experienced managers. Furthermore, it is likely for cost reasons that the acquired company would be in another country, perhaps creating both language and cultural difficulties. Overall, greenTech appears to be a relatively conservative, risk-averse company and so it is the unfamiliarity and risk associated with this proposal that means it should be rejected. In the terms of Johnson, Scholes and Whittington, the Fenix proposal is not a particularly *acceptable* strategy to the existing management because of the risk involved with acquisition.

Professor Ag Wan's suggestion may have won by default; after all the television show has to have a winner! However, it also has two significant strengths. The first, central to his proposal, is that it allows the company to see itself in a new and exciting way. The recognition of these core green technology and know-how competencies and their significance in an important and expanding market should be very motivating to *greenTech's* management and employees. Secondly, it has to be recognised that most of *greenTech's* current business activities are with fellow electronics companies or enthusiasts. Professor Ag Wan's proposal continues that tradition. Transactions will be business-to-business, often at quite a technical level. *greenTech* is comfortable with and experienced in such transactions. Professor Ag Wan's suggestion appears to be suitable, in that the strategy addresses the situation in which the company is operating. It is acceptable because it is in line with the expectations and values of the shareholders. Finally, it appears to be feasible as it does not require excessive funding and most of this funding is focused in one specific area: market research. The proposal is an excellent cultural fit and so was justifiably selected as the winner in the programme.

(c)   (i)   A number of issues can be identified in this process.

First of all, 40% of enquiries do not proceed after the delivery and payment details have been sent to the customer. The scenario suggests that this is of concern to *greenTech* because it wastes time and effort. However, it also impacts upon Xsys and for both of these companies this wastage means the loss of significant selling opportunities. The reason for this high wastage rate is not specified. Three possibilities include:

The cost of the computer was more than expected. In this case it would be useful to supply the cost as soon as delivery details have been completed. This means making sure that the web site has access to Xsys pricing details.

The delivery date was later than required. Although it would be tempting to automatically show the delivery date on the screen alongside cost details, this might not be commercially sensible. It would be better to direct effort at reducing the delivery time so that it was no longer an issue.

Finally, the delay gives the customer time to reflect and change their mind. It would be preferable to get customer commitment much earlier in the ordering process.

The credit check is performed too late in the ordering cycle. 20% of orders are rejected at this point. Hence greenTech and Xsys have wasted time and money communicating with the customer. The suggestion again is to bring payment and credit checking forward to the start of the ordering process. This would remove two processes from the greenTech swim lane: 'request delivery date' and 'e-mail delivery and cost details'.

Bringing ordering, payment and payment checking to the start of the process eradicates the need for Xsys to provide two delivery dates, one on initial ordering and a second on confirmation.

The problem of delivery time could be addressed by using EIM (or a similar courier company) to deliver directly to the end customer. This would remove two further processes from the *greenTech* swim lane – 'agree delivery date' and 'arrange delivery to customer'.

Making the changes proposed above now only leaves 'place confirmed order' and 'test computer' in the *greenTech* swim lane. 'Place confirmed order' can be automatically triggered near the start of the ordering process. If responsibility for testing was given to Xsys (and there are good reasons why it should be), then there would be nothing left in the *greenTech* swim lane. greenTech becomes a virtual supplier and the sales department can get on with making sales rather than processing orders.

(ii)   The design of processes can be viewed as an implementation of strategic planning. This is normally associated with what Johnson, Scholes and Whittington term the design lens. It views strategy development as the deliberate positioning of an organisation through some analytical, directive process. It is often associated with 'top-down' design in that the objectives and goals are determined first and then processes are designed to realise them. In the context of the scenario, the new strategic direction now being followed will required a set of processes designed to facilitate business-to-business transactions with potential new customers. Process is following strategy. As a result process design and associated measures should align with business goals and objectives.

Alternatively, the investigation and potential re-design of the way processes take place within an organisation supports the lenses that Johnson, Scholes and Whittington termed, respectively, experience and ideas. An investigation of current processes might suggest that process goals and measures may not be aligned with strategy. This may be because the processes have diverged from their original specification or it may be because the strategy is not operationally feasible and the people undertaking the processes to implement it know this. Consequently, processes are often modified by employees and managers to make them workable and eventually, strategy is modified to accept this.

The re-design of processes may lead to incremental changes or it may lead to a significant strategic shift. Opportunities discovered while focusing on specific processes may have very significant repercussions. In the case study, the potential role of greenTech as a virtual supplier may be very interesting to the board. It would eradicate delay, reduce operational costs, reduce delivery costs and perhaps provide better (but certainly quicker) customer service. However, this is quite a significant strategic move and the decision to follow the chosen strategy would have to be re-evaluated if the company changed its strategic position.

			ACCA Marking scheme	Marks
(a)			Up to 1 mark for each significant point up to a maximum of	12
(b)			Up to 1 mark for each significant point in the evaluation of each proposal up to a maximum of 4 marks for each proposal. There are three proposals, giving a maximum of 12 marks.	
			Up to 1 mark for each significant point in the justification of the winning proposal up to a maximum of	
			2 professional marks for appropriate tone, recognition of context of scenario, conviction of answer	
			Maximum	20
(c)	(i)		Up to 1 mark for each identified deficiency, suggestion or implication up to a maximum of	10
	(ii)		Up to 1 mark for each significant point up to a maximum of	6
			Up to 2 professional marks for clarity of the analysis	
			Maximum	18
Total				50

Examiner's comments

Part (a) was designed as a gentle introduction to the paper, giving candidates an early opportunity to confidently gain relatively easy marks. It should have also helped candidates prepare themselves for the subsequent evaluation of strategic options (part b of this question). The P3 examination panel decided to restrict candidates to a SWOT analysis so that answers did not use too many alternative models, consuming a disproportionate amount of examination time. Candidates generally answered this question very well with many answers gaining ten marks or more of the twelve on offer. However, despite restricting the question to a SWOT analysis, there was evidence that some candidates spent too long on this part question, writing too much and causing themselves time problems later in the examination.

Part (b) asked candidates to evaluate the three proposals suggested in the scenario and to justify the selection of the proposal from Professor Ag Wan as the best strategic option for greenTech to pursue. This was a significant part question (worth twenty marks). Although it was answered quite well, many candidates did not apply sufficient analysis and evaluation. For example, in considering Fenix's suggestion to buy manufacturing capability, many candidates made the legitimate point that this would secure the supply chain and potentially reduce supply costs. However, fewer candidates recognised that greenTech had grown organically to this point and had no demonstrable capability in acquiring companies and managing these acquisitions. Even fewer candidates pointed out that evidence suggests that few acquisitions (even when made by experienced acquirers) deliver the anticipated benefits. The justification of the Ag Wan selection was also relatively weak. Some candidates felt that it was not the best option and explained why in their answer. Although this analysis might be legitimate it is not answering the question. The question requires the candidate to take a position and to justify this position whether they believe it or not.

The final part of the compulsory question was split into two parts. The first part had not been asked as a compulsory question before. Despite this, most candidates provided good answers, showing good business analysis skills within the constraint of a time-constrained examination.

The second part of this question was poorly answered, with many candidates providing only cursory answers. Some candidates did answer this question using the framework of the Harmon process-strategy grid. Although this is not recognised in the suggested model answer, credit was given for using this approach and relating it to the case study.

79 GET

🔑

Key answer tips

This question involved external and internal analysis, strategy evaluation and critical success factors. Students should be well prepared for these areas and the biggest barrier to success may be time management. There may be a temptation to include too many models in answers and it would be vital to be aware of the mark allocation and the number of points expected to be included in each section. In discussing critical success factors there was scope to bring in areas such as benchmarking and the balanced scorecard. But there should have been enough marks available to students to pass without having to do this.

(a) **An assessment of GET's strategic position**

The answer can be formulated in a number of ways. The following model answer uses an external analysis which forms the basis of the opportunities open to GET and the threats that it faces. The internal analysis summarises the strengths and weaknesses and includes an assessment of the company's financial position. Appropriate models and frameworks would be PESTEL and Porter's five forces (external analysis) and a resource audit (mainly used here in terms of financial terms and internal competencies).

External analysis

The political environment is very important to GET as it was the election of the PNR that effectively brought the company into being with the privatisation of the country's rail network. The attitude of the government to failing franchisees is also very significant. There is a chance that these franchises will be terminated and opened to re-bidding, which should be of interest to GET. However, the stance of the main political opposition has to be monitored and, if possible, influenced. The opposition initially suggested a re-nationalisation of the network, but have modified their view to taking a larger portion of the company's profits. Thus the profitability and perhaps even the continued existence of GET is potentially threatened in the long term.

The government is also enacting more safety legislation which is adding to GET's costs. Further safety legislation is expected concerning the relaying of track and all franchisees will be expected to implement any requirements immediately. These are likely to be costs that GET did not predict when they won the contract and so are almost certain to have an impact on profitability.

The economic health of Rudos is very important to GET as it affects the demand for its services. In the fourth year of the franchise no government subsidies were paid and economic recession led to a fall in passenger numbers. GET needs to monitor the economic health of the country and to bring its passenger number predictions into line with economic indicators.

There is evidence in the scenario that road transport has suffered from a lack of investment under the PNR, resulting in many of the roads becoming heavily congested. Fuel costs are also soaring, which reflects the increasing scarcity of oil and spiralling transport and storage costs of distributing that oil. Rail transport offers a congestion-free alternative to road transport, potentially using power that does not rely on oil. GET needs to reflect this in its strategy and its marketing.

Many industrialised countries have seen the rise of the 'green consumer' who makes ethical choices in the selection of products and services. This will apply to transport, where they may be willing to spend more to use a method of transport which is more energy efficient. Rail services appeal to this consumer group and GET needs to emphasise this in its marketing.

Finally, the principles of privatisation have spread throughout the world. GET needs to monitor the intentions of other countries, such as Raziackstan, who are keen to divest themselves of an expensive public service and, at the same time, raise capital for use elsewhere in the economy. It seems likely that many opportunities will arise in the future.

Within the industry itself, the power of customers is relatively weak, particularly as the potential substitute (road transport) is increasingly expensive and congested. The nature of the franchise means that consumers have no choice at all within each franchise section. All rail users travelling through East Rudos must use GET. The long-term nature of the franchise is an effective barrier to competitors. New entrants are barred until the opportunity arises for them to bid for the franchise.

Internal analysis

The management team of GET has gained important experience in running a newly privatised rail franchise. This team already had significant operating experience (gained with RudosRail) but they have adapted quickly to the new private sector model. The company is the most profitable of the new franchises and it is held up as an example of successful privatisation. These are important internal competences which GET might wish to exploit elsewhere.

The new ticketing system is also an important internal competence. It is so successful that it is used by three of the other franchise operators. GET is paid on a transaction basis for the bookings that it processes on behalf of these other franchisees. As well as providing an important internal competence it must also have brought in unexpected and regular revenue which could not have been foreseen when the franchise was originally won.

The company (GET) reports profitability levels well above industry norms. In 20X4 it returned a gross profit margin of 34% compared with 22% for the industry as a whole. Its operating profit margin of 22% is also significantly higher than the profit margin for the sector as a whole (10%). Overheads appear to be well controlled.

The company also reports good liquidity levels with a current ratio of 2.93 (compared with 2.1 for the sector as a whole) and an acid test ratio of 1.55 which is also greater than the industry average of 1.12. The company can easily meet its short-term liabilities.

The efficiency of the company might be measured in a number of ways. Two potential measures are employee/route kilometre and revenue/employee. In both these measures, GET outstrips the industry norms. Revenue/employee is over $106,000, compared with $85,000 in the industry as a whole. Employee per route kilometre stands at 3.27 compared with 4.1 overall, which means that in these terms the productivity of GET is higher than the Rudos average.

The company has also invested in new trains and its excellent reliability record has meant that it has quickly built up a well-respected image and brand. This brand is rapidly becoming a significant asset of the company, rated highly by both peers and customers.

A clear weakness is the fact that the company is essentially a one-contract (franchise) company and is vulnerable to external factors that can affect the profitability and existence of this contract. The management team is experienced in the rail industry, but has little external perspective. The team would appear unable to bring external ideas and experience from a different industry or different country. There might be a concern that the team cannot think 'outside the box' and this might affect its ability to secure the long-term future of the company.

The company is highly geared, with a gearing percentage of 75% compared with an industry norm of 48%. This reflects the way that the company was initially funded. This might be of concern to their bank if the country is heading into economic difficulties.

Despite its profitability, its Return on Capital Employed (ROCE) is low (2.63%) compared with the industry average (4.5%) and this must be of concern to shareholders.

Tutorial note

A number of financial ratios are calculated above. Marks will be given where legitimate alternative values are calculated, reflecting different ways of defining the ratio. These alternative values may lead to different conclusions, and again credit will be given for this. It is recommended that candidates explicitly show how each ratio has been calculated. The rationale for the ratios given is shown below.

Gross profit margin = Gross profit/sales revenue = 110/320 = 34%

Operating profit margin = Net profit before tax and interest/sales revenue = 70/320 = 22%

Current ratio = Current assets/current liabilities = 585/200 = 2.93

Acid test ratio = (Current assets – inventory)/current liabilities = 1.55

Revenue/employee = Sales revenue/number of employees = $106,312

Employees/route kilometre = Number of employees/route kilometres = 3.27

ROCE = Net profit before interest and tax/capital employed (Share capital + reserves + long term loans) = 70/2660 =2.63%

Gearing % = long term liabilities/(share capital + reserves + long term liabilities) = 2000/2660 = 75%.

(b)

Tutorial note

This model answer is structured around the criteria of suitability, acceptability and feasibility, but this is not required by the question. Answers that take a different approach will be given appropriate credit.

Report name: An assessment of the proposed strategy of GET

Author: Anne Examiner

Report date: 11 November 20X4

Introduction

I have been asked to provide an independent assessment of the proposed strategy of GET to acquire SOFR and the franchise to run the railway services of Raziackstan. My evaluation will use an assessment of the suitability, acceptability and feasibility of this strategic direction.

Management summary

There are powerful suitability and acceptability arguments for pursuing this strategy. However, funding and risk issues may mean that a more conservative strategy might be preferred, perhaps waiting until the failing franchises in Rudos are offered for sale.

Suitability

Suitability is concerned with whether a proposed strategy addresses the circumstances in which an organisation is operating – its strategic position. In the context of this part question, does the proposed strategy of GET, to bid for the rail franchise in Raziackstan and purchase SOFR, correctly respond to influences in the external environment and exploit its internal competencies? As Johnson, Scholes and Whittington ask, does the 'rationale of the strategy make sense?'

There are obvious ways in which the proposed strategy makes sense. Firstly, it provides GET with an opportunity to exploit its acknowledged competencies in running a newly privatised railway. GET has an experienced and respected management team, together with a computerised booking system which is recognised by its peers as effective and successful. The contract in Raziackstan provides an opportunity to quickly implement tested management practices and supporting operational processes.

GET is currently a one-contract company, with a limited life span if it fails to win the Rudos franchise when it is offered again. The acquisition of the Raziackstan contract appears to reduce its dependence on the Rudos franchise and perhaps offers the company greater longevity.

Furthermore, acquiring contracts outside Rudos also appears to make sense. Although the opposition political party in Rudos has slightly modified its stance, it still remains a potential long-term threat to both the existence and profitability of the franchise. In contrast, Raziackstan offers greater political certainty, at least in terms of its commitment to rail privatisation. It also has less stringent employment and safety legislation and so the expensive implications of recent legislation in Rudos will not be incurred.

GET might also be relatively confident about increasing profits in Raziackstan by bringing the rail network up to the efficiency levels it has achieved in the East Rudos franchise. At present, the number of employees employed per route kilometre (5.33) is greater than at GET and revenue per employee significantly less ($22,500 revenue/employee) If GET can cut staffing in Raziackstan to achieve similar levels of productivity as it currently achieves, then profits will improve without the need to raise ticket prices.

The acquisition of SOFR appears to allow the company to spread its risk, buying a company which is in a market which should be expanding as the country begins to upgrade its neglected rail network. GET may also find synergies between SOFR and its franchise operation in Rudos.

However, it must be recognised that the key functionality of its software (allowing franchise cross-charging and Internet booking) is less important in a country where the whole of the railway system will be allocated to one operator and less than 20% of the country's population has access to the Internet. The software application may be an important asset of GET, but it is not of great significance in this particular situation.

Acceptability

The acceptability of a proposed strategy is concerned with the expected performance outcomes of a strategy in terms of return, risk and stakeholder reactions. A consideration of risk is very important here.

There are a number of mismatches that need to be considered. Firstly, GET has experience of operating a rail franchise where it has total control over the track and the trains. In Raziackstan there will be a different model. Punctuality, safety and efficiency will depend on both the railway (running the trains) and the state (maintaining the tracks). Conflicts of interest and responsibility are likely. GET has no experience of working under these terms.

Secondly, GET has no experience of managing outside Rudos. There are clear indications in the scenario that both the social and industrial culture of Raziackstan is very different.

For example, railway employees perceive that a 'railway job is a job for life' and it seems likely that there will be a clash between the management culture of GET and the organisational culture of both the railway operation and SOFR. The apparent improvements in productivity may be hard to achieve. The risk is even greater at SOFR because GET has no obvious internal competencies to bring to bear. It has no experience of running an engineering company, let alone one in an overseas country with a different culture and expectations. Stakeholders in Rudos may also be concerned that the management of GET might be distracted from running the East Rudos franchise, resulting in reduced performance.

Feasibility

Feasibility is concerned with whether an organisation has the resources and competences to deliver a strategy. Financial feasibility is considered under this heading, identifying the funds required and the sources of those funds. This will be an issue for GET. Although it does have some cash, the company is already highly geared and this was identified as a potential weakness in the previous analysis. The franchise in Rudos was financed by the Bank of Rudos, but it seems unlikely that it would wish to increase its exposure, particularly to an investment in a distant country. The financial infrastructure of Raziackstan is immature and so also seems unlikely as a source of funding for GET. There are also potential financial and commercial risks that the government could change its strategy on railway privatisation and GET cannot be sure how profitable or secure its investment in Raziackstan will be in the medium to longer term. Resource deployment considers the feasibility of specific strategies by identifying the resources and competences needed for a particular strategy. For example, is it feasible for GET to establish expertise in engineering, particularly in another country where it has no experience of managing at all?

Conclusion

At first sight, the bid for the Raziackstan rail franchise and the associated purchase of SOFR appears to be a reasonable strategy. However, more detailed analysis suggests that the rationale is not as strong as it could be and there are many risks involved. Eventually, it comes down to the company's ability to find funds and its appetite for risk. In the long term it may be better for the company to await the outcome of the audit report on the failing franchises in Rudos. Bidding for these might be a more profitable and less risky strategy.

(c)

Johnson, Scholes and Whittington defined critical success factors (CSFs) as 'those product features that are particularly valued by a group of customers and, therefore, where the organisation must excel to outperform competition.' In the context of the case study scenario, the competition is represented by alternative forms of transport (car, bus or aeroplane) or indeed perhaps the decision not to travel at all. The marketing message of GET stresses safety and punctuality. These are likely to be important to the customer, although other aspects of service provision might be as important, for example: convenience (timetabling), cleanliness and security. The relative importance of CSFs is likely to vary with the market segment (the group of customers). For example, business travellers may value punctuality, while leisure travellers might value cleanliness and security. Rail companies (such as GET) will have CSFs concerning financial performance and passenger numbers.

CSFs are normally measured through key performance indicators (KPIs). These are targets that the organisation has to achieve. Acceptable punctuality is usually defined by a percentage of trains that have arrived at the scheduled arrival time or before. A certain amount of latitude is usually allowed – for example, in the United Kingdom a train is deemed to have arrived on time if it arrives at its planned destination station within five minutes (i.e. 4 minutes 59 seconds or less) of the planned arrival time. For longer distance operators a criterion of arrivals within 10 minutes (i.e. 9 minutes 59 seconds or less) is used. Critics of this approach have also suggested that it encourages train companies to be conservative in their train timetabling, so ensuring that they meet the target. Safety can be measured in terms of accidents or fatalities per thousand kilometres travelled. Cleanliness might be measured by the number of complaints received about litter and dirtiness. Security might be measured by the number of criminal offences committed on the railway.

The balanced business scorecard was established to help focus companies on non-financial, as well as financial measures of performance. The customer is one of its four perspectives and so this links directly to the critical success factors defined above. However, the other three perspectives of the scorecard are a rich source of KPIs and so many companies have KPIs for financial, internal business processes and learning and growth. Here are some examples from the perspective of GET:

Financial: target return on capital employed

Internal business process: asset utilisation – trains should be used for a target number of hours per day. Utilisation of assets is important

Learning and growth: targets for increasing qualifications in the workforce

Although Johnson, Scholes and Whittington focus their definition of a CSF on the customer, other definitions are much wider. John Rockart originally defined CSFs as:

'The limited number of areas in which results, if they are satisfactory, will ensure successful competitive performance for the organisation. They are the few key areas where things must go right for the business to flourish.'

In practice many organisations use the term CSF for other elements of the balanced business scorecard, even though these are not directly evaluated by the customer when they are making their purchase decision. The concern, here, is that internal CSFs will only be valued by internal stakeholders and not by the customers that they serve.

A consideration of CSFs highlights the significance of Raziackstan's decision to split track provision from rail travel provision. It is easy to envisage a situation where safety is compromised by poor track maintenance and track faults lead to poor punctuality. The Rudos model seems much clearer, where responsibility is for everything within the franchise.

ACCA Marking scheme		Marks
(a)	1 mark for each appropriate point up to a maximum of 20 marks.	20
(b)	1 mark for each appropriate point up to a maximum of 16 marks.	16
	1 mark each for report structure, style, and fluency up to a maximum of 4 professional marks.	4
(c)	1 mark for each appropriate point up to a maximum of 10 marks.	10
Total		**50**

Examiner's comments

The first part of this question was answered well with some candidates getting full marks. Most candidates made good use of the financial data provided in the scenario. However, some answers, despite scoring well, displayed elements of poor examination technique that probably led to later time problems in the examination. Specifically, candidates were not required to describe selected models and frameworks in depth. Some answers described frameworks such as Porter's Five Forces at great length and this was not needed. The question requires application, not description. Secondly, the injudicious selection of frameworks often led to the same points being needlessly repeated (for example, in the PESTEL and the SWOT analysis) and marks can only be given once. Candidates are also reminded that not all elements of a PESTEL analysis are bound to appear in the case study scenario or that relevant points will be evenly spread amongst the six influences. Also, technology (in PESTEL) refers to external technological change, not to the internal technological resources of the organisation.

The second part of the first question was less well answered than the first part of the question. Many candidates struggled to impose a structure on the answer and, although many used the suitability, acceptability and feasibility framework, they often repeated themselves and failed to make enough distinct points to get the marks on offer. Surprisingly few candidates tied their answer to their strategic position analysis, the first part of the question.

The proposed strategy concerns an opportunity, and candidates might have considered this opportunity in the context of the strengths, weaknesses, threats and indeed, alternative opportunities, identified in the previous part of the question. This would have revealed that some of the company's strengths are largely irrelevant in the proposed strategy (for example, the internet booking system) and some weaknesses (gearing and ROCE) might make funding such a proposal impossible. Similarly, candidates might have dwelt on how the proposed strategy addresses the threats to GET identified in their position analysis. Very few candidates identified that the nature of the proposed franchise (trains but not tracks) was fundamentally different to GET's home country experience and raised important elements of risk. Some candidates also made the mistake of perceiving GET as the franchisor, not the franchisee, and hence included much irrelevant comment on its strategy. Candidates must also stay within the bounds of the case study scenario. Nowhere does it say that SOFR will be 'hugely expensive to acquire'. Overall, the answers were average, and they should have been much better.

The final part of this question asked candidates to explain and discuss the concepts of Critical Success Factors (CSFs) and Key Performance Indicators (KPIs). Many candidates appeared to be unfamiliar with this part of the syllabus and this is reflected in the average mark for this part of the question. Some candidates merely changed the sequence of the words; stating that 'critical success factors are the factors that are critical to the success of the business', and then listed the strengths of GET. The focus of the answer really needed to be on what the customer values and where the organisation has to excel to outperform the competition. Some candidates did not consider the rail industry at all, framing their answer in the context of a manufacturing company or a university.

80 MIDSHIRE HEALTH   *Online question assistance*

Key answer tips

This question is a test of learning and knowledge as much as application. The question highlights that not every Section A question will focus on strategic decisions. There were very few strategic elements in this question and instead the focus was very much on strategy in action. The requirements covered project management, culture and the strategy lenses. All three question elements were similar to questions which have been set before (sometimes in Section B), so that each part could be treated almost like an individual question. There is plenty of scope to score marks as long as candidates focus on the actual problems in the scenario and don't make their answers overly theoretical.

(a) (i) Project initiation

It is good practice to establish a Project Initiation Document (PID) or Terms of Reference (ToR) at the start of the project defining the objectives, scope, constraints, authority (owner, sponsor) and resources of the project. In the context of the case study scenario, there appears to be confusion around the objectives, scope and ownership of the project.

Project objectives and project scope: what is the project?

The objectives and scope of the project appear to be at different levels. The project might be 'to establish a formal strategic planning system at MidShire Health', or, it might be more restricted to the development of a 'comprehensive computer-based information system recording the outcomes and activities of the organisation'. Certainly the implementation team set up to undertake the detailed work appears to be primarily concerned with the functionality of the software package and the presence of Eurotek support consultants would tend to support this focus. The assertion from the CEO that the objective of the steering group is 'to deliver health to the Midshire community' adds further confusion. Although this objective is amended later in the project, restricting it to 'effectively and efficiently treating disease', both of these objectives really concern the organisation as a whole, not a specific project within that organisation. It is preferable that the project objectives should be more restricted.

The immediate employment of consultants with a potential software solution will inevitably skew the project towards a particular technical solution designed to support the planning system. There needs to be a distinction at the initiation of the project between the business objectives of the project and the technical objectives of the software system required to support those business objectives. The CEO confuses the two, a confusion accentuated by the early selection of a technical solution, before the business requirements have been defined (see later).

A failure to define a consistent achievable objective often results in projects lacking focus, leading to confusion amongst the project participants about what they are supposed to be doing. Terry Nagov really needed to establish a proper project objective within a formal Project Initiation Document.

The role of the steering group: who owns the project?

All projects should have a sponsor or authority that makes decisions about the project and supports it throughout its lifecycle. Ideally, this should be one person. It is possible for a group of people to play this role, but it is important that they promote a united front. Even if the objectives and scope of the project can be defined (see previous paragraph), the steering group is disunited in the context of project sponsorship. There are clear conflicts within the group and some of these have been made public. Projects without a well-defined committed sponsor are likely to be unsuccessful as they lack clear leadership and support. Furthermore, if the sponsor is a group, then the focus of the project will veer to reflect changes in interest and power in the make-up of the group. The sponsor (owner) role should have been given more thought at the start of the project and responsibility should have been documented in the Project Initiation Document.

Conduct of the project

Two aspects in the conduct of the project deserve scrutiny. The first concerns the procurement process. The second is group and stakeholder management.

Procurement process

The Eurotek solution was selected before the requirements of the strategic planning process had been defined. Once these requirements had been developed, it became clear that the software package was a poor fit and that a considerable amount of bespoke work was needed to make it fit-for-purpose. The cost of these developments effectively led to the end of the project. This was a poor process. The information system requirements of the strategic planning process should have been developed before a potential software package solution was selected. The selection process should have involved more than one company and should have been transparent, so that the reasons for selecting a particular solution were documented and auditable. It is unclear from the scenario why the Eurotek solution was selected so early in the process, particularly as their expertise appeared to lie in the banking industry, rather than health care. Most public sector organisations have to follow strict procurement guidelines and it is surprising that these were not in place at MidShire Health.

Group and stakeholder management

Terry Nagov appears to believe that the three employee sets within the steering group (senior hospital doctors, hospital nursing managers and health service support staff) are equally powerful within the project context. However, this is clearly not the case. The hospital doctors resent the inclusion of the health service support staff in the steering group. The hospital nursing managers side with the hospital doctors at key points. The objectives of the health service support staff appear to be aligned with those of Terry Nagov, but this support is not as effective as it may appear because it comes from the weakest set within the steering group. In Tuckman and Jenson's terms the group is fractional, stuck in a storming stage. Differences in power and culture will make it extremely difficult for the group to move beyond this stage. However, the person who could make it happen (Terry Nagov) undermines possible progress by choosing to openly question the ethics of one of the hospital doctors. This appears to destroy the possibility of group harmony and also brings into play a significant actor (Etopia's health minister) who, although very powerful, had hitherto had no obvious interest in the project.

Project cancellation procedures

The CEO did not explore opportunities for negotiating the $600,000 quoted development cost or look for alternatives. Eurotek might have been flexible on price, particularly if the developed software could have potentially been used in other health authorities. In such circumstances, MidShire Health might have negotiated a royalty fee, to help them recoup their investment. Perhaps this was also the point when alternative suppliers could have been sought, providing solutions which were closer to the requirements of the organisation. This would have led to the investment in Eurotek being written off, but this was also a consequence of project cancellation. No post-project review was conducted, and lessons learned were not fed back into the project management process. In fact, the email sent to the steering group members specifically stated that there would be no further meetings. As someone once wrote, the 'only unforgiveable failure was the failure to learn from failure'.

(ii)   **Organisational culture**

Johnson, Scholes and Whittington suggest that the culture of an organisation consists of four layers. Firstly, *values* which are often written down as statements of the organisation's mission. The visionary objective of the CEO might be an example of a value. The 'mission is to deliver health to the people of Midshire and, by that, I don't just mean hospital services for the sick, but a wider vision, where health is a state of complete physical, mental and social well-being and not merely the absence of disease or infirmity'. *Beliefs* are more specific and concern issues which people in the organisation can talk about. The hospital doctors appear to firmly believe that the visionary objective of the CEO is unobtainable. 'You have to realise that poor health is often caused by poverty, poor housing and social dislocation. You cannot expect MidShire Health to solve these problems. We can advise and also treat the symptoms, but prevention and cure for these wider problems are well beyond us.' *Behaviours* are the day-to-day way in which the organisation operates. Certain aspects of these become clear in the scenario describing the strategic planning project. Finally there are the *taken-for-granted assumptions* that are at the core of an organisation's culture. In the scenario there is a contrast between the CEO's vision of delivering health and the perception of hospital doctors and nursing staff that the real work is really about treating the ill.

The *behaviours* of the organisation can be explored further through selected facets of the cultural web.

The *stories* told by the hospital doctors are primarily concerned with belittling the role of the professional administrator. 'As we know', stated one of the doctors, 'we all agree that efficiency can only be achieved through giving control and budget to the doctors, not to the administrators *who are an unwanted overhead.* This is the first step we should take.' We can assume that the chief administrator (the CEO) present at the meeting could not have missed this slight. Secondly, the planning process does not appear to be perceived as real work. During one of the meetings the hospital doctors stated that they had to leave to get back to their *real job of treating patients.* It almost appears that the hospital doctors have agreed to participate in the planning process as a damage limitation exercise, trying to protect their power and status, rather than because they have any real interest or belief in the planning process and its goals.

A definite hierarchy in the *power structures* appears to exist during meetings. When the senior hospital doctors are present, the nursing representatives side with them and provide a powerful block to any of the initiatives proposed by the CEO. When the hospital doctors are not present, the nursing representatives appear to be more conciliatory, agreeing to actions and objectives that they renege on in subsequent meetings. The opinions of the support staff are clearly not valued by the hospital doctors. The hospital doctors showed their disdain by leaving one of the meetings when the objectives and role of the support staff were discussed. Their ideas, for example for preventative care, are quickly dismissed by the powerful coalition of the hospital doctors and the nursing managers.

ANSWERS TO SCENARIO-BASED QUESTIONS : SECTION 4

The activities of MidShire Health are affected by the hospital doctors who, through their powerful professional organisation, have negotiated very favourable terms of employment. Not only do they enjoy high salaries for full-time positions, but they also have the right to undertake private practice where they deliver services for private hospitals to fee-paying patients. This almost unprecedented degree of freedom is tolerated by the government and is a parameter that the CEO has to work within. As Mintzberg observed, such organisations are 'the one place in the world where you can act as if you were self-employed yet regularly receive a pay check (cheque)'. Such flexibility does not seem to stretch to the nursing staff, but long-term loyalties seem to bond them to the hospital doctors. In contrast, the support workers appear to work under difficult circumstances, expected to serve the whims of professionals, but with little recognition of their contribution and little autonomy in undertaking their work. Probably as a result of this, they appear to be the most receptive group to the changes proposed by the CEO.

The lack of *control* the organisation has over the powerful hospital doctors is shown by the fact that one of the doctors perceives that it is perfectly acceptable to criticise his employer in public, disclosing private information from meetings to the press. This behaviour is excused as being in the 'public interest' and the doctor receives support from his colleagues. The CEO, although appalled by the behaviour, cannot pursue any disciplinary action because of threats from nurses and doctors.

Organisational configuration

Organisations tend to configure in a number of ways. The attributes or building blocks of the organisation relate to each other in different ways.

Terry Nagov was formerly the CEO of a company making mobility appliances. As well as having a profit motive (unlike MidShire Health), the company developed its business strategy through a centralised management structure, with line managers given the power and responsibility to achieve defined objectives and targets. Production itself was heavily automated, administered and controlled through semiskilled employees who followed standards and procedures defined by senior managers. In terms of Mintzberg's configurations, the company appears to exhibit many aspects of a *machine bureaucracy*. The work it undertook appears to be routine, with much of it being simple and repetitive, allowing the company to establish efficient highly standardised processes. Within machine bureaucracies much of the power resides with the managers at the top of the organisation.

To outsiders such organisations can often appear to be an example of a focused, structured organisation which, as Mintzberg himself concedes, 'can be enormously efficient and provide an unmatchable reliability of service'. To a government struggling with rising costs in an economic recession, such organisations contrast starkly with, as the government minister put it, 'the anarchy of the health service'. To an outside agency, such as the government, appointing a CEO such as Terry Nagov to bring order and control must have seemed an attractive step. Nagov had an excellent record in the private sector and bringing such skills to the public sector would seem to have self-evident benefits.

In Mintzberg's terms, MidShire Health is probably *a professional bureaucracy.* Although the work is still relatively standardised, its complexity means that judgements are usually required. The type of work undertaken in the professional bureaucracy is quite different to that of the machine bureaucracy. Considerable discretion is required in the application of skills that have been gained over years of training. MidShire Health depends on its professional staff and, consequently, like all professional bureaucracies, gives them considerable control over their own work. A machine bureaucracy generates its own standards internally and enforces them through its line managers. This is the approach that the CEO is familiar with. However, in contrast, the standards for a professional bureaucracy originate from self-governing associations that the professionals belong to. Hence the intervention of the Institute of Hospital Doctors (IOHD) would be viewed legitimately by the hospital doctors, who believe that authority comes through expertise, not through a management hierarchy. In questioning the legitimacy of such advice, the CEO failed to recognise the central role that professional associations play in such bureaucracies. It was bound to cause offence to the professional staff on the working party.

A recognition of MidShire Health as a professional bureaucracy should also have helped the CEO predict the hospital doctors questioning the value of having support staff on the working party. In such organisational configurations, such employees are seen as largely subservient to the professionals delivering the fundamental activities of the organisation. In fact, many support staff are managed in a machine, top-down way, and so their enthusiasm for the formal planning initiative might be expected. It closely matches their experience, as well as providing an opportunity to potentially undermine what they consider to be the comfortable, capricious existence of the powerful professionals.

Similarly, the request of the CEO for the doctors to consider the 'good of MidShire Health and its image within the community' is likely to fall on 'deaf ears'. As Mintzberg comments, 'most professional focus their loyalty on their profession, not on the place where they happen to practice it.'

The problem of introducing change in professional bureaucracies is explicitly considered by Mintzberg. He states that 'change in the professional organisation does not sweep in from new administrators taking office to announce wide reforms or from government officials intent on bringing the professional under technocratic control'. This, of course, exactly describes the situation at MidShire Health. Rather, he sees change as seeping in through a slow process of changing the professionals themselves, through altering recruitment policies and training. In the short term, he would probably suggest that the government would be better off placing pressure on the professional associations that influence their member (such as the IOHD), rather than tamper with the professional bureaucracies directly.

Finally, it has to be recognised that MidShire Health is a public sector organisation funded by general taxation, rather than by its specific users or customers. In principle the provider of the funds (government) provides resource inputs into a service that is competing with other services funded by general taxation – such as national security. Thus health services, in principle, need to show that they are providing value for money so that politicians support further funding. Such an approach appears to give the government a lot of power. However, the existence of powerful professions and the willingness of press and public to defend health service principles dilute this power, leading to the kind of frustration explicitly articulated in the case study scenario.

(b) The approach to strategy suggested by the CEO is essentially *strategy by design,* based on a logical process whereby senior management devises a clear strategic direction and a system is then put in place to implement this direction throughout the organisation. The overall mission of the organisation is pursued through increasingly specific objectives cascaded down through the organisation, so that all layers of management are pursuing objectives defined and aligned to the determined strategy. This is probably the most popular perception of how strategy is developed. Although it has its critics, such an approach *appears* to be used by many organisations. Perhaps the relatively simple manufacturing environment of the CEO's former company made a rational planned approach a feasible way of managing strategy. Certainly such order often appeals to politicians, as in the case study scenario, particularly when the provided service is funded out of general taxation and where politicians define the resource inputs – how much money is to be spent on health, compared with competing claims of defence, education etc. Politicians increasingly look for *value for money,* and a designed strategy appears to be an orderly and controlled way of delivering such value.

Strategy as experience is based on the premise that organisational strategy is largely based on the adaptation of past strategies. This adaptation is a reflection of the experience of managers and others working within the organisation. As Johnson, Scholes and Whittington suggest, this is 'strongly driven by the taken-for-granted assumptions and ways of doing things embedded in the culture of the organisation'. This is largely the approach of the senior hospital doctors and nursing managers on the steering committee. Strategy as experience resolves different views and expectations through a process of bargaining and negotiation. By participating in the steering group, these two powerful interest groups were increasingly able to negotiate a vision of health care and health care delivery that matched their perceptions. The powerful position of professions in a public bureaucracy and the relative weakness of professional managers and administrators make it unlikely that large shifts in strategy will happen. Such organisations as the IOHD are clearly willing to publicly undermine the value of professional managers and administrators in a public service. They do this by alluding to 'public interest', rather than self-interest and appear to have little problem in rallying public support. The CEO is unlikely to have experienced this in previous posts and so would have been relatively inexperienced in developing strategy from a coalition of vested interests.

Strategy as ideas largely concerns the issues of innovation. This strategic lens emphasises the importance of diversity and variety in and around the organisation which can be harnessed to produce new ideas. Strategy emerges from people working within the organisation who are faced with challenges and issues in their everyday work. Senior management provides the context for strategy, selecting and promoting ideas originally emanating from lower down in the organisation. Elements of this can be seen in one of the health support members of the steering committee stressing a strategy that encourages problem prevention rather than problem treatment. However, even within the constraints of the steering committee, these ideas were quickly dismissed by a powerful coalition of the hospital doctors and nursing managers. It is likely that the CEO will have experienced suggestions from employees in the past. Ideas would have probably emanated from production operators for reducing waste and from sales managers suggesting new pricing ideas and new products. However, the current culture of MidShire Health seems unlikely to nurture many ideas and innovations. Powerful vested interests are in a position to smother innovations that reflects 'thinking outside the box'. Certainly such ideas would need special protection, something that the CEO fails to offer even within the closed environment of the steering committee.

Johnson, Scholes and Whittington see the three strategy lenses as complementary. A certain perspective may fail to see important issues raised by using a different lens. In the context of the case study scenario, the CEO would perhaps be better to develop strategy through experience, perhaps supplemented by new ideas and innovation. The strategy by design appears flawed, particularly given the divergent views on the mission of the organisation. However, despite this, strategy by design is the approach that the CEO appears to prefer and adopt.

ACCA Marking scheme			Marks
(a)	(i)	1 mark for each relevant point up to a maximum of	18
	(ii)	1 mark for each relevant point up to a maximum of.	18
		Up to 4 professional marks are allocated for the clarity, structure and logical flow of the answer.	4
(b)		1 mark for each relevant point up to a maximum of.	10
Total			**50**

Examiner's comments

Question 1a required candidates to diagnose the problems at MidShire Health in terms of project management, organisational culture and organisational configuration. In general candidates were weaker on the last of these, organisational configuration, although a significant number of candidates did reference the Mintzberg stereotypes.

Too many answers followed the sequence of the meetings described in the scenario, repeating the same information and diagnosis, often accompanied by copying out sections of text directly from the scenario. There was a lack of analysis and organisation in many answers. This repetition of the same points also led to long answers which probably contributed to time problems later in the examination. In general, part a) (i), concerning project management was better answered than part a) (ii), on culture and configuration. This was largely because general points made about good project management were accompanied by appropriate illustrations from the scenario. This was less evident in the cultural analysis, where facets of the cultural web were often described in detail, without any supporting evidence that they were relevant to the scenario.

There is an explicit learning objective on the three strategy lenses defined by Johnson, Scholes and Whittington and a very similar question to the part b) question posed here, was set in December 2008, concerning another public sector organisation, the National Museum. However, despite this, very few candidates scored good marks on part b of this question. Many candidates scored less than three marks, with answers that were often very sketchy and just rearranged the key words of the question. For example 'a strategy must be designed' and 'it often reflects the experience of the CEO and the ideas he has brought in from elsewhere'. Prior to the examination, the examination panel believed that this part question would be very well answered, as it is a discrete part of the syllabus which has been asked before. However, this was not the case.

81 MACHINESHOP

Key answer tips

This question has a heavy slant towards the strategic elements of the syllabus. Students have to evaluate different expansion methods and a potential acquisition in particular. Help is given in the form of direction as to which tests to use and this should help even the less well prepared students. Part (c) of the question covers Porter's diamond model which has rarely been examined in the past and may challenge some students. But students have answered this area well in the past and, with only 10 marks available for this part of the question, this shouldn't be the difference between pass or fail on this question.

(a) *Internal growth*, sometimes called organic growth, takes place when the company grows by building on and developing its own existing competencies. This is how MachineShop has grown to date. The frequent opening of new stores represents its organic growth. The company appears to be comfortable and successful in this approach.

As well as being familiar with this approach, internal growth has a number of other advantages for MachineShop.

First, MachineShop is the only company which really understands the market that it has positioned itself in. Consequently, there are no equivalent companies or competitors to target for acquisition and so there is no clear alternative to organic growth. This market knowledge is a core competence, creating and reinforcing competitive advantage.

Second, although the final cost of developing through organic growth may be greater than through acquisition, the spread of cost may be easier to bear. Acquisitions usually require a major expenditure at a certain point in time. A slower rate of change, associated with more gradual expenditure and sustainable growth, may also minimise disruption to other activities within the company. Acquisition can be a significant distraction and it could easily prevent the directors from continuing their successful expansion of the MachineShop stores.

In some circumstances, internal growth may be the only realistic option available to an organisation. This may be the case at MachineShop. It acknowledges that it is having difficulty in identifying companies to acquire or with which to pursue a strategic alliance. FRG, analysed in depth in the second part of this question, is the best fit that MachineShop can find, yet it is a business which primarily deals with trade customers and larger machines and it has no experience of selling to domestic consumers.

Internal development avoids the political and cultural problems arising from post-acquisition integration and coping with the different traditions and expectations of the acquired company. MachineShop has already experienced such problems with LogTrans and EngSup.

However, international expansion is often very difficult to achieve with internal growth. This can be due to government restrictions. For example, the government of Ceeland required, until recently, that firms trading in Ceeland were registered in that country and had at least one Ceelander director. Cultural differences also inhibit organic growth. The company will have little understanding of how business is done in the country, the expectations of stakeholders or the way that business transactions are agreed and executed.

An *acquisition* takes place when ownership is taken of another organisation. A compelling reason to develop by acquisition is the speed of entry it apparently provides into a new product or geographical market. This speed of entry is often associated with scale. MachineShop is considering the purchase of a company which already has revenues of $9m. It would take a long time to build a company of that size. One of the concerns of Dave Deen is that the MachineShop concept will be adopted by emerging competitors in countries where it does not have a presence. A prime motive for considering the acquisition of FRG is that it has a depot network, distribution and sales team already in place. FRG is also familiar with the organisational and social culture of Ceeland. It is aware of its laws and corporate responsibilities, tax and legislative regimes. If MachineShop tried to grow organically in Ceeland, it would be starting from scratch in a country where it had no experience of trading.

The acquisition may provide an opportunity for MachineShop to exploit its core competencies in a new market, as well as satisfying Dave Deen's desire for continuing growth and high profile business activity.

Rapid growth through acquisition may also offer immediate economies of scale. This is one of the attractions to Dave Deen. As the company grows larger, it should be able to reduce product costs, allowing it to raise the barriers to market entry, reducing the attraction of the market to potential competitors. Growth through acquisition is a quick way of delivering the scale and cost efficiency of operations required to deter potential competitors from entering the market that it understands and dominates.

Finally, acquisition may provide an opportunity for an organisation to address a lack of resources or competencies in certain areas. This is what prompted MachineShop's two acquisitions in 20X4. LogTrans was bought to provide the company with internal logistics capacity and EngSup was purchased to assist in post-sales support.

Strategic alliances take place when two or more organisations share resources and activities to pursue a given strategy. Both companies seek to gain benefits through co-operation. In the context of MachineShop and FRG, the prime motive would be what Johnson, Scholes and Whittington term as 'co-specialisation'. An alliance would be used to enter a new geographical market where an organisation needs local knowledge and expertise. One of the features of strategic alliances is the range of alliances that might be pursued. Some alliances are very formal, others involve informal networking between organisations with no shareholding or common ownership involved.

A *joint venture* is an arrangement where a newly created organisation is jointly owned by the parents. In this instance, a new company could be created in Ceeland with the local company providing labour, local expertise and countrywide knowledge. MachineShop would provide the products, marketing expertise and finance. At the other end of the spectrum, MachineShop could consider a looser network arrangement where FRG would provide space in their stores for a MachineShop franchise to operate. In this way, MachineShop would gain depot space which they could use to build their own market. This would be an ideal way of prototyping the MachineShop concept in Ceeland to see if the market really does exist and that parallels with Arboria are not unrealistic. In return, FRG would receive a franchise fee which would help it improve its financial position, as well as it potentially benefiting from cross-purchases by customers attracted to the store by the MachineShop facility. Such a loose arrangement could be put in place very quickly, compared to any formal joint venture, acquisition or organic expansion.

One of the main problems of strategic alliances is the ability of the initiator to find an appropriate partner. It is not known if the company which is currently being targeted (FRG) would be interested in a strategic alliance. Hence a search for a partner would have to take place, which could prove difficult and time-consuming. There may also be a concern, at MachineShop, that once the partner understands the dynamics of the market, they will steal the idea and promote it as their own. Networking also offers a relatively modest and low profile approach to expansion and this may not give Dave Deen and his fellow directors the visible growth they seek. It may be too conservative and not exciting enough.

Summary

A case could be made for adopting any of these three distinct approaches and this is recognised by MachineShop itself. This is probably why it believes that growth will be achieved through a combination of organic growth, acquisition and strategic alliance. The latter two are really quite problematic given MachineShop's internal competencies and the market that it is in.

In the context of risk, a loose strategic alliance with a foreign agent seems an attractive route. However, the company would have to find a suitable partner and the approach may not deliver the visible growth required by the directors. An acquisition is risky, particularly in countries where MachineShop has no experience of trading. Furthermore, MachineShop's limited experience of acquisition to date has not been particularly successful, despite both acquired companies being based in Arboria. Organic growth offers the advantages of being proven and familiar. However, it may be difficult to achieve the rapid growth demanded, and is particularly risky to pursue in countries where the company has little understanding of trading arrangements, organisational and social culture and stakeholder expectations.

(b) **Report**

From: Business analyst

To: The Board of MachineShop

Introduction

This brief report looks at the potential acquisition of FRG by MachineShop. It uses the criteria of suitability, acceptability and feasibility, which is a standard framework for evaluating potential acquisitions. It concludes with my recommendation.

Suitability

Suitability is concerned with whether a strategy addresses the circumstances in which an organisation is operating, the strategic position. In the context of MachineShop, does an acquisition make sense and, in the narrower context, does the acquisition of FRG make sense? Johnson, Scholes and Whittington, noted authors on business strategy, have suggested that an acquisition makes particular sense if speed to market is vital. This appears to be the case at MachineShop, where the board wants the company to grow quickly whilst there are no direct competitors. In terms of capabilities, the delivery of economies of scale is also important and this has already been identified as a key benefit of the acquisition, further raising a barrier to entry to potential competitors. Finally, in terms of growth, acquisition appears to largely avoid the cultural problems that are bound to arise by trying to organically grow a company in a foreign land. Expansion in Ceeland is seen as an *opportunity* for rapid growth, exploiting important *strengths*, in particular the internal competencies of MachineShop. Acquisition, particularly in Ceeland, appears to offer the rapid growth which the company seeks.

Acceptability

Acceptability is concerned with the expected outcomes of a strategy. These can be seen in context of stakeholder reactions, risk and return. In the context of MachineShop, the primary stakeholders, the board, are likely to be excited by a foreign acquisition. It provides you with the high profile and the business excitement that you enjoy. However, in financial performance, the potential purchase of FRG looks less attractive. Any financial ratios calculated for FRG cannot really be compared with MachineShop, because the nature of the customers is quite different, with 65% of MachineShop's sales being made to domestic consumers, and so is the country and culture that the two companies operate in. However, whilst acknowledging this limitation, an analysis of the latest financial figures (Table 1) does not appear to paint a particularly attractive picture. FRG has gross profit and operating margins well below that of MachineShop. FRG also has a relatively low Return on Capital Employed (ROCE) of 6.45%, compared to 17.5% for MachineShop. The gearing ratio is higher (20.16%) and the interest cover is lower (2.67) than MachineShop.

Table 1: Comparison of MachineShop and FRG

	Calculation (1)	MachineShop	FRG
Gross profit margin	Gross profit/revenue	28.00%	16.67%
Operating margin	Operating profit/revenue	17.00%	8.89%
ROCE	Operating profit/capital employed	17.50%	6.45%
Gearing ratio	Long-term loans/capital employed	15.00%	20.16%
Interest cover ratio	Operating profit/finance charges	3.5	2.67

(1)   *Other acceptable definitions will be credited*

Improving the financial performance of FRG might be seen as an *opportunity* for MachineShop, except that the post-acquisition performance has actually worsened at the two companies it acquired in Arboria and these were also marred by management and labour disputes. At present, improving the financial performance of acquired companies does not appear to be a core competence of MachineShop. MachineShop also has no experience of acquiring a foreign company and the scale of the acquisition is much greater than its two acquisitions to date. FRG has a turnover of $9,000,000, almost nine times the combined revenue of the two Arborian companies which MachineShop acquired in 20X4.

Feasibility

Feasibility is concerned with whether an organisation has the resources and competencies to deliver a strategy. Financial resources are in place to fund an acquisition through a combination of loans and retained profit. However, no negotiations have yet been opened with FRG. As a result, no comment on the financial feasibility of the acquisition can yet be made. However, the difficulty of satisfactorily valuing a private company suggests that many months of negotiation might lie ahead, particularly given the number and composition of the shareholders of FRG. Trade unions may require certain post-acquisition guarantees about labour retention and reward. Such protracted negotiations would partly nullify, at least, the speed of growth that acquisition appears to offer.

Overall, acquisitions have a poor record in delivering business success. There are usually problems of integration and cultural fit. MachineShop has experienced this to some extent with both LogTrans and EngSup. At LogTrans, the directors had to be removed post-merger because of personality clashes. At EngSup, there was a problem in instilling in service engineers the need for appropriate customer service.

The post-financial performance of the two acquired companies has also been disappointing. Since acquiring LogTrans, gross profit, operating margin and ROCE have fallen and the company is more highly geared than it was before the merger with a reduced interest cover ratio. The same is true at EngSup. Table 2 summarises the data. MachineShop has to review its competencies in acquisitions, not just its competencies in its market. It must also recognise that both these acquisitions took place in Arboria, a country where it understands the culture, laws and regulations. It might be reasonable to expect that the acquisition of a foreign company would be even less successful.

Table 2: Performance analysis, LogTrans and EngSup (20X3–20X6)

	LogTrans – 20X6	LogTrans – 20X3	EngSup – 20X6	EngSup – 20X3
Gross profit margin	17.86%	21.54%	21.43%	23.08%
Operating margin	9.29%	10.77%	11.43%	13.85%
ROCE	9.56%	13.46%	12.50%	15.52%
Gearing ratio	14.71%	9.62%	9.38%	6.90%
Interest cover ratio	2.17	4.67	4.00	5.63

It also has to be recognised that FRG is not a complete match to MachineShop. FRG is experienced in the business market, but has no experience of selling to domestic customers, a service that accounts for 65% of MachineShop's sales.

Conclusion

In theory, an acquisition would appear to be a suitable growth strategy given MachineShop's strategic position and objectives. However, whether the acquisition of FRG is appropriate is more doubtful. FRG does not appear to be financially performing particularly well and it has no experience of selling to domestic customers. Furthermore, MachineShop has no experience of acquiring a company outside Arboria or, indeed, a company as large as this one. Its two previous acquisitions were within Arboria and were relatively modest in size. Both acquired companies should have represented relatively good 'fits' within the supply chain of MachineShop. However, performance post-acquisition has been disappointing, with both companies reporting drops in profitability. MachineShop would have to improve their competencies in managing acquisitions.

Overall, the proposed purchase of FRG appears to be very risky and MachineShop might be better looking elsewhere for a more suitable acquisition. It might also consider entering into a dialogue with FRG about a strategic alliance of some sort (perhaps followed by acquisition), which might offer an attractive alternative to immediate purchase of the company.

(c)   Michael Porter developed his diamond to explore the determinants of national competitive advantage. Its primary use is at a national and regional level as a framework for exploring the competitiveness of a nation (or region) and as a framework for determining policy initiatives. However, it might also be used in this context to analyse, in a more structured way, the competitive nature of Ceeland, the country which MachineShop is keen to expand into, and also to understand factors that might have contributed to MachineShop's success in Arboria. The diamond has four principal determinants.

The first of these is *factor conditions* which are the inputs necessary to compete in any industry, such as labour, land, natural resources, capital and infrastructure. The case study scenario suggests that the transportation system in Ceeland is cheap and effective and ease of distribution is one of the factors which attracted MachineShop to the country. Furthermore, the country has a well-established digital communications structure, and as MachineShop expects to make extensive use of internet order placement, this is also important. Both of these are examples of *advanced factors* which offer more sustainable advantages than basic factors, such as natural resources and unskilled labour and they would make Ceeland attractive to MachineShop. However, both these factors are also *generalised factors* which do not provide as decisive and sustainable a basis for competitive advantage as other more *specialised factors*.

The second facet is the *demand conditions*, the nature of home demand for an industry's product or service. This appears particularly significant in the context of MachineShop. Porter argues that the home market usually has a disproportionate impact on a firm's ability to perceive and interpret buyer needs. One of the reasons for this is the attention the home market requires. Product development usually takes place in the home market. Pride and ego focus attention on succeeding in this market. Pressure from buyers is immediate and the proximity and cultural similarity of these buyers mean that their needs are well understood.

MachineShop has reaped the benefits of supplying a vigorous, growing and demanding home market in Arboria which, it believes, may allow it to anticipate buyer needs in other countries. Dave Deen believes that macroeconomic factors suggest that Ceeland is quickly beginning to resemble Arboria. MachineShop has to hope that his perception is correct and that consumers' needs are not just idiosyncratic to Arboria. Further research needs to be undertaken to ensure that Ceeland's cultural and social values will really lead to the changes in consumer behaviour that the economic trends are suggesting. If they do, then MachineShop will have definitely benefited from demands placed on it from the sophisticated and demanding buyers in Arboria.

The third element of the diamond is *related and supporting industries*. This concerns the presence in the nation of supplier industries or related industries which are internationally competitive. There is some evidence of this in the scenario (MachineShop already buy from a Ceeland supplier), although the government (see later) is encouraging the production of light engineering and so related, supporting industries may eventually develop in Ceeland.

The fourth element concerns *firm strategy, structure and rivalry*. Porter suggests that there is a strong association between vigorous domestic rivalry and the creation and persistence of competitive advantage in an industry. This has not really been a major factor in the success of MachineShop because it has no obvious rivals in the market in Arboria, particularly for domestic customers. A similar situation is likely to occur in Ceeland and so vigorous domestic rivalry will be lacking.

Porter also considers the nature of chance and the role of the government. The role of government is particularly significant in this scenario and it influences elements of the diamond. For example, it has:

- Invested heavily in transportation systems and information technology (factor conditions)

- Lifted regulations on what type of machine can be used by an unqualified operator (demand conditions)

- Removed the requirement for all companies trading in Ceeland to be registered in that country and to have at least one Ceelander director (firm strategy, structure and rivalry).

Encouraged the production of light engineering (related and supporting industries).

So, although Porter's diamond is probably more relevant to understanding industries and countries, it does provide a framework for understanding the national competitive structure that individual firms compete within. Ceeland appears to be relatively attractive from the perspective of factor and demand conditions. However, the stimulus experienced by a company operating in a country where there are internationally competitive suppliers or related industries, or where there is a great degree of rivalry between competitors, will be missing.

	ACCA Marking scheme	
		Marks
(a)	1 mark for each relevant point up to a maximum of 6 marks for each method. It is possible that candidates will include a financial assessment of the post-acquisition performance of LogTrans and EngSup in this part and so marks given for financial calculations (see part (b)) for these two companies may be allocated to this part question. Up to a total of 18 marks for the question.	18
(b)	1 mark will be allocated for each relevant point and interpretation up to a maximum of 18 marks. It is expected (but not mandated) that this will include a financial calculation for FRG. This will be marked as follows:	
	– Gross profit margin	0.5
	– Operating margin	0.5
	– ROCE	0.5
	– Gearing ratio	0.5
	– Interest cover	0.5
	Financial calculations may also be included for LogTrans/EngSup (refer to part (a)) and these will be marked as follows:	
	– Gross profit margin	1
	– Operating margin	1
	– ROCE	1
	– Gearing ratio	1
	– Interest cover	1
	Maximum	**18**
	Professional marks	
	– Structure of the report: up to	2
	– Clarity of the analysis: up to	1
	– Soundness of the conclusion: up to	1
	Maximum	**4**
(c)	1 mark for each appropriate point up to a maximum of 5 marks for general points made about the model. 1 mark for each appropriate point up to a maximum of 5 marks for points that specifically reference conditions in Arboria or Ceeland.	10
Total		**50**

Examiner's comments

Part (a) was relatively well answered. In fact, in a number of scripts it was over-answered with candidates quickly achieving the six marks on offer for a selected method. Candidates must be aware of this, and keep their answer to an appropriate length. This is part of good examination technique. Although many candidates scored well on this part of the question (many scored 15 marks or over), it was at the cost of time management problems late in the paper.

In part (b) candidate were rather average. In general, not enough use was made of the financial information provided for FRG or the data showing the post-acquisition decline of LogTrans and EngSup. Candidates were clear about what the question required, but they often failed to provide an answer of sufficient depth to reflect the eighteen marks on offer.

For part (c), candidates appeared to be aware of the constituent parts of the diamond, but they were less clear about their meaning. In many instances the diamond was confused with the Five Forces model and so assertions were made that were incorrect in the context of the question. For example; many candidates commented that the absence of competition was a good thing for Machine Shop (from the perspective of competitive rivalry). However, in the context of the diamond this could be interpreted as a weakness, because a strong, vigorous rivalry is required to produce and retain a nation's competitive advantage in an industry. Again, candidate answers were generally average. Most candidates knew enough to get some marks (two or three), but few candidates scored exceptionally on this part question (worth ten marks).

82 ECOCAR

Key answer tips

The largest part of this question (part a) should have been familiar to students and it should be an area that students are comfortable with. A PESTEL model was needed, though it was not explicitly asked for (which may have thrown some students). Part (b) had both a calculation and discussion on a make-or-buy decision. Students must be prepared for a cost accounting calculation so that this part does not cause problems for too many students. As is usual, part (c) will be the toughest part of the question, but any reasonable comments will score marks and students needn't worry with finding an appropriate model.

(a) An external environmental analysis considers political, economic, socio-cultural, technological, legal and environmental (ecological) forces that affect EcoCar.

Although it was external environmental factors that prompted Professor Jacques to develop the original EcoCar, it is primarily socio-cultural forces that are determining its current sales. There have to be customers prepared to pay a premium price for environmentally friendly cars, whose conventional rivals are $2,000 cheaper, and are faster with better acceleration. These customers are prepared to pay this premium because they are concerned about the conventional car's use of non-renewable resources (oil) and the effect of its carbon emissions on climate change. They are essentially 'green' consumers. It is easier to be such a consumer in a developed, growing economy where there is sufficient disposable income to be able to make such choices. Thus the economic health and disposable income of the country are important to EcoCar and should be monitored.

Underpinning the green consumer market is the belief that environmental damage is caused by CO_2 emissions and that preserving natural resources for future generations is important. Any scientific evidence to the contrary could cause problems for the EcoCar, for example, if scientists discover that excess CO_2 is actually necessary for the planet's survival. Similarly, if people become increasingly pessimistic, less concerned about their children's future or resigned to the belief that there is nothing they can do to avert catastrophe then their buying behaviour may become more self-centred and hedonistic, spending discretionary expenditure on more immediate personal, sensory pleasures. EcoCar need to monitor such trends. Individual people do really need to believe that they can make a difference to the world in which they, and their descendants, live in.

Technological innovation is at the heart of EcoCar and the company needs to monitor technological trends for at least two reasons. Firstly, for potential alternatives to lithium-ion batteries that could seriously affect the viability of their whole product. Alternatives do exist (hydrogen for example) and so EcoCar is aware that the potential application of alternative technologies must be monitored. Secondly, the company has to be on the look-out for improvements in lithium-ion batteries that could make them cheaper, lighter or more powerful.

EcoCar has been the beneficiary of government policy which has been aimed at nurturing green technology by giving tax incentives, grants and interest-free loans. It has also placed heavy taxes on cars with high CO_2 emissions. Very importantly, it has also funded the development of 130 charging centres throughout the country where the EcoCar can be re-charged. The company needs to monitor the government's continued commitment to energy saving and the policies of any political opposition within the country.

Finally, the government has enacted a number of general laws on car safety that have to be complied with by EcoCar. Further legislation is expected, so the company must monitor this.

Thus there are a number of threats that EcoCar has to consider, using its risk management approach discussed in part (c) of this question. There are also risks associated with the potential decline of the green consumer and the emergence of alternative technologies.

The external industry analysis could use elements of Porter's five forces framework. Deciding the appropriate scope of the industry to be considered is important. This helps determine the competition facing EcoCar, either from the car industry as a whole, the sector concerned with reduced emissions or perhaps transport as a whole.

The technological environment is driving the threat of substitute products. This threat is relatively high in an industry (car manufacturing) where there is no clear successor to conventional petrol and diesel fuelled cars. A number of alternatives and hybrids are either available or under development. Furthermore, there may be a popular movement to 'do without it'. Cheap, frequent, reliable, safe public transport could lead to lower demand for private cars and indeed may be a better choice for the green consumer. Cycling could also pose a threat, combining a non-polluting alternative with exercise addressing problems of obesity and associated health issues.

In theory, the switching costs of the consumer are relatively low if the industry is perceived as the car industry as a whole. The consumer just purchases a different car. However, the EcoCar appeals to a segment of buyers who are prepared to pay a premium price for the 'cleaner' product. Although the cost of the product is relatively high, the buyer does not actively seek out cheaper alternatives. They know that these alternatives exist but they do not purchase them because of their green ideals. In a sense, the consumers do not wish to bargain for this product.

There is an ever-present threat of new entrants into this market. However, there are considerable capital investment costs which EcoCar have overcome with the help of grants, and interest-free loans. These incentives are unlikely to be available in all countries, or even all regions of Erewhon, given that they are linked to tackling areas of high unemployment. Furthermore, the absence of local car-building expertise, together with the processes patented by Professor Jacques should deter entrants into the market.

It is interesting to note that Universal Motors (the second largest car manufacturer in the world) has decided to enter this sector of car production through acquisition, rather than developing its own product. It has brought further capital investment, which may not be available to potential competitors.

The bargaining power of suppliers in the industry is unclear from the case study. Certainly, it is normally difficult to switch suppliers in such an industry because of the nature of the product and the tightly linked supply chains of this industry. This is not a problem for the large car companies who are powerful and much larger than their supplier companies but it could be a problem for a small manufacturer such as EcoCar, which has little bargaining power. However, the ownership of Universal Motors might alter this. They should be able to negotiate favourable contracts with suppliers, reflecting a reduction in the bargaining power of these suppliers. If labour is seen as a supplier, the problem of skilled labour has meant that labour rates have had to be increased and it is this increase (together with the shortage of skilled labour) that has prompted Universal Motors to consider outsourcing the production of the EcoLite model.

In the car industry as a whole there are many competing firms and buyers can switch easily from one to another. The industry has high fixed costs and the cost of leaving the industry is high. Thus competitive rivalry in the car industry is high. However, in EcoCar's sector there are not as many competing firms and they tend to be fairly well differentiated. Thus competitive rivalry appears to be less in this sector than in the car marketplace as a whole. Whichever perspective is adopted, risks will be identified that need to be dealt with by the company's risk management process.

(b) **In support of outsourcing**

The economic argument for outsourcing the manufacture of the EcoLite is best made if the manufacturing of this model is viewed in isolation. The proposed outsourcing supplier has quoted a cost for manufacture of $3,500. This is $1,000 less than the variable cost of manufacturing the current car at Lags Lane. It is still $750 per car cheaper even when transport costs are taken into consideration. Supporting information is given in Figure 1.

	EcoLite
Selling price per car ($)	6,999
Variable cost per car ($)	4,500
Weekly demand (cars)	6
Production time per car (machine hrs)	8
Contribution	2,499
Contribution/machine hour	312
Production time (hours)	48

Figure 1: Information relevant to the outsourcing issue

One of the reasons for the high variable cost of the car is the high cost of labour and inbound logistics. All evidence suggests that these costs will continue to increase to reflect the shortage of skilled labour in the region (as more people retire) and the high cost of moving goods in the congested roads of Midshire. The high cost of the car means that the most profitable combination of products (see below) produces a relatively small margin. This must be of concern to Universal Motors.

Overall, the Lags Lane site is unable to meet the weekly demand for EcoCar's products. The weekly demand for the three-car range is currently 152 hours (see Figure 2) and so the company (with 112 hours of production capacity) cannot meet product demand. Outsourcing will allow EcoCar to meet the demand for their products as well as increasing overall profitability.

The EcoLite has fewer parts in common with the two other cars. The EcoPlus is essentially a slightly more sophisticated car than the Eco and the delay when switching production from Eco to EcoPlus is probably relatively small. In contrast, the EcoLite has only 70% of parts in common with the two other cars which suggests that it is the obvious candidate to switch to a different plant. Overhead costs at Lags Lane should be reduced as there is no need to build and stock sub-assemblies and parts which are only used in the EcoLite. It has been suggested that there will be a $1,250 reduction in weekly overhead costs at Lags Lane if the production of the EcoLite model is outsourced.

Against outsourcing

The economic argument for outsourcing is weakened if the complete product range is considered.

	Eco	EcoPlus	EcoLite
Selling price per car ($)	9,999	12,999	6,999
Variable cost per car ($)	7,000	10,000	4,500
Weekly demand (cars)	6	5	6
Production time per car (machine hrs)	9	10	8
Contribution	2,999	2,999	2,499
Contribution/machine hour	333	300	312
Production time (hours)	54	50	48

Figure 2: Further information relevant to the outsourcing issue

At present the following production combination represents the best product mix with the limited resources. See Figure 2 for supporting information.

• Six Ecos consuming 54 hours of production contributing $17,994 (6 × $2,999)

• Six EcoLites consuming 48 hours of production contributing $14,994 (6 × $2,499)

• One EcoPlus consuming 10 hours of production contributing $2,999 (1 × $2,999)

This total contribution of $35,987 per week exceeds the estimated $35,000 per week overhead cost.

However, if the EcoLite model is made elsewhere, then the following combination of cars will be made at Lags Lane

• Six Ecos consuming 54 hours of production contributing $17,994 (6 × $2,999)

• Five EcoPlus consuming 50 hours of production contributing $14,995 (5 × $2,999)

This total contribution of $32,989 is less than the forecast $33,750 per week overhead cost.

There are also eight unused production hours. It is possible that the future of the Lags Lane production facility could be in doubt if the EcoLite model is outsourced.

The issue of the capacity of Lags Lane could be addressed by becoming a seven-day week three-shift operation (pushing capacity up to 168 hours per week) which would also allow 16 hours for maintenance, given that total demand currently comes to 152 hours. Whether this maintenance time would be sufficient would have to be investigated. There still remains, however, the problem of finding skilled labour in the Midshire area.

Universal Motors might expect political opposition to the proposed outsourcing of the car even if they maintained production of the remaining two cars. Regional and national grants have been given to the company to help develop and produce the car. It has meant that part of a skilled workforce has been kept on in an area of high unemployment, reducing social costs to the community. The feeling that it is the region's car is reflected in its image and sales. Outsourcing might have a detrimental effect on sales. People who were buying it because it was, in part, some reflection of regional pride may now buy elsewhere.

The motivation of the buyers really has to be considered in more depth. It is acknowledged that people pay a premium for this car because they wish to make a social statement. The car uses less energy, has lower emissions and provides employment in the country where it makes most of its sales. Taking away employment may mean that the car may no longer fit the social buying criteria of some of its customers. However, the realisation that non-renewable energy is being used to transport these cars back to Erewhon where 95% of all sales are made may be even more problematic. Buyers may no longer feel that it represents an ethical choice. Building the car in a country where labour costs are low and then transporting it long distances in ships and environmentally unfriendly car transporters may completely undermine the brand.

(c) Answers to the three internal weaknesses are given below. However, other responses could be just as valid and appropriate credit will be given.

Lack of control and co-ordination

The company needs to implement a comprehensive budgeting system. A rudimentary budgeting system appears to exist, focused on planning rather than co-ordination or monitoring.

The scenario shows a lack of co-ordination between production, procurement, inventory and finance. Recently, car production was halted by lack of an important sub-assembly. This led to the emergency purchase of components and overtime working to minimise the delay in re-starting car production. This raised the cost of production and would have reduced the profit margin on finished vehicles. Furthermore, there is evidence that purchases of bought-in finished inventory items (superior quality seats) have been made at times when there was insufficient demand for them or the money available to pay for them. This led to short-term financing requirements at a premium interest rate to resolve a public row with a supplier. There is also a cost associated with storing unwanted inventory.

What the company needs is a plan which co-ordinates all these activities. This is known as a budget. Budgets would be prepared for production, for raw materials and for bought-in finished goods. The latter two budgets would be linked to the trade payables budget, which in turn is linked to the cash budget. Budgets facilitate planned co-ordination between the departments and activities of the organisation. Because they require planning, budgets also promote forward thinking and should help identify any forthcoming problems. These problems can be tackled in a planned way, for example, putting finance in place, before being prompted to do so by potential legal action from a supplier. A longer planning timeframe should have also helped the company arrange such finance at a better rate.

Finally, budgets facilitate control. Deviations from the plan can be spotted early and appropriate action taken. Ordering excessive components would have been identified as a major deviation from plan and senior management action could have been taken. There is evidence of a lack of proper control at EcoCar (for example, training costs) and budgets would have helped address this.

Research and Development succession and learning

The company needs to consider the principles of Human Resource Development (HRD).

Research and Development has been central to the success of EcoCar. However, Universal Motors have recognised that the senior managers are getting older and that there is no succession planning or development in this area of expertise. Furthermore, they have also identified that although the senior managers may be technically competent, their people management skills are limited, losing key graduates that they failed to motivate or recognise. There is a concern that new technological opportunities are not being recognised or exploited because of an inappropriate culture within R & D.

EcoCar needs to completely re-think its approach to Human Resource Development (HRD) if it is to retain an intellectual lead in the industry. HRD is concerned with investing in the learning of people who work for the company, replacing concern about short-term training costs (as expressed about the graduate training scheme) with the vision of long-term training investment. As well as providing an internal pool of capable employees, proponents of this approach also argue that it engenders loyalty and commitment to the organisation, reducing staff turnover and all the costs associated with it. Consequently, it is a key approach to planning for staff succession from within.

The strategic implications of such an approach should also not be overlooked. EcoCar is working in a challenging leading edge environment. Central to the concept of the learning organisation is the belief that adopting such a concept is one of the best ways of challenging and moving away from the current culture of the organisation. This is necessary at EcoCar. Overall, human resource development has the 'prospect of unleashing the potential that lies within all people, allowing employees to contribute to and indeed transform strategy' (Jeff Gold).

The understanding of risk

EcoCar needs to establish a risk management process that identifies and documents risks and put into place policies for eliminating, reducing or coping with them if they occur. In general, Universal Motors believe that EcoCar often recognise risks but do little about them except discuss them. Overall, it is concerned with the amount of risk that senior managers appear to take. Although individually the senior managers are risk averse, as a group they seem to seem to take increasingly riskier decisions as a way of overcoming their individual fears.

In a risk management system risks would be identified and documented, usually on a risk register. Once they have been documented, risks need to be assessed, both for the probability of the risk occurring and for the impact it has if it does occur. Risk is also related to corporate governance. There is strong evidence to suggest that there is risk-related motivation for monitoring and improving corporate governance. EcoCar needs to consider the establishment of a main board risk committee. Revised corporate guidance, building on the Turnbull Report (FRC, 2005), states that companies 'should, as a minimum, disclose that there is an ongoing process for identifying, evaluating and managing the significant risks faced by the company and that it is regularly reviewed by the board'.

In general, there are four strategies for dealing with risk. Risk avoidance is concerned with removing the factors that give rise to the risk. In the context of EcoCar, the risk of adverse publicity due to poor performance in a rally could be avoided by not running a car in the rally. Risk transference is achieved by passing the risk on to someone else. There is a certain element of this in the outsourcing approach being considered by Universal Motors for the manufacturing of EcoLite. Risks associated with employing and fully utilising staff are passed on to the outsourcer. Risk reduction is concerned with reducing the chance of the risk occurring and is usually associated with a mitigation response which details what the organisation should do if the relevant event actually takes place. For example, the risk of employees passing on technical information about the company's products could be reduced by strict contractual terms with deterrent penalties, reducing the chance of them actually passing on this information. The risk would be mitigated by immediate legal action against the employees and an action plan put in place with company's lawyers. Finally, certain risks are just recognised and absorbed. The potential risk is recognised and accepted as part of doing business in that sector, but the risk is continually monitored.

Risks are linked to the external factors identified in the first part of this question. For example, the risk of consumers losing interest in green issues affects the attractiveness of the industry to potential competitors.

ACCA Marking scheme		
		Marks
(a)	Up to 1 mark for each appropriate point up to a maximum of	16
	Professional marks are given for selection of appropriate models, structure and overall cogency of the analysis up to a total of	4
(b)	Up to 1 mark for each appropriate point up to a maximum of	15
(c)	Up to 1 mark for each appropriate point up to a maximum of 5 marks for each weakness, up to 15 marks for this part question.	15
Total		**50**

Examiner's comments

For part (a) many candidates produced excellent answers that helped them pass the examination as a whole. Most used PESTLE and Five Forces and structured the answer well, leading to many getting all four professional marks on offer. However, despite this praise, specific comments have to be made about the way that many candidates addressed this part question.

- PESTEL is about the future and about external influences largely beyond the control of the organisation (EcoCar). Too many answers strayed into internal strengths (technology used by the company) and weaknesses (problems in budgeting). Furthermore, too many answers focused on issues that were relevant in the past. The existence of a skilled work force was significant when the company was established, but that was in the past. The problem now is finding skilled labour (due to retirement) and so labour pay rates have increased. This could have been identified within the Five Forces analysis, considering the power of suppliers. Too many answers included long, irrelevant social and political observations.

- Too many answers listed all the elements of PESTEL and Five Forces and then tried to find aspects of the case study to fit. When those aspects were missing, answers were simply made up. As a candidate, if you find yourself writing something like 'the case study scenario did not include much information on', then you are probably going down an irrelevant path. There is no reason why a case study scenario should have all elements of the model under consideration, or that those elements should be equally weighted. This was certainly true in the EcoCar scenario.

- Finally, time management for this question appeared to be dreadful. It was only worth 16 marks (20 if you include the professional marks – although no professional marks are given for length) but many answers filled more than half the answer booklet. It seems likely that time pressures later on in the paper were mainly caused by over-answering this part of the question. For example, the examiner marked one script which gained full marks for this question. However, the answer also contained a further four pages of discussion of strengths and weaknesses and a repetition of earlier points, now explored within the context of Porter's Diamond. The candidate only just scraped a pass overall. Time management is particularly important when answering a question you like and recognise. The examiner is aware that many candidates felt that the paper was time pressured, but he believes that much of this was self-inflicted through poor time management.

In Part (b) many answers were too general, giving text book answers which were largely irrelevant in the context of the case study scenario. Little credit could be given for answers that just listed the advantages and disadvantages of outsourcing. Context is critical here. For example; what effect will this decision have on regional sales which are currently boosted by consumer's pride in a locally produced product? Will 'green consumers' still want to buy from a company who have used a significant amount of non-renewable energy to transport cars from the production plant to the primary market place? Some candidates tried to use the Harmon process/strategy grid when answering this question, but this was largely irrelevant in this context. Many candidates also failed to exploit the financial data that was made available in the question scenario. Most recognised that outsourcing was financially attractive because the cost of outsourced production was cheaper than the variable cost of the EcoLite model. Most also suggested that the Ecolite was the best candidate for outsourcing as it produced the lowest contribution. However, this assertion failed to recognise the production time of each car. When this was taken into account the EcoPlus has a lower contribution per machine hour than the EcoLite, and its lower demand might make it a better candidate for outsourcing. Similarly, many candidates recognised the extent to which production capacity was a limiting factor. However, very few performed a calculation to show that even the optimal production mix only produced a modest profit and so this was a powerful argument for outsourcing to meet demand. Furthermore, when EcoLite is taken out of the mix, the Lags Lane production plant makes a loss and has unused production hours, factors that could undermine its long-term future and so could be used in the argument against outsourcing. Overall, marks were disappointingly low for this part question. In part (c) many answers were too general and superficial (for example; get everyone together to have a meeting, improve the effectiveness of the training) and so failed to score the marks on offer. The concept of proper budgeting was the key to answering the first issue considered in this part question. Similarly, human resource development (succession planning, learning organisation, perceiving training as an investment rather than a cost) was the key to the second issue under consideration. The issue of risks and risk management was better answered, perhaps reflecting the overlap between P3 and P1 learning. It was their answer to this issue which lifted many candidates to a pass mark in this part question.

83   2TEL

Key answer tips

This question only had 2 parts to it as opposed to the normal three parts, but it focused on key syllabus areas so this should not have worried too many students. Part (a) covered strategic analysis (worth 30 marks) which is an area in which students typically score well. The key dangers to watch out for were to ensure that appropriate models were used at the appropriate time (PESTEL in the first part and 5 Forces in the second), and that the marks available were used to determine the areas in which to spend more time. Part (a) will also have been very time pressured.

For part (b), four strategies needed to be considered and students need to provide the advantages, disadvantages and a financial assessment. These should not have been too challenging but may have been very difficult to provide in the time available. The calculations were made more challenging by the presentation of the data which scattered about the numbers required for each part of the calculation – so students needed to be clear in what they were looking for and which piece of information fit which piece of the calculation.

(a)   (i)   Introduction

2Tel is one of the largest network operators in the world. It is aware that licences for providing mobile networks in The Federated States (TFS), a densely populated country with 70 million people, are due for renewal in three years' time. It is currently evaluating whether it wishes to bid for one of these licences, either in its own right, or through the prior acquisition of one of the current licensees.

It has commissioned this briefing paper into the business environment which the current licensees operate in. This briefing paper begins with an analysis of the wider macro-environment of the industry, using a PESTEL analysis. The paper then considers the competitive forces within the industry using aspects of Porter's five forces framework.

The briefing paper concludes with, as requested, a summary of the opportunities and threats which 2Tel should consider before it decides to enter this market.

Political perspective

Licences are granted by the government for eight years and so it may, at first sight, appear that licence allocation is an important political factor in the mobile network industry. However, the previous government effectively de-politicised the awarding of licences by defining selection rules based on certain minimum criteria (for example, financial and environmental criteria) and the size of the bid. The licences are awarded to the four highest bidders who fulfil the minimum criteria. So, the current performance of licensees is not currently taken into account in the bidding process. This has implications for 2Tel. From a political perspective, there is no particular benefit to be gained by bidding as a current licensee.

The praise of Ofnet and the gratitude of the government for the network operators' phone and message information used to convict offenders in the recent riots count for nothing in the selection process. At present, under the current rules, 2Tel has as much chance of winning a licence in its own right. Indeed, this is reflected in Professor Tan's research and his suggested bid success probabilities.

However, it has to be recognised that the selection criteria are politically decided and so there is a possibility that the current government will change the selection rules before the licences come up for renewal. Issues with the current scheme have already been recognised and it has been agreed that companies who fail to retain their licence will be paid an exit fee of $100m. This will mean, for example, if 2Tel wins one of the licences in its own right then it will have to compensate the company which has lost the licence. Thus there will be a $100m fee for new entrants, which is additional to the bid for the licence. Furthermore, a possible change in selection rules raises at least two issues. Firstly, the government could change the rules so that incumbent licensees were favoured (as long as they have performed effectively) and so there would be a benefit to be gained from acquiring a current licensee. Again, this has been recognised in Professor Tan's research and his allocation of bid success probabilities. There appears to be some support for this change of rules within the government. One government minister has suggested that 'the help provided to us (by the network operators) during the recent riots, should be acknowledged in some way'. Secondly, in an attempt to raise more money to address the national debt, the government could decide that more than four companies should be licensed in the future, increasing competition in the sector and raising more income for the government. This might affect the profitability of the existing licensees.

A very significant political issue is the presence of a regulator (Ofnet) in the sector, who particularly focuses on pricing, service availability and service transfer. The prices of all the four licensees are negotiated with the Ofnet regulator and, consequently, the prices of all four networks are very similar. Ofnet also requires the four licensees to have arrangements in place which allow customers to easily transfer from one network to another. Ofnet has generally praised the performance of all four licensees, except in this last area. It has suggested that it is still too difficult for customers to move network provider, and it intends to bring in regulations which make it easier. Fines will be imposed on networks which do not follow these regulations. The powerful role of the regulator is of particular significance to 2Tel. 2Tel has traditionally operated in countries where there is little or no government regulation of network operators. In these markets prices can be largely determined by the company itself, free from external influence.

Technology of mobile networks

Two aspects of technology are important to licensees operating in TFS. Firstly, innovations in mobile telephone technology are very important to the network licensee because, as well as encouraging the use of the network, new products also tend to make greater demands on those networks, in terms of speed and bandwidth. Thus there is need for continual investment in the network. Secondly, this investment includes a need to continually review the technology and configurations available for constructing and supporting the network itself.

There is a need to invest in new technologies and technical configurations which offer greater speed, reliability and, if possible, lower costs. However, it has to be recognised that both of these technology factors are not unique to TFS, and are likely to be even more significant in markets which 2Tel is already competing in.

Sociocultural and economic considerations

The possession of a state-of-the-art mobile device remains an important status symbol in TFS. Having the latest features and applications is important to people and so devices are regularly upgraded, hence having features which place significant demands on the network, as discussed in the previous section of this report.

The role of the mobile phone network in assisting organised crime and civil disobedience has posed dilemmas for the network operators. On the one hand, they have been praised for their good citizenship in passing relevant information to the police. However, on the other hand, they have been criticised by civil liberties bodies for making this information available. An influential newspaper, whilst recognising the contribution of the networks to apprehending offenders, also criticised them for not withdrawing the networks at the height of the riots. 'Instead of helping catch offenders, the networks, by making their services unavailable, might have prevented the offences in the first place.' 2Tel has to be aware that TFS is an increasingly socially fragmented country with vocal minority groups representing a wide range of pressure groups and communities.

One of the licensees is currently subject to legal action where people are suing the company for releasing information to the government. The company, and the information it holds, is subject to the Data Protection Act, which exempts information held to prevent or aid the detection of crime, but lawyers for both the company and the offenders are confident of success when the case comes to court.

The election of the current government was prompted by a belief that its policies would address the five years of economic decline presided over by the previous government. In general, the population is suffering from high unemployment, static incomes and, more recently, increased taxes and removal of benefits (this measure provoked the riots already discussed) imposed by the austerity government. However, these economic problems do not appear to have any discernible effect on the use of mobile devices. During this five-year period of decline, the use of the mobile networks has increased significantly. This may, of course, be partly as a result of the regulator, who can reasonably be assumed to exerting a pressure to keep prices low. However, it must also be some reflection of the importance which the population as a whole places on mobile phones and being able to make mobile calls. It is seen as a necessity, rather than a luxury.

Legal and environmental issues

Reference has already been made to the Data Protection Act (sociocultural) and regulation from Ofnet (political). TFS has many laws which are enacted within a complex and expensive legal system. Employees are expensive to employ and are difficult to dismiss. Furthermore, legal outcomes are difficult to forecast due to the unpredictable conduct of judges.

Like all companies operating in TFS, the network operators are expected to comply with environmental regulations. However, environmental issues are more an issue for the mobile phone manufacturers and the environmentally-friendly disposal of these mobile phones is an ongoing problem for the manufacturers, but this is not a problem for the network operators.

(ii) Importantly, from a Porter's five forces perspective, there is no threat of new entrants into the industry during the licence period. However, at the end of the licence period, anyone who meets the bidding criteria can potentially be allocated a licence and enter the market place. So, the licences are an effective barrier to entry during the licence period. At bidding time, it is access to capital which forms the largest barrier to entry, as the success of the bid (at present) is largely determined by the size of the bid. This access to capital is particularly significant to potential new entrants as they will potentially be required to pay a $100m entry premium.

Again, from a five forces perspective, the policy of Ofnet to make network transfer relatively easy theoretically increases the bargaining power of customers, and this should exert a downward pressure on prices. Customers are tied into annual contracts, but it should become increasingly easy for them to transfer supplier with no switching costs. At present, evidence suggests that few customers do actually change operators. This may be because of the difficulty of switching (which is the view of the regulator) or it may be because no great price advantage can be gained by switching provider. Evidence suggests that most move due to poor service or poor reception in their geographical area. The fact that mobile charges are so similar between the four rival companies (mainly due to the regulator) means that there is little incentive to move on price grounds.

Porter's five forces framework has competitive rivalry at its centre. When considering competitive rivalry within the industry, there are certain factors which should contribute to vigorous competition; for example, low switching costs and undifferentiated products. However, competition is limited to four similar size companies competing in a growing market place which is subject to price regulation. Competition on price grounds is very difficult because of the activities of the regulator, who is keen to satisfy the government's wish for no supplier to dominate the market. Thus competitive rivalry is restrained and, to some extent, controlled and competition is based largely on coverage, service, and brand image. It is likely that if one supplier did begin to dominate the market, then the regulator would impose rules to re-balance competition.

At present, it is difficult to envisage any threat of substitute products to the mobile networks. Even the threat of 'doing without' seems unlikely, given people's increased dependence on the mobile phone.

(iii) The conclusion of this briefing paper is, as requested, a summary of the opportunities and threats associated with this market.

Opportunities

The relatively imminent re-licensing of mobile networks provides a significant business opportunity. This business is then largely protected (within constraints imposed by the regulator) for eight years. The licences provide an effective barrier to entry.

Despite the economic decline of the country, sociocultural trends suggest a buoyant demand for network services. As mobile products become more sophisticated, it seems reasonable that this demand will continue to increase for the foreseeable future. There appears to be very little threat of substitutes to the mobile network and people are reluctant to 'do without'.

The current licensees acknowledge that technology has to be continually updated. 2Tel is an acknowledged technology leader with expertise in markets which are, at least, as demanding.

Threats

There is a concern that the government will change the licensing bidding criteria, to favour incumbent licensees, before the next granting of licences. This would be a threat to 2Tel's chance of entering the market in its own right.

The market is highly regulated and pricing has to be agreed with a regulator. 2Tel is inexperienced in working in such an environment and it may be seen as a threat to 2Tel's independence and also to its long-term profitability.

The legal framework in TFS is burdensome and legal outcomes are, to some extent, unpredictable. Threats of legal action and the effects of social disruption may lead to 2Tel to conclude that TFS is not a particularly attractive market to enter. There are threats associated with political interference, public criticism, legal action and legal compensation.

(b) **Scenarios**

Developing scenarios is particularly appropriate where there is a high level of uncertainty and so it is impossible to build a single view of how environmental influences might affect an organisation's strategy. The case study scenario is dominated by two very significant environmental factors. The first is the bidding rules for the mobile technology licences. These rules are decided by government and current rules do not favour the current licensees. However, there is evidence that the government is moving its position on this and it has already introduced one measure which will help current licences, the payment of a $100m exit fee to licensees who fail to get their licence renewed, to be funded by an extra entry fee by the successful licensees. The other factor is the price which competing companies are willing to pay for the licences.

2Tel wishes to evaluate the two options of bidding for a licence. The first option is to acquire T-Me, one of the current licensees. The second option is to bid directly for a licence. It wishes to consider four scenarios.

(1) Acquire T-Me and then failing to gain a licence.

(2) Acquire T-Me and then gaining a licence.

(3) Bidding directly for a licence as 2Tel and failing to gain a licence.

(4) Bidding directly for a licence as 2Tel and gaining a licence.

Buying T-Me

Buying T-Me offers a number of advantages:

(1)   If bidding rules are changed to favour current licensees, then 2Tel (through T-Me) has a better chance of being granted a license. Research by Professor Tan shows that in countries where current licensees are favoured, then a current licencee has a 0.6 probability of being granted a licence, compared with probability of 0.2 for new bidders.

(2)   T-Me has experience of the bidding process in TFS. It has been suggested that the cost of putting the bid together (bid cost), will be half that of a new inexperienced bidder.

(3)   T-Me is experienced in working in the TFS culture and with the people of TFS. It is a country which is heavily regulated and T-Me has worked effectively with the industry's regulator (Ofnet) over the period of this licence. 2Tel does not have experience of operating in a heavily regulated environment. Its main networks are in countries where regulation is weak or non-existent.

(4)   There are short-term opportunities for improving the financial performance of T-Me. 2Tel has suggested that it can raise net profit to $100m per year in the final two years of the contract. This appears to be a very reasonable target. The figures in Table One suggest that T-Me's net profit margin is currently 11.42%, the lowest of the four competing companies. A net profit of $100m (on current revenue) would bring the net profit margin up to 14.29%, still below the average industry performance of 14.7%.

2Tel has been informed that they may be able to acquire T-Me for $400m. Their research (conducted by Professor Tan) suggests that the next eight-year contract can be won for $550m and that a net profit of $120m can be driven out of the company for the next eight years. Here is an analysis for the two scenarios which require the purchase of T-Me. All figures are in $million.

Buy T-Me and fail	*Outflows*	*Inflows*
Purchase of T-Me	400	
Bid cost	10	
Net profit (2 years)		200
Exit income		100
	___	___
Total	410	300
Net gain (loss)		(110)

Buy T-Me and gain	*Outflows*	*Inflows*
Purchase of T-Me	400	
Bid cost	10	
Contract fee	550	
Profit (2 years)		200
Profit (new contract)		960
Exit income (Note 1)		100
	___	___
Total	960	1,260
Net gain (loss)		300

(Note 1) Assumes exit at the end of the licence period and that this exit income is still at current levels.

Bidding directly for a licence

Bidding directly for a licence has a number of advantages:

(1)   If bidding rules are not changed, then 2Tel has the same probability of successfully gaining a licence as T-Me.

(2)   One of T-Me's competitors is currently in a legal dispute concerning the disclosure of information to the government. If they lose this court case (and many anti-government judgements are being made at present), then successful claims may be made against the other network operators. Bidding directly for a licence avoids any potential legal costs associated with contesting claims and compensating potential claimants.

(3)   It avoids the cost of purchasing T-Me. There are likely to be significant costs associated with performing due diligence on T-Me and negotiating and finalising the acquisition.

(4)   It avoids having to impose organisational change at T-Me in an attempt to drive out short-term improvements in net profit. 2Tel has estimated that it can increase net profit to $100m per annum. It does appear to have a successful acquisition record, but it also has to be recognised that there is significant evidence to suggest that planned performance improvements in acquired companies are often not realised, particularly in the short term.

Here is an analysis of the direct bidding scenarios.

Bid and win	Outflows	Inflows
Bid cost	20	
Contract fee	550	
Exit fee (payable to losers)	100	
Profit (new contract)		960
Exit costs (Note 1)		100
	____	____
Total	670	1,060
Net gain (loss)		390
Bid and lose	20	
Net gain (loss)		(20)

(Note 1) Assumes exit at the end of the licence period and that this exit income is still at current levels.

Analysis

From the perspective of risk aversion, the bidding directly for licences appears the best option. Potential losses are minimised ($20m, compared to $110m) and potential returns maximised ($390m compared to $300m). If expected values are used which represent the current bidding rules, then this conclusion remains valid.

Scenario	Net gain (loss)	Probability	Expected value
Buy and lose	(110)	0.6	(66)
Buy and win	300	0.4	120
Bid and win	390	0.4	156
Bid and lose	(20)	0.6	(12)

The buying option has a net expected gain of $54, compared to a net expected gain for the bid option of $144m.

However, if the bidding rules are changed to favour the incumbent, then the buy option has a greater expected return ($136m compared to $62m).

Scenario	Net gain (loss)	Probability	Expected value
Buy and lose	(110)	0.4	(44)
Buy and win	300	0.6	180
Bid and win	390	0.2	78
Bid and lose	(20)	0.8	(16)

However, a number of issues have to be raised.

(1)   The statistical probability values for the changed bidding rules are based on research conducted in other countries where bidding is biased towards the current licence holders. These may not be appropriate for TFS. They could be too high or too low.

(2)   Expected values are really more appropriate for a series of decisions, where, over time, the return will tend towards the expected value. The actual values will occur (subject to forecast errors) – not the expected ones.

(3)   The bid price of $550m is itself an estimate and the probabilities of bid success only relate to this bid price. The analysis might suggest that a higher bid is made, which should have a higher probability of success. For example, a direct bid of $750m from 2Tel would still lead to a net profit of $190m for the contract – a return of over 20%.

(4)   No probabilities have been attached to the chance of the government changing the selection rules before the next licences are allocated.

2Tel might also like to take a second look at the buy and lose option. The unattractiveness of this scenario is largely due to the proposed purchase price of T-Me. It may be possible to reduce or restructure this price, or both. For example, the company could offer $290m now, and $110m on successful gaining of the next contract. However, the possible compensation claims are problematic. They are difficult to predict and at this stage, it would seem unlikely that they can be insured against (risk transfer).

Conclusion

Under the current licence allocation arrangements, the agreed price for T-Me is too high, given the risks involved. So, the recommendation is to bid directly for the licence. However, if the purchase price for T-Me could be re-negotiated or re-structured, then there are advantages of acquiring T-Me and using this as a vehicle for the bid.

However, if the bidding rules change to favour the incumbent licensees, then purchasing T-Me becomes the preferred approach from a financial perspective. However, the spectre of possible compensation payments remains and these might be powerful enough to still persuade the board of 2Tel that a direct bid, unencumbered by the past, might still be preferable, even though the chance of winning the licence might be reduced.

		ACCA Marking scheme	
			Marks
(a)	(i)	1 mark for each appropriate point up to a maximum of 14 marks	
	(ii)	1 mark for each appropriate point up to a maximum of 8 marks	
	(iii)	1 mark for each appropriate point up to a maximum of 4 marks	
		Professional marks will be given for structure, coherence, style and clarity of the report up to a maximum of 4 marks	
(b)		1 mark for each appropriate point up to a maximum of 20 marks; this could include:	
		– Quantitative analysis of acquire T-Me and fail – up to 4 marks	
		– Quantitative analysis of acquire T-Me and win – up to 2 marks	
		– Quantitative analysis of bid directly and win – up to 2 marks	
		– Quantitative analysis of bid directly and lose – up to 2 mark	
		– Expected value analysis – buy – up to 2 marks	
		– Expected value analysis – bid – up to 2 marks	
Total			**50**

Examiner's comments

In part (a) (i), most candidates chose to undertake a PESTEL analysis, or more accurately, a PESTEL listing, because there was often no analysis involved. Many candidates produced long answers which were little more than regurgitated facts from the case study scenario. This is not analysis. Analysis requires putting these facts into the context of the briefing paper for 2Tel. Here is the difference:

Regurgitation

- The presence of a regulator focusing on pricing, service availability and service transfer.

- Legal outcomes are difficult to forecast due to unpredictable nature of judges.

Analysis

- The presence of a regulator focusing on pricing, service availability and service transfer. This is very significant for 2Tel as it has little experience of operating in regulated markets

- Legal outcomes are difficult to forecast due to the unpredictable nature of judges. Due to possible expense and adverse effect on the brand, 2Tel may not wish to acquire a licensee facing potential legal action.

Analysis states why the external factor is significant in the context of that analysis (in this case 2Tel). To their credit many candidates did take the analysis approach. However, many others just listed factors and so did not score as well as they should have done.

In part (a) (ii), most candidates used Porter's five forces and scored relatively well. Indeed, probably because the model forces analysis, answers were often better than the preceding PESTEL analysis. Some candidates used Porter's diamond but, although some marks might be scored, this model lends itself less well to the question and the information given in the case study scenario.

Part (a) (iii) should have been a relatively easy four marks. However, too many candidates did not clearly delimit their answers and others strayed into strengths and weaknesses. This sub-part was about summarising external forces (opportunities and threats) which should have been identified in the PESTEL and Five Force's analysis (or their equivalents).

Part (b) was poorly answered and, indeed, not answered at all by a significant number of candidates. The choice between the options could include an analysis of issues developed from the scenario. For example, T-Me (the potential acquisition) is experienced in working in the TFS culture. It is used to working in a highly regulated environment, which 2Tel is not. Similarly, there are advantages in bidding directly. There is a possibility of legal claims against T-Me as a result of the company giving information to government. This risk would be avoided completely by bidding directly.

The calculations required the organisation of data, but nothing beyond addition and subtraction. For example; Option one: buy T-Me and not gain licence had the following costs. The cost of buying the company ($400m) and the cost of bidding for the licence ($10m), a total of ($410m). The income was $200m profit and the $100m exit fee for failing to gain the licence, a total of $300m. Thus there was a net loss of $110m. Option two: buy T-Me and gain the licence had the same costs, plus the contract fee of $550m. So a total cost of $960m. The $200m net profit was the same for the two years prior to the new contract, plus $960m profit from the contract. An exit fee at the end of that contract might be added, giving a total of $1260m, a $300m profit overall. It was also agreed that candidates who ignored the possibility of the final exit fee (producing an overall profit of $200m) would also be given maximum credit for their answers. So marking was very generous.

Similar, relatively straightforward analysis was required for the bid direct options. In fact, the bid direct and fail option only involved one number; the loss of the $20m bid cost. These options could then be subject to the probabilities described in the scenario. For example; option one has an expected value of ($66m) if the bidding rules remained the same, but a lower expected value ($44m) if the bidding rules were changed in favour of the incumbent. Expected values could be calculated for eight scenarios (four with current probabilities and four with changed probabilities). The options that minimised loss and maximised gain could also be identified. Significant marks could be gained here.

Finally, further marks could also be gained by commenting on the accuracy of such probabilities.

There was a lot of information on offer, and substantial marks could be gained by answering the question in a variety of ways. The quantitative work was very straightforward. Addition, subtraction and a little multiplication, and yet some candidates made no answer at all to a question that they should have allowed themselves thirty minutes to answer. Even when the question was attempted, many answers were disorganised, with simple omissions (failing to include the bid fee), misclassification (adding the exit fee to the costs of acquisition) and simple errors in addition and subtraction.

Overall, this was a very poorly answered question.

84   QTS GROUP

Key answer tips

This question focused on an acquisition – an area that has been regularly examined in the past. Part (a) had a couple of traps for candidates: firstly, only the advantages of the strategy were needed, and, secondly, it required the incorporation of some quantitative analysis to support these arguments. Parts (b) and (c) combined the need for some technical knowledge (such as the contents of the cultural web) as well as then applying this knowledge to the scenario. It is this latter skill that will challenge weaker candidates. It will be important that students do not waste time regurgitating the models and trying to pass the question solely on the basis of knowledge. A pass in these parts of the question will only be achieved if the knowledge can be made relevant to QTS Group.

(a)   **Introduction**

Revenues in QTS Group have grown significantly in the last five years, from $610m in 20X2 to $875m in 20X5. Most of this growth has been achieved through the acquisition of smaller training companies operating in a number of niche markets.

QTS Group is now considering the acquisition of A2K, a training company specialising in business architecture training. One of its companies, QTSBA, is already a market leader in this training sector, with 23.76% market share, compared with the next largest supplier, CompTrain, which has 15.5% of the market. A2K is solely focused on the business architecture training market and currently has a market share of 8.17%.

This briefing paper identifies the benefits and advantages to QTS Group and QTSBA of proceeding with the acquisition of A2K.

Further growth through acquisition

A major reason for growing through acquisition is the speed it offers, both in increasing revenue and in entering new markets and/or offering new products. Further growth is particularly attractive to three sets of stakeholders at QTS Group or QTSBA:

- The sales department of QTSBA: who have customers with impending training needs which need to be successfully fulfilled. Finding experienced trainers is an issue. A2K has an experienced training team which would be immediately available, together with an established pool of sub-contractors.

- The shareholders of QTS Group: who have expressed their desire for the retained profit of QTS Group to be better employed in producing revenue, profit and company growth.

- The senior management team at QTSBA: who are on salary remuneration packages which are directly linked to achieving sales revenue performance targets.

Acquiring a new product, entering a new market

As previously stated, acquisition also allows an organisation to quickly enter a new market and/or acquire a new product. In some circumstances it is the only way of entering an emerging market because internal development is too slow or too expensive. Indeed, this is the situation at QTSBA, where the acquisition of the A2K e-learning team will allow QTSBA to:

- Acquire new, established products which they can offer to the market, immediately generating revenue with a significant unit profit margin.

- Acquire e-learning development expertise which can be used to successfully develop new products. QTSBA has already had a failed project where its own uncontrolled software developers used inappropriate software to develop e-learning solutions which were not attractive to customers. A2K has a successful track record in e-learning development and product sales. Acquisition allows the immediate possession of these competencies.

- E-learning may be a key part in extending business architecture training to areas beyond the continent of Eastaria. It might also be possible to use the e-learning team to develop products for other companies in the group.

Establish a dominant position in the business architecture training market

QTS Group has made a management decision to remain and compete in the business architecture training market. However, it acknowledges that the market growth for business architecture training is slowing, although it is expecting future growth, particularly outside Eastaria. Table A illustrates market growth and market share in the business architecture training market, 20X0–20X5.

Revenue	20X0	20X1	20X2	20X3	20X4	20X5
A2K revenue ($m)	12	14	16	17	17	16.5
Year on year growth		16.67%	14.29%	6.25%	0.00%	−2.94%
QTS revenue ($m)	39	40	42	45	46	48
Year on year growth		2.56%	5.00%	7.14%	2.22%	4.35%
Total market revenue ($m)	175	190	196	200	202	202
Year on year growth		8.57%	3.16%	2.04%	1.00%	0.00%
Market share						
A2K	6.86%	7.37%	8.16%	8.50%	8.42%	8.17%
QTSBA	22.29%	21.05%	21.43%	22.50%	22.77%	23.76%

Table A: Market growth and market share in the business architecture training market 20X0–20X5

Table A illustrates that the market grew by 8.57% in 20X1. However, since then, growth has slowed and by 20X5, there was no market growth at all. A2K's growth outstripped the market in 20X1, 20X2 and 20X3, during which it successfully won a number of contracts which QTSBA also bid for. However, since 20X3 its growth and market share has declined. It seems likely that the company's performance has peaked and that it is now finding it difficult to compete successfully in an increasingly competitive market place. In contrast, after its poor performance in 20X1, QTSBA's growth has continually outstripped the market, suggesting that it is successfully anticipating and serving the needs of the market. In BCG terms, QTSBA looks like a cash cow for QTS Group.

Taking a competitor out of a stagnant market place, and at the same time increasing market share to 31.93% has two advantages to QTSBA. First, it reduces the competition in the market, easing competitive rivalry and downward pressure on prices, and second, it means that QTSBA will become twice the size of its nearest competitor, with the operational advantages and brand visibility which this will bring.

Acquiring A2K appears to be a suitable option for QTS Group because it allows QTSBA to increase its market share in a relatively stagnant market place, and (through e-learning) provides opportunities for product and market development.

Exploiting core competencies

The acquisition of A2K will give QTS Group the opportunity to further exploit its core competencies in acquisition and change implementation. The financial performance of the three training companies which QTS Group has acquired in the past two years has improved after acquisition. The return on capital employed (ROCE) and the operating profit of all three companies have increased post acquisition.

There will be also be opportunities for cost efficiencies, associated with economies of scale (for example, in producing course material) and with sharing centralised services. For example, QTSBA already has well-established and successful sales and marketing departments which should be able to easily absorb the work of the current A2K team. There appears little need to retain A2K's marketing and sales directors and all their team, bringing immediate cost savings (after redundancy costs) to QTSBA.

Assessing feasibility is concerned with whether the company has the resources and competencies to deliver the promised strategy. There does not seem any issue here. Although no price for A2K has yet been agreed, it is unlikely to make too much of a dent in the $30m of retained earnings which QTS Group has earmarked to fund acquisition and post-acquisition change. As stated already, there is evidence to suggest that it has both the resources and competencies to deliver this strategy.

Benefits to shareholders

The acceptability of an acquisition is concerned with the performance outcomes of a strategy. This can be looked at in terms of return, risk and stakeholder reactions. Returns are the benefits which shareholders are likely to receive from the strategy. A number of shareholders have already campaigned for the retained profit in QTS Group to be invested in further acquisitions. They are clearly encouraged by the fact that recent acquisitions have apparently led to increased shareholder value, both in the dividend payout ratio and in earnings per share.

In terms of acceptability, risk is concerned with the probability of the failure of a particular strategy and the impact or consequences of this failure.

Table B summarises the financial performance of A2K. Although there are some concerns about its performance, the company is still trading profitably and has relatively large retained earnings. The risk of an inappropriate acquisition seems very low.

	20X0	20X1	20X2	20X3	20X4	20X5
Share capital ($m)	3.00	3.00	3.00	3.00	3.00	3.00
Other reserves ($m)	0.40	0.40	0.40	0.40	0.40	0.40
Retained earnings ($m)	0.80	0.90	0.80	0.80	0.70	0.60
Revenue ($m)	12.00	14.00	16.00	17.00	17.00	16.50
Net profit ($m)	1.75	1.65	1.65	1.60	1.45	1.40
ROCE	41.67%	38.37%	39.29%	38.10%	35.37%	35.00%
Net profit margin	14.58%	11.79%	10.31%	9.41%	8.53%	8.48%

Table B: Financial performance of A2K, 20X1–20X6

The ROCE is a fundamental measure of business performance, considering the net profit generated by the long-term capital invested in the business. The ROCE for A2K has declined from 41.67% in 20X0 to 35.00% in 20X5, but still remains relatively high (the industry sector average is 25%) probably reflecting the relatively low initial investment made by the founders of the company. The company also has fairly substantial retained earnings ($600,000).

The net profit margin is often regarded as the most appropriate measure of operational performance. Just like the ROCE, the net profit margin has declined from a high of 14.58% in 20X0 to 8.48% in 20X5. This is below the industry sector average of 10.00%. This supports Kath's view that the costs of the company have not been properly controlled in the last few years and that there is a fall in delivery efficiency. However, it seems likely that cost savings and increased sales post acquisition, will quickly return A2K to profitability which is at, or above, the sector average.

Overall, QTS Group shareholders are likely to support a proposed acquisition of A2K. It is a low risk option which fulfils their demand for further investment and the company's past record suggests that the acquisition will quickly contribute to higher shareholder returns. QTS Group is arguably, in corporate parenting terms, a synergy manager, enhancing value across a number of business units. In this instance it is potentially acquiring a company whose market is very well known to the current managers of a company already in the group.

(b) This part of the briefing paper briefly explains five contextual factors in strategic change and explores how these are likely to apply to the situation at A2K, should the acquisition go ahead.

Time: this is concerned with how quickly change is needed. A business facing rapid declines in revenue and profitability may have to be turned around very quickly. This is not the case here. Revenue growth at A2K has slowed, but the company is still profitable, although not as profitable at it used to be. QTS Group has a large 'acquisitions fund' to spend on acquisitions and post-acquisition change in companies which it purchases. Consequently, the pace of change could be quite leisurely, perhaps implemented in an incremental process. However, the problem with this could be the attitude of the three senior managers (the CEO, the sales director and the marketing director) if they remain within the merged company. The point has already been made that there is no apparent need to retain the sales and marketing director. It seems unlikely that the senior managers at A2K will either survive or embrace the kind of change envisaged by QTS Group and so changes to these key positions might have to be made very quickly, followed by reassuring customers that it is 'business as usual'.

Preservation: considers the organisational resources and characteristics which need to be maintained. These are key competencies which must not be lost if QTS Group is to improve (or at least maintain) the performance of A2K. At A2K, the key resources to preserve appear to be the full-time business architecture trainers and the e-learning team. The trainers are perceived as excellent (by customers) and the e-learning team has developed effective and innovative e-learning solutions. In contrast, QTSBA already has established sales and marketing departments and so these do need to be preserved.

Diversity: reflects on the diversity of experience, views and opinions within an organisation. It is concerned with the homogeneity of staff groups within the organisation and how they see the world. It is argued that change is hampered by a lack of diversity because everyone in the organisation sees the world in a similar way. This is likely to be an issue at A2K; although some of the trainers may have some diversity of experience, the views and opinions within the organisation are set and controlled by the CEO. Anyone with different views has left or has had their views publicly rejected. There is little diversity to build upon and so change is unlikely to be welcome or understood. QTS Group has to be aware of this. Change will have to be promoted by managers brought into A2K.

Capability: concerns experience of managing change in an organisation. As far as A2K is concerned, there is little capability in implementing change, and indeed relatively little experience of change. Thus managers employed by A2K are unlikely to have the capability to implement the changes which QTS Group will require. In contrast, QTS Group has experience of post-acquisition change in a number of companies and it is, the company believes, one of its core competencies. It will have to introduce managers into A2K charged with implementing the changes it requires. These managers will have to be appointed at a senior level, probably to replace the current board members of A2K.

Readiness: examines the readiness for change of the workforce. It seems clear that both the trainers and the e-learning team are ready for change. The trainers are disillusioned by their lack of input into business policy and training decisions and the e-learning team is angry at the lack of commitment to e-learning (as against conventional face-to-face training) and the reluctance to give e-learning a voice on the board. So, both of the key resources which have to be preserved are ready and open for change. This is a positive factor for QTS Group. It is likely that there will be pockets of resistance (sales, marketing) but it seems increasingly unlikely that these will be preserved in their current state. The current board is also unlikely to embrace change (and indeed might actively oppose it) and so the importance of acting quickly to replace this team is again reinforced.

(c) This final part of this briefing paper explores the importance of organisational culture and briefly explains the concept and application of the cultural web and organisational configuration in the context of the proposed acquisition of A2K.

Organisations vary in their personality and atmosphere. They have different ways of doing things, different attitudes towards customers and staff, different levels of freedom and responsibility. These things help define its organisational culture. When one organisation wishes to acquire or merge with another, it helps if it has an understanding of the culture of the organisation it is considering acquiring. Understanding that culture will help in diagnosis, perhaps identifying that current problems in the company being acquired are due to cultural issues, and in transition, as the company is moved to the culture which the acquiring company believes it should exhibit.

Johnson, Scholes and Whittington conceive organisational culture as consisting of four layers: values, beliefs, behaviours and paradigm, a set of taken for granted assumptions. The *cultural web* is a way of exploring two of these layers, the behaviours and the paradigm. Behaviours are explored in terms of the stories, symbols, power structures, organisational structures, control systems, rituals and routines, which all surround the central paradigm.

In the context of A2K, the stories told at social gatherings suggest that the CEO looks back with enthusiasm at a simpler, golden age with the two founding directors as heroes delivering training courses with a whimsy and a humour missing from the standardised events which are now delivered by the full-time training staff. The *ritual* of inviting these two founding directors to the annual 'celebration event' further excludes the current full-time staff, as the CEO sits next to these two former directors, and stories are retold all evening. Not only do the full-time trainers feel excluded, they also find it hard to reconcile these stories with the two bald, aging, fragile men sitting next to the CEO. QTSBA can exploit this aspect of culture by ensuring that such events are more focused in the future and that the people telling these stories are removed or not invited.

Power at A2K is invested in the leadership (the CEO) and this power structure is reinforced by an *organisational structure* which is very flat. The main power holders (the CEO, and to a lesser extent the marketing director and the sales director) are potential blockages to the changes which QTS Group is likely to propose. This understanding again reinforces the need to remove these people as part of the acquisition process.

Organisations are usually structured in some way to deliver the products and services they offer. Within this structure there are formal and informal organisational processes which take place within internal and external relationships which the organisation has established. Structure, processes and relationships work together. They have to be appropriate for the situation of the organisation and they have to match each other. This matching means that organisations tend towards a limited set of standard configurations. Henry Mintzberg has suggested six stereotypical configurations.

A2K appears to be a *simple or entrepreneurial* configuration. The organisational structure is simple and there is little middle management. Indeed, two-thirds of the staff report directly to the CEO. The CEO provides strong charismatic leadership and has a tendency to be autocratic. Unwelcome suggestions made by the marketing director have been summarily dismissed in the past. The strategy of the organisation reflects the vision of the CEO. However, the expansion of the company has meant that the CEO has become increasingly concerned with operational issues and problems and has lost sight of the strategy. This has been exacerbated by the need for her to spend more time monitoring the financial situation of the company. Indeed, Mintzberg identified this issue as a potential problem in an entrepreneurial organisation. The CEO becomes so enmeshed in operational problems that they lose sight of strategy.

In contrast, QTS Group displays elements of a *machine bureaucracy* with a centralised bureaucratic management, formal procedures and a functional organisational structure. Due to its size and client expectations, it needs to deliver its products in a standard, controlled, consistent way. It is a large, mature organisation and such organisations often tend towards a machine configuration. QTS Group has to be aware of the implications of bringing such a culture to A2K. There may be a concern that it will introduce a configuration where there is inconsistency between the structure, process and relationships. However, as noted before, they are likely to find allies in the full-time trainers and the e-learning staff who might adapt well to a more formal structure based on meritocracy, not autocracy.

The cultural analysis of A2K again suggests that although the CEO, sales director and marketing director wish to remain in their posts after the takeover, it is unlikely that they will be able to adapt to a transition to a different culture. This is yet another reason for recommending that these three managers are excluded from the post-acquisition company. Consequently, agreeing an appropriate severance arrangement with the current A2K board is likely to be an important part of the acquisition negotiation.

ACCA Marking scheme		
		Marks
(a)	Up to 1 mark for each valid point up to a maximum of 19 marks; this will include marks for appropriate calculations. Such calculations are likely to concern market share, market growth, return on capital employed and net profit margins.	
	Maximum	**19**
(b)	Up to 1 mark for each valid point up to a maximum of 3 marks for each contextual factor. This will include 1 mark for accurately defining the contextual factor. Up to a maximum of 15 marks for this part question.	
	Maximum	**15**
(c)	Up to 1 mark for each valid point up to a maximum of 12 marks for this part question.	
	Maximum	**12**
	Up to 4 professional marks for the tone, clarity, vocabulary and approach of the answer.	**4**
Total		**50**

85 POTS

Key answer tips

This is a challenging question for students. Part (a) covers portfolio analysis which is regularly examined, and students who have attempted similar past exam questions would have found lots of similarities between them. Part (c) covers benchmarking which had been the subject of a recent exam article which well prepared students would have read. Part (b) covers contextual features of change which has been a regularly examined area. So the areas should all have been revised by students, though students may be thrown by the combination of the topics, the lack of further strategy evaluation and the appearance in the compulsory section of topics which have previously been the remit of option questions.

(a)   **Power of the Sun (POTS) Co**

The growth of the EA Group (EA) was largely made possible by the profits produced by POTS Co in its first decade. It provided the funding for such acquisitions as ENCOS and Neach Glass. Since 20X6, the company has become steadily less profitable. Gross profit has fallen in each of the last four reported periods (from 25% to 21%). Net profit has fallen in line (from 11.04% to 7.00%) and is now less than half that of the company's heyday. Market growth has slowed considerably as alternative forms of energy have become available. However, POTS market share remains high as many of its competitors have either ceased business or scaled down their operations. In the last two years, when the market has grown by only 0.5%, the company has increased its market share from 25% to 30%. In Boston Box terms, POTS is probably a cash cow, with its high market share and presence meaning that it should be able to maintain unit costs below that of its competitors. However, there is concern within the Group that the company is being neglected and this is being reflected in its profitability. The best managers have been taken out of the company to work in new acquisitions and this has had a demoralising effect within the company. There is also evidence that the brand has grown tired and is not well recognised or respected. This is probably one of the problems with the cash cow. How can managers in the company be motivated when they see their hard-earned profits invested elsewhere in the Group? If EA is still committed to solar energy as an important energy source, then it would probably be beneficial for it to revisit the brand, review its operation and publically reaffirm its commitment to it.

Neach Glass

Neach Glass was an important supplier of POTS Co in the latter's formative years. The managing director, Kevin Neach, became a close personal friend of Ken Nyg, the managing director of POTS (and later the CEO of EA Group). When Neach was on the brink of going into administration it was purchased by EA to preserve the supply of high quality glass. It also allowed Ken Nyg to help out a personal friend. However, in the past five years substantial financial investment and the transfer of some of POTS' best managers have failed to improve performance. Although market share has increased in the last four years (from 7% to 9%), Neach remains a relatively small player in a declining market (reduced by 2% in the last year). Gross and net profit margins are improving (gross profit from 16.98% to 18.26%; net profit from 7.14% to 9.07%) but, in terms of performance within the Group, they remain stubbornly low.

Despite using some of the Group's best managers, net profit has risen less than 2% since acquisition. In Boston Box terms the company is probably a dog. It seems to have inherent problems which the EA Group cannot solve. It was understandable that EA bought the company to preserve the supply line. But, in retrospect, this should have been a short-term response whilst POTS found a new supplier and the company should have then been sold. There are no obvious similarities between energy management and glass manufacture. Divesting this company from the portfolio remains the most appropriate response.

ENCOS

Acquiring ENCOS appeared to make sense. It was clear that other renewable alternatives to solar energy were becoming more common and that a more rounded approach to alternative energy management was required. ENCOS had expertise in energy control systems, but had little marketing expertise and lacked contacts with the large public sector organisations that were seeking to install such systems. EA could bring this knowledge to the company, together with more experienced managers and a higher profile. The acquisition appears to have been successful. It has an increasing market share (19% to 25.93%) in a growing market (15.71% growth in the four years under consideration). Furthermore, the growth of the company is outstripping the growth of the market. Gross and net profit margins are both growing (net profit margin up from 12.41% to 15.95% in the four years under consideration, gross profit up from 19.17% to 23.81%). In absolute terms, these returns are the highest of the companies considered here and net profitability continues to grow disproportionately, suggesting that operating costs appear to be falling. In Boston Box terms the company is a potential star, although further information would be required to confirm this. It has clear synergy with POTS and EA appear to have brought significant competencies to bear. It could be argued that it is performing much better under EA's guidance than it would have as an independent company.

Steeltown Information Technology

If the industry Steeltown Information Technology is competing in is defined as 'public sector technology', then it seems reasonable to suggest that the potential market growth is relatively high. The present government is committed to privatising non-core services, so it can be expected that many councils will follow the example of Steeltown City Council and outsource information technology. It could be argued that Steeltown Information Technology enjoys a very high market share in this new sector, so again potentially qualifying (in Boston Box terms) as a star. No conventional financial figures are available and although the cost plus contract agreed with the council does mean that profits will be reported for, at least, the last five years, these will be relatively modest. The real question with this acquisition is whether it makes sense. EA does have experience of gaining contracts within the public sector, but in energy and control technology, not information technology and systems. It has no experience of acquiring a public sector organisation and creating the degree of change required to move its culture to a profit-driven private sector company. Overall, EA is trying to broaden its product base, and the acquisition of Steeltown Information Technology is its vehicle for pursuing this strategy. Acquisition is an acknowledged way of entering a new market, but usually the acquired company is established in that market, which is not the case with the newly formed Steeltown Information Technology. Whether the perceived synergies with ENCOS will emerge is debatable. The two companies work in different markets.

ENCOS is focused on technical control systems in the energy sector. In comparison, Steeltown Information Technology develops commercial information processing systems in a public sector environment. The drivers are quite different. ENCOS is focused on complex mathematical algorithms with little user intervention. Steeltown Information Technology deals with developing systems for end users who have difficulty in both defining and implementing the systems they commission.

(b)   The issues explored in this question are four of the eight contextual factors, identified by Balogun and Hope-Hailey, which significantly influence strategic change.

Time refers to the amount of time available for EA to implement the changes at Steeltown Information Technology. In some circumstances, time is a very critical factor, because the perilous financial nature of the organisation requires action to be taken quickly to arrest a decline in turnover or profitability, or indeed just to ensure its short-term financial viability. This was the situation at Neach Glass when it was acquired by EA. However, at Steeltown Information Technology the ten year contract with the city council, only reviewed after five years, means that there is no obvious need for the speedy implementation of change. Sufficient profitability is guaranteed for the next five years to maintain present levels of resources at Steeltown Information Technology and this, potentially, gives EA a long elapsed period to implement the changes that they envisage.

The *Scope* of change can be considered as either largely realignment, or largely transformational. Realignment can usually be accommodated within the current culture of the organisation, whilst transformational change requires a significant cultural shift. It seems reasonable to suggest that the change at Steeltown Information Technology will be transformational. Current work is inwardly focused, budget rather than profit-driven, run by managers with little experience of the private sector. There will have to be a fundamental change in the core assumptions of the organisation. Fortunately, there is no need to quickly implement these changes and so an *incremental* approach to change can be adopted. In the Balogun and Hope Hailey model (adapted by Johnson, Scholes and Whittington) this suggests an *evolutionary* approach to change, where paradigm change is required, but over a relatively long time period.

Capability refers to what experience there is of managing change in the organisation. Does the organisation have managers who have successively managed change in the past? Is the workforce used to change and have they readily accepted changes in their work practices? In the context of Steeltown Information Technology, evidence suggests that employees have little experience of change. In fact, established work practices written into trade union agreements have tended to restrict change and this is one of the reasons why the city council decided that they wanted to separate off the information technology department. Employees have been very concerned and anxious throughout the whole process of outsourcing, from the initial decision, through tender evaluation, to agreeing the sale of the organisation to EA. On the other hand, EA does have experience of implementing change in the organisations that they have acquired. This is probably one of the competencies it perceives that it is bringing to Steeltown Information Technology. However, it has to be recognised that this capability has not appeared to be successful at Neach Glass and so some concern might be expressed about the validity of such a claim.

Readiness for change concerns the organisation's attitude towards change. Is it likely to embrace it or is there widespread opposition to change within the organisation or, indeed, do significant pockets of resistance exist? There is little doubt that, initially, there is evidence that there was considerable opposition to change. However, once the proposal was agreed and the sale made to EA, there appears to have been a greater acceptance of the need for change. Perhaps it is best illustrated by the manager who stated that 'he was against outsourcing in principle, but now the sale has been agreed, let's get on with it'. The resignation of the IT director and his deputy has removed a significant pocket of resistance to change and it should make EA's task easier.

(c) Benchmarking is an attempt to assess the relative performance of an organisation. It is understandable that EA wants to benchmark Steeltown Information Technology. Although the contract with the city council is guaranteed for at least the first five years, it is important for EA to understand the performance of the organisation it has bought and the opportunity for driving out improvements and, hence, profitability.

There has been a tendency for organisations to increasingly attempt to benchmark themselves against the industry or sector they compete in, rather than against their historical performance. However, such historical benchmarking was traditionally used when Steeltown Information Technology was part of the City Council. Examples given in the scenario are the reliability of software as measured by reported faults and the satisfaction of users as measured by internally developed and analysed questionnaires. This evidence suggests that the software produced by the organisation is becoming more reliable. However, this may reflect the fact that fewer new systems were developed in the past two years as the council arranged for the technology department's transition to the private sector. Established software tends to have fewer faults than recently released software. Furthermore, the measure is an absolute one, not a relative one. The apparent improvements in user satisfaction may also reflect the hiatus associated with the transition from public to private sector. Furthermore, the overall figures do not seem very high even though the questions were set, collected and analysed by the technology department. In general, externally measured satisfaction surveys are to be preferred.

Benchmarking against competitors is problematic in the context of Steeltown Information Technology because of choosing what sector to compare it with. It is possible to make comparisons, using published government statistics, with other public sector organisations and indeed it seems to compare relatively well, reporting greater user satisfaction and software reliability. However, again these figures have to be treated with care. Did the user satisfaction surveys in the other councils use the same assessment criteria? Now that it has been privatised, the uniqueness of the Steeltown Information Technology experiment makes it almost impossible to find IT companies providing exclusive services to a public sector client against which it might be benchmarked. EA has suggested benchmarking it against the performance of ENCOS. However, the technology it provides and the nature of the client it serves make such comparisons very tenuous. The focus of development has been quite different. ENCOS reports on profit per contract, but Steeltown Information Technology currently only has one contract and is unlikely to have any relevant data, as profitability was not an objective of the organisation. In any case, a major concern with such industry comparisons is that the whole industry might be performing badly and, in some circumstances, losing out to industries or technologies that can satisfy customers' needs in a different way. For example, poor performing companies providing bespoke software solutions may lose out to an organisation providing a standard off-the-shelf software package solution.

The shortcomings of industry norm comparisons have encouraged organisations to seek best practice wherever it can be found. Johnson, Scholes and Whittington comment that 'the real power of this approach is ... shaking managers out of the mindset that improvements in performance will be gradual as a result of incremental changes in resources or competencies'. They give an example of a police force studying a call centre as a way of improving their response to emergency telephone calls. However, software development is quite specific and it will be difficult to think of any appropriate, innovative comparisons.

Finally, benchmarking has been criticised on a number of accounts. Firstly, it can lead to a situation where you get what you measure, which may not have been the intended strategic outcome. If the strategy is flawed, then the benchmarking will encourage the organisation to continue, perhaps even accelerate, in the wrong direction. For example, a focus on measuring the certification of staff is only valid if there is a proven causal link between certification and software quality.

Secondly, since benchmarking compares inputs, outputs or outcomes, it does not, itself, identify the reasons for good or poor performance. The benchmark does not directly compare competencies. As mentioned earlier, improvements may be due to external environmental factors, not directly linked to what the organisation is striving to achieve.

Although benchmarking seems superficially attractive, it appears quite difficult to use effectively at Steeltown Information Technology. EA might be better focused, in the short term, on successfully implementing change and improving employee motivation and processes rather than trying to establish and measure sensible benchmarks.

ACCA Marking scheme		
		Marks
(a)	1 mark for each relevant point up to a maximum of 5 marks for analysing the strategic position of each company and 1 mark for assessing what to do with each company as part of the portfolio of the EA Group. Four companies in the portfolio giving a total of	
	The mark allocation may include, for each company, where appropriate:	
	Percentage analysis of decline/growth:	0.5
	Market share calculation:	0.5
	Market growth calculation:	0.5
	Correct portfolio classification:	0.5
	Maximum	24
	Professional marks are allocated as follows:	
	Up to 2 marks for the clarity of the answer	2
	Up to 2 marks for the structure of the answer	2
(b)	1 mark for each relevant point up to a maximum of	12
(c)	1 mark for each relevant point up to a maximum of	10
Total		**50**

86   QTP

Key answer tips

In part (a) the examiner is very clear as to how it should be presented and it will be crucial that students apply this approach in their answers. It will also be important not to spend too much time on one area at the expense of others – there are 5 marks available for each area and this means that each area should get the same amount of attention.

In part (b), the calculations should be straightforward if a logical approach is used in order to understand and interpret the volume of numerical information provided. Two calculations are required but it will also be important to notice that there are up to 5 marks available for a discussion of the method used.

Like part (a), part (c) illustrated a required approach for necessary changes to the value chain. If students have left enough time for this part of the requirement it should have been easily linked to part (a).

(a)   Inbound logistics and procurement

Inbound logistics is concerned with activities associated with receiving, storing and disseminating inputs to the production process. It encompasses materials handling, warehousing, inventory control, vehicle scheduling and returns to suppliers. It is responsible for bringing raw materials into the organisation and storing it ready for use. Standard window and bespoke window production pose different problems for the department.

In standard window production components tend to be bought in bulk and stored on-site waiting production. This incurs storage costs and there may also be costs associated with wastage and obsolescence. These costs are exacerbated by the problem of mixing standard and bespoke window production. The scenario suggests that bespoke production often displaces standard production, for example, in order to accommodate a customer's increasingly urgent request. This means that components bought in to fulfil a planned standard production run can be left in storage for longer than was anticipated. However, standard window production does facilitate the bulk buying of components and so raw materials should be cheaper.

In bespoke production, there should be fewer storage costs, as the components are moved quickly through to production to fulfil a customer's order. However, because component lead times are lengthier, buyers often pay more for the windows to secure quick supply and to reflect the lower order quantities normally associated with a specific bespoke order.

AT QTP, raw material costs are significantly higher for bespoke windows than for standard windows and this reflects the premium prices expected to be paid for low-volume urgent supplies. However, storage costs (part of which will be storage of raw materials) are much lower, suggesting that the order quickly moves through the QTP factory. However, the number of complaints raised by bespoke window customers perhaps suggests that for many, the order does not move quickly enough.

For both standard and bespoke production, the supply of timber is a problem. Prices are rising and there is an increasing shortage of specialist timber. However, from the perspective of QTP, inbound transport is not a problem. This is provided by the suppliers.

Production (Operations)

Production is concerned with the activities required to transform inputs into the final product. In this case it is the production line process of QTP, transforming timber, glass and fittings into standard and bespoke windows. As well as assembly, production also considers packaging and equipment maintenance.

In most organisations, production is most effective when producing long runs of standard products to inventory, minimising set up time and set down time (and associated costs). The production of well-understood standard products reduces the need for quality control and also minimises wastage. In contrast, bespoke production is usually associated with relatively short runs (reflecting individual customer order quantities) and higher set up and set down time (and costs). Specialised bespoke set ups have to be carefully quality-controlled and wastage rates (because of the unfamiliarity with the task) tend to be higher.

These general observations appear to be supported by the data at QTP. Set up and set down times for bespoke windows are much longer, meaning that the production line is idle for twice as long. The average production run is also shorter and wastage rates are higher. The number of customer complaints (per thousand units) is also higher. Some of these complaints are likely to be about the quality of the delivered window. Bespoke units have to be exactly to the specification of the customer, whilst standard units are to the specification of QTP. It is the responsibility of the customer to ensure that these standard units are fit for purpose.

The production manager's enthusiasm for standard windows is understandable. It maximises production efficiency, at the same time minimising wastage and complaints.

Outbound logistics

Outbound logistics is concerned with the activities associated with collecting, storing and physically distributing the product to buyers. It encompasses finished goods warehousing, material handling, delivery vehicle operation and order processing. Again, different issues are raised by standard window and bespoke window production.

Standard production leads to higher storage costs as windows are stored waiting to be sold to potential customers. The storage of these finished windows may lead to wastage, as windows are made unsellable due to storage conditions: damp, extremes of temperature, fire, flood. Pilfering from employees and obsolescence, as demand dries up for a standard window, may also affect stored windows.

Once sold, customers expect almost immediate delivery of stored windows, making it difficult to plan the routes of the delivery fleet in advance, particularly as that fleet also has to deal with the urgent delivery of bespoke orders. The effective use and maintenance of its own fleet of vehicles is a clear problem for QTP.

In contrast, delivery for bespoke windows produced to order can be planned well in advance and the customer given a specific delivery date. In general, the windows are delivered as soon as they are manufactured and so storage costs are lower. This is reflected in the QTP data where storage costs of bespoke windows are one third those of standard windows. Transport costs are also lower, reflecting the relative ease of planning the efficient delivery of bespoke orders.

Marketing and sales

These are activities associated with inducing the customers to purchase a product and then facilitating that purchase. It includes advertising, promotion, quotations and pricing.

At QTP, marketing and sales is rewarded on the basis of revenue per window sold. The data suggests that the average revenue per window is higher for a bespoke window than it is for a standard one. Consequently, there is an incentive to steer customers towards bespoke windows rather than standard ones.

Marketing and sales also argues that the bespoke approach means that customers always receive exactly the windows they want, rather than ordering standard windows which do not fit their exact needs. This pre-sales customer design service is perceived as an important strength of QTP and it is what distinguishes the company from its competitors. The marketing and sales director claims that 'we have sales people who really understand the windows and what customers want and need. We are not trying to sell them windows off the shelf, just because we have them' in inventory. Fulfilling exact requirements is an important part of building the customer relationship. It is claimed that some important customers purchase standard windows from QTP even when they could be sourced cheaper elsewhere, because of

QTP's past flexibility in developing bespoke windows for them. Thus there are important cross-selling opportunities between standard and bespoke windows.

However, the bespoke approach causes both internal and external tensions. Pressure from customers leads to the marketing and sales department putting pressure (in turn) on inbound logistics and procurement to secure the quick delivery of the required components. As noted already, this leads to high raw material costs. Once the raw material has arrived, pressure is put on production to expedite the order and postpone planned standard production runs. This leads to machine and labour inefficiency. Marketing and sales contend that bespoke orders are still more profitable than orders fulfilled from inventory, but the production manager disputes this.

The bespoke approach probably also demands the active management of customers. It is possible that the customer is constantly enquiring about the status of their order, and delivery on the planned date is essential if the customer is to achieve its own deadlines and profits.

(b)

Tutorial note

The analysis of standard window production might use the current pattern of machine utilisation or it might use a pattern where the production run is uninterrupted. Credit will be given for either and for both.

Financial analysis

Standard windows:

Machine utilisation (average day)

Set up	Production	Set down	Set up	Production	Set down
10 minutes	4 hours	20 minutes	10 minutes	4 hours	20 minutes

Effective machine time per day: 8 hours

Number of units produced: 8 × 12 (8 hours, 12 units per hour) 96 units Average window wastage per day (96 × 2%): 1.92

Sellable production per day: 94.08 units

Revenue: 94.08 × $85 = **$7,996.80**

Cost of production/window

	$
Storage cost	15
Raw material	20
Transport cost	15
Labour cost	12
Machine cost	8
Total	70

Production cost: 94.08 × $70 = **$6,585.60**

Daily contribution: $7,996.80 – $6,585.60 = **$1,411.20**

Bespoke windows:

Set up	Production	Set down	Set up	Production	Set down	Set up	Production	Set down
15 minutes	2 hours	45 minutes	15 minutes	2 hours	45 minutes	15 minutes	2 hours	45 minutes

Effective machine time per day: 6 hours

Number of units produced: 6 × 10 (6 hours, 10 units per hour) 60 units Average window wastage per day (60 × 5%): 3

Sellable production per day: 57 units

Revenue: 57 × 110 = **$6,270**

Cost of production/window

	$
Storage cost	5
Raw material	40
Transport cost	10
Labour cost	15
Machine cost	10
Total	80

Production cost: 57 × $80 = **$4,560.00**

Daily contribution: $6,270.00 – $4,560.00 = **$1,710.00**

So, on this basis, bespoke production produces less revenue per day, but is more profitable. Given the window mix at the moment, the expected daily contribution would be:

$1,411 × 0.7 + $1,710 × 0.3 = 987.70 + 513.00 = **$1,500.70**

The data is based on a mixed standard/bespoke production cycle where planned production runs are often cancelled or interrupted by bespoke production requirements. Thus the pattern of use in a production facility dedicated solely to standard windows should be different. For example, in a fully standard window production environment it should be possible to increase effective machine time to 8 hours 30 minutes (1 set up, production, 1 set down). This would lead to a production run of 102 units (8.5 hours × 12). Given a 2% wastage rate, this would lead to an average daily production of 99.96 units, producing a revenue of 99.96 × $85 = $8,496.60. Cost of production would be 99.96 × $70 = $6,997.20.

Thus contribution would be $8,496.60 – $6,997.20 = $1,499.40, still below the daily contribution of the bespoke alternative. However, this assumes that all other costs would remain the same in a fully standard configuration.

The data provided only concerns direct costs. There is no consideration of overheads. It may be possible that a production line dedicated to standard window development may allow for a reduction in marketing and sales staff and service employees as the windows need less negotiation and support. In contrast, a production line dedicated to bespoke windows may lead to fewer warehousing and distribution staff. Revenues will also be less, so there may be an opportunity to lose staff from general administrative functions.

(c) **Switching completely to standard windows production**

Inbound logistics: It should be possible to reduce the storage costs of components, as they should be stored for shorter periods as production is now based on a planned cycle, uninterrupted by bespoke work. Less time in storage should also reduce wastage and obsolescence.

There may also be opportunities for exploiting just in time (JIT) supply principles, moving storage costs to the supplier and so reducing inbound storage costs at QTP even further. The company might also consider backward integration, looking to acquire timber production facilities so helping secure the supply chain and also, potentially, reducing raw material costs.

Production (Operations): Production efficiencies should be gained from being able to plan production in advance. If set up and set down times remain the same (and this seems a reasonable assumption), then production can be increased to 102 units per day, before wastage. The calculation for this is shown in part (b) of this solution.

Outbound logistics: Planned production should lead to a better utilisation of the distribution fleet. However, this is an area where QTP might consider outsourcing to a specialist logistics company who can exploit economies of scale which are not achievable with a small fleet of vehicles. It can be argued that distribution is not a core competence of the company and would benefit from outsourcing.

Marketing and sales: There are opportunities for head count reduction in marketing and sales as sales switch to standard windows with specifications available in catalogues and on the internet. The focus is now on promotion and order taking, not the negotiation of individual orders. In standard window production, sales forecasting is paramount. This is an acknowledged weakness of the current marketing and sales team and this would have to be addressed.

Overall: In this approach, QTP is an order-obtaining organisation, obtaining orders from customers for goods which it has already produced. Standard window production to inventory should lead to a more efficient window production. However, it may also lead to the loss of customers who value the company's ability to deliver a mixture of standard and bespoke windows. There is evidence to suggest that such customers currently place orders for standard windows even though they could be sourced more cheaply elsewhere. QTP might lose these customers in the future.

Focusing on standard production may also mean that QTP is focusing on a commodity-type market where there will be continual downward pressure on prices.

Switching completely to bespoke production

Inbound logistics: Because orders are definite, component storage costs should be relatively low, but components cannot be ordered in advance and bulk discounts negotiated. Thus in this case there seems an even stronger case for backward integration. Securing supply is even more vital in bespoke production where supplying the customer at the promised time is paramount. It is also acknowledged that raw material costs are currently high for bespoke windows and so owning the means of timber supply should help reduce this cost.

Production (Operations): Production is driven by definite orders from customers, not 'made to inventory' production runs based on forecasts. Freeing up capacity should allow the quicker production and delivery of bespoke orders. Production planning is now primarily concerned with scheduling definite orders to meet the agreed delivery date.

Outbound logistics: Inventory holding costs should be relatively low as deliveries can be planned around customer order dates. Because these are well known in advance, then a delivery schedule can be planned, although this is likely to be sub-optimal, based around the need to deliver to certain locations on certain dates, rather than planning an optimal route around standard delivery locations. Overall, fewer units will be produced and so it might be possible to reduce the size (and hence cost) of the delivery fleet. The certainty of deliveries might also make this a strong candidate for outsourcing. This could deliver significant cost savings.

Marketing and sales: Moving to bespoke production plays to the strengths of the current marketing and sales department. These could be perceived as core competencies which the company needs to exploit. Furthermore, because they are rewarded on average revenue per window, this will also appeal to the department from a reward perspective. The need to acquire new customers may make other elements of the marketing mix, such as promotion, increasingly important.

Overall: In this approach, QTP is an order-receiving organisation, producing windows for orders it has received. This is the preferred approach of the current marketing and sales team. Bespoke production will still allow QTP to fulfil standard windows (they will just be produced as bespoke items) and so customers' needs will be fulfilled, although they may have to pay higher prices than before for such windows. QTP will be positioning itself as a niche provider, able to charge a premium for a specialised service. So, its market positioning will be quite different.

	ACCA Marking scheme	
		Marks
(a)	1 mark for each appropriate point within each department up to a maximum of 5 marks. Four departments are under consideration giving a total maximum of 20 marks.	
(b)	Up to a maximum of 12 marks.	
	For both standard and bespoke windows (4 marks each) – as below:	
	– Effective machine time per day (1 mark)	
	– Number of units produced per day (0.5 marks)	
	– Wastage per day (1 mark)	
	– Revenue (0.5 marks)	
	– Production cost (0.5 marks)	
	– Daily contribution (0.5 marks)	
	Recognition that this is based on current pattern (1 mark)	
	No consideration of overheads (up to 2 marks)	
	Sensitivity analysis (up to 2 marks)	
(c)	1 mark for each aspect of the value chain/department up to a maximum of 4 marks per department up to a maximum of 14 marks.	
	Professional marks are given for the structure, tone, coherence and clarity of your briefing paper (4 marks).	
Total		**50**

> **Examiner's comments**
>
> In part (a) despite detailed guidance, many candidates analysed the problems and suggested solutions (which were only required in part (c)). This was both time-consuming, leading to long answers that filled pages of the answer book, and pointless, because no marks could be given for these suggestions. Please read the questions carefully and, where examples are provided, please study and follow them.
>
> In part (b) some candidates manipulated the data very accurately and gained most of the twelve marks on offer for this part question. Others failed to understand the data properly before undertaking an analysis that was flawed and imprecise. However, more worryingly, too many candidates resorted to general textual answers that stated the obvious 'the inventory figure of this type of production is higher than the inventory figure of that type of production', 'the raw material cost of production of this alternative is almost twice that of the other alternative'. Very little credit could be given for such disappointing answers. Employers will expect qualified accountants to be able to accurately analyse relevant data, coming up with meaningful values and recommendations. The P5 examination will also require such skills.
>
> Part (c) was well answered, although candidates who had provided solutions in the first part of the question must have realised that they were now repeating a lot of information. However, this time, credit could be given where it was due.
>
> Overall, question one was answered relatively well. The lowest marks were generally for the financial case, with many candidates scoring four marks or less. Many answers were just too long, usually because they focused on solutions rather than issues (in the first part of the question) and description rather than values (in the second part of the question). This undoubtedly contributed to the time management problems that candidates experienced and reported in this paper.

87   LING

> **Key answer tips**
>
> Part (a) of this question should be made easier by the examiner being very clear as to what model was expected to be used. But, many students are likely to ignore the fact that there are only seven marks available and therefore induce undue time pressure for the rest of the question.
>
> Part (b) is more likely to suit student expectations on the marks available for this type of requirement, and, again, the examiner helps by suggesting which model should be used. There will be no marks available for using other models.
>
> Parts (c) and (d) focus on an area that has been regularly examined. The key to success will be ensuring that answers are related to the scenario rather than being a simple regurgitation of study notes.

(a) **PESTEL analysis**

A PESTEL analysis identifies the main drivers in the external environment which are largely outside the control of the company. The relevance of these factors may depend upon whether Ling decides to enter the light bulb market directly or to enter it by acquiring a Skod-based company. In some instances the driver affects the industry wherever it is based.

Political

The government is considering the imposition of import taxes. This would be a threat if Ling decides to enter the market place using the distribution company approach and keep manufacturing in Lindisztan. However, it presents an opportunity if Ling decides to acquire Flick and continue to run it as a Skod-based company.

Economic

Although the country of Skod is in recession and consumer disposable income is falling, it seems unlikely that such a low cost commodity product will be greatly affected. This is an industry which is unlikely to be touched by changes in economic prosperity. The only minor issue may be the effect of switching off street lights. This may lengthen the life span of the bulb. However, overall, this is likely to have very little effect on total light bulb demand.

Sociocultural

There is a growing nationalist movement in Skod who are keen to keep jobs within the country. There have been instances, in other industries, where imported goods have been boycotted. It seems unlikely that a backlash against foreign goods would affect such an unglamorous product as a light bulb. However, it is possible, and any potential consumer backlash can be avoided by buying a Skod-based company and manufacturing light bulbs in the country.

Technical

Ling has so far benefitted from technological innovations which have put it ahead of competitors who have focused on candescent and halogen bulbs. However, other lighting initiatives, such as the tubular daylighting devices discussed in the Lighting Tomorrow article need to be continually monitored. This monitoring is required whether Ling enters the Skod market directly, or acquires a company such as Flick.

Legal

The 'efficient lighting' legislation due to become law in Skod in 2017 is an opportunity for Ling to enter the market with its innovative LED products. This is an opportunity whether the company enters the market directly or buys a home-based company such as Flick.

Environmental

Businesses and consumers in Skod are increasingly aware of energy issues. This is partly due to increasing energy prices as well as more frequent breaks in the electricity supply (such as the power cuts which affected Lal's hotel). The LED bulbs offered by Ling are greener and more efficient than candescent and halogen bulbs, which are still widely made in the home industry. In the case of businesses, many are quickly moving to LED light bulbs to reduce running costs and boost their environmental credentials. The environmental attractions of its products is important to Ling but again this is independent of whether they are made by a home-based company or one based abroad.

(b)   **Five forces analysis**

Bargaining power of buyers

In this scenario, the buyers of the industry's products are large supermarket groups, household product superstores and large electrical chains. These buyers, particularly the supermarket groups, purchase a large volume of the industry's products (90%) and so, on the face of it, they can demand favourable prices. However, the products the buyer purchases from the industry represents a relatively insignificant fraction of the buyer's costs or purchases. A recent report suggested that light bulb sales contributed less than 0.1% of a supermarket's revenue. Light bulbs are much less important to supermarket groups than food and drink. When the product sold by the industry is a small fraction of the buyers' total costs, then buyers are less price sensitive. They are more likely to bargain with food suppliers than light bulb suppliers.

Buyers' bargaining power in the light bulb industry is strengthened by the product being undifferentiated, with low customer switching costs. However, the buyers are extremely unlikely to move backwards in the supply chain to manufacture their own light bulbs and so this potentially limits their bargaining power. Again, their focus is likely to be elsewhere.

Some of the factors which concern the buyer also relate to the consumer (end customer) as well. To the end customer, light bulbs are undifferentiated and there are no switching costs. Light bulbs are an insignificant fraction of their total spend and so they are unlikely to shop around to get the lowest price.

Bargaining power of suppliers

A supplier group is more powerful if it is dominated by a few companies and is more concentrated than the industry it sells to. This appears to be the case in Skod, where 90% of glass production is accounted for by three companies and metal production is largely concentrated in the hands of one very large company, OmniMetal. The customers (such as Flick) are large but they are more fragmented than the suppliers. Furthermore, the supplier group is, by and large, not obliged to contend with other substitute products for sale to the industry. Light bulbs are largely made of glass and metal and it seems unlikely that this will change in the near future. This lack of substitutes increases the power of the supplier.

The industry is not an important customer of the supplier group. Most glass is sold to the construction industry. Most metal is sold to the automobile industry. The light bulb manufacturers use less than 0.5% of the country's glass production and less than 0.1% of its metal production. This lack of importance increases the supplier group's power, because suppliers' fortunes are not closely tied to the industry and they will not need to protect it through reasonable pricing. Another factor increasing suppliers' power is that the products (glass and metal) are a vital part of the buyers' (customers) light bulb business. On the other hand, the supplier group's products are largely undifferentiated and switching costs between suppliers appears to be reasonably low. Finally, it seems unlikely that the supplier group poses a credible threat of forward integration into light bulb manufacture and this will be a factor which reduces supplier bargaining power.

Threat of new entrants

Ling is considering entering this market and so the barriers to entry and the potential reaction of current suppliers is important to consider here. The main barriers to entry appear to be:

Economies of scale: The five large dominant companies in the industry should be enjoying economies of scale which force any potential new entrant to come into the market with large scale production, which carries with it a high risk of failure. This is not an issue for Ling who also currently enjoys economies of scale in its manufacture. However, it will deter many other entrants.

Capital requirements: The manufacture of light bulbs requires new entrants to invest large financial resources into production plants. Although capital may be available, the risk associated with large-scale entry may lead to high premiums on borrowed capital.

Access to distribution channels: This may be very significant, as the distribution channels are very specific (supermarket groups, large home products superstores and major electrical chains). The new entrant will have to persuade these channels to accept its products, perhaps through offering price discounts. It seems unlikely that the new entrant can create a completely new channel. Selling directly to the consumer seems unlikely in this industry where individual purchases are both infrequent and low value.

The reaction to new entrants of existing firms in the industry is likely to be relatively forceful as they have a history of vigorous retaliation to prospective entrants. The upsurge of nationalism in the country will also give them a powerful card to play in this retaliation.

Threat of substitute products

Substitute products are products which can perform the same function as the product of the industry under consideration. It is hard to envisage any potential substitute for light bulbs except for candles which, in the long term, are likely to be much more expensive. Another possible substitute is to do without. This is the approach taken by government policy on street lighting. It is turned off from 2300 hrs to 0500 hrs. However, it seems unlikely that many consumers will prefer to sit in the dark instead of using a relatively cheap lighting product. In the short term, the threat of substitute products seems very low. However, in the long term, the tubular daylight lighting initiative described in Lighting Tomorrow is a possible substitute product as it aims to reduce the need for electric lighting.

Competitive rivalry in the industry

Equally balanced competitors. When an industry is dominated by a few firms and these firms are relatively well balanced in terms of size, it creates potential instability because they may be prone to fight each other. This appears the case in Skod where five fairly similar sized firms produce 72% (20X5) of the light bulbs sold in the country and wage short-term price cutting wars, disrupt competitors' supply lines and react aggressively to potential new entrants.

Slow industry growth. Despite the switch to new technologies, there is little market growth. From 20X0 to 20X5 the market only grew by just over 2%. In such a situation, the only way a firm can increase market share is to take it from one of its competitors. Consequently, slow industry growth increases competitive rivalry.

Lack of differentiation or switching costs. Competitive rivalry is increased where the product is perceived as a commodity. In such circumstances the buyer's decision is largely based on price and service and pressures for intense price and service competition result. Light bulbs are definitely a commodity product in Skod.

High exit barriers. Exit costs are high because of the investment required in plant and the fact that light bulb factories cannot easily be adapted for other uses. When exit costs are high, companies hang on in the industry often resorting to extreme tactics which weaken the profitability of the industry as a whole.

(c) **Evaluation of an acquisition**

One of the elements of **suitability** is a consideration of how well the strategy fits with future trends and changes in the environment. This environment has already been considered in the PESTEL and five forces analysis. Acquiring Flick is particularly appropriate in the context of the government's threat to impose taxes on imported goods. The increasingly nationalistic Skod population can also be acknowledged if the acquisition is carefully handled. Ling can stress that it is investing in Flick to secure its future and to create jobs for the people of Skod. The impending efficient lighting legislation also provides an opportunity for Ling, but this is irrespective of whether the company enters the market directly or acquires Flick. However, it is better placed to quickly meet this demand through acquisition. Direct entry is generally a slower approach to growth, as Man Lal has acknowledged.

Entering the market through acquisition also means that it can use the effective distribution channels which are already in place. There is no guarantee that the established distribution channels would welcome a new entrant into the market and indeed they may demand price reductions in exchange for distribution access. Acquisition also means that no new capacity is brought to the market. Ling can then focus on increasing market share in a competitive, relatively slow-growing market. Entering directly is likely to prompt a hostile reaction from competitors currently in the market. Acquiring Flick might also invoke a hostile reaction, but it is likely to be more muted because it does not immediately alter the balance of power in the market.

However, in the longer term, the worldwide size of Ling may affect the bargaining power of suppliers and buyers in the Skod market. As a group, it has revenues which exceed the Skod market total, so there may be possibilities for negotiating reductions in raw material costs and the profit margins of suppliers. If these savings are not passed on to the end consumer, then Ling's profitability will inevitably improve. If these savings are passed on, then Ling will begin to dominate a commodity market place.

A further element of suitability is whether the acquisition provides an opportunity to exploit the strategic capability of Ling. In one sense it does, as it provides an opportunity for it to exploit its technical capability in LED lighting, before the domestic industry can gear up its production levels. However, in another sense the strategy is not suitable because Ling does not have strategic capability in acquiring foreign companies. All of its growth has been achieved through setting up wholly owned distribution subsidiaries. Its only production factories are in Lindisztan.

Acquisition also has to meet the expectations of the stakeholders. In terms of the institutional stakeholders who hold 49% of Ling's shares, the acquisition promises the rapid growth which they are lobbying for. They have been critical of Ling's slow, cautious foreign growth and the maturity of the Lindisztan market means that there is little opportunity for growth there. The institutional shareholders have also been critical of the high levels of retained earnings and they wish to see a significant portion of it invested back into the company to fuel growth. The size of the retained earnings makes the acquisition financially feasible, although of course there is always the possibility that such funds could be better invested elsewhere.

The acquisition of Flick is also of personal significance to Lal himself. It provides him with an opportunity to show the country where he received his business education that he has succeeded. This tangible proof of his success and ambition is important to him. Acquisition is a speedy approach to growth, but it can raise issues of culture clash. This needs further investigation and will be one of the challenges which Ling faces, because it does not have any previous experience of this method of growth. It seems unlikely that the business culture of Skod and Lindisztan is exactly the same and so cultural issues can be expected. Perhaps this is contributing to Man Lal's unease about the acquisition policy.

The **acceptability** of the acquisition can also be considered in the light of Flick's financial performance in its market sector.

The profitability of Flick is currently below average for the industry sector. Gross profit margin in 20X5 was 21.43% (industry average 30%), net profit margin 15.71% (industry average 24%) and ROCE 4.07% (industry average 5.74%). This may suggest to Ling's shareholders that there are short-term profits to be gained by reducing the cost of sales and overheads to a point where the company at least achieves the average performance of its sector.

In contrast, liquidity is higher than the industry averages. The current ratio is 3.33 (compared with 2.69 for the industry as a whole) and the acid test ratio is 1.83 (1.74 for the industry as a whole). It is possible that the high current ratio reflects a lack of investment in plant and equipment. At Flick, property, plant and equipment accounts for 63.33% of its assets, compared with an industry average of 71.09%. Inventory holding appears unnecessarily high and perhaps shows a lack of good inventory management practice. 15% of the total assets are held in inventory, compared with an industry average of 8.7%. Flick's liquidity is boosted by the amount of money it holds in cash or cash equivalents. This accounts for 11.87% of the asset base, more than double the industry equivalent.

Gearing is relatively low. The gearing ratio is 25.9% (compared with an industry average of 35.9%) and the interest cover ratio is 4.4 (compared to an industry average of 2.4). This points towards a cautious approach to investment and borrowing. It may again suggest that Flick has been reluctant to borrow money to invest in production machines and processes which, in the long term, contribute to more profitable products. It has preferred a lower risk strategy which leads, in turn, to the company making lower profits.

However, one area where Flick appears to excel is in its management of receivables. At an average of 104.3 days this is much lower than the industry norm. Its industry payables is broadly in line with the industry norm (192.5 days compared to 208.6 days).

Conclusion

The acquisition of Flick is, potentially, an excellent way of entering the Skod light bulb market. It appears to be a cautiously run company which has reported lower profitability, perhaps as a result of failing to invest in efficiency initiatives. The threat of import controls makes direct entry very risky and there is sufficient evidence to suggest that Ling's input will improve Flick's position in a very competitive market.

One reservation might be the lack of experience the company has in acquiring and managing foreign companies. Thus a comprehensive due diligence process to purchasing the company and a non-intervention approach to managing Flick when it is acquired is recommended, particularly while Ling gets to grip with the cultural differences which are bound to exist. Such an approach is also likely to partly appease any nationalist critics. Even in the short term, there appears to be improvements which can be made to Flick and profitability will improve by just bringing company performance into line with the national average. Although it is expected that Ling will supply most of the funding for expansion and equipping the factory to produce LED bulbs, liquidity and gearing data suggest that Flick itself has unlocked financing potential which could be used to help finance growth.

(d)   Strategic alliance

There are many documented cases where acquisitions have been unsuccessful and so the caution of Ling's financial director is understandable. Strategic alliances appear to offer a less risky way of entering a market place.

A strategic partnership is where two or more organisations share resources and activities to pursue a strategy. The basis for an alliance between Ling and Flick would be co-specialisation, allowing each partner to focus on their core capabilities. Johnson, Scholes and Whittington suggest that 'alliances are used to enter new geographical markets where an organisation needs local knowledge and expertise in distribution, marketing and customer support'. This is exactly the situation Ling finds itself in. In such an alliance it could exploit a new market, retain all production in its own country and save itself the costs of acquisition and due diligence. In return, Flick would gain new energy-efficient products for its home market which would allow it to fulfil the requirements of impending legislation. Crucially, however, the profit of the alliance would have to be split, on some agreed basis, between the two companies.

There are different types of strategic partnership. In a joint venture a new organisation is created which is jointly owned by the parents. The parent companies remain independent trading companies. This is unlikely to be attractive in the Ling/Flick situation. It seems more likely that Flick would wish to sell the product as its own and not confuse the market place with an offering from a related company. A joint venture is probably more appropriate where the participating companies are entering into a different market place. For example, Ling and Flick combining their expertise to enter the energy management consultancy business. At the other end of the spectrum, a network of firms might collaborate without too much formality. For example, Flick could agree to brand and distribute Ling's products, paying a fraction of the sales price (or profit margin) back to Ling. This is in effect a licensing agreement, and this might eventually stretch to the company making the LED bulbs in Skod under licence, after testing the market first through branding and distributing them.

Different levels of formality of the alliance lead to different characteristics. For example, if speed to market is important, then an opportunistic alliance would be preferred to a joint venture. Indeed a joint venture might easily take longer to agree and legally establish than to complete an acquisition.

The form of the strategic alliance can be shaped to take into account the environmental factors which affect the industry and the different capabilities of the participants. It can also be made responsive to cultural differences. However, in the Ling/Flick situation, it is difficult to see how a strategic alliance will address the needs of the institutional stakeholders for growth and Lal's personal desire for acknowledged success and prestige. Furthermore, there may be concerns about the long-term viability of any such alliance. Trust is probably the most important ingredient of any alliance and it seems likely that Ling will be reluctant to licence a product which could be easily imitated by the licensee. Furthermore, just as Ling has limited expertise in acquisitions, it also has no experience of strategic alliances at all. Success requires expertise in setting up and monitoring clear goals, governance, financial arrangements and other organisational issues. There is no evidence in the scenario that Ling has this expertise.

ACCA Marking scheme		Marks
(a)	Up to 1 mark for each relevant point up to a maximum of 7 marks.	7
(b)	Up to 1 mark for each relevant point up to a maximum of 13 marks.	13
(c)	Up to 1 mark for each relevant point up to a maximum of 18 marks. This will include marks for the accurate calculation of financial ratios and for correctly interpreting their implications.	18
(d)	Up to 1 mark for each relevant point up to a maximum of 8 marks.	8
Up to 4 professional marks for the structure, coherence, style and clarity of the answer.		4
Total		50

Examiner's comments

In part (a) the majority of candidates scored if they adhered to the focus requested. Some candidates simply applied the model without considering the full requirement. It should be noted that this question was worth 7 marks and was over-answered by a number of candidates, who did not seem to take the mark allocation into account.

In part (b) some candidates obtained full marks, and this element was well answered on the whole.

Part (c) received mixed responses. Some candidates scored very highly as they covered only the two elements required (feasibility was not requested) and applied it to the method of growth. Other candidates omitted to discuss the actual method of growth (the focus of the question) and instead discussed the environment alone. This lead to a considerable amount of repetition from questions 1a and b. Financial data was provided in the scenario, which could have been used to make considerable observations within this question. Candidates who did this tended to score highly, with others missing the opportunity for some relatively straightforward marks.

Part (d) required the consideration of a different growth method to that discussed in 1c. A number of candidates omitted to answer this question in its entirety, and therefore were unable to obtain the 8 marks available for it.